THE DOCUMENTARY FILM BOOK

WESTON COLLEGE

D1141787

Weston College LibraryPlus
Knightstone Road

Edited by
Brian Winston

In memory of Richard (Ricky) Leacock (1922–2011), George Stoney (1916–2012) and Peter Wintonick (1953–2013)

THE BRITISH FILM INSTITUTE
Bloomsbury Publishing Plc
50 Bedford Square, London, WC1B 3DP, UK
1385 Broadway, New York, NY 10018, USA

BLOOMSBURY is a trademark of Bloomsbury Publishing Plc

First published by Palgrave in 2013
Reprinted 2015
Reprinted by Bloomsbury in 2018
on behalf of the
British Film Institute
21 Stephen Street, London W1T 1LN
www.bfi.org.uk

The BFI is the lead organisation for film in the UK and the distributor of
Lottery funds for film. Our mission is to ensure that film is central to our
cultural life, in particular by supporting and nurturing the next generation
of filmmakers and audiences. We serve a public role which covers the cultural,
creative and economic aspects of film in the UK.

© British Film Institute 2013
Introduction and editorial arrangement © Brian Winston 2013
Individual essays © their respective authors 2013

The authors have asserted their rights under the Copyright, Designs and
Patents Act, 1988, to be identified as authors of this work.

For legal purposes the Acknowledgements on p. v constitute an extension of this
copyright page.

Cover design: couch
Cover images © (front) Kim Longinotto; *A Diary for Timothy* (Humphrey Jennings,
1945), Crown Film Unit; (back) Dziga Vertov; Robert Flaherty and Ricky Leacock
filming *Louisiana Story* (Robert Flaherty, 1948), Robert J. Flaherty Productions Inc.;
Chronique d'un été (Jean Rouch, 1961), Argos Films; *Vtr St. Jacques* (Bonnie Sherr Klein,
1969), National Film Board of Canada

All rights reserved. No part of this publication may be reproduced or transmitted
in any form or by any means, electronic or mechanical, including photocopying,
recording, or any information storage or retrieval system, without prior permission
in writing from the publishers.

Bloomsbury Publishing Plc does not have any control over, or responsibility for, any
third-party websites referred to or in this book. All internet addresses given in this
book were correct at the time of going to press. The author and publisher regret any
inconvenience caused if addresses have changed or sites have ceased to exist, but
can accept no responsibility for any such changes.

A catalogue record for this book is available from the British Library.

Library of Congress Cataloging-in-Publication Data
A catalog record for this book is available from the Library of Congress.

ISBN: PB: 978-1-8445-7341-7
     HB: 978-1-8445-7342-4

Typeset by Cambrian Typesetters, Camberley, Surrey
Printed and bound in Great Britain

To find out more about our authors and books visit www.bloomsbury.com
and sign up for our newsletters.

Contents

Acknowledgments

Rebecca Barden at the BFI is this book's 'onlie begetter' as she commissioned its writing and held me to the task. So she must head the list of those to whom I owe thanks.

Others, though, have also had considerable impact on shaping my agenda here. Primary among those is the informal grouping of documentary studies scholars around the Visible Evidence series of international conferences on the form. Visible Evidence celebrates its twentieth anniversary this year and this *Documentary Film Book* can be seen, in some sense, as an expression of Visible Evidence's concerns and is offered in honour of the series' survival and longevity. This does not mean that all my contributors are necessarily connected to the conference – they are not. Nor, of course, can I claim that all of the concerns raised at Visible Evidence over the years are here reflected: the agenda and any faults it has are mine alone. Rather, it is that the rising interest in documentaries which has occurred over the last two and more decades has been nowhere (within the academy) better symbolised than by these annual gatherings.

In 1990 Jeanne Hall, whose recent PhD had dealt with *Primary*, took a position at the University of Ohio which had a tradition of hosting single-theme film conferences.[1] Charged with arranging that year's event, she chose to focus on documentary. As I detail in the Introduction below, not having had too much of a platform elsewhere, this opportunity to share ideas and research was very welcomed by the participants – a then small band of scholars who specialised in studying documentary. The conference's papers appeared in a special edition of *Wide Angle*.[2] Informal conversations among the participants – the most focused took place at the airport as some were leaving – suggested that it might be a good idea to meet again the following year. Jane Gaines arranged this at Duke and the Visible Evidence series was born. Such has been the level of interest that at each gathering volunteers have appeared offering to host subsequent conferences. Volunteers, too, have established a series of monographs and a website in the Visible Evidence name but there has never been any need to formalise the organisation. This, for me, speaks volumes as to the genuineness of the enthusiasm which has sustained Visible Evidence and which I hope also is reflected in this volume too.

Some more particular acknowledgments are also due. I must thank Chi Wang and the Communications University of China, Beijing, for affording me the opportunity to think through again this first century (more or less) of documentary. The result is the Introduction (below).

Of course, my biggest debt of gratitude goes to my contributors. The effectiveness of what follows as a *vade mecum* entirely depends on their efforts; but John Corner further helped me clarifying the Introduction and Abé Mark Nornes pointed out some implications of my original plan for the book which needed to be corrected. Bert Hogenkamp, Michael Chanan and Patty Zimmerman also rectified at least some of my egregious errors. I am in all their debts.

The Foreword is extracted and reprinted with permission of the author from his 'Why Documentaries Matter' pamphlet (Oxford: Reuters Institute for the Study of Journalism, 2012).

Chapter 1.1 is reprinted from Bill Nichols, 'The Question of Evidence, the Power of Rhetoric and Documentary Film', in Thomas Austin and Wilma De Jong (eds), *Rethinking Documentary: New Perspectives, New Practices* (Maidenhead: Open University/McGraw Hill, 2008), pp. 28–37, with permission of the Open University Press.

Chapter 1.9 is reworked from the editor's 'Treatment: Documentary as Drama', in his *Claiming the Real II: Documentary: Grierson and Beyond* (London: BFI, 2005), pp. 107–27.

Chapter 4.3 is extracted and reprinted from Pearl Bowser, 'Pioneers of Black Document', in Phyllis Klotman and Janet Cutler (eds), *Struggles for Representation: African American Documentary Film and Video* (Bloomington: Indiana University Press, 1999), pp. 1–33, with permission of the Indiana University Press.

And I thank the Drs Gail Vanstone and Frances Mannsåker, as well as Joy Tucker and (not for the first time) Sophie Contento for their help and attention in bringing this task to completion.

NOTES

1. Jeanne tragically died in 2011, too soon to have her role in assisting the establishment of this current phase of documentary studies properly celebrated. We owe her a special debt of gratitude for having done this.
2. *Wide Angle* vol 13, 1991.

Notes on Contributors

IAN AITKEN is Professor of Film Studies at Hong Kong Baptist University. He is the author of, among others: *Film and Reform: John Grierson and the Documentary Film Movement* (1990), *The Documentary Film Movement: An Anthology* (1998), *Alberto Cavalcanti* (2001), *European Film Theory and Cinema* (2001), *Realist Film Theory and Cinema* (2006) and *The Encyclopedia of the Documentary Film* (2006) (concise edition: 2012).

ANA AMADO has a PhD in Literature from the University of Leiden and is Professor of Theory and Cinematographic Criticism in the Philosophy and Literature School of University of Buenos Aires. She is author of *La imagen justa. Cine argentino y política* (2009) and co-author of *Lazos de familia. Herencias, cuerpos, ficciones* (2004) and *Espacios de Igualdad. ABC de un periodismo no sexista* (1996). She was awarded a Guggenheim Fellowship in 2010.

ANITA BIRESSI is Reader in Media Cultures at the University of Roehampton. Her research interests include popular factual television, tabloid culture and class and culture. She is the co-author with Heather Nunn of *Class and Contemporary British Culture* (2013).

TIM BOON, curator and historian of the public culture of science, is Head of Research and Public History at the Science Museum, London. His first book, *Films of Fact: A History of Science in Documentary Films and Television* was published in 2008.

STELLA BRUZZI is Professor of Film and Television Studies at the University of Warwick and her publications include: *Undressing Cinema: Clothing and Identity in the Movies* (1997), *New Documentary* (2000 and 2006), *Bringing Up Daddy: Fatherhood and Masculinity in Post-war Hollywood* (2005) and *Seven Up* (2006). She was awarded a Leverhulme Major Research Fellowship in 2011 and is researching 'Approximation: Documentary, History and the Staging of Reality', a monograph examining contemporary representations of reality and history.

MICHAEL CHANAN started out as a music critic and made his first films for BBC Two on musical subjects. He is the author of several books on the social history of music, as well as others on various aspects of cinema. He is Professor of Film and Video at the University of Roehampton. He blogs as Putney Debater (www.putneydebater.com), and his latest film is *Secret City* (www.secretcity-thefilm.com).

IAN CHRISTIE is a film historian, critic and curator, currently Professor of Film and Media History at Birkbeck College, University of London. He is a Fellow of the British Academy and Vice-President of Europa Cinemas (which supports exhibitors throughout Europe, Asia and South America that show European films). He has a longstanding interest in Russian film, before, during and after the Soviet period, and has published extensively on it.

JOHN CORNER is currently Visiting Professor in Communication Studies at the University of Leeds and an Emeritus Professor of the University of Liverpool. He has published widely on documentary forms, including in *The Art of Record* (1996), *Public Issue Television* (2007) and *Theorising Media: Power, Form and Subjectivity* (2011). With colleagues, he is completing a book on media genre and political culture.

HELEN DE MICHIEL is a San Francisco-based independent film- and new media-maker and writer. Her most recent transmedia work, *Lunch Love Community*, can be watched and shared at www.lunchlovecommunity.org. She is a recipient of the Rockefeller Intercultural Film/Video Fellowship, and has served as the National Director of the National Alliance for Media Arts and Culture and as a board member of the George F. Peabody Awards for Electronic Media. She is a visiting scholar at the University of Oregon.

JON DOVEY is Professor of Screen Media at the University of the West of England. A programme-maker and video artist before becoming an academic, Jon has published on first-person film-making, camcorder cultures and simulation in factual TV. He has been working with Mandy Rose through the Digital Cultures Research Centre (DCRC), which he set up in 2009. In 2011 DCRC convened iDocs, the first UK academic conference looking at the emergent field of interactive documentary.

TAYLOR DOWNING is an award-winning producer of historical documentaries; he has run Flashback Television for more than twenty years. His history series include *Battle Stations*, *The Lost Evidence*, *Andy McNab's Tour of Duty* and *1983: The Brink of Apocalypse* (winner of the Grierson Award for Best Historical Documentary in 2008). He also writes about television history. His recent books include *Cold War* (with Jeremy Isaacs, 2008), *Riefenstahl's Olympia* and *The World at War* (both 2012).

ZOË DRUICK is an associate professor in the School of Communication at Simon Fraser University, who has published widely on the history of reality-based media. She published *Projecting Canada: Government Policy and Documentary Film at the National Film Board* in 2007 and is currently co-editing a book on John Grierson's international legacy.

NICK FRASER has been editor of BBC *Storyville* since its creation. He is a contributing editor of *Harper's Magazine* and the author of six non-fiction books, including *Why Documentaries Matter* (2012). In 2005, he was the first recipient of the Grierson Trustees' Award, recognising his outstanding contribution to the art of documentary.

ANDY GLYNNE is a director, producer and author. He is currently Managing Director of Mosaic Films. Andy initially trained as a clinical psychologist; he became involved in documentaries around fifteen years ago, when he founded the Documentary Filmmakers Group. He has directed and produced numerous films for broadcasters both in the UK and overseas, including over twenty animated documentaries, including the BAFTA and RTS award-winning series *Animated Minds*.

ANN GRAY is Professor of Cultural Studies at the University of Lincoln. She has published on research methods, new entertainment technologies and audience studies. Her most recent book *History on Television* (2012), co-authored with Erin Bell, is a multi-layered analysis of the televising of history in the late twentieth and early twenty-first centuries. She is a founding editor of the *European Journal of Cultural Studies*.

SUSANNA HELKE is a documentary film-maker (whose films include *The Idle Ones*, 2001; *Playground*, 2010; *American Vagabond*, 2013) based in Helsinki, Finland. She presently works as Professor of Documentary Film at Aalto University.

PAUL HENLEY is a full professor at the University of Manchester, where he has been director of the Granada Centre for Visual Anthropology since its foundation in 1987. Previously, he trained as an anthropologist at the University of Cambridge and as a director-cameraman at the National Film and Television School.

CRAIG HIGHT is a senior lecturer with the Screen and Media Studies Department at the University of Waikato. His current research focuses on the relationships between digital media technologies and documentary practice, especially the variety of factors shaping online documentary cultures.

ANNETTE HILL is a professor of Media at Lund University, Sweden. Her research focuses on audiences, genre and media experiences. Her most recent book is *Paranormal Media: Audiences, Spirits and Magic in Popular Culture* (2011). Other books include *Restyling Factual TV* (2007) *and Reality TV* (2005). Her next book is *Media Experiences: Producers and Audiences of Reality TV* (forthcoming, 2015).

BERT HOGENKAMP works as a media historian for the Netherlands Institute for Sound and Vision in Hilversum. He is also Professor by Special Appointment at the VU University Amsterdam. Hogenkamp has published extensively on the history of the documentary film and the use of film by the labour movement. Currently he is preparing the third volume of his history of the documentary film in the Netherlands.

JONATHAN KAHANA is Associate Professor of Film and Digital Media at the University of California, Santa Cruz, where he directs the Center for Documentary Arts and Research. He is the author of *Intelligence Work: The Politics of American Documentary* (2008) and the editor of *The Documentary Film Reader* (forthcoming).

DOUGLAS KELLNER is George Kneller Chair in the Philosophy of Education at UCLA and is author of many books on social theory, politics, history and culture, including *Cinema Wars: Hollywood Film and Politics in the Bush–Cheney Era* (2009) and the just published *Media Spectacle and Insurrection, 2011: From the Arab Uprisings to Occupy Everywhere!* (2012).

RICHARD KILBORN is Honorary Senior Research Fellow in Film, Media and Journalism Studies at the University of Stirling. His main research interests are in film and television documentary. His most recent book is *Taking the Long View: A Study of Longitudinal Documentary* (2010).

ALISA LEBOW is a senior lecturer in Screen Media at Brunel University. Her research is generally concerned with issues related to documentary film, recently to do with questions of the political in documentary. Her books *Cinema of Me* (2012) and *First Person Jewish* (2008) explore aspects of the representation of self and subjectivity in first-person film.

JULIA LESAGE is co-founder and co-editor of *Jump Cut: A Review of Contemporary Media* (www.ejumpcut.org), Professor Emerita from the University of Oregon and co-editor of *Media, Culture, and the Religious Right* (1998).

RAYA MORAG is an associate professor of Cinema Studies at the Department of Communication and Journalism, The Hebrew University of Jerusalem, Israel. Her research and publications deal with trauma and ethics, and corporeal-feminist film critique. She is the author of *Defeated Masculinity: Post-Traumatic Cinema in the Aftermath of War* (2009), *The Defeated Male: Cinema, Trauma, War* (2011) and *Waltzing with Bashir: Perpetrator Trauma and Cinema* (2013).

MARIA DORA MOURÃO has a doctrate from the University of São Paulo, where she is now Vice-Dean of the School of Communications and Arts and Professor of Editing Theory in the Film, Radio and Television Department. She is co-editor of *O Cinema do Real* [*The Cinema of the Real*], published in Brazil (Portuguese, 2005) and in Argentina (Spanish, 2011). She is President of CILECT (Centre International de Liaison des Ecoles de Cinéma et Télévision [International Association of Film and Television Schools]).

CHARLES MUSSER is Professor of American Studies and Film Studies at Yale University, where he teaches critical studies and production courses on documentary and silent cinema. He recently completed the seventy-two-minute documentary *Errol Morris: A Lightning Sketch* (2013).

BILL NICHOLS's book *Representing Reality* (1991) launched the modern study of documentary film. His subsequent book, *Introduction to Documentary* (2nd edn, 2010), is the most widely used textbook on documentary film. He is also the author of *Engaging Cinema* (2010), the first introductory film studies text to stress film's relation to society. Nichols consults frequently with documentary film-makers on their projects.

ABÉ MARK NORNES is chair of the Department of Screen Arts and Cultures and Professor of Asian Cinema in the Department of Asian Languages and Cultures, University of Michigan. He is author of *Forest of Pressure: Ogawa Shinsuke and Postwar Japanese Documentary Film* (2007) and *Japanese Documentary Film: From the Meiji Era to Hiroshima* (2003). Nornes was also a coordinator for the Yamagata International Documentary Film Festival from 1990 to 2005.

HEATHER NUNN is Professor of Culture and Politics at the University of Roehampton. Her research interests include gender and politics, documentary and reality TV, images of childhood and cultural studies and social class. She is the

co-author with Anita Biressi of *Class and Contemporary British Culture* (2013).

DEREK PAGET is Visiting Fellow in the Department of Film, Theatre and Television, University of Reading, and is the author of *True Stories?: Documentary Drama on Radio, Screen and Stage* (1990) and *No Other Way To Tell It: Docudrama on Film and Television* (2011). An associate editor of *Studies in Documentary Film*, he is also on the editorial board of *Studies in Theatre and Performance*.

CARL PLANTINGA is Professor of Film and Media Studies at Calvin College. Among his books are *Rhetoric and Representation in Nonfiction Film* (1997) and, as co-editor, *The Routledge Companion to Philosophy and Film* (2009). He is currently president of the Society for Cognitive Studies of the Moving Image.

CHRISTOPHER PULLEN is Senior Lecturer in Media Studies at Bournemouth University. He is widely published in the area of sexuality and contemporary media, and is involved in public political activism regarding the representation of LGBTs within the media. He is the author of *Documenting Gay Men: Identity and Performance in Reality Television and Documentary Film* (2007) and *Gay Identity, New Storytelling and the Media* (2009). Also he is the co-editor of *LGBT Identity and Online New Media* (2010).

MICHAEL RENOV, Professor of Critical Studies and Vice-Dean for Academic Affairs, University of Southern California, is the author of *Hollywood's Wartime Woman: Representation and Ideology* (1987) and *The Subject of Documentary* (2004), editor of *Theorizing Documentary* (1993) and co-editor of *Resolutions: Contemporary Video Practices* (1995), *Collecting Visible Evidence* (1999), *The SAGE Handbook of Film Studies* (2008) and *Cinema's Alchemist: The Films of Péter Forgács* (2012).

MANDY ROSE is a senior research fellow at the Digital Cultures Research Centre, University of the West of England. Her practice-led research looks at the intersection between documentary and the social, semantic and open web. Since the mid-1990s Mandy has overseen award-winning participatory media projects including the BBC's *Mass Observation* camcorder project, *Video Nation* (1994–2000) and *Capture Wales* (2001–7), a pioneering digital storytelling project in the UK.

PRATAP RUGHANI is an award-winning documentary film director and writer and is Course Director of MA Documentary Film at London College of Communication, University of Arts London.

DAVE SAUNDERS holds a PhD on documentary film from the University of London and has written and taught extensively on the subject. His previous publications include *Direct Cinema: Observational Documentary and the Politics of the Sixties* (2007) and the *Routledge Film Guidebook: Documentary* (2010).

N. FRANK UKADIKE teaches in the Department of Communication and the Program in African and African Diaspora Studies at Tulane University, New Orleans. He is the author of *Black African Cinema* (1994), *Questioning African Cinema: Conversations with Filmmakers* (2002) and has published many articles in journals and anthologies. He has completed work on the anthology, *Breaking Canons: New Approaches to African Cinema Discourse*.

GENEVIÈVE VAN CAUWENBERGE teaches documentary film at the University of Liège and is former chair of its Communication Department. She holds a PhD in Cinema Studies from New York University. She has contributed to numerous international research projects on documentary (*L'âge d'or du documentaire, Dic Doc*) and her publications cover a wide range of topics, with particular focus on French and Belgian documentary, especially on the work of Chris Marker, Agnès Varda and Edmond Bernhard.

ELENA VON KASSEL SIAMBANI holds a BA from Sarah Lawrence College, as well as a Maîtrise, DEA and doctorate in film studies from the universities of Paris I Sorbonne – Panthéon and Paris X Nanterre. Her work includes *Humphrey Jennings, le poète du cinéma britannique* (2009) – the first book on the film-maker in French. She teaches film and theatre at the University of Paris III Sorbonne Nouvelle and is Associate Research Fellow at CATH Research Centre, De Montfort University.

THOMAS WAUGH is Concordia University Research Chair in Sexual Representation and Documentary, and teaches film studies, queer studies and sexuality in the Mel Hoppenheim School of Cinema, Montreal. His most recent book is *The Right To Play Oneself: Looking Back On Documentary Film* (2011), and he is completing a major monograph on Joris Ivens.

DEANE WILLIAMS is Associate Professor, Film and Television Studies, Monash University. He is editor of *Studies in Documentary Film* and his books include *Australian Post-War Documentary Films: An Arc of Mirrors* (2008) and, with Brian McFarlane, *Michael Winterbottom* (2009).

BRIAN WINSTON is the Lincoln Professor at the University of Lincoln and is chair of the British Association of Film, Television and Screen Studies. He has written extensively on the documentary (*Claiming the Real II* [2005]; *Lies, Damn Lies and Documentaries* [2000]) and has a US prime-time Emmy for documentary scriptwriting (for WNET). He scripted an Irish feature documentary on Robert Flaherty, *A Boatload of Wild Irishmen* (for TG4: winner – Special Jury Award, British University Film and Video Council, 'Learning on Screen' Awards, 2012).

EZRA WINTON is pursuing a PhD (ABD) in Communication Studies at Carleton University, where his research and teaching interests include radical and alternative media, social movements, and documentary cinema, institutions and culture. His dissertation looks at the cultural politics of documentary as seen through the lens of Toronto's Hot Docs film festival. Ezra is the co-founder and Director of Programming of Cinema Politica, the world's largest grassroots documentary screening network, and is the co-founder of Art Threat, a cultural policy and political art blog.

PETER WINTONICK is a Montreal-based film-maker, producer, critic and docmedia operative who works all over the world. As a documentary diplomat, he has his finger in many pies, including *Point of View Magazine*, where he is the international editor. As an award winner of the major Media and Arts prize given by the British Queen's representative in Canada, and as a regular civilian, he encounters many new digital ideas, schemes, initiatives and startups. Most of them fail; many evaporate into smoke and mirrors. Nevertheless, he trundles on.

PATRICIA R. ZIMMERMANN is Professor of Cinema, Photography and Media Arts at Ithaca College. She is also co-director of the Finger Lakes Environmental Film Festival. Her books include *Reel Families: A Society History of Amateur Film* (1995), *States of Emergency: Documentaries, Wars, Democracies* (2000) and *Mining the Home Movie: Excavations in Histories and Memories* (2007).

Foreword: Why Documentaries Matter[1]

NICK FRASER Editor, *Storyville* (BBC)

Reality is Providence.

Al Maysles

But they never said how beautiful it was.

George Orwell
(on reading the reviews of *Animal Farm*)

This is an argument in favour of documentaries. Think of them taxonomically, not as a tribe, but a vast assemblage of variegated fowls or mammals constituting a species whose continued existence everyone finds hard to explain. They're among the least valued, and most interesting, cultural forms of our time. Improbably, however, they have emerged from a cave of unknowing into something like sunlight, enjoying a certain vogue. Greater things are expected of them, as if they had somehow displaced print journalism in our efforts to understand things; and they are now being sold as a means to save the world. I am in part sympathetic to such ambitions, and I regard the current success of documentaries as no more than a recognition belatedly afforded to them.

Nonetheless, the much-hailed triumph of documentary films subsists on the shakiest of foundations. After many years, shoulder to the wheel, I am concerned by the increasing difficulty in funding them. Why are most people who make documentaries, even by the appalling standards of freelance journalism, so poor? Can documentaries be funded as books and print are, by the market? Will they be assisted by new possibilities of payment made possible by the internet? Are the economics of documentaries so hopelessly skewed that this isn't an option? Should they continue to rely on television, with which they enjoy a relationship best characterised as a long, intermittently satisfactory marriage of convenience, in which both partners grumblingly submit, with occasional, overwhelmingly unsuccessful, attempts to change things, or even attempts to get free, dissolving the union? Are documentaries a definitively niche form? Should they be thought of as campaigning tools, as just one aspect of the many efforts to improve the world? Do they really change anything?

Among the relatively small number of people whose job it is to commission documentaries and the larger group who make them, often under forbidding circumstances, such questions are hotly debated. My own conclusions are that documentaries are attractive, sturdy hybrids, capable of survival in adverse circumstances. They do many things for us, most of them good. They will benefit best not by systematised assistance, but by our ability to calculate or guess, with a degree of approximation, what is best for them. We can best do that if we think about how they work for us.

Documentaries began as a casual experiment in seeing what happened when you pointed a camera at the things around you. They never caught on in cinemas, and were displaced by fiction. For a long time the genre was kept alive by a mixture of corporate and government patronage, with mixed results. Broadcast television saved the form, supplying documentaries with a steady supply of funds and enabling films to reach large audiences. Recently, however, broadcasters have appeared to tire of documentaries. They are shown in cinemas, with fitful results, and they are beginning to carve out a place online. The partial liberation of documentaries from television has enabled film-makers to produce a great number of brilliant films, to the degree that it may now be said that the documentary has finally become a recognisable cultural form. But so much success hasn't resolved the precarious nature of documentary film, far from it; and film-makers still struggle to make good work.

Nowadays it's common to hear documentary film described as the new rock'n'roll. It was a documentary that saved Al Gore from political oblivion, winning him an Oscar. Few Hollywood directors have actually made documentaries (Scorsese is an exception, though Werner Herzog has been able once again to make fictions as a consequence of his successful documentaries), but it has become commonplace to see the names of Brad Pitt, Leonardo DiCaprio or Sam Mendes attached to films as executive producers. Patrons such as the Ford Foundation, George Soros, Robert Redford's Sundance Institute, Gucci and Puma lend their blessing, giving funds to film-makers.

And in 2010 Oprah Winfrey bestowed her own special benediction on the documentary form at Sundance, pledging to do for it what she had done for books by creating a documentary club on her brand new cable channel OWN.

Among film festivals, Sundance occupies a special place. It's keenly cutting edge, a bit *recherché*, and it has a record of having been right about the direction taken by film culture. People will keep you abreast of gossip at Sundance, and that tends to be focused on the deals being done that lift the odd, successful film from obscurity to success. But another preoccupation has crept into the Sundance scene. People talk about documentary films now. They don't tend to say how much money these films are about to make. Instead they tell each other how good the docs are, how much better indeed than the fictional offerings. Films that only a few years ago would have been restricted to the smallest audiences are now packed out. They're received rapturously, and audiences are reluctant to let their makers leave the Q&A sessions afterwards.

I've watched documentary films on behalf of my own patron and employer, the BBC. I've reached the point where I can no longer recall how many thousands of films I have seen. The irony is that for a long time I didn't really like documentaries. I had an omnivorous interest in different forms of reportage; specifically, I was interested in the ways in which reporters, while retaining a degree of objectivity, might shift public opinion. But I found many documentaries to be staid and predictable, overliteral in their approach and hobbled by an often unacknowledged left-wing bias. I became interested in them out of a hunch: that they were about to become important, and that I should try and stake some sort of claim in a new field.

On arrival in the BBC, in 1995, I was sent *Hoop Dreams*, a recently completed film chronicling five years in the lives of two black inner-city teenagers who wished to become basketball stars. The film was more than two hours and forty minutes long, and the first time I sat down to watch it I was interrupted after ten minutes. Luckily I persevered. As I had been told, the quality of the images improved after seventeen minutes, when the film-makers began to use a more up-to-date camera. But the story of William Gates and Arthur Agee was engulfing. After an hour you felt that knew them, and you knew all about the Chicago school system after an hour and a half. It was possible to think of *Hoop Dreams* as something new. In the 1960s, Norman Mailer began to refer to something called the 'non-fiction novel' in which the lives of real characters could be displayed in the sort of depth that one might associate with fiction. Although there were many series or long-form films accompanying individuals or communities over a long period of time,[2] no one as yet had attempted the same thing in the medium of film. In this respect, Hoop Dreams was a pioneering work, and an impressive one.

In 2011 one of the directors of *Hoop Dreams* was back at Sundance with *The Interrupters*, a two-and-a-half-hour account of the battles against violence waged by social

On arrival at the BBC, in 1995, I was sent *Hoop Dreams*

workers on Chicago's South Side. The film's premise was simple: violence was a plague. It could never be eradicated unless its root causes – decades of underemployment, a culture of macho, drugs, etc. – were eliminated, and that wasn't going to happen, not for decades anyhow. But it was possible to contain and even arrest the spread of violence. You did this by entering the gangs, persuading each of the members that they would die unless they, too, fought against the plague. Former gang members, often those who had spent time in prison on drug charges or even for murder, formed a cadre of specialists, dressed in a red livery and speaking in street idioms. James followed them as they went about their task, comforting the many bereaved families of murdered teenagers, urging gang members to desist.

I was struck, too, by something else – how used to watching long films the audience had become, and how easily accepted was the slang of the South Side. There was nothing staid or unoriginal about *The Interrupters*. But the passionate applause showed how, courtesy of fictions such as *The Wire*, which were themselves heavily influenced, even dominated by the documentary tradition, with their shaky cameras, their discontinuities and crusading naming names style, films like *The Interrupters* were part of a mainstream now. This was another marker in the wide, general acceptance of ambitious, well-made documentaries.[3]

'Documentary', says the dictionary. 'Noun. Based on or recreating an actual event, era, life story, that purports to be factually accurate and contains no fictional elements'. This is useful, so far it goes, but excessively minimal. Why shouldn't non-fiction contain elements of fiction? And why should something only 'purport' to be factually accurate? When you describe anything, it is altered. The act of seeing plainly modifies what is seen. It isn't necessary to be a visionary to understand this. Plainly, too, the photographic recording of actuality complicates things. I AM A CAMERA, Christopher Isherwood's famous formulation, isn't in the least convincing. We may own or use photographic means of reproduction, but we aren't cameras. But the discussion of documentaries has been dogged, perhaps understandably, by photographic literalism.

In a late, elegiac poem, 'Epilogue', Robert Lowell comes closest to recreating the act of description:

> Yet why not say what happened?
> Pray for the grace of accuracy
> Vermeer gave to the sun's illumination
> Stealing like the tide across a map
> To his girl solid with yearning.
> We are poor passing facts,
> Warned by that to give
> Each figure in the photograph
> His living name.

Lowell died a year after writing this poem, in the back of a New York taxi, clutching a Lucian Freud portrait of his estranged girlfriend. He was only fifty-nine, and his life had been marred by the grotesque deformations of reality caused by a severe bipolar affliction. I like these sad end-of-life lines because they show that there's no real conflict between the desire for accuracy and the spirit of illumination. You might think ('poor passing facts') that saying exactly what happened is a lowly, banal activity. No, Lowell is saying, it isn't, it's far from being banal. Indeed, it is so important that one must pray for it. It does represent a kind of grace, though not of course in any religious sense. But there is no single reliable way of capturing anything, as a second, more careful reading of the poem reveals. The sun steals across our lives. We map its course – but how do we know how this is done? We might conclude that there is some Zen-like secret implied by the art of observing things. In reality, we are changed by the act of observation, as well as the objects and people on which we try to focus. We cannot rely on anything, let alone sight, or any machine as fallible as a camera. Most likely, we will resolve to hope for the best, repudiating both literalism and the excess use of metaphors. At the very least 'documentation' requires a copious supply of guile and stealth, combined with the sort of exactitude that allows one to single out a Cartier Bresson photograph at any reasonable distance. Let's be honest, drudgery is part of it, and rote, as well as obsessiveness. But nothing, as Lowell insists, should rightly be excluded. How else will the names come alive?

Documentaries do have their enemies, conscious or inadvertent, and I can anticipate a degree of opposition to these claims. Why fret about the future of a lowly form, widely considered to be on a par with the other offerings of television? Why attempt to elevate what is no more than the cunning assembly of sound and images into more or less plausible narratives? Documentaries, it will be said, have for a long time occupied a humble position in the television economy, securing audiences reliably for a relatively low cost. Many people, year after year, were comforted by the experience of watching slices of life carved out of familiar material for their distraction. There is no need, surely, to investigate their relationship with reality. My reply to such observations is that the widespread uncritical acceptance of documentaries did damage their prospects. A cultural snobbery still surrounds documentaries. They've been regarded as filler, primarily, alternatively as a form of agitprop – and they are still condescended to, by journalists (though less so recently) and film critics.

We would do well to recall their origins. Take, first, an extreme example of the degree to which the depiction of reality in film was prejudiced by its associations with the state. In 1997 I went to St Petersburg in order to work with the film-maker Viktor Kossakovsky on *Wednesday*, a film in which he rendered in counterpoint the day of his own birth, 19 July 1961, with the lives of others born on the same day in the city that was then part of the Soviet Union, and known as Leningrad. Under Communism, everyone was supposed to be equal and therefore enjoy a similar life, and Viktor's efforts were directed to demonstrating how the contrary had happened. A few of those he found had indeed got rich, but most were poor – some were alcoholics or drug addicts – and the film showed signs of slipping into a contemporary description of the St Petersburg lower depths. We needed to show what had been dreamed of in the days of identical ambitions, egalitarian cribs and Pioneer rallies. So Viktor and I went to Lenfilm, the old Communist archives located in a crumbling Stalinist-era building still decorated with plaques in red and dirty white, and watched archive films for a day. We found footage of identical white beds in which small, newly arrived Soviet citizens nestled silently. We also saw samples of lavishly produced weekly accounts of life in which nothing significant happened. The big event was a visit of a surprisingly svelte Fidel Castro, or Nikita Khrushchev's bulky form, sighted in a Ukrainian dairy farm. And it was in this respect that our visit proved to be revealing – as a revelation of how much that was filmed, recorded, known as documentaries, was in fact wholly impersonal, dictated by forgotten needs, laid down to plan. There was no idea of any independently acquired truth here, no sense that one could go out with a camera, as one might bearing a pad and a pencil, and simply describe what was happening. Everything was pre-arranged, controlled from the top.

A milder form of such attitudes was pervasive among broadcasters. They were obliged to serve mass audiences, and it became part of the job of television executives to vet product, ensuring its acceptability. In response to such actions, and as a revolt against mass culture, experimental films were highly prized. Documentaries, too, must follow the route of experimentation. Briefly, in the 1970s and 80s, it became fashionable within academies to speak of the death of the author. Critics, viewers or readers, writers and directors were merely rummaging around in pre-existing artefacts or habits in a quest to update them. Was it possible to be original? Could one even purport to tell the truth? Observers of the cultural scene would reply with a shrug or a nod implying that the question was a stupid one. Forget about individuals, they said, in one dogmatic article after another. Forget about individuals. All that matters is the pattern in the carpet.

Postmodernism is mercifully out of fashion now, but among film critics the view that documentaries do or should resemble narrative fictions remains widespread. A crop of films mixing fact with fiction prompted these thoughts from Nigel Andrews, film critic of the *Financial Times*:

Think about it. Do we still buy, if we ever did, the notion that non-fiction on-screen is anything other than an artefact? That it is not shot through with point-of-view, with the cultural perspectives and prejudices of the day? That it is not as storied and subjective, in its way, as a narrative feature film?[4]

In the *Guardian*, Stella Bruzzi, author of *New Documentary*, similarly applauds films 'that are all about the fluctuation between what's staged and what's real'.[5] She thinks that audiences can learn to watch films for their capacity to play with our ideas of the truth.

I doubt that this is the case. Mixing fact and fiction is a strategy beloved of film aesthetes and Hollywood producers. It has become routine for fictional narratives to claim to be 'real'. How many mainstream Hollywood films each year pay homage to the conventions of documentary film? Any representation of reality, in any medium, can reasonably be described as an artefact. But that doesn't mean that all representations are false, or that the ability to distinguish between fact and fiction isn't important.

Why are documentaries not always taken seriously when it comes to giving an account of the world? Among British journalists, themselves seasoned practitioners of the fictionalisation of reality, documentaries were for many years regarded with deep suspicion. It was alleged that most documentaries were faked – those who made them decided on the story, and went out and filmed what they needed. Often the belief that documentaries were fictional coincided with an intense attraction to them. In *The Kindness of Women*, one of his autobiographical volumes, J. G. Ballard describes a visit to a Copacabana festival of 'scientific and documentary films'. Ballard is excited by the films that will never 'reach the general public': bizarre footage of stress fractures of ice, hockey players, split septums, but most of all, as one would expect from the author of *Crash*, the sexual imagery used to desensitise habitual sex offenders:

The audience ... gazed at the screen with the same steady eyes and the unflinching gaze of the men in the Soho porn theatres or the fans of certain types of apocalyptic science fiction. Whenever the criminal subjects winced with pain or vomited into their sick basins, ripples of appreciation would move across the audience at some particularly striking camera angle or expository close-up as the Soho patrons might have applauded a telling crutch shot or elegant anal penetration.[6]

In Ballard's novel *The Day of Creation*, French film-makers come to Africa in order to make a 'bogus documentary' about the reclamation of Eden from the desert. When the project they wish to film gets out of hand, defying their expectations, they are swept along in the chaos, caught up in violence. They never finish their film.

Perverse and wonderfully attached to normality, J. G. Ballard was, as one might expect, an aficionado of lenses, light meters, obsessively interested in the details of filming. He also thought that, given the chance, human beings would bend whatever new means of communications to their will, turning its truth-telling capabilities into convenient lies. But it is surely significant that Ballard's masterpiece, *Empire of the Sun*, is constructed like a documentary: rough at the surface, with many shifts of tone and abruptly memorable set pieces depicting young hero Jim's mysterious ability to grow up, despite hunger, the failings of adults and horror of the camp in which he finds himself. One can read the book as a version of a film that Ballard might have wished himself make, and of course never could do. But we know now that such films can be made. Indeed they are made, not every day, perhaps, but certainly every year.

Nonetheless the notion that documentaries are somehow inauthentic lives on. The writer Toby Young once pitched an idea to me of a fake documentary, centred around the efforts of a film-maker to uncover a conspiracy capable of explaining the world. In particular he wanted to capture the moody intensity of film-makers. Journalists had acquired a less sombre, more self-mocking view of their calling. If you worked for a newspaper you couldn't retain so great a sense of your importance, and you would certainly know how to tell lies. Besides, Toby suggested, no one watched documentaries. Why then were documentary film-makers so obsessed with what they did? Why did they sound like mendicant friars, dolefully tolling bells to warn us of their presence?

Film-makers themselves are by and large unable to shed much light on this mystery. They're concerned with the hows of their trade – practical things like access, visas, lenses and suchlike. (Light used to be a staple of their discourse, but following the invention of light-adaptable autofocusing cameras, this has fallen off the agenda.) They may talk about why they were attracted to certain narratives. But they are reluctant to say why one set of circumstances rather than another might make for a better, more involving, more lasting film. For a long time, pressed to explain the impact of their films, they would reply in the idiom of John Grierson, founding father of British documentary. Grierson, in his left-wing Calvinist way, believed that films should supply uplift through their capability of depicting good lives, or at least lives in which people strove for humanity, and into which the rest of us could enter, this seeing our sense of ourselves, as democrats and human beings, significantly enlarged by the experience. Viewing such singular, ordinary lives, audiences would experience a degree of solidarity. Many documentaries, to be sure, must have fulfilled this function, though it remains impossible to say how so many individual encounters with reality could have added up to something more significant. Nowadays, with so many channels, and the reluctance of

television executives to admit to any large-scale educative function of the medium, the idea of the documentary as a binding force in society, viewed by a large number of people and attesting to cultural solidarity, is in decline. It has been replaced, to be sure, by the idea that documentaries can be linked to campaigns and made to change the world. Is this more than a pious hope? On occasions, perhaps they can and do have such effects; but no evidence exists to suggest that film on its own is specially good at social mobilisation. Nor is it evident that film-makers will be well served by seeing their films bundled into social movements and made to serve the interests of NGOs.

There are other reasons why documentaries can be considered captivating, and these have come to the fore in recent years. I was attracted to docs (after my initial misgivings) because I liked them. I still do and I also like the fact that, in my opinion, no serious body of theory exists to legitimate them. They have come to subsist, precariously, at a crossroads of contemporary culture, somewhere between journalism, film narrative and television entertainment. They appear to thrive on contradictions, between the stubborn reality they purport to capture and their necessarily limited means, between the impositions of storytelling and the desire, periodically, to interpret or analyse. They aren't fictional, ever, but they can seem in their attractiveness more real than reality. Ultimately, they remain provisional, snapshot-like; and it helps that they cannot be collected, and are thus immune to the unwelcome attentions of connoisseurs. In fact they appear to be doomed to remain on or outside the perimeters of the culture world, which accounts both for their freshness, and the relative poverty of those who make them.

No one should claim to say what a documentary is or should be. It doesn't seem right to wish to fence in the form, excluding the force fields – dramatic fictions, news, agitprop – that surround it. Nonetheless, here are some graffiti-style ways of characterising the good ones.

First, they should live ... be provisional. You shouldn't know where you are going when you start. Second, somewhere – not in a script, perhaps, or by means of a reportorial presence, but through editing, via the lens, or in a barely paraphrasable way, through what they are – there must be some notion of an author, or at least that the film was guided by an individual hand, or an association of individually motivated hands. Third, they must represent some sort of creative collision – not with reality, because that's a foolish idea, but with the idea of how anything can or should be depicted. Also, and this is rare, they should be occasionally funny. Most documentaries aren't funny. This is a mistake because the shock of the real isn't without its own humorous aspects.

Last, and most important, those who watch documentaries as well as those who make them should realise that, as the film-maker Kevin Macdonald likes to say, anything goes. There are traditions of film-making, to be sure. But the vitality of the documentary resides in the fact that it thrives at a series of crossroads scarred by accidents. You can arrive at the idea of documentary through tabloid journalism or philosophy, out of a desire to change the world, or merely because there is a story you wish to tell.

All you really have to want to do is say what happened.

NOTES

1. Taken from *Why Documentaries Matter* (Oxford: Reuters Institute for the Study of Journalism, 2012).
2. Mailer's masterpiece, *The Executioner's Song*, is 1,000-odd pages of meticulously edited documentary transcript, and many docs, not least *When We Were Kings* (1996) are graced by his presence. In Britain, such works as Michael Apted's *7 Up* series (1964 onwards), Paul Watson's *The Family* (1974), Molly Dineen's *The Ark* (1993) and Phil Agland's *Beyond the Clouds* (1994) are instances of long-form series in which the lives of so-called ordinary people receive intensive, often passionate attention. The vast oeuvre of Fred Wiseman is another example. But these films don't display the qualities of plotting to be found in *Hoop Dreams*, nor do they focus so intensively, in the style of novelists, on the emergence of character through incident.
3. *Hoop Dreams* was never nominated for an Oscar. *The Interrupters*, to the astonishment of people who make and talk about documentaries, failed even to make the short-list of films compiled each year by the committee appointed by the Academy.
4. *Financial Times*, 30 December 2010.
5. Xan Brooks, 'Can "Fake" Documentaries Still Tell the Truth?', *Guardian*, 30 September 2010, www.guardian.co.uk/film/2010/sep/30/fake-documentaries-the-arbor. Accessed 2 March 2013.
6. J. G. Ballard, *The Kindness of Women* (London: HarperCollins, 1991), pp. 240–1.

Introduction: The Documentary Film

BRIAN WINSTON

This volume is not an encyclopedia, dictionary or guide-book, much less a handbook, thesis or (hopefully) tract. Rather, it is a *vade mecum*, a collection of essays that any-body interested in the documentary film will find useful and illuminating to have about their person. It has been designed not to cover the waterfront but, instead, to offer a *tour d'horizon*, an overview of the present agenda of con-cerns in the emergent field of documentary studies. That there will be parts of the horizon which are obscured is inevitable, a function of the limitations of space and the editor's understanding; but its agenda is grounded in more than personal concerns. It reflects documentary studies largely as seen through the prism of a series of annual con-ferences on the documentary film which is now in its twentieth year.

The Visible Evidence conferences were born in reaction to disdain. As the study of cinema was being institution-alised within the American academy in 1970s, Christian Metz's pronunciation that '*Tous film est un film de fiction, et le cinéma en général est happé par la fiction*' became common cur-rency.[1] Although Metz was talking about the 'shadow' of the actor on the screen, the tag 'every film is a fiction film' soon came to constitute something of a roadblock to the study of documentary. It rendered its whole underlying premise sus-pect. The result of this was that, despite any film theory focus on the issue of realism, a body of film which made great claim on the real – documentary – was largely ignored; obviously, if all films were fiction, 'non-fiction' film was an oxymoron. Documentary film was a chimera.

Documentary played into this. For one thing, it could not easily explain what, exactly, it was. As a standard French text puts it, it was '*un objet filmique mal identifié*'.[2] It defied definition. On the European continent the form was subsumed into the category of *Kulturfilm* or the even more procrustean concept of *court-métrage* – a genre defined by duration, not content. In English, the term was considered, even by those who first used it in connection with cinema, as 'clumsy' (John Grierson).[3] And, whisper it not: thanks to the British pioneer Grierson's insistence, necessitated by funding realities that required public education be docu-mentary's primary remit, the films, as a body, could never match the excitements and wonder of the anglophone fic-tional cinema – of Hollywood. Documentary was a min-ority audience taste. Scholarly inattention was not entirely unjustified.

Nevertheless, the documentary was not completely ignored in the growing library of serious texts about the cinema. Leaving aside journalistic criticism which did on occasion pay meaningful attention to documentary, in the USSR in the 1920s there was a somewhat premature but vibrant theoretical debate about the problems inherent in filming actuality (e.g., in *The LEF Arena*, 1923).[4] Untranslated from the Russian, this was of course ignored in the West; but it was there waiting to be discovered. More readily to hand were the writings of the anglophone documentary pioneers themselves (e.g., Grierson, 1932;[5] Rotha, 1935[6]). Now, within rising academic concern with the cinema as a whole, some academic attention was (collaterally, as it were) paid to the form[7] (Barsam, 1973;[8] Barnouw, 1974[9]). Belatedly, in 1963, the Russian debate had been recovered in translation – if only into French.[10] This was, though, rather timely as the coming of the observational style of 1960s, with its enhanced claims to be presenting un-(or minimally)mediated evidence on the screen, encouraged theoretical argument. The prestige of Russian Formalism and the imprimatur of French awareness of it began to shift the logs of scholarly anglophone inattention to docu-mentary. There was even the first glimmer of a concern about the ethics of filming and exposing 'real' people on the screen.[11] But it was the efforts of a few in the 1980s that finally secured documentary studies in English if not a place in the sun, then certainly a seat in the shade. And the Visible Evidence conference can stand as a symbol of that general development.

The received story created by the pioneering writers on documentary had to be interrogated. In occasional critical work, documentary's totemic ancestors – Flaherty, Grierson, Reifenstahl, Lorenz etc. – had enjoyed glowing reputations as documentarists, whatever their far from inconsiderable ideological flaws; but now even the film-making skills were becoming tarnished. From the shadows new auteur heroes were glimpsed. Vertov and Jennings, for example, were better remembered and some contemporary practitioners were also being noticed. Especially after 1960, technological developments occasioned a serious debate about the limits of authenticity. Sixties concerns also resonated in documentary's rhetoric of social relevance which echoed some radical nineteenth-century artistic agendas.[12] Very often documentary's modus operandi could be seen as being close to that of critical investigative journalism. By the later 80s, this radical heritage and context – for all that the form's authenticity was being questioned in some quarters – clearly was of relevance in the face of the increasing neo-liberal assault on the post-World War II social settlement.[13] There was not much imaginary about that attack and, within cinema studies, some turned to documentary as a significant front in the clash. Michael Renov, for example, began worrying about documentary's underlying legitimacy in 1988, an effort which was to produce *Theorizing Documentary* in 1993.[14] By that time Bill Nichols had published his seminal *Representing Reality* (1991)[15] which can be said to mark the foundational moment establishing the agenda reflected in this book. The debate about theory was also beginning to catch up with the ignored sophistications of the Russians decades earlier; and the received history was undergoing significant revision as a result of deeper research into the paper archives.

THE RECEIVED HISTORY
(1895–1921–1935–1960)

The conventional history of the documentary in the West presented a somewhat overly technologically determined account. It had begun by indentifying a pre-documentary phase which lasted from the very first images of real events (e.g., *L'arrivée d'un train en gare de La Ciotat* [*Arrival of the Train at Ciotat Station*][16] in 1895 to the debut of the hit feature film ('of the travelogue kind') *Nanook of the North*, in 1922.[17] This last was said to inaugurate a classic silent documentary period that continued until the coming of synchronous (aka 'direct') sound, which, essentially because of financial limitations, happened in documentary somewhat after its introduction to the fictional mainstream. Synch in documentary was conventionally dated to the mid-1930s (e.g., *Housing Problems*, 1935);[18] but, such was the cumbersomeness of 35mm sound equipment, it was used sparingly. Voiceover narration with added sound effects and music was the norm. In the received account, this classic phase lasted until it was disturbed by the development of the 16mm hand-held synch-sound camera rig in 1960. With that advance, dramatically highlighted (in conventional accounts) by *Primary* (1960),[19] supposedly came a shift to a new, dominant 'fly-on-the-wall' observational, non-interventionist aesthetic best described as 'Direct Cinema'.

During the classic period – in this conventional formulation, from the 1920s through World War II to the Direct Cinema era – a range of techniques and approaches was adopted or developed. The tone of the films was unfailingly serious to the point where it was possible to talk, definitionally, of documentary as a 'discourse of sobriety'.[20] Despite the implicit need for 'objectivity' demanded by documentary's claim on the real, the world was acknowledged as being presented through the prism of the documentarist's own sober sensitivities. They were artists like any other and as a result documentaries could embrace poetic visions or express personal opinions in the form of political analysis – what was termed by the continental European radicals 'agitational propaganda' (agitprop). The documentary film-maker was no mere 'fly-on-the-wall' – even if the technology had allowed for such unobtrusiveness, which (of course) it did not.

Films were shot on tripod-mounted cameras, although during World War II combat cinematographers had begun regularly to hand-hold silent (i.e., unblimped, noisy) cameras. Observational material, even if illustrating personal, poetic or agitprop agendas, was the norm. The characters in the film were not to be 'actors' adopting other personas but 'real' people behaving 'naturally' – that is, as if the camera was not present: 'subjects'. Documentarists were 'allowed' by established practices to have subjects repeat actions so that editable footage (i.e., that which conformed to mainstream fictional film-making practice) could be taken. In short, a level of intervention by the documentary director was permitted and this was not held to vitiate a film's authenticity. Logically, then, the wholesale reconstruction of past events for the camera, on the basis of prior witness, was also legitimated. Films were usually shot on location but accurate duplications built as studio sets were also occasionally allowed. Lighting was permitted; it was especially needed when shooting interiors. With sound, documentarists began to interview witnesses (subjects), journalism-style, on film.

The mainstream's conventions, adopted by the fictional cinema for representing time and space (aka 'Hollywood Grammar'), were easily applied to documentary film. Audience understanding of how to 'read' a film, having been determined by the fictional film, would not have embraced anything much different. Since material had to be editable in this mainstream sense, inevitably no alternative 'film language' was developed for documentary. So, when shooting documentary, repeated actions by these 'real' subjects could be called for and cut into the initially captured shot without loss of legitimacy. Events could be cross-cut. During editing, the sound of a synchronous shot could also be overlaid on another shot, most usually in the form of a voice (i.e., synch in one shot continuing as voiceover in another). An authorial voice was permitted in the form of voiceover commentary. (In the silent period this last had taken the form of explanatory intertitles.) Music, and – after sound – added sound effects, were acceptable; as was the use of the archive of previously shot actuality material.

The conventional history of the documentary in the West: a somewhat overly technologically determined account: *L'arrivée d'un train en gare de La Ciotat* (1895); *Nanook of the North* (1922); *Housing Problems* (1935); *Primary* (1960)

Much of this interventionalism was to be rejected by Direct Cinema, however – and with it overt poetic pictorialism and agitprop etc. Nevertheless, it is possible to ignore the breaks of 1935(sound)/1960(16mm synch) to see the entire documentary effort from 1921 on as a continuous attempt to present reality evidentially. Throughout, the mark of the films was that they made this strong claim on the real but, despite this, at the same time allowed their makers to be considered as 'artists'. This did not change. Thus the documentary project absorbed studio sound technology in 1935 and in effect continued, despite a noisy rhetoric dismissing previous techniques, into the 1960s and beyond. The Direct Cinema style which then came to domi-

nance was not as revolutionary as it might have been – indeed, as it itself claimed to be. Certainly, Direct Cinema stridently denied the legitimacy of many techniques deployed in the classic period. Directing subjects, repeated actions, the use of tripods, extra lights, added sound, commentary, interviews – all were eschewed. Nevertheless, Direct Cinema did not so much remove the observational claim on the real made implicit in Grierson's vision as suggest that, if intervention was removed, it would now realise it, legitimately, for the first time. Documentary, the proponents of Direct Cinema claimed, was put on a new footing because of the new 16mm technology. The era of observational documentary's dominance – Direct Cinema's hegemony – began; but the promise, with its acceptance of the essential scientistic possibility that objective evidence could be presented on film, remained.

THE RECEIVED HISTORY CRITIQUED (1895–1960)

These dates are, anyway, somewhat arbitrary – a fact reflected in more than one of the chapters that follow. Flaherty did not create documentary from whole cloth in 1922. Films which can be indentified as having (in the phrase by which Grierson secured the term for a type of cinema) 'documentary value'[21] pre-exist *Nanook*, or co-exist with it. A variety of non-fiction forms were already in play: newsreel, clearly, but also scientific films;[22] ethnographic films;[23] sponsored films made for charities (e.g., *SOS Russia*, made in 1921 for the Save the Children Fund to raise relief for victims of the famine); official public educational and propaganda movies made by various authorities and governments. Most of these were admittedly shorts, but feature-length non-fiction titles can also be found – *SOS Russia*, *The Battle of the Somme*,[24] or *South*, Frank Hurley's account of Earnest Shackleton's failed attempt to reach the South Pole, released in the UK in 1920.

All these efforts, though, lacked *Nanook*'s dramatic narrative impact. Flaherty's importance therefore lies not with the use of actuality material but rather that he took footage of (albeit exotic) everyday activities which he then consciously organised into a dramatic – indeed a melodramatic – narrative form. It was this dramatising at the editing stage that made him exceptional. What distinguishes documentary from other non-fictional cinema genres is that, in Nichols's formulation, it exists 'in the crease between life as lived and life as narrativized'.[25] Other films had 'documentary value', but the power of narrative – determined not so much by what was filmed but by how that footage was edited – is what *Nanook*'s appearance in 1922 heralded.

As with 1922, 1935 only approximates the date of a change-over – in this instance, the coming of synch sound. Esfir Shub, the Russian who pioneered the long archive compilation documentary with *Padenie dinastii Romanovykh* [*The Fall of the Romanov Dynasty*] in 1927, was shooting synchronous sound as early as 1932 (*Komsomol, Pioneer of Electrification*).[26] (That she does not figure in received histories to the extent this and her overall contribution warrants speaks to the patriarchal bias of that history.) Other pre-1935 synch examples can be found (e.g., *Three Songs of Lenin*, Vertov, 1934).

In the same way, hand-held synchronous shooting can be found before 1960. In Germany, where magnetic tape had been developed in the 1930s, 'magsound' was being used in the form of unsprocketed 16mm reels in the editing of otherwise conventionally shot television news film by the mid-1950s.[27] With this technology, Canada's National Film Board developed 16mm synch equipment

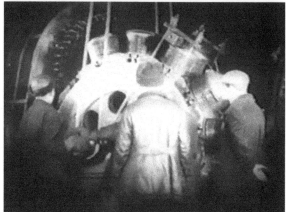

That fundamental breaks in documentary's development occurred in 1922, 1935 or 1960 can be doubted. Consider *South* (1919), *Komsomol, Pioneer of Electrification* (1932), *Les Raquetteurs* (1958)

(using a silent-running – blimped – camera as well as this separate – sprocketed – magnetic tape) in the later 50s for hand-held shooting as well as editing.[28] *Les Raquetteurs* [*Snowshoers*], directed by Michel Brault and Gilles Groulx, was shot by Brault using this rig in 1958 – earlier, then, than *Primary*.

But, as Grierson said of the term 'documentary' itself, let these dates 'stand'. However, that fundamental breaks in documentary's development occurred in 1922, 1935 or 1960 (or, in each instance, thereabout) can be doubted.

Especially 1960.

The American Direct Cinema pioneers in the 1960s raucously insisted on such a break. Direct Cinema practice was encapsulated in a veritable *dogme* that demanded a comprehensive rejection of classic techniques. Documentary could only be a film made with non-professional 'actors' (i.e., subjects), shot hand-held with long synchronous-sound takes, using available sound and light. Most purely and ideally, there should be no interaction between the film-maker and the subjects, no interviews, no commentary, no added sound and/or light. Documentary was, supposedly, thereby transformed. This can be represented schematically:

Griersonian Documentary Practice

	Pre-1960 ('Classic' Silent/ Sound Eras)	Post-1960 (Direct Cinema *dogme* Era)
Pre-production (Aesthetics)		
Sobriety	✓	✓
Poeticism/Agitprop	✓	X
Production (Camera/Sound)		
Tripod-mounted Camera	✓	X
Hand-held Camera	✓	✓
Silent Shooting	✓	X
Synchronous-sound Shooting	✓	✓
Augmented Lighting	✓	X/✓
Production (Direction)		
Directed Action/Repetition (Permitted Intervention)	✓	X
Reconstruction	✓	X
Interview	✓	X
Direct Address (to Camera)	✓	X
Post-production		
Editing	✓	✓
Extra-diegetic Sound	✓	X
Voiceover/Parallel Action	✓	✓
Commentary (Narration)	✓†	X
Graphics	✓	X/✓
Superimpositions	✓	✓
Archive/Compilation	✓	X

†including via intertitles.

The restrictions on practice post-1960 were designed to produce unmediated, or minimally mediated, footage. Films obeying the constraints imposed by Direct Cinema *dogme* were deemed to offer the best – the only – chance for an audience to evaluate (judge) the authenticity of the evidence being presented on the screen.

Lacking such an announced ethic of non-interventionism, previous documentary was considered incapable of providing this. The authenticity of older documentaries was anyway suspect largely because of the use of directed action, repetition and reconstruction. These previously permitted interventions were now deemed to prevent the audience acting as judge. On the contrary, audiences were being told, especially by the commentary, what to think. The evidence such films presented was questionable, manipulative – in short (to use the legal term) 'unsafe'. Nevertheless, despite this rejection of most of classic documentary's tool-box, the Griersonian promise itself was not meaningfully altered by Direct Cinema's dominance. The possibility of capturing, objectively, 'actuality' remained. Direct Cinema *dogme* was a 'New Testament' come to fulfil the Griersonian 'Old'.

As meaningful a development, unnoticed in this history, was another move – not in production technique but in the western exhibition environment. The early Griersonian documentary had never established itself as a viable cinematic form at the box office. It was always marginal and Grierson's defensive rhetoric, stressing the value of alternative non-cinema venues, was facile. During World War II, 18.5 million people in Britain, for example, were claimed as the documentary audience's largest annual figure (1943/4)[29] – but this represented only three days' worth of the mainstream cinema attendance at the time. Official and commercial sponsorship, and Grierson's concomitant insistence on 'public education', ghettoised the form. With the post-war growth of television, this situation was fundamentally transformed. A new, third revenue seam was opened up in addition to official public or private commercial/industrial sponsorship. On the small screen, documentary, although still comparatively a minority taste, found more of a mass audience than it had ever achieved in the cinema.[30]

In the 1950s, non-television films funded in old non-box-office official and commercial/industrial sponsorship modes continued to be made, but television allowed documentary to be relieved of the dead-weight of such support. Grierson might have pontificated about the 'the tyranny of the box office' etc.; and it might well have been true that in church halls and 'other citadels of civic improvement' a dedicated audience might gain a deeper experience from an 'educational' Griersonian short than they would from the products of the Hollywood dream-factory.[31] But, qualitatively different reception was never proved nor even investigated, then or now. In reality, these funding sources had stifled the documentary. Despite some recent misplaced efforts to rehabilitate TV-era Griersonian films, it should not be forgotten that they were, one way or another, still 'official' – consistently betraying documentary's radical potential. As one of the most respected American practitioners, George Stoney, who had worked in the old sponsored style, put it of the post-World War II period: 'We ['classic Griersonians', as it were] lost the respect we once had as documentary film-makers.'[32]

That historical disdain should not be forgotten but with television it changed. Documentary could now inherit the traditions and legitimacy of the 'free' press and it did so with alacrity. Grierson had dismissed the cinema newsreel as exhibiting 'purely journalistic skills' while documentary, he claimed, could do much more.[33] This assertion, though, was essentially more conditioned by funding necessities than by meaningful difference. Making a distinction between news and documentary was demanded by the need to convince sponsors of the latter's value. Now this need was removed by television; but there was a price to be paid, of course. On television, journalism tended to downgrade the documentary's poeticism (and occasional radicalism) by insisting on the (far from ideologically neutral) norms of newsworthiness as the only basis for documentary projects. This did not mean that television documentary necessarily adopted journalism's full investigative potential, but it now was far better placed to tell stories about the world. And this meshed well with Direct Cinema's 1960 rebellion. Indeed it was television's need for lightweight 16mm news-film equipment that forced the development of much of Direct Cinema's new film gear. The move to a journalistic television exhibition environment, though, no more implied a fissure in the Griersonian claim on the real than did Direct Cinema's *dogme* on production procedures. Objective 'actuality' was still being claimed: actually, TV journalism reinforced this.

To reject the coming of Direct Cinema as marking that much of a 'new footing' for documentary, however, is not to deny that it did manage to establish in the public mind that obedience to its *dogme* was the only way to obtain 'documentary value'. Over the last half-century since *Primary*, the technological basis has changed from film to, first, video and subsequently to digital platforms, but the form of the documentary, at its most legitimate in the eyes of the public, remains conditioned by Direct Cinema's rhetoric and aesthetic rules. Because of the flexibility of the new equipment (and the further increased flexibility given by all subsequent technological developments), Direct Cinema *dogme* has been accepted as a corrective to the problems of older documentaries. The Direct Cinema viewer was given, in a phrase of Richard Leacock's, the brilliant cameraman who had shot Flaherty's last major film *Louisiana Story* (1948) and was the senior figure behind *Primary*, 'the feeling of being there'.[34] To all intents and purposes the wide acceptance of the *dogme*

sidelined what had otherwise become an endless debate about the definition of documentary film.

THE PROBLEMATICS OF DOCUMENTARY'S DEFINITION

It had indeed been endless. The first moving images – the Lumières' reel most famously – contained shots which were clearly set up, fictional: *L'Arroseur Arrosé* [*The Watering Gardener Watered*]. Others, equally clearly, were not: *L'arrivée d'un train en gare de La Ciotat*. Some were more ambiguous. *La Sortie de l'Usine Lumière à Lyon* [*Workers Leaving the Lumière Factory in Lyon*] has Lumières' employees, suspiciously well dressed, passing through the factory gates after work with a dog, curiously, gambolling among their number. The shot is not an unmediated image of this everyday occurrence. It is a third take and the dog seems to have been introduced to make it more interesting. But, on the other hand, the workers are the workers, the dog is a dog, the gate is the gate of l'Usine Lumières in Lyon on a day in 1895. Here then is another 'crease' wherein documentary can be said to exist – that between the total manipulations of a fictional set-up (which, without the film-makers' imaginations and preparations, would not exist) and the unmediated observational filming of events (which would have occurred whether film-makers were present on not). Narrativising life involved intervention at more than just the editing stage.

Leaving aside all philosophical questions which influenced Grierson's understanding of the problem (he was a trained idealist philosopher[35]), it was in the creases at the production and the editing stages where he in effect located his famous definition of the documentary in 1933: 'the creative treatment of actuality'.[36] The 'actuality' involved in Grierson's definition can still lay claim to the real – the workers did leave the factory in 1895 etc.; but, creatively, a dog (actual, of course) was also introduced. The result is the mode of signification of the real world seen in documentary; in, exactly, the 'treated' manipulations of *Nanook* – in Flaherty's interventions and reconstructions as well as in his observations. He had the authority of either his own eyes (for the observations) or, for the interventions and reconstructions, he had that of the eyes and memories of various Inuit informants, included Allakarialuk whom he renamed 'Nanook' in the film. It was such mediation which moved the images beyond surveillance, even beyond newsreel, specifically to documentary. To cope with this, Grierson's definition of documentary was necessarily somewhat contradictory. The elements of actuality in documentary were always to be threatened by the need for 'creative treatment'. At a minimum, 'treatment' – manipulation – was needed to create a narrative. Hence the 'clumsiness' of the term 'documentary'. Pragmatically, Grierson could only order: 'let it stand',[37] and by default it had. As a US Supreme

Lumière employees, suspiciously well dressed. *La Sortie de l'Usine Lumière à Lyon* (1895)

Court judge once said of pornography: 'I know it when I see it';[38] ditto the documentary.

The difficulties of definition were exacerbated from the later 1930s on by the needs of synch shooting. Full reconstruction, not only directed repeated actions, became the norm. The equipment for shooting synch had been developed for the fiction film and was essentially designed for use in a studio. It could only be deployed for 'capturing reality' on location with great difficulty. The optical sound camera was as big as a desk. The power needed for it, the film camera (blimped, tripod-mounted and immovable without tracks) and (for interiors) lighting came from a noisy generator mounted on the back of a truck. This had to be parked at a distance from the location, the streets festooned with cables. It was only by careful prior observation, rehearsal and repeated takes that anything of the unmediated original scene could be preserved. It is no wonder that performances in these films whenever synch was recorded tend, especially – given cultural inhibitions – in England, to be stilted. Never mind creative treatment; the very act of filming was drowning actuality.

At a meeting of the short-lived World Union of Documentary at Mariánské Lázně/Marienbad, Czechoslovakia, in June 1948, a definition of documentary was produced which allowed for 'all methods of recording on celluloid any aspect of reality interpreted either by factual shooting or by sincere and justifiable reconstruction'.[39] Synch sound, by requiring reconstruction to one degree or another, was exacerbating the initial difficulties of Grierson's formulation. Now defining documentary involved consideration of the indefinable quality of 'sincerity' on the filmmakers' part. Technical difficulties were deployed to justify reconstructions. In effect, the matter of definition was becoming unmanageable. The Union shortly collapsed, a victim of the Cold War. However, the language used reflects the confusions of those at the heart of the classic phase of the documentary project.[40] At Mariánské Lázně the British were represented by Basil Wright and Donald Alexander, who had worked with Paul Rotha. A young George Stoney was also present among other more prominent, non-anglophone, documentarists from a dozen countries on both sides of the newly descended Iron Curtain, notably Joris Ivens.

Of course, reconstruction was not introduced to documentary practice because of synch sound. It was always present, always legitimated as 'creative treatment'. Stork and Ivens, for example, had made a classic film about the aftermath of a desperate strike in the Borinage, a Belgian coalfield caught in levels of nineteenth-century exploitation and backwardness.[41] Some scenes – notably an eviction – were reconstructed with locals being persuaded to play the role of policemen in costumes hired for the occasion. The film was shot silent so the justification was not synch but, rather, because this was the only way the past event could be filmed. Given the continued unacceptable exploitation of the people involved by the mine-owners, it was a reconstruction easily justified morally; and the progressivist sincerity of the film-makers cannot be doubted.[42]

The problem of 'sincerity' aside, 'reconstruction' is anyway no straightforward threat to documentary value, as it had emerged in the cinema. From the point of view of authenticity and ethics not all reconstruction can be considered suspect. It sits in a continuum from complete non-interventionist surveillance through to totally fictional set-ups. This runs from no contact, either prior to or during shooting, between the film-maker and subject to directed actors adopting personas not their own speaking and acting according to an imagined fictional script.

Beyond non-contact surveillance, the continuum of interactions continues with:

- unfilmed interactions between the film-maker and non-actor ('real') subjects. These can be general arrangements (e.g., permission for access); or, during shooting, directions to delay or immediately repeat actions. Let us call these 'permitted interventions';
- direction could also be justified on the basis of prior witness by the film-maker, or evidence given by the subject or third parties as uncovered during research. In effect, this is a 'filming of history';
- it could include filming typical actions witnessed or evidenced elsewhere being performed by subjects of the same type as those now before the camera: 'filming the typical'.

Should there be sufficiently detailed prior witness (e.g., a word-perfect trial transcript):

- reconstruction could legitimately use actors instead of the original subjects – filming fully documented dramatised history produces 'docudrama' or 'dramadoc'.

Far more problematically, the classic Griersonians allowed themselves to film, on commonsense, experiential grounds:

- possible typical actions by non-actors without the authority of witness – what might be called 'filming the possible'. This is really at the limit of the 'creative treatment of actuality';
- also at the edge is the experimental positioning of non-actors (subjects) in unscripted, previously unwitnessed situations created by the film-makers, who then film the results in an unmediated fashion – 'documenting the artificial' (in what is referred to as 'formatted documentary': aka 'Reality TV').

Finally:

- actors performing imagined actions before the camera have no 'documentary value' in the sense that that term has come to be associated with the moving image: this produces fiction.

INTERVENTION/RECONSTRUCTION/IMAGINATION
FACT ➔➔➔➔➔➔

Subjects +	Witnessed Action	= Surveillence/ Direction/History/ Typicality
Actors +	Witnessed Action	= Docudrama
Subjects +	Unwitnessed Action	= Possible/Artificial
Actors +	Imagined Action	= Fiction

➔➔➔➔➔➔ FICTION

If there is witness, classic Griersonian practice allows all of these possibilities (except the last) as producing 'documentary value' of one sort or another, whose authenticity is accepted to one degree or another. Only the most purely (i.e., totally) fictional is excluded. The crucial element is always witness – obviously the direct witness of the camera observing events as they happened (even if these had been artificially set up, as long as they involved 'real' subjects); but also the possibility of third-party witness being filmed directly as testimony (interviews) or recreated for the camera as reconstruction. Without witness there can be no claim on the real, no 'documentary value', no documentary. Witness – the witness of the camera and/or the film-maker/informant/subject – therefore, is, with narrative, documentary's other essential foundation.

Direct Cinema practitioners accepted the centrality of witness but they insisted that only their own witness via their cameras was legitimate. They were, though, self-deluded in believing if this were done then problems would disappear. After all, only surveillance implicitly suggests non-intervention and Direct Cinema did not limit itself to that. These film-makers understood the need for narrative and it is not, therefore, surprising that their *dogme* did not forbid editing. Despite all the restrictions they imposed on the filming process, the basic contradiction between 'treatment' and 'actuality' was not removed. Editing, as draconian an interventionist technique as any, necessarily persisted. It could do no other. Direct Cinema still had to obey the greater *dogme* of narrativity if the films were to hold the attention of audiences. 'Life' – in effect, filmed witness – if it is to be 'narrativised', almost inevitably demands editing. Documentary's proof of concept was demonstrated by Flaherty, not at the moment of shooting actuality – others had long been doing that – but by his manipulation of the footage on his editing bench. Considerable manipulation was still – necessarily – to be found in the Direct Cinema editing room.

That this need was sidelined in the rhetoric is reflected in the fact that the complex business of shaping a narrative from the footage was in the hands of people who, apart from Frederick Wiseman who edited his own work, are not celebrated: Charlotte Zwerin, Pat Jaffe, Barbara Kopple, for example. That they are all women is surely no accident. The extent of their marginalisation can perhaps be glimpsed in the absurd suggestion of one pioneer, Al Maysles, to a gullible interviewer that the material was actually unedited.[43] More was at stake here than the downgrading of the need for narrative and importance of the woman charged with creating it. The rhetorical failure almost never to discuss editing in effect disguised the inevitable manipulations which that process involved. It was (largely) true that subjects were never directed; but when Leacock said 'We don't cheat', that only applied to the moment of shooting.[44] Although 'cheating' is clearly too strong a word, the creative work of editing undermined Direct Cinema's non-interventionist pretentions. The confusions of 'sincere and justifiable reconstruction' might have been set aside but instead Direct Cinema now tied itself into other theoretical knots. When challenged, the films became 'aspects of the observer's perception of what happened in the presence of the camera' (Leacock).[45] They were nothing more than 'a fair reflection of the experience of making them' (Wiseman).[46]

This rhetoric, though, is disingenuous. Initially, these practitioners – as in the interviews whence these statements – only acknowledged their subjectivity as cinemaphotographers/directors/editors when it suited. Fundamentally, Direct Cinema accepted the cultural positioning of photography as mechanically produced evidence. Objectivity was implicitly 'guaranteed' by the technology. Photography's cultural claim to represent reality objectively, scientifically, meant the film-makers' subjectivity was actually obscured. Audiences are predisposed to ignore the subjectivity of the photographer and 'believe' in the photographic image as (usually) unproblematic evidence. Viewers, of course, were naive to think that a photograph could not 'lie'; it could, and did, from the very beginning.[47] But the Griersonian documentary, both in

its classic and Direct Cinema form, was lost without such naivety. Documentary's claim on the real, 'the difference that made a difference'[48] to fiction, traded on it utterly. Direct Cinema practitioners, offering images to give audiences the actual 'feeling of being there', traded more insistently than most.

Direct Cinema documentarists, happy to share with their Griersonian predecessors the accolades of being film artists, learned to be less strident in their claims. Nevertheless, for all that they came, on occasion, to acknowledge their own partialities, they never addressed – much less attempted to correct – audience reception and the implicit cultural naivety that involved. They might claim, with lawyerly chop-logic, that 'objectivity' and 'truth' were not in play, but their films, with their austere aesthetics including the persistence of black and white, said otherwise.[49]

On one thing, though, they were right: any debate about the truth and objectivity of the image in terms limited by what is seen on the screen alone is sterile – 'a real phoney-baloney argument' as Wiseman once called it.[50] Even if Leacock's formulation is revised to take account of the centrality of editing and documentary is then defined as **narrativised** *recorded aspects of observation*, it is still the case that 'documentary value' cannot be guaranteed by a consideration of the image alone: consideration of the image's reception is crucial. For example, how are we to discuss the meaning of Wiseman's insistence on black and white long after colour was in use except in terms of its meaning for the audiences? And of Wiseman's implicit reliance on their understanding of it as an earnest of authenticity? The audience's reception of the image as authentic is crucial. It does not matter if the film-maker seeks to impose an hegemonic meaning or merely pretends to be presenting evidence: either way, the reception of the image by the audience is the final determinant of its status.

Grierson, of course, was never shy of attempting the imposition of hegemonic readings through editing and commentary. His philosophic acumen rendered complex his notions of what 'truth' the image then presented. Moreover, he implicitly acknowledged this as an issue by constantly attempting to condition the films' reception in the brilliant public relations campaign he conducted in print and in person on their behalf.[51] Explicitly, though, he never overtly sought to deny the cultural positioning of the photographic image as more or less unproblematic evidence, any more than the Direct Cinema practitioners did. For his paymasters and his audiences, documentary still rested on the nineteenth-century saw: 'the camera never lies'. And, despite their later protestations, the Direct Cinema pioneers also relied on a received belief in the evidentiary truth of the photograph. Indeed, their insistence on images speaking for themselves, as it were, ignores even Grierson's largely tacit philosophical subtleties. For Grierson, failing to refine photography's implicit cultural claim on the real was something of a sin of omission. The proponents of Direct Cinema, with their avowed insistence that they were conveying 'the feeling of being there', turned observationalism into a sin of commission. This was enshrined in their practice *dogme* and their confusing rhetorical ventures into print. But, despite all this stridency, 'documentary value' nevertheless does not depend on modes of production *and* the nature of audience reception. More than that: it actually meaningfully depends just on reception, as authenticity can only be confirmed contextually from other sources beyond the limits of the screen. Such confirmation has to be a matter of audience reception.

'Actuality' in the Griersonian sense, as Robert Fairthorne pointed out some eighty years ago, 'is not a fundamental property, but a relation between film and audience of precisely the same order as slow motion which demands previous knowledge of natural motion to give it its peculiar effect'.[52] One must know the speed in experienced reality (or logically deduce it on the basis of that experience) if one is to determine if film footage is in slow motion. The same is true of documentary. Its claim on truth cannot ever be guaranteed by the image alone; it requires audience testing of its authenticity against experience – in reality, or on the basis of other information. Never mind naivety; the claim on the real depends on the audience's prior knowledge and experience of the real. That is why they know it is a documentary when they see it. And the film-makers, however much they refine their procedures, cannot alter that condition of reception. Direct Cinema was thus in fundamental error to think that this could be done.

But there were other, equally vexed difficulties as well.

After all, filming events as they happened did not necessarily mean the subject's filmed behaviour was not influenced by the presence of the camera. Moreover, if this was overcome because the events were so dramatic that a case could be made for the self-absorption of the people filmed, the films might not, of themselves without further additional contextual explanation, inform and explain. The uncaptioned picture, as Barthes assures us, might have an iconic richness but it could well also be semantically opaque.[53] Older techniques were demanded for the contextualisation that is often necessary (e.g., commentary, interviews). The classic style – certainly most elements of it – therefore persisted not only in the rather despised and marginal world of the sponsored film but also, to a large extent, on television. Most documentaries had voiceover commentaries, employed interviews; and they did not completely eschew added lights when filming and/or music and sound effects when editing. The hand-held Direct Cinema long take became just another technique of

the Griersonian cinema. (For one thing, of course, actually obeying the *dogme* required enormously great, economically unfeasible shooting ratios; commonly three times – at least – greater than usual.)

Anyway, few if any films ever completely obeyed all the rules of the Direct Cinema *dogme* – even those of the pioneers such as Leacock who most stridently insisted on them. Such strong claims for authenticity were not being – could not be – matched on the screen. The 'evidence' presented by the films could still be interrogated, doubted even. *Primary*, for example, reveals supposedly unbiased evidence of how candidates in an American presidential election conducted their initial campaigns; but the selection of scenes, it can be easily argued, clearly show the bias of the film-makers towards Senator John Kennedy over his rival Senator Hubert Humphrey.[54] The critic Molly Haskell was able, in connection with *A Married Couple*,[55] perceptively to point out Direct Cinema's tendency to over-claim the value of the evidence it presented. In her view, this film, intimately documenting the breakup of a marriage, promoted 'selected gleanings into self-evident generalisations'.[56] Direct Cinema, whatever it dealt with, tended always to do this. The titles alone lay claim to the general: *A Married Couple, An American Family, Law & Order, Welfare ...*

A Married Couple also illustrates another continuity between the Griersonians and the 1960s Direct Cinema film-makers. It indicates that the ethical difficulties involved in filming real subjects which had dogged documentary from the beginning had not been removed by their *dogme* or practices. On the contrary: although the moral dilemmas of reconstruction were, for the main part, resolved, because of the close observational intrusion made possible by the new equipment, now a new level of ethical challenge confronted the documentarist.

Ethics is the spectre haunting documentary. It is, with narrative and witness, the third leg of the documentary stool. Documentarists, of course, have the right of free expression and, with everybody else, are constrained by the moral requirements its exercise entails. But documentary's moral difficulties also reflect the specific conflict between the assumptions governing the ethics of documenting 'life as lived' (which can be thought of as journalistic requirements of objectivity) and those behind processing this as 'life as narrativised' (which implies creative intervention, that is to say: art). Documentarists seek both journalistic and artistic legitimacy but the ethical frames are different in each case. Objectivity governs the journalistic (however much breached rather than observed) while subjectivity, with no other necessary obligation, suffuses the latter. Indeed, by the nineteenth century in the West, artists were considered in some quarters to be above morality altogether, the right of expression being considered virtually absolute. That position is untenable as there is a societal need that the expression does no harm. Defining 'harm' is, of course, no easy matter but, clearly, in one form or another it can often be in view for a film's participants. Moreover, beyond a limited 'do no harm' constraint, the yoking of 'creativity' (aka art) to the representation of 'actuality' in the context of evidentiary photography results in documentary having to confront, it would seem on a more or less permanent basis, a overwhelming moral morass.

In the dominant context of the Griersonian victim documentary, ethical problems had come to be assuaged by a series of professional shibboleths. Subjects' lives could be disrupted by exposure because, it was assumed, they had given consent to be filmed, and/or because they would be given a voice by the film. Neither of these, however, quite meets the moral case. Documentary subjects can find themselves in hostile public glare or worse. Fully informed consent, needed for any ethically sound film-making, is very often beyond the power of most subjects to give because they cannot fully imagine the consequences of public exposure, never having experienced it before. Given that bald consent is legally sufficient, intentional or inadvertent exploitation by the film-maker is all too common. Informed consent, in fact, is something of a myth.

Nor, if subjects are 'given a voice', does this, almost without exception, ever result in any betterment of their situation. The power of the media is much overstated; seldom do films engender solutions for their subjects' problems. This is not to suggest that documentary legitimacy depends on its effectiveness in resolving the perennial discontents – poverty, injustice, social crises etc. – which are its dominant tropes. So to claim would be naive and it is anyway not documentary's place to solve the problems of the world; rather it is to report on them to ensure they are in the public sphere. The problem with the elusive nature of documentary's social impact is not ineffectualness but that the shibboleths justifying intervention in (and disruption of) people's lives cannot be used as glibly as they tend to be to ground a claim of ethical film-making. The fact is that, almost inevitably, film-makers more obviously benefit from a documentary than do their subjects. This suggests an automatic (as it were) tendency to exploitation in the classic director/subject relationship. It is documentary's 'original sin'; but it is quite specifically limited to matters arising directly during filming or as a consequence of exhibition.

It is, therefore, simplistic to suggest Flaherty had some sort of ethical responsibility for the death of Allakarialuk, who perished in a commonplace Arctic hunting accident a few years after *Nanook* had made Flaherty an international celebrity. Nor does it speak to documentary's ethical quagmires that Flaherty fathered a child, Joseph, with one of 'Nanook's' supposed 'wives' in the film, 'Nyla', Maggie Nuvalinga; and that he abandoned both when he went south for the last time.[57] Flaherty's moral blindness as a film-maker, rather than as man, is more clearly seen in a self-deprecating acknowledgment made in the following decade. He knew he had endangered 'a boatload of wild Irishmen' (as he put it) by bribing them to venture out, as they never would have done without his monetary inducement, in a monstrous roiling sea for the climax of *Man of Aran* (1934). Such reordering reality for the sake of the film is merely an extreme example of everyday practice. (Remember the dog in the shot of the workers leaving the factory.) As Allakarialuk put it when agreeing to make *Nanook*: 'the aggie (movie) will come first'.[58] It almost always does.

Nevertheless, Flaherty, like the vast majority of those who followed, understood that there was a problem but saw it in public relations, rather than moral, terms. He knew, for instance, adverse publicity was a possible consequence of calling for the startling shot in which an elephant steps over an Indian baby in *Elephant Boy* (1937).[59] Harry Watt, another of the first-generation Griersonians, glibly justified the regular need for subterfuge to gain access for filming.[60] Rotha proudly reports his mendacity in misusing his production expenses by giving the money as charity to unfilmed impoverished miners; but he knew that even such a laudable intervention was somehow transgressive.[61]

Documentarists had always been ready to intervene for the sake of the shot but references to this in the written record are hard to find. Ivens, for example, explains how he and Storck moved the camera to mar any possibility of 'picturesque poverty' in *Misère au Borinage*.[62] The sophistication, say, of Esfir Shub questioning her own use of the Tzar's home movies, in *The Fall of the Romanov Dynasty*, to make a case against his autocracy, is of a piece in its rarity.[63] Never mind free expression, documentary could ill afford such honesty. It is no wonder the film-makers have tended to keep their silence. Routinised interventions (down to the everyday level of reorganising the furniture) was clearly part and parcel of 'creative treatment'. In these rare references to the ethics of the production, the impact of morality on documentary's truth claim is never addressed.

With Direct Cinema, though, 'reorganising the furniture' was to be a thing of the past as any form of intervention was seen as illegitimate. That, though, did not mean ethical dilemmas were at an end because, as *A Married Couple* indicates, greater degrees of personal exposure were now possible. The documentarist still held the dominant power; people, subjects, were still supposedly being given a voice; the correction of social ills was still in view; the film-maker was still an artist with a right of free expression. And this could all backfire. The justifications for any endangerments and embarrassments remained unchanged.

In 1967 Tanya Ballantyne, a member of the Canadian National Film Board's unique women's production unit,[64] made an observational documentary about an impoverished Montreal family, *The Things I Cannot Change*. The father's voice is heard but his neighbours' outrage at having all their conditions exposed forced the family to flee. The Board re-examined its protocols ... unlike Fred Wiseman. In the USA the following year, he released *Titicut Follies*, his first documentary, filmed in a prison hospital for the criminally insane. He failed to obtain the consent of all those filmed, arguing they were not anyway mentally competent to give it and, in consequence, after much manoeuvring, the film was banned from public view for decades.[65] When eventually it was widely screened, one inmate, now recovered and in higher education, suffered the humiliation of having to watch the film in class and see

The ethical difficulties involved in filming real subjects: a moral duty of care. *A Married Couple* (1971) and *Titicut Follies* (1968)

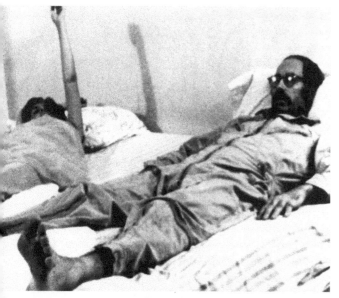

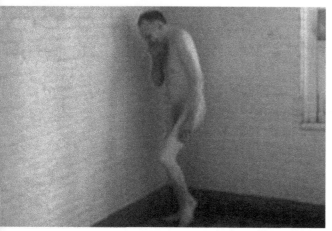

his younger self confess to sexually molesting his daughter. As far as can be known from the public record, Wiseman did not learn from *Titicut Follies* that he had a moral duty of care which might impact on his free speech rights. Rather, the lesson drawn was that all the consent he needed was to record an affirmative 'yes' into his microphone from subjects being asked if they minded being filmed with a possible public screening to follow.

Anyway, there are situations where consent is not needed and, indeed, it might be counter-productive to seek it. Subterfuge and/or the negative consequences of exposure are not the end of the matter as such behaviour and outcomes cannot be automatically condemned. Other factors are in play beyond a black-and-white prohibition against misrepresentation and exploitation. The duty of care owed the subject can be reduced, or in the case of exposing misfeasance or worse, removed. Who is the subject? What are they doing? Where are they doing it? All these are factors affecting the morality of each individual circumstance.

There is always an (albeit unexamined) claim on the public 'right to know' also in play. It, as much as any of the shibboleths above, is there for the film-maker to hide behind. It is a second facet of the film-maker's right of expression. In addition to their right to 'speak', their audiences, in a democracy, have a concomitant right to hear. This duality is reflected in the fact that there are actually two areas of ethical difficulty confronting the documentarist: an ethic of production and an ethic of reception. The right to speak impacts on the production ethic in the form of responsibility to the subject (to which the further justifications of consent and voice also apply); and the consequence of the right to hear (or to know) is reflected in the film-makers' responsibility to the public.

Of course, the public right to know is crucial, part of the paramount human free speech right by which all the others are guaranteed. Documentary shares with journalism a social function to act as a watchdog over society's guardians, a role which demands that a right to hear is in play. This can absolve even the need for consent. It is obvious in *Titicut Follies*, for example, that the mistreatment of the prisoners was clearly a matter of public concern. That Wiseman gained access by claiming the film was for the education of the students to whom he was then teaching law, but then immediately screened it publically, was no reason for official censorship.

Yet, there is a difference between this right to speak and the right to know. The right to speak does not – in fact, cannot if it is to be meaningful – carry within it a restriction as to the truthfulness of utterance. Free speech must be free to lie, to offend. In a free society, 'do no harm' is the only restriction on it; not 'tell the truth'. Suffice to say in this connection, merely hearing an untruth – merely believing (say) a mendacious documentary's truth claim – does not, of itself, damage the hearer if the hearer does no more than listen. In a free society, hearers must exercise autonomy. In fact, a concomitant of free speech is that hearers exercise due caution encapsulated by the old principle *caveat emptor* – let the buyer (the hearer, the audience) beware. However, the enhanced claims of observational documentary to be offering objective evidence tended to weaken the responsibility of the audience for making their own judgments. Any sense of audience *caveat emptor* responsibility was discounted in the discourse on documentary morality. Such was Direct Cinema's triumph that every documentary technique, from commonplace reconstruction to deliberate fraud, could be fanned into moral outrage, scandal and require regulatory sanctions.[66] On one occasion, at least, misrepresentation was even held to be criminal fraudulence on the part of the film-maker.[67]

Direct Cinema's claims were soon coming under less draconian critical attack across a variety of fronts from authenticity to morality, consequences of its strong truth claim which were unassuaged by occasional glib denials of objectivity. Direct Cinema was producing films which of themselves (and inevitably) undercut its claims of limited mediation, authenticity and evidence. The Direct Cinema pioneers 'opened a can of worms and promptly got eaten by them'.[68] Perhaps the final proof that the truth claims had been overstated can be seen in the comparative ease with which observational film could be faked.[69] The long hand-held synch shot, when coupled with maximally naturalistic performances, could produce a compelling simulacrum of unmediated reality.

By the late 1980s, in some quarters, Direct Cinema's 'truth' was being as seriously questioned as the classic Griersonian documentary's had been in the 50s. Despite audiences buying in to the rhetoric (to the point where, popularly, the *dogme* defined the legitimate documentary practice), the austerity of Direct Cinema's self-denying ordnances was chafing against a number of other film-makers' ambitions and intentions. Questioning the *dogme* was beginning to lead to a measure of rejection among film-makers of its constraints. This was being done, though, with less brouhaha than had been deployed when the Direct Cinema pioneers attacked the classic documentary.

In short, within two decades of its introduction, it became clear that Direct Cinema had not replaced the Griersonian documentary. In fact, Direct Cinema had closed off the last reasonable route to deliver indisputable 'objective' evidence on the screen. Deploying fully flexible film equipment was still producing, at best, documentary 'value' rather than documented 'truth'. Direct Cinema documentary represented the last chance to make good on the basic Griersonian vision of 'actuality' as evidence; but the 'New Griersonian Testament' of Direct Cinema, come to fulfil the promise of the Old, had failed to quell oppositional voices. Technology, it turned out, was not capable of silencing those who would deny or limit documentary's evidentiary pretensions. It became increasingly obvious that the goal of presenting audiences with self-evident 'evidence', never mind giving them 'the feeling of being there', was unachievable. In consequence, the shared realist documentary assumptions of the Griersonians and their Direct Cinema heirs came under increasing attack.

CHALLENGING DOGME

The turn of the later 1980s away from Direct Cinema austerities was, in essence, a reaction to its insistent implicit and explicit claim on the real. By the 90s, it was possible to recognise a plethora of possibilities for films not limited by the 'fly-on-the-wall' observational style which could nevertheless still be indentified as documentaries. More and more alternatives were appearing, unheralded, in documentary practice. Amid the uncertainties of the postmodern condition, the stark divide between documentary and fiction, 'real people' and actors, witnessed and imagined events was becoming, as Nichols put it in 1994, 'blurred'. 'A shift of epistemological proportions has occurred,' he announced. 'What counts as knowledge is not what it used to be.'[70] The boundary beaten by *Nanook* had always, anyway, been a shifting line in the snow. 'Nanook' was, after all, actually Allakarialuk, reconstructing events, having been renamed for the occasion. As with the naive belief that the camera could not lie, documentary's claim on the real should never have been uninterrogated; Direct Cinema's rhetoric should never have come to define the limits of legitimate documentary practice. Now its hold was slipping. Narrative, witness and ethical challenges were still documentary's marks but the walls of objectivism, actuality, scientism and facticity, which constituted the Griersonian documentary's realist prison house, were being breached.

Some saw this as the breaking of documentary's boundaries and heralded the arrival of 'New Documentary'.[71] However, much of what characterised the work then emerging reflected less boundary transgression than it did a recovery of the initial freer practices of the realist documentary. The blurring was primarily due to a revaluing of old Griersonian procedures at the expense of Direct Cinema's *dogme*. Of course, the postmodern world of shifting realities provided a fertile environment for challenges to documentary's assumptions, but the term 'hybridity' (from biology), which also came into play at this time, is really not entirely apposite either as far as defining new production modes is concerned. Hybridity, especially in the mixing of the factive and the fictive, was scarcely without Griersonian precedent. 'Real people' (e.g., Allakarialuk) were allowed to act out not only witnessed behaviour but also merely possible realistic scenarios – for example, Bill Blewitt, the hero of a 'story' documentary, *The Savings of Bill Blewitt* (Harry Watt, UK, 1936). (This last was in the mode that can be called 'filming the possible'.[72]) As such procedures were readmitted to legitimacy, anything was becoming possible as long as the twin foundations of narrativity and witness were, more or less, not forgotten. Postmodernism was no necessary condition for this because what was first explored was not so much radical new approaches as a return to older techniques.

'Documentary', Nichols had written, 'offers access to a shared historical construct'; but, he suggested, with documentary, instead of this being in the form of narratives – stories – about '*a* world, we are offered access to *the* world'.[73] This is exactly what classic Griersonian documentary did. Direct Cinema went too far by insisting that it was offering *the* story of *the* world – that is, incontrovertible evidentially confirmed truth. This meant, at a minimum, *the* story of what went on before the camera's lens at the time of shooting. So the first element undercutting the Griersonian/Direct Cinema hegemony involved the abandonment of this 'strong' position. In effect, some documentarists returned to the more limited classical authenticity claim – *a* story. Their films simply reverted to (and refined) older, pre-Direct Cinema, Griersonian techniques.

Errol Morris's *Thin Blue Line* (1988, USA) does this so aggressively that it can stand with *Nanook*, *Housing Problems* and *Primary* as an emblematic marker text. Morris rejected 16mm to return to 35mm. He used the full panoply of film studio technology to shoot a 'miscarriage of justice' documentary. Instead of Direct Cinema's gritty realism, he presented reconstructions of a crime in the lavish, baroque style of a Hollywood film noir. Even the interviews – with the falsely accused man, the actual murderer and the authorities and other witnesses – are lit and shot according to Hollywood norms. Morris re-examines the evidence in the murder case he is investigating using a traditional narrative culminating with the killer's virtual confession. There is little 'new' about any of this.

The Thin Blue Line (1988): an emblematic marker text

The justifications for Morris's aesthetic decisions can best be located in a need to combat perceived audience fatigue. The subject matter (a miscarriage of justice story) was so familiar that filming in the hegemonic Direct Cinema style would not have produced so memorable a documentary. In effect, he was obeying the Russian formalist injunction to seek *ostranenie* – defamiliarisation – as a way of compelling audience attention. Such assumed exhaustion of the viewers speaks to Direct Cinema's ubiquity. The fact the film was made for American public television's premiere drama slot, 'American Playhouse', not its documentary outlets, reflects the extent of Direct Cinema's hegemony. As the persistence of the sponsored documentary and most television documentary indicated, the use of the old techniques had never entirely gone away. Their deployment in *The Thin Blue Line*, however, represents a revived understanding of their legitimacy. Despite Morris's traditional interventions – noir lighting, reconstructions, interviews, music (by Philip Glass) – the film is still a documentary telling *a* story about *the* world, never mind Direct Cinema's *dogme*.

Similarly, dramatised documentary was a development of the reconstructional techniques of the pre-1960 synch-sound era. It had been standard practice to reconstruct witnessed events with the original subjects replaying their roles. Referencing real people in a play does not make it a documentary. (Macbeth, for instance, was, in reality, a king of Scotland. This fact does not make Shakespeare's *The Tragedie of Macbeth* a documentary.) There has to be something more – witness at one level of detail or another; for instance, the re-enactment of a trial using the verbatim transcript as the documentary's script. This came to embrace scripts based on – or, better, constrained by – other not necessarily verbatim but nevertheless highly detailed witness accounts. With such witness, even actors can be used to replace the original non-actors ('real people') involved in an event. The 1974 made-for-television feature *Missiles of October*[74] recreated the Kennedy White House at the time of the Cuban Missile Crisis of 1962, with William Devane playing the President, Martin Sheen as his brother and Howard Da Silva as Khrushchev. The screenplay was sufficiently close to the actual participants' memoirs and other documentation for the piece to be called a 'faction', a term that did not stick;[75] drama-documentary and syllabic abbreviations thereof – 'dram-doc', 'docudrama' – did.

In Britain, the development is best related to the work of a long-running news (current affairs) documentary series, *World in Action*. In the 1960s, it had used, on occasion, extensive reconstruction of some news stories in the fashion of the very first news films, but it seldom essayed dialogue in such circumstances.[76] In 1970, taking 'puritanical' care with the source material, one of the shows' producer/directors, Leslie Woodhead, recreated the prison life of a dissident Soviet Major-General Pyotr Grigorenko (played by Hamilton Dyce): *The Man Who Wouldn't Keep Quiet*.[77] The script was meticulously based on the Russian's *samizdat* prison diaries. The film was shot in a Direct Cinema documentary style but the status of its images and the source of its information were announced in the titles – no subterfuge was involved.

By the early 1980s, dramadocs or docudramas were a regular feature of the television schedules. As the decade progressed, though, they increasingly conformed to the American 'Hollywoodised' fact-based drama model rather than maintaining the British 'puritanical' approach to the minutiae of the material. Like *The Thin Blue Line*, the results spoke documentary's consanguinity to drama; but the Griersonian requirement for witness was still being met. They were indeed 'hybrid', but they had always been so. In the event, they did present a de facto alternative vision of documentary possibilities to the hegemonic Direct Cinema film.

To take a yet clearer example of the persistence of old approaches, consider archive compilation as a type of documented history. Pioneered by Esfir Shub (*The Fall of the Romanov Dynasty*) and successfully transferred to television in the 1950s,[78] this had become so usual a technique in dealing with certain topics – notably the Holocaust – that, by the late 80s, it was in danger of becoming clichéd: recycled footage laden with commentary and burdened with witness testimony. In 1988, with *The Bartos Family: Private Hungary 1* (Hungary), the work of Péter Forgács first came to international attention. He had been collecting and recycling, with amazing sensitivity and minimal manipulation, amateur footage to create a vivid general archive of twentieth-century life mainly, but not exclusively, in Eastern Europe before and during World War II. This was to include, completely unexpectedly, movies made by those who would become Holocaust victims. In so doing he exponentially increased the Holocaust archive adding even everyday images of the background reality to the over-familiar films of the Nazi perpetrators and the Allied concentration camp liberators. Forgács created *ostranenie* with the simplest of techniques (e.g., a superimposed title over a shot of a Dutch family packing, listing what it is they are being allowed to take ... to Auschwitz). At such moments, memory of the overly familiar images is recontextualised and 'Forgács brings us face to face with Arendt's banality of evil'.[79]

But he not only defamiliarises the Holocaust; his refinement of the compilation documentary was far from the predictabilities of its television incarnation. Forgács confirmed the viability and the legitimacy of recycling, and recontextualising, archival material. In doing so, *en passant*, he also offered another de facto demonstration of the limitations of Direct Cinema *dogme*. In contrast to Morris and the dramadoc film-makers, whose challenges to observational techniques were more a reflection of Hollywood,

Forgács – in essence a video-artist – indicates the documentary's openness to avant-garde sensibilities. In doing so he points to a further and yet most profound challenge to the dominance of observationalism.

CINÉMA VÉRITÉ

Documentary had never been limited to Grierson's realist, predominately 'public education' remit. At the outset, in the 1920s, it had been seen as a species of oppositional avant-garde film-making so that there is nothing in, say, Forgács' approach which does not mesh with documentary tradition. The use of 'real people' to appear (i.e., to 'act') on screen also makes documentary an expression of avant-garde cinema (... and in the role of 'Nanook', Allakarialuk; his wife 'Nyla', Maggie Nuvalinga etc.). This alone was sufficiently deviant to allow even *Nanook* itself to be positioned, on occasion, with other experimental variants to mainstream fictional movies. Some films of considerable 'documentary value' have remained so positioned: *Menschen am Sontag* [*People on Sunday*] (1930, Germany) is a 'rhythm of the city' documentary about how Berliners relaxed at the weekend; but it also includes a scripted fictional story, played by non-actors, to sustain its narrative arc. Given that it was written and directed by two filmmakers who went on to distinguished Hollywood careers (Billy Wilder and Robert Siodmak), its closeness to documentary has long been obscured.

Even more overtly avant-garde was *Chelovek s kinoapparatom* [*Man with a Movie Camera*] (1929) which announces itself on screen, with intertitles typical of Soviet manifesto writing of the time, as: 'an experiment in cinematic communication of visible events. ... A film without a scenario. ... A film without sets, actors etc.' The 'author-supervisor' of this 'experiment' was Denis Kaufman, who had taken the *nom de plume* Dziga Vertov.

Vertov refused to be limited by the camera's iconic capabilities, rather seeing it as a tool allowing for new visions of reality to be made manifest. The surface of the world presented on the screen could be penetrated by the camera's eye to produce new film 'truths' – *kino pravda* ... *cinéma vérité*. His project of filming the real was thus at 180 degrees to Flaherty's. Although Flaherty included portrait shots and other acknowledgments of the camera,[80] his procedures were designed to render himself and his film-making invisible (as with mainstream fictional cinema); Vertov's did the reverse. For him, an essential requisite for presenting any 'truth' on the screen was to reveal the processes of filming and then to remind the audience of them constantly. It is this willingness to acknowledge the inevitability of mediation – to luxuriate in it – that positions Vertovian practices as a longstanding alternative to that of Flaherty/Grierson/Direct Cinema.

Man with a Movie Camera offers a de facto political and cultural critique of Soviet urban life during the period of

Man with a Movie Camera (1929): Vertov uses camera tricks and effects – primarily superimpositions – to reinforce his meaning

Lenin's New Economic Policy. At the same time, the mechanisms of film-making are also exposed by including footage of a cameraman (Vertov's brother Mikhail) and film-editor (his wife Elizaveta Svilova) at work. Moreover, Vertov uses camera tricks and effects – primarily superimpositions – to reinforce his meaning. The façade of the Bolshoi Theatre, for example, is made to collapse on itself, transformed into a derelict, ruined site for courtly and bourgeois art – which is how Vertov wanted his audience of (ideally) workers, peasants and soldiers to think of it.

Vertov, though, in making the documentary process visible, abandoned neither witness nor narrative – that much he and the realists shared; and by that sharing 'documentary value' was preserved. *Man with a Movie Camera* is essentially structured, like other realist 'rhythm of the city' films of its era, as a day, starting in the early morning. Nevertheless, by admitting the film-makers'

presence and by rejecting the illusionist underpinnings of mainstream documentary's claim on the real, Vertov spoke to the central problem of creatively treating actuality. With a sophistication unmatched elsewhere, his approach was indeed 'revolutionary', marked by a certain aesthetic violence. This was compounded by his strident rhetorical attacks on the fictional cinema of Eisenstein, Pudovkin and the rest as being inappropriately bourgeois (like the Bolshoi). He was, in consequence, considered by Soviet theorists as 'thoughtless' and his insistence on the unscripted, 'unplayed' film 'a serious mistake'.[81] Eisenstein thought *Man with a Movie Camera* was 'cine-hooliganism'.[82]

In the West, Grierson's group also dismissed the experiment as a dead end – an absurdity; nothing more than camera's filming of other cameras. The film and its maker were marginalised in contemporary Soviet thinking, by western documentarists and, subsequently, by the Russian

Stalinists for whom such formalist investigations had become ideologically suspect. For the next thirty years, Vertov's concerns were ignored and his solutions eschewed but, in fact, *Man with a Movie Camera* stands as more than a mere variant to *Nanook of the North*. Vertov's film was marginalised at the time of its release, but, nevertheless, it threw down an (admittedly latent) gauntlet to Flaherty and all those others who followed after in the West.

It was to be three decades before the challenge was properly addressed and the Vertovian moment was self-consciously and precisely recovered. Just as *Nanook* had been balanced by *Man with a Movie Camera* in the 1920s, so, in 1960, *Primary* was balanced by *Chronique d'un été* [*Chronicle of a Summer*] (1961). Just as Vertov can be positioned against Flaherty (and Grierson/Direct Cinema), so Jean Rouch, the film-maker behind *Chronique*, can be set against the Direct Cinema pioneers.

The guiding intelligences behind *Primary* were Leacock, by training a physicist (who was the first to see how to synch camera and tape-recorder wirelessly), and Robert Drew, a journalist – with Grierson, and his contradictory definition, a ghostly presence behind them. However, Leacock, despite being a physicist, ignored the lessons of the uncertainty principle[83] as to the impact of observation, such obtuseness going against the grain of anglophone pragmatics. Instead, he announced himself and his camera as (his analogy) a voltmeter registering the surrounding reality.[84] Behind *Chronique*, on the other hand, were Rouch, an anthropologist (specifically a film-ethnographer), and Edgar Morin, a leading left sociologist and media theorist. Both were well aware of the difficulties of 'participant observation'.[85] Rouch, less ambitious therefore than Leacock, was hoping, as he announces at the outset of *Chronique*, for only '*un èspese d'un cinéma vérité*' – some kind of Vertovian *kino prava*: film truth.

The division between Direct Cinema and cinéma vérité was, inevitably, subject to some blurring. The Americans, beyond just being merely present, provoked on-camera reaction on occasion, while the French often simply observed without overt intervention. Anyway, less dogmatic than the Americans, Rouch was prepared to use a fuller range of classic techniques than they were. There is almost nothing spontaneously observational (in the sense of surveillance, events happening whether the camera was present or not) in *Chronique*. Rouch and Morin begin by filming themselves interviewing their main subject, Marceline Loridan, about her life. They film her, a market researcher, as she asks random people on the street if they are happy. Thereafter, a seemingly random sequence of people come before their lens, some to be spoken to individually, some invited to dinner or lunch where the topics of conversation are set, on camera, by the film-makers. Rouch and Morin's purpose was to penetrate behind surface reality and illuminate the *mentalité* of their subjects,

'the strange tribe that lived in Paris'. This is not to say that cinéma vérité was better than Direct Cinema at capturing *the* truth; its advantage was simply it was not trying to. The implicit limitation of *a* truth is further reinforced by being only a kind (*espèce*) of truth (*vérité*).

Rouch's self-reflexive modus operandi, the mark of the Vertovian alternative, was just as susceptible to selectivity and partiality as was the Grierson/Direct Cinema approach. The irony in this is that cinéma vérité was facilitated by the same developments of 16mm portable synch film apparatus as had happened independently at the Canadian National Film Board[86] and subsequently in New York. The difference – the advantage – was that cinéma vérité made no implicit or explicit claim to impartiality. The manipulations of the film-makers are seen in plain view – well, most of them.

In fact, the subjects in *Chronique* are connected in largely unstated ways through Morin and many share his radical politics. Significantly, this is never quite revealed on screen. Moreover, the levels of intervention, while arguably being less illusionist than Direct Cinema's practices, were even more vexed ethically. Now documentarists directly caused their subjects to be exposed – not only by the degree of close observation enabled by the equipment, but also by asking them to do things on camera (e.g., 'discuss X'). And, as with Direct Cinema, the style could be faked. Self-reflexivity was even easier to simulate than was transparent observationalism.[87]

Nevertheless, the claim on the real was far more overtly limited; far fewer 'selected gleanings' were promoted into 'self-evident generalisations' than with Direct

Chronique d'un été (1961): the Vertovian moment was self-consciously and precisely recovered

Griersonian Realist (Observational*) Practice v. Vertovian (Reflexive) Practice

| | Griersonian Documentary Practice | | Vertovian Documentary Practice | |
	Pre-1960 'Classic'	Post-1960 Direct Cinema	Pre-1960 *Kino Pravda*	Post-1960 cinéma vérité
Pre-production (Aesthetics)				
Sobriety	✓	✓	✓	✓
Poeticism/Agitprop	✓	X	✓	✓
Archive (Compilation)	✓	X	✓	X
Production (Camera/Sound)				
Tripod-mounted Camera	✓	X	✓	X/✓
Hand-held Camera	✓	✓	X	✓
Silent Shooting	✓	X	✓	X
Synch-sound Shooting	✓	✓	X	✓
Augmented Lighting	✓	X/✓	✓	X/✓
Production (Direction)				
Directed Action	✓	X	X	✓/X
Reconstruction	✓	X	✓	X
Interview	✓	X	✓	X/✓
Provocation	X	X	✓	✓
Film-maker-in-shot	X	X	✓	✓
Direct Address (to camera)	✓	X	✓	✓
Post-production				
Editing	✓	✓	✓	✓
Extra-diegetic Sound	✓	✓	–	X
Voiceover/Parallel Action	✓	✓	X	X/✓
Commentary (Narration)†	✓	✓	X	X/✓
Graphics	✓	X/✓	✓	X
Superimpositions	✓	✓	✓	✓
Special f/x	X	X	✓	X

†including intertitles.
* or '(Transparent)'.

Cinema films. The conditions of the 'experiment', as with Vertov, although not wholly revealed, were nevertheless more overtly on view.

ANOMALOUS PRACTICES

Chronique was to be as ignored by the Direct Cinema pioneers as *Man with a Movie Camera* had been ignored by the Griersonians. In fact, the terms initially used for dismissing it were identical – cameras filming other cameras, a *reductio ad absurdum* etc. It was not until the later 1980s that elements of Rouch's approach began to find anglophone emulators, meshing with some mainstream practices to constitute further challenges to the *dogme*.

In Thomas Kuhn's classic model of the nature of scientific revolutions,[88] experiments designed to support a scientific hypothesis (which Kuhn sees as producing a 'paradigm'), instead, on occasion, throw up 'anomalous' results. In the Kuhnian model, when the weight of the anomalies grows great enough, the paradigm is discarded and a new one emerges – a process he characterises as 'revolutionary'. By analogy, the Griersonian 'paradigm' had suggested films could be made claiming to be evidential, placing audiences in the position of a judge, providing 'the feeling of being there'. This claim ('paradigm') was increasingly undercut as film after film failed to close off questions as to authenticity and objectivity. Instead of proving the paradigm, the instances of the experiment (i.e., the films) produced anomalies (e.g., *The Thin Blue Line*, dramadocs, *The Bartos Family* and numerous other titles with various approaches, tones and techniques) until, in the last decade of the twentieth century, the Griersonian paradigm faltered. *Chronique*, after all, had heralded that its dominance was coming to an end.

The old paradigm's essential promise of providing objective evidence was removed from its capstone position. Film-makers needed no longer to pretend to unauthored scientistic objectivity in order to deliver 'documentary value'. Had Vertov prevailed at the outset, there would have been a cost in terms of surrendering the ideologically powerful claim to be providing 'truth'; but there would also likely not have been such persistent criticism of documentary for failing to deliver this 'objectively'; for making a promise which it had never been able to keep. Not before time, the promise was being withdrawn.

Emblematic to this was seeing a film's director on screen, the crucial marker of the difference between French and North American practice, although, again, one which was not entirely without precedent in the Griersonian documentary. It had long allowed direct camera address. In the classic period, films were often topped and tailed by 'experts' talking to the lens. With television, the 'authored' documentary featuring a reporter, celebrity or expert in shot (often repeatedly) was a commonplace. In the 1970s, independent documentary – encouraged by the zeitgeist (of the 'Me Generation' as it was termed), as well as cinéma vérité and these 'authored' television pieces – also allowed for film-makers to begin to appear regularly on camera. Some made this their trademark and another late 1980s film can stand as an emblematic marker of the turn then underway.

The radical journalist Michael Moore is a scion of carworkers in Flint, Michigan – in their day the most highly rewarded group of industrial workers in the world: or so Moore claims in his 1989 box-office sensation, *Roger and Me*. His documentary investigates the social impact of deindustrialisation as American capital moved its manufacturing base to cheaper industrial environments off-shore. Moore sets off, on camera, to bring the chief executive of General Motors, Roger Smith, to Flint to witness the social damage such company policies had caused. His method is to repeatedly show up at the gates of mothballed GM plants or the corporation headquarters and demand a meeting with the boss. His repeated failure to get to Smith is, of course, a nonsense as is made clear in a climatic sequence when Moore, as a legitimate member of the press, actually comes to confront the executive at a GM PR event. However, the ploy allows Moore to cross-cut his set-up interactions with observational sequences of decline and deprivation. This works most powerfully to bring home

his denunciation of the economic system's amorality. The film's unexpected success in mall cinemas all over America speaks to its effectiveness.

Detractors, made uncomfortable by Moore's polemic, accused him (in the usual way of these things) of fabrication, but could not, in essence, come up with anything more than the fact that these cross-cut sequences, being shot at different times, distorted historical truth.[89] This was to hit Moore formalistically with a supposed rule for documentary veracity that did not exist: it was never part of any documentary procedure. If documentary had depended on sequences in a final film being in the chronological order in which they were obtained, all narrative but plodding sequentiality would be denied. Such a demand would reject exactly what made *Nanook* and practically everything that followed compelling. The form could not have easily survived this. The charge, though, is a measure of how effectively Direct Cinema *dogme* had determined popular understanding of what a documentary ought to be. A rule against non-chronological sequencing is so of a piece with Direct Cinema's actual self-denying ordinances that it sounds plausible.

The authenticity of Moore's sequences, though, was not otherwise susceptible to attack. That reordering affects meaning, the other aspect of this jejune conservative critique, is so ideologically self-serving as to be asinine. Of course, juxtapositioning creates meaning. So what? In fact, Moore did not 'cheat' (well, no more than is usual!); he did not fabricate, did not reconstruct. He selected, in an overt fashion, observational material, gathered with various degrees of intervention at different times, and arranged it to tell a story – quite explicitly from his viewpoint – about the world. Rightist critics can fume, but the Flint he filmed was Flint, GM had moved its factories to Mexico, the city was in acute economic decline by any measure. (The factory gates were Lumières' factory gates. It was 1895 etc.)

Roger and Me is, in terms of Direct Cinema, an anomaly, albeit its protocols are not completely new. Aside from reflecting cinéma vérité's alternative reflexivity, the approach taken also speaks to the persistence and refinement of a number of other classic non-Griersonian documentary approaches – as well as leading to some directions not previously explored.

First, Moore placed an old non-Griersonian documentary tradition of oppositional political engagement centre stage. Documentary propaganda often exploiting (but never, of course, delivering) Griersonian notions of objectivity had long been made by all strands of political opinion. Documentary served the fascist regimes,[90] the Soviets and the oppositional left.[91] Anyway, despite its pretensions to 'education' and objectivity, it is not farfetched to see mainstream Griersonian documentary also as another propaganda tool for the liberal bourgeois democracies.

Roger and Me (1989): an anomaly, albeit its protocols are not completely new

'Objectivity' is a concept scarcely untrammelled by ideology, after all.

The introduction of the Sony Portapak half-inch home-video camera and recorder in 1967 expanded agitprop possibilities by allowing for previously unavailable degrees of access and interactivity – often of a self-reflexive nature. A radical rhetoric emphasising the possible collectivity and interactivity such work could involve emerged. This would come to undercut the very concept of professionalised documentary production. Instead, directors were transformed into 'social-cultural animators ' (to use the language of the time), video activists working as advocates and trainers rather than any species of film artist.

Once again the Canadian National Film Board stands at the forefront of documentary development. Not only did the negative impact of *The Things I Cannot Change* on the film's subjects occasion soul searching at the Board. At the same time, one of its directors, Colin Low, was also making a series of 16mm films with the people of Fogo Island, Nova

Scotia. For these potentially classic studies of deprivation, Low transformed the position of his subjects by relinquishing to them, as much as he could given the high-tech equipment he was using, his directorial prerogatives. To an unprecedented degree, he gave them a voice, unmediated by his vision, to put a case not so much before the general public as before a previously unresponsive and uncaring provincial government. For the first time in documentary film history there was a structured attempt to address the form's 'original sin' by reducing the film-maker to the role of enabler.[92] Consent was an irrelevancy as the films were, much more meaningfully than is usually the case, the work of the subjects. The new protocol became known as the 'Fogo Process' and it instigated a whole strand of film-making for social activist purposes: the Board's Challenge for Change/Société nouvelle programme. The Fogo Process

VTR St Jacques (1968): film-making for social activist purposes

was to be emulated elsewhere; but within the Board the project was carried to another stage when George Stoney, a ubiquitous figure in attempts to democratise North American documentary expression, began distributing Portapaks under the Challenge for Change rubric and arranging the training of the citizenry in their use. Instead of the complexities of film technology, video offered a new basis for documentary production by non-professionals. Instant replay removed the uncertainties involved in exposing celluloid and facilitated collective production and editorial control. Over the next decades, the implication of this slowly pushed itself into professional consciousness – not just a threat to Direct Cinema but also a menace to the very idea of the Griersonian documentary director. The Fogo Process was deeply anomalous in terms of established practice; Stoney's encouragement of non-professional production even more so.

But to return to Moore. His attack on Direct Cinema also highlighted an entirely fresh and unprecedented tone to the documentary, one not prefigured in the form before the 1980s. *Roger and Me* was a hit because, in defiance of the entire Griersonian paradigm, its polemic was bitingly funny. It showed, with very positive box-office results, that documentaries need not always offer a 'discourse of sobriety'. Moore could have made a burning denunciation of the economic situation in Flint, but such social criticism had become hackneyed, overly familiar. Moore's oppositional position was one adopted by many mainstream, 'sober' documentarists. It was possible to see the output of television factual programming, including documentary, as nothing but a sustained radical attack on the status quo, constantly highlighting social problems, its main theme society's victims.

The tendency to make what might be called 'victim documentaries' had been initiated by Grierson's initial 'public education' agenda in the 1930s, in contrast to Flaherty's romanticising of the exotic other in the 20s. In the Depression, anglophone documentary subjects had always tended to be 'poor suffering characters'[93] whose trials, the films suggested, would soon be over thanks to enlightened authorities. With post-war television in the 50s and 60s, the victims remained but the light at the end of the tunnel was dimmer. However, this was less a consequence of the ideology of the personnel involved (much less of the mainstream establishment institutions for which they worked); rather it flowed from the basic anglophone journalistic instinct to comfort the afflicted and afflict the comfortable. Be that as it may, the audience was felt by some professionals to have become anaesthetised to this constant flow of gloom. As with the use of the Holocaust archive, audiences needed anomalies, *ostranenie* – as in *The Thin Blue Line*, *The Bartos Family* or *Roger and Me* – to revive attention. In Moore's case this involved not just being on camera, not only being opinionated, *engagé*, but also being funny – bitingly, satirically funny.

Roger and Me was not alone in undermining documentary sobriety. Its new tone was also heard in the work of Mark Lewis. Lewis's *Cane Toads* (1986), for example, is an ecological disaster movie about the calamitous consequences for Australia of the importation of a large poisonous toad from the South Seas. The animal now infests the entire north-east of the country; but instead of an easily forgettable 'green' film about yet another environmental disaster, Lewis provides an unforgettable, hilarious satire about scientific experts' stupidity. *Cane Toads*, with the toads refrigerated to slow them down for filming, is unforgettable. Documentaries could be amusing, hilarious even, which they had never been before.[94] Given documentary's usual sobriety, satire produced *ostranenie* automatically, as it were.

The question was more than one of tone, though. The use of satire restores documentary's polemical voice, albeit in a new register. This again highlights Direct Cinema's limitations. Direct Cinema could well – if not brilliantly – illustrate what happened in any given situation, but not, necessarily, could it very easily explain the significance of what it presented. Even when it addressed new areas such as intrusive films of family life, the *mentalité* of the subject remained opaque. Rouch's cinéma vérité interventions, being designed to enter the mind of his subjects, addressed this limited ability. So too, in effect, did those works of the avant-garde experimental cinema, which mixed documentary actuality with fiction, although these films were usually seen as being outside the documentary canon.[95] Documentary's established tolerance of such hybridity, however, was key in developing more apposite aesthetics.

Scientistic observation was easily cast, by progressive opinion, as a specifically western, patriarchal mode. As such, it was not necessarily best suited for non-western, non-patriarchal expression. Other voices were not automatically excluded by the aesthetics of Griersonian documentary, although they had, of course, fared badly in sponsorship and commissioning terms. Within the West, ethnic minority and women's voices had sometimes been heard, albeit expressed through this cultural gender-specific aesthetic. For example, aided by rising social sensitivity, women directors managed to mount productions deploying traditional documentary techniques in the service of feminist history. Lorraine Gray's *With Babies and Banners* (1979, USA) or Connie Fields's *The Life and Times of Rosie the Riveter* (1980, USA) would be classic instances of this. But overall neither the classic documentary nor Direct Cinema did much to encourage voices other than its own white, male one.

Illustrating female or ethnic experience had not been facilitated by the Griersonian paradigm. Thus, Michelle Citron's 1979 avant-garde film, *Daughter Rite* (USA), combines her family 8mm archive of her childhood with a fictional encounter between two women. It demonstrates a (necessarily anomalous) feminist documentary aesthetic. The late 1980s marker text of this refusal to acknowledge the Direct Cinema *dogme* is Trin T. Minh-ha's *Surname Viet, Given Name Nam* (1989), with its similar promiscuous melding of archival news and documentary footage and acted (i.e., restaged) interviews. Trin T. Minh-ha's attack on documentary's protocols not only challenged the patriarchal documentary voice; she was also undercutting the Griersonian paradigm.

Another 1989 film was equally anomalous and transgressive. In *Tongues Untied*, Marlon Riggs essayed the creation of a fresh filmic language to document the African American homosexual experience – again defying the paradigm to find a new, more appropriate documentary language. For example, a frame-cut sequence of lips in extreme close-up uttering racist names for African Americans is both literally and metaphorically in the audience's face – and the venom of that experience in life was brought vividly home. Such transgressive levels of intervention for the reconstruction of prior witnessed behaviour more directly delivers some sense of 'the feeling of being there', than does anything done within the constraints of Direct Cinema.

The final consequence of the attack on Griersonian/ Direct Cinema protocols was Reality TV, often termed by its professional defenders as 'formatted documentary'. To much embarrassment in established documentary circles, Rouch's legacy also embraces this. As with *Chronique*, formatted documentary involves the producers placing non-actor subjects in situations of the programme-makers' devising. It can involve a measure of self-reflexivity (e.g., the *Big Brother* format, which allowed for direct address by the subject). With Reality TV's exploitative degradations, however, there is nothing of a Rouchian search for *mentalités*. Its producers, for the most part, are, like eighteenth-century Bedlam keepers, in the business of exhibiting inmates for the entertainment of the public; but not all such interventionism seeks despicable voyeuristic exposure (with added absurdist game-show elements). Far less reprehensibly, programme-makers can place their subjects in more genuine illuminating situations: for example, recreating as accurately as possible the conditions of everyday life in an Edwardian house.[96]

The real distinction between cinéma vérité and formatted documentary more generally anyway has little to do with the intentionality of the producer. It is that formatted television's essence – the basis of its claim of 'documentary value' – is that it provides pure observational footage, surveillance even. Its producers exploit Direct Cinema *dogme* to secure such authenticity as they can command even as they totally ignore its non-interventionist strictures. Therefore, unlike cinéma vérité practitioners, they remain hidden, pretending to the audience that the behaviour filmed is 'real'.[97] It is easy to sympathise with

Surname Viet, Given Name Nam (1989): the refusal to acknowledge the Direct Cinema *dogme; Tongues Untied* (1989): equally anomalous and transgressive

the attempts of Direct Cinema practitioners to distant themselves rhetorically from 'Reality TV' as 'the nadir of human achievement'.[98] Many of these television programmes – away from the historical and towards the game-show end of the production continuum – update the 'attractions' of the fairground freak-show and are clearly ethically indefensible; but, inescapably, all formatted television does document behaviour (however artificial the environment in which it occurs) using established, old-paradigm documentary techniques. Formats assume the same levels of audience belief in authenticity. Thus, what most formatted documentary presents might well be of virtually no value as 'showing us life' (to use an injunction of Vertov's),[99] so unreal are the conditions which produced it; but, nevertheless, it cannot be excluded from documentary's compass. It is yet another anomaly.

These are now so many as to be overwhelming. It becomes possible to reconsider *Man with a Movie Camera*, the template for *Chronique*, seeing it not so much as yet another challenge but, rather, as so thorough an alternative to dominant documentary practice as to institute a new phase. By the late 1980s, the anomalies had piled up to the extent that, despite Direct Cinema *dogme* still determining public understanding of what documentary was, the era of its hegemony was, in practice, coming to an end. The range of options had expanded to embrace the possibilities legitimated by the persistence (or recovery) and refinement of old techniques, including reconstruction, dramatisation, distanciation, reflexivity, political engagement, satire and Reality TV. And, of course, observationalism also persisted. Above all, though, there was *kino pravda*.

Narrative and witness where still in place but the overt interventions of Vertov (and Rouch/Morin) refused the burden of objectivity taken up by Grierson and made even heavier by Direct Cinema. Allowing for the fact of mediation rather than disguising it was, in effect, to put documentary on a whole new footing – a fundamental change of the sort that Direct Cinema had announced itself as effecting but which it had really not provided. For all that the Vertovian approach had been first seen half a century earlier and ignored, it was now, in the context of the recovery and expansion of all documentary's older practices, to provide not so much a challenge as the basis for a new paradigm.

THE POST-GRIERSONIAN DOCUMENTARY

Within documentary circles, already by 2000, the emergence of a new paradigm was firmly enough established to justify, for example, an entire film festival specifically questioning the form. Crossing Boundaries ('for want of a better name') was mounted at the Danish Film Institute,

> not because we have anything against documentary film as such. Quite the contrary. But the films originate from so many different environments and traditions that they transgress the boundaries of traditional documentary film. When we chose, nevertheless, to call it a documentary film festival, we did so because the films, despite their vast dissimilarities, are all connected to reality in a very unique [sic] way ... Reality in the broader sense of the world.[100]

'What counts as knowledge' was, indeed, 'not what it used to be'. And neither was documentary.

But how shall we think of this paradigm shift? It contains enough of the old to be not quite 'New Documentary'.

Conversely, its heterogeneity is not totally captured by the image of boundary blurring or crossing; or by the idea of hybridity. These terms only work if Direct Cinema *dogme* is deemed to contain the whole of documentary, which it never has. Better, then, to focus on the 'connections' to reality that were now broader than Grierson had in view and, therefore, to gloss this current period as being 'post-Griersonian'.

This categorisation is not intended to imply that Grierson was totally discarded in the new paradigm; nor that variations and alternatives to his practice did not pre-exist 1980s practice. Rather, it is to indicate that although Griersonian techniques and agendas (including Direct Cinema's aesthetic) persisted (and persist), the central most salient aspect of the original paradigm – the Griersonian belief that 'documentary value' could be a 'fundamental property' of the image – was no longer in place. It had never actually been a sound foundation for all that it was generally believed to be so; now its misleading character could not be so readily denied.

It is this condition of postmodernity – the evident uncertainties of any document's status in today's context – to which John Corner was in 2000 drawing attention with the term 'post-documentary'.[101] What counts as authentic was, in the face of digital malleabilities, also 'not what it used to be'. After all, never mind anything else, the old paradigm could not withstand digital's destruction of photography's evidential pretentions. Finally, in the age of the digital, it needs must be admitted that photographs can lie. However, acknowledging instead that 'documentary value' depends on 'a relation between film and audience', a matter more critically of reception than of production, means that documentary can survive this destruction of the photograph as evidence.

Documentary was still being determined by narrative and witness, its truths still reflected *the* real (not *a* fictional) world. Now, though, the post-Griersonian documentary paradigm could not be defined any longer as 'the creative treatment of actuality'. Necessarily less succinctly, it could be better described as: *the narrativised recorded aspects of witnessed observation received as being a story about the world*. In effect, a new paradigm matching this description was necessarily coming into being, grounded in the anomalies and further facilitated by the new technology.

Witness was still the glue joining the story to the world, but how it was illustrated is no longer the central issue (at least in forward-looking professional and scholarly circles). In the new post-Griersonian situation any mode of presentation could produce 'documentary value' if underpinned in some way by witness. This means digital imaging has a place. Digitally mapping contour lines onto wartime aerial reconnaissance photographs, for example, produces three-dimensional images into which a viewer can walk or fly; but the virtual topography created is

Griersonian – Vertovian – Post-Griersonian Practice

	Griersonian Practice		Vertovian Practice		Post-Griersonian Practice
	Pre-1960 'Classic'	Post-1960 Direct Cinema	Pre-1960 Kino Pravda	Post-1960 cinéma vérité	Post-1990
Pre-production (Aesthetics)					
Sobriety	✓	✓	✓	✓	✓
Comedy/Satire/Mocumentary	X	X	X	X	✓
Poeticism/Agitprop	✓	X	✓	X	✓
Archive (Compilation)	✓	X	X	X/✓	✓
Formatted Documentary	X	X	X	X	✓
Documusicals	X	X	X	X	✓
Animated Documentary	X	X	X	X	✓
Interactive Documedia	X	X	X	X	✓
Actors (Dramadoc)	X	X	X	X	✓
Hypothetical Documentary	X	X	X	X	✓
Production (Camera/Sound)					
Tripod-mounted Camera	✓	X	✓	✓	✓
Hand-held Camera	✓	✓	X	✓	✓
Digital Imaging	X	X	X	X	✓
Silent Shooting	✓	X	✓	X	✓
Synch-sound Shooting	✓	✓	X	✓	✓
Augmented Lighting	✓	✓	X	✓	✓
Production (Direction)					
Directed Action	✓	X	X	✓/X	✓
Reconstruction	✓	X	✓	X	✓
Interview	✓	X	✓	✓	✓
Provocation	X	X	✓	✓	✓
Film-maker in shot	X	X	✓	✓	✓
Direct Address (to camera)	✓	X	✓	X/✓	✓
Post-production					
Editing	✓	✓	✓	✓	✓
Extra-diegetic Sound	✓	✓	–	X	✓
Voiceover/Parallel Action	✓	✓	X	X/✓	✓
Commentary (Narration)	✓	✓	X	X/✓	✓
Graphics	✓	X	✓	X	✓
Superimpositions	✓	✓	✓	✓	✓
Special f/x	X	X	✓	X	✓

grounded in reality.[102] Unphotographable mental illnesses can be described by patients and illustrated by animation.[103] Imprisoned young offenders can have their experience turned into rap lyrics which they can perform on camera – the documusical.[104] Carefully crafted, 'puritanically' fact-based hypothetical situations shot in established documentary style using actors could yield documentaries about situations yet to happen – for example, a terror attack using smallpox.[105] Call this 'conditional documentary'. All can 'show us life'.

The Korsakow System (2007–11): 'an easy-to-use computer program for the creation of database films'

As can the deployment of the interactive possibilities of new media platforms.[106] The documentarist Peter Wintonik, for example, talks not of documentary but of 'documedia', thus privileging the technology.[107] But, as with Direct Cinema's similar technicist focus, such a position runs the danger of ignoring the social context. The vibrancy of documentary's accumulated aesthetics, techniques and tropes, the strength of realism's grip on the collective imagination, the power of story and the validity of witness will not dissolve in the face of multiple-authored 'documedia' expressions emanating from a cloud of interactivity.

What is significant is not the changes in technology, nor even the removal of the sole, controlling documentarist. The overall, and most fundamental, consequence of the destruction of the old paradigm is that, with the new post-Griersonian documentary, responsibility for determining documentary value is removed from the image and its maker and is passed to the audience (where, in fact, it should have always been). To believe that documentarists ever had any sort of responsibility to deliver 'truth' is to suggest that this could be done – that truth could be, in some way, guaranteed by the image alone. If, on the other hand, 'documentary value' is determined by reception, then the Griersonian ethical burden is removed. A practical case-by-case ethics becomes possible. The post-Griersonian documentary, unlike its predecessors' reliance on viewer naivety, demands sceptical audiences. They reduce the ethical burden and enhance the watchdog justification. The Vertovian injunction to 'show us life' remains, giving the documentary a crucial role in society, one that it is well able to play. Documentary approaches its second century with its value and validity in good order.

NOTES

1. In 'The Imaginary Signifier', Ben Brewster's influential translation of 'Le significant imaginaire' (1975) in Screen vol. 16 no. 2 (Christian Metz, 'Le significant imaginaire' Communications no. 23 [reprinted, 1977] [Paris: Union Général d'Éditions, Trans. reprinted: Imaginary Signifier:

Psychoanalysis and the Cinema, Bloomington, IN: Indiana University Press, 1975]).

2. Guy Gauthier, Le documentaire: un autre cinéma (Paris: Armand Colin, 2011), p. 5.

3. John Grierson, 'First Principles of Documentary', Grierson on Documentary, ed. Forsyth Hardy (London: Faber, 1979 [1966/1932]), p. 35.

4. Osip Brik, Viktor Shklovskii, Esfir Shub and Sergei Tretiakov, 'LEF i Kino' ['LEF and Cinema'] (1927) Novyi LEF vol. 11/12; in 'Novy LEF with an Introduction' (1971) trans. Ben Brewsterm Screen vol. 12 no. 4, Winter

5. Grierson, Grierson on Documentary.

6. Paul Rotha, Documentary Film (London: Faber, 1935).

7. Lewis Jacobs (ed.), The Documentary Tradition: From Nanook to Woodstock (New York: Hopkinson & Blake, 1971). This pioneering collection of comment on the documentary ranges across a wide variety of publications with The Lef Arena, at one end (as it were) and, at the other, around a dozen pieces from mainstream publications, such as Life, Newsweek, the New York Times, New Statesmen etc. The bulk reflects the occasional attention paid to documentary in specialised film publications.

8. Richard Barsam, Non-Fiction Film (New York: E. P. Dutton, 1973.

9. Erik Barnow, Documentary: A History of the Non-Fiction Film (New York: Oxford University Press, 1974).

10. Cahiers du cinéma no. 144, June.

11. Calvin Pryluck, 'Ultimately We Are All Outsiders: The Ethics of Documentary Filming', Journal of the University Film Association vol. 28 no. 1, 1976.

12. Brian Winston, Claiming the Real II: Documentary: Grierson and Beyond (London: BFI, 2005), pp. 31–3.

13. See, for example, Patricia Zimmerman, States of Emergency: Documentaries, Wars, Democracies (Minneapolis: University of Minnesota Press, 2000).

14. Michael Renov (ed.), Theorizing Documentary (London: Routledge, 1993).

15. Bill Nichols, Representing Reality: Issues and Concepts in Documentary (Bloomington: Indiana University Press, 1991).

16. Auguste and Louis Lumière (1895), France.

17. Robert Flaherty (1922), USA/France.

18. Edgar Anstey (1935), UK.

19. Robert Drew and Richard Leacock (1960), USA.

20. Nichols, Representing Reality, p. 3.

21. In a review of Flaherty's second feature-length film Moana (1926), which he wrote for the New York Sun in 1926 (reprinted in John Grierson, Grierson on the Movies, ed. Forsyth Hardy [London: Faber, 1981], p. 24). The connection between graphic representation and the word 'documentary', however, dates back into the nineteenth century at least, as Charles Musser has discovered (see below, Chapter 2.1). The photographer

Edward Curtis followed on from this usage when he coined the term in English in connection with the cinema in 1915. However, it was Grierson's review which brought it into widespread use (Winston, *Claiming the Real II*, pp. 11–13).

22. From Charles Urban's *Cheese Mites*, a sensation in London in 1903, on. See Timothy Boon, *Films of Fact: A History of Science in Documentary Films and Television* (London: Wallflower, 2008). Crucial to the development of the documentary, especially in France, was similar work from the late 1920s on by Jean Panlevé (Guy Gauthier, *Le documentaire: un autre cinéma* [Paris: Armand Colin, 2011], p. 325).

23. For example, Alfred Haddon's 1898 footage of Torres Strait First People performing ceremonial dances.

24. Geoffrey Malins and John McDowell (1916), UK.

25. Bill Nichols, 'Questions of Magnitude', in John Corner (ed.), *Documentary and the Mass Media* (London: Edward Arnold, 1986), p. 114.

26. The film has been recovered from obscurity by Michael Chanan.

27. Ann Martin, '16mm Magnetic Film Sound on TV Newsfilms in Germany', *Journal of the SMPTE* no. 65, June 1956, pp. 336–7.

28. Terence McCartney-Filgate, interviewed by Barbara Evens and Brian Winston, Toronto, 17 May 2012. McCartney-Filgate, a National Film Board cinematographer, was involved in *Primary* because of this prior Canadian experience, although the Americans otherwise ignored the Canadian equipment, insisting on starting from scratch themselves.

29. Paul Swann, *The British Documentary Film Movement 1926–1946* (Cambridge: Cambridge University Press, 1989), p. 85.

30. In the 1920s, successful silent feature documentaries at the cinema box office, following *Nanook*, were not unknown. By the 50s and 60s documentary in the commercial cinema had become more or less limited to Disney's anthropomorphic nature films and intermittent Olympic and World Cup features.

31. Grierson, *Grierson on Documentary*, pp. 69 and 48.

32. Jack Ellis, *The Documentary Idea: A Critical History of the English Language Documentary Film & Video* (Englewood Cliffs, NJ: Prentice Hall, 1989), p. 302.

33. Grierson, *Grierson on Documentary*, pp. 35–6, 73–4.

34. Richard Leacock, *The Feeling of Being There* (Paris: Semeïon, 2012). Leacock's use of the phrase was first recorded in print in 1961 (Gideon Bachman, 'The Frontiers of Realist Cinema: The Work of Ricky Leacock', *Film Culture* no. 19–23, Summer 1961, p. 16).

35. Ian Aitken, *Film and Reform: John Grierson and the Documentary Film Movement* (London: Routledge, 1990).

36. John Grierson, 'The Documentary Producer', *Cinema Quarterly*, 1933, p. 8.

37. Grierson, 'First Principles of Documentary', *Grierson on Documentary*, p. 35.

38. Justice Potter Stewart in *Jacobellis v. Ohio*, 378 US 184 (1964).

39. Huub Jansen, *Inventory of the WUD-AID Collection* (Nijmigen: European Foundation Joris Ivens, 2004); Hans Schoots, *Living Dangerously: A Biography of Joris Ivens*, trans. David Cromer (Amsterdam: University of Amsterdam, 1995), pp. 221–2. (Barsam erroneously gives 1947 which has been widely cited; but that was the date of a preliminary meeting held in Brussels and attended by, among a dozen others, Rotha, Storck and Ivens.)

40. Bert Hogenkamp, 'Definitions and Divisions: The International Documentary Film Movement from 1946 to 1964', *IDFA* (catalogue) (Amsterdam: IDFA, 1999), pp. 160–4.

41. *Misère au Borinage* (1933), Belgium.

42. Joris Ivens, *The Camera and I* (New York: International, 1969), pp. 89–90.

43. Al Maysles (reportedly) to G. Roy Leven, *Documentary Explorations* (Garden City, NY: Anchor Press, 1971), p. 227.

44. Richard Leacock to André Labarthe and Louis Marcorelles, 'Entretien avec Robert Drew et Richard Leacock', *Cahiers du cinéma* vol. 26 no. 140, 1963, p. 26.

45. To Leven, *Documentary Explorations*, p. 163.

46. In ibid., p. 322.

47. Perhaps the most dramatic example of this in the nineteenth stills archive is Andrew Gardener's photographs of the dead after the Battle of Gettysburg in the American Civil War where he recostumed a corpse, in one shot a Confederate infantryman, as a 'sharpshooter' (Kathleen Collins, 'The Camera as an Instrument of Persuasion: Studies of 19th-Century Propaganda Photography', PhD Pennsylvania State University [Ann Arbor: University Microfilms International, 1985] fig. 12).

48. Nichols, *Representing Reality*, p. 7.

49. For example, in old age, Fred Wiseman could admit that his editing: 'is highly manipulative and the shooting is highly manipulative, not in the sense that people do things differently from what they will ordinarily do, but the way that people are shot' (Kaleem Aftab and Alexandra Weltz, 'Fred Wiseman', *Film West*, June 2000, p. 33). Clearly this acknowledgment is more acceptable in tone than his initial dismissal of all questions of 'objectivity' as 'bullshit' (Leven, *Documentary Explorations*, p. 231). Nevertheless, it still says nothing to the main issue, viz.: how the audience reads the film, how much they can be thought to be aware of this manipulation. On that he remains silent.

50. Donald McWilliams, 'Frederick Wiseman', *Film Quarterly* vol. 24 no. 1, Autumn 1970, p. 22.

51. I am grateful to John Corner for this observation.

52. Robert Fairthorne, 'The Principles of the Film', *Film Art*, 1933: quoted in Don Macpherson (ed.), *Traditions of Independence* (London: BFI, 1980), p. 131.

53. Roland Barthes, *Image, Music, Text*, trans. Stephen Heath (London: Fontana, 1977), pp.15–38.

54. Jeanne Hall, 'Realism as a Style in Cinéma Vérité: A Critical Analysis of *Primary*', *Cinema Journal* vol. 30 no. 4, Summer 1991.

55. Allan King (1969), Canada.

56. Molly Haskell, 'The Three Documentaries', Jacobs, *The Documentary Tradition*, p. 475.

57. It is now known that Flaherty fathered a child with Nyla, a women he cast as as one of Nanook's wives in the film, whom he abandoned (Melanie McGrath, *The Long Exile: A True Story of Deception and Survival in the Canadian Arctic* [London: Harper, 2007]). That, however, speaks to a personal moral failing rather than the specifics of film-making ethics.

58. Jay Ruby, 'A Re-examination of the Early Career of Robert J. Flaherty', *Quarterly Review of Film Studies*, Autumn 1980, p. 66.

59. Paul Rotha, *Robert J. Flaherty: A Biography*, ed. Jay Ruby (Philadelphia: University of Pennsylvania Press, 1983), p. 116.

60. An unrepentant Harry Watt explained to Elizabeth Sussex that subterfuge was a normal procedure: 'Being film people, we'd take advantage.' Elizabeth Sussex, *The Rise and Fall of British Documentary* (Berkeley: University of California Press, 1975), p. 89.

61. Paul Rotha, *Documentary Diary: An Informal History of the British Documentary Film, 1928–1939* (New York: Hill & Wang, 1973), p. 104.

62. Ivens, *The Camera and I*, pp. 87f.

63. Vlada Petric, 'Esther Shub: Film as a Historical Discourse', in Thomas Waugh (ed.), *'Show Us Life': Toward a History and Aesthetics of Committed Documentary* (Metuchen, NJ: Scarecrow Press, 1984), pp. 24, 37.

64. Gail Vanstone, *D is for Daring* (Toronto: Sumach, 2005).

65. Carolyn Anderson and Thomas Benson, *Documentary Dilemmas: Frederick Wiseman's Titicut Follies* (Carbondale, IL: Southern Illinois University Press, 1991).

66. Brian Winston, *Lies, Damn Lies and Documentaries* (London: BFI, 2000).

67. The most egregious example of this is the case of Michael Born, a German documentarist/journalist. He was imprisoned in 1996 for four years for fraud because he had repeatedly used actors as 'real' people in a number of television documentaries (Victoria Mapplebeck, 'The Tabloid Formula', *Dox*, 13 October, 1997, pp. 11–12).

68. Noel Carroll, 'From Real to Reel: Entangled in the Non-Fiction Film', *Philosophical Exchange* (Brookport, NY: State University of New York, 1983), pp. 6–7.

69. Jane Roscoe and Craig Hight, *Faking it: Mock-Documentary and the Subversion of Factuality* (Manchester: Manchester University Press, 2001).

70. Bill Nichols, *Blurred Boundaries: Questions of Meaning in Contemporary Culture* (Bloomington: Indiana University Press, 1994).

71. Linda Williams, 'Mirrors without Memories: Truth, History, and the New Documentary', *Film Quarterly* vol. 46 no. 3, Spring 1993.

72. Blewitt was a Cornish fisherman who, in an unlikely fictional tale, looses his smack and uses Post Office savings to accumulate the wherewithall to buy a new one. Paul Swann sees *The Savings of Bill Blewitt* (1936), very much a proto-dramadoc directed (badly) by Harry Watt, as marking the introduction of fictive elements at this level, a critical development for the UK Documentary Movement in the 1930s. (Swann, *The British Documentary Film Movement 1926–1946*). Blewitt went on to appear in three wartime documentaries and in four features.

73. William Nichols, *Representing Reality*, pp. 7 and 109.

74. Anthony Page, *Missiles of October* (1974), USA.

75. Derek Paget, *No Other Way to Tell It: Dramdoc/docudrama on Television* (Manchester: University of Manchester Press, 1998), p. 164.

76. For example, the UK Great Train Robbery of 1963 (in which £2.6 million was stolen) was recreated for one edition of *World in Action* (Mike Wooler, March 1964). Dialogue could to be contemplated only if a verbatim record existed – for example, edited FBI transcripts of bugged conversations in a Mafia boss's office.

    Compare, for example, 'The Battle of Santiago Bay' (1898) which used cut-out models of warships involved. Méliès shot a faked coronation of Edward VII in Paris (1903) and so on (Barnow, *Documentary*, pp. 24ff.; Charles Musser, *History of the American Cinema: The Emergence of Cinema, The American Screen to 1907* {New York: Scribner's, 1990], pp. 200ff. and 287).

77. Paget, *No Other Way to Tell It*, p. 166.

78. Beginning with Henry Salamons' *Victory at Sea* (1952), USA.

79. *A Malestrom [The Maelstrom]* (1997), Hungary. Michael Renov, 'Historical Discourses of the Unimaginable', *Cinema's Alchemist: The Films of Péter Forgács* (Minneapolis: University of Minnesota Press, 2012).

80. Most notoriously he has Allakarialuk ('Nanook') grinning at the camera as he attempts to eat one of the white fur trader's gramophone records, stereotyping the Inuit's supposed technological backwardness. In fact, the Inuit processed Flaherty's negatives for him and were more technologically adept than he at functioning in the hostile Arctic environment.

81. In the pages of *The LEF Arena*. See: Osip Brik and Viktor Shklovsky, 'The Eleventh', trans. Ben Brewster, *Screen* vol. 12 no. 4, Winter 1971, p. 173.

82. In Ian Aitken's citation (Ian Aitkin, *European Film Theory and Cinema* [Bloomington: Indiana University Press,

2002], p. 24). Leyda gives this as 'cinema mischief' in his translation of the original text: S. M. Eisenstein, 'The Cinematic Principle and the Ideogram', *Film Form: Essays in Film Theory*, trans. Jay Leyda (New York: Harcourt-Brace, 1929 [1949]), p. 43.

83. As this concept in advanced theoretical physics is popularly understood: that is, it suggests that the act of observation must inevitably affect the event being observed.

84. To James Blue, in '"One Man's Truth" An Interview with Richard Leacock', *Film Comment* vol. 3 no. 2, Spring 1965, p. 16.

85. A research method where anthropologist or sociologist observers take part in the social processes they are investigating and acknowledge their presence.

86. Just as Terry McCartney-Filgate had joined the team making *Primary*, so Michel Brault joined Rouch for *Chronique*.

87. For example, Jim McBride, *David Holtzman's Diary* (1967), USA; Mitchell Block's ... *No Lies* (1974), USA.

88. Thomas S. Kuhn, *The Structure of Scientific Revolutions* (Chicago: University of Chicago Press, 1962).

89. Harlan Jacobson, 'Michael and Me', *Film Comment* vol. 25 no. 6, 1989.

90. For example, the Nazi *The Eternal Jew*, Fritz Hippler (1940), Germany.

91. For example, *Turksib*, Viktor Turim (1929), USSR; the films of the British and American Workers Film and Photo Leagues. (See Bert Hogenkamp, *Deadly Parallels: Film and the Left in Britain 1929–1939* [London: Lawrence & Wishart, 1986]; William Alexander, *Film on the Left: American Documentary Film from 1931 to 1942* [Princeton, NJ: Princeton University Press, 1981].)

92. Thomas Waugh, Michael Brendan Baker and Ezra Winton, *Challenge for Change: Activist Documentary at the National Film Board of Canada* (Montreal: McGill-Queen's University Press, 2010).

93. Edgar Anstey to Elizabeth Sussex (Sussex, *The Rise and Fall of British Documentary*, p. 63).

94. Humorous stories were a feature of the newsreels but seldom to any great satiric purpose. An exception was the footage from the Nazi newsreel *Wochenshau* and *Triumph of the Will* processed to make the Nazis dance 'The Lambeth Walk'. Although picked up by anglophone newsreels, it was a propaganda short made in 1942 in the British wartime Ministry of Information.

95. Renov, 'Toward a Poetics of Documentary', *Theorizing Documentary*.

96. Nick Murphy and Caroline Ross-Pirie, *The Edwardian Country House* (2002), UK.

97. Some accept this rationale. See, for example: Jon Dovey, 'It's Only a Game Show: *Big Brother* and the Theatre of Spontaniety', in E. Mathijs and J. Jones (eds), *Big Brother International* (London: Wallflower, 2005).

98. Anthony Neilson in Brian Logan, 'The Ouside Man', *New Stateman*, 10 December 2007, p. 39.

99. Quoted in Waugh, '*Show Us Life*', p. 52.

100. Tine Fischer, Arine Kirstein, Arine and Sinnøve Kjae Aerland, 'Welcome to Crossing Boundaries', trans. Paul Bridgewater and Eamann Cosgrave, *Crossing Boundaries 2000* (Copenhagen: Danish Film Institute, 2000), n.p.

101. John Corner, 'What Can We Say about "Documentary"?', *Media, Culture & Society*, 22 September 2002, pp. 687–8.

102. For example, Taylor Downing et al., *The Lost Evidence* (2004), UK/USA.

103. For example, Andy Glyne et al., *Animated Minds* (2004), UK.

104. For example, Brian Hill, *Feltham Sings* (2002), UK.

105. For example, Alex Graham et al., *Smallpox 2002* (2000), UK/USA.

106. See Martin Reiser and Andrea Zapp (eds), *New Screen Media: Cinema/Art/Narrative* (London: BFI, 2002).

107. See Chapter 6.3 below.

PART ONE:
Documentary Values

1.1 The Question of Evidence, the Power of Rhetoric and Documentary Film[1]

BILL NICHOLS

*There are three central issues in the study of moving-image documentary – evidence, narrative and ethics – and of these the first which must be considered is evidence. Without it, the concept of documentary telling, in some privileged way or another, a story about **the** world (rather than being an evidence-less, imaginative fiction about a world) cannot be sustained.*

All discourses, including documentary film, seek to externalise evidence – to place it referentially outside the domain of the discourse itself which then gestures to its location there, beyond and before interpretation. Reference to this external location then names and renders visible what awaited nomination. Evidence refers back to a fact, object, or situation – something two or more people agree upon, something verifiable and concrete – but facts and events only acquire the distinctive status of evidence within a discursive or interpretive frame. Evidence, then, is that part of discourse, be it rational-philosophic, poetic-narrative, or rhetorical, charged with a double existence: it is both part of the discursive chain and gives the vivid impression of also being external to it. In other words, facts become evidence when they are taken up in a discourse; and that discourse gains the force to compel belief through its capacity to refer evidence to a domain outside itself.

The compelling documentary *An Injury to One* (2002) about the history of Butte, Montana, as a mining town and the murder there of a Wobbly (Industrial Workers of the World) organiser, Frank Little, in 1917, demonstrates vividly how facts convert to evidence and how their evidential status is contingent on the discourse to which they attach. At one point Wilkerson recounts the story of a large flock of geese that land on the enormous lake that fills the open pit mine that still dominates the town. The lake is extremely toxic, loaded with copper, cadmium, zinc, nickel, lead, arsenic and sulphates; it has a pH of 2.5, 'roughly comparable to battery acid', Wilkerson tells us in his intense but flatly spoken commentary. A storm takes the geese by surprise and they land on the lake. In the morning 342 geese are dead. They are blistered with lesions, their oesophagi and tracheas corroded, and their livers bloated with toxic quantities of heavy metals. Wilkerson

recounts that representatives for ARCO, the company that now owns the mine, assured the townspeople that the water was actually safe; the geese died 'because of something they ate', not from exposure to the lake water. Wilkerson concludes this section of his stunning film with an observation:

> As the geese help to demonstrate, history, in this case, cannot be so easily expurgated [as the company's original name: Anaconda]. In an act reminiscent of a mass suicide, the geese hurled themselves into the open wound in the heart of the town. Perhaps using the only manner they knew, these creatures were trying to tell us something because it seemed to have escaped our notice. They were directing us to the scene of a crime.

The facts do not, as Wilkerson's sardonic tone suggests, speak for themselves: they must be seen and heard, and thence interpreted, an act that fissures into multiple directions depending on the purposes and goals of the

An Injury to One (2002): in an act reminiscent of a mass suicide, the geese hurled themselves into the open wound in the heart of the town

interpreter. ARCO interprets the death of 342 geese as a case of a bad dietary choice; Wilkerson interprets it as a 'mass suicide' meant to be understood as the silent testimony of witnesses to a crime. The event, however, can only be seen as accidental death, testimony or anything else within the interpretive frame provided for it. Cast back by discourse into the external world, facts take up a place outside discourse and are made to do so in a way that allows their reincarnation as evidence to overlay perfectly the fact to which it corresponds.

The indexical quality of the photographic image is ideally suited to this purpose. A perfect tautology appears to come into being between fact, object or event, on the one hand, and evidence, on the other, so that reference to a piece of evidence marries signified and referent in a single stroke. As the story of the geese suggests, the fact or event does not come into being as evidence; this status accrues later, when it is recruited to a discourse – 'bad food' or 'mass suicide' for the geese, for example – these labels become affixed to that which simple was. And they seem to stick because of an indexical bond between image and referent, that which exists outside the discursive chain.

Sometimes facts speak but in ways not intended by the speaker or film-maker. The viewer, too, may convert fact to evidence, sometimes in ways that run against the grain of their initial recruitment. In Marlon Riggs's powerful documentary about being black and gay in America, *Tongues Untied* (1989), he cross-cuts between a protest march in Selma, Alabama, in the 1960s and a gay pride parade in New York city in the 80s. For Riggs the parallel is evidence of a continuous lineage of protest and struggle for civil liberties and individual rights. But there is a tremendous difference in the two pieces of footage if we examine them not as part of Riggs's stunning visual testament but as visible evidence of two distinct historical moments.

In the Selma march what is most striking is the rich diversity of the marchers themselves: younger and older African Americans, younger and older whites, male and female, primarily but not entirely well-dressed, religious leaders and lay people, all marching to confront a racist society with their visible, demonstrable protest. The two most prominent banners read, 'We March with Selma' and 'We Shall Overcome'. The gay pride march footage features a contingent of young black men, with two bare-chested black males carrying a banner that reads, 'Black Men Loving Black Men Is A Revolutionary Act'. The goal of mobilising a broad, inclusive range of people to confront racism and champion civil rights has yielded to the proclamation of difference, the affirmation of an identity and politics that seeks to embrace the like-minded and gain the public recognition of others. The spectrum of ages, classes and races incorporated into and patently visible in the Selma march has disappeared. Belonging and activism is now predicated on a specific combination of race, gender and sexual orientation. The male and female, mostly younger but occasionally older onlookers, along with a number of primarily white police officers lining the route of the gay pride parade, are a far more diverse group than the marchers themselves. The unity of purpose of an earlier time has yielded to the identity politics of a later one, or so an interpreter could argue just as forcefully as Riggs can argue for a line of continuity.

Careful consideration of this act of converting fact to evidence occurs in R. G. Collingwood's *The Idea of History*, written in 1946, and dedicated to the idea of history as a scientific undertaking.[2] During an extended discursion of 'historical evidence', Collingwood debunks the view that history amounts to citing the testimony of credible authorities whose remarks can be cut and pasted together to provide the requisite history. This outdated method relies on facts drawn from earlier, authoritative accounts – and whose status as evidence can go unquestioned for that reason – that now form the backbone of a new narrative. By contrast, Collingwood argues that good history writing requires making inferences that are always based on questions directed towards a careful examination of the facts themselves. They can only come to serve as valid evidence when freshly taken up into the author's own interpretative discourse. The historian must pose questions that infer what really happened rather than adopt the views of others. Wilkerson's comment about the geese, 'Perhaps using the only manner they knew, these creatures were trying to tell us something because it seemed to have escaped our notice', becomes a standing assumption of critical enquiry: facts and events exist, but their conversion into evidence depends on the analytic powers of the interpreter, be he historian or film-maker.

But in the middle of this call for a methodologically rigorous history, Collingwood suddenly takes a surprising turn. A sub-heading entitled 'Who Killed John Doe?' announces the detour. Contrary to the strictly expository style of all the previous sections, Collingwood now adopts a semi-fictional voice. The section begins, 'When John Doe was found, early one Sunday morning, lying across his desk with a dagger through his back, no one expected that the question of who did it would be settled by means of testimony.' Here is a case where Collingwood can demonstrate the necessity of inferential analysis that, when done properly, will lead to a clear-cut solution.

Using Collingwood's own dictum that 'everything in the world is potential evidence for any subject whatever',[3] and that we should focus not on the content of statements but on the fact that they are made[4] – in other words, that our analysis must not accept what others represent the case to be but must ask, 'What light is thrown on the subject in which I am interested by the fact that this person made this statement?' – we can ask: 'Why does Collingwood tell this who-done-it story in the middle of his disquisition on history? Clearly, it serves as an example, if not allegory, for good historical investigation. It serves Collingwood's goal of giving the impression that history writing can become a science, capable of determining what really happened in an unambiguous manner through an independent examination of the facts and testimony. Inferences lead to knowledge and knowledge leads to the one and only logical solution: the rector did it. Ambiguity is dispelled thanks to the hard, inferential work of the historian labouring in the vineyards of the local, empirically verifiable event. Not all rectors should now be suspected of murder, nor should all murders be attributed to rectors, but in this concrete case, with these facts and statements and with this set of questions to transform facts and statements into evidence, the rector's guilt can be cleanly determined.

By presenting a Sherlock Holmes-like murder mystery Collingwood can arrive at a specific solution to a concrete question. The solution lacks generalising power: it tells us nothing about the behaviour of rectors, or the causes of murder, in general. His example offers a definite conclusion, based on asking questions whose answers generate evidence: a footprint in the wet soil of the lawn becomes admitted as evidence as soon as we ask a question such as: who might have crossed the lawn that fateful night but only after the rain fell?

Though instructive, Collingwood's choice of a murder mystery as metaphor reduces his method to factual determinations that cannot account for historical complexity. He neglects to add to his assertion 'everything in the world is potential evidence for any subject whatever' *and for a wide range of interpretations.* The murder mystery involves facts, questions, evidence and interpretation of a different order from those involved when we ask what brought about the transformation of communism into totalitarianism, why capitalism undergoes cycles of growth and recession, why genocide occurred in Rwanda in the 1990s, or what influence populism has had on American politics. Questions such as these propel us into a realm rather remote from the indisputable evidence, clear-cut verification procedures and singular conclusions that Collingwood naturalises as the common stuff of history through his exemplary fiction.

Collingwood, in fact, builds his conception of proper historiography on the Aristotelian notion of 'inartistic proofs', evidence, that is, that exists outside, or can readily be made to appear to reside outside, the discursive chain. Examples include laws, witnesses, contracts, oaths, and confessions obtained by torture (a practice reserved, in Aristotle's time, for slaves, since citizens would give their own testimony artistically, that is, with benefit of the rhetorical arts). This is the evidence that can most easily be 'thrown out' of the discourse as fact in order to be reeled back in as evidence. Science, like murder mysteries, works with objective facts; the form a precise account of them takes is of minor consequence. Form, for Collingwood, is little more than a question of style; the proof is in facts that serve as evidence. Careful interpretation leads us down a straight and narrow path to the truth, not into a labyrinth of competing interests and interpretations whose relative merits may be decided more by power, or at least rhetoric, than by logic.

Although seemingly the most irrefutable of evidence, inartistic proofs were of minor concern to Aristotle. The 'artistic proofs' that were the heart and soul of rhetorical discourse concerned him much more. Though frequently necessary, inartistic proofs still have to be incorporated into a discourse where they would become convincing. Alone, the inartistic proofs might be necessary but hardly sufficient. Only when such proofs took on their second life as evidence inside a body of signification – discourse – did it become possible for a convincing argument to emerge. *How* inartistic proofs become incorporated into the discourse thus matters more than *what* these proofs reveal in and of themselves.

What concerned Aristotle, and Cicero and Quintilian, among others, were the artistic proofs that strove to guarantee the ethical credibility of a speaker, the emotional response of an audience, and the convincingness of an argument (including the convincingness of inferences or interpretations drawn from inartistic proofs). These are questions regarding rhetorical not philosophic or logical discourse. The protocols of science eschew such discourse. Rhetoric or persuasive speech, it is said, mires us in deception; it lacks a moral compass; it leads to ideology rather than knowledge. Or so it seemed to Plato and to Roland Barthes, the latter of whom, in 1964, wrote the seminal essay, 'The Rhetoric of the Image', and so it seems to those who attack film-makers like Michael Moore for 'distorting' or 'inventing' facts that serve as tendentious evidence, as if there could be any other kind once we enter the arena of human affairs where science no longer reigns supreme.

Barthes's essay, which, for me, marks the beginning of the end for an understanding of the crucial role of rhetoric in contemporary culture (except as handmaiden to ideology), asks questions about the meaning of an image, in this case, an advertisement for Panzani pasta sauce in the form of a photograph of a shopping net filled with fresh vegetables and Panzani products, their labels clearly legible. Like Collingwood, Barthes is moved to question authority, to refuse to accept the advertisement at its word. Barthes asks of the image, as Collingwood did of his suspects: how does it disguise what it says as something natural and obvious?

Like Collingwood's who-done-it, the mystery of meaning is once again carried to one and only one conclusion. The image represents ideology. It does so because it sets out to naturalise Panzani. Products – most importantly, a can of pasta sauce – are equated in the image with the fresh, wholesome bounty of the farm. A perfect tautology exists: fresh vegetables are Panzani; Panzani is fresh vegetables, nothing more or less. Or as he puts it himself,

> To the general ideology, that is, correspond signifiers of connotation which are specified according to the chosen substance [sound, image, gesture and so on]. These signifiers will be called *connotators* and the set of connotators a *rhetoric*, rhetoric thus appearing as the signifying aspect of ideology.[5]

It is no longer the rector who did it but ideology. The power of rhetoric to move an audience by establishing a credible, compelling and convincing case of any kind, on any subject, for any purpose becomes reduced to the power of rhetoric to put ideology into practice.

The linkage of the visual with the ideological through Lacanian imaginary fuelled much of this distrust of the visual. This line of thought returns us to Plato's attack on rhetoric as a corrupting form of flattery, or deception. Plato terms the proper cultivation of the body 'gymnastics' and its corrupt form cosmetics, or *kosmètikè*, those flattering applications of ornament that render appearances false. In an attempt to preserve the centrality of rhetoric as discourse measured by its effects without dismissing it as sheer deception, Quintilian differentiates between the use of cosmetics such as colour, ornament, gesture and emotion for venal and noble purposes. His negative example involves slave dealers who use cosmetics to increase the value of those whom they sell by giving them a flattering appearance. Such an appearance renders the slave overvalued and any subsequent transaction dishonest. This would seem to be the category in which advertisements, and certainly the Panzani ad, would fall.

Venal purposes contrast, for Qunitilian, with the art of the noble orator who sees speech as an instrument for the expression of views strongly believed and compellingly conveyed.[6] 'In place of the cosmetic body Quintilian puts a political body ... As the place of political relations, the body escapes from the moral disdain of metaphysics ... The body – image, passion, pleasure, effect, and affect – gains legitimacy in politics and in rhetoric too ... By all these shifts Quintilian succeeds in justifying the definition of rhetoric as wisdom ... To ensure the victory of justice, eloquence is thus within its rights to apply itself not only to instructing the soul but also to moving the body.'[7]

Rhetoric, in other words, may sometimes be deceptive but it is also the only means we have as social actors, or film-makers, for conveying our beliefs, perspectives and convictions persuasively. Cosmetics, or, more aptly, a rhetoric of persuasion, strives to move others; it shocks, disturbs, provokes, inspires, galvanises or defamiliarises, displaying the old in a new, revelatory manner. In this case, the rhetoric of the image belongs to a struggle for power in which the meaning and effect of an image or film cannot be determined in advance as simply and always ideological in the sense of serving the interests of the status quo by the use of deceptions. Instead, the rhetoric of the image, or film, speaks, as narrative or logic might speak, with multiple purposes and to different ends but in ways that strive to compel belief as much as they might please or prove. Rhetoric gives a distinct voice to those who wish their perspective and their interpretation to enter into dialogue with that of others.

Voice refers to the ways in which a documentary film speaks to its audience. *An Injury to One*, *Tongues Untied*, *The Revolution Will Not Be Televised*,[8] *Fahrenheit 9/11*[9] and *The Maelstrom*,[10] among many others, evidence a voice that speaks probingly and responsively towards others as well as angrily towards injustice, abuse, exploitation, racism, anti-Semitism, cruelty and other barbarisms. It acknowledges its subject, and audience, as its equal not its object, target, victim or tool. This is a voice that speaks through the body of the film: through editing, through subtle and strange juxtapositions, through music, lighting, composition and *mise en scène*, through dialogue overheard and commentary delivered, through silence as well as speech, and through images as well as words. If style turns attention to the one who addresses us, voice turns attention to the audience addressed.

Often, this voice includes the personal but untrained voice of the film-maker herself rather than the impersonal, professional delivery of a voiceover commentator. The film-maker's voice stresses the sense of direct encounter, an embodied perspective, relayed to the viewer. Something personal is at stake, as it clearly is in Marlon Riggs's overall film: his own experience as a black, gay man gave him a distinct perspective on racism that now inflects the voice that speaks to us.

This is no less true of Yervant Gianikian and Angela Ricci Lucchi's *Oh Uomo* (2004), which, without spoken commentary of any kind, nonetheless speaks compellingly through its compilation of archival footage of abandoned orphans, scavenging youths and disfigured veterans from World War I. The eyes of the starving, traumatised and lost engage the camera that encountered them so many decades ago with a vivid openness and acute intensity that cries out for response. The film-makers, through the duration of shots that accumulate into a requiem to catastrophe, offer a delayed response that engages us in a near-hypnotic séance with survivors and victims that are fleetingly reanimated before us.

Such films face the challenge of how to speak of that which escapes our notice, like the 'mass suicide' of the geese in *An Injury to One*. Herbert Sauper confronts this question forcefully, in *Darwin's Nightmare*,[11] when all he can find are the horrific consequences of a highly lucrative industry that air expresses frozen Nile perch from Lake

Victoria to Russia and Eastern Europe. Meanwhile, the massive and accidentally introduced perch are devouring every other species of fish in the lake; women are driven into prostitution, and many of the indigenous residents of the area live off the thousands of rotting fish carcasses left lying in the sun. Like Wilkerson's geese, these carcasses of heads and bones are directing us to the scene of a crime.

Monstration, the act of asking viewers to look at what the film-maker hopes they will convert from fact to evidence, increases in difficulty when the subject lies buried in the past and when the visible signs of a mass political movement flicker uncertainly. Like *Lone Star*,[12] with its discovery of a buried badge that launches a quest to learn the consequences of what happened many years before, films like *An Injury to One* or *The Maelstrom* address the political landscape of past and present but with no expectation that interpretive frames are readily available for application. Voice now functions, in part, to guide the viewer towards an interpretive frame that will be of their own design but still capable of forging consensus about the nature of the evidence provided by facts or events.

The documentary voice that has taken form in recent times is clearly an oratorical voice but not a dogmatic one. It is the multi-dimensional, embodied voice of films that speak to viewers in the hope of moving them, predisposing them, inducing a sense of political and historical consciousness that represents a step towards going beyond established boundaries by means of a truth that had escaped awareness. As Werner Herzog put it, in speaking of the quality he seeks in his documentary work (the particular reference was *Grizzly Man*[13] and what we learn of the horizon at which the animal and human conjoin),

> In great moments of cinema you are hit and struck by some sort of enlightenment, by something that illuminates you, that's a deep form of truth and I call it ecstatic truth, the ecstasy of truth, and that's what I'm after in documentaries and feature films.

Hit and struck. This is a form of knowledge or a way of seeing that is closer to a paradigm shift than the accretion of information, the laborious process of conventional learning, mystery solving, or the marshalling of evidence of a pre-existing form of political activism. Herzog's ecstatic documentary is the work of orators who set out not to show but to move, to establish movement that may come in a flash and extend forward in an altered temporality.

This form of knowing presupposes finding the means to bring to a condition of visibility what has escaped notice. It sets out to identify what may attain visibility and yet still not be seen since what is seen is a trace, sign, symptom or consequence of that which remains beyond the net of words and the reductive aspect of naming. The geese, and perch, and even grizzly bears, speak with their

Grizzly Man (2005): 'the ecstasy of truth' – Werner Herzog

actions. The mining pit turned toxic, the African lake, source of the Nile, turned killing field, the shattered jaws and missing noses of the veterans of World War I in *Oh Uomo*, all speak of consequences that hit and strike us. This is a form of speech that offers the possibility to predispose us to see anew, and, in seeing anew, to make a radical shift in what is both true and yet still a mystery. No words can contain such mystery but some forms of speech can render it recognisable.

A striking example of such speech, one that requires a retroactive reading, occurs in *The Revolution Will Not Be Televised*, about the attempted coup that ousted Hugo Chavez for a period of time. At one point, President Chavez arrives at the Presidential Palace, where the Palace Guard stands at attention and salutes him. Chavez casually starts a conversation with one officer and then, as he enters the palace, playfully rubs his hand on the belly of the soldier standing at attention and guarding the entrance. Chavez was an officer himself and he clearly retains a rapport with these officers and men. Later, after the coup has taken place and Chavez is held captive, the insurgents, remarkably, routed from this very palace. And who was responsible? The Palace Guard. At this point, the viewer may well realise that a fact and prior event – a casual conversation, a pat on the belly – can function as evidence in an interpretive argument about how Hugo Chavez returned to power. The film need not say anything directly; the evidence is in the image, if we can see and interpret it. The film speaks through its imagery as readily as through its verbal commentary.

The voice considered here is often a poetic voice that seeks to convey what it feels like to enter into the past, what it feels like to enter into other lives, what it feels like to experience oppressive, violent conditions and to emerge with an altered sense of self by being placed in relation to others who pass before us. In *An Injury to One*, Wilkerson scans across a long procession of mug shots of the hun-dreds of miners arrested as Wobblies in Butte. This 'night train' of shots moves past in the centre of the frame, with large black borders at top and bottom. The photographs serve as a reminder of the repressive uses of what was a relatively new technology at the time, photography, but they also restore these men to visibility and celebrate them as heroes who, once silenced, are now reanimated in their passage before us.

The oratorical voice of documentary uses previous times and disparate places to establish the multiple points necessary to form a trajectory that moves forward with a utopian desire to uphold a set of principles and expose a series of consequences. It brings these consequences – exploitation, oppression, poverty, destruction, military coups, neo-colonial occupations, economic deprivations, global immiseration, social degradation, torture and murder, injustices to one and all – to a condition of visi-bility, if we can see and understand what this voice brings forth as fact without explaining. This is a voice that can no longer assume we all see things the same way. The politi-cal base in shared experience seen the same way, with shared principles and common goals is too fragile, too pre-carious for that, and, even if it were not, affirming what is already known is different from seeing anew what stands before us.

The voice with which an image or film speaks is capable, of course, of innumerable effects – many of which may well be ideological but not necessarily ideological in the sense of reinforcing the status quo. Speech and images may embody counter-ideologies designed to subvert or reject the status quo.[14] To re-examine the tradition of 'downcast eyes' and suspicion about the rhetoric of the image as ideology invites an investigation of, among other things, representational film practice where speaking on behalf of counter-ideologies is frequently the *raison d'être* of the work in the first place. Documentary film-making, with its strong ties to a tradition of liberal ameliorations and radical transformations of social practices, is one such exercise. The body of the film, and film-maker, with its expressive mix of passion and knowledge, sets out to move us. Such movement can contest the status quo as readily as it can confirm it; such movement is the constitutive domain in which power and pleasure combine to achieve political effect.

THE EVIDENCE IN QUESTION

Collingwood rightfully advocated an approach in which evidence is seen as what is made to appear in response to a question. From this perspective, a fact can become evi-dence despite itself, despite reticence or a lack of any intention of serving as evidence. (Symptoms consistently possess such a quality.) A fact or object can suddenly turn into evidence once we put a question to it. Questions do not stem from the image or the fact, object or event for which it stands, but from what we ask of it. Barthes's own questions had this quality about them, but Barthes seemed content to locate a meaning and effect in the image as if his interrogation exposed what the image itself sought to conceal through its cosmetic application of a 'lustral bath of innocence' to a consumer product. When we recognise that evidence emerges as a response to the questions we pose, we are in a position to recognise the ambiguity of that evidence: with a different question, different evidence, different arguments and different conclusions would have emerged.

The radically different interpretations, resulting from sharply distinct questions, of the Rodney King footage are a vivid example. Rhetorically, these questions retroactively fabricated quite different 'lustral baths of innocence', as it were, for Mr King or for his assailants, members of the Los Angeles Police Department who pursued and arrested him for speeding, fleeing and then resisting them. That is to say, opposing perspectives and different questions led to rad-ically disparate interpretations by the prosecution and the defence at the two trials of the police officers accused of beating Mr King.[15] The voice of documentary is largely given over, as a rhetorical utterance designed to move us, to shaping and focusing the polysemous quality of sound and image. Innocence, and other qualities, emerge after the fact, as that which a rhetorical voice desires to confer on what will be identified as evidence.

Despite the certainty rhetorical utterances wish to confer, images retain a fundamental ambiguity that who-done-it mysteries, advertising and other forms of reduc-tionism efface. Barthes's later writing embraces such ambiguity, although he never went back to revise his earlier writing about the image and its ideological effect. For every social issue, divergent positions emerge, with overlapping forms of evidence used as answers to differ-ent rhetorical questions. No denotative plane of certainty underpins these differences. The voice and gestures of the orator or the film's body seek to move us in relation to those social issues and conflicts that do not lend themselves to scientific determination and unanimous agreement.

Style, form and voice are the heart and soul of persua-sive engagement, and persuasive engagement is at the core of political discourses and social practices, whatever their ideological consequences. We inhabit an arena that remains fully within the shadow of ideology. There is no exit, only the constant effort to pose questions, present evidence and make arguments that advance upon what has come before. Leaving certitude behind moves us into an arena of radical doubt that cannot be dispelled so much as deferred, suspended and, ultimately, embraced as part and parcel of an advance, a movement, whose direction and intensity remain open to all the vicissitudes of history.

NOTES

1. Reprinted from Bill Nichols's chapter of the same name in Thomas Austin and Wilma de Jong (eds), *Rethinking Documentary: New Perspectives, New Practices* (Maidenhead: Open University Press/McGraw-Hill, 2008).

2. R.G. Collingwood, *The Idea of History* (Oxford: Oxford University Press, 1946).

3. Ibid., p. 280.

4. Ibid., p. 275.

5. Roland Barthes, 'The Rhetoric of the Image', *Image, Music, Text*, trans. Stephen Heath (New York: Hill and Wang, 1977), p. 49.

6. This discussion of Quintilian's correction of Plato's apparent condemnation of rhetoric draws heavily on Jacqueline Lichtenstein's discussion (Jacqueline Lichtenstein, *The Eloquence of Color: Rhetoric and Painting in the French Classical Age* [Berkeley: University of California Press, 1993], pp. 86–8).

7. Ibid., pp. 88–9.

8. Kim Bartley and Donnacha O'Briain, *The Revolution Will Not Be Televised* (2002), Ireland.

9. Michael Moore, *Fahrenheit 9/11* (2004), USA.

10. Péter Forgács, *A Malestrom* [*The Maelstrom*] (1997), Hungary.

11. Hupert Sauper, *Darwin's Nightmare* (2004), Austria.

12. John Sayles, *Lone Star* (1996), USA.

13. Werner Hertzog, *Grizzly Man* (2005), USA.

14. See Göran Therborn, *The Ideology of Power and the Power of Ideology* (London: Verso, 1980) for a lucid discussion of the various forms of ideology that are operative in any given social formation. Therborn's treatment of ideology dissolves the Althusserian notion of ideology-in-general, akin to the 'general ideology' adopted by Barthes in 'The Rhetoric of the Image', into its component parts in a given historical moment. A general ideology that constitutes the subject may remain operative, but concrete class ideologies and counter-ideologies are the common sites of political struggle, unless redesigning the subject is our sole and exclusive goal.

15. See my 'The Trials and Tribulations of Rodney King' (Bill Nichols, *Blurred Boundaries: Questions of Meaning in Contemporary Culture* [Bloomington: Indiana University Press, 1994]) for a full discussion of the Rodney King footage and its use in the trials of the police officers charged with beating Mr King.

1.2 'I'll Believe It When I Trust the Source': Documentary Images and Visual Evidence

CARL PLANTINGA

An interrogation of documentary's evidential base lies at the heart of current debates, but there are other views possible on what this means apart from the 'scepticism', exemplified by Nichols's approach. One can adopt a 'critical realist' view and preserve a more optimistic position on documentary's evidentiary possibilities. After all, the popular reception of documentary as some species of evidence or other largely remains, despite occasional scandals, in place.

THE DEFAULT POSITION

Arguably, the default position for most of us is to believe that under certain conditions, both moving and still photographs provide evidence that something looked or occurred in a certain way. We see video of the local weatherwoman standing heroically in a hurricane, and her hat blows off; we believe that it is windy where she stands. We see a news photograph of a favourite restaurant being consumed by flames, and we know that we won't be dining there anytime soon. This belief in the informative and evidentiary power of photographic images[1] holds not only for ostensibly naive audiences, but for media-savvy film and media scholars as well. In 1991, when Rodney King was the victim of police brutality at the hands of the Los Angeles police, a bystander, George Holliday, captured much of the beating on videotape. Yet despite the stark evidence apparently provided by the video, four Los Angeles police officers, after a very public trial during which the videotape was deconstructed by clever lawyers, were acquitted of the charges of police brutality. The official response of the Society for Cinema Studies[2] was telling: 'The verdict to acquit four white Los Angeles Police Department officers contradicts powerful visual evidence – video evidence of excessive police brutality seen globally.'[3]

Most of us tend to believe in the veracity of the photographic image and I will argue that, under certain conditions, we are right to hold such beliefs. Yet we must also acknowledge that all photography is implicated within webs of subjectivity, stemming in large part from the multifarious functions and contexts that inevitably influence the status of motion and still photography as evidence. And just as most of us are tempted to lend a special epistemic

authority to photographs, it is also commonly acknowledged that photographs may mislead as well as inform, and can be marshalled to support dubious arguments and false claims. It is the purpose of this chapter to sort through these conflicting tendencies, and to shed light on whether, and under what conditions, moving photographs can count as evidence within the context of a documentary. And supposing that we decide that photography can provide evidence, we must then ask: evidence of what, exactly?

EVIDENCE AND EPISTEMOLOGY

The position one takes on whether documentary photography can provide evidence for the claims of a documentary depends on two central variables. The first variable, discussed further below, is one's epistemic commitments, that is, one's position on the very possibility of knowledge and its dissemination through discourse. The second variable is one's definition of 'evidence'. It makes sense at the outset to distinguish photographic evidence from proof, on the one hand, and information, on the other. In this chapter I will consider evidence to be any data that lends credence, or warrant, for the belief that something is the case. For example, I see human footprints in the snow. This provides evidence for my belief that someone has recently walked by. According to this definition, photographic evidence would be any still or motion picture or group of pictures that provide(s) data that supports a claim, argument, or assumption that something is the case.

Consider, for example, one such use of images in *Hearts and Minds* (Peter Davis, 1974, USA), the powerful anti-war film produced towards the end of the Vietnam War. In the film we see a shot of a seated General William Westmoreland, US Commanding General in Vietnam from 1964–68, in which he says, '… the Oriental doesn't put the same high price on life as does the Westerner. Life is plentiful, life is cheap in the Orient … Life is not important.' This is juxtaposed, both before and after, with footage of a funeral at which both Vietnamese children and adults grieve vigorously, and in which the mother of a slain soldier, in her destitution, attempts to climb into the grave of her son. If Westmoreland's claims provide an assertion, the images put that assertion to the lie, and seemingly provide evidence for its contradiction.

Photographic images in documentaries have many functions other than the providing of evidence. Moving images can be rich in visual information, such that what one can learn from them potentially outstrips their use to support or deny an implication or explicit assertion in a film. In this way moving images contain visual information that is not explicitly used as evidence. The images of the Vietnamese funeral, for example, can provide information about military funerals in Vietnam at that time, though the images are included for a different, more rhetorical purpose. The unique power of the photographic image, however, is that its informativeness is accompanied by what many take as built-in evidence, supplied by the medium itself and the photograph's means of production. Thus moving images of the funeral will typically be taken as more authoritative about what happened at the funeral than would be a verbal claim by a bystander or a commentator; many viewers will take Westmoreland's assertions to be put into question by the images.

Evidence does not necessarily rise to the level of proof. As I use the term in this chapter, photographic evidence provides additional credence to an assertion or implication, but does not necessarily 'prove' the claim or implication. Within the context of a documentary argument, for example, a moving image may lend support for an argument or part of an argument, but in itself cannot be said to demonstrate or prove that the argument is correct. Thus we may speak of various levels of evidence, from weak to strong. Some moving images may be thought to constitute such strong evidence that they constitute proof, while others might constitute only weak evidence.

With regard to the second variable, epistemology, one's position on whether documentaries can represent reality with truthfulness, accuracy, or objectivity will likely determine, or at least strongly influence, one's position on whether documentary images may count as evidence. Many documentary scholars are sceptics about the documentary in this regard, suspicious of any optimistic or positive accounts of claims to knowledge in general, and in particular of the capacity of documentary films to convey truth or truths. Michael Renov, for example, is suspicious of the mainstream documentary's 'self-assurance', and instead allies himself with 'contingency, hybridity, knowledge as situated and particular, identity as ascribed and performed'. Renov argues that 'all discourse *constitutes* the objects which it pretends only to describe realistically and to analyze objectively'.[4] If all documentary discourse constitutes its subjects, however, then the claims and implications of documentary films are not subject to corroboration or disconfirmation, and all questions of evidence, truth-

telling, falsity, accuracy and deceptiveness become irrelevant. Clearly, if documentaries merely constitute, make up, imagine, or fictionalise their subjects, the question of whether images can serve as evidence becomes moot. All films are fictions, equally reliable – that is, not reliable at all, becoming fabrications expressive of our wishes and desires and reflecting not reality but our self-interest.

What I call a critical realist perspective does not deny that documentaries are often false and misleading, nor does it deny that the concerns of the sceptics are in many cases legitimate. It does hold that in at least some cases, the documentary can be truthful, accurate and informative. In other words, from the critical realist perspective, the claims and implications of documentaries, in some cases, can be judged against standards of evidence. For example, Errol Morris's *Mr Death: The Rise and Fall of Fred A. Leuchter* (1999, USA), provides interviews with and footage of Fred Leuchter, an erstwhile execution equipment designer who, after befriending some holocaust deniers, travels to Auschwitz to perform a series of experiments on the remains of the gas chambers there, concluding in *The Leuchter Report* that the gas chambers had never seen gas in sufficient quantities to kill anyone. Through many means Morris undermines Leuchter's conclusions, using the testimony of historians and scientists to question Leuchter's experiments and findings. Morris's claims and implications about *The Leuchter Report* can be judged against independent evidence only if the documentary reports on, makes claims about, or shows us its objects, but not if it merely constitutes them. The critical realist takes it as a given that *Mr Death* does not constitute its objects, but represents and makes claims about them. The critical realist further assumes that, in some cases, those claims can be confirmed or disconfirmed by evidence. The possibility of photographic evidence, then, can be affirmed only if one holds something like the critical realist perspective on the documentary.[5]

THE CASE FOR IMAGES AS EVIDENCE

The question at hand is whether photographic images in the documentary can count as evidence and, if so, evidence of what? In this section, I will make the strongest arguments I know for taking some documentary images as evidence.[6] In the next section I will complicate and qualify these claims.

C. S. Peirce's well-known distinction between three types of signs[7] he calls icons, indices and symbols, provides an entry into understanding the informative and seemingly authoritative power of photographic images. This tripartite distinction distinguishes between signs according to their relationship with their referent. The first kind of sign, the icon, resembles its referent; the second, the index, is related to its referent by causality or proximity; the third type, the symbol, has a purely arbitrary, conventional relationship with its referent. The photographic image is a complex sign indeed, because it may simultaneously be an icon, index and symbol.

For the purposes of this chapter, the photograph as icon and index are the most important, because they directly relate to the use of images as evidence. It will be useful to briefly describe the use of photographs as symbols, however, if only to highlight differences between photographic and linguistic communication. The symbol is related to its referent by convention alone. Thus a flag may stand for nationhood or patriotism, a cross for Christianity and the word 'cat' for those smallish furry creatures some people choose to keep as pets. Photographs are symbolic in that the image of a symbol carries some of the symbol's meaning, depending on how the image is used in discourse. Photographs may function not only as symbols, but as both icons and indices as well, while language, in contrast, bears a purely symbolic relationship with its referent.[8]

The photograph is iconic in that, under certain conditions, it resembles its referent. Philosophers could spend a lifetime unpacking this claim. Just how is it possible that a two-dimensional piece of paper or celluloid or a flat computer screen can be said to resemble three-dimensional reality? Since my time and space and the reader's patience are limited, let us stipulate that resemblance, for the purposes of this chapter, may best be described as this: the photograph, under certain conditions, offers a visual array that can display (some of) the same visual information as that which was available to a person at the pro-filmic scene when the photograph was taken. Potentially, then, someone looking at the before-mentioned shots of the Vietnamese military funeral could get (some of) the same visual information she would have received had she been present at the scene. This is subject to all kinds of qualifications and conditions, but is true in essence.[9] There is a sense in which we see photographs much like we see the world, through natural visual perception. It is for this reason that not only people, but pigeons, dolphins and other non-human animals are able to glean accurate visual information from photographs and videos.[10]

Photographs are also indices, Peirce's second type of sign, because they are related to their referent by a causal process. There is a sense in which the light rays emanating from the pro-filmic scene, together with various physical processes and the mechanical functions of the camera, cause the resulting image. What I would add to Peirce's formulation is that this causal process renders the photograph *to some extent* independent of human intentionality. This is not to say that photography, cinematography and videography have no creative or intentional aspects. Of course they do. Yet once the image-maker decides how to shoot the scene, the mechanical processes of the camera in relation to the physical properties of light complete the process. This is why the Rodney King video was so compelling as

evidence to many of its viewers. It did not matter what the videographer's politics were. Whether he was drunk or high or angry at the police; whether his stomach had butterflies or his head hurt; whether he had intentionally sought out police brutality or just happened to come upon it – none of this matters much. Once he pointed the camera at the policemen beating Rodney King and switched the machine on, the mechanics of the camera and the physics of light became the relevant factors in determining the evidentiary status of the video. The elements of that video that count as evidence, then, are to an extent independent of human intentionality. We could not say the same for a verbal account or an artist's rendering of the beating. In those cases, human intentionality typically plays a much larger role. Thus the indexical nature of documentary photography lends it evidential authority that is in some cases justified.

This is also the sense in which documentary photography can be said to be objective. The word 'objectivity' is an ambiguous landmine of a term, so it is important to specify how one uses it. By 'objective' I do not mean 'fair' or 'balanced' or 'true'. To call a photograph objective, in the sense that I have been arguing for, is to say that *in one respect* it escapes the subjectivity of the photographer. The photograph is only in part the product of the photographer's imagination. She or he determines framing, focal length, ISO, camera movement, lens and so on, and yet despite all of the subjective and creative decisions that go into taking the photograph, or getting the shot, the final result is to some extent free of the imagination of the maker. Thus when in *The Cove* (Louie Psihoyos, 2009, USA), the film-makers use surveillance cameras to clandestinely record the killing of dolphins for meat in a small cove in Taijii, Japan, they assume (and spectators believe) that the visual record of the killing carries evidential force because it is objective in respect to the mechanistic production of the image.

To claim that the photographic images of the dolphin slaughter in *The Cove* are objective in respect to their mechanistic production is not to deny that the film is subjective in other respects. *The Cove* as a whole obviously takes the point of view that slaughtering dolphins is morally wrong. The shots used in the film as evidence are themselves subjective in the sense that they imply a visual perspective through shot composition, choice of subject, focus and focal length. Yet does this negate the veracity of the visual record produced by the photographic equipment? Hardly. Suppose that I photograph you cooking an omelette. The fact that my photo is taken from a particular perspective has little bearing on the value of the photo as evidence that you are in fact making an omelette, unless the perspective precludes seeing the relevant portions of the pro-filmic event. To presume that only data free of perspective or point of view could count as evidence would constitute an extremist positivism or scientism.

The Cove (2009): hidden cameras capture evidence of the slaughter of dolphins

If we grant that documentary images can count as evidence, this leaves a question unanswered. What are documentary images evidence of? My best answer would be that documentary images can count as evidence (1) when they provide accurate and reliable information about the pro-filmic scene and (2) when they lend credence to, or else undermine, a claim or implication made in a documentary. The shot of the interview with General Westmoreland is an example of the first sort of evidence, since it strongly suggests (along with sound recording) that Westmoreland really said the things we see and hear him saying. The shots of the Vietnamese funeral are examples of the second kind of evidence, since they contradict Westmoreland's claims about 'Oriental' cheapness of life, thus undermining an explicit claim made elsewhere in the film (by Westmoreland).

COMPLICATIONS AND QUESTIONS

So far I have made a positive case for the claim that, in some cases, documentary images count as evidence. Yet there are problems to be addressed and qualifications to be made. We must consider (1) the context in which the images appear, (2) the type of image and the nature of its use and, finally, (3) the difficulty of determining what images are evidence of.

First, consider the context in which documentary images appear. The spectator, sitting before a screen and viewing a documentary, may have little or no knowledge of the film-maker's reputation or methods, of how the documentary images were produced, or of what kind of equipment was used and what the film-maker's persuasive intentions were. Were the film-makers 'flies on the wall' going unnoticed by the film's subjects, or '1000lb gorillas' radically influencing everything that occurred before the cameras? Are the images actual recordings or have they been altered or completely fabricated digitally? Joel Snyder and Neil Walsh Allen claim that photographs cannot provide incontrovertible evidence because spectators typically lack knowledge of the physical processes involved in the making of any given photograph. Only the film-makers have the knowledge of whether manipulative or deceptive techniques were employed in the making of the image. Snyder and Allen write:

> the picture is valuable as an index of the truth only to the extent that the process by which it is made is stated explicitly, and the pictures can be interpreted accurately only by people who have learned how to interpret them ... Needless to say, the explicitness that provides guarantees to the scientist is rarely demanded of most photographs we see, and if demanded couldn't be provided.[11]

Snyder and Allen are right, in my opinion, if we require of the indexical photograph that it supply legally, medically, or scientifically acceptable proof. In the context of the viewing of a documentary, however, audiences do not typically require such rigorous evidence,[12] nor need they do so in most cases.

To understand how images work as evidence in documentary films, we must consider the viewing context. Although some films straddle the ambiguous borderland between fiction and non-fiction, most films come indexed as documentary or fiction. That is, documentaries are identified as such through publicity and various stylistic markers, and the audience brings to bear various expectations when they recognise that a film is identified as a documentary. Audience members expect that a documentary film will bear a different relationship with reality than a fiction film, and that documentary film-makers, in presenting the film as a documentary, presume to make accurate assertions and to present images and sounds that serve as reliable guides to the pro-filmic scenes represented in the film.[13] Thus if audiences take the images of a documentary film as evidence, it is often due to a trust in the film-makers and their methods, a trust that the film-makers are respecting this implicit contract between them and the audience. The kind of evidence documentary images offer, then, isn't legal or scientific, but 'rhetorical'. Rhetorical evidence depends on various assumptions about the trustworthiness of the film-makers, their purposes and claims, and the conditions under which the relevant images were created. It also depends on a congruence between the film's and the viewer's perspective, or on whether the film-makers can persuade the audience to accept their viewpoint. This trust may be warranted or not, but it isn't *necessarily* unwarranted unless the film-makers are deceptive, dishonest, or incompetent. The first condition for documentary images to count as evidence is that the film-makers both produce and employ the images in appropriate ways, what I mean by 'appropriate' to be further discussed below.

Considerations of the image as evidence must also gauge the type of image in question and its function within the film. The use of images of staged, re-enacted, or recreated scenes has generated enormous discussion throughout the history of documentary, but mostly after the Direct Cinema movement, which led film-makers and audiences to consider such techniques to be manipulative or inherently deceptive. Before Direct Cinema, however, staging and recreation were accepted documentary practice. Arguably, staged scenes can provide evidence that something looked or occurred in a certain way, but it is much more tenuous evidence than that provided by footage that 'captures reality unawares'. The staged scenes of the effects and aftermath of nuclear war in Peter Watkins's *The War Game* (1965, UK) may have some evidentiary value. Watkins claims that his staged scenes were knowledgeably designed based on the evidence of Hiroshima and Nagasaki and the best calculations of the scientists of the time, but viewers would nonetheless put much more stock in them, and rightly so, had he been able to use actual footage of a nuclear attack in Britain. (Thankfully, no such footage exists.) In general, footage of re-enacted or staged events should be clearly identified, such identification providing the audience with information about how to understand the footage in relationship to what it is purported to show.

Unstaged footage of events that were not influenced by the presence of the camera and film-makers provides the strongest evidence, under certain conditions, that a pro-filmic scene looked a certain way or that such and such actually occurred. Yet in all of these cases the spectator is wise to consider the type of scene and the film-maker's possible influence. In the case of the Holliday footage of the Rodney King beating, the policemen had no knowledge of the presence of the camera, and thus the fact that the police were being videotaped had no influence whatsoever on their behaviour. Yet in many other kinds of situations, for example a filmed interview with a politician, the presence of the camera means everything. The most difficult cases are films or shots in which the subjects seem to be behaving naturally, but in relation to which there is ultimately no way to judge. Again, whether the spectator takes such images as evidence often depends on the level of trust the spectator invests in the film-makers' methods. Whether the spectator is warranted to take the images as evidence in any particular case is another question.

What about digital imaging technology that makes the manipulation of photographically realistic images so easy, or at least, promises to do so in the future? Brian Winston, for one, has argued that computer-generated imagery threatens to crumble the epistemic foundations of trust in documentaries because it undermines the common assumption that photographs do not lie.[14] Yet Winston's claim underestimates the place of trust in the audience's assent to any communication, and to documentaries in particular. Digital imaging does not change the nature of the photograph in fundamental ways; the digital photograph may still function as an icon, index and/or symbol. The salient change wrought by digital imaging has to do rather with the ease, or at least the future potential ease, of deception through photographically realistic representation. Let us not forget, however, that deception has always been possible and present in documentary photography. What digital photography will make salient is the need to enforce institutional and community standards about the use of digital imagery in documentaries. If I trust the reporting of the *New York Times* or *The Times Online*, it is because I trust that the relevant news-gathering institutions will enforce standards for evidence and use of sources. Similar standards apply to many of the institutions that support and produce documentaries. We lend our trust to the images in a documentary not solely on the base of the images in themselves. Anyone living through the backlash against Michael Moore in the USA understands that his use of photographic images guarantees neither belief nor assent to the claims made in his documentaries. Audiences also consider the source, whether it be an independent film-maker or an institutional sponsor, and whether they believe the source can be trusted.

Moving on to another consideration, suppose that it is true that photographs can provide reliable information similar to what would have been available to a person at the pro-filmic scene. If so, the claim is nonetheless subject to various conditions. For an image to provide such information, it must meet certain conditions. It must be in focus, properly exposed and pointed at the relevant area of the pro-filmic scene. The information the shot provides is subject to considerations of film stock and image resolution, ISO, focal length, colour balance, camera movement, the use of filters or lights and a host of other factors.

Most important, however, is that what the image purports to show is often subject to interpretation, not simply because stylistic choices in making the shot influence how we see that information, but because *seeing itself is subject to interpretation*. Suppose that an audience of diverse political persuasions witnesses the meeting of a governmental political body. Afterwards, they are asked various questions. The audience may agree on certain things, for example, that there were certain parliamentarians or senators present and that they said such and such. They might be able to agree on what the politicians were wearing, or that so-and-so tripped and fell to the floor and another so-and-so banged the gavel two times. But when asked to make generalisations about the meeting, based on what they saw, the level of agreement would drop remarkably. Was it a productive meeting? Did the meeting demonstrate the smooth functioning of democracy or the inertia of a broken political system? Was this an august body of distinguished diplomats or a confederacy of dunces?

Photographic images provide their best evidence for the brute presence of various entities before the camera and, beyond that, that entities looked a certain way or moved through space in a certain way. Yet images cannot make sense of this physical reality. Human beings do that. In the Rodney King video, the images remain mute about the officer's intentions, and about what happened before and after the events that were taped. The defence attorneys for the four police officers were able to exploit the inherent weaknesses of such visual evidence to make a case that convinced jury members that the visual evidence was weak.

Moreover, images show us particulars and do not make generalisations. When we see an image of a grungy dog, it is a particular dog. Yet the image provides only weak evidence for the voiceover narrator's (hypothetical) claim that dogs in general are dirty or grungy. It is very difficult for a particular to provide strong evidence for a generality, since moving from a single instance to a general claim hardly constitutes inductive proof. Yet moving in the opposite direction has more force. A contrary example throws into question a generality, such that Westmoreland's claims about cheapness of life in the Orient becomes questionable merely by an example of life's obvious value to a particular Vietnamese family.

To summarise so far, I have claimed that spectators may be warranted in taking documentary images as evidence of something, but only if the images satisfy certain conditions. The spectator must trust that the film-makers have produced the images using appropriate means for their providing accurate visual information. The spectator must understand the uses of an image in the context of the documentary, and whether it actually constitutes evidence for what the documentary claims. The spectator must be able to gauge the kind of evidence an image provides. Given the fact that certain information in images is available only through interpretation, the image provides its strongest evidence for what it shows of brute visual reality – for example, how something looked or what literally happened – as opposed to generalities – for example, value judgments about an action or attributions of intentions to a person.

There may seem to be a host of conditions to be met for a documentary image to count as evidence. I would argue, however, that many images meet these conditions and do so count. The Rodney King video, in my opinion, is evidence of police brutality towards Rodney King. The images of dolphins being slaughtered in *The Cove* demonstrate that such a slaughter took place, and that it was conducted in a certain way. The images (and sounds) of *Hearts and Minds* provide evidence that General Westmoreland falsely asserted that life is not valued by Asians.

EVIDENCE AND RHETORIC

Whether or not images are good evidence, spectators often take them as such. One can separate the issue of actual evidence, that is, data that gives warrant for believing something, versus the perception of evidence. Thus we might ask what place images have in the rhetoric of documentary films, in contributing to the persuasive force of documentaries. Some documentary theorists have been deeply suspicious of the use of images as evidence and pessimistic about the ability of audiences to make discerning judgments about such use. Brian Winston, for example, has written that a misleading 'scientificity' is built into the photographic apparatus, such that audiences tend to take documentary photography as embodying an unproblematic and transparent truth.[15] While I share Winston's suspicion that audiences are prone to find evidence where they should not, I find the source of this tendency less in the misleading nature of photographic images than in the human tendency to accept and reject evidence based not on epistemic warrant but on self-interest and inertia. Thus if politically conservative audiences reject the overarching messages of Michael Moore's *Sicko* (2007, USA) or *Bowling for Columbine* (2002, USA) (see Chapter 1.4), they are unlikely to take the films' images as evidence of much, while those who already agree with the films' claims will more likely find the images to be persuasive.

Certainly the objectivity of the image is worth something to the persuader or propagandist. A documentary image may provide denotative or literal evidence that something happened in a certain way. But images also have connotations, the word 'connotation' being another way of accounting for the image as a symbol. All of the objects, colours, compositions and camera movements that a film-maker shows bear symbolic or connotative meaning. In *The Thin Blue Line* (1988, USA), Errol Morris films interviews with two men in prison, both of whom have been implicated in the same murder. David Harris wears red, and the scene is bathed in reddish-orange light, while, in a separate interview, Randall Adams wears white, and the background light is colourless. This may be a case in which, as Roland Barthes notes, the 'denotated image naturalizes the symbolic message, it innocents the semantic artifice of connotation'.[16] In other words, the denotative force of the image makes its expressive, connotative and symbolic elements seem natural. Thus if Randall Adams's white clothing makes him seem innocent and David Harris's red clothing and red light make him seem guilty, it may be because symbolic meaning accrues ostensible authority from the images' indexicality.

Images are most persuasive as photographic evidence, however, when the audience trusts the film and, implicitly, the film-maker. 'Trust' is the operative word here. In *On Rhetoric*, Aristotle writes that the perceived character or ethos of a speaker can almost be said to be the 'controlling factor' in persuasion, for 'we believe fair-minded people to a greater extent and more quickly [than we do others]'.[17] We might say the same for a documentary film because audiences understand that documentary films, unlike mere documents, are structured rhetorical discourses. If the film's claims and representations seem reasonable; if the film seems honest and reliable; if it has been indexed as a documentary; if it has been vetted by critics and film-makers and has gained an institutional reputation; if we have reason to trust the film-makers; if all of these conditions apply, we are more likely to take the film's images as evidence. And we are more likely to be justified in doing so.

NOTES

1. I will use the word 'image' in this chapter to refer to both still and moving photographic images in film, video, or digital media.

2. The organisation is now called the Society for Cinema and Media Studies.

3. Quoted in *Jump Cut: A Review of Contemporary Media* no. 37, July 1992, p. 2.

4. Michael Renov, *The Subject of Documentary* (Minneapolis: University of Minnesota Press, 2004), pp. 136–7, and quoted in 'Introduction: The Truth About Non-Fiction,' in Michael Renov (ed.), *Theorizing Documentary* (New York: Routledge, 1993), p. 7, emphasis in original.

5. For a brief discussion of the sceptical and critical realist positions in documentary theory, see my 'Documentary', in Paisley Livingston and Carl Plantinga (eds), *The Routledge Companion to Philosophy and Film* (London and New York: Routledge, 2009), pp. 499–501. For Noël Carroll's vitriolic take on the documentary epistemology debate, see his 'Nonfiction Film and Postmodernist Skepticism', in David Bordwell and Noël Carroll (eds), *Post-Theory: Reconstructing Film Studies* (Madison: University of Wisconsin Press, 1996), pp. 283–306; Brian Winston's equally acrimonious response is found in his *Claiming the Real II* (London: Palgrave Mcmillan, 2008), pp. 226–30. Errol Morris's perspective on issues of epistemology and ontology in the documentary can be found in my 'The Philosophy of Errol Morris', in William Rothman (ed.), *Three Documentary Filmmakers: Errol Morris, Ross McElwee, Jean Rouch* (Albany: State University of New York Press, 2009), pp. 43–60. See also Errol Morris, 'There is such a Thing as Truth', editorial for National Public Radio, 2 May 2005. Text reprinted on http://www.errolmorris.com/content/editorial/npr505.html. Accessed 11 October 2006.

6. The arguments here are abbreviated versions of a more fully developed case, for which see my *Rhetoric and Representation in Nonfiction Film* (Cambridge: Cambridge University Press, 1997), pp. 40–82.

7. A 'sign', in this sense, is anything (a mark on a page, object, sound, gesture, etc.) that can be used to communicate something to someone.

8. One possible exception may be onomatopoeia, in which spoken words are said to resemble the sound of their referent, as in *buzz*, *crack*, or *cuckoo*.

9. Plantinga, *Rhetoric and Representation in Nonfiction Film*, pp. 46–58.

10. Ibid., pp. 54–6.

11. Joel Snyder and Neil Walsh Allen, 'Photography, Vision, and Representation', *Critical Inquiry* vol. 2 no. 1, Autumn 1975, p. 162.

12. This is not to claim that the uses of photography and other imaging technologies in science, medicine, or the law reach some standard of perfection, but rather to assert that if one were to demand such standards of the documentary image, few images in documentaries could ever count as strong evidence.

13. Elsewhere I call the documentary's implied stance towards reality 'asserted veridical representation'. See my

'What a Documentary Is, After All', *Journal of Aesthetics and Art Criticism* vol. 63 no. 2, Spring 2005, pp. 105–17.

14. Winston, *Claiming the Real II*, pp. 7–10.

15. 'The Documentary Film as Scientific Inscription', in Renov, *Theorizing the Documentary*, pp. 37–57; also see Winston's *Claiming the Real II*.

16. Roland Barthes, 'The Rhetoric of the Image', in *Image, Music, Text*, trans. Stephen Heath (New York: Hill and Wang, 1977), p. 45.

17. Aristotle, *On Rhetoric: A Theory of Civic Discourse*, trans. George A. Kennedy (Oxford: Oxford University Press, 1991), p. 38.

1.3 The Performing Film-maker and the Acting Subject

STELLA BRUZZI

Despite the deep-seated cultural attachment to the evidential quality of the photographic image, the authenticity of documentary witnessing, whether by film-makers directly or through the agency of informants, is problematic. What if a witness is giving a 'performance'? 'Inauthenticity' is inevitable if the documentary subject is thought to be 'acting'. And what if the film-makers reveal themselves? What is the impact on 'documentary value' of their 'role'?

The performative documentary is a mode which emphasises – and indeed constructs a film around – the often hidden aspect of performance, whether on the part of the documentary subjects or the film-makers.

When one discusses performance and the real event, this fusion has more usually been applied to documentary drama, where a masquerade of spontaneity can be seen to function at an overt level. It is useful to note the discrepancy between performative documentaries and dramas that adopt the style of a documentary by using, for instance, hand-held camerawork, scratchy synch-sound recording and ad-libbed dialogue as one finds in wide-ranging examples, from Ken Loach's *Cathy Come Home* (1966) to Rob Reiner's 'rockumentary' *This is Spinal Tap* (1984) to Armando Ianucci's faux 'mockumentaries', *The Thick of It* (2005–12) and *In the Loop* (2009). Though divergent in most other ways, all these examples assume proximity to the real to reside in an intensely observational style.

The docudrama and fake documentary output of the past thirty years is predicated upon the assumption that drama can legitimately tackle documentary issues and uncontentiously use non-fiction techniques to achieve its aims. It thus becomes possible for drama to perform a comparable function to documentary: *Cathy Come Home* raised public awareness of homelessness, thereby greatly aiding the charity Shelter, while Granada's *Who Bombed Birmingham?* (1990) led directly to the reopening of the case of the Birmingham Six. Continuing in this tradition, *Hillsborough* (1996), directed by Charles McDougall and written by Jimmy McGovern, dramatised the events surrounding the tragedy at Hillsborough Stadium, Sheffield Wednesday's home ground, where the FA Cup semi-final

between Liverpool and Nottingham Forest was to be played on 15 April 1989. Ninety-six Liverpool fans were crushed to death and another 766 were injured. The drama-documentary adopts a realist aesthetic, within which the role of performance is, paradoxically, to draw the audience into the reality of the situations being dramatised, to authenticate the fictionalisation.[1]

In contrast to this, the performative documentary uses performance within a non-fiction context to draw attention to the impossibilities of authentic documentary representation. The performative element within the framework of non-fiction is thereby an alienating, distancing device, not one which actively promotes identification and a straightforward response to a film's content. There is, however, an essential difference between films that are performative in themselves and those that concern performative subject matter, frequently in conjunction (as in the work of Errol Morris and Nicholas Barker), with an elaborate and ostentatiously inauthentic visual style. My argument is that documentaries are a negotiation between film-maker and reality and, at heart, a performance. It is thereby in the films of Nick Broomfield, Molly Dineen, Errol Morris or Nicholas Barker that this underlying thesis finds its clearest expression.

Bill Nichols, in *Blurred Boundaries*, complicates terminology slightly (considering the familiarity of the term 'performative' since Judith Butler's *Gender Trouble* was published in 1990) when he adopts the term the 'performative mode' (following the didactic, the observational, the interactive and the reflexive modes)[2] to describe films that 'stress subjective aspects of a classically objective discourse'.[3] Diverging from this application of the term 'performative', this discussion will focus on documentaries that are performative in the manner identified by Butler and others after J. L. Austin – namely that they function as utterances that simultaneously both describe and perform an action. Austin's radical differentiation between the constative and performative aspects of language (the former simply refers to or describes, the latter performs what it alludes to) has been expanded upon and relocated many times in recent years, but rarely with reference to documentary.[4] Examples of words that Austin identifies as being 'performative utterances' are 'I do', said within the context of the marriage ceremony, or 'I name this ship the *Queen Elizabeth*', said while smashing a bottle of champagne against the vessel's side, his reasoning being that 'in saying what I do, I actually perform that action'.[5] A parallel is to be found between these linguistic examples and the performative documentary which – whether built around the intrusive presence of the film-maker or self-conscious performances by its subjects – is the enactment of the notion that a documentary only comes into being as it is performed, that although its factual basis (or document) can pre-date any recording or representation of it, the film itself is necessarily performative because it is given meaning by the interaction between performance and reality. Unlike Nichols, who finds it hard to disguise his latent wariness of the performative documentary mode, supposing that the more a documentary 'draws attention to itself', the further it gets from 'what it represents',[6] this chapter will view the performative positively.

The traditional concept of documentary as striving to represent reality as faithfully as possible is predicated upon the realist assumption that the production process must be disguised, as was the case with Direct Cinema. Conversely, the new performative documentaries herald a different notion of documentary 'truth' that acknowledges the construction and artificiality of even the non-fiction film. Many theorists would view this reflexivity as breaking with documentary tradition – but this is only valid if one takes as representative of the documentary 'canon' films that seek to hide the modes of production. This, largely, has been the way in which the documentary family tree has evolved, with the relative marginalisation of the more reflexive documentary tradition exemplified by early films such as *Man with a Movie Camera* (Dziga Vertov, 1929, USSR), *À propos de Nice* (Jean Vigo, 1930, France), *Land Without Bread* (*Las Hurdes*, Luis Buñuel, 1933, Spain) and continuing into the work of Emile de Antonio, Jean Rouch and French cinéma vérité and Chris Marker. Just as legitimate is the view that the new performative documentaries are simply the most recent articulation of the film-makers' unease at this very assumption of what documentaries are about – that, like the popular mainstream docusoaps or Reality TV, the films of Broomfield, Michael Moore and others have sought to accentuate, not mask, the means of production because they realise that such a masquerade is impossibly utopian. The erroneous assumption that documentaries aspire to be referential, or 'constative' to adopt Austin's terminology (that is, to represent an uncomplicated, descriptive relationship between subject and text), is being specifically targeted in performative films, which are thus not breaking with the factual film-making tradition, but are a logical extension of that tradition's aims, as much concerned with representing reality as their

predecessors, but more aware of the inevitable falsification or subjectification such representation entails.

A prerequisite of the performative documentary as here defined is the inclusion of a notable performance component, and it is the insertion of such a performance element into a non-fictional context that has hitherto proved problematic. If, however, one returns to Austin's speech models, then the presumed diminution of the films' believability becomes less of an issue: what a film-maker such as Nick Broomfield is doing when he appears on camera and in voiceover is acting out a documentary. This performativity is based on the idea of disavowal, that simultaneously signals a desire to make a conventional documentary (that is, to give an accurate account of a series of factual events) while also indicating, through the mechanisms of performance and Broomfield's obtrusive presence, the impossibility of the documentary's cognitive function.

Nick Broomfield's films do this quite literally, as the conventional documentary disintegrates through the course of the film and the performative one takes over. The fundamental issue here is honesty. The performative element could be seen to undermine the conventional documentary pursuit of representing the real because the elements of performance, dramatisation and acting for the camera are intrusive and alienating factors. Alternatively, the use of performance tactics could be viewed as a means of suggesting that perhaps documentaries should admit the defeat of their utopian aim and elect instead to present an alternative 'honesty' that does not seek to mask their inherent instability but rather to acknowledge that performance – the enactment of the documentary specifically for the cameras – will always be the heart of the non-fiction film. Documentaries, like Austin's performatives, perform the actions they name.

ISSUES OF AUTHORSHIP IN THE PERFORMATIVE DOCUMENTARY

What has occurred within the last decade or so in both film and television (and performative documentaries are at the forefront of this) is a shift towards more self-consciously 'arty' and expressive modes of documentary film-making. Reflexive documentaries, as they challenge the notion of film's 'transparency' and highlight the performative quality of documentary, will emphasise issues of authorship and construction. Documentary film-makers such as Nicholas Barker in the UK or Errol Morris in the USA make their authorship explicit, not through personalisation but through formulating a consistently obtrusive and flamboyant visual style. The question of authorship has traditionally proved a thorny problem for the documentary, as the recognised intervention of an auteur disrupts the non-fiction film's supposed allegiance to transparency and truthfulness.

As, however, I argue against the uncompromised rendition of the real being an attainable goal for non-fiction, the presence of the auteur is not so problematic, for one of the corollaries of accepting that documentary cannot but perform the interaction between reality and its representation is the acknowledgment that documentary, like fiction, is authored. As with the theorisation of the auteur in the realm of narrative fiction film, what appears to pose particular difficulties where documentaries are concerned is the author-director. A familiar charge levelled at documentary directors – who, through a variety of means such as voiceover, appearance on camera and overt stylisation have signalled their control over their work – is that they are needlessly egotistical in not allowing the subject matter to 'speak for itself'. But, as Nick Broomfield has countered, no one accuses the current affairs presenter-reporter of being egotistical, merely because s/he is dependent on the piece to camera. The signposting of the documentary author-director or his or her overt intrusion crystallises documentary's fundamental conflict between subjectivity and objectivity. One repercussion of the establishment of a documentary canon that has historically marginalised films emphasising the author's presence is that it has been too readily assumed that the repression of the author has been necessary to the implementation of objectivity.

Culminating in the recent work of film-makers such as Michael Moore, Molly Dineen and Nick Broomfield, who are active participants in their films, documentary has an established tradition of the performer-director. These film-makers, to varying degrees, participate in their films because they are interested in discovering alternative and less formally restrictive ways of getting to what they perceive to be the essence of their subjects. The means by which they achieve this are not those conventionally associated with truth-finding post-Direct Cinema as they entail breaking the illusion of film, thereby interrupting the privileged relationship between the filmed subjects and the spectator.

Recently, many more documentaries are emerging that take for granted the existence and inevitable presence of their film-makers, directly demonstrating the inherent performativity of the non-fiction film. The overt intervention of the film-maker definitively signals the death of documentary theory's idealisation of the unbiased film by asking, categorically and from within the documentary itself: what else is a documentary but a dialogue between a film-maker, a crew and a situation that, although in existence prior to their arrival, has irrevocably been changed by that arrival? What author-performer-based documentaries reiterate are the twin notions that a documentary is its own document and that the interventionist documentary film-maker is a fluid entity defined and redefined by every context in which he or she appears. The

Biggie and Tupac (2002): 'it's not the presence of the camera that changes people's behaviour, it's the relationship they have with the people behind it' – Nick Broomfield

author-performer is thereby one constituent of a film's ongoing dialectical analysis. As Broomfield comments in an interview about *Biggie and Tupac* (2002), in Direct Cinema films the audience is not granted any information about the film-makers behind the cameras, going on to conclude about why he abandoned that way of film-making that 'it's not the presence of the camera that changes people's behaviour, it's the relationship they have with the people behind it'.[7] In Broomfield's films the relationship with the people behind the camera is explicit.

THE 'STAR DIRECTOR': NICK BROOMFIELD

Nick Broomfield is a quintessential documentary auteur, whose formulaic style is, to a documentary audience, instantly recognisable – so much so that in 1999/2000 he (with the assistance of his original cameraperson/collaborator Joan Churchill) starred in a series of Volkswagen Passat television ads brandishing his distinctive boom and asking his generic awkward questions. Broomfield is British documentary's 'star director', he is a recognisable face, has had a season of films at the National Film Theatre (1997) and has been a topic for discussion in gossip columns. His trademarks are films built around the tortuous chase after elusive subjects and the collapsed interview that sometimes, as in *Tracking Down Maggie* (1994), fails to materialise. When *Kurt and Courtney* was released in 1998, several journalists expressed their disillusionment with 'the Broomfield film'.[8,9]

The simple fact that there has been a Broomfield backlash – arguably concluded after *Biggie and Tupac* with the release of the more politically significant and serious *Aileen: The Life and Death of a Serial Killer* (2003, co-directed with Joan Churchill) – is testament to his star status. Since

Driving Me Crazy (1988), Broomfield has appeared on camera in his films as the hassling director enacting the process of making a documentary, hounding his subjects and wearing them down until they finally give him a story. Although earlier films likewise explored the performative potential of the interventionist director (in films such as *Behind the Rent Strike* [1974] and *Soldier Girls* [1981], for example, Broomfield is addressed directly by the films' subjects, although he remains largely off camera), Broomfield's later films (despite his indebtedness to Direct Cinema) have become supreme examples of the director-performer model. Alongside the centrality of 'performance' there is, in these later films, a more heavily signposted belief in documentary's 'performativity'; in their very structure they proclaim that, without the intervention of Broomfield and his crew, there would be no film.

The central issue in how one perceives Broomfield's work is the specific persona he performs on camera. Towards the end of *Driving Me Crazy* – a documentary following the rehearsal period and performance of the all-black musical *Body and Soul* – scriptwriter Joe Hindy exclaims 'I don't think you're adorable any more, Nick,' a sentiment echoed in *Heidi Fleiss: Hollywood Madam* (1995) when, once again after some time, Madam Alex, one of the film's three protagonists, shouts at Broomfield down the telephone: 'You're such a greedy f****** pig. I'm so sick of you.' Broomfield's on-screen persona is the sweet, ingratiating, slightly gullible buffoon; it is only late in the proceedings (if ever) that his subjects realise that this is an act, a ploy on Broomfield's part to get the material he wants. In one interview, Broomfield cites an unlikely precursor in Pier Paolo Pasolini, whom he met during the filming of *The Canterbury Tales* in England in 1971. He saw in Pasolini someone who, though ostensibly reserved himself, generated chaos around him, observing that, while other film crews 'were always incredibly ordered, almost military, with a clear chain of command', Pasolini's 'seemed to operate with a purposeful anarchy'.[10] Broomfield's particular admiration for Pasolini's 'ability to use chaos to a creative advantage' could be describing his own post-*Driving Me Crazy* films, for all the documentaries that revolve around his on-screen performance are exercises in controlled chaos. The 'control' aspect relates directly to Broomfield's performance of himself: he remains sweet, dogged, usually unflustered, while around him his films almost implode. The anger of Joe Hindy and Madam Alex stems from their belated realisation that Nick Broomfield the documentary film-maker is not synonymous with 'Nick Broomfield' the charming man with Mickey Mouse earphones and boom who extracts information from them. An interesting aspect of how critics and spectators relate to Broomfield's work is that they too sometimes find it hard to accept the dichotomy: after the screening of *Heidi Fleiss* at the 1995 London Film Festival, one member of the audience during the

ensuing Q&A session asked Broomfield to expand upon the fact that, while he appears a little stupid on screen, he seems intelligent in real life. Broomfield's tactful response was to reiterate that his smiley persona has proved most useful in getting his subjects to open up on camera.

Broomfield's self-performance fuels the debate around 'realness'. Peter Wollen in 1974 used a formula to specifically illustrate this schism in relation to authorship and the fiction film, arguing – from an auteur-structuralist perspective – that the auteur is only the identity discovered within the text and does not pertain to the individual beyond its parameters.[11] Adopting Wollen's equation, Nick Broomfield ≠ 'Nick Broomfield', the inverted commas signifying the version of the auteur to be found within the films. It is over-simplistic to argue that Nick Broomfield, the author beyond the frame, is irrelevant to how one views and interprets the films in which 'Nick Broomfield' appears; rather it is the dialectic between the two that motivates the documentaries and informs our responses to them. The subject 'Nick Broomfield' is constructed on screen from within the documentary frame, whereas Nick Broomfield the auteur remains omniscient and detached (a role that is partly articulated through Broomfield's own narration for his films). Complicating matters is that the two are indisputably the same person, they just perform different functions for the purposes of making a documentary and it is this difference and the dialogue that ensues which informs the films. Quite graphically, Broomfield's dual presence articulates the idea that documentaries are the result of a dialectical negotiation between the reality that existed before he arrived and that which subsequently becomes the subject of his films. Why is the performative documentary problematic? Most importantly, it is problematic because it throws into sharp relief previously held notions of fixity of meaning and documentary 'truth'; in a film in which all reliable significance is generated by and through 'Nick Broomfield' the performer-director, there is necessarily a tension between the subjects before and after his arrival that is never fully resolved. The true stories upon which Broomfield's documentaries are based are compromised, filtered through the structured chaos on the screen.

Nick Broomfield's films could not always be characterised thus, and it is illuminating to compare the later documentaries with those he made with Joan Churchill. Although it is in *Driving Me Crazy* that Broomfield first appears on screen as his films' agent provocateur, it is the earlier *Lily Tomlin: The Film Behind the Show* (1986) about the American comedienne which proved to be the catalyst for a change of approach. Despite its title, *Lily Tomlin* is a straightforward film in the Direct Cinema mould that follows a performer, in this case Tomlin, preparing her one-woman Broadway show *The Search for Signs of Life in the Universe*. Subsequently Broomfield describes the 'nightmare' that filming *Lily Tomlin* became when, following an exchange of writs, the resulting film was severely compromised: 'The film was a very pale reflection of what had been a very miserable experience. But it occurred to me that if we'd had the miserable experience on film it would have at least been amusing.'[12]

Prior to this, Broomfield had collaborated on several observational documentaries, many of which – such as *Tattooed Tears* (1978), about the California Youth Training School, and *Soldier Girls*, about women US Army recruits of Charlie Company, Fort Gordon, Georgia – followed in the Fred Wiseman mould of showing the workings of institutions and official organisations. The films are serious, politically motivated and subject-driven, concentrating on material that is still the standard fare of observational documentaries. Even though (as in both films cited above) Broomfield and Churchill single out a handful of individuals to focus upon, such figures are used as representative characters through whom the workings of the institution/organisation can best be conveyed, so – in a generic sequence repeated a number of years later in *Soldiers To Be* (2000) – a brutal, aggressive sergeant shouts at new recruits for making their bunks sloppily.

The Broomfield–Churchill collaborations use interventionist mechanisms only sparingly and functionally – for example, conveying factual information that assists the spectator's understanding of a sequence through short subtitles. The films' emphasis is on the subjects to such an extent that, at the end of *Soldier Girls* when Private Johnson (one of the film's principal characters) is leaving, she spontaneously turns and bids farewell to Churchill and Broomfield. Although the image of Private Johnson embracing Nick Broomfield is caught on camera and is not omitted from the finished film, he is only glimpsed fleetingly in the corner of a frame as if signalling the filmmakers' surprise and self-consciousness at this violation of a key observational rule. For the most part, *Soldier Girls* and *Tattooed Tears* serve as exemplary illustrations of the vérité-derived tradition: they feature personalised situations that carry with them more general political connotations; they make statements through observation as opposed to through intervention; they sublimate the filmmakers' opinions to those of the people they pursue, although elements such as editing, a greater identification with the 'victims' rather than the figures in authority and the subjective camerawork serve to implicitly convey what those opinions might be.

Both early films contain several moments that could legitimately be termed 'classic vérité', when observation becomes synonymous with insight and the acquisition of knowledge. Sequences that dwell upon Ronnie, one of the youthful prisoners in *Tattooed Tears*, being forcibly restrained or Private Alvez in *Soldier Girls* being punished for lack of motivation by having to dig, well into the night,

an ostensibly useless grave-like hole both manage to imply criticism of the actions they show simply by the length of time that is dedicated to each and the by the manner in which the film-makers focus upon the suffering, victimised Ronnie and Private Alvez. Both sequences offer covert commentary on the events they depict.

Broomfield's subsequent style evolved out of a frustrated awareness of the limitations of the observational mode. He articulates this most directly in relation to *Driving Me Crazy* when commenting 'I'd always wanted to examine the documentary form and I'd become sort of disenchanted with the narrow parameters of this style of film-making. All too often what you look at on TV is very cleaned up and dishonest.'[13] In a later interview he adds: 'There's no point in pretending the camera's not there. I think what's important is the interaction between the film-makers and those being filmed, and the audience is aware of that interaction so they can make decision of their own.'[14] If one examines even the much earlier work, the tensions are visible within the films themselves. During the restraint sequence in *Tattooed Tears*, Ronnie snatches a quick, furtive glance to camera, this transgressive look highlighting the immutable wall between the subjects and the film-makers of observational films. Similarly, throughout *Soldier Girls* there is the suggestion that the film's protagonists are knowingly acting up for the camera and hence unable to mask the film process's lack of spontaneity. Part of the power of *Soldier Girls* results from its enactment of this tension between what should and should not be included in an observational documentary – moments such as Private Hall learning how to perform the role of sergeant by joining in Sergeant Abing's sustained, personalised attack on Private Alvez following her fit of screaming after being made to dig the hole. Abing begins with the groundless intimidation 'you don't deserve to be out there in society, you might kill someone out there, Alvez' (Alvez, after all, was originally accused of lacking motivation as a recruit), to which Hall adds:

> You know Alvez there's something about you that tells me you might be the type that would take a weapon and go up on top of a building and start just picking off people in the street just for the heck of it, because you're so apathetic, sooner or later it's bound to turn to hate.

Besides contradicting herself, Hall delivers this fanciful diatribe in the deliberate, slow manner of someone who is both assuming an unfamiliar role that she is eager to perfect (in this case the part of the brutalising sergeant) and is trying to sound convincing despite having to make up what she is saying as she goes along. This and other similar performances in *Soldier Girls* imply, through their very awkwardness, that they are striving to seem unaware of the film-makers' presence but are finding this impossible.

It is moments such as these that substantiate Broomfield's contention about 'dishonesty'. Not only are his and Churchill's films characterised by such textual cracks and tensions, but they illustrate the unworkability of the observational ideal by striving too hard to mask the necessity for more formally structuring devices such as voiceover or direct authorial intervention.

Broomfield's transition to a more openly authored style also coincided with the termination of his partnership (both personal and professional) with Joan Churchill, although she has continued to operate the camera on some of his later films such as *Tracking Down Maggie* and *Kurt and Courtney* and ultimately returns as co-director of *Aileen: The Life and Death of a Serial Killer*. If one returns to Broomfield's statement about his growing disillusionment with his methods at the time of *Driving Me Crazy*, what also becomes evident is his frustration at not having been able to show (in *Lily Tomlin*, for example) the mechanics and practicalities of documentary film-making. An indispensable corollary of making the shift towards appearing on camera is Broomfield's now proven desire to 'examine the documentary form' by dismantling it. From being good genre films, Broomfield's documentaries become counter-documentaries in that they analyse the non-fiction film from within, constructing a documentary around what a documentary should not be, in this 'post-vérité' age: a film made up of telephone conversations, arguments before and after interviews, discussions between director and crew, chats with incidental characters. Clearly, Broomfield's level of self-reflexivity was not, in the 1980s, new to documentary – an awareness that documentaries existed on the same continuum as fiction films and were also 'constructed' and 'inauthentic' has been a foundational idea of documentaries from the early modernist documentaries of Vertov, Cavalcanti and Siodmak. What was new was what Broomfield, in his post-*Driving Me Crazy* films, chose to do with his reflective awareness, namely to telegraph, via the films' formal and physical marginalisation of their central subjects, the dichotomy between director and performer that Nick Broomfield embodies when appearing in his films. Just as there is a fundamental distinction to be drawn between Nick Broomfield and 'Nick Broomfield', so there is an equally significant differentiation to be made between the documentary and the 'documentary', the former signifying the films' putative subject and the latter the resulting film.

The contrast is most graphically illustrated by markedly unsuccessful films such as *Tracking Down Maggie* and *Sarah Palin: You Betcha!* (2011). Both films, purport to be 'about' their subjects, Margaret Thatcher and Sarah Palin, respectively, but both also contain very little of either Thatcher or Palin, and become instead films 'about' – not just featuring – the peripheral characters such as the neighbour on Flood Street who took Thatcher's old lavatory from the skip in front of her house or the Palins' Alaskan neighbours. There is a suspicion in both cases that Broomfield did not try especially hard to get a solid interview with either female politician (they are both, after all, on book-signing tours and so presumably in the business of courting publicity), and that instead he was enjoying himself getting to know their neighbours, friends and critics. Both documentaries, however, fail because they cannot bring together the two components of the dialectic: the light, frothy veneer and the serious subject matter. The success of Broomfield's performative documentaries is directly dependent upon the collision at some point between the proposed conventional documentary subject (Sarah Palin, Eileen Wuornos, Eugène Terre'Blanche, Heidi Fleiss, Madams and clients of a New York fetish parlour) and the unconventional, ostensibly shambolic performance of that subject on film; the documentary and the 'documentary' must meet as must Nick Broomfield and 'Nick Broomfield'. The interview situation is the usual place for these meetings to occur, and films that lack a substantial interview with their pivotal figures (*Maggie, Kurt and Courtney* or *Sarah Palin*) prove unsatisfying because any serious intent behind the films is lost altogether.

A film in which one can observe Broomfield's constructive use of interview is *The Leader, His Driver and the Driver's Wife* (1991), his first documentary about Eugène Terre'Blanche, the leader of the neo-Nazi Afrikaner Resistance Movement (the AWB) in South Africa, made at a time when apartheid was crumbling but nevertheless a political force. *The Leader* – like his second Aileen Wuornos film, to which I will soon turn – is one of Broomfield's more ideologically committed documentaries, in which occurs a successful amalgamation of political content and performative style. Like *Aileen: Life and Death of a Serial Killer* will do twelve years later, *The Leader* parallels the amassing of the central documentary story with the experience of making a film. The focus of both is the (in conventional terms inadequate) interview that Broomfield conducts with Terre'Blanche, in the words of JP, Terre'Blanche's driver, 'the worst he's ever seen'. For political effect, Broomfield turns into 'Nick Broomfield' the provocateur as he and his crew continue to provoke Eugène Terre'Blanche until he starts shouting at them and telling them off. The centrality of the interview continues in Broomfield's work and is used to potent political effect in the second Aileen Wuornos documentary. The way in which the performative works in *The Leader*, however, ultimately suggests that the pre-existing facts upon which it is based – like the actual Nick Broomfield – do exist. Certain of Broomfield's later films (most notably *Heidi Fleiss*) problematise this simple, reflective interpretation of the performative by not abiding by the simple binary oppositions examined above. Many of these more recent films, however, show a move towards the clichéd Nick Broomfield film that is more about him than about his subjects as the films become more fixated on the 'Nick Broomfield' persona which increasingly dominates the documentaries' action than their purported documentary subject.

Having arguably spent the decade or so after *The Leader* making a series of documentaries (*Heidi Fleiss*, *Fetishes*, *Kurt and Courtney*, *Biggie and Tupac*) more entertaining and self-indulgent than they were either politically motivated or even personally involving, *Aileen: The Life and Death of a Serial Killer* – Broomfield's second film about the notorious American female serial killer – proved to be a welcome return to documentary film-making with a sober purpose. Aileen Wuornos, who committed seven murders between 1989 and 1990, was arrested on 9 January 1991 and finally executed in Florida at the behest of Governor Jeb Bush on 9 October 2002, having been held on 'death row' at Broward Prison. Wuornos's life story inspired the Academy Award-winning Hollywood movie *Monster* (2003), which thanks Broomfield in the credits for his work as consultant.

Since making *Aileen Wuornos: The Selling of a Serial Killer* in 1993, Broomfield had kept in touch with Wuornos, principally via her best friend Dawn Botkins,[15] who wrote to Wuornos every day and to whom (as shown at the end of the second film) her ashes are returned after execution and cremation. The catalyst for this second documentary was Broomfield being served with a subpoena to appear at Wuornos's pre-execution trial, after she had changed her plea for the murders she had committed from self-defence to murder in cold blood. On his official website Nick Broomfield reiterates comments he makes in the documentary's voiceover when saying about *Aileen: The Life and Death of a Serial Killer*:

> This is the most personal and disturbing film I have made. I knew Aileen over the course of 12 years and the barbaric nature of her death had a profound effect on me, and months of nightmares. It was one film I didn't choose to make. I came to it as a witness and ended up attending an execution. The violence of taking a life remains the same whether it is legally sanctioned or not. It introduces murder into our vocabulary of behaviour.[16]

This second Wuornos documentary marks another important moment of transition in Broomfield's career (although, in these terms, *Sarah Palin* shows him regressing again); in it, for instance, there is markedly less Broomfield than in *Biggie and Tupac*, made only a year earlier in 2002, and Broomfield's resurrection of a more sombre, observational style is strongly reminiscent of his more politically committed earlier films, such as *Juvenile Liaisons* (1975) and *Soldier Girls*. *Aileen: Life and Death of a Serial Killer* is also the first time since *Juvenile Liaisons 2* (1990) that Broomfield has shared his director credit with his long-time cinematographer (and former partner) Joan Churchill.[17]

Yet Tanya Horeck, in an article that compares *Life and Death* and *Monster*, argues that the documentary conforms to Broomfield's established authorial style in that, 'as with his other films, Broomfield and his on-screen performance as documentary film-maker take centre stage',[18] it seems to me to be the case that the overtly performative aspects of the director's style are, in the second Wuornos film, significantly diluted. Broomfield does not, for instance, brandish his familiar boom or wear his equally familiar headphones and mischievous smile, and, at a more textually complex level, there are only a few vestiges left of the tonal interplay between the straight Nick Broomfield, director, and his lighter, more flippant on-screen alter ego.

Life and Death centres on a perceived injustice (that the Florida courts sentence to death a woman who Broomfield sets out to prove is visibly mentally disturbed) and in this sense the conventionalised dynamics between the performative director and his subject are suppressed in favour of a more sober investigative approach. As with Michael Moore's films (for example, his relatively restrained and peripheral performance in *Fahrenheit 9/11*), there is, crudely speaking, an inverse correlation between the extent of Broomfield's serious involvement in his subject matter (and indeed the seriousness of the subject matter itself) and the amount he appears on screen; the less he features the more seriously we should take the documentary.

When Broomfield does occupy screen time, it is crucially to underline a substantive point and, even more crucially, to deflect attention *away* as opposed to *onto* himself. The underpinning motivation for *Aileen: Life and Death of a Serial Killer* was Broomfield's conviction that Wuornos in part changed her plea from self-defence to guilty not because she had, when originally convicted, been lying but because she wanted to secure for herself a closer day of execution. Broomfield is of the conviction that Wuornos is insane and should not have been executed; as he states categorically, when being interviewed in the last scene of the documentary by the press corps hovering around on the day of Wuornos's execution: 'We're executing a person who's mad.'

Broomfield's diminished physical presence in front of Churchill's camera functions in tandem with his keenness to articulate his own opinions on the issues raised by the case – a case which, as I have indicated, Broomfield was only involved with again because he was called as a defence witness in Wuornos's pre-execution trial. Broomfield at first does not realise why exactly he has been issued with a subpoena, but it soon becomes clear that the prosecuting attorney is keen to discredit his first film about Wuornos, *Aileen Wuornos: The Selling of a Serial Killer*. *Life and Death* opens with footage from this hearing, during which the prosecution play a video of a key sequence from *The Selling*: Wuornos's then lawyer Stephen Glazer's alleged 'seven-joint ride', during which the lawyer is shown smoking seven joints of marijuana while driving to visit Wuornos in prison. Glazer at some point in the final edited sequence has changed shirt and the prosecuting lawyer insinuates that Broomfield pasted together two different sequences, an allegation that Broomfield, on camera, denies and later refutes outright, after having been able to check his rushes. Although the director's more traditional performance as the jovial 'Nick Broomfield' is minimised, Broomfield's presence at the start of *Life and Death* as a witness within a narrative not of his own construction adds a further performative layer: that the validity of his documentary methods are themselves being scrutinised and critiqued.

Despite the subdued tenor of Broomfield's performance in *Life and Death*, dialectical enquiry shifts to the scrutiny and treatment of its subject, Aileen Wuornos. The internalised collisions within Aileen's portrayal and her self-representation start with her assertions at the outset of the documentary that she is guilty of murder and awaits her execution. This conflicts directly with the director's conviction that her crimes were in self-defence and that Wuornos is insane and, later on, conflicts movingly and exasperatingly with Wuornos's own confession – elicited when she does not realise she is still being filmed – that she had killed in self-defence after all. Tanya Horeck dwells on Broomfield's use of extreme close-up in *Life and Death* and argues convincingly that these are used 'as visual verification of her mental disturbance', contributing 'to her monstrosity' as well as demonstrating 'the degree of her anguish'.[19] Her contention is in part that such intimate images of Wuornos's features compensate to an extent for the lack of information she proffers about herself and her motives; the scrutinising documentary gaze thereby performs an evidentiary function – when 'hard' evidence is lacking. Earlier, Horeck had suggested that Wuornos's media image had been constructed via the repeated use of a finite series of images of her face, most notably the image used for the DVD cover for the documentary – of her handcuffed, with hands raised to the level of her neck, eyes shut and head thrown slightly back. Wuornos is getting her hair out of her face (a gesture she repeats several times through *Life and Death*), but, as Horeck notes, it looks almost as if she is strangling herself.

As I have previously argued in relation to Abraham Zapruder's 8mm footage of the assassination of President John Kennedy, there are examples of documentary or factual footage that, despite having become overwhelmingly familiar and important to the shared public consciousness, remain unable to explain the events they represent. As a consequence, 'The central inadequacy of such images has led to a peculiar canonization of certain emotionally charged pieces of film and video, images that could be termed "iconic".'[20]

The images of Aileen Wuornos function in a similar way to Zapruder's 8mm film, the images of Princess Diana's mangled car or footage of the planes hitting the twin towers in New York on 11 September 2001. In the absence of a clear and non-contradictory statement from Wuornos about why she committed the seven murders, the iconic images of her become substitutes for knowledge and certainty: we are compelled to 'read' into them what we do not know about Wuornos's motives or her state of mind. These images of Wuornos thus perform an evidentiary function that goes some way to compensate for the lack of detailed and consistent information. As Horeck surmises, the 'extreme close-ups of Wuornos ... are presented as visual verification' of her disturbed mental state[21] – and in this also function as corroborating evidence for Broomfield's own conviction that the state of Florida is condemning to death someone who is insane.

There resides, therefore, in the potentially dialectical interaction between images of Wuornos and what she actually says about herself, a performative element: that the 'real' Aileen Wuornos cannot be understood and 'read' through her performance.[22] Horeck argues that the interviews in *Life and Death* offer 'a dramatic staging of reality' for which Wuornos is shown 'preparing herself' and in which she 'delivers performances'[23] with Broomfield, Churchill's camera and the viewer in mind. Although there is, as I have suggested, an inverse correlation between the seriousness of Broomfield's subject matter and the amount he appears on screen, one crucial interview with Wuornos demonstrates how the conventionalised Broomfield performance itself can be used to serious ends.

The interview on which hinges the argument proposed by Broomfield in *Life and Death* (that Wuornos committed the murders in self-defence) is also the one interview when Broomfield becomes the visual focus and when we go some way to being permitted a glimpse of a more authentic Aileen Wuornos. This pivotal encounter takes place six months before Wuornos's eventual execution in May 2002 at Broward Prison, Florida. Wuornos greets Nick Broomfield and Joan Churchill extremely warmly and sits down in a booth the other side of a glass divide through which she and Broomfield talk. Broomfield starts by asking her how she spends her days, to which Wuornos replies that she now remains in her cell '24/7', writing letters to her friend Dawn, reading the bible, thinking and 'preparing for my death'. She no longer smokes or goes out and also refers to 'getting all the tears out' because she does not want to cry in the execution chamber. Aileen Wuornos presents a reasonable, calm, even stoical image here, even when ranting about the corrupt cops – a favourite target – who let serial killers kill. Broomfield then asks her about her family, which is when Wuornos confirms, contrary to what we have seen and others have said, that 'I came from a real and decent family'; her father she portrays as 'so straight and so clean' and her mother as anti-swearing, saying she could have become 'an outstanding citizen of

America' if her own life had been easier. Broomfield then enquires what has been the happiest time of her life and Wuornos cannot think of anything because she 'has been through so much hell'. Her expression here is quite different from the madly defiant, aggressive interviewee of the iconic images or the majority of this film and this statement of weariness concludes with the reflection: 'I want to get in the fucking chamber tomorrow and leave,' a statement we cannot but help interpret via the resignation and unhappiness just expressed. Then, Wuornos turns and starts to have a rant at the Supreme Court, accusing them of 'fucking with my execution' and warning that 'there's going to be bloodshed' if they continue to do so, so 'get that fucking warrant signed'.

Life and Death might not resemble entirely the more narcissistic, trivial documentaries that preceded it, but, like so many of those documentaries, it has a pivotal interview that defines the film and its subject and in which Broomfield poses the critical questions that, whether directly or indirectly, convey the essential nature of his subject and in so doing serves to broadly confirm the director's own perspective on events. Broomfield's documentaries are performative, but this does not make them open to any interpretation. It is as Wuornos concludes her rant against the courts that Churchill's camera turns away and ostensibly stops filming. Turning away, it seems, from Wuornos's violent anger.

However, the camera is not off, although Wuornos thinks it is and Churchill continues to film secretly. As Broomfield explains in retrospective voiceover, this was the only way to get Wuornos to confess that she committed the murders in self-defence. Setting aside the legal issues, the conclusion to this sequence is morally and ethically complex. In vision is first a Sony DV tape sitting on the counter, then Broomfield, his head craning forward near the glass that separates him from Wuornos, straining to hear her words. In a whisper Wuornos states, 'I've got to go down' because 'they'll never do me right, they'll only fuck me over some more, so I have to go to the death.' When asked again whether she killed Mallory and the others in self-defence she responds, without hesitation: 'Yes, but I can't tell anybody. Never.' Broomfield poses this question twice and twice gets the same response. This, for Broomfield and Churchill, is the unheeded testimony that Wuornos should not have been executed, but ethically, how should the viewer process this information? In many ways, this is a classic Broomfield moment: he catches his subject unawares and uses a crafty interview to inadvertently reveal a truth about them and their actions that, hitherto, they had been too alert to divulge.

However, this moment is markedly different in tone to similar moments in *The Leader* or any of the lighter films in between because it is not about Broomfield's superiority being affirmed or his subject being duped; this is a straight investigative moment: wanting to reveal the truth by any means necessary. Broomfield's expression on camera while Wuornos talks is resigned, as if he is trying to think what he can do with the information he is being told. As Wuornos concludes 'so I can only get to the death', Broomfield looks directly into the lens; this is perhaps the most notable instance of him being at a loss. The poignancy of this sequence is crucial and moving as both performative subjects – Broomfield and Wuornos – temporarily drop the personae that have become so intensely familiar. This is a supreme Broomfield scene, a moment of ethically messy authenticity, when the seriousness of his earlier films and the formal dexterity of his later ones converge to make the sort of political point he has not made in a while. Wuornos is then led away and calls over to Broomfield as she leaves: 'I'll always remember you and love you,' looking – as she so often does – into the camera. Broomfield, although he has betrayed Wuornos's trust, honours this tenderness by cutting to a news report announcing Governor Jeb Bush's decision to execute her. This sequence validates Broomfield's performative techniques, ensuring that they are not just a gimmick, but are also capable of teasing out the truth.

This interview, though, contrasts sadly with Wuornos's final interview the day before her execution, which she expressly wanted to grant to Broomfield. This is a ghastly, fraught exchange but one which starts well enough as Wuornos tells Broomfield 'I'm prepared. I'm all right with it.' With her hair swept back, her eerily black irises, the exposed whites of her eyes, her malnourished skin and her bad teeth inside her pinched mouth, she begins her extended, unstable diatribe against the police and a guard who she thinks allowed her to carry on killing, tried to poison her and piped sonic rays into her cell and brain. At this moment of disturbing insanity, Nick Broomfield then reveals that he has visited Wuornos's biological mother Diane, who wants her daughter's forgiveness. This is another classic Broomfield tactic: dropping in information that will goad his subject – often, as here, at a vulnerable point – into getting angry, and what ensues is a traumatic scene, as Wuornos, in extreme close-up and staring at the camera, rails:

> You sabotaged my ass, society. And the cops. And the system. A raped woman got executed and was used for books and movies and shit ... you're an inhumane bunch of bastards and bitches and you're going to get your asses nuked in the end.

Her eyes the colour of crude oil, Wuornos cuts the interview with one final angry flourish: 'Thank you, society, for railroading my ass.' Later Broomfield maintains that, 'I thought, in a way, asking her for forgiveness might be of some solace to Aileen.'[24] With the clank of chains she gets up and Broomfield pleads 'I'm sorry' in his characteristically limp, sweet voice and Wuornos gives him and the world the finger.

As with the earlier interview, this scene relies on some familiar Broomfield techniques – the performance of his slightly sweeter and dippier alter ego, the catalyst question to trigger an irate response – but the effect is different and more ambivalent as he no longer has justice on his side quite so straightforwardly. When asked what prompted him to tell Wuornos he was sorry, Broomfield answered:

> Because I felt that the interview was such a disappointment for her ... Obviously she was disturbed by the fact that she was going to be executed the next day and, frankly, who wouldn't be? But I felt that maybe she thought that I'd let her down, and it just seemed such a sad way to be saying goodbye to somebody.[25]

This has proved to be yet another shambolic and, in conventional terms, unsatisfactory Broomfield interview, but what it also conveys, extremely strongly, is that, on the day prior to her execution, Wuornos was not of sound mind. *Aileen: The Life and Death of a Serial Killer* is Broomfield's least showy film since he began to appear before the camera, and it is also his most sincere and motivating film, at least since *The Leader, His Driver and the Driver's Wife*. The two documentaries are tonally quite distinct, but they serve as oppositional reminders of how effective and affecting Broomfield's authorial involvement can be. Whereas *The Leader* charted the demise of the white supremacist movement in South Africa through irony and humour, the second Aileen Wuornos film offers a more sombre indictment of a justice system that Broomfield considers to be 'primitive' and 'barbaric'.[26] *Life and Death*, though superficially imposing narrative closure at the end with Wuornos's death and burial, also remains open as it raises the whole issue of whether or not a documentary can actually change the course of events; it clearly matters to Broomfield that he failed to prevent Wuornos's execution and so the film's attack on Jeb Bush and the legal system he sanctions continues.

DOCUMENTING 'NICK BROOMFIELD'

Broomfield's very technique encapsulates the idea of documentaries as not necessarily determined or closed, but rather as dialectical and open to reinterpretation. The performative documentary is the clearest contemporary exponent of my thesis that the documentary as prescribed by advocates of observational realism is an unrealisable fantasy, that documentary will forever be circumscribed by the fact that it is a mode of representation and thus can never elide the distance between image and event. It is imperative, however, to acknowledge that this deficiency does not invalidate the notion of the non-fiction film, merely that

the non-fiction film is (and largely always has been) aware of the limitations of the audiovisual media. With this acknowledgment, what ensues when examining documentary output is an awareness that it is predicated upon a dialectical relationship between aspiration and potential, that the text itself reveals the tensions between the documentary pursuit of the most authentic mode of factual representation and the impossibility of this aim. The documentaries of Nick Broomfield express these tendencies through their use of multiple dualities, in particular Broomfield's repeated performance of himself as the benign, chaotic investigative reporter as a means of then undermining or interrogating his documentary subjects. From within such a performative framework, the very notion of a complete, finite documentary is continually challenged and reassessed.

Perhaps as tacit recognition of this, Broomfield's work since *Aileen: Life and Death of a Serial Killer* has spanned both documentary and drama and has exemplified at least three of Broomfield's 'modes'. In terms of documentaries, in 2006 Broomfield revisited the terrain of *The Leader, His Driver and the Driver's Wife* when he returned in disguise to visit Terre'Blanche and his driver for *His Big White Self* and, in 2009, he completed *A Time Comes* about six Greenpeace volunteers who, in 2008, were tried and acquitted for shutting down Kingsnorth power station in the UK. He also, though, made *Sarah Palin: You Betcha!* in his comedy political documentary tradition, a disappointingly flimsy film that never gets gratifyingly close to Palin herself. In among these documentaries, Broomfield made two political dramas: *Ghosts* (2006) about the twenty-three Chinese illegal immigrant cockle pickers who died in Morecambe Bay, UK, and *Battle for Haditha* (2007) about twenty-four men, women and children allegedly shot in Haditha, Iraq, by four US Marines, in retaliation for the death of a Marine by a roadside bomb.

In an interview coinciding with the UK release of *Biggie and Tupac* Broomfield argued:

> There's no point in pretending the camera's not there. I think what's important is the interaction between the film-makers and those being filmed, and that the audience is aware of the interaction so they can make decisions of their own. When I was at the National Film School, Colin Young, who was my teacher, said that the problem with *cinema vérité* [sic] is that you don't know the film-makers behind the camera. The audience doesn't have that information so they don't know what the interaction is. That's the variable that's most influential – it's not the presence of the camera that changes people's behaviour, it's the relationship they have with the people behind it.[27]

Broomfield here articulates the essential importance of his performative style of documentary film-making as well as defining the equally essential difference between this and Direct Cinema, namely that it is not the apparatus that makes the filmed subjects behave as they do but rather the relationship they have with the film-maker. Broomfield's documentaries are constructed around this relationship and although he has been accused of making films about himself, in *Aileen: Life and Death of a Serial Killer* he has made a notable documentary very much about Aileen Wuornos, but which is constructed around her relationship with Broomfield. The interventions of Broomfield himself make this film not only more urgent and politicised than other treatments of Wuornos's case (such as *Monster*), but also more emotionally involving: performative documentary at its most powerful.

NOTES

1. In September 2012, the Hillsborough Independent Panel concluded that up to forty-one of the deaths might have been averted had some of the failings in how the police and emergency services handled the tragedy been addressed more swiftly. The report concluded that 'multiple failures' by the emergency services and others contributed to the death toll. In response, the Attorney General confirmed that he would consider all new evidence with a view to potentially overturning the original verdicts of 'accidental death'.

2. For a discussion of the previous four modes, see Bill Nichols, *Blurred Boundaries: Questions of Meaning in Contemporary Culture* (Bloomington: Indiana University Press, 1994), pp. 32–75; Judith Butler, *Gender Trouble: Feminism and the Subversion of Identity* (London and New York: Routledge, 1990).

3. Nichols, *Blurred Boundaries*, p. 95.

4. Cf., though, the mention of Austin in Susan Scheibler, 'Constantly Performing the Documentary: The Seductive Promise of *Lightning Over Water*', in Michael Renov (ed.), *Theorizing the Documentary* (New York: Routledge, 1993), pp. 135–50, and Caryl Flinn, 'Containing Fire: Performance in *Paris is Burning*', in Barry Keith Grant and Jeanette Sloniowski (eds), *Documenting the Documentary: Close Readings of Documentary Film and Video* (Detroit, MI: Wayne State University Press, 1998), pp. 429–45.

5. J. L. Austin, *Philosophical Papers* (Oxford: Oxford University Press, 1970), p. 235.

6. Nichols, *Blurred Boundaries*, p. 97.

7. Damon Wise, 'Boom Raider', *Sight & Sound* vol. 12 no. 5, May 2002, p. 18.

8. See Megan Spencer, 'Sideshow Alley: The Documentaries of Nick Broomfield', *IF* no. 15, July 1999, p. 63.

9. For a critical response to *Kurt and Courtney*'s depiction of love, cf. Caitlin Moran, 'You Give Love a Bad Name', *Time Out* no. 1077, June 1998, pp. 18–21.

10. Nick Broomfield, 'Heroes and Villains: Pier Paolo Pasolini', *The Independent Magazine*, 6 February 1993, p. 46.

11. Peter Wollen, *Signs and Meaning in the Cinema* (London: Secker & Warburg, 1972).

12. Maggie Brown, 'Fetishes', *Daily Telegraph Weekend Magazine*, 10 August 1996, p. 42.

13. Elaine Paterson, 'Heller Let Loose', *Time Out* no. 1007, 1989, p. 53.

14. Wise, 'Boom Raider', p. 18.

15. Jason Wood (ed.), *Nick Broomfield: Documenting Icons* (London: Faber and Faber, 2005, p. 228.

16. www.nickbroomfield.com. Accessed 19 September 2012.

17. Until the mediocre *Sarah Palin: You Betcha!* it was tempting to equate commitment and sobriety in Broomfield's documentaries with the presence of Churchill, but in light of this latest film, such demarcations work less well.

18. Tanya Horeck, 'From Documentary to Drama: Capturing Aileen Wuornos', *Screen* vol. 48 no. 2, Summer 2007, p. 143.

19. Ibid., p. 144.

20. Stella Bruzzi, *New Documentary* (London: Routledge, 2006), p. 21.

21. Horeck, 'From Documentary to Drama', p. 144.

22. Cf. Judith Butler's discussion of Jennie Livingston's documentary *Paris is Burning* in Judith Butler, *Bodies that Matter: On the Discursive Limitations of 'Sex'* (London and New York: Routledge, 1993), pp. 136–8.

23. Horeck, 'From Documentary to Drama', p. 155.

24. Wood, *Nick Broomfield*, p. 231.

25. Ibid.

26. Ibid., p. 229.

27. Ibid.

1.4 On Truth, Objectivity and Partisanship: The Case of Michael Moore

DOUGLAS KELLNER

Performance and subjectivity inevitably impact on documentary objectivity. However, documentary is positioned culturally as offering objective accounts of the world and all the subjectivities involved – of film-makers and of their witnesses – is discounted. Yet might it not be better to acknowledge that documentary objectivity must always be suspect? Better, in fact, to expect nothing more than that a documentary clearly reveal these inevitable subjectivities – even partisanships?

Documentary film has long been a contested terrain, with different film-makers exposing conflicting normative ideals of presenting their representations of the world. Broadly speaking, one can classify documentary/non-fiction films as either openly *partisan*, seeking to address a specific issue and offer a political intervention, or claiming to be *non-partisan*, seeking to objectively represent a situation by minimising biases, presuppositions, or a political agenda.[1] Thus, within the documentary tradition, there are film-makers who aspire to a norm of maximum objectivity, contrasted to those who insert themselves in their work in a non-objective partisan camp. The films of Michael Moore obviously fall into the latter category and have given rise to assaults on his work – largely by supporters of the concept of documentary he opposes, or those opposed to his politics.

A partisan tradition thus tends to reject the ideal of objectivity and to present subjective and politically charged representations of the world, while affirming documentary film as an important tool for representing social reality and promoting progressive social change. In this chapter, I present Michael Moore as an exemplar of a partisan documentary tradition which rejects what it sees as a 'myth of objectivity'. Yet Moore claims that his work breaks through official government and ideological mystification and lies to tell the truth about specific historical situations and problems. I interrogate specific films of Michael Moore to discuss the ways in which his films and cinematic discourse reject the concept of objectivity, yet seek and claim to be truth-telling, and that situate Moore in a partisan documentary tradition that privileges politics over canons of documentary objectivity.

I argue that Michael Moore has created a unique documentary style that combines partisan and interventionist cinema with his personal voice and vision, combining the personal with the political, pathos and humour, expository argumentation with strong point-of-view critique.[2] Emile de Antonio, Moore and others in a left-wing partisan tradition reject the ideal of so-called 'objectivity', admitting they are making committed and interventionist political films.[3] De Antonio and Moore both sharply criticised cinema vérité's[4] aesthetic, which held that documentary itself would reveal the truth if the film-maker simply used the camera to capture events without intervening with a narrative voice or point of view.[5] Against this aesthetic, de Antonio claimed that choice of subject matter, framing and editing created a construct that contained a film-maker's vision and politics and that pure objectivity is both impossible and undesirable. De Antonio spoke frequently of the 'myth of objectivity', noting:

> The very idea of *cinéma vérité*[6] is repugnant to me. It is as if the film-maker owned truth of some kind. I have never felt that I owned truth. I tried to be as truthful as I can but I know I am a man of deep-seated prejudices and many assumptions about the nature of society which color all my thinking and feeling and the work that I do. For me, there is no concept of objectivity. Objectivity is a myth.[7]

The normative ideal of objectivity in the documentary film came from a variety of sources, including a tradition of photography that saw the camera as a mode of reproducing reality; journalism schools which reacted against the tradition of yellow and political journalism dominant in the USA in the nineteenth century and held objectivity as an ideal; and documentary film-makers who followed a realist aesthetic and objectivist notion of truth.[8] Moore appears to agree with de Antonio that objectivity is a spurious ideal, often making clear his biases, point of view and politics,[9] although, as we shall see, Moore is guided by a normative ideal of truth, but his critics attack his 'bias' and 'distortions'. Interestingly, a left-partisan tradition was dedicated to truth, including Lenin whose paper *Pravda* claimed to represent the truth of Russian politics. Following Lenin's affirmative concept of truth, Dziga Vertov called his early documentary team 'Kino Pravda,' although he would later use the concept of 'Kine Eye' to describe his project.[10]

For the left-partisan tradition in which I suggest Michael Moore's work should be situated, truth is subjective, complex and often elusive, and the quest for truth is guided by a point of view and partisan politics.[11] This tradition seeks to inform and persuade, and to use a broad and comprehensive notion of truth which includes telling the bigger story, unveiling lies, revealing often unnoticed connections and documenting facts often not perceived. The partisan documentary tradition necessarily privileges perspective, interpretation, critique and political intervention, and is thus roundly dismissed by a documentary tradition and critics who have a more conventional and objectivistic notion of truth.

Michael Moore's most significant films deploy three types of documentary strategy to seek contextual and situational truth: personal witnessing, exploratory and confrontational quest dramas and partisan political interventions. These categories, to be sure, are ideal types and to some extent overlap and characterise all of his work, which provides sharp critique of the regnant institutions of the era in highly partisan cinematic attacks on the dominant ideology and ruling powers and institutions of contemporary US society.

ROGER AND ME AND THE DOCUMENTARY OF PERSONAL WITNESSING

A proliferation of documentary films of personal witnessing emerged in the 1960s and 70s when members of the civil rights, women's, gay and lesbian and other social movements told their personal stories to bear witness to injustices and explore social problems. Emile de Antonio's *Mr Hoover and I* (1989), his most overtly personal work, exemplifies this category in which the personal becomes a vehicle for the political, and in which de Antonio tells his life story through use of material from his FBI files.

Michael Moore's first documentary film, *Roger and Me* (1989), puts on display the hardships that the closing of the Flint, Michigan, auto plants caused for working-class people, including his own neighbours. The film opens with images of Moore growing up in Michigan in a working-class family, with his father employed in a Flint General Motors (GM) auto plant.[12] Moore quickly cuts from home movies showing him clowning in a Popeye suit and happily playing with his family to montage of Flint in the post-World War II era of prosperity. The sequence establishes the filmmaker and his locale as the centre of the film.

Roger and Me unfolds with a fast, kinetic pace, intercutting home movies, newsreel footage of the Flint plant and TV footage of Pat Boone and Dinah Shore singing ads for GM cars. Like de Antonio, Moore chose resonant music and a soundtrack that is as rich and evocative as the visuals. Throughout the film, the soundtrack provides a strong counterpart to the visuals and Moore's own voice confirms his involvement in the events he is narrating.

Newsreel footage establishes Flint as the birthplace of GM and portrays the giant automobile plant, assembly lines, crowds of workers, parades and images of the good life in Flint. After a quick look at his work as a journalist for ten years in the Flint area and a brief sojourn in San Francisco to edit *Mother Jones* (one of Moore's few failed projects), the film changes tone as Moore returns home to Flint in the mid-1980s in the midst of GM's closing of automobile plants and the subsequent decline of the town's fortunes.

Moore's central focus in *Roger and Me* is class and the impact of corporate restructuring and downsizing on the working class. The film presents illuminating contrasts between the rich and poor, the working class and the corporate elite, continually cutting from images of working-class devastation and despair in Flint as GM continues its closures to upper-class prosperity and obliviousness to the plight of the workers and the poor.

The narrative hook for the film, expressed in the title *Roger and Me*, is Moore's quest to talk to Roger Smith, president of GM, and convince him that he should visit Flint to observe the consequences of his corporate restructuring. The quest takes Moore to a variety of offices, clubs, elite restaurants and hotels where Smith is allegedly to be found, interspersed with images of people in Flint thrown out of their houses, neighbourhoods deteriorating and dejected workers losing their jobs and homes.

Moore's personal involvement in the lives of the rich and the poor bears witness to and illustrates class differences and growing working-class oppression. As a long-time inhabitant of the area, Moore manages to obtain access to a wide range of local characters, from poor blacks and whites and a number of laid-off workers, to public officials, PR functionaries and visiting celebrities. The film establishes Moore as a major portrayer of Americana, an astute analyst of class and capitalism, an advocate for the poor and someone personally involved in presenting the effects of class oppression.

In retrospect, *Roger and Me* is a remarkable first film. When he began, Moore reportedly did not know anything about film production. Documentary film-maker Kevin Rafferty served as one of his cameramen and taught Moore how to set up a shot. Rafferty himself made the successful and engaging *The Atomic Café* (1982) and an exposé of the white supremacist movement in *Blood in the Face* (1991) that Moore himself participated in, indicating a growing interest in documentary film-making.[13]

Moore's satirical and biting critical representations of the upper-class elite in Flint, enjoying life while misery engulfs the underclass, brilliantly capture the decadence, shallowness and class privileges of the rich during the Reagan era. Moore proves equally effective at getting celebrities and public officials to hang themselves with their own words in front of the camera, presenting Flint native and TV's *The Newlywed Game* host Bob Eubanks in a bad light, telling a horribly anti-Semitic joke about Jewish women and AIDS. *Roger and Me* skewers as well local politicians in Flint, attacking their efforts to bring a Sheraton Hotel, a convention centre and an Auto World theme park to town when obviously the city needed programmes that would provide better housing, jobs and human services to its working and underclass. There is also a brief segment in which Ronald Reagan comes to Flint, has pizza with workers and provides his usual upbeat patter.

On this point, critic Harlan Jacobson – in one of the first detailed interviews with Moore – took him to task for reordering the historical sequence of events, as Reagan actually campaigned in Flint in the early 1980s, while the (later bankrupt) Sheraton, failed convention centre and Auto World were begun in the mid-1980s. By contrast, Moore's narrative is focused on footage from around 1986 to the late 1980s. Yet it appears from Moore's sequencing that the Reagan visit and building campaign came after the lay-offs that Moore presents.[14] Moore protested to Jacobson that he was telling a story, condensing hours of footage to present Flint's tragic recent history, and that his story about Flint was largely accurate.[15] As Moore and de Antonio claim, all films are constructs, editing is highly subjective and there are other criteria besides objectivity and accurate historical sequencing by which to judge documentaries.

Since Jacobson's critique, however, there has been a cottage industry of Moore critics who have attacked his editing and alleged distortions. In fact, Moore's films are of a unique genre, often departing from standard documentary conventions. Moore readily admits that he is engaging in polemics and satire, and, as he often insists, he presented his first film as entertainment as well as a political engagement.[16] By the time of *Fahrenheit 9/11*, however, Moore had published entire books documenting statements and claims made in his films, and used his website to attack his critics and defend his work on a factual and documentary basis, suggesting a clear commitment to claiming that his films were truthful.[17]

From a critical perspective, *Roger and Me* puts on display the class privilege, racism and sexism of the upper classes and their lack of social conscience and humanity. Privileged corporate and political figures deserve satire and critique, and the public deserves to see their unguarded and revealing moments. Yet, *Roger and Me* provoked questions as to whether Moore does or does not exploit the working-class characters and lower-echelon functionaries in his film. One example of this accusation focuses on his portrayal of the 'pets or meat' rabbit lady, Rhonda Britton,

a young woman struggling to pay her bills by raising rabbits that could be sold either as pets or meat.[18] Moore returns to her in a short follow-up documentary showing her raising snakes and rats as well as rabbits, providing a poignant picture of how the struggle for survival in predatory capitalism drives people to engage in bizarre occupations – a theme that would later frequently reappear in his TV series.

In the absence of Roger Smith, Deputy Fred Ross becomes one of the major figures in the film, appearing early on as the casual and lighthearted evictor of poor people who cannot pay their rent. He claims he is just doing his job, knows many of the people he is evicting and serves as an engaging middle man between the town elite and the poor. In one striking scene near the end of the film, Roger Smith spouts banalities about Christmas and reads from Dickens as Deputy Ross evicts a family during the holidays, carrying out a Christmas tree as a distraught woman shouts obscenities, using audiences' associations with Christmas to highlight the inhumanity of the town's socioeconomic and political structure.

Moore's mode of personal witnessing and intervention in *Roger and Me* goes beyond standard compilation film documentaries in a highly condensed, fast-moving and entertaining montage of sequences which express a clear point of view in a well-constructed narrative about capitalism and class in the USA. This topic is seldom addressed in mainstream media and rarely has a documentary on this topic provoked so much interest and discussion. Moore managed to take political documentary film out of the ghetto of a marginalised cinematic form and into mainstream film. His innovative and successful film, however, propelled Moore into a life of public controversy.

Roger and Me began the construction of a unique genre: the Michael Moore film. Moore emerges from his first film as a storyteller, fabulist, satirist and witness to the corporate downsizing and devastation of his beloved Flint. Yet, in retrospect, Moore does not appear as a rigorous documentary film-maker concerned about historical sequence, strict documentation of facts, or objectivity. Moore positions himself instead as an entertainer and provocateur who raises questions, attacks wrongs and wrongdoers, and speaks up for the oppressed and against the oppressors. Despite critiques of inaccuracies of historical sequences or 'facts' in his films, much of what Moore says is 'true' in the wider sense. Certainly his films strained certain conventions and traditions of documentary film-making that uphold 'objectivity' and eschew political partisanship as norms, and elicited ferocious debate. As we shall see, by the time he made *Fahrenheit 9/11*, Moore would be more concerned about standard documentary conventions. Yet he would continue to develop his own unique, controversial, and hard-to-classify film-making in *Bowling for Columbine* (2002) and subsequent films.

INTERLUDE: *BOWLING FOR COLUMBINE* AND EXPLORATORY DOCUMENTARY MONTAGE

An exploratory documentary tradition on the political left uses film as a medium to probe social problems, as with the work of Emile de Antonio, discussed above. In *Bowling for Columbine* Moore explores connections between guns, militarism and violence in American history and contemporary society, and investigates the question of why there has been so much violence in the USA. *Bowling for Columbine* took Moore's documentary aesthetic to new levels of complexity and controversy, eliciting both widespread praise and condemnation. By now, Moore was a genuine American celebrity, and he uses his strong persona once again to engage his audience in a quest narrative, this time to try to find out why there is so much violence with guns in the USA today. Moore's voice is again the narrative centre of the film and it is more confident, self-assured and insistent than in his earlier work.

Bowling for Columbine suggests that one of the major effects of the media is to generate fear that ruling politicians can exploit. While Moore makes connections between US history and military actions, guns, the media and violence, he does not attribute causal relationships between these forces. Instead, he suggests that they interact in a complex social environment. It's not just one thing, but many things that cause Columbine shootings

and violence in the USA. *Bowling for Columbine* thus provides a multi-dimensional and multi-causal view of violence in the USA, gun culture and teen shootings. It is open and non-reductive and does not provide simplistic answers.[19]

This openness is apparent in one revealing sequence in which Moore interviews Tom Mauser, father of one of the Columbine victims, about why the USA has more violence and gun victims than other industrialised countries. Mauser passionately asks: 'What is it?!' The scene then cuts rapidly back and forth, with Moore and Mauser repeating the query, ending with Mauser saying: 'I don't know.' Neither is obviously able to answer the unanswerable question, and Moore's exploration of the issue does not offer simplistic or easy answers. However, his queries are able to ferret out responses like Charlton Heston's, who in the film's penultimate sequence blames violence on American history and then the country's 'mixed ethnicity', suggesting a racist response.

Moore's film closes with his infamous confrontation with Heston and a montage demonstrating fear in the USA. Moore concludes: 'Yes, it was a glorious time to be an American,' cutting to the titles and an upbeat version of 'What a Wonderful World'. Moore has not really found the answer to the question why there is so much gun violence in the USA. Nonetheless, *Bowling for Columbine* suggests connections between US gun culture, history, the media,

Bowling for Columbine (2002): by now, Moore was a genuine American celebrity

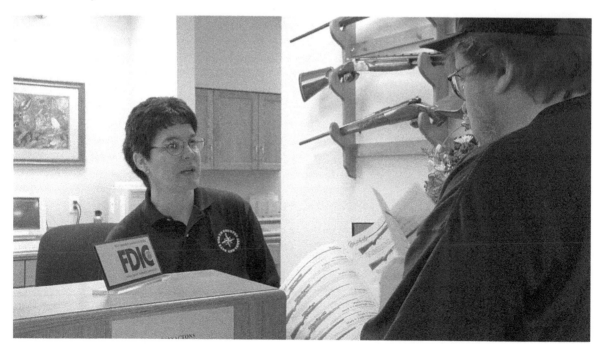

political organisations and policies, US military interventions and the weapons industry, deteriorating families and living conditions, and violence. Frighteningly, as divisions increase between the rich and the poor, and alienated youth cannot find meaningful jobs, this matrix of factors is likely to produce more violence, and will require systematic social change and transformation.

The standard conservative critique of Moore and his films, however, is that 'Michael Moore hates America' and presents a wholly negative view of the USA.[20] This conservative critique misses the point of who Michael Moore is and what he is doing. Moore presents a new type of personal interventionist documentary that combines personal witness to wrongdoing and an exploratory quest for answers to social problems with satire and humour and the development of his own crusading character. Moreover, he shows the USA as it is rarely seen on film and television, which tend to idealise the USA as a beacon of affluence and prosperity, or as a highly functional system where (TV) cops get the bad guys and (TV) lawyers prosecute wrongdoers. Moore shows typical Americans who are overweight, undereducated and not beautiful or glamorous. He puts on display the more freakish and bizarre aspects of Americana and the significant differences between a corrupt upper class, its political apparatus, mid-level functionaries and operatives, and the culture of class, race, gender and age oppression. Rarely before have so many common people, so many forgotten people, but also so many varied and interesting characters, appeared on the screen in a documentary film.

Michael Moore's films thus run counter to the dominant ideology that idealises the 'American dream', and his work undercuts the fantasy representations of life in the USA as shown in countless TV series, films and the whole apparatus of advertising. In Michael Moore's probing explorations, the USA appears as a very strange country with a lot of bizarre aspects to its economy, politics, culture and everyday life. In putting on display the underside of American life, Moore is similar to his fellow documentary film-makers Errol Morris and Ross McElwee.[21] And like Emile de Antonio, Moore would take on a sitting president and highly controversial war in his most widely discussed film to date, Fahrenheit 9/11.

FAHRENHEIT 9/11 AND PARTISAN INTERVENTIONIST CINEMA

Bowling for Columbine grossed almost $60 million, making it the most successful documentary in history through 2002. While it received top honours at the Cannes Film Festival and Academy Awards, and was voted the top documentary of all time by the International Documentary Association (IDA), it also received fierce criticism. Moore was now identifying himself as a documentary film-maker making non-fiction films in an era with a fictive president in a specious war undertaken for false reasons. Upon receiving the Academy Award for best documentary in 2002, Moore invited the other documentary film-makers nominated for best documentary on the stage with him and announced:

> I've invited my fellow documentary nominees on the stage with us ... because we like non-fiction. We like non-fiction and we live in fictitious times. We live in the time where we have fictitious election results that elect a fictitious president. We live in a time where we have a man sending us to war for fictitious reasons, whether it's the fictions of duct tape or the fictions of Orange Alerts.[22]

During a period marked by one of the most mendacious presidents and administrations in US history, Moore felt it was important to provide an all-out assault on the Bush–Cheney administration, including evoking the stolen election of 2000,[23] and George W. Bush's limitations and failures as president. Hence, Fahrenheit 9/11 stands as Moore's most interventionist film, taking on the sitting president, George W. Bush, and his Iraq War during the 2004 election season. While Roger and Me bore witness to the assault on working-class jobs and lives in the Flint, Michigan, area and implicated General Motors in socioeconomic deterioration, the film did not carry out actions or recommend a specific activist agenda. Likewise, Bowling for Columbine came up with no answers or proposals to deal with the problem of gun violence in the USA; in fact, Moore seemed genuinely surprised and delighted when Wal-mart executives announced they would no longer sell 17 cent bullets, following Moore's visit to their Michigan headquarters with two surviving victims of the Columbine shootings.

It is clear, however, that Moore intended Fahrenheit 9/11 to be an important and perhaps decisive influence on the highly contested 2004 presidential election. These exalted aims are made clear in the foreword by John Berger and introduction by Moore to The Official Fahrenheit 9/11 Reader (2004), which contains the film script, reviews and documentation of some of the controversial claims and segments in the film.[24] Berger asserts Fahrenheit 9/11 'may be making a very small contribution toward the changing of world history. ... What makes it an event is the fact that it is an effective and independent intervention into immediate world politics.'[25] Moore described the tumultuous response to the film, the thousands of emails that poured into his website, and claimed: 'In an election year where the presidency could be decided by a few thousand votes, these comments were profound – and frightening to the Bush White House.'[26]

While the film was immensely popular, it also evoked fierce criticism, perhaps unparalleled in documentary film history, unleashing the entire right wing against Moore, as well as many mainstream critics.[27] In Fahrenheit 9/11

Moore continued to develop his own unique form of documentary film, serving as narrator and intervening occasionally in the action. While *Bowling for Columbine* examined a complex of issues centred around guns and violence, *Fahrenheit 9/11* focused more intensely on the personality and politics of the Bush–Cheney administration and in particular its exploitation of 9/11. As in his earlier films, there was a centrepiece villain who was the target of Moore's scorn and critical animus: this time, it was the president of the USA. In taking on George W. Bush and the American presidency, Moore was going after his biggest target so far. The controversy over the film, as well as the fact that it became the largest-grossing and arguably most influential documentary in history, provided an index of Moore's success in provoking his audience and promoting debate over issues of key importance.[28]

Playing on the title of Ray Bradbury's novel about book-burning, *Fahrenheit 451*, *Fahrenheit 9/11* refers to 'the temperature at which truth burns'. The first section of the film takes on George W. Bush, beginning with his stolen presidency after the Florida election fiasco of 2000, and then going back through his chequered career and failures in the oil industry, investigation by the securities exchange for insider stock trading, failure to fulfil his National Guard service, and his family connections with the Saudis, followed by Bush–Cheney administration neglect of warnings about terrorism prior to 9/11, and Bush's slacking at his ranch and family vacation sites before 9/11. Other segments document Bush–Cheney administration responses to the 9/11 attacks, how they and the media generated fear, and how the administration manipulated that fear.

The film opens with fireworks exploding and Moore musing 'Was it just a dream?' A sudden camera movement cuts to Al Gore campaigning in Florida. After a quick review of the Supreme Court intervention for Bush, a contested inauguration and the appalling failure of the US Senate to support black congressional calls for investigation of election irregularities, an astonishing title sequence unfolds, showing members of the Bush–Cheney administration – Bush, Cheney, Rumsfeld, Rice, Ashcroft and Wolfowitz – being made up for a televised statement or photo-op. The sequence suggests that the administration is a product of artifice and scripted theatre (and, in the case of Wolfowitz, unseemly hair management). Although the images are comic and deflating, sinister music and off-centre close-ups help convey the threat and danger of the highly secretive and rarely exposed mechanics of Bush–Cheney administration image production. In this sequence, Moore unveils the truth about the artifice involved in political media performance, shows Bush laughing and clowning just before he is announcing his Iraq War intervention and positions his audience against the members of the Bush–Cheney administration who are presented as artificial and sinister.

Moore chose to represent the 9/11 attack on the World Trade Center with a black screen and horrified voices responding to the tragedy, before cutting to show how it affected a wide range of ordinary people. He then intervenes as narrator, describing 9/11 and revealing that he had a friend killed that day. Moore presents highly revealing images of Bush, such as those of him sitting aimlessly for seven minutes after being told that the nation was under terrorist attack, while 'My Pet Goat' was read to a grade school class. Bush is later shown making a statement to reporters on fighting terrorism and then seamlessly shifting to take a golf shot, telling the group to 'watch my drive'. Moore shows him clowning and smirking before announcing to the nation that he'd just attacked Iraq. These images of Bush were shocking because most audiences had not seen such negative or revealing images of him before, portraying Bush as superficial, smug and smirkish, arrogant and incompetent. After 9/11, criticism of the presidency was taboo and the media served as a propaganda machine for the Bush–Cheney administration's 'war on terror', a point Moore makes with a montage of media clips.[29]

Moore thus purports to tell the truth about the Bush–Cheney administration and breaks the taboo against criticising the US government that served as a norm following the 9/11 terror attacks. The right wing went on ferocious attack, screaming that Moore was making false claims about connections between the Bush and bin Laden families and other Saudis, and about connections between oil companies, Bush–Cheney administration officials and US foreign policy. For *Fahrenheit's* critics, the film was a pack of lies.[30] However, Moore did not make specific causal claims, but instead pointed to connections and raised questions for the viewer to unravel and interpret. While his critics generally had a reductive and positivist mindset that claimed Moore was making specific dogmatic claims and arguments, in fact his vision is more dialectical, focusing on connections between factors that interact in overdetermined and complicated ways. Moreover, Moore was raising issues that had not been discussed: US support for bin Laden and Saddam Hussein in the 1980s, relations between the Bush family and the Saudis, the failures of the Bush–Cheney administration to address terrorism before 9/11, and its problematic policies in the aftermath. While the film does not follow a chronological sequence (the second half especially jumps back and forth between different time periods), Moore does not noticeably juggle time sequences to make narrative and political points, as he sometimes did in his earlier films. While admitting that the film was highly partisan, Moore also published *The Official Fahrenheit 9/11 Reader* to document claims made in the film.

Closing sections of *Fahrenheit 9/11* show a Halliburton ad touting its role in Iraq, revealing that the company, of which Dick Cheney was a former CEO, was garnering billions in no-bid contracts. Businessmen are seen at a conference on how to make money in Iraq, getting 'a piece of the action'. In a memorable sequence, the audience is shown George W. Bush addressing a group of 'the haves and the have mores', telling them: 'Some people call you the elite, while I call you my base!' Although this self-mocking humour is characteristic of the traditional Alfred E. Smith memorial dinner held to raise money for Catholic charities, it reveals the anti-populist thrust of the Bush–Cheney administration. The film ends with a flustered Bush trying to finish the old 'fool me once' saying, finally blustering, 'Fool me, can't get fooled again.' Michael Moore concludes: 'For once, I agree with him.' The film then cuts to the credits, accompanied by Neil Young's 'Rocking in the Free World'.

Moore's film is thus a fierce assault on the Bush–Cheney administration, using satire and parody to mock the president and his administration, to raise questions about its connections to corporate elites, the military-industrial complex and Middle East oil interests, and to demonstrate the horrific effects of the Iraq War. Moore's intervention was highly ambitious: while it failed to attain its political dream of removing an incumbent president, it was recognised as one of the most popular, daring and controversial documentary films of all time.

THE PARTISAN INTERVENTIONIST

As we have seen, Michael Moore's work is highly partisan and interventionist, asserting specific political positions, as well as attempting to inform and entertain. The partisanship of Moore's films has helped to generate assaults on his work largely by supporters of the concept of documentary he opposes, or those opposed to his politics. In Moore's films there is also more of an interaction between documentary and entertainment, fact and narrative, and archival/shot footage and creative editing than in non-partisan documentaries. His films' entertainment value obviously accounts for their success, while many people identify with and applaud the Michael Moore character and love to see him confront the bad guys and uncover corporate or political wrongdoing. Moore is one of the few US film-makers who is consistently critical of corporate capitalism and who explore class differences and oppression in the USA. His personal witness to problems and his presentation of them from his own point of view produces a much more subjective and interventionist text than is found in a non-partisan and 'objectivist' documentary tradition.

Moreover, while one can quibble with some facts and editing sequences in Moore's films, his cinema portrays larger truths neglected by other film-makers and the media industry, such as the fact that corporate restructuring and downsizing has been creating great misery for the working class and devastating communities. Moore was also one of the first to raise questions about George W. Bush's competency, an issue that entered the mainstream after his inadequate response to Hurricane Katrina and the economic collapse of 2008.

Moore's most recent films, including *Sicko* (2007), *Slacker Uprising* (2008) and *Capitalism: A Love Story* (2010), indicate that there is now clearly a Michael Moore genre in which Moore inserts himself into social problems and narratives and serves as a gadfly and provocateur against what he considers mendacious and pernicious forces and institutions and presents himself as the voice of truth. His films as a whole are rich with detail, information and insights into relations between often-overlooked economic, political and cultural forces, and in an accessible and entertaining format. Michael Moore is an American original, combining the crusading idealism of JFK liberalism with left-wing anti-corporate populism; the comic antics of the Yippies with the more performance-oriented left, still visible in the anti-corporate globalisation and Occupy movements. Moore is as American as apple pie with his baseball caps, oversized body and ego, often dishevelled appearance, and ability to continually redefine himself and come out on top. While Moore exposes some of the seamier and more freakish aspects of American life, and takes on major institutions and the corporate and political elite, he also embodies and presents in his films good, decent, common people, confused people overwhelmed by circumstances – a whole panorama of American characters portrayed in the tradition of Diane Arbus, Errol Morris and R. Crumb.

While Moore's films are highly controversial, intensely polarising and extremely partisan, his works raise important questions, make connections overlooked in conventional media, provoke discussion and enquiry, and rarely fail to entertain those willing to enter his cinematic universe. They clearly exhibit in the contemporary moment a partisan tradition of film-making that eschews traditional norms of objectivity yet aspires to speak and show truth to power, to carry out radical social critique and to propose radical political transformation. For Moore, objectivity is a myth but truth remains a normative ideal to which his films attempt to aspire. The passionate criticism of his films and the ongoing debates they provoke confirm that truth itself is a contested terrain and that truth-telling which goes against the grain will often provoke intense controversy. Moore's films have consequently received adulatory reception from those who believe he is telling the truth about the contemporary US and global capitalist system while eliciting fierce criticism from those who defend the system that Moore attacks.

NOTES

1. In *Michael Moore Fahrenheit 9/11* Robert Brent Toplin makes a similar distinction and has a chapter on the partisan and engaged documentary tradition ([Lawrence:

University of Kansas Press, 2006], pp. 71–90) in which I am suggesting Moore's work should be situated and interpreted.

2. In this chapter, I draw on a study of the entirety of Michael Moore's work found in Douglas Kellner, *Cinema Wars: Hollywood Film and Politics in the Bush/Cheney Era* (Malden, MA: Blackwell. 2010). My focus in this chapter, by contrast, is on interpreting Moore in relation to notions of partisanship, truth and objectivity in his cinema. I am drawing on several books that provide overviews of Michael Moore's life and work including the accessible introductory study by Emily Schultz, *Michael Moore: A Biography* (Toronto: ECW Press, 2005); Jessie Larner, *Moore & Us* (London: Sanctuary, 2005), which provides both critique and good political contextualisation of Moore's biography and work; Larner's subsequent book on Moore, however, *Forgive Us Our Spins: Michael Moore and the Future of the Left* (New York: Wiley & Sons, 2006), presents a highly problematical critique of Moore. In addition, I draw on a vast amount of film scholarship and internet material on Moore, as well as his own books. In fact, Moore appears to be one of the best-documented and controversial documentary film-makers in history.

3. There is no evidence that de Antonio had a direct influence on Moore, although the similarities are striking. Moore has reportedly said that Kevin Rafferty's *Atomic Café* is the only film that influenced him (see Schultz, *Michael Moore*, p. 64), and has never, so far as I know, discussed de Antonio's work; Rafferty himself was influenced by de Antonio and thanked him in credits on *The Atomic Café* (see below). In Michael Moore, *Here Comes Trouble: Stories from My Life* (New York: Grand Central, 2011), Moore himself notes that he saw de Antonio's *Point of Order* at Detroit's Art Institute, along with other radical documentaries (p. 409), but does not discuss de Antonio's work or possible influence on him. On de Antonio, see the Introduction to Douglas Kellner and Dan Streible (eds), *Film, Art and Politics: An Emile de Antonio Reader* (Minneapolis: University of Minnesota Press, 2000).

4. American usage at this time privileged this term over Direct Cinema and it is still widely used to describe the observational style (ed.).

5. On cinéma vérité see note 6 below. See also Stephen Mamber, *Cinema Vérité in America: Studies in Uncontrolled Documentary* (Cambridge, MA: MIT Press, 1974).

6. De Antonio is obviously concerned more with the claims of observationalism than with Rouchian reflexivity. It seems reasonable to suggest Direct Cinema would better describe the object of his 'repugnance' than the reflexivities associated with Rouchian cinéma vérité (ed.).

7. See Emile de Antonio, 'Conversation with Bruce Jackson', at www.sensesofcinema.com/contents/04/31/emile_de_antonio.html. Accessed 18 August 2006.

8. On photography and mechanical reproduction in film and photography, see Walter Benjamin, 'The Work of Art in the Age of Mechanical Reproduction', in Benjamin, *Illuminations* (New York: Schocken, 1969), pp. 217–52. On how the documentary ideal of objectivity is grounded in pretensions to science, see Brian Winston, 'The Documentary Film as Scientific Inscription' (1973), in Michael Renov (ed.), *Theorizing Documentary* (New York: Routledge, 1993), pp. 37–57. On the rise and function of the norm of objectivity in journalism, see Michael Schudson, *The Power of News* (Cambridge, MA: Harvard University Press, 1996).

9. Moore has said: 'There's a myth of objectivity out there, whether it's a documentary or the *Philadelphia Inquirer*. We're subjective beings by nature. Even the decision of what to put in the paper, where to place it – it's all subjective.' (Ken Lawrence, *The World According to Michael Moore* [Kansas City: Andrews McMeel, 2004], p. 98.)

10. For an overview of Vertov's life, work and influence, see Jeremy Hicks, *Dziga Vertov: Defining Documentary Film* (New York: Palgrave Macmillan, 2007). See also Kevin O'Brien (ed.), *Kino-Eye: The Writings of Dziga Vertov* (Berkeley: University of California Press, 1984).

11. In discussing the normative ideal of truth in Michael Moore's work, I am also drawing on Charles Musser, 'Truth and Rhetoric in Michael Moore's *Fahrenheit 9/11*', in Matthew Bernstein (ed.), *Michael Moore: Filmmaker, Newsmaker, Cultural Icon* (Ann Arbor: University of Michigan Press, 2010), pp. 79–104.

12. For later richly textured stories of his youth, see Moore, *Here Comes Trouble*.

13. Ibid. Moore presents a detailed account of how Rafferty helped him create *Roger and Me* (pp. 401ff.).

14. Harlan Jacobson, 'Michael and Me', *Film Comment* vol. 25 no. 6. This text is the mother-lode of the anti-Michael Moore industry. For example, later critique of the sequencing of Moore's Flint narrative following Jacobson's argument, see Schultz, *Michael Moore*, pp. 61ff.; Larner, *Forgive Us Our Spins*, pp. 66ff.; David Hardy and Jason Clarke, *Michael Moore is a Big Fat Stupid White Man* (New York: Regan, 2004), pp. 17ff. For a sharp critique of Jacobson's failure to grasp Moore's documentary aesthetic and Jacobson's rather old-fashioned perspective on documentary, see Toplin, *Michael Moore Fahrenheit 9/11*, pp. 26ff.

15. See Michael Moore in Jacobson, 'Michael and Me'.

16. In an interview at the time, Moore explained, concerning *Roger and Me*: 'It's not an NBC White Paper, not an episode of *Nova*. To the guardians of documentary, I apologize that the picture is entertaining.' Michael Moore, *Australian Financial Review*, 4 May 1990. Cited in Lawrence, *The World According to Michael Moore*, p. 110.

17. See Michael Moore, *The Official Fahrenheit 9/11 Reader* (New York: Simon and Schuster, 2004); and Moore's website,

which documents some of the facts in his films, http:// www.michaelmoore.com/books-films/facts/ fahrenheit-911. Accessed 23 March 2012.

18. For critique of Moore's depiction of some working-class people in the film, see Pauline Kael, 'Melodrama/Cartoon/ Mess', *The New Yorker*, 8 January 1990, pp. 90–3.

19. Moore's right-wing critics and Larner, *Forgive Us Our Spins*, constantly claim that Moore is making reductive causal claims, whereas in fact his dialectical cinema makes connections between different phenomena and in good modernist fashion forces viewers to raise questions and make connections themselves.

20. See the anti-Moore films by Mike Wilson, *Michael Moore Hates America* (2004), *FahrenHYPE 9/11: Unraveling the Truth about Fahrenheit 9/11 and Michael Moore* (2004) and Larry Elder, *Michael and Me* (2004), or the attacks on Moore in Hardy and Clarke, *Michael Moore is a Big Fat Stupid White Man*.

21. Morris has made nine highly acclaimed documentaries, including *The Thin Blue Line* (1988), *Mr Death* (1999) and *The Fog of War* (2003), www.imdb.com/name/nm0001554. McElwee's twelve documentaries include *Sherman's March* (1986), *Time Indefinite* (1994) and *Bright Leaves* (2003), www.imdb.com/name/nm0568478/. Accessed 28 September 2008.

22. Michael Moore, 2002 Academy Awards ceremony, quoted in Lawrence, *The World According to Michael Moore*, p. 51.

23. For my take on the 2000 election and first nine months of the Bush presidency, see Douglas Kellner, *Grand Theft 2000: Media Spectacle and a Stolen Election* (Lanham, MD: Rowman and Littlefield, 2001). Toplin provides a judicious and balanced appraisal of Moore's claims about the Bush presidency, conservative critiques and counter-arguments in *Michael Moore Fahrenheit 9/11*.

24. Moore, *The Official Fahrenheit 9/11 Reader*.

25. Ibid., p. ix.

26. Ibid., p. xv.

27. After his 2002 Oscar acceptance speech Moore stated: 'For the next couple of months I could not walk down the street without some form of serious abuse. Threats of physical violence, people wanting to fight me, right in my face, "F— YOU! You're a traitor!" People pulling over in their cars screaming. People spitting on the sidewalk. I finally stopped going out.' *Entertainment Weekly*, 9 July 2004, cited in Lawrence, *The World According to Michael Moore*, p. 52. In *Here Comes Trouble* Moore goes into excruciating detail concerning the threats and even assaults on him during the Bush–Cheney era, pp. 1–32.

28. Toplin, *Michael Moore Fahrenheit 9/11*, even-handedly presents the conservative critique of the film and deals with criticisms in terms of the failure of many conservative critics to understand Moore's unique brand of film-making and the partisan reaction against his left-wing politics. Moore presents his own defence of the film and answers to his critics in *The Official Fahrenheit 9/11 Reader*; see also his website, which addresses critiques of the film, at www.fahrenheit911.com/library/book/ index.php. Accessed on 23 March 2012. See also Musser, who presents a detailed dissection of right-wing criticisms of *Fahrenheit 9/11* in 'Truth and Rhetoric in Michael Moore's *Fahrenheit 9/11*'.

29. For my take on the 9/11 terror attacks and how the media promoted Bush–Cheney administration policy without raising serious questions or debate, see Douglas Kellner *From September 11 to Terror War: The Dangers of the Bush Legacy* (Lanham, MD: Rowan and Littlefield, 2003).

30. See the attacks in Hardy and Clarke, *Michael Moore is a Big Fat Stupid White Man*, and the right-wing films attacking Moore cited in note 20.

1.5 CGI and the End of Photography as Evidence

TAYLOR DOWNING

Partisanship aside, the film-maker's subjectivity has always impacted on photography's evidential status. Despite the foundational positioning of the photographic camera in the 1840s as a species of scientific instrument (like the thermometer), photographs were never meaningfully 'physically forced to correspond point by point to nature' as Charles Peirce erroneously thought. However much it was (and is?) believed that the 'camera cannot lie', any necessary evidential connection between the world and photographs of it is now utterly dissolved.

A few years ago, a Canadian director told me a story that just about sums it all up. He had been a CGI graphic artist for many years and some time previously he had worked for a broadcast company on a documentary about the Battle of the Atlantic in World War II. The researchers at the broadcaster had sourced excellent authentic archive film of convoys at sea and of the convoys coming under attack from German U-boats. However, they had very little genuine archive film of the U-boats in the Atlantic and almost nothing of the U-boats below the surface of the sea. So they asked him to create CGI images of U-boats at sea preparing to attack and firing their torpedoes at a distant merchant ship. The CGI artist did as he was asked, was pleased with the look and the effect of the images he created and the delighted producers intercut his CGI images with the archive film to create some great sequences.

A few years later, after he had moved on from being a CGI artist, he returned to the same broadcaster as a director to make another World War II documentary. On his first day back he was given a list of archive film held in the broadcast company's archives that he could use in his new film and there on the list was 'Shots of U-boats under the sea'. He asked to see the shots and, of course, they were his own CGI images made some years before! He pointed out to the producers that these images were not archive film but were in fact CGI. But none of the people he had worked with a few years before at the broadcaster were still there and the producers he was now working with insisted that the images in question were historic footage as they came from the archive collection held

by the broadcaster ... and the archive catalogue could not be wrong. In other words, the CGI images had gone into the broadcaster's archive and as far as they were concerned were now genuine archive film. No one else in the broadcast company knew of the origins of the images and as they looked authentic they had effectively become real.

There are several levels to this story that point up the lack of good record keeping, the shortness of the corporate memory, the assumption that an archive catalogue will always be correct in what it says it contains and so on. But more than anything it shows how easy it is to blur the 'real' world of genuine photographic imagery with the 'fake' world of digitally generated imagery. Shots and sequences that ten years ago would have required feature film budgets to create can now be put together at modest cost by broadcast graphic teams or by a production company with a set of good fast computers and some easily accessible software. It is easy to acquire digital 'models' of most objects, from U-boats to battleships, from jeeps to racing cars, and from dinosaurs to wild animals. With these models digitised in to the graphics software, a good CGI artist can, within hours, bring them alive, animate them, provide a background against which they appear and make them look very realistic. We've all seen documentaries in which two Tyrannosaurus Rex fight each other, Vesuvius erupts over Pompeii, an ancient Egyptian pyramid is built before our eyes ... or a U-boat attacks an Atlantic convoy. Most of the time we can suspend our disbelief and enjoy the digital artefacts for what they are. I have produced many documentaries in which two fighter aircraft fight it out in a dogfight high in the skies, or a tank fires at close range into a building and brings it down – all created by talented CGI artists. But when images like these become confused with the 'real thing' then surely alarm bells should start to ring. Where is the use of all this CGI leading us and is it the death of photographic evidence?[1]

My particular area of interest and the focus of this short chapter is in the combining of CGI with archive film or other newly generated imagery in the production of

The Lost Evidence (2004): Omaha Beach on the morning of 6 June 1944, D-Day. 'We joined several aerial photographs together on a graphics computer to create a mosaic that never existed ... We had great fun'

historical documentaries.[2] I believe that producers have a responsibility to present an accurate view of the history they tell. Historical truth is, of course, illusory. The very process of writing about or constructing the past and what has gone before is subjective. But that does not mean that producers of historical documentaries that are going to be seen by millions of people, who possibly derive their principal view of the past from these history programmes, should not struggle to use the artefacts they have at their disposal accurately and honestly. If a producer uses a piece of archive film completely out of context or has an eye-witness relating a story that is demonstrably wrong or incorrect, then that producer is, in my book, not doing a good job. If a viewer cannot believe that the producer has used the archive film or the oral testimony honestly and properly then how can that viewer believe anything that the producer tells him or her in the historical narrative?[3]

I produced a series for the US History Channel a few years ago in which we used genuine World War II aerial photographs taken over the field of battle by reconnaissance aircraft as the combat was raging below. We sourced the wartime aerial photographs from a variety of specialised libraries in Britain, the USA and Germany. We joined several aerial photographs together on a graphics computer to create a mosaic that never existed when the aerial images were first used for photographic interpretation during the war. We then overlaid these mosaics with a 3D contour map of the area in question. And, hey, we then had

a three-dimensional model of the battlefield at Monte Cassino, or at Iwo Jima or Stalingrad, or of the Normandy beaches, or wherever the aerial photos had been taken. We could then simulate the process of flying over and moving around these digital models, looking down on an image of the actual battle taking place below. We could even zoom in to the very spot where one of our eye-witness interviewees had been at the time he described in his interview. We had great fun, the series was a huge success and several follow-on series were commissioned. Rarely did we stop to ask ourselves what it was we had created. Authentic aerial photographs taken as events really were happening below had now been turned into digital models to play with, fly around and zoom into. We had created some sort of digital hybrid – half photographic evidence and half computer game.[4]

Of course, pretending that the viewer is watching the real thing is all part of the purpose of using CGI. Sometimes it is just impossible to create something in front of a camera, or rather it is far too expensive to do so. There is barely a feature film made today that doesn't blend digitally created backdrops with live action. It is far cheaper to create a digital castle, a space machine or a battlefield and insert your actors into it, than it is to build a convincing set of the same thing. This is merely another level of the creativity that goes into making a drama. Is there any inherent difference between building a set which is entirely artificial and in creating a digital backdrop which is fabricated by the manipulation of digits? But when it comes to documentaries, should we expect a different level of authenticity?

Of course, it's far too simplistic to say that the photographic image is always real in a way that the digital image is not. Anyone who has studied archive film knows how the camera can so easily lie, or at the very least mislead. Archive images can be staged, set up or manipulated during production. The very well-known and widely used shot of soldiers appearing to go 'over the top' in *The Battle of the Somme* documentary produced in 1916[5] as the battle raged, were not filmed at the Front but at a training camp. The key moments at the Battle of El Alamein could not be filmed because they took place in the dead of night when the film cameras could not get an exposure, so for the popular documentary *Desert Victory* (1943) they were staged in a studio in north London. But *The Battle of the Somme* and *Desert Victory* were powerful wartime documentaries that were much admired when they were first made and have been used as authentic archive footage by dozens of filmmakers for decades. Indeed *The Battle of the Somme* has achieved the status of being entered on the UNESCO Memory of the World Register. So even distinguished international recognition is not a guarantee of authenticity (although most of the rest of the film is indeed authentic, if rather stagey).

So, it is not the case that moving images and photographic records are always authentic and CGI is always a fake. But no matter how they have been set up or manipulated archive film is always a form of historical evidence – of what the original film-makers were trying to achieve or to get across. In the editing of the *Battle of the Somme* film, it was realised that the cameramen operating on the Western Front had not been able to film the critical moment of going 'over the top'. It was simply too difficult to set up their large cameras and cumbersome tripods in the confined space of a front-line trench. And setting up the camera on the ground above the trench to film men advancing into battle would have been suicidal for the cameraman. But the editors realised that this moment was crucial to the impact of the film and that with so much authentic footage recorded it would be necessary to stage this scene in as realistic a way as possible, including getting a soldier to fall down wounded as he clambered forward into the smoke. They certainly made it look real and audiences at the time were particularly impressed by this memorable shot. When Rider Haggard went to see the film a woman in the audience screamed out 'They've got him, the bastards!' when the soldier fell.[6] As a piece of historical evidence this sequence shows what people expected and feared was happening up and down the front line. And millions of viewers of television documentaries have been equally impressed with the scene over recent decades.

And it is certainly not the case that the fakery of CGI is always simplistic or cheesy. There is without doubt a truly creative use of CGI imagery. When Simon Schama records a piece to camera about the beauty of the medieval cathedral walking down the nave of a church which is slowly painted in by CGI around him with colourful frescoes to show how magnificent the interior of even a standard village church would have looked, we can all marvel at the spectacle.[7] When a Channel 4 documentary on the history of a domestic house stripped away the layers of the house era by era to realise how the interior had been shaped and the rooms decorated over the last 150 years, the effect is fantastic.[8]

But CGI is, after all, what it says it is – computer generated, the manipulation of digits by a powerful processor. It is certainly not real or authentic in any normal sense. I leave it to others to debate the meaning of truth in documentary studies. But, as a producer of historical documentaries for many years now, I offer up a few thoughts of my own. First, I feel less awkward about digital 'fakes' than I do about other sorts of 'fakery' – for instance, re-enactment (I use the words 'fake' and 'fakery' in a deliberately provocative sense). Re-enactments or dramatisations have been used in historical documentaries for years to represent the court of Elizabeth I, the deck of HMS *Victory* at Trafalgar, a Spitfire squadron during the Battle of Britain or troops on patrol in Afghanistan. Even presenter-led series from Simon Schama, David Starkey or Niall Ferguson include re-enactments. Rarely are they convincing. The details are often wrong and the twenty-first-century re-enactors are nearly always too healthy, too large or have much better teeth than the historical figures they portray would have had. They can effectively illustrate an interviewee's recollections, or a written account of an event. But they are usually pretty corny and inevitably feel rather cheap – documentary budgets never allow for the resources that go into a real drama. So *Band of Brothers*, a high-value HBO drama produced by Steven Spielberg in 2001, is more real in its portrayal of what it was like to be under fire and caught up in combat in World War II than almost any documentary that has tried to show the same. In documentary, the line between re-enactments that have any validity and those that are purely risible is a thin one.

However, digital 'fakes' at least can convey a reasonably accurate illustration of what we think a scene might have looked like seventy, a hundred or 400 years ago – particularly when we have a photographic model to start from, or when there is some form of visual evidence to build on, as in my series using aerial photographs. Another example that I would argue has more authenticity about it than the use of re-enactments is the digital colourising of black-and-white film. Personally, I love black-and-white film and I have no enthusiasm for colourising it. When classic black-and-white feature films have been colourised, like *Casablanca* (1942), for instance, the result is a disastrous concoction that should never be let out of the computer suite in which it was created. However, the colourisation of black-and-white documentary archive film, in my view, has been done very effectively in the last few years in series like *World War One in Colour* and more recently by a French production company in a World War II series called *Apocalypse*.[9] We do know the authentic colour of uniforms, of weapons and of landscapes and these can be digitally painted in. By digitally adding colour to faces and to people it does help them look more 'real' and makes them feel closer to us today rather than being more distant historic figures. This appeal of making the past look closer to the present is especially strong among the younger demographic, who are attracted to historical documentaries far more when they are in colour than in black and white.

Another aspect of this is the digital restoration of archive imagery, whether this is done in colour or in black and white. *The Battle of the Somme* film referred to above, originally made in 1916, has deteriorated markedly over the last ninety years. Although it had been stored in relatively benign conditions at the Imperial War Museum custom-made nitrate film vaults, the chemicals in the film had degraded and, despite frequent copying by the IWM film archivists, the picture quality was far from what it had been. In 2006, each frame of the original negative was digitally copied and cleaned up frame by frame by a specialist company in Wales.[10] The effect when the film was re-shown on the big screen was literally stunning. Parts of shots and sequences, particularly wide shots of the landscape of the battle, that had not been seen on the film copies for decades had come back to life and were there again in pristine clarity. We saw long-forgotten elements in some shots that we had never been able to see before. For me, this was a victory for digital restoration over the chemistry of the original film evidence. *The Battle of the Somme* courtesy of computer-aided treatment was more 'real' than it had been before – despite the fakery of the staged 'over the top' sequence.

My argument is not that there is a clear distinction between a 'real' and a 'faked' world in television historical documentaries. I'm not arguing that photographic evidence is always 'real' and that other forms of reconstruction or digital creation are always 'fake'. My case is simply that there are grades between all these extremes and that CGI can sometimes be a liberating force for the producer to generate something that although it might be new and of today can give us an authentic insight into the past and be as real as most other more conventional artefacts used by the makers of television history. My concern is when these two separate elements are confused, when the digital realm is sold as the real world, when the CGI U-boats under the Atlantic become archive footage of real U-boats filmed in 1942. This is dangerous and misleading. I believe we

should welcome CGI, but we have to be very wary of this form of deception.

NOTES

1. The capacity of the computer to generate images was demonstrated early. A 'drum scanner' allowing the digitisation of a photographic image was in use by 1957 and the applicability of the technology to feature film production in, first, title sequences and then in special effects was being increasingly explored from the 1960s on. The use of CGI in post-production image creation is dated to *Terminator 2* (James Cameron, 1991, USA) and *Jurassic Park* (Steven Spielberg, 1993, USA) (Leo Enticknap, *Moving Image Technology: From Zoetrope to Digital* [London: Wallflower, 2005], pp. 222–3). The impact of the digital on photography's evidential status was also noted early, in the 80s. The widespread adoption in newspaper offices of a dedicated image-manipulating system, the Scitex, produced a series of 'scandals' involving fabrications, such as moving the position of one of the pyramids at Giza (Brian Winston [ed.], *Claiming the Real: The Documentary Film Revisited* [London: BFI, 1995], pp. 5–6).

2. See also Chapter 5.3.

3. There has been a long debate about the need for the accurate use of archive film in television history documentaries, see, for instance, Paul Smith (ed.), *The Historian and Film* (Cambridge: Cambridge University Press, 1976), pp. 121–85, and Taylor Downing, *The World at War* (London: BFI, 2012), pp. 31ff. and 153–6.

4. The series called *The Lost Evidence*, produced by Taylor Downing for Flashback Television, was made for the US History Channel from 2004–07 and was shown around the world on history channels and on several terrestrial channels.

5. For a rather grand account of how *The Battle of the Somme* was shot, written by the cameraman himself, see Geoffrey Malins, *How I Filmed the War* (originally published 1920 and reprinted by the Imperial War Museum and the Battery Press, n. d.). For the staging of scenes for *Desert Victory* see Peter Hopkinson, *Split Focus* (London: Rupert Hart-Davis, 1969).

6. Stephen Badsey, 'Battle of the Somme: British War Propaganda', *Historical Journal of Film, Radio and Television* vol. 3 no. 2, September 1983).

7. Simon Schama's *A History of Britain*, executive producers Janice Hadlow and Martin Davidson; episode 6 *Burning Convictions*, BBC, 2001.

8. *No 57: History of a House*, produced by David Edgar, Charles Wace, Jill Lourie and Hannah Wyatt; a six-part series on the history of a house in Bristol, Flashback Television for Channel 4, 2003.

9. *Apocalypse* was a six-part series made by CC&C Productions for France 2 in 2009; a lot of care was taken

in the selection of shots and sequences to colourise. The process took about one day to colourise one minute of black-and-white film. *Apocalypse* was shown in a British version on Channel 4, 30 October–4 December 2010.

10. The digital restoration was carried out by Dragon Digital Intermediate and is available, with special features on the film about its importance in the development of documentary and on the music accompanying it, on DVD as *The Battle of the Somme* (IWM, 2008).

1.6 Drawn From Life: The Animated Documentary

ANDY GLYNNE

Paradoxically, far from its 'claim on the real' being wiped out by the digital, the documentary can be liberated from its traditional prison-house of photographic observationalism. If documentary value is more a matter of witness than of a supposed evidential quality of the photographic image (anyway in the digital era a totally unsustainable proposition), then witness can be illustrated by non-photographic (as well as photographic) means: even – say – by animation.

Over the past few years, I've found myself in the increasingly uncomfortable position of being asked to be a spokesperson for 'animated documentaries', which seem to be all the craze these days; both the documentary and animation communities seem intent on celebrating this ostensible foray into each other's domains. I am the reluctant participant in these discussions, not because I'm inherently grumpy or averse to such debates, and not because I don't believe in the power of the form (because I do, very much, as I shall discuss below), but because I'm not sure I share the same intractable belief in the status of animated documentary as a genre that others do. I consider myself a documentary film-maker, or more probably a storyteller who is interested in the experiences of real people. Sometimes, where and when it's indicated, I use animation in my films; sometimes I don't. I am no more an advocate for animated documentaries than I am for any other documentary form; I guess I'm a creative pragmatist, if there is such a thing, in that I believe the form, or genre, should suit the subject matter, rather than imposing a certain form for the sake of it.

There are those films for which the pairing of animation and documentary can result in something unique, compelling, thought provoking and truly original. There are, however, many films for which the pairing doesn't work, and yet, due to the increasing presence of the form in cinema and television, more and more of these films are made to which the latter applies. This chapter is an attempt to talk about what animated documentaries are; how, why and when they work; and how, why and when they sometimes don't.

But let's start by looking at what all the fuss is about! Animated documentary, if defined as a genre which combines both documentary and animation, isn't particularly new. During World War I there were a number of documentaries that used the format as pro-war propaganda.[1] The format has been used for many public service information films, including such subject matter as how the stock market works.

And animation has been used heavily in live-action documentaries too. In recent history, we have films such as Michael Moore's *Bowling for Columbine* (2002, USA), which has various bespoke animated inserts, used to great comic effect. Jessica Yu's *In the Realms of the Unreal* (2004, USA) uses animation to bring to life the amazing art of the Outsider Artist Henry Darger. And *The Corporation* (Jennifer Abbott and Mark Achbar, 2004, USA) cleverly uses animated sequences and animation archive as cutaways to great effect, often highlighting the absurdity, hypocrisy and disingenuousness of multinational corporations. We could even say that the series *Walking with Dinosaurs* (Tim Haines and Jasper Holmes, 1999, UK) is an 'animated documentary' in the sense that it used CGI throughout and has as its subject matter the history of dinosaurs and their contemporaries.

Given that twentieth-century film history is littered with examples of animated documentaries, why does it seem so significant now? A renaissance of the form? Perhaps. But probably what's got people's interest is that, whereas before, documentaries may have used animated segments or have used animation juxtaposed with third-person narration, now there are films being made which feel a little bit more 'documentary' in their constituency, and by that I mean that they deal with real people, real testimony and first-person thoughts and feelings. It is this type of fully animated documentary which draws from real-life experience, which can offer a witness to subjective experiences and offer the viewer a novel way of looking at a particular theme or subject matter. It is this type of documentary that feels new, innovative, exciting – something I think offers a unique way of examining certain issues. And it's this kind of 'character-oriented' animated documentary that I'd like to talk about for the rest of this chapter.

Ari Folman's *Waltz with Bashir* (2008, Israel) is perhaps the best-known example of a fully animated, character-oriented documentary. It tells the story of the director's lost memories from the 1982 Lebanese Civil War. The audio we hear consists of Ari Folman's thoughts, recollections and meetings with various people from his past, as he tries to piece together what happened to him during the war and, more specifically, on the day of the Sabra and Shatila massacre. The film uses animation to evocatively capture a past for which there is little archive; it is also a past of forgotten and half-formed memories, of trauma. And it's this representation of subjectivity in which animation can come into its element. For, unlike live action – which does, of course, have pacing, music and a whole host of other devices to create mood – animation can do so much more; it can, at the very least, add another dimension to a narrative and give it a way to start to build bridges between the external world (of things, people and objects) and the internal one (of memories, thoughts and feelings). *Waltz with Bashir* begins to do this, but there are also other examples where the use of animation-as-metaphor is used with great skill.

The Nazi Holocaust has become an obvious context for animation, partly because it's something that's historical and unfilmable (very little archive exists to show what actually happened), but also because what occurred is so horrific, so unimaginable and so full of inner thoughts, feelings and sensibilities that audiovisual testimony alone cannot convey, that it seems an obvious breeding ground for the two forms of animation and documentary to meet. *Silence* (Orly Yadin and Sylvie Bringas, 1998, UK) is a short animated documentary in which Tana Ross, a victim of the Holocaust, tells her story of survival; it uses archive mixed with animation to give a rich and immersive sense of both the Holocaust and its aftermath as perceived by the protagonist. Another film that deals with similar subject matter is *I Was a Child of Holocaust Survivors* (Ann Marie Fleming, 2010, Canada), in which Fleming takes an excerpt from Bernice Eisenstein's autobiographical book and animates it into a coherent, but shortened, story of the author's experiences growing up in a family of Holocaust survivors.

There are instances where animation also works in a documentary context because you need to protect the identity of the protagonist(s). An example of this is the powerful series *The Wrong Trainers* (Kez Magrie, 2006, UK) made for the BBC, which takes the testimony of young children talking about their experiences of living in poverty and creates a cartoon-esque style to make the subject matter accessible for its intended younger audience. *Hidden*, one of the first animated documentaries to focus on the testimony of a principal character, and made by Hanna Heilborn and David Aronowitsch with Mats Johansson (2002, Sweden/Finland), takes as its main narrative a recorded interview with a hidden refugee child in Sweden. The young child has no permit to stay in Sweden and he describes how it is to be persecuted. The use of animation is not particularly rich in metaphor here, most of the film is simply an animated

character being interviewed. But it's powerful in its simplicity, in the rawness of the way the child talks about his experiences and, of course, the deliberate irony of his being hidden, and the film-makers hiding him through animation. The same film-makers also made another animated documentary about child slavery in Sudan, which is equally powerful. A final example of using children comes from a film I produced some years ago called *Leona Alone* (2004), directed by Rani Khanna and animated by Benji Davies, which tells the story of a young girl with sickle cell thalassemia (the girl died shortly after from the disease). The use of animation allows an audience to sense the isolation of Leona, as well as giving a sense of what the disease is like, ending with a stark image of her loneliness.

To me, as I mentioned earlier, the choice of pairing animation and documentary is not just a stylistic choice, but rather comes from a sense that it's the best (or one of the best) ways to represent the subject matter. With the above examples of films about children, not only does animation provide a way of making them anonymous, it also allows us to perceive their experiences in a way that we might not be able to do if we were simply faced with a live-action interview, a film composed of interview and cutaways, or a dramatised re-enactment.

ANIMATED MINDS

The emerging theme for me is the way in which animation can give us an increased sense of access into subjective experiences, memories, emotions, thoughts and perceptions. As someone who was originally trained as a clinical psychologist, I had a natural predisposition to being interested in the workings of the mind, and I had a constant agenda of trying to get a sense of what someone's inner experience is like – a trend which continued into my career as a documentary film-maker. I'm frustrated by the notion that thoughts and perceptions are often incommunicable, especially when it comes to inner experiences, which are so different from our own. People with mental health problems have often attempted to communicate their experiences – whether this has been done through poetry and literature, through painting, through sculpture, or through music. A challenge, for me, was to see if there was a way film, with its tapestry of audio and visual layers, could also help to convey something about one's inner world. Using animation and documentary seemed a perfect fit.

So *Animated Minds* (2004), a series of short animated documentaries, was conceived as an attempt to communicate the subjective experience of mental health problems to a wider audience. The idea was simple: to take the testimony of a variety of people who have experienced mental distress, and then to try to animate this experience. Particular attention was given to metaphor; the people we interviewed often were encouraged to use metaphors to explain what they were experiencing, and this helped the

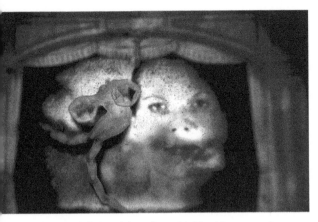

Animated Minds (2004): 'I can't cry. My blood is my tears'

animation. Examples of this include 'I can't cry. My blood is my tears' when talking about self-harm; 'I wasn't eating to make myself thin, I was eating to disappear' when talking about eating disorders. When describing coming down from a bipolar high into profound depression, one woman stated, 'my fingernails think that time has passed but it hasn't. It's like the thing that turns you on, the light bulb thing that's not there any more.' The combination of an honest and open discussion of the experiences of mental illness with well-articulated and metaphorical language provided an excellent canvas on which to use animation.

I'm terrible at judging my own films, but it seems that this series was very successful, not only due to the accolades and awards they received, but more from the feedback we got from people with mental health problems, doctors, carers and other professionals – all of whom claimed that the films served as important communication tools. The best feedback of all was a patient who wrote to me and said, 'At last. I've been trying to explain to my consultant [psychiatrist] for years what it feels like to live with and experience this disorder. Now I can show him!'

There was something else very important about the *Animated Minds* series which could have only been achieved with animation. Part of our aim was to make sure that each film tried to address a specific mental health condition, such as depression, bulimia, Asperger's Syndrome and so on. If we'd made these as live-action films and had seen one person talking, then suddenly the film becomes more about a particular individual rather than a 'condition'. In contrast, we wanted the words spoken to represent what it is like to suffer form a particular illness, so that people (like in the example of the patient above) can use the film as a tool for communication. The difference is perhaps subtle, but nonetheless important; animation helped shift focus onto the experiences rather than the individual.

My involvement with animated documentary has perhaps led to a sense of the instances when animation and documentary make a logical pairing, and give rise to a certain gestalt. In my opinion, a non-exhaustive list of these instances would include:

- When you're trying to give some kind of representation of individual's internal processes; that is, trying to capture a sense of what the world looks like from within, whether this be mental illness, sorrow, memories, deafness, being a child – anything in which we, as an audience, are given some kind of window into inner experiences.
- When you're trying to film the unfilmable. There are certain things we can't film, either because we were not there at the time, or because it's not the kind of thing that a camera could have been present at. Whether this be the story of someone caught up in a tsunami, a narrative of the Holocaust or other genocide, or the victim of an assault, animation, when paired with a single-person narrative, can often be extremely powerful – often more powerful than dramatisation.
- When you're trying to protect someone's identity, either because they're a minor, or they want anonymity, animation can offer far more in the way of rich landscapes than simply filming someone against a window, or pixelating their face.

There are, of course, instances when animation doesn't work, when its put into a film as an afterthought or simply because a director thinks it might look good. It's not perhaps fair to pick on specific examples, but perhaps it's good to talk generically about the ways in which it might be used in the wrong context. Just as, time and time again, documentaries are conceived that don't necessarily lend themselves to the visual form – they'd be far better as a radio documentary or a magazine feature – so too there are those who are intent on making an animated documentary, without being able to answer adequately the question 'Why? Why bother?'. I've come across filmmakers who approach me with a 'great idea for an animated documentary', which often are single-character-based films. My first question is 'Why? Why animation?' and often there's no real explanation, other than a preferred aesthetic or sense that this is somehow the new zeitgeist. My argument here – and its not just me being a humbug – is that one has to ask whether the subject matter lends itself to the art form, and not whether the art form should mould around the subject matter, just for the sake of it. Hopefully, in this short rant of mine, I've made the case for supporting the former and being very wary of the latter.

NOTE

1. For example, *The Sinking of the Lusitania*, Windsor McKay, 1916, USA.

1.7 Dramadoc? Docudrama?: The Limits and Protocols of a Televisual Form

DEREK PAGET

Digital and animated imagery are not the only alternatives to observational footage of events available to the documentarist. From the very beginning of photography, reconstruction has always been a possibility and, as with the digital and animation, if an evidential base is available to legitimate it, in this instance full dramatisation – with actors, script, sets etc., etc. – it can still have 'documentary value'.

DRAMAS OUT OF CRISES

The idea of docudrama emerged from television, which from its earliest days incorporated news and information with entertainment. Because of its inherent mix of the informational and the performative, docudrama was almost purpose-built as an occasional form that could exploit the mass medium's synergising for mass audiences of the factual and fictional. But the very proposal to amalgamate apparently antithetical modes has often been taken as a provocation, and docudrama can be seen as the 'ambulance chaser' of televisual form. In seeking a space between 'straight' drama and documentary 'proper', docudrama inevitably generates debate about ethical permissibility, practical usefulness, even the social and psychological danger involved in this hybrid. One manifestation of anxiety is the frequent assertion that docudrama simplifies issues and 'blurs boundaries' between fact and fiction.

Whenever there is a crisis that finds a place in the public sphere, there tends to be a docudrama. This in itself is important, and reason enough for docudrama to feature in a book about documentary. Its persistence in TV schedules, and its current attractiveness to movie-makers, is the result both of a residual rationalism in western societies and the ongoing appeal of the dramatisation of human behaviour. 'How does it *feel?*' is a characteristic question of a tabloid century obsessed with the individual and the personal, and dramatic performance can offer compelling answers to the question. Two screen cultures, British and American, have key places in docudrama's development. While the presence in Britain of a public service broadcasting ethos shaped the British 'dramadoc', American 'docudrama' has been shaped by an equal and opposite propensity to put entertainment first. But both traditions enshrine the assumptions that *facts* matter and that *truth* will out, along with the conviction that individual human agency is central to the understanding of larger historical currents. In the twenty-first century's screen ecology, British and American approaches have fused and globalised. The new dispensation partly explains docudrama's continued potential, and not just on television and in the cinema, to examine issues and to occasion controversies.[1]

THE DIFFICULTY OF DEFINITION

Definition has been a problem for docudrama. Andrew Goodwin and Paul Kerr noted in 1984 the plethora of terms, including the obvious 'drama-documentary', 'documentary drama', and their shortened versions 'dramadoc' and 'docudrama'. They concluded that the form was 'not a programme category, it is a debate'.[2] My own neologism 'dramadoc/docudrama' (the subtitle of the first edition of *No Other Way To Tell It*), sought to highlight the practical difficulty of disentangling the two words. The coinage enabled me to stress comparisons and correspondences between Anglo-American television histories and practice, both highly influential worldwide. Although 'docudrama' is now the more recognised word in general discourse, owing to American dominance of screen markets, explanation of terms used over the fifty-odd years of the form's existence can still tell us a great deal.[3]

'Drama-documentary' or 'dramadoc', then, refers to a television programme (even if made on film) and a British context. A dramadoc looks and sounds like a fiction film, but references known events. The claim for documentary status rests on pre-film research into those events. Dramadocs follow events taken from real situations, and major characters bear actual names of real protagonists. Telescoping events and compositing minor characters facilitates narrative structures familiar from television drama and fiction film. These conform to the demands of TV schedules and audience expectations. Naturalist or realist performance and filming techniques are the norm. Insertion of documentary material occasions the least possible narrative disruption. Audiences' prior knowledge is a factor to be exploited by writers and researchers.

Much of what I have just said about 'dramadoc' can equally be said about the generality of modern screen 'docudrama', but the label 'documentary drama' is different. It again derives from British TV practice, especially of the 1960s, and nominates films in which invented events and fictional protagonists provided illustrations of real situations and problems. A celebrated example is the BBC's *Cathy Come Home* (1966). Writer Jeremy Sandford took situational and behavioural elements from the lives of several women he interviewed during research to make the iconic fictional homeless mother 'Cathy'.[4] Direct use of documentary film devices – voiceover, archive footage, caption and graphic, direct address – are more often to be found in documentary drama. 'Documentary' functions as adjective describing the noun 'drama': the film/teleplay is a fictional drama that looks more like a documentary in order to enhance its claim to represent real events and people.[5]

Whatever the label, these films and TV programmes have a lot in common. They retell events from national and international histories, thereby reviewing and/or celebrating (and/or memorialising) them; they re-enact aspects of the lives of historical and contemporary public figures or tell the stories of 'ordinary' citizens; and they portray issues of concern to local, national and occasionally international audiences. The effort to define the form, and the debate about its stylistic manifestations, are important and interesting because they articulate deeper cultural concerns about the nature and status of factual material, the extent and reliability of any 'facts' presented, and the ethics behind the style of dramatic representation. The attempt to incorporate many of the values and some of the aesthetics of documentary film and television enables the best docudramas to seek the kind of serious attention sought historically by documentary film.[6]

The fact that the form is accused of 'blurring boundaries' between fiction and non-fiction indicates above all that docudrama tests the limits of what can be achieved by applying the secondary powers of drama to the primary facts of real events. The form is ultimately best seen, as documentary itself is, as an ongoing response to technical, institutional, historical and political pressures to *represent reality*. Especially during the twentieth century, western cultures became hypnotised by the holy grail of the *real*. The possibility of privileged access to real life through the agency of the camera seemed very possible. This continuing but troubled quest has become more and more complicated by aesthetical, ethical and philosophical considerations that outweigh technical advance. Focused further by doubts about the very status of a documentary image now itself subject to digital manipulation, the grail seems less not more realisable in the twenty-first century.[7]

EARLY HISTORY: COMPENSATING FOR LACK

The use of drama in documentary has a screen history that pre-dates any of these terms. Early twentieth-century documentary and historical film, constrained by technology, dramatised precisely because it could so rarely witness. Cameras could not easily be where anything was actually happening, and sound synchronisation was many years away. Action was therefore routinely recreated, and if audiences believed what they saw they seem to have done so willingly enough. As audiences became more sophisticated, film-makers became engaged – some would say ensnared – in a century-long quest for the authenticity that could inspire belief. 'Documentary' began to be distinguished from 'actuality' and 'newsreel' as some non-fiction film took on narrative shape and thus encouraged more complex audience interest. Ur-definitions, like John Grierson's 1933 claim that documentary was 'the creative treatment of actuality', facilitated this. But it is worth pointing out that Robert Flaherty's 1922 *Nanook of the North*, sometimes hailed as the first documentary, is highly docudramatic. Action and *mise en scène* alike were to an extent fictions, and real Inuits acted in role as their forebears. Grierson's Empire Marketing and GPO Film Units routinely rehearsed and re-enacted in films like *Night Mail* (1936). The argument for 'creative treatment' represented an attempt both theoretically and ethically to legitimise practices pragmatically indispensable.[8]

Documentary film was the beneficiary of a wider interest between the two World Wars in the real. Mixing fiction and fact became accepted as a means of heightening realism and increasing social and political relevance. In Europe and America the idea of the documentary, linked to a politics of the left, offered a way to demonstrate art's relevance to society. With the worldwide Depression and issues of labour rights prominent in western democracies, with the (apparently) shining example of Soviet revolution available, and with events such as the Spanish Civil War a focus for political activism, there was no shortage of subjects for 'creative treatment'. Fiction film, too, borrowed techniques honed in documentary to heighten the realism of, for example, the Hollywood 'biopic' and Warner Bros. social problem movies.[9] The match between serious fiction film and documentary was even more evident during World War II, when sound and vision technology was also in the process of improvement, and when Hollywood directors such as William Wyler and George Stevens were behind the cameras. Films providing information and/or propaganda in all combatant countries were grounded in realistic styles, with documentary devices common stylistic features, but often required dramatisation (the war situation making access difficult).

POST-WAR: ACCESS THROUGH TECHNOLOGY

Post-war, sound synch became an established 16mm film technology by the 1960s. With camera and microphone present more often at real-world events, documentary film made perhaps its most plausible claim yet to represent the real. Things were different, however, in the fledgling television industry. Here the access offered to observational cinema by new technology was impossible because television's electronic cameras were even more unwieldy than pre-war film ones. The 'outside broadcast' of sporting events and public occasions was possible, but speech-based programming like drama – and documentary – was live and studio-based. The occasional telecine cutaway reinforced the idea of 'a world out there', but in general the real world had to be brought into the studio.[10] The television 'story documentary' of the early 1950s, for example, was docudrama in all but name. Factual information was mainly conveyed in scripted and rehearsed dialogue and actor voiceover. The focus, as with 'human interest' journalism, was on the individual-as-representative. Producer Caryl Doncaster defined story documentary as 'a method of translating complex social problems into human terms'. Mixing documentary and drama was an accepted feature, too, of American television in the 1950s. NBC/CBS's *Armstrong Circle Theatre* drama anthology series (1955–63) parallels the story documentary. It presented informational and historical material through a mixture of devices, studio-bound dramatisation being prominent.[11]

The technological improvements evident in American Direct Cinema films like *Primary* (1960) marked a breakthrough for location action. The practices of its makers Robert Drew, Richard Leacock and D. A. Pennebaker inspired Canadian TV executive Sydney Newman. Taking over the BBC's flagship series 'The Wednesday Play' (1964–70) in the early 1960s, he introduced a policy of 'agitational contemporaneity' designed to match observational cinema. He sought to bring a reality-based social relevance into television drama, and tapped into the wider cultural revolution that was sweeping the arts in Britain and America. Television drama, current affairs and science departments alike used documentary drama as part of this drive for relevance.[12]

THE GOLDEN AGE REVISITED

The 'Wednesday Play' and 'Play for Today' (1964–84) strands broadcast a number of teleplays that, like *Cathy Come Home*, had a documentary base – *Up the Junction* (1965), *In Two Minds* (1967), *Edna the Inebriate Woman* (1971), *The Cheviot, the Stag, and the Black, Black Oil* (1974), *Days of Hope* (1975), *The Spongers* (1978) among them. They are often cited as evidence of a 'golden age' of British television drama, and all but two were produced by Tony Garnett and directed by Ken Loach.[13] Loach and Garnett, in particular, redrew the

boundaries of the mixed form. They were energised by a radical politics that interrogated the post-war break-up of the British class system. Their films dealt with problems of sexuality, poverty and homelessness, and illuminated tensions within a working class newly interesting in the post-war dispensation. The films convinced partly through a presentational style, partly through a documentary provenance derived from observational cinema (location rather than studio action, hand-held cameras, dialogue that appeared improvised, 'wild track' voiceover).

Peter Watkins's 1965 *The War Game* went even further in testing the boundaries of the possible in documentary drama. The film provocatively took its informational base from actual British government preparations for nuclear war. Using an invented scenario in the conditional/subjunctive tense, the film asked what would be the effects on a small town in Kent, according to the government's own (and other) experts, after a nuclear strike on central London? Mixing newsreel with documentary drama, amateur performers and real individuals, the film vividly demonstrated the potential horror of nuclear war. It was too vivid for its time, and the BBC came under government pressure not to screen it. BBC governors effectively banned it, with the resultant storm of protest ensuring its fame. It is a key marker of the differences between censorship approaches to film and television.[14]

If the Loach/Garnett documentary dramas were dramas in a documentary style, Granada Television's *World in Action* team made dramas they prepared and regarded as documentaries. Citing problems of access and/or political sensitivity as their reason for making their current affairs 'drama-documentaries', producer Leslie Woodhead saw the them as a journalistic last resort. He said in 1981 that 'taking up the dramadocumentary [sic] trade was simple, pragmatic ... I came across an important story I wanted to tell but found there was no other way to tell it.'[15] Granada dramadocs (1980's *Invasion*, 1981's *Strike*, for example) set a standard both for other programme-makers and for critical commentary. The meticulous use of captions explaining the provenance of factual material was one much admired feature. ATV's 1980 *Death of a Princess*, in contrast, caused political difficulties, indeed offence, in the Arab world it depicted. This could be attributed partly to its more fictionalising 'documentary drama' approach, but was more to do with the sensitivity of British–Saudi relations. Granada's films could be accommodated more easily as part of the West's political campaign for change in the Communist Bloc.

In America, the big shift to docudrama occurred after the major film studios began to produce 'made-for-TV' movies' in the 1960s. Once the film and television industries no longer regarded each other as rivals, films with factual narratives offered significant advantages all round. The docudrama *Brian's Song* (ABC, 1971) proved popular

Invasion (1980): the meticulous use of captions explaining provenance of factual material

enough not only for repeat television showings but also for theatrical release. Steven N. Lipkin contends that docudramas achieved such success in America by being 'rootable', 'relatable' and 'promotable': 'rootable' in the sense that plots are, literally, rooted in current events well known through the news and high school history lessons; 'relatable' because audiences can empathise with the experiences of protagonists either ordinary like themselves or made to seem ordinary by realist acting; 'promotable' because, with their framework of events and issues made accessible through other media, docudramas promote themselves and are thus very cost-effective.[16]

CURRENT STATE OF PLAY: ACCOMMODATING PLENTY

For fifty years, and whatever the label, docudrama fitted well enough into terrestrial television in post-World War II Britain and America, broadly serving the purposes described above and benefiting from its occasional place in

habitual television viewing. The periods of 'scarcity' (few channels) and 'availability' (more channels) saw a consolidation to the point where docudrama became as recognisable to viewers as soap-opera and sitcom. In the current period of digital 'plenty' (cheaper equipment, proliferating channels, technologically facilitated 'viewing on demand', vast amounts of air-time to fill) docudramas have burgeoned to become a staple for film companies, television networks and cable and satellite channels alike. The merged industry is well positioned to exploit television's tendency to cannibalise existing forms and make new ones. Not only has docudrama flourished in this period, it even begins to look respectable when compared to 'Reality TV'.[17]

At the 'low-concept' end of the market a tendency towards melodrama stems primarily from the commercial priorities of American television. Low-concept docudrama tends to focus on the sensational, as in the 'Long Island Lolita' trilogy of the early 1990s. Here NBC, CBS and ABC,

the terrestrial dinosaurs of America's 'golden age', all produced docudramatic treatments of a notorious attempted
murder case.[18] Thrust into the news through special, often
traumatic, experiences, protagonists in such docudramas
can be seen as representative in terms of suffering or victimhood, or they can simply be offered as freakshow.[19]

This contrasts with 'high-concept' docudrama, generally regarded more highly, especially when associated with
the British investigative tradition imported into America
through the co-production deals that obtained from the
1990s. Granada and Home Box Office's 1990 'co-pro' docudrama *Who Bombed Birmingham?*, for example, can claim to
have contributed to the campaign to free the 'Birmingham
Six', Irishmen wrongly convicted of a 1972 IRA bombing
incident.[20] Like *Hillsborough* (1996, about a football stadium
disaster) and *No Child of Mine* (1997, about the sexual
exploitation of children), controversy about the film raged
around content issues, with the form dragged into public
attention as a by-product. Docudramas like these have the
potential to contribute to public debates. The 1993 murder
of Stephen Lawrence inspired the 1999 films *The Murder of
Stephen Lawrence* and *The Colour of Justice* – extending the
opportunity to debate racism in Britain. In 2002, a fresh
inquiry into the infamous 1972 'Bloody Sunday' incident in
Northern Ireland provoked *Sunday* and *Bloody Sunday*. The
post-internet factor of supporting websites – evident
especially alongside high-concept television docudramas
like these – increases the possibility of such docudramas
animating wider debate.[21]

Because the docudrama's claims to the real are so
provocative, worries about form reveal much about the
media's general claim not just to represent the real, but,
further, 'to be real'. It also, perhaps, explains the proliferation of new, reflexive forms trailing new descriptive
terms. Thus 'mock-documentary' ('mock-doc', 'mockumentary') was coined for films that are actually highly fictional but which satirise documentary's pretensions (for
example, that it is possible to observe the real without
interfering with it). Films like *This is Spinal Tap* (1984) ape, in
knowing ways, documentary's most obvious conventions
in order to deconstruct them. Channel 4's *Feltham Sings*
(2002) and Penny Woolcock's 2002 Channel 4 film version of
John Adams's 1991 opera *The Death of Klinghoffer* are
examples of reflexive hybrids, 'documusical' and 'docu-
opera'. Music and song add their potential emotional grasp
to the informational reach of these films.[22]

'Historical-event docudrama', meanwhile, has shifted
the formal qualities of films dealing with 'anniversary'
moments in history. For example, in the BBC/HBO's *D-Day*
(2004) and *Hiroshima* (2005) there are mixes of archive film,
witness statement to camera and acted reconstruction
that reveal reflexively the architecture of the docudrama.
They hark back, with more self-consciousness, to earlier
newsreel features such as *The March of Time* (1935–51).

Conditional-tense/subjunctive-voice docudramas like the
BBC's *If …* series (2004–06) continue the reflexive tradition
inaugurated by *The War Game* by projecting docudramatic
material into imagined futures. The major contemporary
historical moment of 9/11 saw a plethora of films dealing
with 'terror attacks' (for example, the BBC's 2004 *Dirty
War*). Even elderly terms like 'biopic' continue to have a
purchase, treatments of famous people's lives having
become more formally docudramatic.[23]

Especially in high-concept co-production, films are
increasingly being made for both cinema release and television broadcast. This was true of Paul Greengrass's films
about Stephen Lawrence and Bloody Sunday, and it is true
of Michael Winterbottom's *The Road to Guantanamo* (2006),
for example.[24] HBO is particularly associated with such
product, striking deals with a number of British and
European production companies and achieving critical
acclaim and impressive audience reach without necessarily surrendering grasp of issues or production values.
Hollywood's own use of real-world material for films from
Schindler's List (1993) to *The Hurt Locker* ('based on fact' and
a 2010 Oscar winner) is also, I would argue, part of the
current burgeoning docudramatic continuum and ecology.

Like the literary adaptation and the 'biopic', the docudrama is now a major part of commercial fiction-film culture
as well as of television production. Ultimately, the question
of whether docudramas are fact or fiction, true or false, signals a cultural fascination with the very concept of *truth*
and *lie*. At present there is a widespread lack of public trust
in agencies with duties of care – government, the law, the
professions – and the webs of deceit that have grown up
around hierarchical authorities have ensured plenty of
material for docudramatic treatment. By 'making mischief',
as they sometimes do, docudramas offer radical alternatives to official accounts where the dark art of 'spinning'
news, good and bad, is endemic. At their best, docudramas
offer the potential to shed new, critical light on contemporary issues. 'True stories' in the cinema and television challenge viewers' understanding of the real, test their sense of
the limits of representation and raise important ethical
questions about access to and representation of reality,
about the precarious balance between the private and the
public and about the personal and the political.

NOTES

1. Documentary modes have burgeoned in the theatre, too –
   see Alison Forsyth and Chris Megson (eds), *Get Real:
   Documentary Theatre Past and Present* (Basingstoke: Palgrave
   Macmillan, 2009). In academic writing on documentary
   the notion that documentary has a hold on truth has
   been problematised to an extent that enables a
   'both/and' claim to be made for docudrama. Its
   documentary research base enables a bid for the moral
   high ground of the documentary while dramatic

structures of 'make-believe' open the emotional terrain. The 'porosity' that currently obtains between drama and documentary occurs in a period when trust in public figures and bodies, particularly in western societies, is at a low ebb. 'Porosity', a concept first promulgated by Walter Benjamin, seems a more useful notion to me than the 'blurred boundary', suggesting as it does something organic rather than perverse (Walter Benjamin, *One-Way Street and Other Writings* [London: Verso, 1985]); and see also Derek Paget, '"Acting with Facts": Actors Performing the Real in British Theatre and Television since 1990. A Preliminary Report on a New Research Project', *Studies in Documentary Film* vol. 1 no. 2, October 2007.

2. Andrew Goodwin and Paul Kerr, *BFI Dossier 19: Drama-documentary* (London: BFI, 1984), p. 1.

3. On definition, see also Janet Staiger, 'Docudrama', in Horace Newcomb (ed.), *The Museum of Broadcast Communication Encyclopaedia of Television, vol. 1* (Chicago: Fitzroy Dearborn, 1997); Steven Lipkin, *Real Emotional Logic: Film and Television Docudrama as Persuasive Practice* (Carbondale, IL: Southern Illinois University Press, 2002); and my own *No Other Way To Tell It* (Manchester: Manchester University Press, 1998, 2010). I rephrased the subtitle for the 2010 second edition to read 'Docudrama on Film and Television', recognising that 'docudrama' has become the preferred term in terms of general use. British practitioners, however – and to some extent British academics – hang on both to 'drama-documentary' and to 'dramadoc'.

4. A measure of the film's success is that the character of Cathy (played by Carol White) is iconic not only in the history of British television, but also in Britain's fifty-plus years of wrestling with the housing problem. See my 'Preface' to the 2003 edition of Sandford's play (Derek Paget, 'Preface' to Jeremy Sandford, *Cathy Come Home* [London: Marion Boyars, 2003]). See also John Corner, *The Art of Record: A Critical Introduction to Documentary* (Manchester: Manchester University Press, 1996), pp. 90–107.

5. John Caughie's important *Screen* article, 'Progressive Television and Documentary Drama' (vol. 21 no. 3, 1980: republished in Goodwin and Kerr, *BFI Dossier 19*) inaugurated much of the subsequent academic discussion, with its adumbration of a documentary and a drama 'look' to the fact-based TV dramas of British television's 'golden age'. In John Caughie (2000) *Television Drama: Realism, Modernism and British Culture* (Oxford: Oxford University Press, 2000), he returns to the subject, pointing out appositely that docudrama's balance between the literate and the visual tends to be weighted more heavily in favour of the former than is the case with fiction film.

6. For more detail on all these points, see Corner, *The Art of Record*, pp. 31–43.

7. Brian Winston's *Claiming the Real: The Documentary Film Revisited* (London: BFI, 1995) was first in the field to examine the implications of the digital revolution for documentary's always-already dubious claim to unmediated truthfulness. All claims to authenticity are thrown into doubt as a result both of digital technology and postmodern scepticism. Latterly, more media-literate audiences have also come to question the old wisdom that 'the camera cannot lie' (see Annette Hill, *Reality TV: Audiences and Popular Factual Television* [London: Routledge, 2005] for audience research that illustrates this).

8. Grierson is credited with the first, adjectival, use of the word 'documentary' in a review of Robert Flaherty's *Moana* in the *New York Sun*, 8 February 1926 – see Forsyth Hardy (ed), *Grierson on Documentary* (London: Collins, 1946), p.11. Grierson wrote that the film had 'documentary value'. The definition was made in his 1933 article 'The Documentary Producer', *Cinema Quarterly* vol. 2 no. 1, pp. 7–9.

9. 'Between the Wars' was a period not unlike the present one, with documentary attaining prominence across the arts. Writers like John Dos Passos and John Steinbeck incorporated factual material into the plots of their novels; 'photo journal' magazines such as *Life* used documentary photographs as intensifiers for articles on social problems, and 'Living Newspaper' documentary theatre became a staple mode in Europe and America. 'Biopics' have been a constant for the film industry from early days. The best book on this, in my view, is still George Custen, *Bio/pics: How Hollywood Constructed Public History* (New Brunswick, NJ: Rutgers University Press, 1992).

10. Sporting events like the FA Cup Final, the Boat Race and the Grand National were early 'outside broadcasts', and the 1953 Coronation of Queen Elizabeth II drew huge audiences. Much of the drama of the time has been lost, but where it has been preserved, 'real' is not a word that springs immediately to mind when watching its staginess now.

11. Paul Rotha's 1956 collection has several essays by story documentary personnel, including Arthur Swinson and Caryl Doncaster. His 'Writing for Television' and her 'The Story Documentary' can be found in Paul Rotha (ed.), *Television in the Making* (London: Focal Press, 1956). William Bluem, *Documentary in American Television: Form, Function, Method* (New York: Hastings House, 1979), has the best account of *Armstrong Circle Theatre* – see pp. 192–4.

12. *Primary* followed the campaigns of American presidential candidates John F. Kennedy and Hubert Humphrey; camera operators shouldered their cameras through crowds and meetings, finding a raw edge for their footage. By comparison, and bizarrely, even studio-based soap-opera series like ITV's *Emergency – Ward 10* (1957–67)

and the BBC's *Z Cars* (1960–78) were sometimes categorised as 'documentary dramas' in the same period. Science departments like the BBC's *Horizon* (from 1964) also turned to docudrama at this time.

13. For more on the 'golden age', see Jonathan Bignell, Stephen Lacey and Madeleine Macmurragh-Kavanagh (eds), *British Television Drama: Past, Present and Future* (Basingstoke: Palgrave, 2001) – in particular, Shaun Sutton's 'Sydney Newman and the "Golden Age"', pp. 54–7.

14. *The War Game* was given a kind of controlled release to cinemas via film societies, but was not shown on British television until 1985, by which time the nuclear threat had become less of an issue.

15. Leslie Woodhead's *Guardian* lecture is reprinted in Alan Rosenthal (ed.), *Why Docudrama?: Fact-Fiction on Film and TV* (Carbondale, IL: Southern Illinois University Press, 1999), pp. 101–10. I took the title for my book from this remark of Woodhead's. See Peter Goddard, John Corner and Kay Richardson, *Public Issue Television: World in Action, 1963–98* (Manchester: Manchester University Press, 2007), for more on *World in Action*; Brian Winston, 'Introduction: The Filmed Documentary', this volume.

16. See Lipkin, *Real Emotional Logic*, especially pp. 56ff.

17. See John Ellis, *Seeing Things: Television in the Age of Uncertainty* (London: I.B.Tauris, 2000), for this useful periodisation of television into times of 'scarcity', 'availability' and 'plenty'. The latter, of course, refers to the digital revolution of the late twentieth century which makes obsolete old assumptions about how television is produced and consumed.

18. For more on the 'Long Island Lolita' docudramas, see Allan Rosenthal, *Writing Docudrama: Dramatizing Reality of Film and TV* (Boston: Focal Press, 1995), p. 19; and Rod Carveth, 'Amy Fisher and the Ethics of "Headline" Docudramas', *Journal of Popular Film and Television* vol. 21 no. 3, September 1993. For more on 'high-' and 'low-concept' television, see Gary Edgerton, 'High Concept, Small Screen: Reperceiving the Industrial and Stylistic Origins of the American Made-for-TV Movie', *Journal of Popular Film and Television* vol. 19 no. 3, July 1991.

19. 'Movies of the week' have attracted particularly uncomplimentary labels that betray a tendency for critical condescension – 'headline docudrama', 'disease-of-the-week docudrama' and, more generally, 'trauma drama' (see Thomas Hoffer, Robert Musburger and Richard Nelson, 'Docudrama', in Brian Rose [ed.], *TV Genres: A Handbook and Reference Guide* [Westport, CT: Greenwood Press, 1985]; Carveth, 'Amy Fisher and the Ethics of "Headline" Docudramas'; Jane Feuer, *Seeing Through the Eighties: Television and Reaganism* [London: BFI, 1995]).

20. In America the HBO title was *Investigation: Inside a Terrorist Bombing*.

21. *The Colour of Justice* was a televised version of one of the Tricycle Theatre, 'Tribunal' stage plays, first produced on stage also in 1999 (in London). The vastly costly 'Bloody Sunday' inquiry finally published its report in 2010.

22. Documentary film theorists have for some time been discussing documentary's shifting status in culture – see inter alia Bill Nichols, *Representing Reality: Issues and Concepts in Documentary* (Bloomington: Indiana University Press, 1991); Bill Nichols, *Blurred Boundaries: Questions of Meaning in Contemporary Culture* (Bloomington: Indiana University Press, 1994); Michael Renov (ed.), *Theorizing Documentary* (London: Routledge, 1994); Stella Bruzzi, *New Documentary: A Critical Introduction* (London: Routledge, 2000). On mock documentary, see Jane Roscoe and Craig Hight, *Faking It: Mock-documentary and the Subversion of Factuality* (Manchester: Manchester University Press, 2001). Jane Roscoe and I have written on 'documusical' in our 2006 online essay 'Giving Voice: Performance and Authenticity in the Documentary Musical', *Jump Cut: A Review of Contemporary Media* 48, www.ejumpcut.org/. Accessed 29 September 2012.

23. See Tobias Ebbrecht, 'Docudramatizing History on TV: German and British Docudrama and Historical Event Television in the Memorial Year 2005', *European Journal of Cultural Studies* vol. 10 no. 1, February 2007, where the form has been instrumental in that country's coming to terms with reunification in particular. Recently, I came across 'monumentary', coined to cover memorialising docudrama like 2004's *Omagh*. See Brian McIlroy, 'Memory Work: *Omagh* and The Northern Irish Monumentary', in Brian McIlroy (ed.), *Genre and Cinema: Ireland and Transnationalism* (London: Routledge, 2007). This film about an IRA atrocity seems to me much better described as docudrama, however.

24. It is worth pointing out that Greengrass and Winterbottom – also Peter Kosminsky – are, to an extent, all heirs to Ken Loach. Several of the high-concept docudramas mentioned in this section were the work of these directors. Winterbottom is also responsible for *A Mighty Heart* (2007), the feature film docudrama about Daniel Pearl.

1.8 Ambiguous Audiences

ANNETTE HILL

Ultimately, documentary's truth claim rests not on the image alone but also on its reception. The debate about the nature of evidence speaks to the intrinsic qualities of the image – to the authenticity of the image, however it is produced. If the truth claim is grounded not on the image alone but also on the reception of the image, then questions as to audience understanding of documentary's claim on the real – which until recently were seldom examined – become crucial.

'DOCUMENTARIES ARE AN ILLUSION'[1]

To say documentaries are an illusion suggests audiences are entertained by the way films, or programmes, speak in a playful way to them about fact and fiction. It's a mixed-up media environment where images and sounds of the world around us are reproduced and reconstructed on television, radio, print media and the web. It can be difficult to know what is fact or fiction. Documentaries are an illusion in the sense that audiences actively collaborate in the construction of reality in film, television, or the web. They know just enough about how the media works to be sceptical of it. Despite this complicity, the 'd' in documentary does not stand for deception in the minds of audiences. Documentary stands for rational and critical engagement with truth and evidence. It also stands for emotional engagement with the value of these ideals in society and culture. Audiences expect a magician to be skilled in the art of deception as a performative act. But they expect documentary-makers to tell the truth within the process of representing reality. The trickiness of documentary as an objective and subjective genre is not lost on audiences. They use the ambiguous associations of reality and illusion to be sceptical of truth claims in the media and to believe in the truth as they see it. In this way, audiences are engaging through documentary with a wider set of issues regarding evidence and ideas of truth in contemporary culture and society.

MULTIMODAL RESPONSES

Research on audiences has tended to focus on distinct modes of engagement with the genre and various categories of documentary within it. For example, one common mode shows how viewers know the genre is part of public service media where the remit is to inform audiences.[2] The public expect to learn something about the world when watching nature documentary series produced by the BBC. Another mode of engagement with documentary is to understand it as representing reality. Such a response indicates audiences perceive the genre as factual, which means there is a direct relationship with the image and actuality.[3] For example, the public expect hard-hitting current affairs series to depict real events, or social problems, as they are happening now. These distinct modes of engagement can also overlap so that audiences can expect a documentary to give them some knowledge about events as they are caught on camera. This way of understanding audiences shows how viewers respond to documentary as part of a knowledge and reality project.

In previous work on documentary audiences, I suggested there was a double mode of engagement with documentary, where viewers both watched factual content and reflected on the process of watching.[4] This is like seeing yourself in a dream and thinking 'that is me dreaming'. Other researchers also noted something similar in the way this genre draws you 'inside the documentary experience, with its distinct mix of objective and subjective dynamics'; Thomas Austin described the 'seeing, feeling and knowing' of documentary film audiences.[5] To reflect on the centrality of ambiguity to this genre adds further dimensions to understanding audiences. Other kinds of ambiguous cultural experiences are opportunities for audiences to have not one response, or a double mode of engagement, but multimodal responses to audiovisual content.[6] We experience the world as multimodal, drawing on sight, hearing, smell, taste or touch. Why should a documentary experience be any different?

Documentary is a genre that invites a rich range of responses from audiences. Cognitive engagement is one mode of response. This is the kind of thinking where viewers know that documentary is a construction rather than a direct record of reality. These same viewers will also rationalise that there is some degree of reality within certain kinds of documentaries. Psychological engagement can include an understanding of other people's personalities within a documentary, their motivations and personal dynamics, the way their mind works. This psychological mode can also link with a self-reflexive style of response by audiences, where they are aware of their reactions as well. There are emotional responses to a style of documentary, specific event or person. For example, Thomas Austin[7] found that audiences spoke of an emotional truth within certain documentary films. There are sensory modes of engagement with documentary. These responses can be linked to aesthetics, such as a nature documentary that appeals to the visual sense. Or they can be associated with memories or places, such as a food documentary that reminds viewers of a particular taste. And related to this mode are physical responses. This is where a mock documentary horror film can make you jump.[8] We may draw on one mode of engagement over others, but we have this repertoire of responses at our disposal.

In the following analysis of audience research on factual genres, including documentary and its wayward offspring Reality TV, there is a repertoire of responses to audiovisual content. This analysis focuses on why someone would say 'documentaries are an illusion'. This is a deceptively simple statement. Just as illusions are complex constructions of artifice and evidence, so too documentary challenges us to question what we know, see and feel to be true.

To understand this statement it is necessary to analyse audiences of documentary and other kinds of factual genres at this juncture in time. What we shall see is that cultural practices associated with documentary are in tune with other sociocultural trends related to reflections on reality. Audiences draw on their full repertoire of responses to documentary in order to deal with these issues.

DOCUMENTARY AS ILLUSION

Titles for influential books on documentary signal an underlying concern with issues of reality and illusion within the genre as a whole. *The Art of Record* indicates by its title 'a widely recognized and problematic duality in documentary work – its character as both artifice and as evidence'.[9] *Claiming the Real* analyses the realist documentary idea and asks 'What can or will be left of the relationship between image and reality?'.[10] *Blurred Boundaries* critiques realism within documentary film.[11] In a review of documentary studies, Corner writes: 'scholarship will never "resolve" the issue of definitions and borderlines, these will actually become more uncertain and "thin" as audio-visual culture becomes more inter-generically fluid'.[12] Documentary is an ambiguous genre operating at 'the margins of reality'.[13]

To say documentary is an illusion means viewers understand the generic fluidity of the genre. Indeed, the statement indicates viewers start out in a default critical mode towards the truth claims within documentary. In a 2003 survey, 53 per cent of respondents claimed that documentaries (of all kinds) were true to life (from a total representative sample of 4,516).[14] When asked if it was very important that documentaries were true to life, 32 per cent said yes. News and journalism scored far better, with around 90 per cent of respondents claiming the genre was true to life and its truth claims were important to them.[15] For reality game-shows, as few as 10 per cent of respondents perceived these as true to life and said the programmes' truth claims were important to them.[16] Clearly, documentary has suffered from its association with Reality TV, a hybrid genre that is not what it claims to be.

Such criticism of documentary is closely linked to changing trends in Reality TV and factuality as a whole. Back in 2000, when the reality game-show format *Big Brother* (Endemol for Channel 4, UK) first arrived in Britain, the most dominant types of Reality TV at the time were the hybrid genres of docusoaps and infotainment. Viewers were already flocking to Reality TV in peak-time schedules, leaving documentaries to graveyard slots.[17] In a representative survey of around 9,000 viewers (8,216 adults aged between sixteen and sixty-five plus and 937 children aged four to fifteen) taken from the industry Broadcaster's Audience Research Board (BARB) sample, Reality TV was popular with 70 per cent of all respondents. Before *Big Brother*, what people liked most about Reality TV were people's stories caught on camera. Of all respondents, 75 per cent claimed to like informative elements and 68 per cent liked observational elements in Reality TV. Their tastes matched viewing preferences, with observation and information-style programmes more popular (around 65 per cent) than the new reality game-shows (35 per cent).[18]

Performance and authenticity were part of the way people evaluated the reality of these shows. Over 70 per cent of adults in the survey thought that stories about ordinary people in Reality TV were made up or exaggerated. And this was mainly because of the perception of people overacting for the cameras (70 per cent of adult respondents) rather than an understanding of editing techniques, or digital manipulation. Even though audiences were aware of the performative and entertaining aspects of the genre, at that time what people valued most was the ability to represent the public in a popular way. Among adult respondents, 55 per cent claimed that Reality TV 'gives you all sorts of information about life' and 48 per cent thought these shows 'give people a chance to speak on TV about what matters to them'.[19]

Such a perception of Reality TV changed with the more dramatic elements that came to characterise game-shows such as *Big Brother*, life experiment and lifestyle series such as *Wife Swap* (RDF for Channel 4, UK) and talent shows like *Popstars* (19 and Fremantle for ITV1, UK) in the 2000s. People started to see many kinds of representations of reality as tricks of the mind. The panel of viewers in 2003 treated the genre as entertainment. Reconstruction shows that actually contained actors were thought to be more real than Reality TV. A third of respondents (31 per cent) thought people acted up for the cameras in reconstruction shows, compared to nearly the entire sample for reality game-shows (88 per cent). What is more, people stopped caring about whether Reality TV represented the public in a popular way. Less than 40 per cent claimed it was important ordinary people did not act up for the cameras.[20]

The fact that audiences stopped caring about the authenticity of people and their experiences in these reality formats was, to a large degree, a result of their increasing cynicism that these were ordinary people at all. The people that came to characterise Reality TV participants were wannabes, hungry for celebrity status. The perception of Reality TV offering members of the public a chance to tell their story and for audiences to learn a little something about life gave the genre some public value in 2000. But, three years later, this style of factuality was to become known as 'Humiliation TV', with little public value beyond that of entertainment. The fact that audiences talked up the genre in 2000 is an indication something significant happened to perceptions of its reality status over a short period of time. By 2003 people were taking great delight in trashing the genre and the people who took part in the shows.

This conversation about changes within factuality highlights connections between documentary and Reality TV:

> NINETEEN-YEAR-OLD FEMALE SALES CLERK It really did start there, with that kind of idea of let's follow someone around and see what they do with their lives.
> TWENTY-SIX-YEAR-OLD MALE OFFICE WORKER Yeah, cause it's actually documentaries …
> NINETEEN-YEAR-OLD FEMALE SALES CLERK Yeah. And then it broke down to let's follow people around, or let's put them somewhere where we actually don't have to follow them.
> TWENTY-FOUR-YEAR-OLD FEMALE CIVIL SERVANT Yeah, I was going say that, definitely. You could almost break it down in the middle. You've got a situation where you follow the ordinary around, you follow people's lives, record it, document it. Then you've got an almost experimental Reality TV, where you force people into a situation to get, you know, the reaction you want, I suppose.
> TWENTY-FIVE-YEAR-OLD MALE BUYER It's not even that reality based is it? It's contrived.

The notion of factual evidence as something you record and document changes within the experimental nature of this hybrid genre. Reality becomes a matter of misdirection.

What is significant about modes of engagement with Reality TV is this emphasis on psychological and emotional issues. How people act in a Reality TV show is a framing device for evaluating truth claims within the genre. In *Seeing Through Self-deception*, Barnes[21] comments on the difference between intentional and non-intentional accounts of deception. There is a widespread understanding that when the cameras roll people deceive others for all sorts of reasons, both intentional (in the case of politicians) and non-intentional (in the case of some types of Reality TV participants). Indeed, seeing through self-deception is one of the reasons audiences like to watch Reality TV because they try to judge different degrees of deception. Reality shows use a dizzying array of evidence, hand-held and hidden cameras, video diaries, observational footage, staged set-ups, surveillance and live studio set-ups, to name but a few. Audiences like to have these multiple perspectives where they can cross-reference sources and assess other people within these shows.

Peter Lunt has noted how Reality TV has been dominated by a theme of social interaction where the ways individuals react to a problem or event is a means of reflecting on reality.[22] Such a dominant theme within Reality TV has schooled audiences in psychological and emotional modes of reflecting on reality in other genres. For example, nearly 40 per cent of viewers in the 2003 survey claimed that ordinary people acted up for the cameras in documentaries.[23] A similar percentage thought people acted up in political programmes. Given the high degree of cynicism in political performances and distrust in modern politics, this comparison between the way people act in documentary and political programmes is cause for concern.[24] In a separate category for nature documentaries, less than 10 per cent said people acted up for the cameras, which is what we might expect from programmes about animals and the environment. Clearly audiences distrust other people and their motivations for being on camera.

A dominant trend within contemporary audiences is to be cynical of the media in general. As one person commented: 'our media culture makes us more sceptical' (twenty-two-year-old male student). Another viewer explained:

> It seems to me that TV doesn't have the same kind of trustworthiness as it used to have … you kind of think 'oh yes, yes, yes', you believe what you see. But you don't know whether you get all of it, like, a full range. (Forty-five-year-old male primary school teacher.)

There is a strong association with artifice and distrust: 'the problem is we are so used to seeing things on television having been carefully orchestrated beforehand … you think what is true or what isn't?' (thirty-eight-year-old female consultant). Factual evidence within the media, from a photograph, or web cam, to a newspaper article or blog, is usually treated with a certain degree of cynicism: 'I think we're all aware shows and any sort of media tries to manipulate us one way or another' (twenty-six-year-old male office worker).

The identity position of sceptic is very attractive to media audiences. A sceptical identity serves a useful purpose in positioning audiences with a collective understanding of themselves as media critics. Bill Nichols[25] comments on the problem of evidence: 'when we recognize that evidence emerges as a response to the questions we pose, we are in a position to recognize the ambiguity of that evidence'. It is certainly the case that audiences recognise the ambiguity of evidence as presented in the media and as experienced in social life. How to assess evidence in the news, or documentaries, who to trust as a credible source, how to tell if someone is deceptive, are problems audiences are aware of, although this doesn't mean they know how to resolve them.

With regard to Reality TV these sceptical trends towards representations of reality have made the genre shift more towards entertainment. Shiny-floor shows like *Strictly Come Dancing* (BBC Worldwide for BBC1, UK), or *The X Factor* (Syco and Fremantle for ITV1, UK) have come to dominate Reality TV of today. It is no accident that the days of *Big Brother* are over, as formatted reality shows cannot make claims for some kind of social experiment when their target audience perceives the genre as entertainment. But audiences do not want documentary producers to make variety shows. Eighty per cent of respondents in the 2003 survey claimed it was important documentary was shown on television. And the same amount said it was important ordinary people did not act up for the cameras in documentaries. In the next section, the statement 'documentary is an illusion' is turned upside down. While documentary can be criticised as an illusion, at the same time it also stands for an idea of truth.

DOCUMENTARY AS TRUTH

Truth is not a fixed and knowable thing, although that is an attractive idea for many of us. Rather it is an idea that is put into practice and interpreted in context. Truth within documentary is an idea that materialises as a programme or film based on real people, events and places. Paul Ward notes that in a genre that has undergone many changes 'the only unchanging thing about documentary is that it is a form that makes assertions or truth claims about the real world or real people in that world'.[26] As we have seen, the idea of truth within documentary does change in relation to scepticism of representations of reality.

It can be tricky to talk about truth when everyone sees themselves as a media critic. There are different strategies audiences use to assess and reflect on truth claims. John Corner notes two protocols of truth in documentary. The first relates to the origination of the image – how far was the image captured and how far was it constructed?[27]

And the second relates to the organisation of the image – how does editing, music, speech, or narration, frame the image? A protocol of truth based on the organisation of an image can be used as a strategy for assessing documentary. As this viewer said: 'I think it is essential that it seems and feels authentic and that you can believe in it and that you are not too aware of the editing processes' (thirty-six-year-old female personal assistant).[28] To draw on the other protocol positions documentary images as truthful because they are perceived to originate from a natural setting. This strategy is important to documentary audiences because it allows them to differentiate the genre from others: 'Reality TV is, they are more like sort of caged animals ... whereas in documentaries I think there is a tradition of respect and humanism in documentary-making' (thirty-year-old male gardener).

The notion of humanism is central to understanding audience engagement with documentary as truth. When viewers watch documentary they can assess its truth claims with regard to people and their social interaction. The psychological and emotional modes of response that are so dominant in Reality TV are also at work in documentary. While in Reality TV people seem less human, in documentary people seem more natural and true to themselves. This conversation about the documentary film *Spellbound*[29] highlights the humanism that viewers perceive as integral to the genre:

THIRTY-EIGHT-YEAR-OLD FEMALE OFFICE ASSISTANT The kids had really different, diverse backgrounds, with weird parents, and the kids were cute and weird and interesting. They didn't get ten little dolls, you know, perfect American suburban spelling kids. They got a mixed bag of really interesting kids. That's one of the things, though. You know, as you sit down as a viewer: it is real. If you trust it, it's real. THIRTY-THREE-YEAR-OLD FEMALE BAR WORKER You're not necessarily going to get exactly everything you exactly want. That's right, it makes it more real, you know, to draw you into it. Although you're dealing with a factual thing, you want to be taken in there.

The diversity of people and their experiences is a framing device for trust in the truth claims of this documentary.

In the following discussion of *Capturing the Friedmans*,[30] these viewers reflected on ideas of truth and evidence as part of individual experience and action:

NINETEEN-YEAR-OLD FEMALE SALES CLERK Did anyone see *Capturing the Friedmans*? TWENTY-SIX-YEAR-OLD MALE OFFICE WORKER No, I didn't see that. NINETEEN-YEAR-OLD FEMALE SALES CLERK It was a very good documentary. It's good because they don't tell you that these people were convicted of child abuse. You don't know whether these people had done it or whether they were innocent. And you find out in the end that they were both convicted. And that's very interesting, because this family obviously allowed the documentary to happen and to be shown. But they treated them with so much respect – respect for the family, and respect for the people who had been through all of that.

TWENTY-FIVE-YEAR-OLD MALE BUYER Was that because they allowed you to form your own opinion?

NINETEEN-YEAR-OLD FEMALE SALES CLERK Yeah, I think a documentary should allow you to form an opinion, even if it's a documentary that's got an agenda.

TWENTY-SIX-YEAR-OLD MALE OFFICE WORKER But which documentaries don't have an agenda?

NINETEEN-YEAR-OLD FEMALE SALES CLERK *Capturing the Friedmans*. Watch it!

TWENTY-SIX-YEAR-OLD MALE OFFICE WORKER OK. So it doesn't have an agenda. Doesn't it even have the agenda to portray what people normally think of as beasts?

NINETEEN-YEAR-OLD FEMALE SALES CLERK No, because they don't even necessarily show … you have absolutely no idea whether they were guilty or not. … It's a perfect documentary in a way.

This is 'a perfect documentary' not because of the subject matter but rather the way the film invites a range of responses – psychological, emotional – to this difficult issue. For this person, the film deals with a fluid notion of truth and evidence where the viewer is asked to decide for themselves what happened to this family.

There is a way of understanding documentary as truth where an idea of truth is embedded in individual experiences. This is a pragmatic response to a difficult issue in a tricky genre. Peter Lunt explains:

> the adoption of the idea that truth resides in events or process is an important part of pragmatism. The argument is that it is better to judge the character of individuals through their actions just as the motions of objects reveal the operation of physical forces.[31]

Viewers use different notions of truth within various contexts and put these into practice through the process of watching. For example, the idea of truth as personal integrity is put into practice through the context of documentary production. In this way documentary-makers are understood as more humane than Reality TV producers. Or, the idea of truth as derived from diversity of experience is understood within the context of different characters within a film.

This pragmatic approach to truth partly explains why people say different things about documentary as artifice and evidence. If audiences reflect on evidence within factuality then truth becomes an idea that is rooted in media processes. Criticism of media techniques becomes part of discourses surrounding documentary experiences. But if audiences reflect on a specific event or persons depicted in a documentary then an idea of truth resides within an individual and their reactions to social processes. In this case, documentary experiences tend to be more associated with discourses of the self. Although the idea of truth may seem like a moving target, this pragmatism works well for documentary audiences. Faced with the problem of image and reality in society and culture, people judge the character of documentary through their experience of it.

MIXING FACT AND FICTION

Documentary is a genre that mixes up fact and fiction. As such, documentary is rich in ambiguity – is it real or not? And it is rich in layers of meaning for audiences – what is reality or illusion? Documentary audiences respond to the genre in multiple ways, drawing on cognitive, psychological, emotional, physical and sensory modes of engagement with fact and fiction. At this moment in the development of documentary, other kinds of factuality are impacting on modes of engagement with the genre. A default critical position is common to audiences who are generally sceptical of the media and question representations of reality in audiovisual culture. Audiences like to see themselves as critics. This means they tend to appropriate discourses of scepticism when talking about documentary alongside other hybrid genres such as Reality TV. A comparative response has its down sides as documentary can get caught up in talking trash about factual entertainment. But critical discourses can also highlight what viewers value about a genre that is more about fact than fiction. They like how documentary leaves the question of reality open, compared with Reality TV, which has moved from the borderlands into entertainment.

Documentaries can feel natural and true to life compared with the artificiality of much media today. An idea of truth becomes significant to understanding the development of the genre and how audiences engage with documentaries in more psychological and emotional ways. The problematic duality of image and reality has led audiences to use a pragmatic approach to issues of authenticity and truthfulness. This is an idea of truth as part of individual experiences and something to be understood in the context of specific events or social contexts. For a genre so rooted in knowledge and learning, this emphasis on truth as a social process shifts an understanding of documentary towards individual experience rather than a public knowledge or reality project. Ways of engaging with documentary to some degree change the character of the genre as a cultural experience. As this person said: 'I don't know if documentary actually teaches you, or if it's more about your response to it' (twenty-six-year-old female librarian).

RESEARCH NOTE

The data cited in this chapter is taken from two studies. The first was an Economic and Social Research Council (the former regulatory body Independent Television Commission) and Channel 4-funded project that used a quantitative survey, semi-structured focus groups and in-depth interviews during the period 2000–01 (see Hill, *Reality TV* [see note 18], for full details). The second was funded by the former regulatory bodies the Broadcasting Standards Commission and Independent Television Commission, Jönköping International Business School, Sweden, and the Society, Opinion and Media Institute, Göteberg University, Sweden. This was a multimethod and comparative study, using quantitative surveys, semi-structured focus groups and in-depth interviews during the data collection period of 2003–05 in Britain and Sweden (see Hill, *Restyling Factual TV* [see note 2], for further details).

NOTES

1. Quoted from a thirty-year-old male gardener. Please see Research note regarding all sources in this chapter (unless otherwise specified).

2. See John Corner, Kay Richardson and Natalie Fenton, *Nuclear Reaction: Form and Response in Public Issue Television* (Academia Research Monograph, 1990); Annette Hill, *Restyling Factual TV: Audiences and News, Documentary and Reality Genres* (London: Routledge, 2007); Thomas Austin, *Watching the World: Screen Documentary and Audiences* (Manchester: Manchester University Press, 2008).

3. See Dai Vaughan, *For Documentary: Twelve Essays* (Berkeley: University of California Press, 1999), and Paul Ward, *Documentary: The Margins of Reality* (London: Wallflower Press, 2005).

4. Annette Hill, 'Documentary Modes of Engagement', in Thomas Austin and Wilma de Jong (eds), *Rethinking Documentary: New Perspectives, New Practices* (Maidenhead: Open University Press/McGraw-Hill, 2008).

5. John Corner, 'Television Documentary and the Category of the Aesthetic', in Alan Rosenthal and John Corner (eds), *New Challenges for Documentary* (Manchester: Manchester University Press, 2005), p. 56; Thomas Austin, 'Seeing, Feeling, Knowing: A Case Study of Audience Perspectives of Screen Documentary', *Participations* vol. 2 no. 1.

6. See Annette Hill, *Paranormal Media: Audiences, Spirits and Magic in Popular Culture* (London: Routledge, 2011).

7. Austin, 'Seeing, Feeling, Knowing'.

8. See Jane Roscoe and Craig Hight, *Faking It: Mockdocumentary and the Subversion of Factuality* (Manchester: Manchester University Press, 2001).

9. John Corner, *The Art of Record: A Critical Introduction to Documentary* (Manchester: Manchester University Press, 1996), p. 2.

10. Brian Winston, *Claiming the Real: The Documentary Film Revisited* (London: BFI, 1995), p. 6.

11. Bill Nichols, *Blurred Boundaries: Questions of Meaning in Contemporary Culture* (Bloomington: Indiana University Press, 1994).

12. John Corner, 'Documentary Studies: Dimensions of Transition and Continuity', in Austin and de Jong, *Rethinking Documentary*, pp. 26–7.

13. Ward, *Documentary*.

14. Hill, *Restyling Factual TV*.

15. Ibid.

16. See ibid.

17. See Brian Winston, *Lies, Damn Lies and Documentaries* (London: BFI, 2000).

18. Annette Hill, *Reality TV: Audiences and Popular Factual Television* (London: Routledge, 2005).

19. Ibid.

20. Hill, *Restyling Factual TV*, p. 125.

21. Annette Barnes (1998) *Seeing Through Self-deception* (Cambridge: Cambridge University Press, 1998).

22. Peter Lunt, *Stanley Milgram: Understanding Obedience and its Implications* (London: Palgrave Macmillan, 2009), p. 141.

23. Hill, *Restyling Factual TV*.

24. See John Corner and Dick Pels (eds), *Media and the Restyling of Politics* (London: Sage, 2003).

25. Bill Nichols, 'The Question of Evidence, the Power of Rhetoric and Documentary Film', in Austin and de Jong, *Rethinking Documentary*, p 37 (reprinted in this volume, Chapter 1.1).

26. Ward, *Documentary*, p. 8.

27. Corner, 'Documentary Studies, p. 23.

28. Hill, *Restyling Factual TV*.

29. Jeffrey Blitz (2002), USA.

30. Andrew Jarecki (2003), USA,

31. Lunt, *Stanley Milgram*, p. 133.

1.9 Life as Narrativised[1]

BRIAN WINSTON

The second central issue in documentary is the need for narrative. Importing this into actuality footage is the essence of Flaherty's breakthrough in Nanook of the North (1922). It is with narrative that Grierson located the essence of 'creative treatment' as the basis of the distinction between documentary and other forms of non-fiction cinema.

Grierson wanted the term 'documentary' reserved as an exclusive description of a particular form of factual cinema, set aside from and above newsreels, travelogues, educationals and the like. What really was to make the documentary different, beyond a certain quality of observation, was its need for 'very different powers and ambitions at the stage of organising'.[2] These 'powers and ambitions' came into play via the second term in the Griersonian definition – 'treatment'.

'Treatment' was used as a synonym for 'dramatisation'. 'The creative dramatisation of actuality' was one of the first 'demands of the documentary method', as Rotha put it.[3] 'Treatment' or dramatisation (also sometimes referenced as 'interpretation') reflects the documentarist's desire and willingness to use actuality material to create a dramatic narrative. Grierson knew that the 'actual world of our observation' could be filmed and structured to be dramatic along such lines. Dramatically structured actuality was exactly what he had seen, perspicaciously, in Flaherty's work. It was the very thing which distinguished the Flaherty films from previous efforts in factual filmmaking.

I think Flaherty's reputation is overblown but, curiously, his apologists – such as Richard Barsam[4] – never seem to make as much as they might of his one real and indisputable contribution to the development of the cinema. In what seems to have been a flash of genius, while reshooting his Inuit footage (the first rushes having been lost in a fire), Flaherty understood the need to make a drama arise from the life being observed (or better, being constructed through the process of observation). This was very different from imposing a drama from without, as Curtis had done in *In the Land of the Head-Hunters* (1914). Instead of a fictional Western melodrama, Flaherty, by contrast, filmed the supposedly everyday life of a single Inuit family. He imposed no external melodrama, and that is crucial. The first two reels of *Nanook* are a series of single-shot 'postcards', multi-shot vignettes and two longer sequences. The 'postcards' are portraits of Nanook and Nyla or one or two shots of such things as 'The Mysterious Barren Lands' (as the intertitle has it); building a moss fire; walking to the river; the children being fed by the fur trader; Nanook clowning with the gramophone and so on. These vignettes consist of from three to eleven shots. For instance, there are the three shots used to cover the arrival of Nanook's kayak at the shore; the three shots showing how a kayak is covered with skin; the shots showing fur pelts at the trading post; or the eleven shots which show the large, open four-oared omiack boat being launched, crossing a body of water and landing by the post.

There are also two full-scale sequences. In the first, which lasts for five minutes twenty seconds, Nanook goes fishing among the ice floes. There are thirty-three shots including six intertitles. In the second sequence, Nanook and his comrades hunt walrus. This lasts for five minutes and has forty shots, including seven intertitles.[5]

The 'postcards' and vignettes together establish the environment of the film. There are the beginnings of a narrative in the way Flaherty deployed some of these proto-sequences. Take Nanook's arrival in his kayak: this establishes the fur trader's post, which is the location for a number of other events – trading, feeding Nanook's children and Nanook's clowning. There is, though, little sense of temporal continuity and certainly no causal relationship between these elements. In other words, there is a chronology if only because all films in the act of projection are necessarily chronological; but there is no causality.[6] The bulk of these 'postcards' and vignettes are, to use a term of Gérard Genette,[7] iterative: that is, they represent a narrative instance or an event or activity which can be read as a typical instance of that event or activity.

In a realist text, the iterative is a crucial element contributing to the reader's sense of the text's representation of reality. We see Nanook light a moss fire, for example, but that stands for his regular fire-lighting activity. Of course,

Nanook of the North (1922): the supposedly everyday life of a single Inuit family

in film 'the concrete expression of the unique texture of every moment'[8] makes the idea of the iterative difficult; but, nevertheless, such shots are too brief to be seen as singular and specific. Moreover, their iterative effect is sometimes reinforced by the generalised titles, for example, 'This is the way Nanook uses moss for fuel'.

The two longer sequences, on the other hand, are straightforward narratives with a clear hermeneutic, as Barthes uses the term. Barthes defines the hermeneutic code in narrative as 'a variety of chance events which can either formulate a question or delay its answer'.[9] Will Nanook succeed in his hunt for food? In each of these two sequences, Nanook leaves by sea. We witness his arrival at a hunting site and his preparations. He then kills the prey and makes a start on the return journey. The answer each time is 'Yes! He succeeds'.

But these sequences are not integrated into the iterative material which surrounds or precedes them in any

way. Overall, the first two reels of the film are a more or less random selection of scenes of Inuit life, some more specific than others, featuring Nanook and his family.

What happens some twenty-three minutes in, after the title 'Winter …', is very different. Bill Nichols has said: 'Documentary operates in the crease between life as lived and life as narrativised.'[10] And it is 'life as narrativised' that, for the first time, we now witness in *Nanook*.

At first sight, it might seem that Flaherty is simply continuing with his previous film-making strategy. We see Nanook and his family begin a journey by land. He traps a fox, builds an igloo, hunts a seal, loses control of his dogs, gets caught in a blizzard and, finally, finds a disused igloo. There is a difference between these sequences and the earlier mélange, though, and it is considerable. First, all these events are quite firmly part of one journey. There is a strong temporal sense governing the progress of this journey, with at least two days and nights being very carefully delineated. Even the iterative vignettes of life in and around the igloo – for example, Nanook playing with his son, teaching him to shoot with bow and arrow – are integrated into this narrative.

Moreover, and in absolute contrast to the first part of the film, these sequences depend on each other causally. It is in order to hunt that the family makes the journey. They cannot feed on the fox Nanook captures so they need to hunt seal. The seal meat causes the dogs to fight, which delays Nanook's search for shelter. The blizzard then endangers them and they have to race to find shelter in a disused igloo. This diagesis can be read as an example of Tzvetan Todorov's notion of 'transformation' as a main principle of narrative.[11] The equilibrium of the family's life at the post, where food and shelter are provided, is broken by the approach of winter and the need to make a journey.[12] Nanook then repairs the disruption by providing food and shelter once again.

Or Barthes's analytic system can be used. His concept of the hermeneutic is as easily applied to the last fifty-odd minutes of *Nanook* as it is to the two earlier sequences. Questions, raised in part by the visuals but more directly by the intertitles, create a series of textual enigmas to engage the spectator's interest. Within the large question of the family's overall chance for survival, as the film progresses, more specific questions are posed. Will the family eat? Will the dogfight mean a fatal delay? Will they find shelter? As is not the case with the first fishing and hunting sequences, such questions now extend across a number of discrete episodes. There is even a closure when, after their race against the blizzard, the family settle down, fed, in safety for the night.

Nanook also exhibits that 'logic in human behavior' which Barthes[13] makes into the proairetic code of narrative. From the series of events he chose thus to string together in these reels, Flaherty constructs a perfect melodramatic climax, brought on by Nanook's successive activities in hunting the seal and feeding his dogs as a storm blows up. These become 'a series of actions, natural, logical, linear'.[14] Further, we can note that a third system of narrative analysis also 'works' for *Nanook*. William Guynn's conclusion[15] is that Christian Metz's syntagmatic system, developed for the fiction film, can be readily applied to it.

This demonstration of how to construct out of (supposedly) observed material a text which exhibits all the characteristics of a fictional drama is Flaherty's major contribution to the cinema. This must not be underestimated, for he put it together, at the 'stage of organising', out of various discrete elements which he had filmed at different times and in a different order, perhaps even for different story purposes. Understanding not just how to manipulate his 'everyday' material, but also what dramatic necessity imposed on that manipulation, is the essence of Flaherty's contribution. He was obeying the generally understood requirements of structuring a multi-reel fiction film at this time. As the sub-headings for a chapter in an early screenwriting manual put it: 'Sequence and Consequence; Logical Cause and Complete Solution; Sustained Climax; All Expectations Fulfilled'.[16] That is exactly what happens in *Nanook* after 'Winter ...'.

This, then, is 'treatment'. Grierson's understanding of the need for dramatisation, though, immediately takes us far from a vision of documentary cinema as being in stark opposition to a cinema of fiction. Indeed, for Grierson, it is exactly the fictionalising quality of narrative – 'dramatic form' – that is the distinguishing mark of documentary. Because it shared dramatic narrative, however, documentary thus slipped, almost without friction, into the fiction cinema as a species of genre. Grierson's taxonomic triumph was to make his particular species of non-fiction film, *the* non-fiction genre while at the same time allowing the films to use the significant fictionalising technique of dramatisation.

'CHRONO-LOGIC'

The development of the documentary, then, critically depended on the discovery of dramatic formulations to turn the everyday into drama. Flaherty used the model of the journey to accomplish this. Charles Musser suggests[17] that a journey to China was the ur-documentary subject in a sequenced late-seventeenth-century illustrated lantern-slide lecture. This should not surprise. Journeys and narratives go together: 'To depart/to travel/to arrive/to stay: the journey is saturated. To end, to fill, to join, to unify' – one might say that is the basic requirement of the *readerly* where the 'readerly' is glossed as 'what can be read ... a classic text'.[18]

The despised but popular travelogue was in essence based on filming journeys; but the journey also figures in many diverse 'higher' documentaries – from the epic march of the Bakhtiari in *Grass* (1925), through the voyage of the fishermen in *Drifters* (1929) to Buñuel's alienated and ironic wanderings across the *Land Without Bread* (1933) and beyond. Journey films solved actuality's big narrative problem – closure. How should such films finish? Obviously, a journey film ends with the end of the journey. Another quite simple solution was to construct the film to run apparently for the duration of a period of time with a well-defined culturally determined closing – a day, most commonly.

This became documentary's preferred way of capturing the urban experience on film. Shots (often taken over a period of months or even years) were organised into thematic clusters and those clusters into a chronological progression. The chaos of the modern world was thereby shaped into a day in the life of a city – 'an event-oriented, vaguely chronological approach'.[19] As in Walter Ruttman's *Berlin: Die Symphonie der Großstadt* [*Berlin: Symphony of a City*]

(1927), the trajectory of the film is from the early morning through the working day to the entertainments of the evening. Even Dziga Vertov, who stridently opposed the idea of fiction film on ideological grounds and claimed he was escaping from narrative, made a city documentary, *Chelovek s kinoapparatom* [*The Man with a Movie Camera*] (1929), which still puts 'Waking' before 'The Day and Work Begin', which is itself before 'The Day's Work'. The film's 'day' concludes with 'Work Stops, Leisure Begins', although it must be admitted that many of these last activities also take place during daylight.[20] Vertov proves the rule. For most documentarists, the diurnal was as seductive an organising principle as the journey.

Take the wartime work of Humphrey Jennings.[21] There is a denseness about the ways in which Jennings, and his editor Stewart McAllister, wove images together, an associative intuitiveness, which is apparently capable of confusing some into believing that films such as *Listen to Britain* (1942) exhibit a 'non-narrative style' or an 'absence of narrative editing'.[22] Yet, for one thing, shots within the sequences of this film are classically edited. There are matched cuts on the couple sitting out the dance in the dance-hall sequence; on the soldiers singing in the night train; and on Dame Myra Hess playing the piano at a concert. It is a little strong to claim no narrative here, even before the overall structure of the film is considered.

Sorenssen notes, following Dai Vaughan's observation, that the film 'is organised around a 24 hour time cycle';[23] but somehow the implication of this is resisted. The chronological element was not something added at 'the stage of organising' in the cutting room. The film was conceived around time, as the treatment reveals: 'It is half past nine – the children are already at school ... and at 10.30 the BBC comes "Calling All Workers". ... At half past twelve, the clatter of typing in the Ministries and offices in London lessens.'[24] Moreover, this was a response to the brief, which was to make a film about the lunch-time concert series in the National Gallery, which was considered by itself to be 'too dreary'.[25] The time-cycle was the key to dramatisation.

This is extremely important:

As has been clearly established in recent narratology, what makes Narrative unique among the text-types is its 'chrono-logic', its doubly temporal logic. Narrative entails movement through time not only 'externally' (the duration of the presentation of the novel, film, play) but also 'internally' (the duration of the sequence of events that constitutes the plot).[26]

The internal 'chrono-logic' of *Listen to Britain* arises from its strongly inscribed diurnal pattern, in this case from afternoon to afternoon. The pattern compensates for the film's admittedly weakened proairetic.

This is often the case. The diurnal is not simply another major way in which documentarists dramatise actuality; it also works to reintroduce the narrative logics of the proairetic code in films such as this, where single characters give way to a changing series of individuals who collectively represent the mass. Guynn argues:

The documentary text rarely exhibits [the] functional economy characteristic of the fiction film. ... Motivation, the causal alibi that seems to emerge effortlessly from the narrative telling, is precisely what is lacking at certain jointures of the text; the segmental units do not call each other into being in an inexorable logic of time. Rather segments tend towards closure, the short circuiting of their narrative potential.[27]

He suggests that these gaps are normally filled by spoken commentary (or, one can add, previously by intertitles). More than that, though, they are also filled exactly by an 'inexorable logic of time'; to wit, the diurnal pattern. It is because of this, as Guynn notes, that Jennings here 'takes pride' in avoiding commentary or 'any sort of mediating language of this kind'.[28]

Designed in part for US and Commonwealth consumption, *Listen to Britain* poses big hermeneutical questions about the state of Britain's morale in the blitz, including the issue of how well the very fabric of the country is surviving. (London, implicitly, is 'not being left in ruins', wrote Jennings in his treatment.[29]) Each shot and each sequence are evidence for the viewer of how such questions are to be answered. The propaganda importance of offering positive answers to these enigmas is clear. And this element of narrative is expressed in, as well as being considerably bolstered and strengthened by, the use of time.

In Jennings, the poet/painter's imagination struggled with the inevitable chronological prison of the cinema. For instance, in the summer of 1940 he was planning a short film in which the theme of men leaving for war would be told through the family images found on the walls of a remote rural home:

On the walls are portraits, photographs, watercolours of men – predominantly men – engineers and soldiers going back to the days of Robert Stephenson and the Crimea – little framed fragments of regimental colours – photographs of railway bridges – men in uniform and men as children.[30]

Jennings knew that this needed to be made to work as drama; so, deftly, he suggested that these images be cut-aways seen in the after-dinner calm of a day, the children asleep and the adults listening on the radio to Haydn's 'Midi' symphony *while* he cross-cuts 'the bombers going out from a neighbouring airfield'. The film and the music climax as 'The bombers are already over the white coast line.'

In the film he actually realised that year, *London Can Take It!* (1940, made with McAllister and Watt), there was not only a diurnal pattern, from evening to morning, but the added structure of an American journalistic report, written by Quentin Reynolds of *Colliers Weekly*, as the soundtrack. Building these sound-picture complexities against a temporal logic became the Jennings hallmark, seen most clearly in *A Diary for Timothy* (1945) (edited by McAllister's one-time assistant Jenny Hutt).

The visual complexity of his mature style is held together in this film by a perfectly simple 'chrono-logic'. *Diary* takes the events of the last winter of the war – essentially the Arnhem raid and the Battle of the Bulge – and weaves them around the first weeks in the life of the eponymous baby. The film's commentary, by E. M. Forster and arguably the most elegant yet written for a British documentary, is less Timothy's diary than a chronology of avuncular conversation and observation:

> In those days before Christmas the news was bad and the weather was foul. Death and darkness, death and fog, death across those few miles of water for our own people and for others, for enslaved and broken people – the noise of battle getting louder, and death came by telegram to many of us on Christmas Eve.

Jennings's strategies well illustrate the strength of the prison of narrative into which the Griersonian demand for 'treatment' locks the realist documentary. His is the most poetic, impressionist oeuvre and yet it is usually strongly time-based. All the significant war films but one are structured in this way, and his two 1943 films (*The Silent Village* and *Fires Were Started* ...) were actually scripted fictions which maintained their documentary connection only because they used non-actors going through actions supposedly historically (and/or typically) determined (and, of course, because they were produced by documentary film units).

NON-NARRATIVE: WORKS BETTER IN THE HEAD THAN ON THE SCREEN

It could be objected that, Flahertian melodramatics apart, these 'simple' narrative shapes – journeys, days – are in fact too simple to be recognised as such. Actually, they are nothing more than a sort of automatic consequence of film's fundamental temporality (its internal 'chrono-logic') and nothing more. I would rebut this. In the Jennings oeuvre, there is a short film which, despite its brilliance, is nevertheless a vivid demonstration that narrative hegemony cannot be easily overturned.

In *Words for Battle* (1941), Jennings 'sets' seven texts, spoken by Laurence Olivier, against film images, in the fashion of a composer setting words to music for a song. My point is that Jennings and McAllister here abandoned causality and 'chrono-logic' (or at least reduced them to a bare minimum) while still producing an effective film. The roster of writers quoted is chronological (by order of birth) from Camden to Churchill, with only Lincoln out of place. Hillier hints at a movement in the film from an introduction which gives a general description of Britain (Camden) as a land which prizes liberty and tolerance (Milton) to more specific references to the war; children first – being evacuated against Blake; next, adult activities – against Browning; and then death and destruction in the form of blitz damage and a funeral against Kipling.[31] This last, 'When the English began to hate', cues the defiance of Churchill's 'We shall never surrender' speech, while Lincoln's Gettysburg address in some fashion returns us to the Milton. All this suggests that the sequences are secured in their places by something more than the birth date of the author of the words and that they could not be easily rearranged, but this logic is not bolstered by any sort of further chronology or other pattern in the visual track. For instance, a sunset occurs in the middle of the film because the poem being quoted (Browning's 'Home Thoughts, from the Sea') makes reference to it, not because we are in the middle of a dusk-to-dusk structure of the sort Jennings elsewhere favoured.

Words for Battle represents the end of a rather short road. It followed a similar effort, *The First Days* (1939), which Jennings co-directed with Harry Watt and Pat Jackson. This has neither 'chrono-logic' nor the sustained word/image density of *Words for Battle*, and, therefore, as Watt said, 'There was no shape. It wasn't a good film.'[32] *Words for Battle*, although more successful than this, nevertheless did not become a model, not even for Jennings himself. Instead, as we have seen, Jennings and McAllister turned to chronological structures and *Words for Battle*, with its extremely tenuous chronology, remains an exception. Despite this, for some, the film is a piece of 'extraordinary bravura' whose 'effect is irresistible', largely, I would argue, because of the words (and Olivier's delivery of them).[33] Essentially, though, reducing the organising potential of time this much was too dangerous a strategy. It turned out to be easier to create a safety net in the form of a chronology.

Words for Battle, insofar as it is a non-narrative, represents a barely effective form and unsurprisingly, as I have said, it is one that has never been much exploited. Nevertheless, the possibility of such films being effective has been insisted on as a demonstration of documentary difference. The examples given of 'non-narrative' never quite meet the case, however. They are often more simply badly structured rather than a compelling example of an alternative 'non-narrative' form. For instance, one standard text book proposes *Gap-Toothed Women* (Les Blank,

Words for Battle (1941): 'works better in the head than on the screen' – Dai Vaughan

1987, USA) as lacking narrative, but it does have an obscured narrative trajectory.[34] At the end of the day:

> we cannot say that documentary demands a separate semiotics, because we are faced with the simple fact that documentaries are full of narratives and that in telling their stories these texts quite 'naturally' call on signifying structures that the fiction film created for its own uses.[35]

While it seems obvious that documentaries tell stories, not least because that is what the documentarists said they were doing, this was often hidden. But they were also making a claim in a de facto PR campaign of lasting effectiveness that they were different from fictional filmmakers. Thus, of *Nanook*, *Grass* and *Chang* (1927), an early historian could write, curiously, 'None of these pictures told a story in accordance with the accepted patterns of the studios',[36] when in fact that was exactly what they did. Time has not brought greater insight.

Instead, a trope has developed which tends to assume that the documentary does indeed demand separate formal structures. Documentary difference in this regard is almost tacitly accepted. It is assumed that documentaries are 'non-narrative' and, therefore (in some quarters), not even 'real' films. Metz, for example, asserts: 'Remove "drama", and there is no fiction, no diagesis, and therefore no film. Or only a documentary, a *"film exposé"*.'[37] The 'only' comes neatly in. In such a climate, it is no wonder that documentary is deemed to lack all narrative requirements – even, for instance, closure:[38] 'Endings are not supposed to be "neat" in the genre of the documentary.'[39]

Scholarly analysis suggesting various formalist taxonomies of documentary sub-genres such as the 'categorical film' and 'rhetorical film' do not make an effective case that such forms have much meaning to either film-makers or audiences; or indeed that in most circumstances they actually produce watchable films at all. Such claims for documentary exceptionalism have a *post hoc ergo propter* hoc feel. Since documentary is recognisably different in broad terms from fiction, then it ought to differ formally, including being different in its narrative strategies. This allows for these 'automatic' (as it were) readings of this difference – seeing no closures where there are closures; seeing no temporal schemas where there are temporal schemas; even seeing no drama, only 'exposés'; and so on.

A 'non-narrative' documentary is an oxymoron; but that is because narrative – albeit not necessarily narrative limited to traditional concepts of chrono-logical causality – is unavoidable. Current expanded concepts of narrative allow a film, such as *Words for Battle*, to eschew almost all traces of temporality and causality and still 'work' as a species of narrative. Narrative is seen as an organising tendency within any text and between it and the consumer of it. This, then, accommodates much more than simple or even complex time-based storytelling. After all, Barthes's 'hermeneutic code' allows for 'a variety of chance events which can either formulate a question or delay its answer', thereby engaging readers'/audiences' attention in exactly the same fashion as traditional narrative is held to do.[40] Meir Sternberg goes so far as to see narrativity as 'the play of suspense/curiosity/surprise between represented and communicative time'.[41] Monika Fludernik 'disqualifies the criteria of mere sequentiality and logical connectedness' as being central to narrative.[42] For her, shared understandings of the world, social perceptions, narrative and reception conventions – what audiences bring to the business of deconstructing any text – can create narrative.

The presence of narrative in documentary, being inevitable, means that it is no marker of fictionality: documentaries cannot be held to be identical to fiction because they are narratives. Narrative is, if you will, a shared inherited characteristic for both fiction and non-fiction. I join those who hold that the narrative seems to express a fundamental human impulse to tell stories. Some believe that 'a narrative voice pervades virtually every genre and medium of human discourse, ranging from novels and television dramas to sermons, political campaign orations, advertisements, journalistic reports, historical treatises, and everyday conversations'.[43] If narrative is unavoidable, it cannot of itself subvert truth claims *because it is not limited to fiction*. Bill Nichols is therefore correct to castigate those who use the fictionalising requirements of narrative to make a case against documentary's truth claims.[44] For such an argument to have force requires the existence of a mode of discourse that does not tell stories. If such a mode does not exist, and I incline to believe that it doesn't, then clearly documentary's narrativising propensity is beside the point as regards its truth claim. Narrative is unavoidable and, therefore, the truth claim has to be, and is, located elsewhere – in reception, not production. The point is that all efforts to deny documentary narrative result in films, as Dai Vaughan observes, which always work 'better

in the head [of the film-maker] than on the screen [for the audience]'.[45]

I rather take the position described by Guynn:

> We are thus led to the conclusion that what distinguishes documentary from the fiction film is not the simple presence or absence of narrative. Narrative is never absent in documentary films, even if its presence is more or less marked. Nor can we ascribe a particular mode of narration to documentary, given the heterogeneity of [its] texts. ... Certain documentaries closely resemble the fiction film in that they deploy its basic signifying structures at many textual levels; others mark out their distance by adopting these structures episodically or by restricting them to certain textual functions.[46]

The bottom line is: 'Narrative is never absent in documentary film.' It is the essential factor demarking documentary from surveillance; it is a crucial determinant of documentary creativity.

NOTES

1. Reworked from the editor's *Claiming the Real II: Documentary: Grierson and Beyond*, Part III 'Treatment: Documentary as Drama' (London: BFI, 2005), pp. 107–27.

2. John Grierson, 'First Principles of Documentary', in Forsyth Hardy (ed.), *Grierson on Documentary* (London: Faber, 1979 (1932), p. 145.

3. Paul Rotha, *Documentary Film* (London: Faber, 1966 [1935]), p. 105.

4. Richard Barsam, *The Vision of Robert Flaherty: The Artist as Myth and Filmmaker* (Bloomington: Indiana University Press, 1988), pp. 20–3.

5. These counts refer to a Films Incorporated print of the 1976 restoration (by David Shepard) with a specially composed soundtrack for modern classical sextet added (see Ruby's note in Paul Rotha, *Robert J. Flaherty: A Biography*, ed. Jay Ruby [Philadelphia: University of Pennsylvania Press, 1983], p. 2). A fuller history of the various versions of Nanook, including a description by Shepard of his work, can be found in Steve Dobi, 'Restoring Robert Flaherty's *Nanook of the North*', *Film Librarians Quarterly* vol. 10 no. 1/2, pp. 6–18.

6. David Bordwell, *Narration in the Fiction Film* (Madison: University of Wisconsin Press, 1985, pp. 80–7; Edward Branigan, *Narrative Comprehension and Film* (London: Routledge, 1992), pp. 11–12; Seymour Chatman, *Coming to Terms: The Rhetoric of Narrative in Fiction and Film* (Ithaca, NY: Cornell University Press, 1990), p. 9.

7. Gérard Genette, *Narrative Discourse: An Essay in Method*, trans. Richard Howard (Ithaca, NY: Cornell University Press, 1980), pp. 113–60.

8. Robert Stam, Robert Burgoyne and Sandy Flitterman-Lewis, *New Vocabularies in Film Semiotics: Structuralism,*

Post-structuralism and Beyond (London: Routledge, 1992), p. 122.

9. Roland Barthes, S/Z, trans. Richard Miller (Oxford: Blackwell, 1990), p. 17.

10. Bill Nichols, 'Questions of Magnitude', in John Corner (ed.), Documentary and the Mass Media (London: Edward Arnold, 1986), p. 114.

11. Tzyetan Todorov, Introduction to Poetics (Minneapolis: University of Minnesota Press, 1981), pp. 41–5.

12. In the endless debate about Flaherty's 'reconstruction' of a romanticised Inuit past, this essentially improbable plot point – celebrating the arrival of the Arctic winter by taking a trip – is overlooked. Formulated in this way, the plot of Nanook seems somewhat unlikely, but this is indeed what Flaherty explicitly tells us is happening. In its way, though, the taking of the trip is no more unlikely than the fact that the Arctic winter does not apparently alter the light conditions. Winter comes but not the Arctic dark – for obvious reasons. Of course, substituting another title for 'Winter ...' would solve these problems.

13. Barthes, S/Z, p. 18.

14. Ibid., p. 158.

15. William Guynn, A Cinema of Nonfiction (Rutherford, NJ: Fairleigh Dickinson [Associated Universities] Press, 1990), pp. 50–1.

16. Eileen Bowser, History of the American Cinema: The Transformation of Cinema, 1907–1915 (New York: Scribner's, 1990), p. 257.

17. Charles Musser, History of the American Cinema: The Emergence of Cinema, The American Screen to 1907 (New York: Scribner's, 1990), p. 21.

18. Barthes, S/Z, pp. 105, 4, emphasis in original.

19. William Uricchio, 'Object and Evocation: The City Film and Its Reformulation by the American Avant-Garde (1900–1931)', unpublished paper given at the Society of Cinema Studies, Montreal, 1987.

20. Vlada Petric, Contructivism in Film: The Man with a Movie Camera (Cambridge: Cambridge University Press, 1987), p. 73.

21. Grierson grudgingly admitted to Sussex that Jennings was a minor poet (Elizabeth Sussex), The Rise and Fall of British Documentary [Berkeley, CA: University of California Press, 1975], p. 110). The documentary movement really did not like Jennings. Grierson became characteristically opaque when commenting further on him: 'Jennings was a very stilted person. ... He hasn't got this inner feeling for movement that Basil Wright has. ... The word is that he didn't have a sense of smell' (ibid., p. 110). Whatever this might mean, one thing is certain: Jennings really was a published poet, albeit posthumously. It can be added that Jennings reciprocated the animosity. In a letter he could refer to 'Rotha and other of Grierson's little boys' (Mary-Lou Jennings [ed.], Humphrey Jennings: Filmmaker, Painter, Poet [London: BFI, 1982], p. 27).

22. Alan Lovell and Jim Hillier, Studies in Documentary (New York: Viking, 1972), p. 89; Bjorn Sorenssen, 'The Documentary Aesthetics of Humphrey Jennings', in John Corner (ed.), Documentary and the Mass Media (London: Edward Arnold, 1986), p. 57.

23. Dai Vaughan, Portrait of An Invisible Man: The Working Life of Stewart McAllister, Film Editor (London: BFI, 1983), p. 89; Sorenssen, 'The Documentary Aesthetics of Humphrey Jennings', p. 57.

24. Jennings, Humphrey Jennings, p. 30.

25. Vaughan, Portrait of An Invisible Man, p. 85.

26. Chatman, Coming to Terms, p. 9.

27. Guynn, A Cinema of Nonfiction, pp. 76–7.

28. Ibid.

29. Jennings, Humphrey Jennings, p. 30.

30. Ibid., p. 26.

31. Lovell and Hillier, Studies in Documentary, p. 84.

32. Sussex, The Rise and Fall of British Documentary, p. 117.

33. Geoffrey Nowell-Smith, 'Humphrey Jennings: Surrealist Observer', in Charles Barr (ed.), All Our Yesterdays: Ninety Years of British Cinema (London: BFI, 1986), p. 320; Lovell and Hillier, Studies in Documentary, p. 85.

34. David Bordwell and Kristin Thompson, Film Art (New York: McGraw-Hill, 2004), p. 123.

35. Guynn, A Cinema of Nonfiction, p. 70.

36. Benjamin Hampton, A History of the Movies (New York: Dover, 1970 [1931]), p. 422. [Originally: A History of the American Film Industry: From its Beginnings to 1931 (New York: Covicim Friede).]

37. Christian Metz, Film Language: A Semiotics of Cinema (New York: Oxford University Press, 1974), pp. 94, 194.

38. This is claimed not to be an absolute necessity for a documentary, for example, by Dudley Andrew in Concepts in Film Theory (New York: Oxford University Press, 1984), p. 45. The film Dudley Andrew is discussing is Babet Schroeder's biographical documentary General Idi Amin Dada (1975). Andrew suggests that Schroeder was 'under little compunction to achieve formal closure' because it was not only a documentary but also a biography of a living subject. But first-person narratives, eye-witness accounts (which begin in the European tradition with Odysseus's story – significantly – of his journey, told to the Phaeacians), always had this problem. Such personal stories, which came to include both Dante's Commedia and Cellini's Vita, nevertheless become 'the natural form of the mimetic narrative' (Robert Scholes and Robert Kellogg, The Nature of Narrative [New York: Oxford University Press, 1966], pp. 73 and 250). As such, they are certainly capable of achieving formal closure; so much so that even the in medias res last words of Cellini ('da poi me n'andai a Pisa'/'and then I went to Pisa') work as a Barthesian 'final stroke' (Barthes, S/Z, p. 188). I cite this observation of Andrew's as an example of how, en passant,

documentary narrative difference is (almost) taken as read by film scholars.

39. Branigan, *Narrative Comprehension and Film*, p. 98.

40. Barthes, *S/Z*, p. 17.

41. Meir Sternberg, 'Universals of Narrative and their Cognitivist Fortunes (1)', *Poetics Today* vol. 24 no. 2, 2003, p. 28.

42. Monika Fludernik, *Towards a 'Natural' Narratology* (London: Routledge, 1996), p. 19.

43. John Lucaites and Celeste Condit, 'Re-constructing Narrative Theory: A Functional Perspective', *Journal of Communications* vol. 35 no. 4, Autumn 1985, p. 90.

44. Bill Nichols, *Representing Reality: Issues and Concepts in Documentary* (Bloomington: Indiana University Press, 1991), p. 107.

45. Vaughan, *Portrait of An Invisible Man*, p. 75.

46. Guynn, *A Cinema of Nonfiction*, p. 154. In general, Guynn offers an application of Metz's syntagmatic system to a variety of documentaries. This allows him to make an argument (ibid., p. 48) as to how many narrative, as opposed to non-narrative, syntagmas are present in a variety of classic documentaries. The persuasiveness of this obviously depends on the degree to which one is persuaded in the first place by the efficacy of Metz's approach.

1.10 'The Dance of Documentary Ethics'

PRATAP RUGHANI

The last of the three central issues in documentary is the question of ethics: the ethics of filming subjects who are not professional actors – an ethic of production; and the ethics of presenting the results to an audience as something other than fiction – an ethic of reception. Although the documentary has long been questioned on the basis of its authenticity – its claim on the real – it is only in the current century that these issues have been seriously addressed by scholars and practitioners as a – if not 'the' – central issue in documentary film.

It used to take a row or a lawsuit to flush out questions of documentary ethics. All of that has changed. Today, UK media ethics are regularly the nation's leading story as, for example, the Leveson-inspired legislation[1] proposes legal responses to eradicate the corrupted relationships of police and politicians with swathes of the mass media, especially the Murdoch press. Parallel questions are unravelling in the USA and elsewhere. A new settlement is needed, if large parts of the media are to recover a way of talking about ethics without being laughed out of the room.

For documentary, what do 'ethics' mean? Ethics flow from principles such as accuracy or honest dealing with contributors. Yet such principles unfold within a context, configured by the shifting mores and morality of a culture and influenced by the economics and politics of production. They interweave personal and institutional responses which create the 'soil' in which documentary culture grows. Documentary practices range from film to writing; sound to still images with important differences in medium and discipline. Documentary film is an event unfolding in time. Narrative or sequencing is central to it, whereas the viewing duration of a still documentary image is consciously chosen by the viewer. Although the focus here is on documentary film, it is valuable to draw on abiding experiences in documentarists' encounters with their subjects' lives in photography. While these are distinct (though parallel) traditions, their preoccupations are too often separated and there is much to be gained in sharing insights that emerge from common challenges in each form of documentary practice.

The first half of this chapter explores examples of ethical pressures on documentary practitioners and how some respond. All creative documentary work must also navigate the tension between artistic ambition and the responsibilities that attend working with real lives. To bring this into focus, the second half of the chapter asks how artists working in documentary modes serve the gods of free expression. Following a different trajectory into documentary practice, what do artists' insights reveal about the culture of documentary, especially in work that reflects on TV documentary? As Reality TV evolves into 'structured reality' and both absorb resources traditionally spent on documentary, is there a point at which 'actuality' is so confected that the idea of documentary observing rather than inventing life no longer makes sense?[2]

Choices of what and where to shoot, whose stories to tell and how they are conceived, framed, directed and edited, embody ethical decisions for the chameleon documentarist, often striving to please disparate constituencies, from contributors to commissioners, in order to construct the film. Selection of angle, light, subject, questions asked and length of shot sustained deliver meaning and therefore imply judgment. Why *this* shot? What is being said? In whose interests? Ethics are central. Is there a place in documentary innocent of filming choices? Their implications unfold, whether we are alive to them or not – as makers, subjects or audiences. Far from being an added extra, documentary's principal questions of whose story signifies what to whom – whose 'truth' to privilege – are more urgent now in a new century for the documentary as its forms become mobile, interactive and online, alongside their linear ancestors in television and cinema.

UK law marks out a working arena, protecting a broad notion of free speech at the same time as excluding hate-speech or requiring due care to vulnerable people. These laws are codified by the regulator Ofcom in its Broadcasting Code[3] and applied within the culture of particular organisations as with the BBC's editorial guidelines[4] or the National Union of Journalist's (NUJ's) twelve principles in its Code of Conduct.[5] Roughly speaking, the government requires regulators to observe these in broadcast contexts, though they are regularly flouted in the tabloid press where practices can be light-years away from the

NUJ's code. Key themes include: avoiding plagiarism; providing a non-partisan culture in the coverage of politics; privacy; harm and offence (including nudity, sex and violence); fairness and consent; protection for children and minors; conflicts of interest; accountability; commercial interests; religion and terrorism. These legal frameworks are explored in detail in industry judgments and case law.[6] There are strict rules for covert or secret filming (a kind of theft) and compliance with this is 'a big deal'.[7]

For some practitioners, ethics are rarely made conscious, surfacing periodically as an annoying constraint served up by high-minded people, remote from the realities of filming. For others, the opposite is the case and their work is marked by an openness to reframe and a sensibility to see the dangers and limits of what the camera can do, alongside its many opportunities.

Which individual human judgments enable documentary-makers get the killer interview, and at what cost? In the trade-off of the documentary encounter, a contributor's pain can be a documentarist's opportunity. This chapter explores such tensions in order to distil questions which can help point towards a relational frame for the ethics of documentary-making.

Discussion of personal ethics is attractive to humanist readings of the world because it insists on the individual's decisions, role and conscience. Some examples here draw on documentary practices during the Third Reich, an extreme that made individual ethical choices horribly clear. Didn't Nazi propaganda rely on individuals, such as the notoriously celebrated director Leni Riefenstahl, with her *Triumph of the Will* (1935), to create a climate where train drivers delivered the demonised to concentration camps? What if more had refused? Yet to over-focus on the individual risks losing sight of the *structuring* dynamics of politics, institution and culture in delimiting what's possible. If the surrounding culture legitimises hatred, deception or routine invasions of privacy, then the individual documentarist's decisions are lost to all but those with courage and a higher moral compass, whatever the public rhetoric of documentary principles.

The choices and connections of individual documentarists in their portrayal of subjects dovetails with the values and power relations inscribed by institutions or commissioners in much documentary work. Such parameters are typically naturalised into 'how documentaries are'. Cultural and institutional ethics (or lack of them) configure much of what most documentarists do and don't do. This is easier to see in totalitarian societies, harder to own in liberal democracies where cultural pressures to deliver narrative styles are often internalised by documentarists, demanded by commissioners and rarely made visible in industry codes or law.

Occasionally, documentarists reflect on tensions and competing impulses in their thinking and emotional responses and how these shape a film. The moments when ethics become visible are valuable in revealing the partial and constructed nature of the work even when a 'seamless' illusion is sought. This could be a moment of reflexive honesty where a practitioner questions what's expected, or refuses to do what's expected even when under pressure from investors or commissioners for 'the money shot' that might exploit a subject. Some, like Morgan Spurlock in *The Greatest Movie Ever Sold* (2011), surface with a documentary where the story becomes the very struggle to navigate industry and commercial pressures.

Ethical questions can address the practitioner holistically – in mind, body and spirit – and touch the ground of a bigger philosophical enquiry. What, after all, is documentary for? Responses to this are as plural as documentaries themselves. Underlying them all is an ambition to communicate something significant in the world to others. In philosophical terms an ambitious vision for human communication was given by the European philosopher Emmanuel Lévinas. Having survived Nazi occupation in France, Lévinas mapped out a radical view of human connectedness, insisting on *relational* ethics. He rejects much in western philosophy and asks us to pay close and deep attention to the person before us – to look into the face of the Other. Lévinas insists on considering the Other first, that is to say that our first duty is an ethical one of realising our relatedness. For Lévinas, this is ethics as first philosophy, the primary responsibility, which implies questions for makers and audiences alike, which this chapter works towards.[8]

DOCUMENTARY PRODUCTION

UK broadcast documentaries mostly live in a regulatory environment, where a culture of recognising some responsibilities to contributors is normal, though by turns strained. Many broadcasters work within a liberal model of 'balanced opinion' across output, aspiring to give 'fair representation' to most views. This notion of balance is attacked (from many perspectives) for excluding significant voices from debate while claiming to define the spectrum of opinion. For some in TV, the test of 'balance' is whether attacks from different sides are about even, as though alienation of many is proof of occupying a putative 'centre ground' in the argument.

A dominant aesthetic of 'balance' is naturalism. Documentary sequences for TV are typically shot and edited in a flow of imagery to advance a story and conceal aspects of the production process. Commentary typically straps it together, directing attention at a chosen meaning, often settled at the commissioning stage, long before the first frame is shot.

Much of this effaces the journey of a documentary, from idea through research, commissioning, filming and editing to upload or broadcast. As the tools of documentary production democratise – at least for those on the wealthy side of the digital divide – the ethics of documentary-making have never been more central – or more contested. Even when hidden or un-considered by the maker, choices can become discernable in the film itself by close reading, or even by watching 'against the grain' of the maker's intention. In this way, the maker is at least partly revealed along with her or his subjects.

Documentary ethics turn on at least two axes: (1) the documentarist's relationship to subjects in the film and (2) relationship to the audience. The key word with each is *responsibility*, a term handled gingerly and often avoided in the world of documentary artists' film. For artists' documentary (discussed later) the primacy of the individual's artistic freedom – or at least not being bound by convention – can be in tension with responsibilities to the subject.

At the same time, the relationship between filmer[9] and filmed is being recast as camera, editing and upload tools become standard software on smart phones. These tools are quickly naturalised in the hands of generations used to being both (wo)man with the phone camera and the filmed. Rushes or rough edits are quickly uploaded to filtered or open distribution networks, where intimate aspects of life are staple performances on social media. Increasingly, people experience themselves as filmer, filmed and viewer, creating a new and lived familiarity with key stages of the documentary process. This step-change brings UK culture further in line with the USA, where saturation of TV and media production means that contributors often know what they seek to achieve in their encounter with the documentary camera, as performance or portrayal.

CONSENT

Broadcast documentaries regulate their relationships with contributors by acquiring release or consent forms from people, who typically sign over rights to the use of the rushes for the project 'in all media in any territory in perpetuity'. This blanket agreement leaves the contributor taking a step in good faith that the filmers will deal honestly with the rushes in a way that fits the explanation of the project to them. The notion of informed consent derives from the Nuremberg protocols, but their application in documentary contexts would be hugely problematic and such a crude instrument that much laudable documentary work would also be snuffed out.[10] In documentary contexts, makers need to explain carefully to subjects what their involvement means, if subjects are to understand how the documentary process works and how it differs from social media. Consent forms give institutions a way of regulating the filming relationship with contributors even if the results of their appearance cannot be predicted.

For Fred Wiseman and others in the Direct Cinema movement, consent is assumed through the filming process, often through negotiation with institutions rather than individuals filmed. Wiseman feels free to use all material shot unless the person filmed objects *at the time*.[11] Direct Cinema was a sensation for documentary in the 1960s. It saw itself as (and appeared) less constructed than the narrative-driven staples of Griersonian documentary and documentary steered by voiceover. Direct Cinema's strong feeling of 'unmediated' actuality was a significant development aesthetically, leading to new ethical claims for a 'cinema of truth'.

At key moments, however, the illusion of access behind closed doors turned out to be overblown, even a mirage.[12] Today such claims sound disingenuous even when access appears to be open. Viewers now, familiar with the insights of observation, question not just the treatment but also the consent of participants in landmark Direct Cinema works such as Wiseman's *Titicut Follies* (1967), shot in the Bridgewater, Massachusetts, state institution for the 'criminally insane'. Here, the nature of what is being filmed and the conditions of inmates mean that it is hard for a subject to give informed consent. Anderson and Benson argue that this catches the documentarist between a rock and a hard place: 'without informed consent of the subjects the form lacks ethical integrity; without freedom for the film maker, it lacks artistic integrity'.[13]

A film-maker may observe the letter of the law by, for example, producing a consent form signed by a contributor, but how that contributor is handled and what s/he understands by their involvement is key. Conversely, in the crucible of documentary exploration, where there is no guarantee that a contributor may not change their mind about involvement, a consent form at least shows that some kind of agreement existed at one point. Ethics cannot be fully captured in legal and industry codes. Codes provide some legal context but a broader conception is needed to consider documentary ideals and potential for exploitation.

The emphasis in debates on documentary ethics is typically on the responsibilities of documentarists to people in their films, but, as Henry Joost and Ariel Schulman find in *Catfish* (2010), this can cut both ways. In *Catfish*, actor Nev Schulman decides to meet his Facebook fantasy Megan. Megan is exposed as an avatar and when flirtation turns to the prospect of meeting she evades Nev. He pursues her with each step filmed by his brother Ariel and friend Henry. On the path to an eventual meeting, each seek to manipulate the other to such a degree that the documentary becomes an exploration of the fantasies of both subjects *and* film-makers in an age of virtually constructed personae. From a Facebook profile, Megan becomes a complex flesh-and-blood painter called Angela.

At the moment of their eventual meeting, which seals the film with a live encounter, Angela's lies and the documentarists' drive to nail a story, place two sets of needs stage-centre. Who is exploiting whom more in *Catfish* has troubled audiences[14] and this debate embodies the frustrated search for 'truth' amid the performances of Angela and film-makers (with acting credits) who pursue their quarry with an eye on how their deception delivers a useful sequence. Judging Angela and the film-makers' ethics in their deceptions as well as their more honest moments depends on how you read their motives. Some (following Deleuze) find an ethic in deliberate falsification in order to examine and reveal layers of understandings.[15]

This takes ethical codes from abstract principle into the individual film-maker's mind and heart. The path to getting there in *Catfish* creates a tension between what the filmers say are their motives and what some audiences think they smell and see unfolding on screen: something much stranger. Increased familiarity with filming choices and an enduring fascination with the filming process makes the filmers' tracks more visible. Responses to *Catfish*'s ethics turn on whether audiences read the film-makers as dealing straight with their main subject, especially when her ability to be anything but straight with Nev becomes the story-line.

How to weigh these nuances is the very texture of ethical enquiry. Shades of meaning and response are drawn through delicate relationships where what the *documentarist* represents to contributors is increasingly explored – a mirror to the more familiar dynamic of the documentarist choosing who s/he will film. The documentarist seeks genuine responses to advance a story, selecting what to reveal and structuring when this happens in order to tell that

story. How these choices are made and justified is shaped by which gods the documentarist serves – and there are many.

DOCUMENTARY MODES AND SITUATIONAL ETHICS

The flourish of a camera-magician's hand cranked 1890s life into actuality, leaving us film-documents like *Roundhay Garden Scene* (1888) and, more famously, *La Sortie de l'Usine Lumière à Lyon* [*Workers Leaving the Lumière Factory in Lyon*] or the *L'arrivée d'un train en gare de la Ciotat* [*Arrival of a Train at La Ciotat Station*] (both 1895). This iconic footage embodied (and anticipated) abiding tensions for the development of documentary as a factual record *and* as an emerging art practice. The documentarist (as Barnouw observes) quickly started appearing in many guises – as prophet, explorer, reporter, painter, advocate, bugler, prosecutor, poet, chronicler, observer, catalyst and even guerrilla.[16]

These figures work in different documentary modes,[17] described by Bill Nichols as expository; observational; participatory or interactive; reflexive; performative; poetic. Each form implies a singular approach to documentary, depending on the genre or style it cherishes. Its practitioners emerge from distinct subcultures and their room for expression or manoeuvre is shaped substantially by the commissioning and economic structures in which their films are cut. The ethical norms and instincts of the maker are contextually shaped and lead to different gut (and institutional) responses. A couple of examples illustrate this:

- No respectable current affairs or investigative documentary would consider giving contributors editorial rights, in part to protect the project's putative impartiality. In collaborative documentary, by contrast, many practitioners find it unthinkable to show a film without the explicit approval of a fine cut by key contributors.
- If an investigative documentary has an approved public interest case for pursuing its quarry – typically, exposing the corrupt and powerful – then the human effects on those exposed by it are not a concern. In other documentary contexts the opposite is more often the case: the effects on the individual are central in weighing up the purpose of a project and arriving at an ethic of how contributors are handled. The public interest is absolutely not a licence to pursue anything about which some may be curious, but is a way of testing probity rather than indulging prurience.

Casually filming beggars, impoverished or vulnerable people and most kinds of violence all need a carefully considered rationale that serves a bigger context – for example, in exploring an issue or story which is necessarily

Catfish (2010): responses to *Catfish*'s ethics turn on whether audiences read the film-makers as dealing straight with their main subject

informed by such sequences. In these circumstances special attention should be given to the experiences of contributors as *people*, not just as cyphers for a filmer to make a point. As the film moves from an assembly edit to a rough cut, storytelling dynamics take over. As João Moreira Salles puts it, the pressure here is that the director submits to a tyranny of narrativisation: 'After a few weeks in the editing room, the director too becomes hostage to the film. The theme imposes its priorities, and the structure leads the narrative along paths that allow no diversions.'[18]

DOCUMENTARY JOURNALISM'S PARTISAN STRENGTH

Documentary journalism in the broadcast sector speaks less of 'objectivity' (conceptually flawed and increasingly impossible to defend) and more of the aspiration to 'impartiality'.

This framework, rooted in current affairs, does not map easily onto authored documentaries, which largely fall outside the news arena and are more analogous to features, editorial or artistic expression. Three of the world's top-ten grossing documentaries, *Bowling for Columbine* (2000, USA), *Fahrenheit 9/11* (2004, USA) and *Sicko* (2007, USA) are works by Michael Moore, who films from a clear anti-establishment, activist stance where status quo positions appear (or are) ridiculous.

The story structure of Moore's breakthrough documentary, *Roger and Me* (1989), follows his hapless search to interview Roger B. Smith, former CEO and President of General Motors, about the exploitation of workers and the social cost of GM's collapse in Flint, Michigan. The conceit of seeking Roger Smith shows Moore's determination to follow the journalistic priority of interviewing the other side. Here, the search for the interview follows journalistic norms only to ambush them and reveal something other than the ritual TV interviewer/interviewee encounter. This approach bears an implied critique of 'impartiality' as it stakes out a new centrality for marginalised voices – figures whose perspectives would be more fully engaged if self-described 'impartial' networks were to cover a fuller range of perspectives. Campaigns against Moore focus on factual inaccuracies to discredit the larger project, but these typically miss the point of authored performances in documentary, which are designed to get at a partisan truth, rather than conform to a fantasy of 'objectivity'. Moore's vision was to expose the ruthlessness of GM's corporate governance with the simple device of repeatedly being refused a chance to ask Roger his questions. Controversy attends some of Moore's methods, just as it does the practices of much mainstream media; the difference here is that Moore's sleights of hand are anti-establishment and his personae include the bumbling innocent, looking for answers rarely pursued in the fleeting attention span of most mainstream journalism.

Nick Broomfield, likewise, plays innocent while laying traps to great effect in *The Leader, His Driver and the Driver's Wife* (1991, UK). Broomfield successfully annoys Eugène Terre'Blanche, leader of the Afrikaner white separatist AWB Party, with the simple ruse of being late and, thus, manipulates him into letting his mask slip. In a chilling interview, Terre'Blanche's threat of violence is clear, a point in the film from which he cannot recover.

The rise of Moore and Broomfield's personae in documentary produced landmark sequences, confected to reveal another story. Their power comes from the ability to create surreal actuality from unfolding events, such as Moore's visit to the North Country Bank in *Bowling for Columbine*. Moore sees an ad offering a hunting rifle as a promotion for opening an account and decides to follow up. Moore ends the sequence where he successfully opens an account with a killer question to bank staff 'Do you think it's a little dangerous handing out guns in a bank?' He makes an emotive case that specifies the madness he seeks to expose in an America still bewitched by guns in the wake of the high school massacre in Columbine, near Denver, Colorado.

The attraction and impact of this kind of authored documentary is the unfolding of a particular perspective, from a specific point of view, becoming filmic precisely through the craft of editing sound and image to heighten and distil the viewer's experience of a single argument. Many would be neutered, bleached of colour and become unwatchable (or unmakeable) if hamstrung by an idea of impartiality.

PERSUASION AND PROPAGANDA

Audiences understand that a closely argued, persuasive point of view is part of the attraction of what documentary can do so well. Crossing a line into 'propaganda' is a litmus test by which notions of persuasion shade into accusations of making ideologically bound work, impervious to counter-argument or the complexities of life. A key feature of this zone is whether opposing facts and perspectives are ignored or misrepresented.

Leni Riefenstahl, Hitler's favourite film-maker, went to her grave insisting that her two-hour long hymn to Hitler, *Triumph des Willens* [*Triumph of the Will*] (1934), was not a political work even as she polished her memories of creating the visual ur-text of Nazi ideology. Her complicity was clear as she choreographs aspects of the Nazi rally featured in the film. Her tenacious protestations of ignorance helped her when on trial but are simply absurd. Wide shots of the parade ground reveal cutting-edge filming platforms built into its structure, thus intervening to create the event even as she recorded it. Speaking of a sequence featuring Hitler's appeal to a mythic national 'race', Riefenstahl says: 'I was not concerned with what he [Hitler] was saying. He could have been talking about vegetables or fruit.'[19] But he wasn't – he was addressing the aftermath of the purging of the SA in the 'Night of the Long Knives'. Despite her denials, it is barely credible that she knew as little as she claimed. Virtually every synch word in the film addressed the same issue.

Riefenstahl thus failed to answer the core ethical (and in her case political) concern of documentary: what power does a film-maker have to promote either a progressive culture of connection, or one that points in the opposite direction, towards hatred and violence?

It's only possible to 'appreciate' Riefenstahl's 'genius' for location shooting and for evolving a grammar of film if audiences overlook other contemporaries and separate form from content; text from context; ethics from aesthetics; film from politics – as Hitler recommended – and international critics agreed, when showering awards on *Olympia* (1936), her film of the Berlin Olympics.

For many viewers, seeing one's preferred ideas or opinions presented approvingly on screen often means approval for the film-maker. But is there not a deeper responsibility for both makers and audiences to challenge their preferred perspectives, honestly engaging with counter-arguments? In fact, should they not try to obtain greater understanding even as they are in the process of coming to a conclusion? The documentarist – like the dramatist – seeks to take challenges seriously and hold these within a bigger picture of thinking and making: to be open to cross-currents within a situation or perspective. The success or even integrity of a documentary turns on this ability to notice counter-point and generate insights into the situation through the filming experience. This is the ethical core of what might be called 'open'[20] documentary, a hallmark of which is some openness to how life is inevitably 'other' than apriori views (even views that secure commissions). As Errol Morris emphasises 'never go in with a fixed agenda because otherwise you learn nothing'.[21]

Context influences the way a documentary is judged. Al Gore's Oscar-winning environmental film *An Inconvenient Truth* (2006, USA) argues a compelling case for recognising the human role in climate change and global warming. It was fêted and its success led to the UK parliament's ordering its distribution to schools. In 2007, a case was brought by an activist of the neo-liberal New Party to stop the film's school distribution. The High Court ruled that the film could still be shown but only with nine 'inaccuracies' corrected through guidance notes.[22] Despite widespread international acclaim on broadcast and theatrical release, it was not deemed fit to show in schools without correction.

PRACTITIONER JUDGMENTS

Peter Kosminsky is widely regarded for work that unpacks the human dimension of crises in British culture and politics, in extensively researched docudramas and dramas like *Warriors* (1999), *Britz* (2007) and *The Promise* (2011). His earlier documentary work includes *Afghantsi* (1988, UK), an account of the Soviet army during its withdrawal from Afghanistan – an invasion that cost more than a million lives.

Afghantsi unfolds with the Soviet Empire on the brink of collapse. Kosminsky interviewed a senior army officer who voiced doubts about the war that eventually cost him his job. Kosminsky knew that the officer's indiscretion was a gift for the film, providing the perfect ballast for the high emotion of its closing sequences. But should he have worried that what was good for the film might have been bad for the contributor? 'You must think it through,' Kosminsky says. 'They were well aware of the risks they were taking. It would be patronising and insulting not to edit it in [in a way that respected their risk].'[23] Neither filmer nor filmed can fully know how the path will unravel when the film is shown, but it was clear to Kosminsky that a senior army figure would not make the decision to blow the whistle without calibrating the risk.

Sometimes the ethics are less clear. In *Afghantsi*, Kosminsky interviews a distraught Soviet soldier's mum, Nina Penchukova, as she tries to fight back tears at the thought of the danger her son faces. Kosminsky had filmed with her conscripted son, Valodya, on operations in Afghanistan and is party to a crucial piece of information that his mother does not yet know: that her son's tour of duty in Afghanistan is to be extended. Breaking this news to her on camera could advance very nicely the exploration that *Afghantsi* seeks to follow in the human cost of a futile war. Her face might reveal heart-felt emotion. Such interviews are the life-blood of documentary. Or he could have chosen not to tell her, knowing how much she worried about her son already.

Working with a Russian journalist (who translated), Kosminsky agreed a third approach: to tell Nina off camera and then ask whether she would continue the interview with a response to the news. This was less invasive than telling her on camera and filming her shock, however much that might capture a heightened response. The strategy worked. Nina was shocked and upset but agreed to speak. For audiences, the film includes a moving (and tearful) reflection on the human trauma of war for an occupying army, juxtaposed with the funeral of a soldier killed on duty.

The filming team had faced dangers in Afghanistan that drew them closer together, but for the recordist, it was a manipulation too far. Kosminsky says,

> After we wrapped the interview, the recordist – with whom I'd worked for many years – had me up against the wall. He was furious I'd told Mrs Penchukova her son would be staying on in Afghanistan. He thought I was totally out of order.

This section of the interview with Nina undoubtedly heightened the emotional pitch of the film, but on reflection Kosminsky describes himself as unsure about whether he did the right thing. It's easier to raise such doubts after one has shot the sensitive material, but is such a lack of clarity intrinsic to documentary film-making? Experienced practitioners know the challenges of weighing up the different needs of contributors, broadcasters, narratives, audiences and production teams. There are contradictory impulses too in the vision and vanities of contributors, seeking out or acquiescing in the attentions of a documentary film crew in their lives. Documentarists blend sensitivity and reflection with a relentless desire to probe, whether through an observing presence or direct questioning. Their challenge is to refine an ethical sensibility while pursuing a story, to know when to keep pushing and when to step back with good grace as necessary, even if it means losing a compelling sequence. As in life, making such judgments can be a close call, to be weighed in the context of relationships with people in the film.

Practitioners navigate this responsibility variously. Some insist on the supremacy of the freedom to narrate and create, insisting that this is the defining ethic. Others offer a more participatory model, including offering participants a right to withdraw. Trinh T. Minh-ha describes her own emphasis as restoring proximity of the subject:

> In the context of power relations, speaking for, about, and on behalf of is very different from speaking with and nearby ... Making a film that shows and speaks with the subject of your enquiry as if they are listening and looking next to you would shift subtly but radically your mode of address, of framing and contextualizing ... what has to be given up first and foremost is the voice of omniscient knowledge.[24]

Some collaborative documentarists go further, sharing the power to create stories from contributors' lives, sharing copyright and emphasising a right to withdraw from the documentary, as in the case of the Prisons Memory Archive, developed by Cahal McLaughlin and team.[25] This takes the notion of consent beyond the filming moment and its bureaucratic proof in consent forms to something mutually navigated and profoundly relational. The filmer would not want to proceed without dialogue and understanding, out of which the film and its mode of exhibition could emerge. This approach takes time and attention – far more research time than is typically invested in broadcast projects – in order to build confidence, through which deeper levels of trust and fuller stories can surface.

DOCUMENTARIST OR ARTIST?

The embrace of documentary modes by key artists and the migration of documentary practice to gallery spaces is opening a fertile period of new hybridity in the relationship of documentary to art. With it, comes a new phase in the relationship of ethics and aesthetics and what this means for the maker's responsibility.[26]

Many documentary-makers are wary or even nervous of describing themselves as artists, preferring to stay closer to the resonance of grittier social realities that 'documentary' more often signals. This wariness of many documentary-makers is instructive, since the techniques of framing and aesthetic convention can be just as considered or even mannered in documentary forms as any 'fine art' practice.

The compliment, however, is returned as many artists currently working in documentary modes are reluctant to call themselves 'documentary-makers', cautious perhaps that such a category may problematise the primacy of the individual's artistic freedom, his or her authorial voice and the pre-eminence of subjectivity and aesthetic considerations before social ones.

This tussle over language – artist or documentarist? – is crucial as it offers a key to the structural tensions between two clans. John Ellis argues that: 'The discovery and communication of *truth* is what motivates a documentary maker, and the desire to make something new comes as a consequence of it.' For artists, he says, it's the other way around.[27]

Whatever they call themselves, the division between 'documentary-maker' and 'artist' is eroding. It was never sealed in the first place. Early creative practitioners, from Jean Painlevé to Dziga Vertov or Alberto Cavalcanti, leave bodies of work that inhabit both spaces, through a sense of wonder, constructivism and by turns surreal and expressionist influences, respectively. The exploration of documentary modes by artists continues in festival and gallery contexts, adding a new frisson to the relationship of documentary and art worlds and reviving a structural tension between recording actuality and using it to serve an agenda or vision far distant from the consent of people whose images are the very texture of documentary film.[28]

LAND WITHOUT BREAD

In the extensive output of documentary film history it is rare to find documentary films featuring people with physical or neurological disability. An early exception is *Land Without Bread* (1932, Spain) – also known as *Las Hurdes* or *Terre sans Pain*[29] – the only documentary work of celebrated surrealist film-maker Luis Buñuel. The film takes the form of an ethnographic travelogue to the impoverished villages of Spain's High Hurdes and its late sequences feature a number of people with mental disabilities or neurological disorders.

Land Without Bread's shocking alienation from key subjects described as 'village idiots' invites some to locate a 'sardonic'[30] tone or even a surreal undermining of documentary convention, especially of the authoritative commentary voice, arguing that its crassness exposes the pomposity of what was later called documentary's 'voice of God'.[31]

The film announces the putative poverty, disease and passivity of the area: 'In the High Hurdes midgets and idiots abound ... Generally they look after the goats. ... Some are dangerous.' This increasingly hostile tone is accompanied by shots calculated to distance audiences from any counter-intuitive empathy with those dubbed as 'idiots'. Catherine Russell describes Land Without Bread as 'shocking for its profound lack of sympathy', and that its 'formal playfulness is inappropriate to its subject of lived poverty'.[32] Surrealists' interest in non-rational and irrational associations of mind intertwine with a fascination in people with complex neurological conditions. This preoccupation makes it all the more important that the ethics of such encounters are thought through, especially in agreeing with subjects how actuality featuring them is shot and used.

Can the artist's creative ambition trump ethical questions? Even in its own terms, does Land Without Bread's ridicule or contempt succeed in undermining the documentary travelogue form itself? Can it not be argued that the documentary subject is a rich place to push the limits of alienation? To sustain a reading of this work as successfully undercutting documentary conventions that were not yet crystallised, it would need to do more than rehearse commonplace prejudices against the excluded, marginalised or derided. Audiences in many societies were already largely alienated from most people with advanced neurological disorders. Do these sequences do more than simply reinforce such alienation? The film claims many revelatory moments, like capturing the chance fall of a goat from a high mountain. Can this be read as a surrealist's intervention in travelogue or another example of documentary's routine deceptions in many modes? Trims of this shot, reveal Buñuel himself shooting the goat in order to dramatise the sequence,[33] a technique also used by some wildlife film-makers of the period.

Though banned by left- and right-wing authorities, Land Without Bread may be more shocking to us now in its handling of disabled people. Ramón Gieling, in his film Buñuel's Prisoners (2000, the Netherlands), visits the region, gathering testimony of Buñuel's inventions, manipulation and unreliability. A more surreal project of this time – more shocking to convention – might have been an attempt to cultivate some sort of rapport and dare to empathise with how this land without bread looked to the so-called 'idiots': to cultivate empathy with people we can only glimpse, from the long end of the lens, and never hear from.

Unfortunately, examples of how hard it seemed for early documentarists to identify with the excluded are common and lack of empathy is more the norm, as in Martin and Osa Johnson's Congorilla, also released in 1932

(USA). Today these films tell us more about the film-maker's projections and the imperial culture of their times than they do about the putative subjects of these films, where marginalised or colonised peoples figure, at best, as objects of exoticism or romance, or, in the case of Land Without Bread, passing contempt. As such they become documents of Empire, either geographical as in the Congo or cultural, as the empire of the so-called able-bodied colonises and subordinates the putative experience of the disabled Other.

The figure of the 'cretin' is significant for Buñuel and it can be argued that by the time we see them in Land Without Bread, Buñuel has effectively undermined any authority that the (yet to be invented) form of travelogue documentary may have adduced. This may well be and there is much to admire in this work, but the use of people with neurological disorders or disabilities in this case is the opposite of 'relational' (in Lévinas's sense) as they only exist in Land Without Bread as cyphers for strangeness in an experimentation with documentary meaning. In this sense they function only as raw material for the documentary artist's making of meaning, not as people with their own sensibilities, let alone agency. It begs the question: why, in the history of documentary film, are so many Others routinely marginalised, excluded or subjected to what Lévinas describes as a 'totalising vision'[34] that is a subsuming gaze, enslaved by ego, incapable of truly meeting difference?[35]

If the primacy of artistic vision can be seen as de-politicising in its preoccupation with aesthetics and ethically troubling in the hands of some artists, the rigorous pursuit of a single vision has, paradoxically, been used by others to expose the limits of narrative documentary practice and shock audiences into new sights.

Some artists have turned to gallery spaces as a site to interrogate the ethics of documentary processes. For Phil Collins's Turner Prize exhibit The Return of The Real (2006), the often exploitative experience of appearing on Reality TV is related by former participants in a gallery video. The installation included a working TV production office, Shady Lane Productions, as researchers contact people to recount their experience. In this way, the invisibility of production ethics are revealed and interrogated, recasting the ethics of documentary production as an exhibit in its own right. The gallery offers a space to recover fidelity to contributors as subjects who talk back in a way disallowed by TV conventions.

Avant-garde artists have pushed at the boundaries of taboo in documentary practice, such as Stan Brakhage with his seminal work The Act of Seeing with One's Own Eyes (1972, USA). This work sustains the camera's gaze insistently on the human corpse, further dehumanised through autopsy (the literal meaning of which gives the film's title). Audiences were shocked into a kind of revulsion that questions prevailing attitudes to death.

At other moments, artists' interventions have had a pivotal political effect, recovering smothered histories and excluded experience. The achievements of *Handsworth Songs* (1986, UK), directed by John Akomfrah of Black Audio Collective, and *Territories* (1984, UK), directed by Isaac Julien of Sankofa, forced a nascent recovery of black British experience, implicating the stereotyped and derogatory fragments of what passed for recognition of black experience in mainstream British cultural life. With an interior gaze, Mona Hatoum's *Measures of Distance* (1998, UK) opened windows on unseen experience, turning on the axis of mother–daughter/migrant–memory which placed the subject and her subjectivity at the heart of the documentary. In each of these films, authors draw the work through their lived responses – not talking *about* objectified Others, but modelling their own experience, alongside the kind of talent and autonomy rarely acknowledged in broadcast documentary contexts.

Television today has long retreated from engagement with artists' film, after some proud moments that brought significant work to new generations. It is partly this retreat that has made the 'documentary turn', with its ethical and political edge in fine art spaces, all the more significant. Historically, there have been moments of crossover between artists' film and crevices in the UK broadcasting schedule. Similar flickers emerged on PBS in the USA, such as Marlon Riggs's *Tongues Untied* (1989), but Riggs's work – passionate, ground-breaking in form and politics – was vilified by the right and itself became a symbol of the 'culture wars'.

Documentary's lightning-rod relationship to life continues to draw practitioners to refashion our way of looking at actuality. Isaac Julien's nine-screen installation film *Ten Thousand Waves* (2010, UK) opens with thermal imaging actuality footage of Morecambe Bay, UK, where twenty-three migrant Chinese workers drowned when sent to pick cockles by gangmaster Lin Liang Ren. Here the raw records of this tragedy preface and anchor highly stylised sequences – of saturated colour and fictive beauty. Julien heightens the impact of the thermal imaging footage by combining it with audio of an emergency call from a woman who witnessed the events: 'It was a *bricolage* approach, to ignite a frisson between actuality and the constructed materials the incongruousness of the event and a fictional event. *Ten Thousand Waves* breached and sutured these elements together.'[36] Julien's installation weaves the view of an infra-red kino-eye in Morecombe Bay to open out onto succeeding screens which navigate other waters, leading back to the mother-culture of China and her filmic myths.

Amar Kanwar's *The Lightning Testimonies*, installed at *Documenta 12*, features interviews with survivors of sexual violence on the Indian subcontinent since Partition in 1947. Key ethical considerations include the challenge of how to document the unspeakable, how much to show of 'reality' yet honour the memory of people so dehumanised that such violence was possible. Representation of such violence is reshaped by cultural and political context, sometimes leading to a reckoning with the practitioner's own conscience, as with Magnum co-founder George Rodger's response to his photography in Bergen-Belsen.[37]

> I'd be talking to somebody, a prisoner there. It actually did happen. Cultured man. He was so happy to be liberated and he'd been a long time in the camp and in the middle of a sentence he suddenly fell down dead ... I actually photographed him. To my absolute horror I found I was getting the dead into photographic compositions to make good pictures and I thought 'My God, I'm getting as though this doesn't mean anything to me' and I couldn't accept this – such absolute horror really didn't affect me as much as it should. And so I decided then and there that I was going to quit. I'm not going to take another picture and I just felt it was the end for me. I couldn't take any more.[38]

Faced with such extremes, Rodger had the human decency to no longer combine an aesthetic response with an ethical one.

Away from such extremes, practitioners find ethics and aesthetics are woven fine into the structure of response. Can Vertov's *Man with a Movie Camera* (1929) separate its artistic and documentary impulses? It is *the* urtext to trouble industrial and academic distinctions, which try to delimit practices by cultural contexts such as 'gallery' or 'broadcast' sectors.

Whatever the trajectories of artists and documentary-makers in forming their practice, a central area obtains in the creation of work that generates five essential ethical questions. Rather than try to define a 'moral' code for documentary ethics, appropriate responses are more likely to emerge through close attention to these questions:

- Is there a problem if the potency of actuality becomes just another colour on the artist's palette?
- What is the maker's relationship and responsibility to subjects?
- How do contributors' thoughts, feelings and responses to their representation resolve in the making of the work?
- What rights and duties obtain as an art work circulates or becomes a documentary film in another sector – for example, for broadcast?
- When there is a tension between the author's artistic or editorial freedom and a subject's response to it, how is this resolved? That is, how much editorial control is offered or artistic independence taken in the passage of actuality to documentary art?

TRANSPARENCY

And what of the second axis: the documentarist's relation-ship to audience? Audiences expect film-makers to engage honestly with their subjects and to distil what they find. These are straightforward aspirations to visit on complex and often intractable controversies. Indeed, it is often the complexity and controversy of a situation that attracts documentary-makers. Audiences recognise that the trans-lation of a story or experience into a documentary film involves choices, so the key question for documentary becomes: what kind of manipulation is 'ethical'? The resulting film will have a perspective, but most expect that the route to this perspective has not gone beyond a thresh-old of manipulation (in a neutral sense) towards manipu-lation (in the pejorative sense of practising a deception). The fundamental bond endures: documentary audiences expect factually rooted work that aspires to exploration rather than propaganda.

A central ethical question thus becomes the trans-parency that film-makers show to audiences and from it the bond of trust that is nurtured. Trust is not now depend-ent on the rhetoric of neutrality (so often a mirage), but on being straightforward, or at least not misleading an audi-ence.

This is particularly important for access-based docu-mentaries, like documentaries filmed inside the military. The Channel 4 series *New Model Army*[39] (2000, UK), about the experiences of black and Asian soldiers in the British Army, opened with a sequence of shots and commentary revealing the presence of the military 'minders' who were incompetent enough to stray into shot. 'His is no token presence', the commentary says of an army project officer attached to the film crew. 'He is at our elbow at all times when we are on military premises, in the camp, on manoeuvres and even when we tried to give him the slip.'

Minders were sometimes joined by other officers during the filming of *New Model Army*, who stood within sight or even the direct eye-line of the interviewee, listen-ing and even staring intently as black soldiers talked about their experience of army life. At times, it was a near-comic attempt to intimidate, encourage soldiers to self-censor and to keep the documentary series on-message. Footage shot under such conditions is supplemented throughout by interviews and sequences where the Army has no con-trol, but revealing the conditions of access was essential so that audiences have a fair chance to judge for themselves the context of what they are seeing.

The legal principle *caveat emptor*, let the buyer beware, offers a useful caution to audiences – it's *our* own responsi-bility to look carefully before trusting anything we see. As Brian Winston writes, 'the central issue is where the point of balance lies between socially necessary controls and the demands of freedom'.[40]

The recent arrival of 'structured reality' programming offers the latest challenge to documentary notions of trust. Emerging from docusoap and Reality TV, 'structured reality' hones a story-line and sets out to deliver it. Daran Little, story producer on the first series of *The Only Way is Essex* (TOWIE) (2010–) and *Made in Chelsea* (2011–) says:

> They tell me what's going on in their own lives. They tell me things they want to do, or hope to do. I structure, scene by scene, what should happen in each episode to draw out the drama and the comedy. Then we schedule the scenes.[41]

Filming includes stopping scenes to direct the conversa-tion, encouraging dramatic revelations and a ruthless focus on characters' romantic lives. The shows don't so much follow events as lead them, confecting scenarios which strain credulity. Results are by turns so self-con-scious that it's hard to think that audiences would not wonder how much reality is left when the structure has defined so much of the show. TOWIE carries the following health warning (dressed up in PR) in its opening titles: 'The tans you see might be fake, but the people are all real, although some of what they do has been set up purely for your entertainment.'

Rather than a backlash over fakery, TOWIE won BAFTA's YouTube audience award. The degree of producing and complicity that coaxes 'structured reality' into being marks a new genre where the camera is not effaced or nat-uralised by documentarists seeking to look below the skin, but rather the camera creates a staged space for characters to confect and perform versions of themselves that suit TV's perceived demands.

THE FILMER AND THE FILMED

As documentary forms evolve, the way ethical issues play out has morphed. This is not a technicist argument – the ethical questions remain simple, profound and relatively unchanged since the birth of film – but there are new con-texts for old tensions. The technology of meta data, for example, means that filmers need to be aware of digital opportunities and dangers. Meta data is a digital trace of filming details recorded by the camera and can be used to identify key information, like when a shot was taken. This leads to action such as recovery of a time-line of abuse within Abu Ghraib, as described in Errol Morris's *Standard Operating Procedure* (2008, USA). It can also leave activists and their subjects dangerously identifiable, when protest-ing government abuse. Witness, the human rights cam-paign group, is working to help activists scramble meta data to help protect the identities of protestors or dissidents who may be pursued by authoritarian regimes.

Documentary history has advanced by attempts to deepen understanding (however imperfectly) between filmer and filmed – for example, in Rouch's *Chronique d'un été*. Sometimes it fails even as it aspires, as David MacDougall asserts in his dismissal of anthropological documentary's ability to understand Otherness in its own terms or to acknowledge the encounter with the film-maker.[42]

Documentary practices now appear in many modes and contexts. It is rare for people not to know that media is mediated. The question is no longer 'Is this film a series of selections?' but more: 'How are these selections made?' The situational ethics (economic, political, institutional and personal) that configure the filmer's creative space influences whether the documentary achieves an honest exploration and distillation of what unfolds or whether it is seen to distort or subjugate in a totalising vision. At best, as Lévinas argues, an insistence on understanding the experience of the Other can challenge all egos in the encounter and bring documentary practices towards an empathic, expansive vision, for filmer, filmed and their audiences.

NOTE

Thanks to Deborah Cherry, Tony Dowmunt, Cate Elwes, Zoe Forster, Catherine Lupton, William Raban, Jennie Savage, James Swinson, Lizzie Thynne, Brian Winston, students of MA Documentary Film at London College of Communication, the Sheffield International Documentary Festival, IDFA, IFFR, the Whitechapel and Hayward Galleries and especially to Thea Ellora.

NOTES

1. Lord Leveson's Report on 'the culture, practices and ethics of the press, November 2012, http://www.official-documents.gov.uk/documents/hc1213/hc07/0780/0780.pdf. See also inquiry submissions at http://www.leveson inquiry.org.uk/T. Accessed 1 September 2012.

2. Molly Dineen argues that 'structured reality' is becoming 'basically fiction' in BAFTA TV debate: 'Is Structured Reality Corrupting Documentary?', 17 April 2012, http://www.bafta.org/press/bafta-tv-debate-is-structured-reality-corrupting-documentary,191,SNS.html. Accessed 29 July 2011.

3. Ofcom's fairness code applies to the BBC. In many matters the BBC Trust and editorial guidelines are primary. http://stakeholders.ofcom.org.uk/binaries/broadcast/831190/broadcastingcode2011/pdf

4. http://www.bbc.co.uk/editorialguidelines/guidelines/. Accessed 1 September 2012.

5. http://media/gn.apc.org/nujcode.html. Accessed 1 September 2012.

6. Mark Hanna and Mike Dodd, *McNae's Essential Law for Journalists* (Oxford: Oxford University Press, 2012); Brian Winston, *Lies, Damn Lies and Documentaries* (London: BFI, 2000).

7. Key fault-lines between some newspaper attitudes to privacy in the UK and broadcasters' views are usefully explored in BAFTA debate, 5 December 2011, 'Investigating the Investigators: Ethical Dilemmas in TV Journalism', http://guru.bafta.org/investigating-investigators-ethical-dilemmas-tv-journalism. Accessed 1 September 2012.

8. Michael Renov, *The Subject of Documentary* (Minneapolis: University of Minnesota Press, 2004), pp. 150–1; Libby Saxton, *Haunted Images* (London: Wallflower Press, 2008), pp. 104–5.

9. John Ellis suggests this term to describe 'anyone who films, whether within the film and television industries or for other uses'. *Documentary, Witness and Self-revelation* (London: Routledge, 2012), p. 2.

10. Winston, *Lies, Damn Lies and Documentaries*, pp. 148–9.

11. F. Wiseman, interview with the author at IDFA, Amsterdam, 21 November 2009.

12. Brian Winston, *Claiming the Real* (London: BFI, 2008), pp. 153–60.

13. Carolyn Anderson and Tom Benson, *Documentary Dilemmas: Frederick Wiseman's Titicut Follies* (Carbondale: Southern Illinois University Press, 1991), p. 101.

14. See, for example, http://movieline.com/2010/01/29/does-sundance-sensation-catfish-have-a-truth-problem/. Accessed 1 September 2012.

15. B. Massumi, *Realer than Real: The Simalcrum According to Deleuze and Guattari*, first published in *Copyright no. 1*, 1987, pp. 90–7. http://www.anu.edu.au/HRC/first_and_last/works/realer.htm. Accessed 30 December 2012.

16. These roles were outlined by Erik Barnouw in *Documentary* (London: Oxford University Press, 1974).

17. Bill Nichols, *Introduction to Documentary* (Bloomington: Indiana University Press, 2001); Stella Bruzzi, *New Documentary: A Critical Introduction* (London: Routledge, 2000).

18. João Moreira Salles, 'The Difficulty with Documentary', Lúcia Nagib and Cecilia Mello (eds), *Realism and the Audiovisual Media* (Basingstoke: Palgrave Macmillan, 2009), p. 231.

19. Riefenstahl's frustration with this line of enquiry is clear in Müller's documentary portrait *The Wonderful, Horrible Life of Leni Riefenstahl* (Ray Müller, 1993, Germany).

20. I use 'open' in the sense coined by Karl Popper of a culture that can accommodate dissonance in Karl Popper, *The Open Society and Its Enemies* (London: Routledge [1996, 1962]). A secondary resonance of 'open documentary' is openness to interactivity and community collaboration in the creation of narrative.

21. David Lean lecture, BAFTA, 2011, http://guru.bafta.org/errol-morris-annual-film-lecture. Accessed 1 September 2012.

22. http://www.bailii.org/ew/cases/EWHC/Admin/2007/2288.html. Accessed 1st September 2012.

23. From Q&A session following screening of *Afghantsi* at Sheffield International Documentary Festival, 2005.

24. Eva Hohenberger, 'Vietnam/US', an interview with Trinh T. Minh-ha in Gail Pearce and Cahal McLaughlin (eds), *Truth or Dare: Art and Documentary* (Bristol: Intellect, 2008), pp. 118–19.

25. Cahal McLaughlin, 'Inside Stories: Memories from the Maze and Long Kesh Prison', *Journal of Media Practice* vol. 7 no. 2, November 2006, pp. 123–33.

26. See Chapter 5.5 for Michael Renov's further explication of this relationship.

27. John Ellis, 'Dancing to Different Tunes', in Pearce and McLaughlin, *Truth or Dare*, pp. 118–19, emphasis added.

28. McLaughlin, 'Inside Stories', p. 60.

29. *Terre sans Pain* circulates in versions with some variation in commentary. Quotes are from the English version.

30. Barnouw, *Documentary*, p. 131.

31. Jefferey Ruoff, 'An Ethnographic Surrealist Film: Luis Buñuel's *Land Without Bread*', *Visual Anthropology Review* vol. 14 no. 1, XVIII, Spring/Summer 1998, pp. 45–57, http://www.dartmouth.edu/~jruoff/Articles/EthnographicSurrealist.htm. Accessed 15 January 2012.

32. Catherine Russell, *Experimental Ethnography:The Work of Film in the Age of Video* (London: Duke University Press, 1999), p. 34.

33. Described by Brian Winston in interview with the author, London, 4 May 2012.

34. Emmanuel Lévinas, *Totality and Infinity*, trans. Alphonso Lingis (Pittsburgh: Duquesne University Press, 1969); see also Seán Hand (ed.), *The Levinas Reader* (Oxford: Basil Blackwell, 1989).

35. Project ArtWorks, under Director Kate Adams, is pioneering an exploration of partnership with people with advanced neurological disorders, examining the ethics of consent, including notions of 'assent' and 'dissent' in actuality filming, www.projectartworks.org. Accessed 1 September 2012.

36. Interview with the author, London, 2 July 2012.

37. See fuller discussion of practitioner responses to this challenge in Pratap Rughani, 'Are You a Vulture? Reflecting on the Ethics and Aesthetics of Coverage of Atrocity and its Aftermath', in Richard Keeble, John Tulloch and Florian Zollmann (eds), *Journalism, War and Conflict Resolution* (Oxford: Peter Lang, 2010).

38. G. Rodger, *A Life in Photography*, 1987 [VHS], The Photographers' Gallery, London.

39. Roger Mills and Pratap Rughani (directors), Channel 4, *New Model Army*, August/September 2000.

40. Winston, *Lies, Damn Lies and Documentaries*, pp. 3, 63–110.

41. Julia Raeside, 'A Different Kind of Reality TV', *Guardian*, 1 June 2011, http://www.guardian.co.uk/tv-and-radio/2011/jun/01/reality-tv-only-way-essex. Accessed 30 July 2012.

42. David MacDougall, 'Beyond Observational Cinema', in Paul Hockings (ed.), *Principles of Visual Anthropology* (The Hague: Mouton, 1975).

1.11 Deaths, Transfigurations and the Future

JOHN CORNER

Authenticity, narrative and ethics delimit the field of the moving-image documentary but these disputatious terrains have always meant that its fertility as a film and television form is a question of constant concern; especially when compounded by the persistent fragility and volatility of its audience appeal. Worries about documentary's health are in no way alleviated by the current proliferation of documentary forms.

In this chapter, I want to examine some questions concerning the contemporary situation of documentary and about what is involved in attempting to predict its future. This is a topic which has seen a great deal of dispute over recent years, with judgments as to the 'health' of work in the area and its prospects showing at times an astonishing degree of variation. Documentary, having been pronounced to be dying or even dead by some commentators, was seen by others to be enjoying a renaissance. Among other things, I want to explore some of the reasons for this diversity of assessments. In doing so, it will be necessary to register the diversity of documentary production itself, within changing economic, technological and cultural settings, and the extensive use of documentary approaches in many formats which would not themselves be easily or comfortably identified under that label.

Although it is a matter that will receive more intensive discussion elsewhere in this volume, the question of the working criteria being used in describing a piece of work as a documentary is something that should be brought into the picture right from the start. Whereas for several other types of media production, contemplation of their future might make initial progress without too much by way of explicit definitional criteria, in examining documentary the issue of precisely *what* is the object of historical tracking and forecasting needs immediate attention.

CORES AND NORMS

The grounding emphasis I want to place here is on the way in which Grierson's own (highly strategic) accounts of 'documentary' position it as a distinctive form of non-fiction film-making. Brian Winston brings this out provocatively in his major critical and historical study.[1] I discuss

it myself in my own brief discussion of founding ideas[2] and it is given detailed attention in relation to its intellectual context by Ian Aitken.[3] One dimension of this distinctiveness is seen to be its commitments to 'civic' improvement, the precise political character of which together with the broader working assumptions have rightly been the subject of scrutiny and debate. Another dimension, variously weighted across the range of Grierson's writings, is aesthetic ambition, pulling the project away from the more expressively restricted uses of film and sound to record, inform and instruct (as in the newsreel and the lecture-film) and placing work under the documentary heading as an important contribution to cinematic art.

It is worth noting straight away that if the principal elements of Grierson's definition, its imprecision, variants and downright contradictions notwithstanding, are used as core criteria, then a great deal of work which gets called 'documentary', including by its makers, would not be found to warrant the label quite so easily, if at all. Among this range, a large amount of television production over sixty years would look questionable. However much it might conform to aspects of Grierson's recipe, it is generally organised within orientations towards the world as an object for factual film-making essentially outside of those within which Grierson grounded his advocacy for a documentary cinema.

As, again, Brian Winston, along with many other commentators, has observed,[4] a mode for 'core' documentary strongly rivalling that of Grierson's emerged in the 1960s around the varieties of observational film-making and their selective but expansive take-up into versions of television 'fly-on-the-wall'. Rather than the awkward combination of civic (in fact, mostly state-supportive) purposes with self-conscious aesthetic development, this model emphasised the specificity of the relationship between the images and sounds of the documentary and localised realities. Using technological developments to do so, it placed a tight referential fidelity to *occurrence* at the centre of the documentary idea, with consequent implications for the organisation of time and of narrative structure within film-making. In this model, the social utility of documentary lay in the sustained scrutiny of particular interactions which it offered for viewing contemplation and for the making of inferences by viewers. To use Winston's resonant term, its 'claim on the real' generally rejected both the artistic self-consciousness recommended by Grierson and the overt (often declamatory) propositional structure which his model frequently required in order to work as a form of public address and as stimulating civic education.

We can identify a third major 'core' too, although it has exerted influence mainly over broadcasting. This is the journalistic model (again, well represented in Winston's scholarship), extensively revising the Griersonian as work for television developed across a range of variants, including those using frameworks of enquiry, interview and presenter exposition drawn adaptively from press and radio reporting. The interview becomes the staple sequence of the journalistic model, shot and employed in various ways. One of the consequences of its particular kinds of realism and modes of address is to displace the framing 'dramatic' realisms by which Grierson sought to immerse viewers in orchestrated aspects of reality and to stimulate their feelings as well as offer knowledge. The journalistic model frequently takes documentary down to a multi-sourced, 'ground level' view of what is happening that is out of keeping with the primary aims of Griersonian aesthetics (see the account in Goddard et al.[5] of how one current-affairs series developed from diverse documentary and journalistic coordinates).

All of these models have, in different pragmatic contexts, worked as very different 'cores' (sometimes explicitly so, sometimes not) against which other kinds of documentary work have been placed and accorded significance in relation to the past, present and future. This has not been a big problem for discussion and study of documentary, primarily because in practice the term has developed a more inclusive usage and has not been referred back strictly to Griersonian precepts, however much these have exerted a rhetorical pull (see Winston and also the introduction to this book for a provocative account of 'post-Griersonianism').[6] This usage has recognised, if sometimes reluctantly, the impact of work using very different models and methods. Allowing for the play of dispute, of which that persistent strand of documentary scholarship obsessed with 'definition' is one indicator, the classification has been applied in such a way as to cover, if messily, all the core areas indicated above, as well as others. For instance, in the USA, the work of those in independent, radical cinema attained something close to a defining role in marking the continuation of the 'core' documentary project in a way which preserved strong links with the Griersonian strand of experimental aesthetics at the same time as it rejected any location within the framework of official public information. Here, the critical retrospectives in Nichols[7] and Renov[8] have been among the most influential accounts. Another interesting example is provided by the long history of the wildlife documentary, particular in series television. Here, a whole range of non-fiction film-making about aspects of reality, some of it informed by scientific enquiry, has been placed on the edges, if not beyond, the sphere of 'documentary proper' largely because it does not concern itself with the 'human social subject' and the 'social issue' in the way that many other dominant models have done. One indication of this is the minimal attention, at least until recently,[9] paid to wildlife filming in the publications and conferences of 'documentary studies'.

At times, indeed, use of the category has become so inclusive as to incorporate much of that wider (and constantly growing) range of non-fictional production from which Grierson was rather keen to differentiate the kind of cultural practices he wished to advocate. Nevertheless, despite this expansiveness, in many arguments about documentary the issue of the *normative*, of value and commitment by the film-maker, emerges. In doing so, it raises doubts about the degree to which what is at issue is really *descriptive*, a matter of identifiable thematic or formal factors, however varied in their combination. Therefore, among the questions we need to ask are those about the particular kind of 'core' being assumed in any given stance or position being taken up and the kind of normative framework it might entail. As I shall suggest below, the play-off of different assumptions about the 'core characteristics', including the 'core values', of documentary have been brought out with unusual sharpness in the diverse assessments made of 'reality television' and its likely impact upon its 'parent' genre (in those cases where genealogical connections have been recognised at all!).

IN SICKNESS AND IN HEALTH

I noted earlier that the health and direction of work in documentary has been a perennial subject of debate. However, the last twenty years have seen that debate increase markedly both in its intensity and range of articulation. The growth of a 'Documentary Studies', initially out of Film Studies but with quite rapid connections to Media and Cultural Studies[10] has provided an academic forum for discussion, running alongside and sometimes in nervous combination with, the continuing strand of debate within sectors of film production and the television industry.

In Britain, the view that documentary was a category of work in decline was expressed frequently from the 1990s, although there had been earlier anxieties. Of significance here was the use of documentary journalism on television as the primary reference point. With changes in the television economy, following intensification of market imperatives and competition for viewers, documentary television journalism was seen to be under threat. It often required large budgets to support extensive periods of primary investigation and, with few exceptions, it did not bring in popular audiences in anything like the numbers required in order to justify high levels of funding within a changed industrial setting. Using documentary journalism as the core form, and its values as central, a generalised picture of regrettable decline was often presented. The 'winners' in this transition were seen to be forms of popular drama and light entertainment which could work across a wider, and younger, demographic profile.

Within this context, of a perceived growing risk to documentary in one of its major television variants, there then emerged through the 1990s what would become in many countries, at different rates and with varying impact, the most significant single development in discussion of what documentary was and where it was headed – 'reality television'. The growth, across its several phases, of what is perhaps best termed 'popular factual entertainment', borrowing from a range of documentary approaches but with an emphasis on observational structures, has radically complicated the context in which discussion of contemporary documentary can occur. At the heart of the complication is the division both within the industry and within academia about how various examples of the new programming stand in relation to the 'idea' of documentary. Some commentators have regarded a good proportion of the new programming as essentially an expansion of documentary work, bringing refreshed ideas about organisation and styling and winning an unprecedented and very welcome level of popular audience interest. Others have seen it as nothing less than generic subversion, the application of selected elements of documentary practice for ends lacking in integrity and social value and framed entirely by new commercial imperatives to present audiences with diverting spectacles rather than engage with them as citizens. Nichols provides an early and strong account of this perspective.[11]

Not everyone has come down uncompromisingly on one side or the other. There has been a good deal of 'sieving' work carried out, in which the increasingly wide range of reality formats has been checked in relation to 'core' criteria and items placed (sometimes cautiously) either side of the notional line that separates the bold, innovative continuation of the documentary project from its unworthy, when not socially and culturally injurious, Other. Among the many forums in which this debate has been played out, the annual Genre Audits of the journal *Broadcast* and the sessions of the annual Sheffield International Documentary Festival provided opportunities for vigorous exchange.

A quotation which I have used in teaching to illustrate something of the ambivalence across different positions comes from John Willis (a former Channel 4 Commissioning Editor for Documentaries), writing in 2000. Willis, who at the 1997 Sheffield Festival had responded to the growth of reality television programmes by talking of documentary 'surfing on a new wave of success',[12] here adopted a more cautious, if still very positive tone:

> our own schedules are full of documentary soaps about airlines or hotels, doctors or vets. As one BBC producer inelegantly told me, 'We're drowning in a tidal wave of vets with arms up cow's bums.' Now, to some commentators, this renaissance is a disaster. Documentary soaps are more akin to entertainment and can be intrusive, sometimes dishonest. They're the Big Macs of documentary – bland and rather tasteless, a symbol of the terrible commodification of factual television. And I think that's partly true. But for those of us who've seen years of documentary budgets being cut and documentaries pushed to the edges of the television schedule, it's a pleasure to see so much factual programming, at peak time.[13]

A number of the key terms are brought together here, sometimes revealing evaluative tensions beyond those that are made explicit. The term 'documentary soaps' serves to align at least some of the new programmes with the core idea, in a relationship both of continuity and renewal. What is happening can be seen as a generic 'renaissance', but it can also be seen as a 'disaster'. 'Entertainment' may be regarded as part of the problem, allowing in the 'dishonest' and the 'tasteless'. Such programmes can be viewed as the Big Macs of documentary, but within this judgment they remain part of documentary, if a dubious part. Nevertheless, in the context of recent budgets cuts in the broad area, the idea of 'factual programming' at peak time is a pleasure to note (it is revealing that 'documentary' is *not* the term used in this affirming comment).

The play-off of different tones and positions in the passage is instructive. Conflicting positions are brought into the account as part of the considered appraisal, but one line of judgment ('commodification') is admitted only through the jokey displacement that 'terrible' performs upon it. The idea that in some way the success of the new formats reverses the years of cuts in documentary budgets clearly runs counter to the widely aired view that it was precisely the growth of the 'reality' models that had increased the economic threat to 'core' activities.

This view had been trenchantly put forward by the celebrated documentary-maker Paul Watson two years earlier:

> What saddens me about such stuff is that it's pushing better programmes to the margins. Why pay a fortune to put on original drama, or invest in a serious, investigative documentary, when you can get away with a cheap series simply by pointing a camera at someone wanting self-promotion.[14]

Such uncertainty about where to position the extensive range of popular factual entertainment in relation to the idea of 'documentary' has continued for over a decade. It has worked, as I have observed, to confound a clear sense of what is being taken into account, and what not, in any readings of tendencies and futures.

A further major development with consequences for ideas of 'what was happening' to documentary was a phase of successful feature documentaries in the cinema, discussed at several points elsewhere in this volume. Michael Moore's *Bowling for Columbine* (2002, USA) and *Fahrenheit 9/11* (2004, USA) have to be central to any assessment here, along with the huge success in Britain of Kevin MacDonald's *Touching the Void* (2003) and the continuation of box-office success of films such as Morgan Spurlock's *Super Size Me* (2004, USA), Andrew Jarecki's *Capturing the Friedmans* (2003, USA) right through to Luc Jacquet's *March of the Penguins* (2005, France), James Marsh's *Man on Wire* (2008, USA) and beyond.

This development received a good deal of deserved attention both in the press and within documentary studies, although in the former the familiar dangers of exaggerating a 'trend' into an awesome phenomenon were apparent. While in the process offering some perceptive judgments, Blake Morrison partly fell into this trap in his long article in the *Guardian*, 'Back to Reality'.[15] Morrison describes how he delayed for a while before going to see *Touching the Void*, since it was a documentary, and: 'the word suggests something earnest, pedagogic, propagandist, short on colour and narrative excitement, and more suited to the small screen than the big'.[16] So this is another articulation of 'core' documentary, clearly referencing elements of the Grierson model but projecting these in a strongly negative light. Documentary is 'boring' and (in a rather ahistorical twist) better suited to television than cinema.

As he surveys the other recent cinematic work, either in distribution or about to appear, Morrison reflects on a trend reversal:

> The resurgence of documentary is a phenomenon few could have predicted. The battle for a place in mainstream cinema outlets was lost half a century ago, and in recent years, as reality TV has taken over the schedules, the question has been whether documentary can survive even within mainstream television.[17]

Evaluative ideas are thus worked into a narrative, just as they were in the Willis quote cited above. The present 'resurgence' is placed against the recent fight for 'survival'. Importantly, reality programming is now regarded principally as a threat to television documentary rather than, as in Willis's account, the main route taken by its 'renaissance'. This view is confirmed in later comment:

> But since the mid-90s, the space for documentary on television has increasingly been given over to programmes about self- or home-refurbishment – how to improve your cooking skills or your life. *So marginalised have documentaries become* that the idea of them attracting large cinema audiences, or being borrowed as DVDs and cassettes from video stores, seems wildly implausible.[18]

So, in 2004, television documentary is still 'marginalised' according to Morrison, a judgment running entirely counter to that of Willis and one which is perhaps greatly aided by the omission from his account of that extensive range of reality formats then being screened with popular success (including docusoaps) which were not concerned with cooking and self-improvement.

What discussion of the 'new wave' of cinema documentary also often failed to notice adequately was the way in which many of the successful films drew extensively on the repertoire of 'brighter' approaches, including in presentation, narrative design and on-screen action, which had been employed in the development of diverse reality series like the BBC's *999* (1992–2003) and Michael Moore's *TV Nation* (1994–95), as well as many others. Morrison shows himself to be partly aware of this in his comment that: 'Now that documentaries (Michael Moore's apart) are no longer politically engagé, pleasing an audience, rather than trying to improve it, seems less of a crime.'[19]

In the context of my earlier discussion, this is an interesting comment to make about 'core' values and it may not be an over-reading to see evaluative uneasiness at work in the very awkwardness of its formulation. The popular value of 'pleasure' is placed approvingly against the elitist one of 'improvement', but the sentence only really works because of the rhetorical ploy by which the idea of the criminalisation of pleasure is introduced ironically to underpin the judgment made.

I have wanted to outline some of the very different factors at work in the changing culture of documentary over the last two decades. These have, of course, varied considerably internationally and I have mostly concerned myself with the shifts as they have occurred in Britain and (within cinema at least) in the USA. What I have wanted to bring out is the very different perceptions of change which they have generated. These perceptions have often worked with different notions of what 'documentary' essentially is, what its core values are and whether these values are to be celebrated or regarded as due for revision when assessing the indicators of change. In the next section, I want to look briefly at some aspects of my own reading of the situation, made first of all at the end of the 1990s, and at the way this reading has variously been subject to discussion and to dispute by other commentators.

CHANGING GENERIC COORDINATES: 'POST-DOCUMENTARY'?

In 1999, I gave a paper at a seminar in Florence for the European Science Foundation project, 'Changing Media/Changing Culture'. It looked at the changing settings for doing documentary work, particularly on television, and attempted to assess the continuing adequacy of the term 'documentary' as a category in circumstances where audiovisual culture, including digital culture, was displaying an increasingly diverse range of ways of recording and representing the real for different purposes. The paper appeared as a working paper[20] on the project website. Some of its arguments were incorporated into other conference papers and formal journal articles. Among the latter was a piece taking as its initial reference point *Big Brother*, but moving more widely across the field of non-fiction television. This was published under the main title 'Performing the Real'.[21] In the papers and then this article I made openly speculative use of the term 'post-documentary' culture, picking up on an earlier passing use of it in a book review to give a more dramatic and provocative focus to the questions of generic transformation, and indeed of generic dispersal, which seemed to be raised by current tendencies.

By working with a contrasting, even paradoxical, duality in the phrase 'documentary in a post-documentary culture' (the title of the earlier web paper, followed by a question mark), I wanted to signal a sense of a growing disalignment between the established, if unstable, terms of reference and the changing patterns both in perception of non-fiction work (including the perceptions of audiences) and in non-fiction practice. It seemed to me that the broad cultural coordinates upon which the documentary project had (precariously) sustained itself and been strenuously championed across its different phases were in quite radical transition. What I did not want to do was suggest that an assembly of approaches and practices which many people might want to go on calling documentary was 'finished'. Nevertheless, some people took my comments, despite the duality noted above, as declaring such a termination and then (understandably) moved to champion its continued existence (although in a few cases they celebrated what they took to be an overdue announcement of its demise!). Just *how* continuity of development would occur, alongside the transitions, in *what* adaptive relationship with the new dynamics of the audiovisual economy and the changing culture of popular viewing, was a matter of speculation in the paper – not of any firm verdict.

Part of my interest was in the shift in documentary *purposes*, and in the claim to documentary 'authority', brought about by many of the newer forms, but particularly by modes of popular factual entertainment. Unlike some other commentators, I wanted to recognise the way in which many aspects of what was bundled up, politically

and socially, within established ideas of 'documentary' were in need of a healthy dose of subversion and rejection and so I welcomed certain elements of reconfigured practice. What I did not bring out as strongly as I might have done was the way in which my concern, as well as being about changed practices within a reconfigured media economy, was also about the terms for *classifying* practice and for allotting to those classifications particular orientations and values. The transitions I discussed were both at the level of practices and of classifications, the former increasingly, it seemed, moving out from the 'reach' of established versions of the latter. As an indicator, usually applied approvingly, of an approach to making and using audiovisual recordings, 'documentary' was becoming quite radically resituated by a range of technological, economic and cultural developments in the representation of reality.

My comments have caused a good deal of discussion, most of it welcoming the contribution to what was already a lively debate about shifts in mediations of the real, one which has since developed in its range and intensity.[22] Apart from those who misread me as declaring the 'end' of recognisable documentary, there were those who wanted to introduce some qualifications, some 'pulling back', on taking the notion of a 'post-documentary' culture as by itself an adequate, final verdict on the contemporary context of production and viewing (among those making this point cogently were Kilborn,[23] Bruzzi,[24] Beattie[25] and Winston).[26] This response was welcome as far as I was concerned, since the aim of my comments, and therefore the manner of their expression, had been self-consciously polemical, an attempt to set up a position for dialogue about the terms of transition. When used of ideas or classifications, 'post' is an interesting and often rather tricky prefix, of course. In many such uses it indicates a degree of continuity (in the sense of having recognised, and developed in relation to, that which it is 'post'), as well as the idea of moving beyond and of marking a shift. This, rather than a notion of total 'break', is the sense in which I put forward the notion as one worthy of debate.

In the continuing dispute about these matters, I am struck by the way in which many of those who seek to affirm generally what they want to continue to call 'documentary' (as well as affirming the qualities of particular films and programmes) often find themselves faced with a choice. This is between a kind of strategic, *normative* closure around certain values and functions taken by them to be defining (at least for what they want to write or talk about) and a *descriptivism* so inclusive across highly varied territory that the category becomes gestural and rather question-begging. I have been in this rather uneasy position myself and will doubtless find myself there again. Those working in documentary studies will also know how almost no conference is complete without what seems now a ritual questioning of 'what we mean by documentary'. This questioning can come from genuine bewilderment in those outside the area or as an opportunity for sophisticated display from specialists who have turned the impossibility of a definitive answer into a key part of their conferencing and publication repertoire.

DOCUMENTARY FUTURES

Given the above outline, what are the implications for the future of 'documentary'? Well, we can be sure that the issue of definition will continue, as new variants are perceived to lie either within or without the boundaries, however generous these become (debates surrounding documentary animation, as in Ari Folman's *Waltz with Bashir* [Israel, 2008] or the use of actors miming recorded interviews, as in Clio Barnard's *The Arbor* [UK, 2010] are ample testimony to this, alongside many other instances). Academic debate about the terms of transition, some of it using 'post' and 'trans' prefixes, will continue too.[27] A number of practitioners in factual film and television will want to use the category in primary self-definition, while others will not find this level of generic identification necessary or even attractive. The strong presence in popular culture which the versions of Reality TV have provided mean that at least elements of documentary work are likely to develop rather than to recede, along with the confident sense that this broad new area can now look after its own self-classifications without either being seen as definitively Other than documentary or as an inferior, degraded sub-generic variant. As formerly, but perhaps with an increasing variety, 'documentary passages' will occur in films and programmes conceived and delivered within diverse aesthetic and discursive recipes at some distance from any conceivable sense of documentary's 'own' generic space.

The coordinates in relation to which the making of specific types of factual film and programmes is undertaken will continue to change. They can be seen to include six key lines of interconnected relationship – political, social, economic, institutional, technological and aesthetic, all referred to variously at other points in this volume. Their combined tendency will be such as to produce a further sense of generic dispersal, notwithstanding clear strands of continuity. Insofar as core documentary values involve serious engagement with the physical and social real for the purposes of some discourse of 'critical civics', whatever the political orientations by which this is framed and delivered, the economics of production and of distribution will clearly be of importance. Audiences' generic expectations perhaps deserve emphasis once again here, lest the matter of generic continuity and transition be seen to be principally one of production perspectives, on the one hand, and academic commentary, on the other. A new

generation of audiences for film, television and web-based productions will be placed in circuits of knowledge and entertainment, cut across by options for habitual disregard as well as for cross-referral and combination, in which the whole generic system as it presently exists may be subject to radical shifts.

The tendencies I discussed earlier might be seen as comprising in part something of a 'documentary diaspora', a process which will undoubtedly develop further. There will be much to celebrate in what is to come. Of this, I am sure. However, there will also be much that will provoke critique and condemnation. 'Documentary' is a term which, as well as indicating a range of representational practices, has regularly been used to mark out in different ways certain ethical and social commitments in the use of audiovisual recording. For a variety of reasons that I have outlined, that 'marking out' will prove even more challenging in the future than it has been in the past.

NOTES

1. Brian Winston, *Claiming the Real II: The Documentary Film Revisited* (London: BFI, 2009 [1995]).
2. John Corner, *The Art of Record: A Critical Introduction to Documentary* (Manchester: Manchester University Press, 1996).
3. Ian Aitken, *Film and Reform: John Grierson and the Documentary Film Movement* (London: Routledge, 1990).
4. See also Dave Saunders, *Direct Cinema: Observational Documentary and the Politics of the Sixties* (London: Wallflower, 2007).
5. Peter Goddard, John Corner and Kay Richardson, *Public Issue Television: World in Action, 1963–98* (Manchester: Manchester University Press, 2007).
6. Winston, *Claiming the Real II.*
7. Bill Nichols, *Representing Reality: Issues and Concepts in Documentary* (Bloomington: Indiana University Press, 1991).
8. Michael Renov, *The Subject of Documentary* (Minneapolis: University of Minnesota Press, 2004).
9. See, for instance, Richard Kilborn, 'Animal TV', *Jumpcut* no. 28, 2006.
10. See the account in John Corner, 'Documentary Studies: Dimensions of Transition and Continuity', in Thomas Austin and Wilma de Jong (eds), *Rethinking Documentary* (Maidenhead: Open University Press/McGraw-Hill, 2008, pp. 13–28.
11. Bill Nichols, *Blurred Boundaries: Questions of Meaning in Contemporary Culture* (Bloomington: Indiana University Press, 1994).
12. Andy Fry, 'Factual's New Soft Sell', *Broadcast*, 17 October 1997, pp. 20–1.
13. John Willis, 'Breaking the Boundaries', in John Izod, Richard Kilborn and Matthew Hibbard (eds), *From Grierson to the Docusoap* (Luton: Luton University Press, 2000), p. 100.

14. Paul Watson, 'When I made "The Family", Viewers Were Shocked To See Real People on TV. Today, These Cheap, Pernicious "Fly-on-the-Wall" Shows Just Treat Us Like Fools', *Daily Mail*, 17 February 1998, p. 9.

15. Blake Morrison, 'Back to Reality', *Guardian*, 5 March 2004, http://www.guardian.co.uk/film/2004/mar/05/1. Accessed September 2012.

16. Ibid.

17. Ibid.

18. Ibid., emphasis added.

19. Ibid.

20. John Corner, 'Documentary in a Post-Documentary Culture?', working paper Number One on Loughborough University website for 'Changing Media/Changing Europe' (2000), European Science Foundation project 1999–2004. Site removed in 2010.

21. John Corner, 'Performing the Real: Documentary Diversions', *Television and New Media* vol. 3 no. 3, August 2002), pp. 255–69.

22. See, for example, N. Carpentier and S. van Bauewel, *Trans-Reality Television* (Lanham, MD: Lexington, 2010).

23. Richard Kilborn, *Staging the Real* (Manchester: Manchester University Press, 2003).

24. Stella Bruzzi, *New Documentary* (London: Routledge, 2006).

25. K. Beattie, *Documentary Display* (London: Wallflower, 2008).

26. Winston, *Claiming the Real II*. See also Winston's comments on the 'post' question in his introduction to this volume.

27. As in J. Mast, 'Documentary at a Crossroads: Reality TV and the Hybridization of Small Screen Documentary', *Sociology Compass* vol. 3 no. 6, December 2009, pp. 884–98, and Carpentier and van Bauewel, *Trans-Reality Television*.

PART TWO:
Documentary Paradigms

2.1 Problems in Historiography: The Documentary Tradition Before *Nanook Of The North*

CHARLES MUSSER

However defined; whether cinematic order, genus or species; whatever the questions of authenticity, the demands of narrative and the quagmire of ethics, moving-image documentary has persisted as a potent type of cinema. It has a sturdy history. Given a general western addiction to realistic modes of representation (validated by the scientism of photography), coupled with a mature conception of the nature of evidence, this is scarcely surprising. Nevertheless ...

The beginnings of documentary have been underconceptualised and underexplored. Even now, many sources see the documentary film as having an early, promising pre-history with the short films of Auguste and Louis Lumière, but the mode itself only appearing with Robert Flaherty's *Nanook of the North* (1922).[1] This is already a retrospective assertion, a striking anachronism, since the term was coined, according to Anglo-American mythology, by John Grierson in 1926, when he wrote that, 'Of course *Moana* [1926], being a visual account of events in the daily life of a Polynesian youth and his family, has documentary value.'[2] Both of these elements have a special relevance in explaining the history they constitute, but each is also symptomatic of problems that have impeded a proper history. The Lumières' achievements, to which we will return, gives documentary a media-specific cast and implicitly asserts that it was with the beginning of cinema (motion pictures) that the first glimmers of its documentary potential were recognised. In fact, this media-specificity has had to give way in the current era of digital video in which video documentaries are seen as straightforward continuations of the documentary film tradition.

The privileging of *Nanook of the North* and its retrospective association as the starting point of documentary obfuscates much more than it illuminates. Underneath a nonsensical embrace of an extraordinary auteurism, there is perhaps one underlying logic: that this moment follows closely upon the formation of the classical Hollywood cinema in the USA. Documentary has been defined against Hollywood cinema and fiction film by critics and theorists such as John Grierson and Dziga Vertov, but also by the French. So the moment when motion pictures achieved a particular stability and status with the vertically integrated studio system (c. 1919–20) and the international dominance of American productions contributed to the generation of a non-fiction counterpart defined as documentary.[3] This may help to explain why the term 'documentary' was so quickly embraced, but it works within an historical paradigm that this chapter rejects.

The early history of documentary requires an exploration of several strands, one of which is the history and etymology of the term itself. The term 'documentary' dates back to the late eighteenth century, where it appeared in a judicial or governmental context. London newspapers were using the term 'documentary evidence' as early as 1786.[4] News coverage of the lengthy trial of Warren Hastings in the House of Lords and Parliament from 1788 to 1791 generated numerous references to 'documentary proof' and 'documentary and oratory testimony'.[5] 'Documentary' was thus an adjective referring to documents in a legal context. By the mid-nineteenth century, the use of the term 'documentary' was broadened beyond the legal framework to include scholars and others looking at documentary evidence.[6] The 'documentary value' of photography was heralded by the 1850s.[7] Likewise, Richard Harding Davis's book, *The Cuban and Porto Rican Campaigns* (1898), consisted of a hundred illustrations from photographs, which were said to have documentary value.[8] By the 1890s, the term 'documentary photograph' was beginning to be used with some frequency: the French photographer Leon Vidal (1833–1906) was trying to establish a Museum of Photographic Archives and Documentary Photographs[9] by the early twentieth century.[10] 'Documentary' as a term was also associated with non-fiction film. In a brief article on a Pathé news film of a 1922 horse race, C. R. G. remarks that 'Many people will find it interesting not only as a vivid reproduction of the spectacle but also as a piece of documentary evidence.'[11] By the 1920s commentators were often referring to the 'documentary interest' or 'documentary values' of photographs, reproductions, illustrative material and even film.[12] The term 'documentary' or 'documentary films' was imported to the USA from French-speaking parts of Europe. *New York*

Times correspondent Martha Gruening, writing from Paris, refers to the 'documentary travel film'.[13] Meanwhile, the Catholic Church applauded 'instructive documentary films' being made in Belgium.[14]

'Documentary' was a term that was more or less quickly applied to well-established non-fiction screen practices and typically embraced or superseded terms such as 'travel film', 'educational film' and 'illustrated lecture'. The term 'illustrated lecture', which had been standard nomenclature for documentary-like programmes in the nineteenth century, had become inadequate and antiquated: a new term was needed and 'documentary' filled the bill. Between the 1850s or 60s and the 1920s or 30s, the illustrated lecture was a cultural form that was fundamentally connected to audiovisual presentations involving projected images using lantern slides and then film. It might, therefore, be tempting to trace documentary back to the origins of photography and the emergence of photographic techniques (the development of photographic glass slides) and practices, which soon came to characterise the illustrated lecture using photographic slides – what was frequently called 'stereopticon lectures' in the USA. As we have seen, the term 'documentary' was sometimes associated with photography, giving this some appeal. However tempting as this formulation might be, this would merely push backwards in time a reliance on a form of media-specificity that an adequate delineation of the form's long history cannot sustain. (Indeed, in recent years the animated documentary has enjoyed something of a boom.) In the early nineteenth century, in the era before photography, there were exhibitors who gave lantern-slide lectures that operated within what Bill Nichols refers to as the discourse of sobriety. On topics such as astronomy and travel, they operated within a non-fiction framework while using painted lantern slides. On the other hand, there were also illustrated lectures that used other kinds of visual aids besides projected images (science demonstrations, artefacts and so forth). Granted that such practices were less clearly delineated, recognisable strands of the documentary clearly go back much further. Where to begin?

THE HISTORY OF NON-FICTION SCREEN PRACTICE

The history of documentary might be said to begin with the introduction of projected images on the screen for non-fiction purposes, in short with Althanius Kircher and Christiaan Huygens in the 1640s and 50s. Although Kircher's exhibitions with his catoptric lamp – which relied on the sun rather than a candle or other light source – were generally used to depict fictional tales, there were two ways in which his presentations were aligned with the documentary tradition: first, stressing the importance of demystifying the projected image, Kircher presented the apparatus within the framework of

a technological demonstration or lecture illustrated with various apparatuses; second, anticipating later science-oriented presentations involving projected images, he often showed live flies: 'smear honey on the mirror and behold how the flies will be projected on the wall through the surface of the mirror with extraordinary size'.[15] If Kircher enjoyed presenting satirical scenes and theatrical tragedies, his fellow Jesuit Andreas Tacquet used a catoptric lamp to give an illustrated lecture about a missionary's trip to China.[16] The lantern was also used to present illustrated lectures on the life of Christ – certainly seen as part of the discourse of sobriety – dealing with history, biography and religion.

My goal is not to present an unbroken genealogy from Kircher to the present day, even assuming this was possible. By the early nineteenth century, the illustrated lecture was becoming a more established presence in Anglo-American public culture. As Richard Altick has shown, illustrated lectures on astronomy had become quite common.[17] In 1825, a London optician was advertising his instructive lectures on astronomy using a 'Phantasmagoria Lantern'.[18] The following year in Philadelphia, J. L. Rhees was offering a series of lectures on geography and natural history, which were 'illustrated by magic lantern representations'.[19] In 1842 at London's Kensington Hall, Joshua Coffin delivered an illustrated lecture on Palestine using fifty-five paintings projected by the magic lantern.[20]

Illustrated lectures could use a variety of visual aids and sometimes involved the demonstration of new technologies, such as Alexander Bain's illustrated lecture on 'The Electro-magnetic Printing Telegraph' at the Royal Polytechnic in London.[21] In 1861, Mr Rarey gave an 'illustrated lecture on his power over the horse at the Brooklyn Academy of Music ... when several vicious horses were effectively subdued'.[22] Dr Robert A. Fisher lectured on 'Gunpowder, Cannon and Projectiles' using large diagrams, models, shells and chemical experiments.[23] Early exhibitions of the phonograph, like the one that occurred at Chickering Hall in New York City on 23 March 1878, also functioned in a similar way.[24] The extensive use of illustrated lectures and the balance between those using lantern slides versus other illustrative material is suggested by an 1855 report by the Pennsylvania Hospital for the Insane: 132 events were held in the lecture room for its inmates. Dr Lee delivered forty lectures: one on the construction and uses of the magic lantern, four on Canada and the fur trade, two on the Arctic regions, two on the polar regions and two on ornithology. These were undoubtedly among the fifty presentations that used the magic lantern and dissolving views, while others – one on the telegraph in operation, two on electro-magnetism and four on electricity – probably involved scientific demonstrations.[25] This underscores an important conceptual tension that an understanding of documentary and the documentary tradition requires. On one hand, there were many illustrated lectures that could (in theory) be transferred to digital formats with striking continuities and produce something one would describe as a documentary. Nevertheless, 'illustrated lecture' as a term was more flexible and expansive.

The development of photography did not give lanternists initial access to projected photographic images: this had to wait for the development of the albumen and collodion processes in the late 1840s. These new photographic techniques enabled a photographic image to be transferred to a glass surface, while earlier processes (daguerrotypes and talbotypes) had used either a silver-plated copper surface or paper as a base. When John A. Whipple and William B. Jones of Boston patented an albumen process (using egg whites as an adhering agent) in June 1850, they had apparently been using it for several years.[26] The Langenheim brothers, William and Frederick, had also been working with the albumen process and played an important role in the introduction of photographic lantern slides.[27]

During the 1840s, the Langenheims facilitated the introduction of several new photographic processes into the USA. Interested in the process of paper photography developed by William Henry Fox Talbot, they became its exclusive agents in the USA. While licensing the talbotype process was not commercially rewarding, the venture encouraged them to adopt and to improve the albumen process. Employing glass as a support for the emulsion, the Langenheims began making photographic lantern slides. In introducing these new slides, the brothers claimed:

> The new magic-lantern pictures on glass, being produced by the action of light alone on a prepared glass plate, by means of the camera obscura, must throw the old style of magic lantern slides into the shade, and supersede them at once, on account of the greater accuracy of the smallest detail which are drawn and fixed on glass from nature, by the camera obscura, with a fidelity truly astonishing. By magnifying these new slides through the magic lantern, the representation is nature itself again, omitting all defects and incorrectness in the drawing which can never be avoided in painting a picture on the small scale required for the old slides.[28]

By 1851 they were exhibiting slides at London's Crystal Palace Exhibition, where these hyalotypes received extensive praise.[29] Views were of buildings and landmarks in Philadelphia (US Custom House, Penitentiary of Pennsylvania), Washington (Smithsonian, the Capitol) and New York (Croton Aqueduct), as well as portraits of well-known Americans. Their early positive pictures on glass slides were mounted in rectangular wooden frames that were 3⅝ x 6⅞ inches with a 2¾ inch or 3 inch circular opening for the image. Many were hand coloured and they cost

$4–5 apiece. The Langenheims thus saw their introduction of photograph slides as an extension of existing magic lantern practices.

The progress made in photographic processes moved back and forth between Europe and the USA as the Langenheims' innovations were adapted to the stereoscope, The move from daguerreotypes to more modern photographic images for the stereoscope was not straightforward. Writing for the *Philadelphia Photographer*, M. A. Root reported that:

> Mr Niepce's process of making negative pictures by using albumen in combination with iodide of potassium, was published in the early part of 1848. In this, his process, he states distinctly that the *positive* pictures are always best taken on paper.
>
> Mr Langenheim informs me that he, 'by modifying Niepce's process, obtained the *first positive pictures on glass* to be viewed by transmitted light, in 1848. And in 1849' he says, 'I exhibited for the first time such positive glass pictures by means of the magic lantern in the Merchants' Exchange at Philadelphia.
>
> 'While in Paris, in 1853, I was introduced to the celebrated optician Dubosque-Soleil, to whom I showed some of my magic lantern pictures, made by me in Philadelphia. He was delighted with them, and asked my permission to show them in a scientific magic lantern exhibition, which he had to give in one of the public institutions, and during this exhibition he showed these pictures, stating to the audience that they were the *first pictures* of the kind ever shown in Paris.'
>
> In conversation, Mr Dubosque told me that when he was engaged in 1851, to arrange the display of his articles for the 'World's Fair' in London, he saw my photo magic lantern pictures, the first he had ever seen, and thinking that such photo-positive pictures on glass might be used to supersede the daguerreotype pictures, until then manufactured for him by Mr Ferrier; he had at once written to Mr Ferrier, to come over [from] London to examine my transparent positive pictures taken on glass, and that since then they had tried and made such transparent positive pictures on glass for the stereoscope.[30]

Photographers in France and England soon enjoyed a booming business in making glass slides for the stereoscope, but this innovation happened somewhat later in the USA. It was again the Langenheims who responded to European developments by making the first stereoscopic glass slides in the USA during the summer of 1854.[31] Nevertheless, in the latter part of 1858 the production and sale of stereoscopic glass slides was still getting started in New York City, with landscapes on paper selling from $6–9 per dozen and landscapes on glass from $15–30.[32]

Antoine Claudet tried to project individual halves of a stereoscopic slide and retain or re-create a 3-D effect in 1857.[33] The resulting achievement, which he called the stereomonoscope, received significant attention in the press and among scientific journals. The *Chicago Press and Tribune* reported,

M. Claudet, the veteran photographer, has accomplished a particularly [impressive] result in his art, enabling him to produce the stereoscopic illusion by the agency of a single picture. In the centre of a large black screen, there is a space filled with a square of ground glass, upon which, by some light managed behind the screen, is thrown a magnified photographic image representing a landscape, a portrait, or any other object. When the observer looks naturally at the object or picture, with the two eyes, without help of any optical instrument, an extraordinary phenomenon takes place – the picture is seen in perfect relief, as when two different pictures are looked at through a stereoscope. ... By this remarkable discovery, M. Claudet has solved a problem which has always been considered an impossibility by scientific men – for the stereomonoscope, by its very name, must sound like a paradox to the ears of those who are versed in the knowledge of the principles of binocular vision, until they have had the opportunity of repeating the experiments by which M. Claudet has found a new fact which they had not noticed or explained before.[34]

In fact, although projecting a single photographic image did not produce a 3-D effect, viewers did experience a visceral sense of depth that was much stronger than if a photograph was merely viewed on paper or a metal surface. Claudet believed (wrongly) that projecting a photographic image onto a ground glass was the key to retaining a three-dimensional sense of depth.

Chemist John Fallon of Lawrence, Massachusetts, apparently acquired one of Claudet's lanterns and, after refiguring and discarding elements, offered what was referred to as an 'improved stereopticon', which he exhibited in the 1860s. According to one press report,

Although the stereopticon was exhibited for a time in the Polytechnic Institute, and in the Hall of Illustration, Regent's Park, London, yet it did not advance beyond the first discovery. J. Fallon, Esq., of Lawrence Mass, the chemist of the Pacific Mills, who has devoted thirty years to photology, imported from England one of these instruments for his own family. But under his hands it was developed into something so perfect that his friends desired that others might have the pleasure which he enjoyed. He has sent it forth on a charitable mission, and for churches, Sabbath schools, and sanitary commissions its charities can be counted by thousands. In

Massachusetts, such men as Prof. Agassiz, Longfellow, Hillard, Holmes, Rev. Dr Park, and many other leading representative men 'assisted' with delight at many of the exhibitions, and the first two aided in delineating the scenes.[35]

By January 1861, announcements for the 'stereopticon' were appearing in such American periodicals as the *Saturday Evening Post*, which remarked that 'It produces in a wonderful degree the impression that you are gazing upon the real scenes and objects represented.'[36] *Arthur's Home Magazine* hailed this 'triumph of science and art combined' and declared,

No picture or dioramic view is comparable with the 'Stereopticon' in giving a just idea of scenery or architecture. You seem to stand in the very place that is represented, and to see everything just as it exists, in all its true portions.[37]

After being exhibited in the Boston area and in non-theatrical venues, Fallon's stereopticon opened at Toro Hall in Hartford, Connecticut, on 23 December 1862, where the effects were declared to be 'brilliant and startling, and the representations singularly truthful'.[38] It then moved to Hartford's larger and more prestigious Allyn Hall for a week in mid-January.[39] Exhibitor J. Leyland supervised the Brooklyn, New York, debut of this 'scientific wonder of the age' at the Atheneum on 14 April 1863. Although audiences were embarrassingly small at first, the city's leading citizens (including Mayor M. B. Kalbfleisch and Charles J. Sprague) urged Fallon and Leyland to remain 'so that all may enjoy its beauties and profit by its instructions'.[40] It ultimately ran almost continuously for six weeks with a 25 cent admission fee. The evening debut consisted of 'a choice selection of landscapes, architectural views and sculptures gathered from travels in the most illustrious parts of Europe, Asia and our own country'.[41] The mistaken belief that 'half of a stereoscopic view could be made to present a solid (i.e., stereoscopic) effect' persisted.[42] The *New York Journal of Commerce* commented that the stereopticon,

has been developed into something so brilliant and beautiful that the pictures produced are as much beyond the ordinary photograph as that, in fidelity and beauty, is beyond the old fashioned engraving. In short, the delight which one person has in looking through the stereoscope, a thousand persons can have at once – so that there is sympathetic and social pleasure. The Stereopticon, as it is called, takes the ordinary glass stereoscopic view, and by fine lenses and the most intense of artificial lights, throws and magnifies the miniature view upon a canvas to such an extent that every one in a building as vast as the

Academy of Music can see with distinctness each scene. There is no straining of the vision; there is no wearying of the eye as in the stereoscope, but one merely sits and gazes upon the sublime scenery of the Alps, the renowned old abbeys, the busy streets of London, Paris, Naples, and Grand Cairo; the grand, awe-striking remains of Egypt, and the solemn instructive scenes of Palestine. In the same manner and with the same ease that we look upon a real landscape from the deck of a Hudson River steamer. The distant and the rare are brought to us – or rather like a magic mat of the Arabian tale we are borne on swift and brilliant wings to the ends of the earth. The treasures of statuary art from the Louvre, the Vatican and the Museo Borbonico are ours. Nothing seems so dream-like as the Apollo Belvedere, the Venus de Medici, and the *chefs d'oeuvre* of the great Thorwalden, which appear upon the scene in all their roundness and beauty.[43]

Another reviewer echoed many of the same sentiments, remarking that 'you can imagine yourself borne away on the enchanted carpet of the Arabian tale, and brought where you can look down upon the veritable Paris, and Rome, and Egypt'.[44] Leyland soon made almost daily programme changes, devoting each illustrated lecture to a specific country or region: *Great Britain, France, Switzerland and the Rhine*, and *Italy*.[45] For another popular programme, the 'wall photographer' exhibited photographs of statuary. These evening shows – with Wednesday and Saturday matinees at reduced fee – were 'attended by the learned and scientific portion of society as well as others'.[46] Within a few weeks, P. T. Barnum had introduced the 'Great English Stereopticon' as his principle attraction at the American Museum, with 'photographic views of scenery, celestial and animated objects, buildings, portraits, &c, &c.'[47] It was soon followed by Fallon's stereopticon at Manhattan's Irving Hall for a five-week run.[48] The stereopticon was launched with an array of competing exhibitions that anticipated in some ways cinema's novelty year thirty-three years later.

A combination of factors contributed to the sense that the stereopticon was a new and important media form. The powerful illusory effect of the stereopticon was similar to the experience that spectators would have with the first projected films – the sense of being transported to a different place (and time). Commentators were impressed by the realism and the immediacy of the image – with the sense of 'being there'. These 'wonderful exhibitions' produced 'brilliant and startling' effects as well as representations that were 'singularly truthful'. 'The Old World and the New, are brought in all their beauty and grandeur to our very doors.'[49]

Programmes were initally composed of a miscellaneous collection of slides – the stereopticon of attractions, to coin a phrase, but exhibitors quickly gathered together enough photographic views of particular subjects so that

they could be forged into coherent non-fiction programmes. One could say that the novelty of such slides momentarily disrupted the established practices of the illustrated lecture, but then reaffirmed and expanded them. Although photographic slides would eventually be used for fiction – Bamforth and York & Company were prolific producers of life-model lantern slides – photography and photographic slides were a boon to the documentary tradition in that photography generated images that were more detailed, objective and (soon) cheaper to produce than the painted slides on which showmen had had to rely previously. It would be a mistake to refer to the resulting programmes as 'documentaries'. They went by various names – names that varied from country to country – but they were certainly part of what we must recognise as the documentary tradition. Their ressemblance to the heavily narrated, expository documentaries of the 1930s and beyond should be obvious to all. Moreover, we can recognise a number of genres, which were already well established in the 1880s, if not before, for which there is remarkable continuity even to this day. They would include the war programme, the science programme, the religious programme, the 'city symphony' programme (to use an anachronism), the political programme and so forth. The travel genre quickly broke down into a number of popular sub-genres focused on exploration in the polar regions, the African Safari, the travelogue of Europe, Asia and the Americas and so forth. Almost without exception, each has its own complex, rich genealogy. The documentary tradition flourished in the late nineteenth and early twentieth century with 'documentary-like' programmes. To not see this, takes an incredible act of blinding willpower.

War has been a prominent and recurrent subject in the documentary tradition as can be seen by simply focusing on the Anglo-American tradition. There were illustrated lectures on the Crimean War (1854–55), though it does not appear that Roger Fenton's photographs – or photographs in general – were used. David Francis reports that slides for illustrated lectures on the Crimean War at the Royal Polytechnic were hand painted.[50] In New York, by June 1864 Fallon's stereopticon devoted its final programme to the Civil War with *The Army of the Potomac*:

> The views illustrate the army from the first battle of Bull Run up to its present position under the commands of Gen. McDowell, Gen. McCellan, Gen. Burnside, Gen. Hooker, Gen. Meade and Lieut. Gen. Grant are vouched for by all our generals, and bring the battle fields, their incidents and localities, before us in the most faithful and vivid manner, each view being reproduced on a canvas covering a surface of over 600 square feet.[51]

Stereopticon lectures on the Civil War became immensely popular in the USA and remained common until the late nineteenth century. Very soon after the arrival of cinema, cameramen began to take films in war zones and also make re-enactments closer to home. These were shown as individual news films or in small groups but they were also combined with lantern slides to give illustrated lectures on the war. In his examination of early war films, Stephen Bottomore notes that Frederic Villiers took more than a dozen films of the 1897 Greco-Turkish War and used them for lectures on his return to England (the images on the screen almost certainly included lantern slides since Villiers also brought a still camera with him).[52] In the USA, the Spanish-American War was an immensely popular subject for the screen. The Eden Musee offered *A Panorama of the War* while Lyman Howe devoted his Autumn 1898 programme to a sustained narrative treatment of the War.[53] Dwight Elmendorf gave illustrated lectures such as *The Santiago Campaign and the Destruction of Cervera's Fleet – War Through a Camera* at New York's Carnegie Hall and on some occasions integrated films into his programmes.[54] Soon after showmen in Britain were offering extensive programmes on the Boer War, complete with lectures and sound effects – again integrating slides and films.[55]

Exhibitors began to integrate slides and films into their illustrated lectures to create a documentary-like programme; this was already the case in the late 1890s and the practice continued into the 1920s and beyond.[56] Burton Holmes used it for his presentation *Manila* (1899–1900) on the Filipino-American War and *Port Arthur: Siege and Surrender* (1905–06) for his treatment of the Russo-Japanese War.[57] The same approach was used in many cases for the Balkan War of 1912. British war correspondent Angus Hamilton visited the USA in early 1913 an gave a series of lectures on *The Balkan War* in New York, Pittsburgh and other cities – again interweaving slides and film.[58] The reasons for this practice were multiple. Illustrated lectures were generally assembled and exhibited by individual showmen. It would have been prohibitively expensive to fill an evening-length programme with films, which were expensive to produce or to buy. The motion-picture camera was bulky. Still images were not only much cheaper, they were much easier to produce so there were many more images to choose from. Moreover, lantern slides were often hand coloured and quite beautiful. Although projection technology was improving, problems with flicker persisted for many, even after 1903 when the three-blade shutter was introduced. The alternation between stills and motion pictures was also an alternation between colour and movement. Clearly one feature of all this was that the lecturer was in charge of post-production – the gathering and organisation of material, the writing and delivery of a lecture, the choice of music and so forth – and the author of the programme. Many lecturers continued to use only slides but the combination of the two became very

common around 1906, at the time of the nickelodeon boom.[59] Not surprisingly, these illustrated lectures tended to be presented outside the network of commercial motion picture theatres or nickelodeons.

The emergence of the feature film in 1912–13 would have a significant if complex impact on the documentary tradition. At first, films were often being shown in legitimate theatres during the summer months when they were normally dark, providing the theatre owners with extra income. Many of these early feature-length programmes were non-fiction. Some were in Kinemacolor, such as *Actual Scenes of the Balkan War*, which was paired with *Making the Panama Canal* (both 1913) in many venues.[60] These programmes were now composed exclusvely of motion pictures, though they still generally had a lecturer. However, there was often more than one set of the same films being shown and it was not the lecturer so much as the programme itself that was being promoted. *Paul Rainey's African Hunt* (1912), for instance, was showing at New York's Lyric Theater in the spring and summer of 1912. There was generally still a lecturer and while s/he was mentioned in reviews, s/he was no longer seen as the author. In any case, documentary-like programmes composed exclusively of motion pictures were major contributors to the ascendency of the feature film.

With the onset of World War I in 1914, the English, French and Germans began to produce feature-length non-fiction films (as well as shorter news films) to present their side of the war. These were meant to inspire each nation's populations, but they were also used to win over the hearts and minds of citizens in neutral countries such as the USA. At the very end of 1915, Official French Government War Films were released under the title *Somewhere in France*. From Great Britain there was *Britain Prepared* (December 1915).[61] At about the same time, the Germans offered *Deutschwehr War Films*, with proceeds from admissions going to German War widows and babies. As one reviewer remarked:

> While the pictures linger on the details behind the lines which play so important a part in modern war, they have some elements of novelty and are not without interest. But showing pictures of a noble church razed almost to the ground with the explanation in a subtitle that it had been used as a fortress, and showing a pasture on which cows are grazing to prove that Germany suffers from no lack of food, smacks too much of propaganda and too little of entertainment for the observer who is neutral either in fact or desire.
>
> As a matter of fact they are cleverly designed to warm the hearts of those who love the fatherland, to bolster such hearts with confidence and to disprove widespread statements as to conditions in Germany. But they shed no new light on any phase of modern warfare.[62]

In New York City, the Commissioner of Licensees, Mr George H. Bell, had declared that there must be no pictures of victories or defeats and that films displaying partiality would be suppressed.[63] However, his concern focused on fiction films where manipulation seemed more obvious. Because these films were non-fiction, it was assumed at first that they would be objective. Many officials believed that non-fiction programmes would provide information rather than fan emotions, but war documentaries soon challenged those assumptions.

The first great non-fiction war film – and one is tempted to argue the first landmark war documentary – was The Battle of the Somme. The completed five-reel film (approximately sixty-three minutes) premiered on 10 August 1916 at London's Scala Theatre while the battle itself was still being fought. On 21 August the film was shown simultaneously in thirty-four London movie houses and in provincial cities the following week.[64] It was screened privately (but widely reviewed) in New York City in late September and then presented in a succession of major pictures houses the following month. Under these circumstances, it was no longer possible to train and assign lecturers to the screenings. Intertitles had to do all the work of communicating verbal information, and this was desirable because it assured a standardised presentation – an important consideration in the propaganda effort. In short, if Paul Rainey's African Hunt was still in some sense an illustrated lecture, The Battle of the Somme was not.

The British followed The Battle of the Somme with The Battle of the Ancre and the Advance of the Tanks (1917). With the USA's entry into war in April 1917, the Committee on Public Information, or Creel Committee, produced a wide variety of motion pictures for informational and propagandistic purposes. Among them were three feature-length films: Pershing's Crusaders (May 1918), America's Answer (to the Hun) (August 1918) and Under Four Flags (November 1918). While there were often brief introductory talks by 'four-minute men' before the films, these films were screened without lecturers and depended on

The Battle of the Somme (1916): intertitles had to do all the work of communicating verbal information

their intertitles for a standardised presentation in all parts of the country.

The above sketch of non-fiction war programmes could be done for all the other genres and sub-genres of the documentary tradition that flourished in the nineteenth and early twentieth centuries. With *Nanook of the North*, for instance, Robert Flaherty creatively engaged a genre that goes back, at least, to the late 1880s when Robert Peary gave illustrated lectures on the Eskimos or Inuit, after one of his early efforts to reach the North Pole. One might appreciate (but also analyse) the sentiment that has led to the designation of *Nanook* as the first documentary, but which is at best an honorary *and* retrospective labelling. Of course, *Nanook* possesses many remarkable qualities that make it ground-breaking, such as the loving, respectful treatment of a superficially ordinary, fourth-world indigenous man and his family. But these are not criteria that define the documentary as such.

Bill Nichols has offered a number of criteria for conceptualising documentary, but, from a historical point of view, the consolidation of creative control within the production company in the non-fiction arena, which is to say the emergence of the non-fiction *film-maker* who produced a standardised product that did not depend on his/her physical presence at the point of exhibition, seems a key element or shift. In this respect the role of non-fiction in the emergence of the feature film in 1912–13 was an important moment, but it was World War I and the demands for massive, rapid dissemination of a standardised non-fiction work of propaganda that led to the systematic application of innovations that characterised documentary as a practice. Some might have once objected that these films are propaganda not art, but, as we now recognise, many subsequent films in the documentary tradition are propaganda – and one cannot help but recognise the many parallels between *The Battle of the Somme* and John Huston's *The Battle of San Pietro* (1945, USA). Of course, the arrival of recorded sound ironically meant that documentaries often looked and sounded more like the illustrated lectures of the pre-World War I era; nevertheless, the mode of production was further centralised – extended to embrace sound (music and other forms of sound accompaniment had remained outside the control of the documentarian). In this respect, we can think of the documentary tradition, a particular strand of non-fiction audiovisual practice, as originating in the seventeenth century and developing through a remarkable series of technological innovations until it assumes a series of characteristics of modern mass media and modern mass culture. That this should happen in the midst of World War I and, in fact, concurrent with the development of the Ford assembly line should hardly be a surprise.

NOTES

1. Erik Barnow *Documentary: A History of the Non-fiction Film* (New York: Oxford University Press, 1993 [1974]), pp. 2–48; Jack C. Ellis, *The Documentary Idea: A Critical History of English-Language Documentary Film and Video* (Englewood Cliffs, NJ: Prentice Hall, 1989), pp. 9–27.

2. John Grierson, *New York Sun*, 8 February 1926.

3. One weakness of this chapter must be acknowledged upfront: the Anglo-American myopia of my own research and knowledge. There are histories that are emerging of documentary in other national cinemas and some may be taking an approach similar to what I am offering here, but they have not been integrated into the Anglo-American scholarly apparatus. The Goethe Institute, for instance, offers a brief English-language history of German documentary, which begins with Walter Ruttmann's *Berlin. Berlin: Die Sinfonie der Großstadt* [*The Symphony of the City*] (1927), see: http://www.goethe.de/kue/flm/fmg/en43803.htm. Accessed 2 September 2012. Perhaps for this early-ish, pre-1922 period, this failing can also be a strength because it allows us to focus on language in the English-speaking realm. For instance, the fact that the term 'documentary' was borrowed from the French allows us to see the ways in which French documentary practice has a particular place in the Anglo-American tradition.

4. Anon., 'St Eustatia Prize Bill', *London Chronicle*, 4 July 1786, p. 23.

5. Anon., 'House of Lords', *London Chronicle*, 1 March 1788, p. 215; Anon., 'House of Lords', 12 April 1788, p. 359; Anon., 'Account of the Trial of Warren Hastings, Esq.', *American Magazine*, July 1788, p. 516; Anon., 'Sketch of Mr Hasting's Trial', *Connecticut Courant*, 22 August 1791, p. 2. Hasting, who had been Governor General of Bengal, was charged in Parliament with high crimes and misdemeanors and impeached in 1787. His trial ran from 1788 to 1795.

6. Anon., 'New Greece', *Observer*, 6 October 1878, p. 6. These conclusions are based on a sampling of periodicals dating back to the late eighteenth century using random word search engines (in particular the London *Observer* and the *Hartford Courant*).

7. Anon., 'Exhibition of the Photographic Society', *Observer*, 9 January 1859, p. 5. See also Anon., 'Miniature Painting', *The Crayon*, 1 August 1860, p. 228, in which photographs enable painters to depict a scene with topographical accuracy that generates 'documentary value'.

8. Anon., 'Stories of War and Peace', *New York Tribune*, 10 December 1898, p. 4.

9. Anon., 'Notes and News', *Photographic Times and American Photographer*, 27 April 1894, p. 267; see also Anon., 'On the Ground-Glass', *Wilson's Photographic Magazine*, 1 May 1894, p. 192.

10. A review of Arnold Wright's *Twentieth Century Impressions of Hong Kong, Shanghai and other Treaty Ports of China* (1908)

characterised it as 'all hard fact and documentary photograph'. (Anon., 'New Books', *The Scotsman*, 4 February 1909, p. 2).

11. Anon., 'The Grand National Film', *Manchester Guardian*, 4 March 1922, p. 6.

12. Anon., *Merchantmen-at-Arms* [book review], *The Scotsman*, 15 December 1919, p. 2; Anon., *Old English Sporting Books* [book review], *The Scotsman*, 3 November 1924, p. 2; Anon., *Col Charteris and the Duke of Warton* [book review], *The Scotsman*, 2 March 1925, p. 2.

13. Martha Gruening, 'European Revolt Against Our Films', *New York Times*, 31 October 1926, p. X6.

14. Anon., 'Vatican Repudiates Attack on Our Movies', *New York Times*, 29 July 1927, p. 17.

15. Athanasius Kircher, *Ars magna lucis et umbrae*, Amsterdam, 1671 (1646), pp. 792–4.

16. H. Mark Gosser, 'Kircher and the Lanterna Magica: A Re-examination', *Journal of the Society of Motion Picture and Television Engineers* vol. 90 no. 10, October 1981, p. 975.

17. Richard Altick, *Shows of London* (Cambridge, MA: Belknap Press of Harvard University Press, 1978), pp. 364–5. But these exhibitions were not limited to the UK or prestigious lecture halls. In Charleston, South Carolina, a church sponsored a series of lectures on astronomy, illustrated with the magic lantern, to the disapproval of a church periodical. (Anon., 'Church Desecretation', *Episcopal Recorder*, 12 April 1845, p. 14.)

18. Advertisement, *Observer*, 27 March 1825, p. 3.

19. Advertisement, *Philadelphia Recorder*, 9 December 1826, p. 147.

20. Anon., *Episcopal Recorder*, 20 December 1842, p. 151.

21. Anon., 'Electro-Magnetism', *New York Mirror*, 25 September 1841, p. 312.

22. Anon., 'The News', *New York Herald*, 24 January 1861, p. 4.

23. Anon., 'Brooklyn Items', *New York Tribune*, 11 January 1862, p. 3.

24. Anon., 'The Phonograph Exhibited', *New York Times*, 24 March 1878, p. 2.

25. Anon., 'Report of the Pennsylvania Hospital for the Insane: For the Year 1855', *New Hampshire Journal of Medicine*, 1 May 1856, p. 47.

26. Patent No. 7,458, Improvement in Producing Photographic Pictures upon Transparent Media, issued 25 June 1850.

27. Louis Walton Sipley, 'The Magic Lantern', *Pennsylvania Arts and Sciences*, 4 December 1939, pp. 39–43ff.; Louis Walton Sipley, 'W. and F. Langenheim – Photographers', *Pennsylvania Arts and Sciences*, 1937, pp. 25–31. The crucial work on the magic lantern in the USA remains Xenophon Theodore Barber, 'Evening of Wonders: A History of the Magic Lantern Show in America', PhD thesis, New York, 1993.

28. Langenheims, quoted in *The Art-Journal*, London, April 1851, p. 106.

29. See Anon., 'The King of Arms', *Observer*, 4 May 1851, p. 3.

30. M. A. Root, 'The Magic Lantern: Its History and Uses for Educational and Other Purposes', *Philadelphia Photographer*, 1 December 1874, p. 11, emphases original.

31. Frederick Langenheim to H. H. Snelling, 19 September 1854, in 'Personal and Fine Art Intelligence', *Photographic and Fine Arts Journal*, 1 October 1854, p. 319.

32. Anon., 'The Stereoscope', *New York Tribune*, 9 November 1858, p. 3.

33. Anon., 'Photographic Inventions', *Scientific American*, 25 May 1861, p. 326.

34. Anon., 'New Inventions', *Chicago Press and Tribune*, 14 May 1859, p. 3.

35. Anon., 'An Optical Wonder', *Louisville Daily Journal*, 29 April 1863, p. 1. The same basic review was also reprinted in *The Merchants' Magazine and Commercial Review* vol. 48, May 1863, p. 430.

36. Anon., 'The Stereopticon', *Saturday Evening Post*, 5 January 1861, p. 2.

37. Anon., 'The Stereopticon', *Arthur's Home Magazine*, April 1861, p. 17. Whether all these stereopticons can be attributed to Fallon is unclear: a stereopticon was shown at Temperance Temple in Baltimore on 4 February 1862, but it was quite possibly a renamed magic lantern and not Fallon's. (Anon., 'Temperance Temple', *Baltimore Sun*, 4 February 1862, p. 2.)

38. Anon., 'Amusements', *Hartford Courant*, 18 December 1862, p. 2.

39. Advertisement, *Hartford Courant*, 12 January 1863, p. 3; 'The Stereopticon', *Hartford Courant*, 14 January 1863, p. 2.

40. Mayor M. B. Kablefleisch et al. to John Fallon, 25 April 1863, reprinted in *Brooklyn Eagle*, 4 May 1863, 17.

41. Anon., 'The Stereopticon at the Atheneum', *Brooklyn Eagle*, 15 April 1863, p. 3.

42. Anon., *New York Journal of Commerce*, as quoted in *Louisville Daily Journal*, 29 April 1863, p. 1. Bertel Thorvaldsen (19 November 1770–24 March 1844) was a Danish/Icelandic sculptor.

43. Anon., *New York Journal of Commerce* as quoted in *Louisville Daily Journal*, 29 April, p. 1.

44. Anon., 'Modern Miracles', *Brooklyn Eagle*, 15 April 1863, p. 3.

45. Anon., *Brooklyn Eagle*, 29 April 1863, p. 1; Anon., *Brooklyn Eagle*, 15 May 1863, p. 1.

46. Anon., 'The Stereopticon', *Brooklyn Eagle*, 7 May 1863, p. 3.

47. Anon., *New York Daily Tribune*, 4 May 1863, p. 7.

48. Anon., 'Irving Hall', *New York Times*, 18 June 1863, p. 2.

49. Anon., 'Touro Hall', *Hartford Courant*, 24 December 1862, p. 2.

50. David Francis, email correspondence, 23 July 2012.

51. Anon., *New York Daily Tribune*, 27 June 1864, p. 3.

52. Stephen Bottomore, 'Filming, Faking and Propaganda: The Origins of the War Film, 1897–1902', PhD dissertation, University of Utrecht, 2007, chapter 3.

53. Charles Musser, *Before the Nickelodeon: The Early Cinema of Edwin S. Porter* (Berkeley: University of California Press, 1991); Lyman H. Howe, programme, Autumn 1898, reprinted

in Charles Musser, with Carol Nelson, *High Class Moving Pictures: Lyman Howe and the Forgotten Era of Travelling Exhibition* (Princeton, NJ: Princeton University Press, 1991).

54. Anon., 'War Through a Camera', *New York Times*, 18 January 1899, p. 7; Anon., 'The Santiago Campaign', *Brooklyn Daily Eagle*, 4 April 1899, p. 3.

55. Bottomore, 'Filming, Faking and Propaganda', chapter 11.

56. Henry Evans Northrop integrated Lumière cinematographe films with lantern slides for his illustrated lecture 'A Bicycle Trip Through Europe' in March 1897. (Anon., 'An Illustrated Lecture', *Brooklyn Eagle*, 9 March 1897, p. 7.)

57. Anon., 'Historic Siege', *Milwaukee Sentinel*, 11 October 1905, p. 4, reprinted in Musser, with Nelson, *High-Class Moving Pictures*, pp. 311–12.

58. Anon., 'Hamilton Praises Turks', *New York Times*, 20 Februrary 1913, p. 20; Anon., 'Lecture on the Balkan War', *Pittsburgh Press*, 3 April 1913, p. 3.

59. Edward Curtis, for instance, gave a series of illustrated lectures on American Indians, combining slides and films, in 1906–07 (Brooklyn Institute of Arts and Sciences, Ticket No. 31, 27 April 1907, reprinted in Musser, with Nelson, *High Class Moving Pictures*), p 181.

60. Anon., 'New England', *Moving Picture World*, 3 May 1913, p. 502; Anon., 'Novelties in Kinemacolor', *New York Times*, 2 March 1913, p. X8.

61. Luke McKernan, 'Propaganda, Patriotism and Profit: Charles Urban and British Official War Films in America during the First World War', *Film History* vol. 14 no. 3–4 2002, pp. 369–89.

62. 'Pictures at Chestnut German Propaganda', *Philadelphia North American*, 9 May 1916, p. 8.

63. 'Facts and Comments', *Moving Picture World*, 3 October 1914, p. 35.

64. https://en.wikipedia.org/wiki/The_Battle_of_the_Somme_%28film%29. Accessed 3 March 2013.

2.2 John Grierson and the Documentary Film Movement

IAN AITKEN

The field for the reception of the moving-image documentary might well have been well tilled by the established taste for optical devices in illustrated lecture presentations, but it was still some decades before Flaherty's crucial narrativising breakthough in 1922. It was not until his second film, Moana, in 1926 that John Grierson was inspired to recognise a new form of cinema and provide both a theoretical and institutional foundation for it.

Somewhat anachronistically, the founding intellectual source of the tradition engendered by John Grierson can be located in classical, idealist German philosophy. This philosophical tradition was, among many other things, preoccupied with the notion that the modern world had become an increasingly inhuman place, and that society had grown too fast and too large to be any longer congruent with optimal personal or social conditions. This tradition also questioned both western materialist assumptions founded upon a belief in capitalism and progress, and foundational ideas concerning the possibilities of democracy; and, in place of these, put forward the notion that society – including the capitalist economy – should be governed and administered by an elite network of semi-autonomous, über functionaries, who would be associated with, though also partly autonomous from, the state apparatus and its more habitual agents. These influential elite functionaries would set themselves stoically above sectarian interests, and would be dedicated to both consolidating the existing coherence of the social order, and promoting the sorts of reforms necessary to achieve such consolidation and, also, advancement. In effect, they would guide the historical development of the social formation. However, and as this model suggests, the idea of 'reform' involved here largely indicates a desire to move society into a greater condition of integration and stability, rather than, for example, into a greater condition of equality, justice, or democratic constitutionality. It can also be argued that this idealist tradition had both negative and positive aspects: negative, in that it was relatively corporatist, bureaucratic and elitist in disposition; positive, in that it also offered a thorough intellectual critique of capitalist modernity; and both of these features were to leave their mark on Grierson's thought.

This, in brief outline, is the foundational intellectual model which influenced John Grierson; for Grierson, the principal philosophical source of this model was Hegel's conceptions of the state, the spirit and the absolute – and the movement of the spirit and the state towards the absolute over the course of social-historical evolution. Following this Hegelian model, Grierson conceived of the state as a compilation of institutions which possessed fundamental value because those institutions had evolved progressively over the long course of historical time as meaningful collectivities and in the face of a destructive sectarianism, which Grierson, following his idealist disposition and Scottish Presbyterian background, deemed to be both engrained within the human condition and exacerbated by the forces of capitalist modernity.[1] In this Hegelian model, therefore, the agents of the state are seen as dedicated to the preservation of social unity, and to fending off the various destructive self-interested drives of other agents within the social formation, whose activities might shatter that social cohesion.

As argued, however, in addition to those who might be described as the ordinary, run-of-the-mill agents of the state, there would also be a semi-autonomous level of figures who, like their more pedestrian counterparts, also understood clearly the need to ensure social stability, but who, in addition, comprehended the overall principles of the movement towards the absolute. This was where Grierson believed his mission to lie, and he regarded himself as one of these torch bearers.[2]

Following this idealist tradition, Grierson came to believe that what had been achieved thus far in the development of the state must be both preserved and advanced, because, in his view, 'The State is the machinery by which the best interests of the people are served.'[3] Grierson's perennial bête noir was also apparent to him from an early age: group-based sectarianism and self-seeking individualism. Somewhat ironically, however, given his idealist roots – roots which are, to say the least, not entirely compatible with classical accounts of democratic accountability – the notion that corrupt power groups might manipulate the state and society for sectarian ends led Grierson to repeatedly emphasise, in a very unidealist manner, the importance of democracy and universal suffrage as a counter-balance to the influence of such self-interested power elites. But, on the other hand, if authentic power was to be placed in the hands of the 'ordinary' person through democratic franchise, that person would also have to be appropriately 'educated', from above, as it were; in order that such education act as a counter-balance to self-seeking individualism, misunderstanding, or even ignorance; and this was where Grierson and, eventually, elements of the Documentary Film Movement, presumed to play a role.

The idealist, Hegelian tradition that eventually came to influence Grierson was revived in Europe between the 1880s and the 1930s and became particularly influential in Central and Eastern Europe, where it influenced figures such as Georg Lukács and Max Weber, among many others; and evolved into a tradition of what has been referred to as 'romantic anti-capitalism'.[4] The tradition was also introduced into Britain towards the end of the nineteenth century and became influential in some universities, notably at Baliol College, Oxford, and Glasgow; and it was at Glasgow University that Grierson encountered the tradition when he attended the University between 1914 and 1919, and where he studied philosophers such as Kant, Hegel and the British philosopher W. H. Bradley.[5] It was the sense of mission involved in this tradition, which, when combined with the sense of vocation which Grierson inherited from his Scottish Presbyterian background, endowed him with the sense of purpose that was to drive him obsessively throughout the course of his career.

However, it was not only philosophy which led Grierson to the conclusion that sectarian forces were deflecting modern society and the modern individual from the course set by the absolute, but also what was happening around him, in central Scotland, at that time. After World War I, the capital goods industries of shipping, coal and steel more or less collapsed in the greater Glasgow and central Scotland area, plunging the whole region into a recession which created social deprivation on a frightening scale, and which brought about what has been referred to as an 'intensive exploitation of working people' by means of wage cuts and fierce competition for employment.[6] During this period, the fast-expanding metropolis of Glasgow, close to where the young Grierson lived, had some of the worst housing conditions in Western Europe, while disease, alcoholism and infant mortality were endemic. Grierson was an intimate witness to this unfolding social catastrophe, and it left in him both an ingrained hostility to unfettered capitalism and individualism, and a desire to ensure that such a collapse of the social order would not occur again in the future. Indeed, the sense of modernity being in, or almost being in, a state of crisis, and

John Grierson

the idea that there was little time to waste, was to charge up Grierson throughout his career. Motivated by the authoritative intellectual tradition he had absorbed while at university, Grierson came to believe that he knew what the problem was, and also how to resolve that problem; and, throughout his career, he did not spend too much time taking alternative – and therefore, in his view, mistaken – opinions into account over-much, even though he was always happy to enter into any argument that came along. After all, there were many who still had to be convinced, so Grierson never stopped talking. As he put it when giving a sermon – as a lay preacher – to a small Presbyterian congregation in 1920:

> Those who take no part in the fight never realise, and the whole secret of it is that each one of us must take part in the establishment of good things, before good things can come to pass ... it is for each of us to live and live strongly for the community of men, and to act according to the light that is in us.[7]

Grierson's concerns over the extent to which, in the modern situation, society had grown too extensive, chaotic and unregulated, were further reinforced when he travelled to America in the early 1920s. Here he was faced with an unexpected intellectual challenge which, to his credit, he eventually managed to overcome. When he arrived in America, Grierson found himself unwittingly caught up in an extensive right-wing political project which was ultimately designed to under-cut and roll back the American democratic system and, in particular, the voting franchise. Grierson went to America on a Rockefeller scholarship, and his original research remit was to study 'Immigration and its effects upon the social problems of the United States'. The objective of the conservative grant providers was, of course, to use the findings of the project to prove that immigration was indeed causing social problems and that, as a consequence, the immigration of the poor into America should be cut back, and the vote even withheld from the under-educated and ignorant masses then flowing into Ellis Island from Ireland, Greece, Poland, Italy and elsewhere.

The underlying thesis of this right-wing political project was that traditional conceptions of democracy – based, for example, on the Rousseauesque model of *The Social Contract* (1762) – were no longer appropriate to the new 'big society', in which it was impossible for the individual citizen to understand – and then vote on – every important issue of the day. The 'big society' thesis was pedalled particularly strongly at the time by the self-appointed 'public opinion' guru Walter Lippmann, who, in his book *Public Opinion* (1922), argued that society should be run by functional power elites, and not by democratic structures and a universal franchise at all.[8] However, Grierson soon came to reject what he referred to as 'the intellectuals' case against the people', because the Hegelian and neo-Hegelian traditions he hailed from had implanted within him the conviction that such power elites would inevitably behave in a sectarian and corrupt manner.[9] Thus, democracy was essential, in order to foil such sectarianism. From this position, contra-Lippmann, Grierson then came to the conclusion that the coherence of society could be better consolidated by the emergence of new media systems which would provide the citizen with social information, show the interdependence of the individual subject and the social formation, and promote necessary reform. But all of this would have to be under-written by democratic constitutionality.

This, then, provided the basis of Grierson's conception of the role which a progressive and enlightened mass media should play within the contemporary 'big society'. Such media organs would be charged with: (1) providing information to the citizenry, (2) showing how society was a social entity, rather than just a conglomeration of autonomous and selfish individual interests and (3) striving to promote the kind of reforms which would enhance the stability and advancement of democratic society. This eventually led Grierson to change the focus of his research from a study of immigration to a study of the mass media and, in particular, the press and the cinema. However, Grierson soon abandoned the idea that the American popular press could ever fulfil a genuine social function, given the extent to which he believed it to be dependent on the whims of both market forces and interested parties of all sorts; and it was this belief which then led him into an engagement with the cinema. Initially, Grierson felt that progressive branches of the commercial cinema might be able to carry out such a social function, so he developed a nascent theory of filmic social-realism which was premised on the assumption that feature films might be able to convey their romantic tales against the backdrop of some social institution or other; thus uniting the particular with the general and serving a socialising function. However, Grierson eventually came to the negative conclusion that Hollywood would never make the sorts of films which he believed to be required, and one consequence of this conclusion was that his embryonic theory of cinematic social-realism fell quickly by the wayside.[10]

THE DOCUMENTARY FILM MOVEMENT

When he arrived back in Britain in 1927, Grierson had the good fortune to be appointed to an organisation whose remit fitted fully with his developing aspirations. The role of the Empire Marketing Board (EMB) was to augment marketing relationships within the then British Empire, and it aimed to achieve this, in part, through the production of publicity, much of which was highly accomplished in terms of design and imagination. The EMB was, of course, a government organisation, manned by career civil servants, and one potential problem for Grierson here was that he might be considered to be something of an outsider – though, of course, given his idealist inclinations, Grierson never wanted to see himself as a traditional civil servant anyway. However, the EMB was an unusual government organisation for the time in that its director, Stephen Tallents, chose to appoint a substantial number of people from outside the civil service to important creative positions within the institution. Grierson was one of these and was, therefore, not alone. Like Grierson, Tallents had also had an idealist education, this time at Balliol, Oxford, and his vision of what he wanted at the EMB matched with Grierson's idealist-utopian aspirations well, as the following quotation illustrates:

> What we wanted to sell was the idea of the Empire as a co-operative venture between living persons interested in each other's work and in each other's welfare. Our task was not to glorify the power of the Empire but to make it live as a society for mutual help, a picture of vivid human interest, as well as of practical promise.[11]

Such comments also underscored Grierson's developing thoughts on the social mission of the mass media.

Grierson's first role at the EMB was to write a series of reports on how the institution might develop. One of these took the form of a long memorandum, written in 1927, entitled 'Notes for English Producers', which eventually turned out to be the foundational constitution of the Documentary Film Movement.[12] In this memorandum, Grierson advised the EMB to embark on the production of documentary films which would differ from those already in existence, in that they would maximise the use of cinematic means in order to portray the interconnection of individual and society. In a further memorandum written the same year, entitled 'Further Notes On Cinema Production', Grierson also argued that such films could not be made by the commercial sector and would, therefore, have to be made within the state system.[13] Later, in 1928, Grierson set out more proposals for the first configuration of what later became known as the Documentary Film Movement, and these consisted of suggestions on how to establish a film library, hire a small team of film-makers, create distribution and exhibition outlets and set about making two films in the first instance.[14] One of these was to be a short film on the herring industry, and this eventually became *Drifters* (1929), possibly the most revolutionary film to be made in Britain at that point.

Drifters exhibits the influence of then highly controversial (in fact, banned) Soviet montage films such as Sergei Eisenstein's *Battleship Potemkin* (1925), and also combines that formalist influence with a highly symbolic homage to nature, the sea and the toil of humble fishermen. The officials at the EMB who saw the film at its first screening were bewildered by what they saw, as they had been expecting to sit down before a straightforward public relations short. However, the critical and commercial success of the film enabled Grierson to squash any move those officials may have been contemplating to rein in his ambitions; and he went on to establish the EMB Film

Drifters (1929): possibly the most revolutionary film to be made in Britain at that point

Unit and gather disciples around himself. The 'movement' had been inaugurated, and Grierson now had the instrument through which to put his neo-Hegelian vision of the movement of the spirit towards the absolute into practice: the documentary film would, henceforth, be the instrument through which sectarianism would be held in check and a high-minded socially cohesive ideal be promulgated.

What then come to pass around Grierson's Documentary Film Movement over the 1930–52 period can best be characterised in terms of a continuing displacement between Grierson's Hegelian-oriented vision and civil service functionaries who, for the most part, had no understanding whatever of what he was after. The strategy of the 'movement' over these years was to carry out routine commissions, while stealthily engaging in more experimental and socially meaningful work. Important films certainly emerged from this strategy. However, the result of this strategy was, in addition, a continuing series of misunderstandings and, at times, genuine antipathy between the various parties. Grierson also came to realise fairly quickly that the central premise of his Hegelian-inspired plan – that he and his film-makers would be ceded substantial authority and autonomy to guide the actions of the state through the production of films – could never come into reality against a context of the highly conservative English civil service of the inter-war years. In fact, to such traditionalist functionaries, schooled in free-market orthodoxy, the idea of a publicly owned documentary film movement was always an anachronism anyway, and even a vaguely (or even explicitly, as some of them thought) 'socialist' initiative. After all – as numerous official memos concerning the EMB and later film units would enquire – why could the commercial sector not be allowed to make such films?[15] And if a public film unit, staffed by capricious outsiders, *must* exist, these functionaries would and did ensure that strict controls and restraints were placed on its activities.

Up till the mid-1930s the Documentary Film Movement was still largely unified behind Grierson and his ideals. But, of course, the movement cannot merely only be identified with Grierson, and what we have here is much more in the nature of a documentary film movement, albeit one founded by Grierson, rather than a 'Griersonian tradition'. This distinction is a crucial one, for it is paramount that the movement not be exclusively identified with Grierson. Others were involved too, and had substantial roles to play. For example, when the Brazilian Alberto Cavalcanti joined the movement in the mid-30s, he brought with him the experience of having worked within the French cinematic avant-garde of the 20s, an area of which Grierson himself had little knowledge. Cavalcanti was to have a major impact on the movement during the 30s and 40s, and was largely responsible for some of the most important films which emerged there, including Basil Wright's *Song of*

Ceylon (1934), whose innovative and experimental use of sound reveals Cavalcanti's influence. However, Cavalcanti was also often at odds with Grierson and his close associates, including, for example, John Taylor, who believed that 'It was a great mistake to have Cavalcanti really, because he didn't understand what documentary was supposed to be doing.'[16] In fact, by around 1936, and after the movement had moved from the EMB to the General Post Office, with the establishment of the GPO Film Unit, a definite rift had begun to open up between Grierson and his closest associates, such as Taylor and Stuart Legg, and film-makers who wished to place more emphasis on the aesthetic quality of the films being made – film-makers such as Alberto Cavalcanti, Harry Watt and Humphrey Jennings, who would all go on to lead the movement into important new directions during the late 30s and the war years. By 1936 Grierson had also moved away from the idealist-modernist position he had adopted over the making of *Drifters*, and was now becoming much more hard-headed in insisting that the films of the movement must be primarily educative and socially purposive. The row boiled over in 1941, when Grierson criticised his successor at the GPO Film Unit, Alberto Cavalcanti, for being a 'fellow traveller', a term which, given its use in the Stalinist purges of the 30s, carried rather weighty and unfortunate overtones (i.e., of treachory and betrayal).[17]

In any case, though, by 1936 Grierson had already decided to leave the state sector when it became clear that even more restrictions were about to be placed upon the GPO Film Unit. When he came to the firm conclusion that the British state would not be the sort of home for the movement of socially purposive film-makers that he had originally envisioned it might be, he moved out of its confines and initiated an enlargement which took on a momentum of its own, which eventually came to span the globe. In 1936 Grierson left the pay of the state to help establish film-making units in various corporate concerns, such as the Shell oil company. The objective here, once again, was to obtain commissions, but this time from the corporate sector, and to make films which would satisfy the needs of the sponsors, but also, where possible, go beyond such requirements in order to attain higher levels of aesthetic quality and social representation. Thus, by 1936 the 'movement' had come to consist of the sole remaining state-controlled film unit: the GPO Film Unit, plus the Shell, Realist and Strand film units, and an organisational body entitled Film Centre. Films were also commissioned from bodies such as Shell, Imperial Airways and other corporate organisations by film-makers such as Paul Rotha and Basil Wright. Revealingly, however, after Grierson left the GPO Film Unit in 1936, and under the leadership of Cavalcanti, the unit went on to produce some of the most important films to emerge from the Documentary Film Movement as a whole.

In 1940, shortly after the outbreak of war, the GPO Film Unit became the Crown Film Unit, and also took up position as the central state documentary film-making unit of the war period, charged with making films largely for home consumption. In 1939 Grierson left for Canada to found the National Film Board of Canada, and both 'Griersonism' and the 'movement' now spread beyond the shores of Britain. But Grierson lost his way during the war years, as indicated by his unfortunate 1941 attack on Cavalcanti, and he became increasingly confrontational in his attitude, denigrating 'aesthetic' film-making and insisting that, at that time, in the midst of world war, only socially purposive forms of film-making were warranted. Grierson took a number of people with him from Britain to develop film-making in Canada, including Stuart Legg, Stanley Hawes, J. D. Davidson, Basil Wright, Evelyn Spice and Raymond Spottiswood; and these individuals had a significant impact upon the development of Canadian film culture, at least during the 40s.[18] However, Grierson himself was also responsible for the development of two tendentious and bombastic film series: *Canada Carries On* and *World at War*, series of films as far removed from the ground-breaking *Drifters* as could be imagined – and films which even Jack Beddington, Head of the Films Division of the Ministry of Information in Britain, found to be too crudely propagandistic for British film propaganda purposes.[19]

In Britain, the war years marked the apotheosis of Grierson's ambitions for the Documentary Film Movement, though, paradoxically, he was not to play any part in such supplementation. Now, at last, documentary film was playing a central role at the heart of the state apparatus, and tapping into vast fields of emotion against the context of the war effort. Now, themes of national unity, the consequential heroism of ordinary people, the necessary assimilation of the classes and the incorporation of the individual with the collective and the institutions of state, received powerfully emotive embodiment in films such as Humphrey Jennings's *Words for Battle* (1941), *Listen to Britain* (1942) and *Fires Were Started* (1943). During this period, therefore, it can be argued that Grierson's original vision became realised to a considerable degree. However, wartime is not normal, ordinary time and, after the war, there was a return to the pre-war ante in terms of the relations which obtained between the film-makers and the civil servants who employed them. The most radical leftist government in British history may have come to power in 1945, but, against a background of post-war austerity, the Treasury and civil service remained as they had ever been: bastions of cautious, conservative orthodoxy.

After the war ended, the Ministry of Information, the home of the Crown Film Unit, was disbanded and then replaced by the less potent Central Office of Information. Grierson returned in 1948 to take up the rather grandly titled post of 'Controller, Film', and thus became head of the Crown Film Unit. In theory, the great work of the wartime Documentary Film Movement should have continued smoothly into the radicalised post-war environment. After all, the post-war context, in which there was a felt need to establish a sense of cooperative unity in the face of Cold War antagonism suited Grierson's integrationist ideology perfectly. Now, Grierson, the self-proclaimed post-war 'internationalist' – 'I am entirely a person who is concerned with the establishment of good international understandings' – could preside over a film apparatus which might show how the whole world of nations should move towards an essential international unity, rather than be divided by ideology, politics and opposing economic formations.[20]

Unfortunately, however, this did not come to pass, as escalating restrictions were forced upon the film-makers in what turned out to be a post-war period marked by austerity and budgetary prudence, and as those same film-makers also began to age and become less productive. The unfortunate early death of Humphrey Jennings in 1950 was also an important factor in this decline, robbing the Documentary Film Movement of possibly its best film-maker. In 1950, Grierson resigned his post as Controller, Film, and the Crown Film Unit itself was eventually abolished in 1952. This was, undoubtedly, a great reverse for Grierson and the movement. However, by 1952, civil servants had become intent on cutting back government-produced film-making and, in any case, the post-war advent and growth of television in Britain had created a far more effective public relations avenue for the dissemination of official publicity. On the other hand, it has been argued that Grierson himself was partly responsible for the demise of the Crown Film Unit, in that 'Once again he created his own opportunity, mesmerised and enthused people with his plans, but when it came to it he failed to carry them through.'[21]

The abolition of the Crown Film Unit began the latest, and final, chapter of the movement founded by John Grierson in 1930. The major figures, such as Grierson, Harry Watt, Basil Wright, Paul Rotha, Alberto Cavalcanti and others, continued to work in various capacities up till around the mid-60s, after which most of them went into retirement. However, the influence of the movement also spread far during the 1952–70 period. In Britain, that influence could be felt in television from 1950 onwards, and particularly in Granada Television, where both Harry Watt and Denis Forman worked; Forman – who worked under Grierson at the Crown Film Unit in the late 40s – acted as managing director there between 1964 and 1974. In addition, Grierson's consensualist approach influenced current affairs policy in the BBC and ITV – but that is another story, which cannot be covered here.

A COMMONWEALTH OF DOCUMENTARY FILM[22]

Beyond Britain, the movement, and 'Griersonism', also had a considerable influence over this period. For example, between 1954 and 1961 J. B. Holmes produced films for Shell in Africa and Asia; Stanley Hawes became Head of the Australian Film Board in the mid-50s; Ralph Keene worked as an advisor and producer for the Government Film Unit in Ceylon between 1955 and 1963, while Alexander Shaw worked for UNESCO, advising on documentary film-making until 1970. New Zealander Len Lye also worked in America for the *March of Time* series during the 50s, while Evelyn Spice, Norman McLaren and Stuart Legg worked at the National Film Board of Canada up till the late 50s and beyond. Other members of the Documentary Film Movement also worked abroad during this period, but the general picture remains unclear; much research still needs to be carried out, both in relation to the figures mentioned here and others who remain in the shadows.

The period from 1945 till the emergence of television in many of Britain's overseas colonies around the late 60s was also the heyday of the colonial film units. While the Crown Film Unit had been belatedly established in 1940, following much pressure from the Griersonians, the Colonial Film Unit had been established slightly earlier, in 1939, on the outbreak of war, and under the sometimes brittle joint governance of the Colonial Office and Ministry of Information. The remit of the unit was to help official film-making in the colonies work more effectively for the war effort. So, for example, the Colonial Film Unit provided personnel, equipment and funding to official film-makers and local film-makers until, by 1955, most of the thirty-five registered colonies of the Commonwealth received aid in one form or another. The initial objective here, from the point of view of the Colonial Office, and from the early 40s onwards, was to assist colonial governments in official film-making until each country was able to establish and manage its own film unit; and it was initially expected that it would take some time before this would take place. However, such expectations were quickly undermined when various administrations took the initiative, and set up their own units, New Zealand paving the way in 1941. Other colonial administrations quickly followed suit and, given this context of rapid self-governing development, a decision was eventually taken in 1953 to disband the Colonial Film Unit, which had more or less ceased making its own films by 1951 anyway and had downsized considerably from its mid-40s peak.[23] Although, therefore, the Colonial Film Unit was finally abolished in 1955, surviving the Crown Film Unit by only some three years, the decision to close it was made around the same time that the Crown Film Unit was abolished, clearly signalling the general direction of official intent at the time vis-à-vis government film-making.

Thus, although the final period of the core 'Grierson tradition' and Documentary Film Movement in Britain might be dated up to 1952, the final period of the movement elsewhere, and particularly in the colonies, must be dated from 1941 and up to the late 60s. This is the era of the colonial film units. The films that were made in these units during this period could not, of course, hope to match the landmark output of the earlier British film units. Usually, supervision by colonial civil servants was tighter than had been the case with Britain during the 30s, and the civil servants were now wiser to the film-makers' covert tendency to innovate. In many respects, the colonial civil servants of this period were also – and perhaps not surprisingly – even more conservative and traditional in their outlook than Grierson's bête noirs of the 30s had been. However, in some cases this was actually not so and the film units sometimes managed to work as small, relatively autonomous bodies, able to make significant films from time to time. The influence of the Documentary Film Movement also continued to make itself felt here, both in terms of personnel and the character of the films made. The situation was, therefore, quite variable and a considerable amount of research still remains to be carried out in order to clarify these matters.

It will be helpful at this point to further explore the influence of the movement and tradition during this period by looking in more depth at one of the colonial film units, the Hong Kong Film Unit, in order to see how some of the principles of the tradition and movement were carried on into this later period. Following the demise of the Colonial Film Unit in 1955, the colonial Hong Kong government belatedly established the Hong Kong Film Unit in 1959. Between 1959 and 1969, when it was closed down, the film unit made some seven hundred short films which were shown regularly (and under compulsion) in the Crown Colony's sixty-eight cinemas. As was the case with the overall history of the tradition, many of these films were relatively routine and low-budget. However, some were made in a more innovative manner in an attempt to raise levels of quality. What is interesting about these films, as they are viewed today, is the extent to which the film-makers involved attempted to introduce a higher level of quality into even the most routine of films. Of course, these films could not be directly critical of the government, as, by the way, had also been the case with the films of the EMB and GPO Film Units. Nor could they be particularly critical of social conditions, in the way that films such as *Coal Face* (1935), *Housing Problems* (1935) and *Enough to Eat?* (1936) *had* been. However, what they could show, in considerable detail, was the social condition of the colony, including problems such as drug abuse, the poor quality of housing and poverty. What is also striking is the way in which these films are highly visually realistic in the extent to which they portray the rich texture of the local, ethnic

culture and society. Apparently, during this period, the civil servants in charge of the film unit 'trusted' the film-makers and afforded them a relatively long leash, which the film-makers then used to make intermittent, indirect points concerning issues of social reform.[24]

The links between the Documentary Film Movement in Britain and its later spread to the colonies can be seen in some of the work of the Hong Kong Film Unit, and in that of the other colonial film units. However, it is not always readily apparent to what extent the Colonial Film Unit can be associated with the Documentary Film Movement. Between 1940 and 1942, the Crown and Colonial film units actually worked together to a certain extent, and even shared the same premises, in Soho Square, central London.[25] However, after 1942, the Crown Film Unit moved to Pinewood Studios; the Colonial Film Unit then expanded into the premises in Soho Square. Subsequently, while the influence of the Documentary Film Movement can be seen in the early work of the Colonial Film Unit, the two units appear to have worked increasingly apart, a division exacerbated by the fact that, while the Crown Film Unit was controlled by the Ministry of Information (later Central Office of Information), the Colonial Film Unit was largely controlled by the Colonial Office. What is not entirely clear, therefore, is how these two units, and their films and personnel, intersected over the 1940–52 period – a problem made worse by the fact that the Colonial Film Unit films often have no credits – and a considerable amount of research remains to be carried out in this area.

However, in addition to the tentative links which might be established between the Documentary Film Movement, the Colonial Film Unit and the film-making activities within those colonies which were directly serviced by the Colonial Film Unit (particularly those colonies in Africa), much stronger connections can be established between the influence of the movement and those colonies which developed their own, fully fledged production units. Here, the Grierson influence was extensive. For example, Grierson himself travelled to Australia and New Zealand between 1938 and 1940, representing the Imperial Relations Trust and making suggestions as to how official film-making might develop in these countries – suggestions which eventually influenced the formation of the New Zealand Film Unit in 1941 and both the Australian National Film Board and Australian Commonwealth Film Unit in 1945.[26] People who had worked with the movement in Britain were also employed in these colonial film units. For example, Margaret Thompson worked for Grierson at both Crown and Group Three before going on to work at the New Zealand Film Unit. That link is quite clear, while others are more indirect. For example, one concerns Hugh Greene, brother of novelist Grahame Greene (who had worked with the Documentary Film Movement during the 30s). Greene, who was familiar with the activities of the movement himself and who would later go on to become a modernising director general of the BBC during the 60s, found himself working with the Malaya Film Unit in the late 40s, thus establishing a link here between the movement and a film unit serviced by the Colonial Film Unit. The role played in Australia by Stanley Hawes has already been mentioned. Other examples could be given; one commentator has even argued that 'the achievements of the Grierson movement were eventually to influence the documentary production of no less than ten nations'.[27] Grierson's memorandum to the then prime minister of Australia, Robert Menzies, on the development of official film-making in Australia could also well sum up the work of some of the Griersonian-influenced and Documentary Film Movement-influenced film units of the 1941–69 period. In his memorandum, Grierson argues that the role of official film-making should be to: 'Break down sectionalism and induce a national viewpoint. ... Bring the disparate elements ... together and create ... an integrated view. ... Bring[ing] into the public imagination the problems, responsibilities and achievement of Government'.[28] All of this can be seen in much of the work of the colonial film units.

A PECULIAR TRADITION

At one level, the Grierson 'tradition' can be viewed as an idiosyncratic attempt by one man to establish a new form of power-grouping within society, one which would take over responsibility for some of the processes of social mass communication currently managed by government functionaries and the commercial market. Grierson believed that these agents could not understand the historico-philosophical development of society as he could, so he felt the necessity to build a 'movement' which would embody that understanding within the medium of the state-commissioned, official documentary film. In Grierson's time, in the normal course of events within traditional civil service practice, government policy and the various activities of the state apparatus would be communicated to civil society and the media through a variety of means, including briefings to the media, the granting of interviews and the publication or production of documents and artefacts. This material might then be interpreted and debated by the mass media, including the press, radio, etc. However, Grierson trusted neither the role of official agents in this process, nor that of the free-market media, whom he considered to represent sectarian, rather than the national interest. What the Grierson tradition attempted to do, therefore, was to take over partial responsibility for this process of mass communication and structure it in terms of Grierson's key ideas concerning the portrayal of the intersection of the individual and social spheres, and the historico-philosophical movement of society. In this approach, agents of the state and the free-market media

would be pushed aside as a new class of social-idealist intellectuals, film-makers and producers hoved into view. This attempted displacement did, of course, have as a consequence the creation of a lasting distrust towards the 'Grierson men' on the part of both the civil service and the commercial documentary film sector.

Another reason for that distrust, however, at least on the part of government officials, was that the programme of Grierson and the Documentary Film Movement encompassed both a belief that that social stability was threatened by an inequitable distribution of wealth and resources and a conviction that such inequality had to be put right. Grierson, in particular, wished to raise the condition of the ordinary man and woman because he believed that, if this did not occur, the constancy of the social order might eventually be put at risk. Grierson did not wish to raise the condition of the poor on the basis of any socialist agenda, but on the basis of his idealist conception of the historico-philosophical development of society. Nevertheless, this aspect of Grierson's thought kindled a definite social-reformist consciousness within the Documentary Film Movement as a whole, and a concomitant suspicion among government and the commercial film sector that the 'Grierson men' were closet socialists, or communists. This suspicion reached a high point in 1947, of course, when Grierson was refused a visa to enter the USA, apparently because of concerns raised by the FBI.[29]

Grierson's vision, and his sense of a potential impending collapse of democratic society during the inter-war period, led him to believe that the Documentary Film Movement must expand quickly, and this explains the rapid expansion of the movement prior to the outbreak of World War II. After the war that expansion continued because various countries required public relations film-making to be established. However, the intellectual and creative direction and motivation which had informed the Documentary Film Movement during the 1930s – which had not only come from Grierson, but also from Cavalcanti, Jennings and others – was no longer really present, and the post-war development of the movement can best be characterised more in terms of an onward, increasingly disconnected progression, which was eventually brought to a halt by the establishment of television. Of course, elements of the movement then moved into television, in Britain, Australia and in many other places, and continued to have an influence of sorts. However, the period of the film units, inaugurated by Grierson in 1930 with the founding of the EMB Film Unit, had more or less come to a close by 1970.

In final conclusion, it can be said that the Grierson tradition was a rather *peculiar* tradition, based, as it was, on a combination of neo-Hegelianism (stemming only from Grierson), progressive reformism, conceptions of national identity filtered through an idealist disposition (as in Jennings), European modernism and rather eclectic conceptions of mass education and the role of the mass media and public relations. However, this same peculiarity also generates ambiguities which provide the foundation for future research into the tradition. As has already been argued here, 'Griersonianism' should also not be conflated with the Documentary Film Movement, which is made up of many persons, films, publications, ideas, institutions and events – not just Grierson. Finally, much more research into the movement is also required, in relation to the intellectual foundation and substance of the movement, the development of the movement within Britain from 1930 to 1952 and after, and further development outside of Britain between 1939 and 1970.

NOTES

1. John Grierson, *Grierson on Documentary*, ed. Forsyth Hardy (London: Faber, 1979), p. 130.
2. Ian Aitken, *Film and Reform: John Grierson and the British Documentary Film Movement* (London: Routledge, 1990), p. 186.
3. Grierson, *Grierson on Documentary*, p. 139.
4. Ferenc Feher, 'The Last Phase of Romantic Anti-Capitalism: Lukács' Response to the War', *New German Critique* no. 10, Winter, p. 139.
5. Aitken, *Film and Reform*, pp. 37–47.
6. Janet Glover, *The Story of Scotland* (London: Faber, 1960), p. 362.
7. Grierson Archive papers, 'The Contribution of Poetry to Religion', G1.5.2: 3 (1920).
8. Walter Lippmann, *Public Opinion* (New York: Allen and Unwin, 1922), p. 146.
9. Grierson Archive papers, G4.19.21: 2.
10. Aitken, *Film and Reform*, pp. 64–74.
11. Ibid.
12. Grierson, 1927, PRO BT 64/86 6880.
13. Grierson, 1927, PRO CO 760/37 EMB/C/4: 16.
14. EMB Film Committee Memorandum, 1928, PRO/CO 760/37 EMB/C/9: 8.
15. Commons Select Committee Report on Expenditure: Government Cinematographic Films, 1934, HMSO, pp. 9–15.
16. Ian Aitken, *Alberto Cavalcanti: Realism, Surrealism and National Cinemas* (Trowbridge: Flicks, 2001), p. 73.
17. Grierson, *Grierson on Documentary*, p. 112.
18. Gary Evans, *John Grierson and the National Film Board: The Politics of War-time Propaganda* (Toronto: University of Toronto Press, 1984), p. 55.
19. Ian Aitken, *The Documentary Film Movement: An Anthology* (Edinburgh: Edinburgh University Press, 1998), p. 29.
20. Ibid.
21. Nicholas Pronay, 'John Grierson and the Documentary: 60 Years On', *Historical Journal of Film, Radio and Television* vol. 9 no. 3, September 1989, p. 241.
22. The phrase is Jane Landman's (ed.).
23. 'Colonial Film Unit, Report of the' HKRS 41–1–7190, 1952.
24. Ian Aitken, unpublished interview with Peter Moss of the Hong Kong Government Information Service, May 2010.
25. Rosaleen Smyth, 'The British Colonial Film Unit and Sub-Saharan Africa, 1939–1945', *Historical Journal of Film, Radio and Television*, vol. 8 no. 3, September 1988, p. 287.
26. G. Shirley and B. Adams, *Australian Cinema: The First Eighty Years* (Sydney: Currency/Angus and Robertson, 1989), p. 165.
27. Ibid.
28. A. Moran and T. O'Regan (eds), *An Australian Film Reader* (Sydney: Currency, 1985), pp. 72–3.
29. Forsyth Hardy, *John Grierson: A Documentary Biography* (London and Boston: Faber, 1979), pp. 162–3.

2.3 Challenges for Change: Canada's National Film Board

THOMAS WAUGH AND EZRA WINTON

In 1936, Grierson famously stated: 'I look upon cinema as a pulpit'; but the effectiveness of Griersonian documentaries as sermons can be readily disputed. What cannot be questioned is the evangelical zeal which fired Grierson and his followers to spread his vision of documentary across the British Commonwealth. Of nowhere is this more true than of Canada.

NFB 1939–2010
Warclouds, 1939–45

On 2 May 1939 the Parliament of Canada passed an act creating the National Film Board of Canada (NFB). One year prior, Canadian diplomats in London had hatched a plan to hire British documentary pioneer John Grierson to assess the obsolete Canadian Government Motion Picture Bureau, which he argued needed a tune-up in order for Canada to properly sell itself for commerce and tourism overseas. Grierson, still on the payroll of the Imperial Relations Trust, was soon appointed the first Government Film Commissioner, and undertook to move state film-making towards the contemporary information goals he had learned at the knee of his teacher, Walter Lippmann, in the USA in the 1920s. At the same time, Grierson was 'working for the British', and when war broke out five months after the Act of Parliament it was clear that the NFB pro-British propaganda films were to play a vital role in bringing the then neutral American neighbours into the conflict.

Any assessment by Canadians of this institution cannot help but reflect the ex-colonial's resentment. The reader might even sense a smug gratification that the output of the colonial branch plant, originally set up as a temporary propaganda outpost for the imminent Battle of Britain, refused to wrap up after war's end and persisted to surpass by far the mother country's own documentary achievement of the second half of the twentieth century. This can be said to embrace six major 'innovations' of the Board which have shaped world documentary and can be found exemplified in the huge institutional stockpile of over 12,000 documentaries made between 1939 and 2010. As the NFB has sought, over the seven plus decades of existence, to fulfil its original mandate: 'to interpret Canada to Canadians and to other nations', these are suffused with the documentary vocations of propaganda, nation-building, civic education, entertainment, art and advocacy to a degree unmatched elsewhere.

The authors will first only briefly set out a skeletal chronology of the studio's history, which readers can otherwise easily access in the bountiful literature on the subject. We shall then consider six major 'innovations' of the Board, offering an inventory of such achievements considered historically, artistically and politically: public arts funding; geopolitical intervention; domestic political intervention; advances in dissemination and accessibility; programmes around diversity; experiments in aesthetics and technology.

Officially, the NFB was charged with producing and distributing films about Canada, for Canadians and the world. The first 'documentary' made under the auspices of the Board was an eighteen-minute uncredited gem called *A Study of Spring Wild Flowers* (1939). Somewhat more pertinent to American isolationists were the newsreel shorts that the NFB wartime image factory began to pump out and successfully place in international theatrical distribution for the duration of the war, a unique moment in the history of an institution better known for parallel non-theatrical distribution.

Making Peace Exciting, 1945–56

After war's end and the departure of both its founder and its raison d'être, the Board had a momentary identity crisis but soon shifted its mandate to no-nonsense peacetime citizen education. Films, produced in both 35mm and 16mm, exploring a host of topics – many chosen by Canadian governmental departments – from foreign aid to hockey to mental health, were sent to screens across Canada and abroad. In 1947 the NFB stepped up its educational services, choosing subjects meant to 'meet the needs of teachers and school curricula'.[1] To replace its wartime circuits, the Board developed a growing number of regional film councils (250 in 1948) to accommodate non-theatrical screenings (facilitated by itinerant projectionists – almost 300,000 in 1953 alone), while film libraries grew to 305 across the country.

Meanwhile, the international 'Red Scare' came to Canada and undermined the Board's autonomy (even Grierson had departed under a cloud). A refurbished Film Act in 1950 that defined an arm's length relationship to the state would forestall further political encroachments – though never completely. The Board approached the emergent television market equipped with a new TV studio, and programming such as the anthropological series *Faces of Canada* (1952). The once robust theatrical circulation of newsreel films and shorts was steadily declining, alongside that of commercial theatrical newsreels everywhere.

Catching Up with a Turbulent and Changing World, 1956–67 and Beyond

In 1956 the NFB officially moved to Montreal, appeasing language and cultural tensions and inaugurating the golden age of in-house directed films. Stylistic and thematic diversity were the watchwords, and the Board became increasingly known for its technical innovations. The Direct Cinema style of portable hand-held cinematography and synch sound became the NFB signature around the world, and the *équipe française*'s elaboration of this breakthrough over the next dozen years was perhaps the most sustained creative spurt in NFB history. On the English side, Studio B (the 'experimental' unit) became known for quirky and reflective essay-film-making deploying the new Direct style and also challenging the hegemony of voice-of-God exposition. For example, animation techniques grafted onto still archival photography led to the Oscar-nominee *City of Gold* (Wolf Koenig and Colin Low, 1957) and a whole new documentary genre. The influential *Candid Eye* series (1958–61) consolidated the orientation towards a spontaneous, subjective way of filming actuality (seen most famously in the portrait of Paul Anka, *Lonely Boy* [Wolf Koenig and Roman Kroitor, 1962]). Geopolitics was not entirely off the agenda during these years, and trouble brewed over a twelve-part series called *The Commonwealth of Nations* (1957), due to its critical focus on apartheid in the sister dominion of South Africa.

Quebec's 'Quiet Revolution' was underway, leading not only to the burst of creativity mentioned above, but also to structural changes (a bicephalous institution with almost autonomous English and French programmes) and a quantum leap in French-language production and versioning.

Quebec nationalism was in synch with New Left political awakening from coast to coast, and social-issue documentaries came to the fore after a generation of post-Red Scare quiescence. *River with a Problem* (Graham Parker, 1961), about pollution in the Ottawa river, had anticipated activism work later in the decade, as did, on the French side, acute attention to urban space and class in *September Five at Saint-Henri* (Hubert Aquin, 1961). But the energy of New Left idealism crystallised most in the Board's radical Challenge for Change/Société nouvelle (CFC/SN) programmes, an initiative

launched in 1967 by Ottawa's new anti-poverty line, pursued in collaboration with various federal ministries until 1980. In 1967 the controversial exposé of poverty *The Things I Cannot Change* (Tanya Ballantyne Tree, 1967) symbolically inaugurated this experiment in media democracy. Colin Low's landmark series on Newfoundland's Fogo Island (1967–68) was just as influential, tackling social issues by involving communities in the documentary film-making process; the Fogo Process spread around the world. The semi-autonomous Société nouvelle had a distinct sensibility, more open both to social science rigour and to New Wave aesthetics, and set up the storefront video coop Vidéographe in 1971 to harness and disseminate the new portable video equipment that was rivalling 16mm as the official CFC/SN technology.

The 1970s reinforced tendencies towards dissent and minority enfranchisement, including the maintenance of a strong presence of *indépendantiste* voices in the French studio: several were censored but star in-house poet-director Pierre Perrault's was not (*Un pays sans bon sens!/Wake up Mes Bons Amis*, 1970). In 1971 a training programme for 'Indians' was begun and four years later women artists were officially recognised with the monumental creation of Studio D (the women's movement had been heralded by the first female-directed film in 1964).

Retrenchment, 1980–96

As the era of Liberal Party hegemony under Pierre Elliott Trudeau drew to a close, signs of retrenchment, cutbacks and downsizing were in the air even before the inauguration of the Tory regime under Brian Mulroney in 1984. The 1982 Applebaum-Hébert Report, for example, recommended almost total cession of the production mandate to the private sector, and even if this report was mostly shelved, production greatly decreased as the institution advanced warily through the years of Canadian-style Reaganomics.

Despite a restored political somnolence signalled by the CFC/SN closing in 1980, Studio D continued its surge,[2] joined in 1986 by a francophone counterpart, Regards de femmes. The box office and the controversies around several women's productions became the NFB's best argument against privatisation, since such risks could only be taken within the publicly funded institution.

Meanwhile, Quebec's two unsuccessful sovereignty referenda took place at the start and the tail end of this period, and Denys Arcand's bitter, literally Machiavellian post-mortem *Le confort et l'indifférence/Comfort and Indifference* (1981) signalled the decline of Quebec nationalism as the predominant issue in the French programmes. Otherwise, this was the period devoted to expensive epics by other in-house big names as well, from Perrault to Donald Brittain and Paul Cowan, but also to smaller-scale explorations of the politics and cultures of diverse identities, from aboriginal (*Incident at Restigouche*, 1984) to the emergent LGBT community that finally acceded to visibility in the 1990s.

More heavy-handed cuts to the NFB throughout the 90s led to the now permanent fear that complete closure was imminent (Studio D closed its doors in 1996). Yet auteurs continued to lift the mood, from staff director Tahani Rached's under-recognised musical documentary about the welfare class's hunger and resilience *Au Chic Resto Pop* (1991) to freelancers Peter Wintonick and Mark Achbar's imaginative epic *Manufacturing Consent: Noam Chomsky and the Media* (1992) to Alanis Obomsawin's *Kanehsatake: 270 Years of Resistance* (1993), an introspective yet angry epic situated behind the Mohawk barricades at the Oka Crisis of 1990. On the technological front, the Board officially entered the future with the digitisation of film and tape and with new modes of distribution to supplant the long-vanished councils and 16mm collections – for example, the flagship Montreal storefront CinéRobothéque.

Holding Fast, 1996–2010

Against all odds, and by 1997 operating at 30 per cent less capacity than before the cuts, the NFB kept production up, but not without a hit to quality. An increasing focus on marginalised communities in Canada, especially aboriginal and visible minority communities, was evident, as was the necessity to continue the digital push to maintain its mandate and save its identity. Digital experiments were soon consolidated – NFB.ca, digital film-making and digital distribution and exhibition (e-cinema). The year 2009 saw the single most significant innovation in terms of access in public culture: the online screening room, where more than 700 productions were made available for free streaming. Cable TV was not neglected: the Aboriginal Peoples Television Network and the Documentary channel were launched and more outlets for NFB documentaries were tapped.

Co-production activity picked up, often along international lines, relationships that also produced new platforms and new international envelopes for documentary, such as the World Documentary Fund. The environment, globalisation and international human rights were fortified as the emerging generation's major preoccupations: *Wal-Town*[3] (Sergeo Kirby, 2006), a grassroots road movie about big-box economics, got less play than the 'international' hits, the undercover Tibet exposé *What Remains of Us* (Francois Prévost and Hugo Latulippe, 2004) and two prize-winning China epics, both with eco-resonance, *Manufactured Landscapes* (Jennifer Baichwal, 2006) and *Up the Yangtze* (Yung Chang, 2007). On a smaller scale, a successful effort to revive Challenge for Change was the Film-maker in Residence project – an award-winning multi-media project involving subjects in the media-making process that explores the spaces and people around an inner-city hospital in Toronto.

PUBLICLY FUNDED ARTS

Perhaps the NFB's most significant innovation as an institution of public film production and distribution over the seven decades that saw the liberal welfare state established and then slowly privatised and chipped away has been its very survival. Few state film institutions in the world match the NFB's stature and influence,[4] or its prolific library and its model of access to publicly funded documentary. Despite this, the NFB has had to perform a continuous and precarious balancing act between debilitating cuts and federal sustenance since the 1980s. Despite a track record of over 13,000 works and 5,000 awards, the NFB has been unable to sustain a critical mass of employees (from 800 in 1945 to 490 in 2009), migrating after 2000 towards public-private co-productions and (relatively inexpensive) digital dissemination frameworks. In earlier years the NFB's staff film-makers trailblazed an architecture for state arts institutions that prioritised the not exactly novel idea that creators deserve secure livelihoods and secure work spaces for long-term research and project development (supported by producers, administrators and technicians). But, beginning in the 90s, most were let go (in 2010 only the unstoppable Obomsawin remained) and many more technicians followed, some ominously replaced by lawyers.

In 2009, film-maker Jacques Godbout characterised the NFB as 'an institution on the road to extinction',[5] with its in-house directors and its institutional memory endangered species in the public mediascape. The prevailing ideological climate under the post-2006 Conservative minority regime, hand-in-hand with corporate elites, favoured axing 'hand-outs' for the arts while buttressing corporate welfare with the public purse. Disabling structural changes have transformed the legendary production hothouse into an enervated arts agency leveraging dwindling funds towards a bureaucratic centre that facilitates co-productions and concentrates on diffusing its library to the public via new media. Still the NFB has shown great innovation in 'making do' with the scarce resources at hand.[6]

Numbers should help illustrate: for the fiscal year of 1957–58, the Board's budget was over $33 million in 2010 dollars. By 1994–95 the budget had proportionally increased to $81 million. Those numbers drop to $67–8 million a year by 2010. This equates to roughly $2 per citizen per year spent on the NFB, in contradistinction to the estimated $60 per citizen spent bailing out Canadian banks in 2009.

Despite pressures of privatisation in a neo-liberal economy, the NFB has survived, (most) principles intact. Despite the constant anxiety of the threat of reduced support (or extinction) and arts-phobic ruling political parties,[7] the NFB continues its legacy of innovating public-funded arts institutions – reinventing itself and arguing its relevance as much as is needed along the way.

The sheer persistence and unbroken continuity of the world's leading state cinema institution is an important model. The NFB has evolved as a powerful creator and disseminator of images at arm's length from the government, yet acquitting reasonably well the confounding task of reflecting Canada back to itself and the world while fostering new talent and facilitating experimentation.

The NFB's legacy thus includes not only its enormous library of documentaries, fiction and animated films, it also includes a model for public arts institutions,[8] providing citizens with another of the ineradicable rights of democratic societies, beyond health and shelter and education, and in spite of hostile governments and unfavourable economic contexts: the right to public, non-commoditised cultural memory, resources, tools, stories, self-images, political challenges and utopias.

GEOPOLITICS

In the first six years of its existence, the National Film Board's contribution to the evolution of the documentary art form is inseparable from both the career of its founding commissioner John Grierson and the international political arena in which it established its mandate. For the institution the legendary British pioneer of documentary set in motion and its support by the Canadian government not only provided a crucible for testing and developing his model of the public-interest documentary, teaching the citizenry the lessons of contemporary liberal democracy, but also tested his ambitions to make it a factor in a world order in crisis. That this test was in fact carried out on a war footing, a baptism by fire within the geopolitical struggle against fascism, made it all the more urgent for Grierson and Canada. Few doubt that the Board rose to the occasion, becoming the most prolific public institution of moving-picture wartime information in the world, in some ways becoming a mouthpiece for the Allies, even after the USA had entered the war, and reading an audience by war's end of 30 million in twenty-one countries, a stunning accomplishment even allowing for more recent claims that the Board's own audience figures were exaggerated.[9]

The major vehicles for this access were the Board's two flagship theatrical series Canada Carries On (1939–59) and The World in Action (1941–45).[10] The approximately seventy films produced between the outbreak of war and the end of 1945 look both outward, towards the geopolitical front or what Grierson analysts have called the 'new internationalism',[11] and inward, towards the land and the people that Grierson unexpectedly discovered as he encouraged their war effort, founding a national cinema in the process. The pressure of the Ottawa assembly line may well have resulted in what a consensus of film historians have termed a lack of artistic staying-power: indeed, the films, modelled by director-editor Stuart Legg on the successful American newsreel series The March of Time (1935–51), often do not hold up as

well as, say, the British works of Humphrey Jennings – mostly because of their stentorian voiceovers. However, their considerable virtues are clear beyond their success in the international exhibition system, pushing the archival compilation genre to its maturity (in comparison to the sensationalist commercialism and populist condescension, respectively, of March of Time and the other US series, Why We Fight [1942–45]) and the mission of political education to a level that successfully spelled out the ideals of the Atlantic Charter and future United Nations to diverse audiences. From Canada Carries On, for example, High over the Borders (Raymond Spottiswoode, 1943) elegantly joins the themes of kids and migrating birds, the genres of dramatisation and nature documentary, and the locations of rural Canada and Argentina, for an eloquent advocacy of hemispheric solidarity beyond borders and, prophetically, of planetary health. From The World in Action, War for Men's Minds (Stuart Legg, 1943) appeared late in the war, and self-reflexively focused on propaganda itself, an ambitious effort to counter fascist and democratic uses and values (some would say not clearly enough[12]), but was Grierson's most ambitious and justifiably his favourite 'internationalist' project in Canada.

This first fruitful period of the history of the NFB, 'the largest and best coordinated government film operation in the world'[13] has had its hagiographers as well as its detractors.[14] However, through its consolidation of one of the most important and least examined documentary genres, the compilation film, it innovated 'a new concept of film journalism' and a programme of citizen education ('progressive film propaganda of education, inspiration and promise of a better tomorrow'[15]), based on both unprecedented theatrical distribution and on a pioneering network of non-theatrical distribution. This stirringly productive moment left a legacy of innovation and commitment, one that turned out to be collective, well beyond the individual imprint of the British envoy who stayed six years and left the country (but in fact never really left Canadian cinema).

The wartime newsreel series set the political and artistic precedent and the prerogative for the Board to continue throughout the post-war decades to address international audiences and examine international issues, attracting as much controversy as praise. Many films – for example, If You Love This Planet (Terre Nash, 1982), the Oscar-winning intervention into the Reagan-era arms race – blatantly targeted the US audience and reaped the benefits in terms of both political and box-office impact. Others – from The People Between, Grant McLean's prophetic 1947 film on the Chinese revolution that became a brickbat of the Red Scare, to the gently partisan Vietnam exposé Sad Song of Yellow Skin (Michael Rubbo, 1970) to Abortion: Stories of North and South (Gail Singer, 1984) to the current decade's China blockbusters – became principled, often daring, independent gestures on the frontiers of international affairs.

NATIONAL POLITICS

The NFB not only laid the groundwork for what would become a national cinema and operated throughout the decades as a political bellwether, it also acted more or less efficiently as a kind of political conscience for the nation, and sometimes as a political catalyst. Throughout the war and the first decade of the post-war years, the National Film Board had managed and maintained the inherent tensions between the regions of Canada and their political colours, between the various points on the ideological spectrum in the Canadian political arena, weathering censorship brouhahas and outcries from parliaments and provinces – and even the Red Scare – with diplomatic overtures to both the working class and the bosses. That it was able to do so through the ever-reliable bureaucracy, a cosy relationship with the long-ruling Liberal Party, and the occasional ritual bloodletting, adds to the paradox of this role.[16]

If Canada had its cinematic May 1968, it lasted from 1956 to 1980. Politics became more volatile in 1956, when the Board's headquarters shifted from sleepy Ottawa to turbulent Montreal, about to become the crucible of Quebec's Quiet Revolution. A new generation of Québécois film-makers, ardently both nationalist and leftist in orientation, accelerated the Board's shift towards a bicephalous, bilingual institution, and spearheaded the institution in its flirtation with the left throughout the 60s. The *équipe française* explored rapidly changing Quebec society in the first part of the 60s, and with the tools of Direct Cinema in their hands pioneered a vision of class and national politics in the increasingly industrialised and urbanised population with both an ethnographic and personal, ironic eye. Denys Arcand and Gilles Groulx summed up this entire historical chapter with their respective feature-length Marxist mega-epics, *On est au coton/Cotton Mill Treadmill* (1970) and *Vingt-quatre heures ou plus/24 Hours or More* (1973), both of which languished in the censors' drawers for years. Nevertheless the distinct voice and political sensibility of the 'French studio' would remain distinct and autonomous thereafter.

Meanwhile, the technological and political utopias pushed both sides of the Board in less auteurist directions, towards the legendary media democracy experiment Challenge for Change/Société nouvelle.[17] Using both 16mm and the new Portapak half-inch video systems and inspired by the Canadian version of the US 'War on Poverty' and hand-in-hand with the ongoing regionalisation restructuring of the over-centralised behemoth, young media artists like Dorothy Hénaut and Maurice Bulbulian made their expertise and equipment available to communities confronting their economic and political problems (allegedly abdicating their artistry in the process[18]). Between 1967 and 1980 they brought out about 225 films championing community empowerment and social change, enfranchising voices that had seldom been heard, from aboriginals to slum-dweller welfare recipients. *You Are on Indian Land* (Mike Mitchell and Mort Ransen, 1969) and *P'tite Bourgogne* (Maurice Bulbulian, 1968) may be among the most enduring, speaking both aesthetically and politically. Dupes of the contradictions of liberalism embodied in state-funded dissent, or prophetic experimenters with the still-living ideal of media democracy, the CFC/SN civil servants, citizens and film-makers left an undeniably rich legacy of empowerment and protest in the NFB catalogue.

In subsequent decades the Board's political relevance may have occasionally seemed too contained by its perennial scraps with veterans' organisations, but just as often a Board production packed a critical wallop – for example, the recent brave interventions on Monsanto and frankencrops[19] (*The World According to Monsanto*, Marie-Monique Robin, 2008), on government and media apathy towards missing and murdered First Nations women (*Finding Dawn*, Christine Welsh, 2006) and on the petro-apocalypse of Alberta's tar sands (*H2Oil*, Shannon Walsh, 2009).

DISSEMINATION AND ACCESSIBILITY

Distribution hasn't always been the NFB's forte. Despite bureaucratic dysfunction, the Board has often excelled at distributing its arsenal of documentary works in four distinct areas: theatrical shorts, community screenings, educational sales, and new media and accessible archives.

Theatrical Shorts

Wartime NFB distribution boomed, with commercial contracts with powerhouse theatrical distributors like Columbia Pictures and France Film. The ambitious newsreel series *Canada Carries On* and *The World in Action* became familiar to audiences across North America and the world (see above).[20] By 1944 the Board had outpost offices in several countries which, combined with diplomatic missions and private distribution deals, facilitated nearly 2,000 films screening in theatres in thirty-one countries.

Community Screenings

During the early years at the Board a philosophy of citizenship-through-documentary inflected a widespread NFB matrix of 'churches, community centres, factories and trade union halls'.[21] This unique network reached 385,000 people per month through 3,000 screenings at its high point.[22] After the war, film circuits gave way to film councils – community screenings no longer administered by the Board, but organised by labour, educational and civil society groups.

During the 1950s, expenditures on distribution at the Board were almost equivalent with production,[23] an ephemeral budgetary characteristic that reflected the Board's investment in grassroots-style film circuits which were 'adapted from the imperial practice of mobile cinema [and] corresponded to the Canadian state's work on integrating immigrant communities through public information, which became entrenched in government during the Second World War'.[24]

Non-theatrical distribution continued through the 60s and 70s with the aforementioned NFB's Challenge for Change programme, where the goal of ongoing dialogue between documentary-makers and subjects ensured regular community screenings. Despite a declining distribution budget, many success stories occurred, such as a 1971 four-walling of a third of New Brunswick for Léonard Forest's Acadian manifestos. From the 80s on, community screenings have continued to be the life-blood, although with less centralised resources and administration from the Board and typified more by collaborations between the NFB and other stakeholder groups within subject and audience networks.

Educational Sales/Views

The National Film Board has continually strengthened its brand at educational institutions in Canada and abroad as a purveyor of high-quality pedagogical materials. From the post-war filmstrip craze to the web resources of the 2000s, the education market ranks high among the Board's bread-and-butter revenue streams – for instance, during 2008–09 there were over 31 million Canadian views of NFB productions across all platforms and '46% of this Canadian audience was achieved within the educational market'. As of 2009, one third of the Board's nearly $6 million annual revenue is achieved through educational sales.[25]

New Media and Accessible Archives

In 2009 the Board began a monumental project of digitising swaths of its enormous film library.[26] From the iPhone application that gives access to NFB docs on-the-go to the labyrinthine cornucopia NFB.ca (over 1,000 titles available for streaming at time of writing), the NFB continues to pioneer public access to documentary. NFB documentaries are increasingly available to any computer or mobile user, facilitating easy access to a rich chronicle of politics, culture, documentary movements and moments, and the shifting plates of Canadian history – in both official languages. While the production and dissemination of celluloid, tape and DVDs has taken a major hit in this new turn, the implication for public access via online platform dissemination is enormous and unprecedented. Commuters can watch the latest NFB short, fans can build their own lists, guest curators can fashion their own playlists, educators can open NFB.ca and stream a veritable audiovisual tsunami for pedagogical spaces devoid of such finger-tip documentary access.[27]

While the NFB continues to fend off criticism for their declining production activity (from 308 films in 1944 to ninety-four in 2009), as well as the disappearance of in-house directors, as a public access model for documentary dissemination and accessible archives, the NFB is once again providing an exemplary example.

DIVERSITY

During the Grierson era, his team of mostly British white male film-makers, with a few Canadians (including at least four proto-feminist directors), mingled in apprenticeship positions and occasionally captured the images of Canadian demographic diversity (at least one glimpse of Japanese-Canadian internees and considerably more of French-Canadian habitants joined a modest series of ethnographically cast aboriginal subjects). But by and large the first generation of NFB directors sought out mirror images of themselves – images, not voices. Although French-Canadian producers and directors began to emerge in the post-war years, it was only after the move to Quebec and the commissionership of Guy Roberge (1957–66) that the institution enabled the full emergence of a coherent and autonomous francophone voice.

As for other minority identities within Canada's mosaic, whether racial, religious, cultural, or sex/gender, their participation on screen or behind the camera was at best sporadic until after 1970. A few notable exceptions include Crossroads (Don Haldane, 1957), a docudrama on an interracial marriage – nuanced and bold in comparison to US work on similar themes of the Eisenhower era. It is really only in the late 60s that diversity began to supplant benignly passive and tokenistic multi-culturalism as the predominant framework. Challenge for Change/Société nouvelle's experiment in putting the technology in the hands of citizens frequently led to the discovery of difference as a integral element of everyday life. For example, Encounter at Kwacha House – Halifax (Rex Tasker, 1967) exceptionally offers a lively conversation among black youth about African American militancy and its application to local conditions of racism and unemployment.

Twenty-five years later it was no longer a novelty to hear black voices on screen and from behind the camera – due in no small part to diversity initiatives from within the women's Studio D. Second-wave feminism had first emerged in the CFC/SN programmes, where women communities increasingly claimed representation on both the French and English sides, in particular with the remarkable 'En tant que femmes' series of widely televised hybrid features and the 'Working Mothers' series. This momentum led directly to the two prolific and distinct women's studios, respectively Studio D (1975–96) and 'Regards des femmes' (1986–96), and it was in Studio D that the most significant venture in 'visible minority' diversity unfolded: the 'New Initiatives in Film' (1991–96). Studio D was also the setting for the most important breakthroughs around sexual diversity, having produced lesbian works as early as 1977, albeit discreet (Some American Feminists, Margaret

Wescott), and opening the floodgates with the 1992 hybrid megahit *Forbidden Love: The Unashamed Stories of Lesbian Love* (Lynne Fernie). Male and francophone producers and directors tried to catch up, but by the new millennium the queer gush had dwindled to a trickle, perhaps because the now realised utopia of same-sex marriage removed all political urgency from sexual politics, but important works continued to emerge around the still undomesticated topics of queers of colour (*Solo*, Atif Siddiqi, 1993, beneficiary of a successful 'Reel Diversity' competition) and sex-work *Hommes à louer/Men for Sale* (Rodrigue Jean, 2009), the latter interview epic prevailing over a censorship battle that echoed the good old days.

Representations of and voices from within Canada's aboriginal communities have their distinct history, gradually superseding earlier colonial, folkloric or ethnographic impressions of Canada's first peoples, most two-dimensional. The shift to the documentary depiction of on-screen individuals and communities with complex identities, political voice (and agency) and diverse cultures is commonly correlated to Challenge for Change/Société nouvelle. Here several films were made, successful in terms of both impact and representation: from the musical compilation lament *Ballad of Crowfoot* (Willie Dunn, 1968) to the implicitly contestatory, poetico-observational 'ethnography' *Cree Hunters of Mistassini* (Boyce Richardson and Tony Ianzelo, 1974). The groundwork was laid and the prolific Obomsawin became the flagbearer of subsequent decades, seconded by younger documentarists like Gil Cardinal, Loretta Todd and Tracey Deer; meanwhile the docu-flavoured fiction of Inuit prize-winner Zacharias Kunuk was another landmark (*Atanarjuat the Fast Runner*, 2000). The NFB is justifiably proud of this history of the development since the 1960s of state-funded First Nations cinematic enfranchisement, and the heritage has been sustained by recent innovations such as the First Nations 'Studio One' in Edmonton (1991–96), the youth-oriented web-based project 'Our World', in British Columbia and the Yukon, and Wapikoni Mobile, a prize-winning travelling audiovisual studio in Quebec and Labrador, founded in 2004. Nevertheless some would argue that the NFB's contribution may have co-opted voices of struggle rather than enabled agency.

In recent years, with the disappearance of in-house directors and the growing importance of co-productions and sponsored indie work, the institution has paradoxically seemed more open to a mosaic of voices (especially low-budget ones!). But, of course, all gains are precarious as queer film activists discovered when the important classics of the 1990s were suddenly yanked out of circulation without notice.

AESTHETICS AND TECHNOLOGY
In its seventy-year history, the NFB has innovated countless contributions to the aesthetics of documentary film,

often in tandem with – and often inspired by – technological developments in cinematography, sound recording, processing, editing, etc. In this limited space, two exemplary instances of the NFB's major techno-aesthetic innovations are profiled.

Direct Cinema
The slow transition from 35mm to 16mm as the principal format of documentary production in the post-war gave NFB film-makers, cinematographers, technicians and producers a golden opportunity that they seized to make a world historic contribution: the development of Direct Cinema.[28] It was only around the mid-1950s that documentary film-makers saw the potential of the new 16mm equipment developed largely for home movies, military uses and television – portable hand-held 16mm cameras and portable tape devices cable of synchronised-sound recording, like the Nagra, as well as newly sensitive microphones and film stocks, often 'pushed in the processing' – for finally escaping the heritage of the voiceover, voiceless documentary, sedentary and expository, objective and impersonal.

Cameramen such as Michel Brault and Terence Macartney-Filgate worked internationally and contributed to US and French developments, as well as Canadian. Operator-directors like Claude Jutra, Gilles Groulx, Pierre Perrault, Marcel Carrière, Roman Kroitor and Wolf Koenig invented a versatile and sensitive idiom of observing and listening to everyday life as well as participating and even intervening in the real world – its social problems and cultural transformations, its inhabitants and the flux of their lives. The Québécois tradition, as with Rouch and their other contemporaries in France, developed more interest in the realm of language and ideas (*Pour la suite du monde*, Pierre Perrault and Michel Brault, 1963) than the more visual North American anglophone peers, but both English and French Canadians insisted on interactivity (including interviews), keeping away from the observational purism that Americans like Leacock and Wiseman adhered to. Both also largely eschewed the event- and personality-focused journalistic style of fellow American pioneer Robert Drew. The aesthetics and technological applications of Direct Cinema, pushed in collaboration with other national cinemas – principally French and American – constituted the bedrock of observational and interactive currents of not only the NFB but also international documentary over the subsequent half-century, and remains one of the NFB's – and Canada's – main contributions to world cinema.

(Digital) Hybridity
Bhabha describes hybridity as 'neither the one, nor the other' but an 'in-between space, that innovates and interrupts the performance of the present'.[29] Refusing categories

and drawing from multiple forms, genres and practices has always been a celebrated part of the NFB's procedures – though not heralded as such.

In the post-war era, discussion-catalyst 'trigger films' and prize-winning dramatised documentaries (*Mental Mechanisms*, series, 1947–50) deployed actors performing clinically developed case-study scenarios. The late 60s inaugurated a fertile stream of major experimental 'essay' feature documentaries by auteur directors that played out over the rest of the century, buoyed up by the studio's generous budgets and the leisurely research pace available to in-house creative people, from the French studio's New Wave-inspired features *Les Filles du Roi* (Anne Claire Poirier, 1974) and *Passiflora* (Fernand Bélanger and Dagmar Gueissaz-Teufel, 1985) to Paul Cowan's original mix of dramatisation and document in his experimental biopic of Canada's pioneer abortion-provider *Democracy on Trial: The Morgentaler Affair* (1984). The NFB's cross-pollinations, too often unrecognised by world cinema gatekeepers, were in the forefront.

Since the 1990s, when the game-changing digit arose, the documentary world has been undergoing a dizzying phase of growing pains – as a genre, and as a set of aesthetics, ideas, practices and platforms. New tools for making documentaries and new circuitries of delivery and display are inclining makers and purveyors towards new convergences and collaborations the likes of which were not seen in the world of celluloid, tape and couriered canisters. Hybrid documentarists like Katerina Cizek argue for a new way of approaching documentary that abandons exclusivity clauses with the words/concepts 'film' and 'theatre' in favour of 'media'. Her output includes two multi-media, multi-platform NFB projects called *Filmmaker-In-Residence* (2005–) and *Highrise* (2010–). The first deploys digital photography, video and sound to explore the spaces around an urban hospital in Toronto, putting process over product but still yielding a very slick DVD box set, a fine blog and a website (or, as the NFB calls it, 'immersive online documentary'). The latter project, with a similar aesthetic and technical arsenal, tells the stories of the people who live in suburban high-rises in multiple cities across the globe. Cizek points to the importance of working with a public institution and 'the liberty we've been given to experiment, to not worry about "product" but rather to focus on process'.[30] Despite enforced penury, the NFB continues to forge a new hybrid vision for documentary process in the vastly interconnected multiverse of the digital mediascape.

INTERPRETING CANADA

Evans writes that 'the Film Board record will show just who Canadians were, and like history itself, its film documents will convey to future generations the priorities and passions of the era from which they emanated'. Future documentary audiences, administrators, policy-makers,

National Film Board of Canada: the little colonial branch-plant that could. And did documentary for seventy years

film-makers and scholars will look back at a time when the 'leaner' NFB first reflected 'a corporate image consonant with the era of privatisation',[31] and will experience the same loss and confusion as those who experienced its slow, dwindling demise in the 1960s and 70s. But, in addition to the problematic of a national cinematic endowment plundered, they will also see a heritage that is unassailable. They (the post-YouTubers?) will see also, despite the ups and downs of bureaucracy, governmentality, censorship, internecine resentment, star egos and erratic marketing, an exemplary contribution to world documentary – its formal trajectory, its political systole–diastole, its technical and aesthetic discoveries, its implantation of public culture and conscience. They will see Grierson's little colonial branch-plant that could. And did. And did documentary for seventy years.

NOTES

1. http://www.NFB.ca/hi.storique/1940-1949. Accessed 3 September 2012. For a detailed and engaged account of the NFB's relationship to institutional education, see Zoë Druick, *Projecting Canada: Government Policy and Documentary Film at the National Film Board* (Montreal: McGill-Queen's University Press, 2007).

2. Studio D produced two of the Board's most controversial and internationally famous documentaries of the decade:

Bonnie Sherr Klein's *Not a Love Story: A Film About Pornography* (1981), acclaimed and denounced when it opened theatrically in London and New York, and banned in Ontario; and the irreverent Oscar-winner, the filmed lecture *If You Love This Planet* (Terre Nash, 1982), an intervention in the nuclear arms race. (Gail Vanstone, *D is for Daring: The Women Behind the Films of Studio D* [Toronto: Sumach Press, 2007]; Elizabeth Anderson, *Pirating Feminisms: Film and the Production of Post-war Canadian Identity*. [Diss: University of Minnesota, 1996].)

3. Disclaimer: in another life Winton was the impetus for this documentary, and appears as a main character.

4. With a respectful nod to *television* networks PBS and the BBC.

5. http://cupe.ca/culture/jacques-godbout-onf. Accessed 3 September 2012.

6. At time of writing the NFB was under the wing of the Ministry of Heritage, whose budget was slashed by the Conservative minority government in 2008.

7. To wit, rumours of the infamous 1982 Applebaum-Hébert 'final solution' recommendation resurfaced in 2008 with Prime Minister Harper at the helm, as Canada's arts communities reeled from millions in cuts across the sector.

8. Australia's sixty-year-old board (recently swallowed by something called Screen Australia) and India's still active Films Division were both modelled after the NFB – to name two.

9. The NFB's traditional claims of audience statistics are passed on by Rodney James, *Film as a National Art: NFB of Canada and the Film Board Idea* (New York: Arno Press, 1977 [1968]), and D. B. Jones, *Movies and Memoranda: An Interpretative History of the National Film Board of Canada* (Ottowa: Deneau, 1981), but are questioned by Peter Morris, 'Re-Thinking Grierson: The Ideology of John Grierson', in Pierre Véronneau, Michael Dorland and Seth Feldman (eds), *Dialogue: Canadian and Quebec Cinema* (Montreal: Mediatexte, 1987), and Joyce Nelson, *The Colonized Eye: Rethinking the Grierson Legend* (Toronto: Between the Lines, 1988).

10. This last title was bought by Granada Television, UK, for its long-running path-breaking news-documentary series in 1963 (ed.).

11. Gary Evans, *John Grierson and the National Film Board: The Politics of Wartime Propaganda* (Toronto: University of Toronto Press, 1991); Jack Ellis, *John Grierson: Life, Contributions, Influence* (Carbondale: Southern Illinois University Press, 2000).

12. Nelson, *The Colonized Eye*, p. 110.

13. Ellis, *John Grierson*, p. 206.

14. Ellis and Evans belong to the former category, Morris and Nelson to the latter.

15. Respectively James, *Film as a National Art*, p. 80, and Evans, *John Grierson and the National Film Board*, p. 6.

16. See Malek Khouri, *Filming Politics: Communism and the Portrayal of the Working Class at the National Film Board of Canada, 1939–1946* (Calgary: University of Calgary Press, 2007), on the Board's relationship with the labour movement and the left during the war.

17. See Thomas Waugh, Michael Brendan Baker and Ezra Winton (eds), *Challenge for Change: Activist Documentary at the National Film Board of Canada* (Montreal: McGill-Queen's University Press, 2010).

18. Jones, *Movies and Memoranda*, pp. 157–75.

19. Known as GM (genetically modified) crops in the UK (ed.).

20. http://www.NFB.ca/history/1940-1949/. Accessed 3 March 2013.

21. Druick, *Projecting Canada*, p. 80.

22. Ibid., p. 82.

23. Gary Evans, *In the National Interest: A Chronicle of the National Film Board of Canada from 1949 to 1989* (University of Toronto Press: Toronto, 1991), p. 62.

24. Druick, *Projecting Canada*, p. 80.

25. Departmental Performance Report 2008–2009, pp. 24, 31.

26. Although it should be noted the Board has not provided its blueprint for title selection, a seeming contradiction of its mandate of transparency as an accountable public institution.

27. In the first year of the NFB's online adventure, 3.7 million film views were logged and over half a million views were counted on the iPhone alone (NFB.ca).

28. Nomenclature is still confusing and sometimes controversial: Canadians, following Quebec francophones and the French, most often see Direct Cinema as a stylistic spectrum derived from the new lightweight synch technology of the late 1950s, of which American-style 'vérité' is one sub-category. The authors use either term only in very specific and narrowly defined historic contexts and otherwise avoid confusion by eschewing them completely, preferring 'observational' and 'interactive' to refer to the two historic branches of Direct Cinema. (See Chapter 2.10.)

29. Homi Bhabha, *The Location of Culture* (London: Routledge, 1994), p. 7.

30. Katerina Cizek, email to the authors, 7 July 2010. (See also Chapter 6.3 below [ed.].)

31. Evans, *In the National Interest*, pp. xi, xiii.

2.4 Grierson's Legacies: Australia and New Zealand[1]

DEANE WILLIAMS

Even as, back in the UK, journalistic values, rather than a public education agenda, were sharpening documentaries' edge on television, the Griersonian paradigm was promulgated beyond Canada by Grierson himself and many of those who had worked with him. This effectively directly secured his vision of the documentary – sober, official and educative in the name of forging national identities – across the rest of the white Commonwealth.

In the international histories and accounts of documentary film John Grierson is a substantial figure. Numerous books on documentary film attribute to Grierson the first use of the term 'documentary' in relation to film,[2] while others trace the complicated term, 'the creative treatment of actuality' to him. Grierson was a major contributor to the early writing on documentary. His essays in *World Film News*, *Cinema Quarterly* and *Documentary Newsletter* not only served his purpose of drawing attention to the films; they also became part of the fledgling international network of cinema journals. Grierson's forcefulness in 'First Principles of Documentary', 'The EMB Film Unit' and 'The Course of Realism' were prominent contributions to the discourse of realist film and, of course, to the figure of John Grierson.[3] For film communities outside of Britain, such as Australia and New Zealand, these essays often preceded the availability of the films Grierson had been involved in or associated with and proffered a particular reception of the films. Not only were the films made by Harry Watt, Edgar Anstey, Basil Wright, Arthur Elton, Alberto Cavalcanti and Robert Flaherty understood as Grierson films, they were often understood through the vision for them that Grierson proposed.[4]

One prominent way that Australian and New Zealand documentary (and, to some extent feature) film production has been understood is in relation to a legendary trip made by Grierson to these countries in 1940 on behalf of the Imperial Relations Trust to advise on these countries' use of documentary film.[5] Undoubtedly, the majority of documentary films made in Australia have been produced with the aegis of government sponsorship and there has been a lineage established between the various incarnations of government documentary-making. From the moment in 1911 when the Australian Federal government appointed its first cinematographer within the Department of External Affairs, on to the Commonwealth Cinema and Photographic Branch of the Department of Agriculture, to the Films Division, Department of Information, to the Commonwealth Film Unit and then Film Australia, and now Screen Australia, documentary production in Australia has provided an institutional continuum conducive to the writing of historical accounts which are introduced by turning to Grierson. For example, Albert Moran explains the 'metamorphosis' of the Film Division of the Department of Information into the Australian National Film Board (ANFB) in 1945 writing 'to understand this change, we must begin with the 1940 visit to Australia of John Grierson, the "father of the British documentary film"'.[6] The setting up of the New Zealand Film Unit in 1941, immediately following Grierson's visit, is understood to be a watershed for documentary film history in that country. Similarly, Jack Ellis writes how, prior to Grierson's visit,

> New Zealand had its own Government Film Studios ... in Wellington, and the Publicity Division of the Tourist and Publicity Department made the same kind of tourist films as Canada had done. But now the war had cut the overseas tourist trade to the bone, and the government film staff was being whittled down to an unarticulated skeleton. Grierson's visit produced a shift in emphasis and, on the basis of a report he submitted at government request, a National Film Unit was created.[7]

Underpinning Moran's and Ellis's understanding is a reliance on the figure of Grierson as a foundation upon which the discourse of documentary film in these countries has been built.

Grierson's visits to Australia and New Zealand in the period 1938–40 need to be contextualised, partly in relation to the Canadian situation. Joyce Nelson writes that Grierson's initial visit to Canada was in 1931 for the Empire Marketing Board and was 'to report on the strength of the nationalistic spirit in Canada and especially the strength of the English spirit in Toronto'.[8] From this visit he gleaned that not only did Canada have a government-sponsored film unit which 'reached 25 million in North America each year' and from which the EMB could learn a great deal about equipment and organisation, but also that French-Canadian nationalism was, in his view, anathema to the assimilation of ethnic minorities because 'the dominant ethnic-cultural identity had encouraged the other groups ... to maintain theirs'.[9] Yet his second visit, in 1938 on behalf of the Imperial Relations Trust, according to Nelson, must be understood in relation to the possibility of war.[10] Britain was concerned with strengthening its ties with the dominions, so Grierson was sent to Canada, then to Australia and New Zealand, to 'survey the possibilities of setting up a film centre in each of these countries'.[11] Nelson quotes Gary Evans, who asserts that the 'specific goal' of Grierson's assignment for the Imperial Relations Trust was 'to set up a North American propaganda base to urge Canada and (more important) the United States into an active partnership with Britain at war, if war came'.[12] It doesn't seem unreasonable to assume that Grierson's role in Australia and New Zealand was not to be much different. Also, as Jack Ellis points out,

> Grierson's work has arrived before him. By the mid-thirties there had been established an Australian-New Zealand British Film League, and it was reported that in New Zealand 'British documentary and educational films [had] a greater chance of distribution than anywhere in the Empire'.[13]

As we have seen Australia also had a fledgling documentary film system ready to be employed in the cause of empire.

Grierson had adapted the British model for documentary film to the Canadian system (presumably bringing to it a degree of 'creative expertise' if there already existed distribution and technical know-how that Grierson saw as superior to his own at the Empire Marketing Board). For Australia and New Zealand, Grierson's visit to Canada can be understood as the first employment of the Documentary Movement model where 'it is possible to see in Grierson's activities in Canada an extension of the ideas and experiments he was developing in Britain'.[14] This extension meant that Grierson obtained full support and didn't have to deal with the kinds of divisions between countries that existed in Great Britain. In Canada, the Grierson model was an attempt to represent 'what Canadians need to know and think about if they are going to do their best by Canada and themselves'.[15] Nevertheless, these sentiments were 'to unite the country and serve national purposes without advocating nationhood'.[16] More importantly, the Canadian National Film Board 'was to serve as a North American propaganda base,

encouraging the United States to abandon its isolationist neutrality and reinforcing Canada in its partnership with Great Britain'.[17]

Post-war Australia and New Zealand were envisaged as needing reconstruction as nations and documentary film was to play a major role in this nation-building. Sounding a lot like the words employed in Canada, Grierson's 1940 letter 'Memorandum to the Right Honourable, the Prime Minister', written at sea on his way to New Zealand from Australia, has been understood as a kind of manifesto for the Australian National Film Board and for New Zealand and includes these words:

1. The film is a powerful medium of information and if mobilised in an orderly way under a determined government policy, is of special value to the Australian Government at the present juncture.
2. It could do much in the following vital matters:
   (a) Break down sectionalism and induce a national viewpoint, by bringing a love of Australia to itself in terms of films describing national effort and constructive contributions to the more important fields of national activity.
   (b) Bring the disparate elements of the war effort together and create in the Australian mind an integrated view of the national war purpose and war effort.
   (c) Bring into the public imagination the problems, responsibilities and achievements of Government.
   (d) Project to other countries a view of Australia as a powerful and progressive people, fulfilling its responsibilities to a large new territory – a matter of great importance today in international information.
   (e) By projecting Australia, contribute substantially to the 'projection' of the British Commonwealth of Nations.[18]

As we can see here, Grierson's proposals rely on the twin emphases of empire and nation to meld a sense of cohesion and public-mindedness as these contribute to a vision for the British Commonwealth of Nations.

This repetition of ideas used in Britain and Canada represents Grierson's position on Australia as a representative of the Imperial Relations Trust and as a member of the British Commonwealth, clearly containing the dual sentiments of empire and nation. For Australian documentary it is the latter that has been understood to be the primary legacy of Grierson's recommendations, yet it also has much in common with the earlier nationalistic New Deal model of the Roosevelt administration of the 1930s in the USA, which can provide a mirror to Australian government initiatives. In distinguishing between the British, Canadian and US models it is important to consider two factors: that the Australian National Film Board was not set up until

1945 and that Grierson's proposals should be seen in the light of the changes brought about by Australia's post-war governments.

The setting up of the Australian National Film Board in 1945 must also be understood in relation to a number of initiatives in wartime Australia performed by this Department of Post-war Reconstruction. These initiatives included the Commonwealth Universities Commission, the Australian National University, the Snowy Mountains Authority (a hydro-electric scheme administration) and the Australian Broadcasting Control Board.[19]

In this cultural, economic and administrative reshuffle the Australian National Film Board is sometimes misunderstood as providing a break or at least a 'new hope' for documentary in Australia and for this reason is often positioned separately from the long tradition of government film-making that had in one form or another been in existence since the turn of the century.[20] However, a significant number of the personnel who moved from what was the Department of Information's Film Division were involved in government propaganda and were to form the initial group of film-makers at the Board.

A larger consideration is a political and economic one. The models proposed for Canada, Australia and New Zealand were war-effort models; the dominions were being encouraged to participate in the production of propaganda – that is, newsreels – as part of an imperial project combined with the nationalist viewpoint that Grierson saw as a component of a National Film Board. The Australian Conservative government of the day, in particular Prime Minister Robert Menzies, is said to have initially 'agreed to co-operate with Grierson and provide him with whatever information he needed for his report to the Trust'.[21] However, upon his arrival, Grierson is said to have been 'puzzled and frustrated at the politely distant reception and the difficulty of obtaining an interview with the Prime Minister'.[22] Given Grierson's Canadian model it seems reasonable to suggest that the Australian government considered itself already committed and active in the area of propaganda production in the service of empire and were less appreciative of the imperial sentiments that Grierson was bearing: sentiments that jarred with the nationalist spirit emerging from the Australian war effort. Most accounts of the frosty reception afforded Grierson have put this down to a clash of personalities, Menzies possessing a similar gruff assertiveness to Grierson's persona. Yet it seems that, by attending to Joyce Nelson's emphasis on the imperial impetus of Grierson's visit, it may be that Grierson was simply providing a model which was, to some extent, already in existence.

However, as we have seen, when the Australian National Film Board was set up in 1945, it occurred in a post-war culture closely related to the institutional initiatives of the post-war governments in the cause of nation-building. That

is, as early as 1945 the Labor Government was understood by some to be 'draining the blood of the Empire' in the pursuit of a 'parochial nationalism'.[23] The ANFB emerged from a culture conducive to its aims of representing the nation to itself. One of the most prominent of lobbyists was Professor Alan Stout, who wrote, in words recalling the New Deal,

> The film can help us to look at ourselves, and can bring home to us vividly how different sections of the community live, the problems they have to face, and how they are facing them … Its special power lies in the appeal to the imagination, and in its ability to simplify issues, focus attention and bring contrasts into sharp relief.[24]

Yet these aims were implicit in Grierson's proposals, which allowed the various lobbyists for a national system of production and distribution to employ these proposals while addressing them to the resurgent nationalism of late-war and post-war Australia. This tendency in Grierson's proposals, while paralleling similar New Deal sentiments, remains at the heart of the history of how Grierson influenced Australian documentary.

One film that has become emblematic of this period of documentary film-making in Australia is Stanley Hawes's *School in the Mailbox* (1946). Hawes was appointed Producer-in-Chief of the National Film Board and was an experienced film-maker and production teacher, having worked directly under Grierson.[25] Essentially, *School in the Mailbox* is a film about the correspondence school education system

School in the Mailbox (1946): a Grierson model for documentary adapted to local conditions

in outback Australia. The problem for the film is that of distance and how the Federal government caters for the children of farming families. As Ina Bertrand points out, the film is a 'classic' documentary, with traditional relations between image, narration and music, utilising what we might call a Griersonian model for documentary adapted to local conditions.

> The social problem addressed is again distance – specifically the difficulties of access to education for children living in remote and isolated areas. The solution illustrated by the film is the correspondence school, welding parents and teachers and transport workers into a well-oiled team. This is an idyllic picture of a country where the sun always shines, where the nuclear family is unchallenged, where racial and familial harmony is unthreatened, where the community looks after everyone regardless of age or location, where parents recognise that education is (in the words, again, of the peroration) 'The future of their children, their country and the world'.[26]

In New Zealand, the film culture into which Grierson arrived was similar to that in Australia. New Zealand documentary pioneer John O'Shea recalls that the first producer of the New Zealand National Film Unit, Stanhope Andrews, was one of the members of the 'small but lively Wellington Film Society' and that films such as Grierson's own *Drifters* (1929), Basil Wright's *Song of Ceylon* (1934), Elton and Anstey's *Housing Problems* (1935) and Turim's *Turksib* (1931) were 'irresistibly impressive' to him and 'conveyed ... some idea of what a film could be'.[27]

In their articulation of an alternative documentary film tradition in New Zealand, Annie Goldson and Jo Smith understand Grierson's visit in relation to a similar tradition in governmental film-making. Prior to 1940, government film-making, in the main, consisted of 'scenics' which emphasised landscapes 'to cultivate New Zealand as a brand on the international market (as well as nurture national pride)'.[28] Grierson's arrival in 1940 coincided with a shift in the emphasis evident in these words from an address he gave while in New Zealand:

> So when you send us your films never send merely the scenic ones. Put in something about the real things you do. Do not be ashamed to describe your problems, and what you are doing about your problems. Remember we are pretty imperfect ourselves, and if you appear always in the spit and polish of perfection we know very quickly that you are either inhuman or you are liars. Above all your country must send us films about people so that we can see their faces and remember that New Zealand is not just a couple of spots on a distant map but a real place with a flash of the future in its eyes and a beat in its heart.[29]

The Coaster (1948): fulfilled the template of Grierson's model regardless of the suitability of that form for its subject

In Grierson's words here it is possible to see a coincidence with his agenda in his memorandum, but also a shift to a more nationalist tone while maintaining the inclusive tenor of empire. While it is unclear exactly whether Grierson's visit resulted in or merely coincided with the setting up of the National Film Unit (Jonathan Dennis claims 'the suggestions in his report were never implemented'),[30] the output of the unit, principally the *Weekly Review* (1943–50) series of newsreels and short documentaries, focused more on the war effort.

Like *School in the Mailbox* in Australia, Cecil Holmes's *The Coaster* (1948),[31] one of the *Weekly Review* series, is one of the most derivative of films of the time, utilising poet Denis Glover's rhythmical, rhyming narration to render the journey of a transport ship along the coast of New Zealand in a maritime tribute to Watt and Wright's *Night Mail* (1936).[32] In this regard, *The Coaster* fulfilled the template of Grierson's model regardless of the suitability of that form for its subject. Goldson and Smith write,

> The *Weekly Review* exactly fulfilled Grierson's goal of civic education. The filmmakers, as civil servants themselves, were to work in tandem with other Government departments. During the war, the *Weekly Review* concentrated on the New Zealand war effort at home and abroad, while in the post-art period, the spirit of nation-building took over.[33]

In this shift from war effort to nation-building it is possible to see a movement from the tenets of empire to those of nation-building after the end of World War II. While it is possible to see the Grierson priorities of realism, locationism and nationalism as they are elucidated in part (a) of the memorandum, written before Grierson's visit to New Zealand, as part of a documentary tradition, the same

tenets come out of a call to belong within the empire. As
Goldson and Smith point out, Grierson's vision,

> was prescriptive rather than reflective. At this point in the
> development of a national film culture, the New Zealand
> Government used documentary to narrate a particular
> imagined community based upon tropes of virile white
> masculinity and a benevolent and paternalistic form of
> governmentality.[34]

Goldson and Smith make this point to contextualise an
'alternative tradition' of left-wing and union-based documentary film 'evident from the beginnings of documentary' in New Zealand.[35] While principally focusing on
post-war documentary films, Goldson and Smith are keen
to undermine the notion that documentary film in their
country commenced with Grierson. In fact, since that post-
war period New Zealand documentary film has become
synonymous with a tradition at odds with the vision for it
prescribed by Grierson. As Goldson and Smith write:

> Filmmakers such as Barry Barclay, Merata Mita, Gaylene
> Preston, Annie Goldson and Peter Wells have produced
> works that continue a vital and sustaining style of
> documentary that articulates real social critique, that
> experiments with aesthetic convention and emphasizes
> disruption, dissension and difference. These filmmakers
> reveal the nation as a contested construct, made up of
> peoples and viewpoints that often resist and confront
> prevailing and orthodox views of New Zealand Society.[36]

Within the Commonwealth's white dominions, Grierson's
proposals for government film, based on the model taken
up in Canada, were built on the dual foundations of
empire and nationalism; foundations that he deemed
appropriate to the wartime service of Great Britain.
Australia and New Zealand already had some forms of
governmental film-making by the time of his visit in 1940;
the Menzies Government, in particular, believed it was
serving the empire and therefore had no need for this
component of Grierson's model. By 1945, when the post-
war Labor government began nationalising institutions, it
included in its raft of initiatives the ANFB, whose tenets
have been historically tied to the nationalist components
of the Grierson model. The nationalist component has,
because of the way it was conducive to the resurgent
nationalist movements in Australia, provided an immediate delimited filmic model for government propaganda.
In New Zealand, the so-called Grierson model of the
Weekly Review, while directly related to the issues of
nation and empire, sat alongside the beginnings of
an alternative tradition in documentary film that still
flourishes today.

NOTES

1. This chapter is a reworked version of my 'Between
   Empire and Nation: Grierson in Australia', *Screening the
   Past*, 7 July 1999, http://www.latrobe.edu.au/screeningthe
   past/firstrelease/fr0799/dwfr7e.htm
2. Grierson wrote that 'of course *Moana*, being a visual
   account of events in the daily life of a Polynesian youth
   and his family, has documentary value' (John Grierson,
   'Flahery's Poetic *Moana*', *New York Sun*, 8 February 1926,
   quoted in Lewis Jacobs (ed.), *The Documentary Tradition*
   (New York: W. W. Norton & Co, 1979), pp. 25–6.
3. John Grierson, 'Documentary', *Cinema Quarterly* vol. 1
   no. 2, Winter 1932, and vol. 1 no. 3, Spring 1933; John
   Grierson, 'The EMB Film Unit', *Cinema Quarterly* vol. 1
   no. 4, Summer 1933; John Williams, 'The Course of
   Realism', in Charles Davy (ed.), *Footnotes to the Film*
   (London: Lovat Dickson, 1937).
4. Harry Watt writes that Grierson 'had the quality of an
   evangelist, which made it difficult to question his
   theories and beliefs'. (Harry Watt, *Don't Look at the Camera*
   [London: Elek, 1974], p. 189.)
5. See Chapter 2.2, this volume.
6. Albert Moran, *Projecting Australia: Government Film Since
   1945* (Sydney: Currency, 1991), p. 2.
7. Jack Ellis, *John Grierson: Life, Contributions, Influence*
   (Carbondale: Southern Illinois University Press, 2000),
   pp. 137–8.
8. Joyce Nelson, *The Colonized Eye: Rethinking the Grierson
   Legend* (Toronto: Between the Lines, 1988), p. 37.
9. Ibid., p. 39.
10. Ibid., p. 43.
11. Ibid.
12. Ibid., p. 33
13. Ellis, *John Grierson*, p. 138.
14. Forsyth Hardy (ed.), *Grierson on Documentary* (London:
    Faber and Faber, 1966), p. 26.
15. Ibid., p. 27
16. Nelson, *The Colonized Eye*, p. 57.
17. Ibid., p. 58.
18. John Grierson, 'Memorandum to the Right Honourable,
    the Prime Minister', in Albert Moran and Tom O'Regan
    (eds), *An Australian Film Reader* (Sydney: Currrency, 1985),
    pp. 72–3.
19. Geoffrey Bolton, *The Oxford History of Australia, Volume 5.
    The Middle Way: 1942–1995* (Melbourne: Oxford University
    Press, 1996), p. 29.
20. In Shirley Graham and Brian Adams, *Australian Cinema:
    The First Eighty Years* (Sydney: Currency-Angus and
    Robertson, 1989), the section on the setting up of the
    Board is entitled 'Documentary Hopes' (p. 174), while in
    Moran and O'Regan, *An Australian Film Reader*, the chapter
    on documentary is called 'Documentary Hopes' (p. 67)
    and the first entry is Grierson's 'Memorandum to the
    Right Honourable, the Prime Minister'.

21. Ina Bertrand and Diane Collins, *Government Film in Australia* (Sydney: Currency Press, 1981), p. 98.

22. Ibid.

23. Robyn Gollan, *Revolutionaries and Reformists: Communism and the Australian Labor Movement 1920–155* (Canberra: Australian National University Press, 1975), p. 146.

24. Professor Alan Stout, quoted in Bertrand and Collins, *Government Film in Australia*, p. 99.

25. Ina Bertrand, 'Theory into Practice: Stanley Hawes and the Commonwealth Film Unit', *Screening the Past*, 7 July 1999, http://www.latrobe.edu.au/screeningthepast/firstrelease/ fr0799/ibfr7d.htm. Accessed 25 July 2012; Ina Bertrand, 'Stanley Hawes and the Commonwealth Film Unit', *Australian Journal of Communication* vol. 24 no. 3, 1997.

26. Bertrand, 'Stanley Hawes and the Commonwealth Film Unit'.

27. John O'Shea, 'A Charmed Life: Fragments of Memory ... and Extracts from Conversations', in Jonathan Dennis and Jan Bieringa (eds), *Film in Aotearoa New Zealand* (Wellington: Victoria University Press, 1996), p. 16. For an account of the Wellington Film Society see Simon Sigley,

'How *The Road to Life* (1931) Became the Road to Ruin: The Case of the Wellington Film Society', *New Zealand Journal of History* vol. 42 no. 2, 2008.

28. Annie Goldson and Jo Smith, 'The Contested Nation: Documentary and Dissent', in Ian Conrich and Stuart Murray (eds), *Contemporary New Zealand Cinema: From New Wave to Blockbuster* (London: I.B.Taurus, 2008), p. 157.

29. John Grierson, 'The Face of a New Zealander [From a Talk by John Grierson]', in Jonathan Dennis (ed.), *'The Tin Shed': The Origins of the National Film Unit* (Wellington: New Zealand Film Archive, 1981), p. 22.

30. Jonathan Dennis, 'Introduction', *'The Tin Shed'*, p. 5.

31. *The Coaster* [Weekly Review 374], 1948, http://www. nzonscreen.com/title/the-coaster-1948

32. Even director Cecil Holmes described the film as 'a bit derivative'; see my *Australian Postwar Documentary Films: An Arc of Mirrors* (Bristol: Intellect, 2008), p. 54.

33. Goldson and Smith, 'The Contested Nation', p. 157.

34. Ibid., pp. 157–8.

35. Ibid., p. 158.

36. Ibid., p. 157.

2.5 New Deal Documentary and the North Atlantic Welfare State

ZOË DRUICK AND JONATHAN KAHANA

That it did not require the ties of empire to demonstrate how apposite was Grierson's vision of the value of documentary to the anglophone liberal democracies can be seen in its parallel development in the USA. Similar social pressures produced a virtually identical response.

Is documentary an enduring, even timeless, form or manner of image-making, an attitude that may be applied across various situations and media of social observation? Or is it a historically specific style or genre, one that works on and in certain times and places better than others? The so-called New Deal documentary is a good test of this problem, which has determined the course of documentary history and criticism since the 1930s. Documentary has, of course, persisted beyond this formative 'classical' period of the 30s and early 40s, and has thrived even apart from the confluence of factors that made social documentary first possible as a national endeavour: government support; a progressive ideology widespread among artists, intellectuals, politicians and bureaucrats; and a public appetite for social and economic reform during periods of revolution, reform, or crisis. Under these conditions, photographers, writers and film-makers developed a now-familiar aesthetic of poverty, pathos and authenticity, the visual and rhetorical code for a popular structure of national feeling that helped establish the urgency, the necessity and the morality of the sweeping changes attempted, in the USA and elsewhere, under the mantle of the welfare state.

In this chapter, we argue that New Deal documentary might be productively put into a broader context to which welfare legislation and certain realist cultural forms owed their provenance. This is hardly a bold or original move: John Grierson himself suggests as much in his preface to the 1952 edition of Paul Rotha's book *Documentary Film*, where, arguing that documentary was always interested in more than just new kinds of pictures, he includes among its possible foundations,

Clydeside movements, I[ndependent] L[abour] P[arty]'s, the Great Depression, not to mention our Lord Keynes, the L[ondon] S[chool of] E[conomics], P[olitical and] E[conomic] P[lanning] and such. Documentary was born and nurtured on the bandwagon of uprising social democracy everywhere: in Western Europe and the United States, as well as in Britain. That is to say, it had an uprising majority social movement, which is to say a logical sponsorship of public money, behind it.[1]

Perhaps it seemed necessary to Grierson, in the wake of World War II, during which the national production, marketing and circulation of non-fiction film had been a cultural and military priority of every Allied and Axis state, to remind post-war readers of Rotha's book of a different, earlier efflorescence of documentary. As documentary entered an uncertain and unstable period in the 1950s, the government use of film in the 30s to promote reforms and social policies – which coincided, in Europe and North America, with a new emphasis on social planning – would have seemed to Grierson and others of his generation like a golden age. (A reporter for the *Washington Post* captured the power of this conjunction in an article about a Washington screening of *The Plow That Broke the Plains* in a 1936 programme of government films from different countries, including the Soviet Union and Nazi Germany; commenting on the Russian example, the reporter enthused 'it was more than a movie, this product of the Soviet government, it was an idyll'.[2]) This social organisation took a number of forms, from welfare state provisions to publicity campaigns thought by many contemporary social theorists to be essential for the spread of information in an expanded public sphere. Education itself was being reimagined as a universal institution and documentaries were linked by a generation of policy-crafters to the functioning of mass democracies. The New Deal can act as shorthand for the promise made by numerous governments to their populations to trust a semi-socialised state in difficult times, despite challenges by both left- and right-wing factions. In particular, we believe the American case should be reconnected to the British documentary tradition, which itself was influenced by American social theory, and to the growth of state-funded documentary in the USA's northern neighbour, the 'Dominion of Canada', during the inter-war period. Educational film was used extensively by governmental agencies across the western world during the inter-war period.[3] What was unique about the New Deal films was their scope and scale, in particular their narrative emphasis on the nation.

As with industrial films, whose beginnings may be tracked back to the same period, state documentaries might best be regarded as 'interfaces' between discourses and forms of social and industrial organisation.[4] In fact, it is possible to trace the genealogy of government-sponsored films to communication forms that emerged first in the private sector: journalistic forms of reportage and publicity forms that manifested in a variety of social formations, from politics to corporate communication. In new mass societies, the state was adopting corporate forms of governance. Documentary film was only one of many forms of communication adopted by corporations and states alike to plead their case and trumpet their accomplishments in the public sphere. The difference was that state-sponsored films had to devise a rhetoric that would include the audience members and film subjects alike as stakeholders in a grand project. While the centralised planning of the state didn't totally determine film content, it certainly was a significant force in the realisation of these film projects. Nevertheless, despite the national context for the New Deal documentaries, their connection to international currents in social politics and film-making should not be overlooked. In what follows, we trace John Grierson's connection to American social theory and attempt to sketch out the lines of influence that criss-cross North American welfare state documentary of the inter-war period.

THE NEW DEAL AND STATE PUBLICITY

The set of American social and economic policies enacted during the Depression and encapsulated in the moniker given to the welfare state in this period – the 'New Deal' – are associated with a series of iconic images from the mid- to late 1930s, photographs taken by the likes of Dorothea Lange and Walker Evans and titled according to their ordinary subjects, like 'Migrant Mother' and 'Alabama Tenant Farmer's Wife, 1936'. As is made plain in the flat, denotative captions given these sombre, frontal portraits of tough Midwestern women staring poverty – and the viewer – in the face, the ethos of New Deal documentary photography was that of an honest confrontation with grim socioeconomic conditions and painful political necessities. The idea that documentary in all its forms and periods 'tells it like it is' owes much to these silent, stoic images, and their moving-image counterparts, *The Plow That Broke the Plains* and *The River* (1938), Pare Lorentz's films about the drought and flooding that devastated the American plains and the Mississippi delta, not least

because, in the photographs and the films alike, the people do not speak. They cannot represent themselves, as Marx said in another context, so they must be represented.

This double sense of representation depends upon a kind of political trompe l'oeille that dates to this period, but has been useful to liberal documentarians (and their ideological sponsors) ever since. What we think we see in these pictures – the evidence of a crisis too big to be handled as a routine, local emergency; the character of anonymous but exemplary individuals struggling bravely through difficult times – is apparently there by virtue of the fact that the photographer or film-maker simply positions him or herself in (or in front of) reality, capturing it in black and white, warts and all. The documentary quality of these famous images, however, owes as much to what is *not* apparent in them, but which made their appearance possible: the vast, multifarious programme of government support for the ruined American economy and the social and cultural institutions that depended upon it, a political-economic structure commonly and somewhat reductively known as 'welfare' or 'the welfare state'. Under the auspices of the Farm Security Administration, one of many new agencies among the 'alphabet soup' of economic assistance and stimulus programmes created by Franklin D. Roosevelt during his first two terms as president, photographers like Lange and Evans were hired to document the situation of farmers and other workers left jobless or homeless by natural and economic disaster, and to capture as well the efforts of the federal government to give them food, shelter, work and hope. For some cultural workers (including many of the artists, writers, actors and musicians hired through the several cultural branches of the Works Progress Administration), government contracts constituted their primary or only means of income during the worst years of the Depression. Thus, one could say that Roosevelt's New Deal made possible both the forms of public assistance documented by some of these images and the production and circulation of the images themselves.

By the same token, some historians have even gone so far as to claim that the term 'documentary' – which comes into broader use in the 1930s and 40s, in the USA and elsewhere in the North Atlantic welfare states – is not really appropriate outside of this period, in relation to which it names not only a realist and socially conscious use of photography and cinema, but a political-economic condition and an associated cultural infrastructure conducive to the production and circulation of pictures and stories of ordinary people, struggling with the problems of everyday life and demanding our attention, sympathy and action.[5] And insofar as documentary presumes an 'us' – a particular 'people' who can be both the object and the subject of concern – it would also seem necessary to describe each documentary project by its place in the world, as well as its place in history. But even when it seems natural to describe

The River (1938): a powerful icon of a utopian progressivism

a documentary 'project' as a national one by the location of its subjects, its production, its creative personnel, its message, or its intended audience, we should remind ourselves that nations do not occur naturally: they must be produced and constantly reproduced through ideology. With its verisimilar pictures and its messages of concern, documentary was, during the Depression, one means for binding 'the people', through an image of themselves at work, at rest and at risk, to the idea of the nation, on the one hand, and the apparatus of the state, on the other. The photographs and the films – and especially Lorentz's films, *The Plow That Broke the Plains* and *The River* – support such an argument: with their stories of failures of past land use planning (or complete lack thereof) and of the possibility of crafting a just and equitable society, these works appear in retrospect to stand as a powerful icon of a utopian progressivism thought to be specific to the USA during the Great Depression. Versions of this argument are found in other countries in this period, and could certainly explain the popularity of and support for documentary discourse at the highest levels of government, across the globe, during the 1930s.[6] But it could not explain so well the migration of forms, both cultural and political, across borders and decades: while it is certainly possible to argue that the 'welfare state' has a classic period of emergence, historians continue to disagree about where and when it starts and ends.

DEVELOPMENT OF THE WELFARE STATE IN THE NORTH ATLANTIC ECONOMY

By the late nineteenth century, the North Atlantic economy was beginning to form and an 'Atlantic era in social politics was taking shape'.[7] Arguably, by the 1930s a half-century of internationally circulating social reform ideas were poised to emerge; the Depression was the crisis that invited them out of policy proposal form and into application. Although

this eruption of reforming sentiment took place in different forms in different places, it was a force felt around the North Atlantic economy in the 30s.

These ideas were matched by new forms of public expression. The nation-state projects that occupied Europe and North America during the nineteenth century were projects of governmentalisation and rationalisation with affective dimensions. Nationalism, the sentiment that would motivate citizens to give their lives to their nation, was, above all, just that: a feeling. Rousing this feeling and channelling it towards aims deemed desirable by social planners became one of the dominant problems of the age. Democracy's rise, in other words, was shadowed by theories of publicity. As influential political theorist John Dewey argued, 'there can be no public without full publicity in respect to all consequences which concern it'.[8] Paradoxically for a polity supposedly built on citizen deliberation, spin became one of democracy's most important tools. Put differently, one could say that the organisation of the state took on an inherently mediated form in the early decades of the twentieth century. As soon as film technology became available, cinema became one of the numerous practices connected to forming and sustaining national identity.

Industrialisation of agriculture and the establishment of energy mega-projects, such as dams and power plants, were defining features of early twentieth-century planned economies. These themes are clearly reflected in the burgeoning form of documentary film in the late 1920s and 30s. From images of Vertov's man with a movie camera traipsing across electrical generators in the film named for him (*Man with a Movie Camera*, 1929) to the British Empire Marketing Board and General Post Office film units' celebration of coal mining in numerous films about industrial Britain, the organisation of the food and energy needs of immense populations was the theme of international films across the political spectrum during this period. *The Plow That Broke the Plains* and *The River* are no exception. Both films consider mistakes made in the industrialisation of agriculture and the need to rationalise and control nature more effectively.

Like Grierson, Lorentz began his work in the cinema as a film reviewer, and turned to film-making out of a desire to shape public opinion and influence public policy: in Lorentz's case, the impetus was to help the government convey the events of the dust bowl. *Plow*, his first film, attained Resettlement Association funding and was a great hit in theatres and internationally on the film society circuit. (A more radical film had been scripted by Nykino members Ralph Steiner, Paul Strand and Leo Hurwitz, indicting capitalism for the current ills, but Lorentz rejected their perspective in favour of his preferred angle, which focused on natural disaster and its roots in agricultural practice.) The final version of the film steered clear of politics, opting instead for a 'melodrama of nature – the tragedy of turning grass into dust'.[9]

The idea to use film to tell the full story behind current events that had inspired Grierson was also the animating factor behind Lorentz's depiction of the dust bowl. Both wanted documentary to be able to convey the particulars of social experience in national terms that would convince viewers to support targeted state policies. Although progressive in some ways, these films reflected a set of influences that were concerned with social engineering and centralised planning and that were careful to avoid criticism of either the current government or the dominance of the market as a social and political force. This tension between modernism and tradition was perhaps most noticeable in the films' soundtracks: both the British and American productions experimented with sound effects and voiceover in ways that surpassed, in creativity, anything being attempted in Hollywood at the time; and Grierson and Lorentz both employed important avant-garde composers to write scores for their productions: one only has to hear Benjamin Britten's clanging, industrial music for *Night Mail* (1936) or Virgil Thomson's modernist updating of folk themes in *The Plow That Broke the Plains* and *The River* to understand how far ahead of their respective national film industries both producers wanted to be, and how the aesthetic of their respective cinemas – despite the obligation each felt to national institutions and patriotic mythologies, and despite the reputation each has gained for being a cultural stick-in-the-mud – drew not only from local and vernacular traditions of culture, but also from international flows of artistic innovation.

TRAVELLING THEORY: GRIERSON AND NORTH AMERICA

John Grierson was a scholar and journalist with an interest in new media when he travelled extensively in North America in the mid-1920s. There he came into contact with Walter Lippmann, the American magazine and newspaper editor and political pundit. Lippmann was a prominent public intellectual who bemoaned the state of modern democracy in which citizens were ill educated. Lippmann advocated for civic education so that citizens might be able to deal critically with information reported in the daily news. It was Lippmann who encouraged Grierson to turn his interests in public education from newspapers to films. (The anonymous review of Robert Flaherty's 1926 film *Moana*, in which Grierson is supposed to have used the term 'documentary' in relation to cinema for the first time in English, was published in the *New York Sun*.) However, it is worth noting that Grierson's ideas about documentary can be traced to American social thought more broadly. Indeed, Grierson notes that Lippmann's pessimism was precisely what prompted him and others in his generation to apply themselves to projects of public information.[10]

In 1924, Grierson took up a Rockefeller scholarship to pursue graduate work in sociology and political science at the University of Chicago. He was keen to study public opinion formation in a city of immigrants. Placing himself at the centre of the new scientific study of society, at Chicago Grierson studied with Charles Merriam and Robert Park, men who later came to be known as architects of the New Deal. From Merriam, Grierson was influenced to think about citizenship training as the bedrock of a functional democracy. Merriam advocated that the school system was the most important way to inculcate youth into a feeling of national belonging, and away, if necessary, from ethnic affiliations to bygone motherlands. Schools were also the place to iron out eccentricity and build up physical prowess. Strong minds and bodies could and should be regulated, according to Merriam, by active state-run systems of pedagogy, both inside and outside the classroom.

Robert Park contributed to modern social scientific thought the vision of society as a system made up of subcultures. Also interested in the timely questions of social integration that dominated the North American academy, Park utilised the biological metaphor of human ecology to study the shifting social organism. Like Merriam, Park saw modern life as an experiment in which motivated social scientists could affect the outcome. Grierson's ideas about the role documentary film could play in mediating between state and citizen were an amalgam of ideas gleaned from Lippmann, Merriam and Park. Typical of this view, he would later write: 'education is the process by which the minds of men are keyed to the tasks of good citizenship'.[11]

Grierson also spent time travelling across Canada and the USA, making a number of personal and professional connections. He was especially interested in the Hearst newspapers and *Time* magazine, both of which featured writing different from anything he had seen in the more sober English press. Upon his return to the UK in 1927, Grierson introduced ideas from American social science, journalism and public relations to the British civil service. He became involved with the formation of the Empire Marketing Board (1928–33), an agency that aimed, as its name suggests, to combine political allegiance with industry and trade. Grierson's involvement with the British Documentary Movement (see Chapter 2.2) allowed him to combine his thoughts about national publicity with ideas about citizenship training. But he maintained a number of ties to North America through the 1930s.

Canada was a special link in the British Empire. Situated next door to the USA and sharing its language, Canada represented the most obvious battleground between American and British influences. Britain did not want Canadians to lose their emotional and economic affiliations with the motherland, and Hollywood films, it was feared, might inspire Canadians to shift their allegiances. In 1930 Grierson went to Canada to study the model of the Canadian Government Motion Picture Bureau and the Ontario Government Film Service, both of which had become quite well developed over the 20s, especially by comparison with other state-run film services in the western world. Five years later, Grierson was sent by the Imperial Relations Trust to advise the National Film Society – an organisation funded by the Rockefeller Foundation – on national film matters (see Chapter 2.3). In 1938 he was invited to write a report on film in Canada, which resulted in the recommendation to form a National Film Board (NFB) to serve the growing nation's film needs outside of theatres, beyond the marketplace (but not, of course, unrelated to the economy). Not only would the NFB consolidate the film work previously undertaken by the Government Motion Picture Bureau, it would also provide visual materials for education, whether the venue was the factory, the classroom, the community hall, or the church basement. Perhaps most importantly, the National Film Board would provide a Canadian perspective on Canada and the world to combat American screen dominance and to contribute to the flow of films around the British Empire.

Yet even before the establishment of the National Film Board, Canada was producing films that might be characterised as having a 'New Deal' flavour. The film *Heritage* (1939), made by the Canadian Government Motion Picture Bureau, was inspired by *The Plow That Broke the Plains* 'to make a national case for a federal government program that concerned a regional issue'.[12] Made in the same year as his assignment in Canada began, and as soon as he accepted the post of National Film Commissioner, Grierson began to promote *Heritage*.[13]

NATIONAL PROJECTIONS/TRANSNATIONAL PROJECTIONS

Lewis Jacobs once said that in the 1930s Americans 'made films to show up the bad side of the country', while the British 'made films to show up the good side of the British government'. American films, he said, were interested in the element of reportage, while the British films tended to be acted and staged.[14] Although there is a grain or two of truth in this characterisation, it tends to obscure the similarities between state-sponsored documentary filmmaking across the North Atlantic, as well as the differences within national documentary 'movements'. Indeed, just as it has been argued that the New Deal itself was a compromise intended to suppress revolutionary energies coming from left of the Democratic party, New Deal documentary found a way to soften sharper voices of proletarian dissent and incorporate more radical perspectives on the socioeconomic crisis facing the nation into individual figures of the long-suffering people. (Even when the working class appeared in New Deal documentary as a collectivity, as it does briefly in the Lorentz-produced film about rural electrification, *Power and the Land* [1940], directed by

the itinerant socialist Joris Ivens between films in Spain and China, it does so in literally muted form.[15]) Certainly, in North America documentary was developed as a promising new educational experiment, an interface between citizens and state in national economies with budding welfare provisions. So, rather than see these films as unique to the USA or as part of an impetus that was prematurely truncated, we have tried to encourage the possibility of seeing the New Deal documentaries as one episode in a much longer trajectory of state reorganisation of economies and populations that began in the nineteenth century, reached its peak in the 1930s and arguably continued with some vigour after World War II in international bodies such as UNESCO.

Inherently political and state-funded though it was, one of the defining features of North American New Deal documentary is its careful avoidance of reference to politics. The films invoke trust in the state regardless of who might be in office at the moment they were made and screened – despite mis-steps of the past. This belief in the state, if not in the government of the day, reflects the interface of these films with a welfare state discourse that had been developing for decades. Democracy now could be expressed as a set of plans for the population seemingly counteracting but simultaneously facilitating the growth of the North Atlantic economy. And welfare state documentary cinema – a fully realised, if frequently reinvented, version of the propaganda apparatus that Sir Stephen Tallents termed, in 1932, 'national projection' – would prove, in North America, the UK and other mass industrial societies, a key cultural force in the embattled persistence of the welfare state ideal, through the middle and late twentieth century.

NOTES

1. John Grierson, 'Preface', in Paul Rotha, *Documentary Film* (London: Faber and Faber, 1952 [1935]), p. 16.
2. Edward Folliard, 'Tugwell Farmer's Lot is Sad Compared to Soviet Idyll', *Washington Post*, 11 May 1936.
3. Standard accounts of educational non-fiction cinema production in North Atlantic welfare state agencies are provided in Richard Dyer McCann, *The People's Films: A Political History of US Government Motion Pictures* (New York: Hastings House, 1973); and Rachel Low, *Documentary and Educational Films of the 1930s* (London: Allen and Unwin, 1979). More recent film historians have taken renewed interest in the concepts of education, government and documentary as they apply to and appear in state-produced non-fiction cinema in this period. See, for example, Alison Murray Levine, 'Projections of Rural Life: The Agricultural Film Initiative in France, 1919–1939', *Cinema Journal* vol. 43 no. 4, Summer 2004; Charles Tepperman, 'Digging the Finest Potatoes from their Acre: Government Film Exhibition in

Rural Ontario, 1917–1934', in Kathryn Fuller-Seeley (ed.), *Hollywood in the Neighborhood: Historical Case Studies of Local Moviegoing* (Berkeley: University of California Press, 2008); Gregory Waller, (2008) 'Free Talking Picture – Every Farmer is Welcome: Non-theatrical Film and Everyday Life in Rural America during the 1930s', in Melvyn Stokes, Robert Allen and Richard Maltby (eds), *Going to the Movies: Hollywood and the Social Experience of Cinema* (Exeter: University of Exeter Press, 2008); Jennifer Zwarich, 'The Bureaucratic Activist: Federal Filmmakers and Social Change in the Department of Agriculture's Tick Eradication Campaign', *Moving Image* vol. 9 no. 1, Spring 2009.

4. Vinzenz Hediger and Patrick Vonderau, 'Introduction', in Hediger and Vonderau (eds), *Films That Work: Industrial Film and the Productivity of Media* (Amsterdam: Amsterdam University Press, 2009), p. 11.

5. See Martha Rosler, 'In, Around, and Afterthoughts (On Documentary Photography)', in *3 Works* (Halifax: Press of the Nova Scotia College of Art and Design, 2006 [1981]), p. 73; John Tagg, *The Burden of Representation: Essays on Photographies and Histories* (Amherst: University of Massachusetts Press, 1988), pp. 8–11.

6. See Zoë Druick, *Projecting Canada: Government Policy and Documentary Film at the National Film Board* (Montreal: McGill-Queen's University Press, 2007), pp. 45–9; Jonathan Kahana, *Intelligence Work: The Politics of*

American Documentary (New York: Columbia University Press, 2008).

7. Daniel Rodgers, *Atlantic Crossings: Social Politics in a Progressive Age* (Cambridge, MA: Belknap Press of Harvard University Press, 1998), p. 4.

8. John Dewey, *The Public and its Problems* (Denver: Alan Swallow, 1954), p. 167.

9. Lorentz, cited in Blaine Allan, 'Canada's *Heritage* (1939) and America's *The Plow That Broke the Plains* (1936)', *Historical Journal of Film, Radio and Television* vol. 19 no. 4, 1999, p. 450. Lorentz effectively fired Hurwitz, Steiner and Strand before the end of the shoot, finishing the film with cinematographer Paul Ivano. The conflict is reflected in one of the on-screen versions of the film's production credits, which lists all four names, but relegates Hurwitz – in non-alphabetical order – to the bottom of the list.

10. John Grierson, 'The Course of Realism', in Forsyth Hardy (ed.), *Grierson on Documentary* (London: Faber and Faber, 1946), p. 78.

11. John Grierson, 'Education and the New Order', in Forsyth Hardy, *Grierson on Documentary*, p. 122.

12. Allan, 'Canada's *Heritage*', p. 440.

13. Ibid., p. 466.

14. James Beveridge, *John Grierson: Film Master* (New York: Macmillan, 1978), p. 111.

15. Kahana, *Intelligence Work*, pp. 122–35.

2.6 The Triumph of Observationalism: Direct Cinema in the USA

DAVE SAUNDERS

Post-World War II, documentary legitimacy increasingly came under fire. Questions as to the authenticity of the image more and more focused on the issue of film technology itself – cumbersome, intrusive, demanding intervention. 16mm synchronous-sound film was adopted as a potential solution, one that would confirm the documentary's evidentiary power and thus make good on Grierson's original agenda.

> It is now possible to film with a simplicity that has been little more than a dream in the past. Taking the camera off the tripod is like being cured of a paralysis.
>
> Ian Cameron and Mark Shivas[1]

One of the most significant and influential developments in non-fiction film's tortuous history was sparked on the North American continent during the early 1960s. Blooming to a short-lived but definite movement that burst forth from humble, journalistic beginnings into a theatrical phenomenon, Direct Cinema – an ethos of more-or-less purely hand-held, synch-sound filming coupled with classically continuous editing techniques – arose from the directed intersection of technological and personal imperatives, and within a serendipitous epoch of sometimes illusory, sometimes genuine, sociopolitical upthrust. Out of the 60s (by which I mean the cultural epoch, rather than the strictly numerical decade), of course, emerged much art: famously from the sphere of counter-cultural cinema, if perhaps less so from the silver screen's insidiously domestic rival the television set, whose Eisenhower-era monotony served as a catalyst for what became American documentary's tendency towards 'reactive observationalism'.

The birth of the 'fly-on-the-wall' documentary, its visual traits still commonly employed as shorthand for 'authenticity' and its stylistic ticks ubiquitously absorbed across virtually every genre, at one time seemed, at least for those intimately involved, like little short of the call to a film-making revolution. Even if such retrospectively naive dreams quickly died down to a more cautious appraisal of the possibilities at hand, those relatively few exemplars of true Direct Cinema, all in all a remarkable body of work that comprises something of a minor canon,

deserve continued attention by anyone seeking to grasp fully the nebulous methods and functions of the documentary form as a whole. Although the French exponents of cinéma-vérité (chief among these were Jean Rouch, Edgar Morin and Chris Marker) independently pursued roughly analogous aims at around the same time (as, indeed, had the fleeting British Free Cinema movement a few years previously), their trans-Atlantic counterparts were less concerned with ideas of overt anthropological validity, sociological study and self-reflexivity, being more interested in the visual telling of dramatic stories in order to secure popular acceptance in a way that would potentially supersede conventional forms of reporting.

The now largely forgotten experimental work of the Canadian National Film Board's B Unit, in particular the television series *Candid Eye* (1958–59), deserves mention in this context as another, similarly parochial attempt at roving reportage much in the tradition of Free Cinema; but, crucially, the American films foreshadowed to the north have one overwhelming advantage: notwithstanding early difficulties, they successfully married their footage (of carefully chosen subjects in inherently dramatic situations) to continuous, *properly synchronised sound*, while simultaneously managing to create works that chimed with the times' hopes and anxieties. At once, the Direct Cinema pioneers seemed to offer unprecedented access to political or cultural icons and a sympathetically composed antidote to the prevalence of what they regarded as staid, overly verbal commentary on current events. Contrary to histories that describe Direct Cinema's genesis as a chance coming together of happily mutual personnel armed with the necessary gadgets, it would in reality take one man, ideally placed within the media and with a determination to remodel television along the above lines, to set things in motion by developing a singular idea *in tandem* with the tools needed to realise it. Moreover, far from amounting only to politically disengaged chroniclers operating in a supposed vacuum[2] from the start, the American Direct Cinema practitioners worked – away from protest, the avant-garde and *obvious* commitment, but very much as products of their epoch – in symbiosis with prevalent modes of thought vis-à-vis the purposes and problems of candid film-making.

Former fighter pilot Robert Drew, an ambitious young picture editor at *Life* magazine, was by the mid-1950s beginning to imagine ways in which he might bring the candid vibrancy of *Life*'s 'photo-essays' to the ideologically drifting, politically stilted and scandal-tainted 'wasteland' of US television: a burgeoning market that Drew's employer, media magnate Henry Luce, was naturally eager to exploit, both to compensate for the photographic press's dwindling sales (thanks to the increased popularity of television) and to promote ideas of what he called a 'national purpose', or a programme of aspirational guidance and global improvement designed broadly to forward middle-class, consumerist American interests during the Cold War era. Drew considered himself 'a cog in a large, corporate machine',[3] but nonetheless proposed an alternative to the likes of Edward R. Murrow's widely acclaimed but in some ways highly limited (and mostly studio-bound) current affairs show *See it Now* (1951–58). Sent to Harvard in order to study new means of newsgathering, Drew, in 1955, set about drafting a research paper, entitled 'See it Then':

> Grierson's documentaries were instructional in nature. That is, he, as a teacher, which he viewed himself [sic], would come up with a thesis for information people ought to have ... And Grierson's school of documentary filmmaking on reality, I thought, was propaganda ... And propaganda doesn't work, for real people ... If Grierson was at heart a sociologist and a propagandist, then Flaherty was at heart a naturalist ... and his aim was to discover. [*Nanook of the North*, 1922] was a strange cross of realism and naturalism, of form from the novel, but more than that, from real life. Grierson remained cut off from real life on one hand and the great currents of story-telling on the other ... I know that Flaherty set up and posed ... but as a theoretician it was to me a compatible, better way of viewing the potential of film for enlightening people ... drama would be the spine and strength and power of this particular reporting medium.[4]

In other words, Drew, by this time immersed in the work of the great novelists, wanted to combine Flaherty's use of narrative conventions and footage based on notions of 'discovery', with the kind of unobtrusive, 'candid' methods favoured by his still-photographer colleagues at *Life* – notably the veteran Albert Eisenstaedt, whose vibrant images of an America becoming increasingly comfortable with cameras and their presence struck a chord central to Drew's ambitions. 'Voice of God' narration, a sonorous staple of existing news formats, was, ideally, to be eschewed in favour of 'picture logic'; natural light and sound were to be used whenever possible; there would be minimal prompting of and interference with subjects;

interviews were to give way to conversational exchanges, fostered in an atmosphere of implicit awareness regarding the undesirability of verbally or visually acknowledging the camera; and events in general, though they may, for narrative convenience, have to unfold around a carefully selected, pre-existing situation, should appear unstaged and spontaneous.

It would, enthused Drew, always mindful to downplay the influence of the montage-reliant Dziga Vertov and the interventionist Jean Rouch (of whom Drew claimed never to have heard), be a 'theatre without actors'.[5] All this would be undertaken via Time Inc.'s Broadcast Division in the name of 'furthering film as a journalistic practice' (a phrase that sums up Direct Cinema's intrinsic quandaries, loaded as it is with numerous, complex connotations apropos the slippery concepts of 'fairness' and 'objectivity' – never, it should be remembered, ideals towards which documentary film, as opposed to news and current affairs output, ought to strive).

To implement his 'theatre without actors', and to surmount the technological frustrations presented by bulky, noisy cameras and notoriously hard-to-synchronise tape machines – all that was commonly available at the time – Drew, himself a film-making tyro but nominally 'executive producer', brought together a like-minded team, later to operate under the banner 'Drew Associates', of hardworking, multi-talented young cameramen and engineers. Donn Alan Pennebaker, recently graduated from MIT and competent in every aspect of portable recording, filming and editing, his friend Richard Leacock (who had filmed Robert Flaherty's swansong, *Louisiana Story* [1948]) and David and Albert Maysles (the latter coined the term 'Direct Cinema') made up the nucleus of the organisation, and remain the most famous original exponents. Under Drew's guidance, Pennebaker and Leacock devised an umbilical cord that connected a small, modified tape recorder to a 16mm Auricon camera; eventually appropriating a quartz-based regulator from a wristwatch, they succeeded in freeing themselves to rove and record the speech of those on camera without fear of endlessly haphazard, manual synchronisation at the post-production stage. Their efforts, though at first unreliable, were a source of great excitement: 'It was freedom! Screw the tripod! Screw the dolly!' said Leacock.[6] All that was now required was a subject, and a story, to suit both Drew and Luce.

In January 1960, John Kennedy, a young senator from Massachusetts whose urbane manner, glamorous family and general air of political freshness made him a long-standing darling of the Luce press, was contesting the Democratic nomination for presidential candidate. 'Jack', extolled his influential father Joseph, 'is the greatest attraction in the country today ... Why is it that when his picture is on the cover of *Life* or *Redbook* that they sell a record number of copies?'[7] Norman Mailer, conversely, took the

Primary (1960): a flawed but fascinating landmark in the history of non-fiction film-making

more cynical view that JFK was a 'hero. And yet he is a void.'[8] Still, Drew astutely sensed that Kennedy's media-friendly attitude and rock star-like effervescence, superficial or otherwise, fitted perfectly with the needs of the Drew Associates for a character who would embody the kind of newness, and astuteness, represented by the new filming techniques. When Kennedy and the more down to earth, traditionally left-wing Hubert Humphrey fought the 1960 Wisconsin Primary, the situation was ideal in terms of offering a narrative frame (in this case an archetypal 'crisis', something upon which Direct Cinema, in its first phase, would often rely), contrasting *characters* (though with markedly similar policies) acting out an easily construed filmic popularity contest, and a Luce-friendly demonstration of the benefits of democratic civics via the ballot box.

The resulting film, *Primary* (1960), is a flawed but fascinating landmark in the history of non-fiction film-making, which, while lending a 'progressive' sense of privy to the workings of an American election – if at the same time not offering any kind of penetrative comment whatsoever – ultimately turns its appearance of fairness to the promotion of the 'cooler' candidate over Humphrey's rustic charms. Kennedy gets tighter shots, in addition to more controlled, longer and hence implicitly deferent coverage (see, especially, Albert Maysles's eighty-second, wide-angle trailing of JFK through an adoring crowd of voters); and the serenely elegant 'Jackie', a *Photoplay* cover-star with whom the plain-looking Muriel Humphrey cannot compete for media attention, provides Drew and company with an obvious locus of sellable sex appeal.

On a technical note, the sound is still a little temperamental, with the result that Drew occasionally must fall back on expository voiceover (or 'lecture logic') to convey information; yet *Primary*, which through its often virtually

silent visual compositions seems tacitly to endorse Kennedy ('whose responsive and engaged style', notes Stella Bruzzi 'mirrors that of observational documentary itself'[9]), bears useful testament to Drew Associates' long endeavours to escape the 'yak, yak, yak, one cigarette after another'[10] approach of Murrow et al. Due to the film's air of basic impartiality, something that partly arises from Drew's beguiled desire not to be ostracised from JFK's media clique, and partly from the tradition of journalism in which its creator was schooled, it ends up as politically compromised, and arguably stymied rather than helped by its total rejection of Griersonian 'propaganda' or didacticism.

In fact, *Primary*'s relatively intimate access, twinned with a Boswell-esque, quiet veneration of its main human focus, provides a televisual analogue to the gently pro-Kennedy sentiments of print journalist Theodore White, who likewise covered the Wisconsin election. As Bernard Cohen observed: 'The more "neutral" the press is – that is, the more it tries faithfully to transmit a record of "what transpires" … the more easily it lends itself to the uses of others.'[11] Quite simply, Drew, in common with many in the media, had found in John Kennedy (a man liable to exclude from his circle anyone who elicited unfavourable information) his muse and inspiration: Kennedy, as Drew well knew, was a new breed of political star whose favour was to be courted via the power of the image.

After Kennedy's election to the White House, Drew and his Associates continued to produce work in general accordance with both the Fairness Doctrine (a passive-aggressive means by which the Federal Communications Commission ensured that broadcasters produced edifying, controversially themed but never seditious material) and Kennedy's brand of globally minded, 'New Frontier' liberalism, which sought to use the airwaves in 'the service of the people and the causes of freedom'.[12] Syndicated under the name 'The Living Camera', and made in an environment that encouraged Drew's apparently disinterested approach, these subsequent films, mostly funded by ABC-TV and Time Inc., include: *On The Pole* (1960), like *Primary*, a story of masculine contest, this time featuring racing driver Eddie Sachs's competition in the Indianapolis 500; *Yanki No!* (1960), which saw the crew travel to Cuba and give a bravely considered appraisal of Castro's personality and regime (and to which was added, to Leacock's disgust, an ABC-authored voiceover emphasising the leader's cultish, 'Messianic' appeal); *The Children Were Watching* (1961), an exploration of educational integration and subsequent racism in New Orleans; *Football* (1961), another film demonstrating Drew's preoccupation with noble competition; and *The Chair* (1962), a crisis narrative about black convict Paul Crump's fight to have his death sentence commuted.

Returning to his favourite subject, JFK, three times after *Primary*, Drew made what amounts to a series of officially sanctioned puff-pieces for Kennedy's 'Camelot'.

These are of varying quality and insightfulness, but the highlights are perhaps *Crisis* (1963), following John and Robert Kennedy's bid to stop Governor George Wallace blocking the entrance of two black students into the University of Alabama, and 1963's *Faces of November*, a post-assassination eulogy to Drew's fallen hero. Wallace, a 'sleazy, strutting Alabama redneck'[13] was a gift to *Crisis*, whose handsome, righteous heroes could not be more at odds with the piece's bulldoggish antagonist, filmed brooding in his mansion and slobbishly gobbling down food while the Kennedy brothers engage in conversely upstanding endeavours – including, in a remarkable instance of simultaneous, geographically separate coordination, during a phone call between Robert and his deputy Nicholas Katzenbach, both sides of which are shown. (The two students, however, are effectively sidelined, appearing once in a while merely to serve as pleasantly countenanced MacGuffins to facilitate the Kennedy vs Wallace show.) *Faces of November* constitutes Drew's most poetic work; entirely doing away with voiceover (something Drew's films, any 'picture logic' therein usually only semi-comprehensible to the average viewer, perpetually required to satisfy commissioning editors' needs for clarity), it presents an elegiac, multi-racial, pan-societal depiction of a nation unified in loss. At this moment, Drew forgets himself to a newfound poesis and visual panache that rises above the strictly narrative tendencies of his previous work; in so doing, he arguably gets closest to his stated goal of bringing the nuanced imagistic properties of the *Life* essay to film. Sadly, however, the networks demurred, having already broadcast a flood of Kennedy tributes produced in a timelier manner.

At around this time, fed up with the repetitive nature of their assignments, the Associates abandoned their chief: a figure, as his charges saw it, unable to move on and embrace truly fresh ideas in sympathy with a growing sense of cultural liberation, spurred on in the wake of Kennedy's killing by intensifying struggles for equality and the disturbing situation in Indochina. (Arguably, the 1960s proper begin not with JFK's election, but with his martyrdom to the liberal cause and its entwined efforts to create a better America while containing the spread of communism.) 'More and more', complained Pennebaker, 'we were becoming like *Life* photographers; just story, story, story. That didn't seem like a helluva lot of fun.'[14] Drew, in essence, was a good citizen of Eisenhower's 50s, excited most by post-war ideals of applied technology, a well-informed, conscientious middle class and trust in the power of the vote. Leacock, Pennebaker and the Maysles brothers, however, frustrated by an inability to gain access to the truly private lives of Kennedy and his ilk, wanted to move on, to forget any idealistic faith in their equipment to offer magical omniscience, and above all to stay relevant and young by addressing, albeit in their own obliquely

observational ways, the artistic issues pertaining to Lyndon Johnson's 'Great Society' and its inherited quests, the contradictions and dreams of which were giving rise to a 'counter-culture' predicated on challenging the unquestioningly patriotic ideals of its parents. 'In my opinion', explained Leacock, 'it is the nature of broadcast television that posed a problem for Bob Drew … Drew's dream, to put twenty to fifty, whatever, hour-long shows on broadcast TV was our nightmare.'[15] If Drew was an unrepentant 'square', somewhat ossified in deference to the needs of Time-Life's consensus-building formulas, then his erstwhile colleagues, by contrast, were getting 'hip' to the underground scene and utilising the portable camera-sound crew as means to facilitate an appropriately transcendental reworking of journalism in opposition to what Pennebaker called 'prosaic, predictable bullshit'.[16] As Peter Graham germanely noted, just after the Drew Associates broke up: '[The Maysles brothers, Drew and Leacock] present not *the* truth, but *their* truth. The term *cinéma-vérité*, by postulating some absolute truth, is only a monumental red herring. The sooner it is buried and forgotten, the better.'[17]

Drew, undeterred, continued to adhere to his principles, over the years making a great many sponsored programmes with titles like *Saving Energy: It Begins at Home* (1974) and *Build the Fusion Power Machine* (1984). This now comparatively forgotten torchbearer's greatest artistic attainments, though, are to be found not in his ultimately futile crusade for a civically upstanding 'theatre without actors' (the 'red herring' of a supposedly revelatory discourse predicated on austerely 'truthful' cinema), but in the vastly more liberated work – and tremendous legacy – of his breakaway disciples, who happily added to Drew's soberly conceived 'picture logic' a revivifying element of authorial brio.

In September 1963, ABC sent Leacock to cover a quintuple birth in rural Aberdeen, South Dakota. The resulting film, *Happy Mother's Day*, is an extraordinarily sarcastic critique of conventional journalism's tendency to exploit and commodify its human subjects in the name of educing middle-class romanticism about the lives of the 'salt-of-the-earth' poor. Leacock's camera, only one among many, works to create a commentary with which the stressed and scrutinised mother, Mary Anne Fischer, appears verbally and physically to sypathise. While hacks from the *Saturday Evening Post* set about their task of forcing Aberdeen's new celebrities into acting out a Norman Rockwell painting, Leacock posits himself as one of 'us', pitted against the thronging 'them' represented by the numerous, haranguing photographers and writers sent by the local and national press to pose, set up and elicit predictable responses – and hymns to vulgar consumerism – ad infinitum. *Happy Mother's Day*, its stance shared with the contemporaneous New Left's view of American materialism as 'a glaze above deeply felt anxieties'[18] shows nothing but disdain for scoops, deadlines and the shoehorning of reluctant individuals into an aspirational mould whereby newsworthy tricks might earn even impecunious farm-folk the supposedly universally desired totems of American wealth. Gifts pour in; fur coats are borrowed; crowds of strangers descend: all to the evident annoyance of the Fischers. 'It is at this moment', writes William Rothman, 'that [Direct Cinema] itself is born, or reborn as a movement of independent film.'[19] So heavily ironic and contemptuous was the film's aloof, sardonic narration (and indeed general attitude) that ABC felt compelled to produce its own, neutered and innocuous version for public consumption.

The following year's *What's Happening! The Beatles in the USA* (1964, made by the Maysles brothers[20]), marked the beginning of Direct Cinema's obsession with musical celebrities – and the ready-made situations, soundtracks and personalities that come with such subjects. Following the adored band on its first tour of the USA, the film acted as a documentary prototype for Richard Lester's *A Hard Day's Night* (1964) and, while not without charms, is just as grating. The Fab Four, impeccably practised in the art of acting up for the camera – or, in other words, never letting their Brian Epstein-schooled, cheeky-chappy guards down for a second, even while 'off duty' (on this evidence, are they *ever*?) – are captured in trains, hotels and in concert, always chased and drowned out by screaming girls desperate for a piece of the Beatles' undeniable if sometimes inexplicable magic. Deadpan wisecracks come thick and fast: from Lennon and cohorts, as expected, comes a nonstop barrage of amplified Beatleness that the film-makers have no hope of overcoming. Several scenes, though, offer a sympathetic joy, as the privately weary Scousers clearly regard the Maysles brothers as both 'in on it' and allies: and, thanks to the band's total familiarity to audiences of whatever stripe, the film has the distinction of being the first Direct Cinema production to use no voiceover whatsoever. Nobody, it's safe to say, really needed any explanation as to who, exactly, the Beatles were (notwithstanding the fact that elders were baffled by their hairstyles [a running joke throughout] and genetically immune to their sometimes rapturous music).

Meanwhile, D. A. Pennebaker secured a minor coup: access to the wedding of LSD guru Timothy Leary, a former academic whose mission to 'turn on' America to the virtues of psychedelic experience was making for alarmist headlines. 'Any action', said Leary, with accidental relevance to Pennebaker's split from Drew, 'that is not a conscious expression of the turn-on-tune-in-drop-out rhythm is the dead posturing of robot actors on the fake-prop TV studio stage set that is called American reality.'[21] Going to Leary's ramshackle New York mansion to sit among the none-more-60s paraphernalia of fifty-seven-variety syncretism, 'enlightened' hedonism and sybaritic indulgence – and just to absorb – Pennebaker never actually films the wedding. For this reason as much as any, the resulting short, *You're Nobody 'Til Somebody Loves You* (1964), is a good example of observational film-making's digression from 'story, story, story', and its subsequent progression into counter-cultural allegiance via more musically inspired, free-form rhythms of editing and visual composition. 'I filmed [*You're Nobody ...*] as a kind of pageant and edited it as a mystery,'[22] said the director, slightly bafflingly, his 'turning on' increasingly evident.

Maybe the ultimate realisation of Direct Cinema's aims at this time, however, came in 1965, with Pennebaker's epochal *Dont Look Back* [sic]. The techniques and attitude at play in the 1964 short about Leary are again evident, this time in a feature-length, voiceover-free account of Bob Dylan's final acoustic tour of England. From its famous, prompt card-tossing introduction (a much-referenced precursor to the pop video) in a back alley by the Savoy Hotel, to its fervent clashes with the press and tense meetings with Dylan's less talented young rival Donovan, *Dont Look Back* proffers Dylan as Pennebaker's muse and co-conspirator. Equally hateful of conventional journalists, Dylan continually throws them off the scent with obfuscatory or surrealist responses to inane questions, all the while brewing up the best songs of his career: a career that was about to 'go electric', outraging the folk purists who had made his name and forwarded him, largely unwillingly, as a nominal successor to Woody Guthrie.

Dylan, though, never happy with the role of 'spokesman for a generation', had no sense of obligation to the nascent, generically folkie self he had just left behind, just as Pennebaker had dismissed the tenets of Time-Life. Neither Pennebaker, nor Dylan, wanted to look back to schematic politics or inherited narratives: the film follows Dylan around, as he performs and marks time with his entourage (which intermittently includes the singer's aggrieved ex-girlfriend, Joan Baez, Dylan's ursine manager, Albert Grossman, and a drunken and dejected Alan Price); yet it tells no real story, nor attempts to explicate or explain Dylan's appeal. But then, why should it? In perhaps the film's most celebrated exchange, Dylan meets with the esteemed journalist Horace Judson, from *Time* magazine (and hence a representative of the Luce/Drew ethos so rankling with Pennebaker). Endlessly and cruelly berated by Dylan, fundamentally for being a 'square' who isn't attuned to what Dylan is trying to do, Judson has no choice but to remain calm and take it: to face facts and accept that the times are a-changin', whether he likes it or not. As Pennebaker has made clear: '*Dont Look Back* has a kind of responsiveness to Dylan, born of Dylan coming very close to things I've been thinking about for a long time. It's sort of an epiphany that took place.'[23]

The epiphany led Pennebaker, in 1967 and in the midst of the 'Summer of Love', to the Monterey Pop Festival. America's first three-day musical event seduced

Dont Look Back (1965): the ultimate realisation of Direct Cinema's aims

the film-maker; like thousands of other dreamers flocking to the West Coast in search of love-ins and flower-power, Pennebaker, though rather older than his hippie subjects, sought spiritual unity through music, drugs, art and sex. Taking along a crew that included Richard Leacock, the entranced former Drew Associate lingers lovingly on 'liberated', leggily beautiful women, worryingly spaced-out attendees and somewhat indulgent performances: *Monterey Pop* (1967) is thus as replete with sexism, turgidity and naivety as it is with bursts of genuinely electrifying talent: witness, for the latter, Jimi Hendrix demolishing 'Wild Thing' (and his amps) as a hypnotised Mama Cass looks on; Janis Joplin, in a gold lamé suit, wrenching 'Ball and Chain' from the bottom of her heart; and soul man Otis Redding winning over a very white, very middle-class crowd of predominantly twenty-something dropouts from the world of work and adult obligation.

(As evidence of the former, the film features eighteen minutes of Ravi Shankar's microtonal meanderings: however

virtuosic, beautifully framed and steeped in the Indian's deeply held beliefs, these prove hard to endure, with the result that it is Hendrix and Joplin, the consummate, three-minute rock performers with everything to prove, who stick longest in the mind.) *Woodstock* (Michael Wadleigh, 1970) takes the Monterey concept to epic lengths, presenting a three-hour, split-screen, panoramic spectacle taking in what appears to be more-or-less the whole Woodstock experience. Wadleigh (not one of Direct Cinema's pioneers, but at least a bona fide hippie) mixes interviews, performances and observational purism to create a massively hewn canvas of colour, exuberance and, ultimately, a lot of mud and litter. Half a million people attended (roughly the same number of GIs were in Vietnam) Woodstock's 'Aquarian exposition', a for-profit event that sanctified and crystallised the counter-culture's less politically astute hopes; while America was putting men on the barren Moon, many on Earth were looking for harmony closer to home, but trampling fields into sludge as they congregated in such numbers that even the self-provision of food and sanitation were impossible.

In a remarkable show of magnanimity, US Army helicopters airlift drug casualties and drop food parcels; Hendrix reappears, exhausted by creative burnout and addiction, to warp 'The Star Spangled Banner' into a distortion-fed musical simile for exploding napalm; and opportunistic capitalists move in to sell cigarettes to a captive clientele of nudists whose Eden is not all it seems. Wadleigh's portrayal, unlike *Monterey Pop*, is sagacious and considered. The ironic absurdities of the situation evidently do not escape him, despite his film's overall thrust: that the hippie dream's eventual efficacy might depend on an appreciation of our world as a 'garden', whose fruits must continually be cherished and replenished in order to return humankind to a prelapsarian state of innocence and peace. As the film ends, on a mournful note of trash-collection among the desolately ruined alfalfa crops, one gets the feeling that the party – or, in other words, the high 60s Dionysian impulse towards hedonistic abandon – is running out of time.

'With the "explosion into reality"', wrote Christopher Booker in *The Neophiliacs*, 'every fantasy, if pushed far enough, must inevitably bring about its own self-destruction.'[24] If Woodstock, on balance, had been the youth movement's crowning glory, then the same year's festival at Altamont – organised by the Rolling Stones, with the Hell's Angels as security – would prove Booker's point and bring down the guillotine. Intended as 'Woodstock West', the festival instead summoned the worst in its intoxicated attendees, and culminated in the stabbing, by furious bikers, of a gun-wielding concertgoer: an event the Maysles brothers capture with unflinching and brave acuity in the resultant film, *Gimme Shelter* (1970), the last of the four truly great music docs to come out of the observational movement.

Shown footage of both their often-brilliant performances and a frame-by-frame rerun of the killing, Jagger and band are seated at an editing machine and forced to contemplate the results of their cynically hubristic hijacking of the hippie movement. An overwhelming feeling of doom hangs over the film, and in particular its contrite ending, in which, silhouetted against a jaundiced sky, dazed-looking partygoers shuffle disconsolately away from Altamont's 'bummer' – and from the 60s summers of love.

The decade's societal flip side (a facet that left-wing political scientist Michael Harrington had long identified as 'the other America', or the socially dispossessed, underprivileged mass that remained immune to liberal and hippie ideals) was covered extensively: not, however, by the ex-Drew Associates, but by a former lawyer and Yale graduate. Frederick Wiseman, who remains the most high-profile adherent to purely observational Direct Cinema (he resolutely uses no voiceover, prompting, interviews or over-dubbed sound whatsoever), continues to produce austerely composed and ever more protracted films annually; Wiseman's most concise attacks on the malaise afflicting the other America, though, are to be found in his early works, all of which use public-funded institutions to critique the wider macrocosm: *Titicut Follies* (1967), *High School* (1968), *Law and Order* (1969), *Hospital* (1970) and *Basic Training* (1971) take the New Left's ideas apropos the alienating tendencies of a federal administration working in service to the 'military-industrial complex', and site them within a series of non-narrative portraits illustrative of a broken society.

The 'machine' of American healthcare, schooling and policing is dissected, not by overt activism – something Wiseman viewed as at best ineffectual, at worst part of the problem – but by a considered, highly manipulated and intelligent body of work that builds to make a case for grassroots reform in sympathy with those such as Herbert Marcuse, who argued that, 'Contemporary society seems to be capable of containing social change ... the struggle for the solution has outgrown traditional forms.'[25] In disavowing these forms, and the related structural manifestations at play within storytelling conventions, Wiseman transcends orthodox methods of social protest in order to reject any kind of mechanistic authority while at the same time offering a voice to the nameless, yet for Wiseman certainly not faceless, inhabitants of a rich nation plagued by Dickensian disparity. (In this way, Wiseman is perhaps a quasi-anarchic product of the 60s 'expressive individualism' as much as is Bob Dylan, who likewise moved rapidly away from explicit reformism to embrace oblique modes of subversion.)

As the 1960s petered out, so did the heyday of Direct Cinema. Not just a dispassionate mirror, but a movement that sharply traced the decade's joys and frustrations while finding therein its purpose, reactive observationalism burgeoned, blossomed and withered within an astoundingly short period of time. 'I had a sense that we had opened up a whole new world', said Leacock, 'and that horizons were limitless. Somehow it ran out of steam. I still don't understand.'[26] Its aesthetic influence, of course, is seen every time a hand-held camera moves to follow or reframe, whether through contrivance or otherwise: from feature films to low-budget docs posted on YouTube, the Direct Cinema look still says 'gritty', 'real' and 'out there with the action' (no matter how such inferences, and their implications, might in fact point to a profusion of thorny issues). Most of the originators have continued in their chosen field, albeit sporadically, into extreme old age; but the time is not as ripe, nor the call for a 'new consciousness' (which is, after all, a concept closely tied to the Direct Cinema ethos) as loud.

NOTES

1. Ian Cameron and Mark Shivas, 'New Methods, New Approach', *Movie*, 8 April 1963, p. 12.

2. David E. James, *Allegories of Cinema: American Film in the Sixties* (Princeton, NJ: Princeton University Press, 1989), p. 213.

3. Quoted in P. J. O'Connell, *Robert Drew and the Development of Cinema Verite in America* (Carbondale and Edwardsville: Southern Illinois University Press, 1992), p. 11.

4. Ibid., p. 35.

5. Dave Saunders, *Direct Cinema: Observational Documentary and the Politics of the Sixties* (London: Wallflower Press, 2007), p. 1.

6. Leacock, interviewed in Peter Wintonick's film *Cinéma Vérité: Defining the Moment* (2001), Canada.

7. Seymour Hersh, *The Dark Side of Camelot* (London: HarperCollins, 1997), p. 8.

8. Norman Mailer, *The Presidential Papers* (Harmondsworth: Penguin, 1968), p. 55.

9. Stella Bruzzi, *New Documentary: A Critical Introduction* (London: Routledge, 2000), p. 131.

10. Leacock, quoted in O'Connell, *Robert Drew and the Development of Cinema Verite in America*, p. 67.

11. Bernard Cohen, *The Press and Foreign Policy* (Princeton, NJ: Princeton University Press, 1963), p. 28.

12. Newton M. Minow, *Equal Time: The Private Broadcaster and the Public Interest* (New York: Atheneum, 1964), p. 64.

13. Dan T. Carter, *The Politics of Rage: George Wallace, The Origins of the New Conservatism, and the Transformation of American Politics* (Baton Rouge, LA: Louisiana State University Press, 1995), p. 142.

14. O'Connell, *Robert Drew and the Development of Cinema Verite in America*, p. 167.

15. Ibid., pp. 238, 236.

16. G. Roy Levin, *Documentary Explorations: 15 Interviews with Film-Makers* (New York: Doubleday, 1971), p. 236.

17. Peter Graham, 'Cinéma-Vérité in France', *Film Quarterly*, Summer 1964, p. 36, emphasis in original.

18. SDS, 'The Port Huron Statement', in Massimo Teodori (ed.), *The New Left: A Documentary History* (London: Jonathan Cape, 1970), p. 165.

19. William Rothman, *Documentary Film Classics* (New York: Cambridge University Press, 1997), p. 142.

20. From the footage they shot for director Dick Fontaine, which was shown in the UK as a Granada TV *World in Action* special 'Yeah, Yeah, Yeah: New York Meets the Beatles' (Peter Goddard, John Corner and Kay Richardson, *Public Issue Television: World in Action, 1968–1993* [Manchester: Manchester University Press, 2007]), pp. 21–2.

21. Timothy Leary, *Turn On, Tune In, Drop Out*, ed. Beverly Potter (Berkeley, CA: Ronin, 1999), pp. 3, 5.

22. Levin, *Documentary Explorations*, p. 229.

23. Ibid., p. 262.

24. Christopher Booker, *The Neophiliacs* (London: Collins, 1969), p. 72.

25. Herbert Marcuse, *One-Dimensional Man: Studies in the Ideology of Advanced Industrial Society* (London: Routledge & Kegan Paul, 1964), pp. xii, 256.

26. O'Connell, *Robert Drew and the Development of Cinema Verite in America*, p. 209.

2.7 Soviet and Russian Documentary: From Vertov to Sokurov

IAN CHRISTIE

At the outset, when documentary was first indentified as a separate cinematic form and the Griersonian paradigm emerged to dominate the anglophone version of it, in the Soviet Union an alternative approach was being essayed by Vertov. Although dismissed in the West and stifled by Stalinism in the USSR, it was to prove a significant, if latent, factor in documentary's development.

The name Dziga Vertov still has extraordinary currency today, perhaps more than any other member of the early Soviet film avant-garde, or even any other silent-era filmmaker. Yet few of those who prize Vertov for his reflexive treatment of the film-making process have seen more than his 1929 manifesto *Chelovek s kinopparatom* [*Man with a Movie Camera*], 'an experiment in the cinematic communication of visible events without the aid of intertitles [or] scenario'.[1] Once accused of 'formalism' and considered unsuitable as a model for documentary proper, this virtuoso 'day in the life of a cameraman' is now widely admired for dealing imaginatively with the film process, from shooting to editing and screening, and has even been proposed as a pioneer of the montage and 'compositing' involved in contemporary 'new media'.[2] Vertov is also responsible, indirectly, for the continued use of the term 'cinéma vérité' to refer to unrehearsed filming of people and situations, which came from the title of his earlier newsreel series, *Kino-Pravda* (1922–25, literally: 'cinema truth').

To say that this is all misunderstanding – of Vertov and of the course of Russian documentary – is probably beside the point. The fact is that a French ethnographic filmmaker, Jean Rouch, adopted the phrase cinéma-vérité to describe what he and Edgar Morin had attempted in their influential *Chronique d'un été* [*Chronicle of a Summer*] (1961).[3] Vertov's title for the newsreel represented a bid to claim the same status for a film chronicle as the Party newspaper *Pravda*, although more relevant to Rouch and Morin's approach would have been Vertov's theory of the 'cine-eye', which argued that the camera can see what the unaided eye does not, 'as a microscope and telescope of the times'. Vertov's first feature-length film, titled *Kino Glaz* [*Cinema Eye*] (1924), would have been a better model for cinema vérité investigative film-makers of the 1960s, but, like most

of his work apart from *Man with a Movie Camera*, was and remains little known.

Vertov was born Denis Kaufman in 1896 in Bialystok, then part of the Russian empire, with a predominantly Jewish population. His brothers Mikhail and Boris would both become leading cameramen, while Denis became involved in futurist avant-garde poetry and sound experiments in Moscow before the 1917 Revolution. In 1918, he became editor of the newsreel *Kino Nedelya* [*Film Weekly*] before launching the more experimental *Kino-Pravda* in 1922. This made considerable use of fast and slow-motion, reverse-action and animated titles, as constructivist devices intended to reveal 'communist truth' during the early Soviet years in a modern way. Vertov's first feature *Kino Eye* (1924) assembled coverage of everyday life in Moscow, anti-religious demonstrations and a Young Pioneers camp, intended as a manifesto in favour of 'life caught unawares' and against the 'opium' of film drama, which Vertov believed Eisenstein and other Soviet filmmakers were producing.

As Vertov's polemics became more strident, he abandoned newsreel for feature-length films, beginning with *Shagai, Soviet!* [*Stride Soviet*] and *Shestaya chast mira* [*One Sixth of the World*] (both 1926), the one a lyrical celebration of the breadth of Soviet achievement and the other an equally kaleidoscopic promotion of its exports. Industrial development was the theme of his next feature, *Odinnadtsatyi* [*The Eleventh Year*] (1928), made in the Ukraine as his relations with the Soviet film authorities deteriorated. And it was thanks to Ukrainian support that Vertov was able to make his two greatest achievements in the transitional period between 'silent' and sound cinema. *Man with a Movie Camera* was a project Vertov had been long preparing as a manifesto, and it follows a reflexive arc in which a cinema audience is shown watching the film that we, and they, also see take shape, thanks to the bravura exploits of the cameraman (his brother, Mikhail Kaufman), seen in a variety of action sequences, filming from a moving car, under a speeding train and from high buildings. Also described as a '*ciné-feuilleton*', the film was intended to prove that non-fictional film could be as

Man with a Movie Camera (1929): 'an experiment in the cinematic communication of visible events without the aid of intertitles [or] scenario' – Dziga Vertov

entertaining, even suspenseful, as the fictional film that Vertov despised.

The film did little to rehabilitate Vertov with Soviet film bureaucrats, who were moving sharply against Leftists and 'Formalism'. But he was able to catch the tide of support for 'construction' themes that accompanied the launch of the first Five Year Plan, and shot *Entuziazm* [*Enthusiasm*] (1931), subtitled *Simfoniia Donbassa* [*The Donbas Symphony*], in the eastern Ukraine amid the crash development of the Donets coal basin. While others hesitated over the impact of synchronised sound on visual montage aesthetics, he also seized the initiative to combine recorded sounds boldly, recalling his early interests in sound art and radio.[4] However, Vertov would complete only two further personal films, the lyrical *Tri pesni o Lenine* [*Three Songs of Lenin*] (1934) and *Kolibelnaya* [*Lullaby*] (1937), before being sidelined by Stalin's demand for 'revolutionary romanticism'.

Although Vertov's work was known in Western Europe at the turn of the decade, the leader of the British documentary movement, John Grierson, dismissed it as irrelevant to the serious task of proving documentary's value. Most influential at this time was Viktor Turin's *Turksib* (1929), which celebrated the completion of the rail link between Turkestan and Siberia with a gritty portrayal of life in both regions, before reaching a rhythmically edited climax that recalls the opening of Ruttman's *Berlin: Die Sinfonie der Großstadt* [*Berlin: Symphony of a Metropolis*] (1927). Many other Soviet documentaries of this transitional period remained unknown for decades, until the 1960s and 70s led to a revision of the earlier Soviet canon that had focused almost exclusively on Eisenstein, Pudovkin and Dovzhenko. One unseen film-maker was Esfir Shub, a critical friend of both Vertov and Eisenstein (whom she taught to edit). Shub had gained experience in re-editing imported films in the early 20s, which no doubt

The Fall of the Romanov Dynasty (1927): pioneering example of the 'compilation' documentary

prompted her project to assemble surviving footage from the pre-revolutionary era in *Padenie dinastii Romanovykh* [*The Fall of the Romanov Dynasty*] (1927). This pioneering example of the 'compilation' documentary was rapidly followed by *Velikii put* [*The Great Road*] (1927), covering the decade since the October revolutions, and *Rossiya Nikolaya II i Lev Tolstoy* [*The Russia of Nikolai II and Lev Tolstoy*] (1928). Shub next turned to the present, with a film about the international situation, *Segodnya* [*Today*] (1930, known abroad as *Cannons or Tractors?*) and a Five Year Plan film, *Komsomolya – shef elektrifikatsii* [*Komsomol: Patron of Electrification*] (1932), which is as boldly experimental in its demonstration of the new sound-film techniques as Vertov. Shub would later make a compilation documentary about the Spanish Civil War, *Ispaniya* [*Spain*] (1939) and collaborate with Pudovkin on a film about the history of cinema in 1940.

Another film-maker whose early documentaries would not be discovered until decades later was Mikhail Kalatozov, best known for his breakthrough 'Thaw' film, *Letyat zhuravli* [*The Cranes Are Flying*] (1957) and for the baroque epic *Soy Cuba* [*I Am Cuba*] (1964). Among a handful of documentaries that Kalatozov made in his native Georgia in the late 1920s, *Sol Svanetii* [*Salt for Svanetia*] (1930) is remarkable. Suggested by the avant-garde writer Sergei Tretyakov, this reveals the harshness of life in a remote part of the high Caucasus with a fascinated precision that reminded the historian Jay Leyda of Luis Buñuel's view of *Las Hurdes* [*Land Without Bread*] (1933) in Spain, except that Kalatozov's restless camera and virtuoso editing were already apparent at this stage (and would not reappear in Soviet documentary until Peleshian fifty years later).

Films that showed the scale and variety of life across the Soviet Union were popular in the 1930s, and Yuli Raizman's *Zemlya zhazhdet* [*The Earth Thirsts*] (1931), about

an expedition to Turkmenistan that has to combat local superstition, could be considered an early example of drama-documentary. But the film-maker most associated with taking cinema to remote regions was Alexander Medvedkin, who directed the Soyuzkino 'film-train' on a number of expeditions during 1932–33. Established to introduce 'new methods and forms of mass work in technical propaganda ... using the cinema to mobilize the working masses around the tasks of socialist construction', the train carried a crew of thirty and full (silent) production facilities.[5] Their basic task was to make instructional films to address local problems, such as ensuring that winter conditions did not delay construction projects. Beyond this, Medvedkin brought his satirical sense of humour to bear on issues of morale, with acted films attacking bureaucracy and nepotism, and promoting personal hygiene. A surviving example of his health films shows how poor hygiene could decimate a Red Army platoon. Medvedkin's train films were never seen abroad at the time of their making, but became the subject of Chris Marker's widely shown documentary *Le Train en marche* [*The Train Rolls On*] (1971), which made a connection between this initiative of the first Five Year Plan and the earlier Civil War era, when short propaganda films were first made. The idea of 'mobilising' film in the service of the revolution had a powerful appeal to radical film-makers in the West, and helped inspire many post-1968 projects to 'take film' to workers and communities.[6]

After Soviet sound production produced its first popular successes in 1934–35, documentary played a less prominent role than entertainment films. But as the threat of war grew, an idea originally proposed by Maxim Gorky was realised. For *Den novogo mira* [*A Day in a New World*] (1940), Mikhail Slutsky gathered material shot by dozens of cameramen stationed around the USSR and edited this into a feature-length portrait of the country in what proved to be the months before invasion. Eighteen months later, the sequel, *Den voyny* [*A Day of War*] (Slutsky, 1942), recorded action on many fronts and was widely shown in Allied countries, as evidence of the Soviet Union's resolve to resist Hitler. Other wartime documentaries chronicled the sieges of Leningrad and Stalingrad, while *Razgrom nemetskikh voysk pod Moskvoy* [*The Defeat of the German Army Near Moscow*] (Alexander Varlamov, Ilya Kopalin, 1942) was adapted as *Moscow Strikes Back* for US release, with a commentary by Edward G. Robinson, and one by Wilfred Pickles for its British screenings.[7] Among the many such films, Leyda singled out *Bitva za nashu Sovetskuyu Ukrainu* [*Battle for Our Soviet Ukraine*] (1944), as 'quite unlike the organised and efficient wartime documentaries from other Soviet filmmakers', on account of its 'passionate lyricism' instilled by Aleksandr Dovzhenko, acting as supervisor and commentator.[8]

It has been claimed recently that some of these films included 'staged' scenes, in order to produce more impressive images – which may well be true, since this has been relatively common practice, especially in war conditions, ever since the official British film of the Battle of the Somme in 1916, and before.[9] Whatever their exact provenance, Soviet wartime documentaries clearly played an important propaganda role, within the USSR and perhaps even more crucially abroad, when they provided Allied countries with inspiring evidence of Russia's ability to contain and eventually roll back the Nazi invasion.

The Cold War that set in during the late 1940s sharply reduced international interest in Soviet culture of all kinds for a decade, until a small group of fiction films in the late 50s – all dealing with the human impact of World War II – heralded a 'Thaw' in cinema, matching the liberalisation already seen in literature and the other arts. A Soviet New Wave emerged in the early 60s, with Andrei Tarkovsky, Sergo Paradjanov, Andrei Konchalovsky, Elem Klimov and Larissa Shepitko among its leading lights. All of these would suffer interference, censorship and even imprisonment in Paradjanov's case, when the Soviet regime reasserted a hardline orthodoxy in 1967. Before this, however, Mikhail Romm's *Obyknovennyy fashizm* [*Ordinary Fascism*] (1965) made a serious and imaginative effort to explain the roots of German fascism to audiences in the USSR and abroad.[10] Starting with images filmed in contemporary Moscow, Romm and his team drew on captured German newsreel and amateur film to create a surprisingly non-propagandist interpretation of National Socialism's appeal. Although dubbed into many languages and widely shown, *Ordinary Fascism* would eventually be withdrawn during the period of cultural repression and 'stagnation' that lasted from the late 60s to the early 80s.

During this period, working in documentary and far from Moscow or Leningrad offered a solution for film-makers seeking more freedom. In Armenia, Artavazd Peleshian (b. 1938) began making short documentary-based films in the mid-60s, before *The Beginning* (1967) revealed him as drawing inspiration from the montage tradition of the 20s. This thrillingly edited meditation on the legacy of the October revolution used an uncontroversial excuse (the fiftieth anniversary) to produce a film that could easily have been condemned as formalist, if it had had a higher profile. Instead, Peleshian was able to continue making lyrical short films such as *Menq* [*We*] (1969) and *Vremena goda* [*The Seasons*] (1975), both celebrating Armenian landscape and culture, before producing his remarkable *Mer dare* [*Our Century*] (1983). Drawing on montage technique and Shub's compilation form, this medium-length exploration of man's ambition to fly and eventually reach outer space manages to celebrate Soviet achievement, while also reflecting the mystical tradition of Fedorov's 'philosophy of the common task'.[11]

In Latvia, Herz Frank (b. 1926, as Gercels Franks) was able to carve out a career as a distinctive documentarist

over the same period, until his 1978 short *Par desmit minutem vecaks* [*Ten Minutes Older*] brought him wider attention. This single-shot film shows a boy watching a puppet show that we don't see, but can follow through the changing expressions on his face. Twenty-four years later, Frank's film would inspire two international collections of ten-minute films on the theme of time. Meanwhile, the dramatic loosening of censorship and central control that began in the USSR in 1986 under Mikhail Gorbachev allowed Frank, along with many other documentarists, to tackle subjects that were previously impossible. *The Final Verdict* (1988) investigated the case of a young man convicted of murdering a Latvian union leader, awaiting imposition of the death penalty; and *Reiz dzivoja septini Simeoni* [*Once There Were Seven Simeons*] (1989) dealt with a tragic aircraft hijacking carried out by members of a Siberian family jazz band who were desperate to escape from the USSR.[12]

Herz's cameraman on *Ten Minutes Older* and other films, Juris Podnieks (1950–92), made a major contribution to demystifying, and perhaps ultimately dismantling, the Soviet Union in his feature documentary *Vai viegli būt jaunam?* [*Is It Easy to Be Young?*] (1986). Beginning with a rock concert, followed by interviews with individual young punk-rock fans, Podnieks's film explores the anomie and pent-up anger of a generation that has lost faith in all Soviet institutions. Rebellious punks, would-be artists and traumatised army conscripts serving in Afghanistan all bear witness to their disillusion, and when the film was given a wide release under Gorbachev's *glasnost* [openness] policy, it helped to spark a national debate about the failure of Soviet society. Five years later, another feature documentary, *Solovki Power* (1990), by Marina Goldovskaya would expose the long history of the use of prison camps by the Soviet regime, dating back to the establishment of a corrective prison on a remote White Sea island under Lenin.

Documentary and fiction film-making had remained relatively separate under the Soviet regime, but one film-maker who was 'discovered' during the revolution that overtook the Film-makers Union in 1986 has consistently worked in both genres – and become post-Soviet Russia's best-known film-maker internationally. Aleksandr Sokurov (b. 1951) began his career working in regional television, in Gorki, in the 1970s. For a routine assignment, to portray a 'typical' collective farm worker, he interviewed Maria Voinova in 1978 and displayed impressionistically various aspects of her life. Sokurov's own life would become difficult after he entered the national film school (VGIK), and, when his graduation film was rejected, he substituted *Maria* instead. When the Film-makers Union under Elem Klimov announced in 1986 that previously banned films could now be submitted for clearance, Sokurov was singled out as an example of a film-maker who had been all but silenced during the previous six years, and he was encour-aged to complete and show for the first time many films begun earlier.[13]

In the case of *Maria*, Sokurov returned to the same vil-lage to discover that Voinova had died while still young, and he filmed a second part, now in black and white, piec-ing together her life as a typically exploited peasant and revealing what pressures had contributed to her family breaking up and her early death.[14] Now entitled *Peasant Elegy* (1988), this two-part film could stand as a symbol of Russian documentary before and after the Gorbachev watershed; and it joined a continuing series of 'elegies' that Sokurov has made. Several of his early archive-based documentaries had musical structures (*Sonata dlya Gitlera* [*Sonata for Hitler*] [1979/89]; *Altovaya sonata. Dmitriy Shostakovich* [*Sonata for Viola, Dmitri Shostakovich*] [1981]), and in *Elegiya* [*Elegy*] (1985) he used the occasion of the great opera singer Fedor Chaliapin being reburied in Moscow, having died in exile in Paris, as an occasion to reflect on the Soviet attitude towards Russia's artists. Formally, the film is striking: Chaliapin's surviving daugh-ters are filmed in slow-motion and seem like ghostly par-ticipants in a séance, while the history of the Soviet treatment of artists is presented in jagged montage style.

Sokurov's elegies and other documentaries have con-tinued to break new ground, both formally and in their atti-tude towards their subjects. *Zhertva vechernaya* [*Evening Sacrifice*] (1984/87) showed the traditional May Day cel-ebrations in what was then still Leningrad as a distanced fresco of crowds surging and swaying in the streets, punc-tuated by the firing of a military salute and accompanied by an eerie combination of wailing police sirens and Orthodox Church singing. *Moskovskaya elegiya* [*Moscow Elegy*] (1986/88) paid tribute to the recently dead Tarkovsky, who had championed Sokurov's work. But *Sovetskaya elegiya* [*Soviet Elegy*] (1989), in Sokurov's own words, 'can hardly be called a documentary film in the proper sense', although it provides an extraordinary portrait of the future president Boris Yeltsin, at a time when he was out of office at the end of the Soviet era.[15] Seemingly intimate footage of Yeltsin morosely alone at home is contrasted with an extended Warhol-like sequence of official portraits of Soviet leaders, producing another invitation to reflect on the weight and meaning of the Soviet tradition.

So prolific is Sokurov that even listing his films becomes difficult, but he has maintained the distinction between 'documentary' and fictional approaches to his subjects, even though the former are often highly subjec-tive, or 'lyrical' in the film-maker's terms, while the fic-tional films often offer substantial documentation – as in what is probably his most widely seen work, the unbroken tour through the Hermitage Museum in *Russkiy Kovcheg* [*Russian Ark*] (2001). In two extended documentary mini-series, *Spiritual Voices* (1995) and *Povinnost* [*Confession*]

(1998), this son of an army family has explored the lives of Russian troops stationed on the Tadjik–Afghan border and the inner feelings of a naval commander. In other films, he meditates in highly personal terms on the great art of the past and our relationship to it (*Hubert Robert: A Fortunate Life* [1998]; *Elegy for a Voyage* [2001]), and a cycle of films col-lectively known as *The St Petersburg Diaries* about historical figures associated with the city.

While Sokurov remained the senior figure at Lendoc Studios in St Petersburg, his younger colleague, Viktor Kossakovsky, was reinventing observational documentary of the everyday in a series of films that began with *Belovy* [*The Belovs*] (1993). In a very different vein from Sokurov, this shows another archetypal Russian peasant woman, Anna Belova, stoically continuing to run the family farm, in spite of being twice widowed and having a feckless brother, who provides much of the film's gentle humour. Subsequently, Kossakovsky has continued to document the ordinary lives of Russians, in *Sreda* [*Wednesday*] (1997), and in two films about his neighbours in St Petersburg, *Tishe!* [*Hush!*] (2002) and *Russia From My Window* (2003). Widely seen at festivals and on television, these have offered a window onto ordinary Russians' lives, recalling the films of Dziga Vertov's brother and cameraman, Mikhail Kaufman, *Moskva* [*Moscow*] (1927) and *Spring* (1929).

The other key figure in post-Soviet documentary is Sergey Dvortsevoy, who gained international recognition with his first film, *Schastye* [*Paradise*] (1995), about a nomad shepherd and his family in the mountains of Dvortsevoy's native Kazakhstan. *Trassa* [*Highway*] (1996) followed a trav-elling circus in the same region, before Dvortsevoy turned his attention to elderly people eking out their lives on the outskirts of St Petersburg, in *Chlebnyy den* [*Bread Day*] (1998), and Moscow, in *V temnote* [*In the Dark*] (2004). His widely acclaimed fiction feature *Tulpan* (2008) returned to the steppes of Kazakhstan, making use of the sensitive obser-vational style and sympathy for the marginal that charac-terise Dvortsevoy's documentaries. As the former components of the USSR struggle to establish their new independent identities – often claiming back figures long considered 'Soviet' (such as the Ukrainian Dovzhenko) – Dvortsevoy's Kazakh identity may turn out to be an import-ant part of his appeal for wider audiences. Indeed, one of last works by Juris Podnieks before his premature death in 1992 was a series, *Hello, Do You Hear Us?* (1990), co-produced with the UK's Central Television, which vividly chronicled the collapse of the Soviet Union and the emergence of its newly independent states. Just as documentary had borne witness to the traumatic early years of Soviet power, with films about the famine that accompanied the Civil War of 1917–23 made by the Workers International Relief to raise charitable donations abroad,[16] so too documentary film-makers recorded the ignominious end of the Soviet experiment, and continue to bear witness to its aftermath.

NOTES

1. From the original opening titles. See Yuri Tsivian, 'Man with a Movie Camera, Reel One: A Selective Glossary', *Film Studies* no. 2, Spring 2000.

2. By Lev Manovich. See his 'Digital Constructivism', at http://www.manovich.net/Vertov/digitalconstruct.html. Accessed 1 September 2012; also Lev Manovich, *The Language of New Media* (Cambridge, MA: MIT Press, 2002).

3. See Rouch's preface to Georges Sadoul, *Dziga Vertov* (Paris: Champ Libre, 1971). See also Chapter 2.10 below (ed.).

4. See John MacKay, 'Disorganised Noise: Enthusiasm and the Ear of the Collective', in *Kinokultura*, http://www.kinokultura.com/articles/enthusiasm-sound.pdf. Accessed 1 September 2012.

5. Text of the order establishing the film-train quoted in Jay Leyda, *Kino: A History of Russian and Soviet Film* (London: George Allen and Unwin, 1960), p. 286.

6. See Richard Taylor and Ian Christie (eds), 'Introduction', *The Film Factory: Russian and Soviet Cinema in Documents, 1896–1939* (London: Routledge, 1988), p. 12.

7. Roman Karmen, 'Soviet Documentary', in Roger Manvell (ed.), *Experiment in the Film* (London: Grey Walls Press, 1949).

8. Leyda, *Kino*, p. 377.

9. The claim about Russian wartime documentaries was made by the director Evgeny Tsymbal in a lecture in London on the use of war footage in several films, 'Witnesses to Time Regained', Apollo Cinema, London, 23 September 2008. I am grateful to John Riley for this information.

10. See the recent study of this ground-breaking film: Wolfgang Beilenhoff et al. (eds), *Der Gewöhnliche Faschismus* (Berlin: Vorwerk 8, 2009). *Ordinary Fascism* is also viewable on YouTube.

11. Nikolai Fedorov (1827–1903) was a Russian Orthodox philosopher and mystic who taught that mankind would achieve ultimate salvation by being 'reborn' in distant worlds. His teaching encouraged scientific research to prolong life, and played a part in inspiring early Russian interest in rocketry and space exploration.

12. See Ābrams Kieckin, 'Herz Frank: Dialogue with Epoch, People and Oneself', *Films in Latvia* (n. d.), http://www.latfilma.lv/history/9rig03.html. Accessed 2 February 2011.

13. Ian Christie, 'The Cinema', in Julian Graffy and Geoffrey Hosking (eds), *Culture and the Media in the USSR Today* (London: Macmillan, 1989).

14. See the film-maker's own account of the film at his website, *The Island of Sokurov*, at http://www.sokurov.spb.ru/island_en/documetaries/mariya/mnp_mar.html. Accessed 3 February 2011.

15. Sokurov's note on the film appears in *The Island of Sokurov*, http://www.sokurov.spb.ru/island_en/documetaries/sovetskaya_elegiya/mnp_sel.html. Accessed 1 September 2012.

16. See Vance Kepley Jr, 'The Workers, International Relief and the Cinema of the Left, 1921–1935', *Cinema Journal* vol. 23 no. 1, Autumn 1983.

2.8 The Radical Tradition in Documentary Film-making, 1920s–50s

BERT HOGENKAMP

Although Vertov's formal agenda was rejected, Soviet state concern with film was widely emulated. Necessarily this resulted in official propaganda films from the fascists as well as Griersonian documentaries from the bourgeois democracies. But there was unofficial, oppositional work as well. Before World War II, there was widespread, if intermittent, activity on the left across the world – not contained by Griersonian reformism, nor limited to only documentary production.

Looking back at his early years as a film-maker, Dutchman Joris Ivens (1898–1989) describes in *The Camera and I*, his first autobiography dating from 1969, how he was offered the opportunity to experiment in 'idea editing'. In 1930 he was given charge of the monthly film programmes of the VVVC (*Vereeniging voor Volks Cultuur* [Association for Popular Culture]) which were held on Sunday mornings in an Amsterdam film theatre. Ivens says:

> On Friday night we would borrow a number of commercial newsreels. On Saturday we would study the material in the newsreels in relation to the international and national situation of the week, re-edit them with any other footage we happened to have available to us giving them a clear political significance, print new subtitles (the films were still silent) showing relationships between events which the newsreel companies never thought of, and which would certainly have shocked them if they had ever seen our uses of their 'innocent' material. After our Sunday morning show was finished we would take the film apart again, restore its original form and return it to the newsreel companies who were none the wiser![1]

Ivens was not the only person who was convinced that the left had to have its own newsreels acting as an antidote against the 'poison' administered by the 'official' newsreels. Neither was he alone in his interest in 'idea editing', the juxtaposition of (a series of) images in order to highlight contradictions in the capitalist world and raise political awareness.[2] There were both pragmatic and ideological reasons for the centrality of these two categories in the late 1920s and early 30s. Certainly in Europe

the left had hesitated to tackle the problem of a film production of its own as a result of the premise stated by Karl Marx that the (economic) base determines the (cultural) superstructure. The implication was that the production of socialist (or proletarian or any other suitable epithet) films in a capitalist society simply would not work, for reasons such as lack of capital, boycott and censorship. As the German communist Willi Münzenberg (1889–1940) mentioned in his pamphlet *Erobert den Film* [*Conquer the Film*] (1925), this sometimes resulted in a Luddite approach to the film. He recalled how some Leipzig workers after seeing an anti-Soviet film, stormed the projection room, destroyed the equipment and burned the film.[3] Münzenberg's solution to the base-superstructure dilemma was to give priority to the distribution and exhibition of Soviet films. After all, these were socialist films, as they were made in a socialist society. Programmes with Soviet films as the main attraction could be complemented with newsreels or short documentaries emanating from what Münzenberg called the 'revolutionary workers movement' in Europe or Northern America.

Willi Münzenberg was the director of the aid organisation Workers' International Relief (WIR) – nicknamed the 'Workers' Red Cross' – which was operating from Berlin and Moscow and had national branches in most industrialised countries. When he wrote *Conquer the Film*, he had already gained considerable experience in distributing Soviet films in Germany, mainly as means of collecting funds for the many causes supported by the WIR. As a next step, he established in 1926 Prometheus Film, a limited company that catered for the theatrical distribution of Soviet films and later the production of German 'proletarian' films. To help the often destitute political organisations in Germany and abroad, Weltfilm, a company for non-theatrical distribution of Soviet films and German 'revolutionary' newsreels, was set up in 1928. Probably the most famous of the many other enterprises initiated by Münzenberg was the illustrated weekly *AIZ* (*Arbeiter-Illustrierte-Zeitung*), which made use not only of the photo montages of John Heartfield but also of the work of German worker photographers. The idea of worker photography was soon emulated in a number of other countries.[4]

The workers' film societies that were founded in the late 1920s as a way to avoid the boycott by the commercial cinema circuits or the outright banning of Soviet films, offered a stage for the kind of alternative newsreel that Joris Ivens referred to. For the German Volksfilmverband Ernst Angel and Viktor Blum compiled *Zeitbericht – Zeitgesicht* [News of the Times – Face of the Times] (1928) from old newsreel footage that had already obtained a censorship certificate. But this exercise in 'idea editing' did not please the censor and he banned it. So it was only through the report of their chairman, the writer Heinrich Mann, that the members of the Volksfilmverband were informed of the existence of *News of the Times – Face of the Times*. Béla Balázs later recalled some of the items shown:

> For instance in the 'Dogs' beauty contest', overwhelmingly glamorous ladies held expensive lap-dogs in their arms. Next to this was 'One who did not take part in the contest': a blind beggar and his 'seeing eye' watchdog, watching over his miserable master in the cold of the winter.'[5]

Ivens was involved in the production of five further newsreels for the VVVC (1930–31) which did not have to be taken apart after the screening but circulated among the various branches of the VVVC. The *VVVC-Journaals* covered issues that were topical at the time in the communist movement, such as the commemoration of the three L's (Lenin, Liebknecht and Luxemburg), the socialist construction in the Soviet Union and a clash between police and workers at an International Labour Defence demonstration in Amsterdam. Making use of footage taken from existing films and new material shot by Ivens and his colleagues, they aimed to show contradictions like the peaceful construction in the Soviet Union as opposed to the war preparations in the capitalist world.[6]

Workers' Topical News, the newsreel made by Atlas Film for the Workers' Film Societies in the UK, covered subjects like Unemployment Day, the Hunger March, May Day, the Charter Demonstration and the Lancashire weavers' dispute. These were seen as 'matters of vital importance to the workers' that, as Ralph Bond (1904–1989) – cameraman and director of *Workers' Topical News* – put it, were 'either ignored or falsified' by the bourgeois newsreels. Three issues were released, two in 1930 and one in 1931. Bond felt though that they were 'mere recordings of actual events', that there was not enough analysis – or 'idea editing' – in them. As a next step he realised a half-hour documentary *1931 – the Charter Film* that formed an integrated part of the ill-fated campaign for the Workers' Charter, organised by the Communist Party of Great Britain and its trade union affiliate, the National Minority Movement.[7]

A similar development from the mere recording of actuality to a more analytical approach could be discerned in the USA.[8] There was no workers' film society movement in the USA but the Workers' Film and Photo League played an active role in producing, distributing and exhibiting films from its New York headquarters. The League produced some sixteen *Workers' Newsreels* from its foundation in 1930 to 1934, covering protests from the unemployed and the National Hunger Marches. The coverage of some subjects warranted longer films, like *Bonus March* (1932). Local Leagues too – for example, those in Detroit, Chicago, Los Angeles and San Francisco – produced their own actualities. As a successor to the *Workers' Newsreel*, the League started the production of *America Today* (1933), a news review for which footage shot by League cameramen and material from commercial newsreels was edited in a Soviet-inspired style that highlighted the contradictions in society.

All these workers' newsreels were silent films on inflammable 35mm stock, meant to be shown either in licensed cinemas or with the aid of portable projectors in halls that were hired for the occasion. But by the mid-1930s the much more expensive sound film had become the norm. Moreover, the workers' newsreels had been made collectively, without any credits for those who had contributed. Those who wanted a professional career in film opted for 35mm and sound; others chose sub-standard (i.e., 16mm) film and a collective form of production and exhibition. In an article in the German periodical *Arbeiterbühne und Film*, Heinz Lüdecke and Koreya Senda had coined the latter approach as 'the agit-propisation of the cinema'.[9] They proposed a left cinema movement that made use of the simple and relatively cheap 16mm equipment and organised screening at locations where working-class people could be found, instead of using existing cinemas for people to go to. Their example was the agitprop theatre that had abandoned the professional stage and instead performed on street corners or at factory gates. Senda, an actor of Japanese origin working in Weimar Germany, had picked up many of the ideas in the aforementioned article from the work of the Prokino organisation in his country of birth. Prokino used 16mm, 'because the white terror in Japan forces the comrades there to do their filmwork (shooting and exhibition) almost always illegally'.[10]

In the UK, censorship legislation helped to make the choice in favour of sub-standard film, as non-inflammable stock did not come under the 1909 Cinematograph Act. Thus, a 16mm print of Eisenstein's *Battleship Potemkin* (1926), which was banned on 35mm, could be screened in any hall that was not licensed under the Act. The left-wing distribution company Kino was established in late 1933, offering 16mm copies of Soviet and other films. Kino had its own production unit, making *Workers' Newsreel* and, inspired by the Soviet examples, even a short fiction film, *Bread* (1934). After a year, it continued as Workers' Film and

Photo League, profiting from the good reputation of its American namesake. In France, however, *Humanité* film critic Léon Moussinac, whose authority in film matters had earned him the respect in much wider circles, torpedoed any attempts to adopt the sub-standard format. In 1932, for example, he savagely criticised the camerawork, editing and illegible captions in a handful of films produced by Huma Films. Under this name, a group of young communists had been making 16mm films, tackling issues like warmongering, unemployment and poverty in the countryside. Moussinac effectively killed off Huma Films, which disappeared without a trace.[11] In a similar way the Dutch communist writer Jef Last castigated, in 1934, the Arbeiders Film Collectief [Workers' Film Collective] for its choice of the 16mm gauge. The collective model was not only adopted by communist-oriented groups. In Belgium the Association of Socialist Amateur Film-makers (ASCA) was active in the mid-1930s, while in France the Revolutionary Left, led by Marceau Pivert, had its own Film Service, which could produce 35mm films thanks to a number of sympathising film professionals.

The 'agitprop' sub-standard films were usually made on a shoestring budget covering only the bare necessities: film stock and laboratory costs. None of the film-makers involved – usually unemployed workers, youngsters still supported by their parents, teachers or full-time activists – was making a living from these films. Left-wing professional film-makers, on the other hand, needed budgets that covered more than the basic expenses. After all, their films were their main source of income. Hardly any managed to earn a living from overtly radical films only. Even Joris Ivens, the most successful radical documentarist in the 1930s, needed the income from bodies like the Rockefeller Foundation and the Rural Electrification Administration.[12] The Dutch director succeeded in finding private sponsors who enabled him to make his films about the Spanish civil war (*The Spanish Earth*, 1937) and the Chinese–Japanese war (*The 400 Million*, 1939) according to his own, sometimes unorthodox views on documentary film-making. The film about the 1932 Belgian mining strike (*Misère au Borinage*, 1933), which Ivens realised with his Brussels colleague Henri Storck, was only possible thanks to anonymous subscriptions (including a substantial contribution from a maverick maecenas who passed away one day before the premiere of the film). The film raised plenty of dust because of the reconstructions to which the two resorted.[13]

During their stay in the Borinage, Ivens and Storck heard a number of stories that were so powerful they decided to ask those involved to 'replay' them in front of the camera. In some instances – for example, the demonstration in Wasmes in commemoration of the fiftieth anniversary of the death of Karl Marx with a painting of the philosopher being carried at the head – this worked very well. As Ivens would put it later, 'the reconstruction

Misère au Borinage (1933): 'the reconstruction was absorbed by reality' – Joris Ivens

was absorbed by reality'. But to demand that unemployed coal miners put on policemen's costumes and act naturally in the reconstruction of an eviction was asking too much. The reconstruction of events in documentary films was a disputed issue. The Soviet documentarist Dziga Vertov (1896–1956) was the leading representative of the non-intervention school. His credo was that life had to be caught unaware of the camera. For this reason Vertov's supporters in the Soviet Union had criticised an earlier film by Ivens, *Komsomol* (1932), about the construction of a blast furnace complex in Magnitogorsk. The film ended with a 'storm night', a volunteer night shift by the young communists on the site – except that the one shown in *Komsomol* was staged by Ivens and his crew. The Dutchman felt justified in doing this because this was the only way to get the right shots that would faithfully reflect the 'integrity and enthusiasm' of these storm nights.[14]

Illusions about the sponsorship of working-class organisations were not unknown and every so often shattered the ambitions of the film-makers. Trade unions, political parties, cooperative societies and other working-class bodies were simply extremely reluctant to commit themselves to the production of a film. For example, Paul Rotha's (1907–1984) appeals for funds at a number of Labour Party congresses in the mid-1930s only resulted in a pamphlet, *Films and the Labour Party* (1936), instead of the film(s) he had hoped for. There were a few exceptions. In the Netherlands it became a tradition from the late 1920s for working-class organisations – whether catholic or protestant, socialist, communist or syndicalist – to have their own films, not necessarily, however, produced by a filmmaker sympathising with the cause. Norway and Sweden were other countries where working-class organisations regularly commissioned films.

Still, occasionally financial support for the production of films could be found. In France, collaboration between the Trade Union Confederation (CGT), the Maison de la Technique and Ciné-Liberté resulted in three documentaries presenting the work of, respectively, the Railwaymen's, Builders' and Steelworkers' Union. Boris Peskine – a railway man and trade unionist himself – directed *Sur les Routes d'Acier* [*On the Iron Tracks*] (1938), which started with a superbly edited, fast-moving hymn in modernist style to the railways. In *Les Batisseurs* [*The Builders*] (1938), Jean Epstein, who had made a name in the 1920s with his avant-garde films, presented a history of building, told by two building workers who are having a break high up on the scaffolds of Chartres cathedral. *Les Métallos* [*The Steelworkers*] (1938), directed by the communist cameraman Jacques Lemare, put down-to-earth, concrete trade union activity at the centre, instead of exalting the profession in a hymn of images and sounds. In the UK, Ralph Bond managed to coax the London Co-operative Societies into sponsoring a series of documentaries, presenting their history, educational work and cultural and political activities. Bond himself directed *Advance, Democracy!* (1938) and *People with a Purpose* (1939), while acting as a producer for *The Voice of the People* (1939). In Belgium, Henri Storck made two newsfilms for the Belgian Labour Party, covering the funeral of the popular socialist leader Emile Vandervelde (*Le Patron est Mort* [*The Boss is Dead*], 1938) and the socialist answer to the celebration of the famous Flemish victory over the French in 1302, which had so far been monopolised by the right (*Voor Recht en Vrijheid* [*For Justice and Liberty*], 1939). Lastly, Frontier Films, a company set up by former members of the American Workers' Film and Photo League, produced *People of the Cumberland* (1938), which showed the importance of the work done by the Highlander School for the poverty-stricken mining community.

These films were a welcome addition to the catalogue of left-wing films. Stylistically, they closely resembled mainstream documentaries, which, given the fact that many of the radical film-makers had found refuge in a 'regular' documentary unit, was not all that surprising. Thus, former members of the US Workers' Film and Photo League acted as assistants to Pare Lorentz, motion picture consultant to Roosevelt's Resettlement Administration, during the making of *The Plow That Broke the Plains* (1936) and *The River* (1938). Ralph Bond was employed by John Grierson's GPO Film Unit and subsequently joined Strand and the Realist Film Unit. Henri Storck established his own film company Cinéma-Edition-Production (CEP), producing documentaries for a wide range of sponsors.

A subject that enormously appealed to radical documentary film-makers was the war in Spain. The insurgents led by General Franco had the support of Nazi Germany and Fascist Italy. The left felt that it had to make strenuous efforts to help the Republic defeat these reactionary forces. Therefore young men travelled to Spain in order to enlist in the International Brigades. Film-makers followed in their track. The English zoologist/film-maker/journalist Ivor Montagu (1904–84) was among the first. Together with Norman McLaren, he filmed the defence of Madrid in November 1936, when it was generally expected to be only a matter of days before Franco would conquer the capital. But the Nationalist attacks were repelled and Franco had to wait until the end of the war in 1939 before he could enter Madrid. The film *Defence of Madrid* (1936) raised almost £8,000 for Spanish Aid, even though it was a rather amateurishly made, half-hour, silent 16mm film. Not only were twenty prints of the film in circulation in the UK, *Defence of Madrid* was also shown abroad, in Ireland, for example, and even further away in Australia.

Defence of Madrid was the first of a series of films, that were used in different countries to reinforce solidarity with Republican Spain and collect money for Spanish relief.[15] *Heart of Spain* (1937), a Frontier Films production made by American director Herbert Kline and Hungarian photographer Geza Karpathi about Dr Norman Bethune's blood transfusion work, was not only released in the USA but also in Canada, France and the Netherlands. Ivens's *The Spanish Earth*, famous for the commentary written and spoken by Ernest Hemingway, had possibly an even wider international release. In the Netherlands, however, the censor demanded that all references to Germany's involvement were deleted, including Hemingway's biting remark 'I can't read German either', accompanying the shot of a German aeroplane that had been brought down. In France, a French version was made by the well-known feature director Jean Renoir and released in April 1938. Unfortunately, it did little justice to the careful balance between the images and Hemingway's sparse but powerful commentary in the original. *Return to Life* (1938), another Frontier Films production, directed by Herbert Kline and French photographer Henri Cartier-Bresson, was shown in the USA and France. It focused on the medical care given to soldiers and civilians.

Apart from these documentaries, newsreels and films – dubbed or subtitled – made available by the information bureau of the Spanish Republic were circulating widely. Lastly, films were also made to suit national or even local circumstances. The British documentary *Modern Orphans of the Storm* (1937) and the Dutch documentary *Camarada* (1938), for example, both dealt with the relief of Spanish refugee children in, respectively, the UK and France. The Dutch Committee for Spanish Aid had its own campaign film, *Een medicus over Spanje* (1937), made by a close collaborator of Ivens, Joop Huisken, and featuring the popular medical practitioner Ben Sajet. There were films on the presence of fellow countrymen in Spain – for example, *Attlee in Spain* (1937) or *With the Lincoln Brigade in Spain*

(1938). Even amateur films made during a visit to the Republic mattered, like *Spain To-day* (1938) by Labour MP G. R. Strauss. Of course, the return of the members of the International Brigade – provided they were allowed to re-enter their native country – was filmed. In the UK, the Association of Cine Technicians was present with a 35mm crew at the welcome rally in the Empress Hall (the film was never completed though), while Ernie Trory, the Communist Party's Sussex organiser, welcomed three returning local volunteers, accompanied by a cameraman proudly handling his 9.5mm camera (the footage was included in the *People's Scrapbook 1939*).

The most original work done by radical film-makers in the 1930s was in the twilight zone between fiction and non-fiction. The Nykino production *Pie in the Sky* (1935), featuring members of the Group Theatre, was a satire on religion and unemployment that was fully on the side of fiction. *Hell Unltd* (1936), the witty anti-war film by Norman McLaren and Helen Biggar, was made up of fiction, non-fiction and animation material. In *La Vie est à nous* (1936), the election film of the French Communist Party (PCF), made by a collective under the leadership of Jean Renoir, a wide range of cinematographic modes – newsreel footage, educational film, fiction sequences, drawings and direct address – was used. The film forcefully puts the case that only the PCF can undo the wrongs from which the ordinary people of France are suffering. The interaction between the different modes is remarkable: at the start, for example, it is revealed that the commentary to a sequence of images showing the riches of France, in a way characteristic of educational films, actually emanates from a teacher (played by Jean Dasté) who is giving a geography lesson to a poor-neighbourhood school class. At the end, fictional characters from the film, such as the unemployed engineer René (Julien Bertheau) and his girlfriend Ninette (Nadia Sibirskaia), appear in an audience which is listening to election campaign speeches by real Communist leaders. Remarkable, too, was a sequence where Colonel De la Rocque, Adolf Hitler and Benito Mussolini were ridiculed by the creative use of editing and sound: the leader of the right-wing Croix de Feu is shown speeding up his steps so that he marches like a Nazi, the German leader is barking like a dog, while the only thing that comes from the Duce's mouth is the sound of gun fire. When the film was banned by the French censor after its premiere in April 1936, the association Ciné-Liberté was founded to enable its members to see the film.[16]

There were two films that were clearly inspired by *La Vie est à nous*. In the Netherlands, John Ferno, another collaborator of Ivens, directed the election film *Land in Zicht [Land Ahead]* (1937) for the Dutch Communist Party. This thirty-minute silent 16mm film used the same approach as *La Vie est à nous*: a mix of newsreel, non-fiction and staged material. A shot of the Dutch National Socialist leader Mussert is manipulated so that it looks as if he is making a Hitler salute. Instead of the comrades selling the party paper being saved from fascist thugs, in *Land in Zicht* the canvassers of the National Socialist newspaper are made to run by the ordinary people. Like the French film, the Dutch one ends with Communist leader Louis de Visser addressing the audience, although his oratory power is lost because of the lack of sound.

The next election film was Ivor Montagu's *Peace and Plenty* (1939), made for the Communist Party of Great Britain. Unlike the Dutch film, it was a professionally made sound film, with a musical score composed by band leader Van Phillips, camerawork by Arthur Graham and actors from the Unity Theatre Mobile Group. *Peace and Plenty* was an outright indictment of the Chamberlain government. Montagu used still photographs in particular to great effect, as well as a puppet of Chamberlain which had been made by the mother of actress Elsa Lanchester. The film ended with a short speech from Party general secretary Harry Pollitt, exhorting the spectators to get rid of the Chamberlain government. Montagu had filmed it in colour, in order to startle the spectators. But it proved too expensive to include the colour stock in the prints, so the film was shown in black and white from March 1939 onwards. The general election for which *Peace and Plenty* was made never took place because of World War II. By then the film had become obsolete as a result of the German–Soviet non-agression pact.

This pact also hampered the completion and release of the feature-length film in which Frontier Films had invested so much energy, time and money: *Native Land*. The film was meant to be an illustration of the Popular Front ideology with its emphasis on the democratic traditions and the struggle against the reactionary, fascist forces. Its episodic structure was made up of non-fiction, drama and animation, linked by Paul Robeson's narration and Marc Blitzstein's musical score. When *Native Land* was finally released in May 1942, the political situation had changed fundamentally – the USA was at war – and the arguments that it presented had lost a good deal of their validity. Still, the film was an impressive achievement.[17]

The radical film-makers who were trapped in countries occupied by the German or Japanese forces tried to lie low by making 'innocent' films or preferably finding other, less conspicuous sources of income. Although outright collaboration with the occupying forces was rare, doubts have been cast on, for example, Joop Huisken's decision to go and work at the Ufa studios in Babelsberg as part of the forced employment (in fact, he used it as a front for his resistance work) or Henri Storck's eagerness to continue film-making during the occupation and particularly realise the film *Symphone Paysanne [Peasant's Symphony]* 1944) with its sacralisation of the earth – a theme dear to National Socialism and Fascism.[18] Radical film-makers elsewhere supported the war effort – certainly after the German invasion of the Soviet Union they did so whole-heartedly – and placed themselves at the service of propaganda bodies like the Ministry of Information in the UK, the National Film Board of Canada, the US War Department and others.

The hope that there would be a better climate after the war for left-wing film production was soon dashed. What happened to Joris Ivens was typical. Appointed in 1944 by the Dutch government as a Film Commissioner of the Dutch East Indies, he was supposed to film the liberation of Indonesia and then make educational and informational films in collaboration with the Indonesians. However, after he arrived in Australia, awaiting the defeat of Japan, he found out that the Dutch government had no intentions to make Indonesia an independent country; instead the pre-war colonial administration was to be restored, if necessary by military violence. Ivens resigned from his post and made *Indonesia Calling* (1946). It was clandestinely shot in the harbours of Sydney, where the dockers' unions boycotted the Dutch ships filled with military supplies destined for Indonesia. As a film, *Indonesia Calling* was a simple twenty-minute political pamphlet – not surprising given its minimal budget – but it introduced the theme of the anti-colonial struggle in the radical post-war documentary. This was later taken up by the young French film-maker René Vautier, who ended in prison for making *Afrique 50* (1950), and later joined the Algerians in their war of liberation against the French.

Typical of the embittered post-war climate that developed in the late 1940s was the fate of the World Union of Documentary (WUD).[19] This organisation had been founded in June 1947 in Brussels by a dozen documentary film makers from West and East, among them Ivens, Rotha and Storck. The Union's first congress took place in Mariánské Lázně/Marienbad in 1948. After long deliberations a common definition was agreed upon:

> By 'documentary' is meant the business of recording on celluloid any aspects of reality, interpreted either by factual shooting or by sincere and justifiable reconstruction, so as to appeal either to reason for emotion, for the purposes of stimulating the desire for and the widening of human knowledge and understanding, and of truthfully posing problems and their solutions in the sphere of economics, culture and human relations.

This definition was the WUD's only lasting legacy, for the tensions of the Cold War soon put an end to the organisation.

New recruits joined the ranks of the radical cinema in the post-war years. Together with the 'veterans', they were responsible for the production of a wide range of actualities, newsfilms and documentaries, both on the standard and sub-standard gauge. Although the 'agitpropisation' of the cinema would have fitted very well in the Cold War climate, it was not reintroduced. Still, plenty of amateur films were shot on themes like protest meetings, marches and demonstrations, May Day and other celebrations, holiday camps, youth festivals, etc.[20] An exceptional development was the establishment of a film unit by the Waterside Workers' Federation of Australia in the early 1950s.[21] Among the professionally made documentaries only a handful stood out because of the urgency of their subject, like Louis Daquin's film on the French miners' strike (*La grande lutte des mineurs*, 1948), Robert Ménégoz's film on the politically motivated dockers' strike in the French ports (*Vivent les Dockers*, 1950) or the collective production on the first Aldermaston march for nuclear disarmament (*March to Aldermaston*, 1959). These three titles contained powerful images, but their makers felt that they would not work without a voiceover narration, which made them fit in what Bill Nichols has called the 'expository mode'. By the end of the 50s there was a feeling that the radical documentary was in need of other 'modes', offering both new political and new cinematographic perspectives. In the course of the 60s these two demands would be met.

NOTES

1. Joris Ivens, *The Camera and I* (Berlin/GDR: Seven Seas, 1969), pp. 96–7.
2. Bert Hogenkamp, 'Worker's Newsreels in the 1920s and 1930s', *Our History* no. 68, 1977.
3. A reprint of *Erobert den Film* can be found on http://www.trend.infopartisan.net/trd1099/t351099.html, 8 November 2010. Accessed 1 September 2012.
4. See Jorge Ribalta (ed.), *The Worker Photography Movement (1926–1939)* (Madrid: TF Editores, 2011).
5. Béla Balázs, *Theory of Film: Character and Growth of a New Art* (London: D. Dobson, n. d.), pp. 155–6.
6. Cf. Bert Hogenkamp, 'Workers' Newsreels in the Netherlands (1930–1931)', in Armand Mattelart and Seth Siegelaub (eds), *Communication and Class Struggle 2: Liberation, Socialism* (New York/Bagnolet: IG/IMMRC, 1983), pp. 157–64.
7. See Bert Hogenkamp, *Deadly Parallels: Film and the Left in Britain, 1929–39* (London: Lawrence & Wishart, 1986).
8. See William Alexander, *Film on the Left: American Documentary Film from 1931 to 1942* (Princeton, NJ: Princeton University Press, 1981); Russell Campbell, *Cinema Strikes Back: Radical Film-making in the United States, 1930–1942* (Ann Arbor, MI: University of Michigan Press, 1978).
9. Koreya Senda and Heinz Lüdecke, 'Agitpropisierung des proletarischen Films', *Arbeiterbühne und Film*, May 1931, pp. 8–11.
10. Koreya Senda, 'Proletarische Film-Bewegung in Japan', *Arbeiterbühne und Film*, February 1931, pp. 26–7.

11. Cf. Bert Hogenkamp, 'Léon Moussinac and the Spectators' Criticism in France (1931–1934)', *Film International* no. 2, 2003, pp. 4–13.

12. For Ivens's career see Hans Schoots, *Living Dangerously: A Biography of Joris Ivens* (Amsterdam: University of Amsterdam Press, 2000).

13. See Bert Hogenkamp and Henri Storck, 'Le Borinage: La grève des mineurs de 1932 et le film de Joris Ivens et Henri Storck', *Revue Belge du Cinéma* no. 6/7, 1984.

14. Ivens, *The Camera and I*, p. 76.

15. Cf. Bert Hogenkamp, 'Le film de gauche et la Guerre d'Espagne', *Revue Belge du Cinéma* no. 17, 1986, pp. 3–27.

16. Jonathan Buchsbaum, *Cinéma Engagé: Film in the Popular Front* (Urbana: University of Illinois Press, 1988).

17. See Alexander, *Film on the Left*, pp. 206–42.

18. Cf. Günter Jordan, 'The Film-worker Joop Huisken (1901–1979)', *The Ivens Magazine* no. 16, October 2010, pp. 26–41; Bruno Benvindo, *Henri Storck, le cinéma belge et l'Occupation* (Brussels: Université de Bruxelles, 2010).

19. See Bert Hogenkamp, 'World Union of Documentary', in Ian Aitken (ed.), *Encyclopedia of the Documentary Film* (New York/London: Routledge, 2006), pp. 1475–6.

20. Cf. Bert Hogenkamp, *Film, Television and the Left 1950 to 1970* (London: Lawrence & Wishart, 2000).

21. Cf. Lisa Milner, *Fighting Films: A History of the Waterside Workers' Federation Film Unit* (North Melbourne, VIC: Pluto Press, 2003).

2.9 *Le groupe des Trente*: The Poetic Tradition

ELENA VON KASSEL SIAMBANI

Grierson had hitchhiked on Flaherty's reputation, declaring that his style of official realist documentary was of a piece with Flaherty's romanticism. This was a public relations masterstroke but it was achieved at the cost of disguising the real differences in approach and intention between them. Griersonian documentary, despite occasional pictorialism, largely eschewed the impressionistic and the poetic. These characteristics were – as was agitprop production – better reflected in non-anglophone documentary.

The *groupe des Trente* is all about definition.

The 'Thirty' were a group of film-makers in France who came together in 1953 in order to defend short films – *court métrage*. They wrote a manifesto and signed a petition calling for a law making shorts mandatory at all commercial cinema screenings. The demand had been provoked by a new ordinance, passed on 7 August 1953, removing a long-standing legal obligation, imposed on exhibitors, to include a short film in every programme.[1] The situation had been that double features had long been prohibited – both in the German Occupation during World War II and immediately afterwards. The result was an abundance of shorts produced in the 1940s and 50s. They had proved popular with audiences and were an asset aiding the emergence of *ciné-clubs* as well. Thirty people signed the petition initially, hence le *groupe des Trente*. Among them were established figures and some who were to make a name later: Alexandre Astruc, Yannick Bellon, Jacques-Yves Cousteau, Georges Franju, Pierre Kast, Alain Resnais, Georges Rouquier and Nicole Vedrès. The government could not ignore them, nor the shorts they produced.[2]

The Group of Thirty's rationale, as expressed in their manifesto, reflected neither Grierson nor Vertov:

> The poem, the short story and the essay have always stood side by side with the novel or other more extensive literary works. The shorter pieces have often served as the germ, the bringing of new ideas or new blood. It is the role that short films have taken on incessantly. Their death would mean the death of cinema. For an art that does not renew itself is an art that is dead.[3]

The key word is *essay*, because this is how most of the film-makers regarded what they were doing. Their 'essays' could take on different forms. They could be documentary, fictional or even animated films. The fact/fiction division underlying the dominant anglophone Griersonian concept of the documentary was, therefore, not in play. Defining *court métrage* was not a vexed philosophical matter; it was merely a question of duration. The *groupe des Trente* did not just represent a certain kind of film-making, such as documentaries.

Some of the shorts, however, were documentaries, albeit more in the poetic Flahertarian than the Griersonian mould. Rouquier, for example, was making films about traditional vocations and farming life; Alain Resnais began with films about art and artists; Georges Franju filmed, poetically, the abattoirs of Paris; and Jacques-Yves Cousteau aquatic life in the Mediterranean. Others were short dramas: for example, *Un Chant d'amour* [*Love Song*] (1950) by Jean Genet is an avant-garde fiction film dealing with the then taboo topic of homosexual desire. Either way, the films could be controversial. *Les Statues meurent aussi* [*Statues Also Die*] (1953), the Resnais documentary, made with Chris Marker, was about African art being underestimated and excluded from the museums. It thereby implicitly addressed the vexed issue of racism. What brought the films and film-makers together, then, was not that they were similar, but that they were all so different. As one of its founding members, Pierre Kast, wrote: 'The group did not come together to defend a particular ideology, but to preserve a certain quality for short films.'[4]

Short films brought in new ideas. It was not only their themes, but also the experimental styles and forms with which these were treated. They embraced innovation. It was much easier, for example, to try new techniques with colour, music, sound and commentary on a short film. They did not – and still do not – require the expense and funding of a long film. Shorts film-makers were mostly of an artistic and liberal disposition and less 'establishment' than were the feature directors. Their goal was not to make money; it was a love of cinema that animated them. And it had done so from before World War II. For example, it was what drove Georges Franju and Henri Langlois to make *Métro* (1934). Two years later, in 1936, they created a *ciné-club* and their obsession with the restoration of old silent films led them to found, with Jean Mitry and Jean-Paul Harlé, the *Cinémathèque française*. This love of film persisted and was the cement holding the group together – even when the enthusiasms of some members, such as Jacques-Yves Cousteau's obsession with the sea or Jean-Jacques Languepin's for the mountains, were focused outside cinema.

Avant-garde and modern ideas (films on music – Paul Paviot's *Django Reinhardt* [1957], for example) would, moreover, also attract a young audience. The short films raised social and cultural issues of direct interest and concern to students. Short films were central to *ciné-clubs* all over France: their length and diversity easily allowing for post-screening discussion. The clubs were sprouting by the dozen in the immediate post-war period. In the town of Dijon alone, the film historian Jean-Pierre Jeancolas remembers, there were five *ciné-clubs*. He started out organising one in his *lycée* and then did the same when he went to university. This young generation of cinephiles most easily identified with the shorts and their makers. The more established feature-film directors – Autant Lara, René Clément or Henri-Georges Clouzot – were not, to put it simply, that much fun.[5] After all, they were producing what would be called, in the 1960s, the 'cinéma du papa'.

As film historian François Thomas points out, from the early 30s to the early 40s there was a rich background of what came to be referred to at the time as the era of the 'école française du court métrage' and, in retrospect, 'l'age d'or du court métrage'. Although the term 'court métrage' carried, of itself, no implication of non-fiction, in French texts of the 40s and 50s – official government publications and journalism – 'court métrage' and 'documentaire' are employed as synonyms.[6] The 1915 definition of *film documentaire* or *documentaire* in the *Petit Robert* dictionary is: 'a didactic film presenting authentic documents and not elaborated for the occasion':[7] not John Grierson's 'creative treatment of actuality', but no less vexatious.

British films, and particularly documentaries, were made known through the *Cinémathèque* by Henri Langlois, as well as with the film journal *Ciné-Club*[8] founded by Jean Painlevé. He and Georges Sadoul would also be pioneers of the *groupe des Trente*. Perhaps, if it had not been for World War II, when cultural ties were impossible to maintain, the British and French definitions would have merged to find a precise meaning of documentary. As it is, up to the present, the British term 'documentary' is synonymous with the French 'court métrage', although the claim on the real implicit in English is not present in the French.

During World War II, British documentary film-makers were given not inconsiderable artistic freedom to make films for a just cause, while in Occupied France the French documentary film-makers had to find a way to keep their country's history and culture alive through defeat and occupation. Throughout the Occupation, Germans supported short films because they also wanted to show Nazi newsreels. The first law prohibiting double features was issued, under their aegis, on 26 October 1940.[9] No programme was to screen any feature longer than 1,300 metres and the programme in its entirety was not to exceed 3,800 metres. This allowed room for the newsreels, as well as creating space for a couple of propaganda shorts. A committee for organising the film industry, the COIC, was put in place at the same time to ensure that such regulations would go into effect. This encouraged the production of *court métrage* films, including documentaries in the anglophone sense.[10] The exhibitors played the reels because they were free of charge. It was left to French film-makers to turn this situation to their advantage. In doing so, they also had the advantage of not suffering from American competition.

The law appeared to be beneficial, according to documentary film historians Luce Vigo and Emile Breton, because 3 per cent of the box-office receipts were reserved for *court métrage* production.[11] René Lucot, one of the Thirty, at whose house the meetings of the group would later take place, wrote that during the Occupation many short films were produced, but not all of them were propaganda. On the other hand, the regulations certainly made asinine propagandistic French documentaries possible. Nevertheless, on balance, some – many – of the shorts were an outlet for legitimate French cultural expression.[12] Memorable documentaries, able to address a cultural agenda without overt compromise, were made. There were enough of them to mount a festival in April 1943. René Lucot's *Rodin* won the first prize; but it was not unique in tone, technique or subject matter.

The wartime archive includes: Jean Lods's film on the sculptor Aristide Maillot (*Maillot*, 1943); *Le Tonnelier* [*The Barrel Maker*] (1942) and *Le Charon* [*The Cartwright*] (1944) by Georges Rouquier; *À l'assaut des aiguilles du Diable* [*Attacking the Devilish Peaks of Mont Blanc*] (1942) by Marcel Ichac; *À la poursuite du vent* [*Chasing the Wind*] (1943) by Roger Leenhardt. All these titles constitute something of a canon of classic documentary work made in very difficult circumstances. It was an area of permitted expression, overtly safe, its messages being nothing more than a de facto reflection of independent French cultural life.[13] The Germans ensured that the shorts were well to the fore in the coverage of *Le film*, a bi-monthly magazine controlled by the German services.

In liberated France, the COIC was replaced by the OPC (*Office professionel du cinéma*). From 19 August 1944 on it was presided over by Jean Painlevé, who had continued making science films during the war. Painlevé created a committee to encourage government funding for short

film production. In the peace, many months after liberation, a system for doing this was eventually announced in
the *Journal Officiel* (25 October 1946). The CNC (*Centre
National de la cinématographie*) was operational from 1
January 1947.[14] (It is still the main government-funded
body.) The October 1946 law also continued the prohibition
of double features, assuring the exhibition of what it refers
to as '*documentaires*'. The more general terms '*court métrage*'
and the even more amorphous 'non-commercial films'
would appear in the *Journal Officiel* a year later, in 1948.[15]

After the Occupation, from 1945 and 1950 *le court* was
not fighting a battle to exist, but a battle to maintain its
own identity.[16] As François Thomas explains, in the second
half of the 1940s and 50s the *court métrage* was not used as
a stepping stone for directors to make feature films. It
existed on its own terms in parallel to the feature film
industry. Making documentaries, after all, did not prove
that a film-maker could direct actors and did not confer on
such directors feature film-making status.[17] On the other
hand, many others in the industry did cross over between
short and full-length film and between production, distribution and exhibition. Pierre Braunberger, for instance,
founder of Pantheon Productions, was both distributor and
exhibitor, with stakes in distributing both lengths, and also
had a hand in running several cinemas.[18]

French documentary would find a wave of inspiration
as soon as the war ended and France was liberated. It is an
irony or a kind of predestined fate that it was at that time
the Crown Film Unit, which had replaced the GPO Film Unit
during the war, was dismantled. The freedom of expression
that had been suppressed in France during the war was
about to burst out. And the French documentarists picked
up where the British left off (or left it, journalistically, to
television).

In the last year of the war, *Aubervilliers* (1945) was a
documentary about a poor district of Paris, or the other side
of what the tourists see. Directed by Eli Lotar, with a script
by Jacques Prévert, it was one of the first clear signs of
where French documentary was going and it created a stir.[19]
Like most shorts, it was a commission, in this instance by
the local mayor, Charles Tillon. For the first time, a French
short was widely reviewed in the press, receiving both
praise and criticism, and creating publicity for other short
films.[20] It dealt with the same kinds of issues that Edgar
Anstey's *Housing Problems* had raised in 1935, but it
preserved, and overtly celebrated, human dignity.

Eli Lotar was well qualified to master such a topic. He
had worked as stills photographer on Cavalcanti's *Le Petit
Chaperon rouge* [*Little Red Riding Hood*] (1929), but Cavalcanti
had also been responsible for *Rien que les heures* [*Only the
Hours*] (1926), a socially aware poetic 'rhythm of the city'
documentary about life in Paris. Lotar must have been
aware of what Cavalcanti had been doing in Britain since
joining the GPO unit in 1933. Most significantly, Lotar had

been the cinematographer on Buñuel's sardonic, surreal
documentary *Las Hurdes* [*Land Without Bread*] (1933). In
Aubervilliers, he does not forget Jean Vigo's poetic and social
legacy (as in *À propos de Nice*, 1930[21]) either.[22] Among the
depictions of slums and shots of rubbish gathered up
under bridges near the wall of the river, there are melancholic scenes of barges floating down the Seine, reminiscent of Vigo's *L'Atalante* (1934). Lotar, though, goes a step
beyond straightforward observation: he brings in a reflexive dimension which was alien to the British tradition.

Towards the end of the film a slum family – complete
with a tail-wagging dog – assembles to have their picture
taken. The action freezes and the family snapshot is next
seen framed on the wall. Then the scenes in the frame
change, showing the impoverished images of Aubervilliers,
while the commentary says that even the walls from which
this picture is hanging are crumbling. Just when we
thought that this is it and these people are condemned to
living this way, the last images in this frame within the
frame show new buildings and construction. It is in the
hands of the workers to change the future. '*L'avenir doit
changer et il va changer.*' The last scene returns to the snapshot within the frame and the family disperses, going off
into different directions to build a better future.

Commentary was another aspect developed in many
of these documentaries. In *Aubervilliers*, for example,
a song, '*Gentils enfants d'Aubervilliers*', specially written
for the film by Joseph Kosma, was used as part of the
commentary, a descant on the spoken narration.

Prévert's influence on the film was not only the poetry
of his commentary, it was also that he had been a member
of *Le groupe d'Octobre*, an avant-garde theatre company that
performed 'short pieces' spreading Marxist values – in the
streets and, especially, to striking workers. Its directors
were his brother, Pierre, and Paul Grimault, Yves Allegret
and Claude Autant-Lara. Although *Le groupe des Trente*
espoused no particular political ideology, it shared with *Le
groupe d'Octobre* a commitment to short forms.

Yet no formal documentary movement coalesced in
France, for all that the film-makers were often very close
and supportive of each other: take Painlevé the pedagogue,
Rouquier the realist and Franju the gothic poet.

Through his science documentaries, Paul Painlevé had
gained a reputation which gave him the opportunity to
write articles for reviews and accounts of his own films for
journals both popular (*Pour Vous*) and specialised (*La Revue
du cinéma éducateur*).[23] Painlevé had shown the same poetic
sensibility which characterised much of the emergent
French documentary tradition in his own films despite
their scientific nature. In *Assassins d'eau douce* [*Freshwater
Assassins*] (1947), for example, jazz is used on the soundtrack to accompany the images of microscopic aquatic life.
But, most importantly, Painlevé was the President of the
Fédération Française des Ciné-Clubs (FFCC); and with

Georges Sadoul, who was its secretary, he was one of the founders and a prolific writer for the journal *Ciné-Club*. Launched in 1947, this was a platform where many film-makers had the opportunity to explain their films.

Painlevé was an admirer of Georges Rouquier and helped him obtain the film stock to begin shooting *Farrebique*, Rouquier's classic elegiac study of rural life. Painlevé also lent him his Debrie camera. *Farrebique* was released in 1946. It is a poetic study of a farming family. Whether it can be labelled a documentary is something that Rouquier said was of no consequence when he wrote about the film in *Ciné-Club* shortly after its release. What he always set out to do was to show real life, he explained. It was history, customs and habits that interested him. Although about modernisation, *Farrebique* does not really illuminate what the farm was like at the time of filming. It is more a 'souvenir' of how things were and the eternal values of *La France profonde*.[24] Some, though, considered *Farrebique* long and boring and it was not selected for the 1946 Cannes Film Festival.[25]

In the September issue of *Ciné-Club*, Painlevé penned a strong defence of the film; and it was finally shown to the public in Cannes in 1947. When he was commissioned by Ciné-France to make a film that same year on the life of Louis Pasteur, he asked Rouquier to co-direct it with him. As Rouquier explained, in *L'oeuvre scientifique de Pasteur*, the film-makers wanted to show the achievements of the great scientist, but they did not want a dry didactic film that ignored Pasteur, the man.[26] This pattern of mutual support in production and in print is an example of how things worked with the documentary film-makers of that period.

Painlevé also helped Georges Franju with *Le Sang des bêtes* (1949). This was Franju's first film and he had little chance of obtaining permission to film in the Parisian slaughterhouses.[27] Both Painlevé and Franju had been close to the surrealists in the 1930s and this film echoes that influence. Despite its subject matter, the film establishes the by-now usual romantic tone, beginning by showing fields on the outskirts of Paris. A young blonde woman walks into the frame with her back to us, and we hear her

Farrebique (1946): a 'souvenir' of how things were and the eternal values of *La France profonde*

dreamy voice as she talks about how poor and desolated the area is, only of interest to 'brocantes' and lovers. Then her beau joins her. The voices of the man and the woman alternate in the commentary. Images of antique dealers' shelves are filmed in surreal isolation: a dining table in the middle of nowhere being polished by its seller; an ornate lamp made for an interior hangs from a branch of a tree; there is a broken mannequin. Children are dancing in a circle amid old barbed wire fences. A lady's fan opens up to cover the lens and the first sequence ends. The actual subject matter is reached in the next sequence as a horse is led to an abattoir; but, for those who can bear to watch, slaughtering animals for meat is as aestheticised as the selling of antiques, as innocent as child's play.

Although the films do not reflect the same ideology, there is a rotation of production personnel with the same names constantly turning up on the credits of different films. Chris Marker wrote and spoke the commentary for *Django Reinhardt*. He later co-directed *Les Statues meurent aussi* with Alain Resnais. As for the music, the prolific Joseph Kosma, who provided many scores, had been a student of Béla Bartók in his native Hungary. After he established himself in Paris, he composed the music for a number of features including Jean Renoir's *La Bête humaine* (1938) and *Les Enfants du paradis* (Marcel Carné, 1945). He is ever present in the credits of the *groupe des Trente* – versatile enough to score Paul Grimault's fictional animated cartoon, *Le Petit soldat* (1947), a love story between a toy soldier and a wind-up ballerina in a toy shop,[28] as well as Georges Franju's horrific *Le Sang des bêtes*. Many composers wanted to produce musical scores for short films because that gave them a small income, as well as a reputation as film music composer; their work became known.[29]

For directors, though, it could lead to major international renown. Alain Resnais directed his first professional film, *Van Gogh*, in 1948, and for the next ten years he only made shorts. *Van Gogh* was written by Robert Hessens and commissioned by Gaston Diehl, president of the art club *Les Amis de l'Art*. Resnais's limited budget of 5,000 francs meant the film was shot silent on 16mm in black and white. He showed it to the producer Braunberger, hoping to get finance for a soundtrack. Braunberger was so impressed that, instead of just financing this, he suggested they shoot the film again in 35mm, albeit still in black and white. It won the 1949 two-reel short-subject Oscar.

The artist's life is documented through a montage of his paintings, with dramatic narration and rapid editing. There is no sight or hint of any picture frames – it is as if they had been painted for the film. Resnais wrote at the time that he wanted to see if painted trees and people, for example, could take the place of real trees and people within a narrative. He wanted to see if film could provoke a response similar to one made by looking at paintings themselves.[30]

Alain Resnais was one of the founders of the group and was its vice-president from 1954–58, before being named honorary president in 1959. As Paul Paviot later remembered, Resnais 'was a conscience for us all'.[31]

After a biographical film on the painter, *Paul Gaugin*, in 1950, Resnais and Hessens, again with Braunberger as producer, made *Guernica* (also 1950) on Picasso's 1937 painting. The history is told in voiceover. Again, the editing is rapid. The stills from the painting are cross-cut with clips from newspapers about the destruction of the town. The combination of the poetic and the political, but also the juxtaposing of poetry with the industrial and the everyday, imports elements of the British documentary tradition (as exemplified by, say, Jennngs).

In 1951, on the initiative of the review *Présence Africaine*, Resnais, with Chris Marker, began work on *Les Statues meurent aussi*. The film was completed in May 1953. Because it asked why African sculpture etc. was not in the Louvre alongside Greek and Egyptian art, the film was deemed to argue a politically live anti-colonialist attitude. It was banned until a short version was finally released in 1961. The full version only followed in 1968.

Nuit et brouillard [*Night and Fog*] (1955) is the seminal film on the horror of Nazi concentration camps. Resnais felt that, independently of the subject matter, this is the film where he came closest to solving the difficulties of commentary writing.[32] Jean Cayrol, a concentration camp survivor, provided the text. It is probing, yet at times it takes a distance. The distancing is punctuated with a switch from black-and-white archival images to contemporaneous exterior shots of the concentration camp in colour. The idea is to show that there can be some hope for the future of mankind, showing that green grass can still grow. The music also helps the spectator to deal with the horror of the subject. As Resnais explained in an interview, 'the more violent the images, the more the composer Hanns Eisler wanted a music that was light in tone in order to show that optimism and hope were always in the background'.[33]

Tout la memoire du monde [*The World's Memory*] (1956) was a commission for the Bibliothèque national. It begins by showing the staff at work on the cataloguing and conservation of the collection. It then switches to a long shot of the readers consulting the books in the library. The voiceover talks of 'la traversée du miroir', and the camera takes us 'through the looking glass'. Before the switch from the cataloguers to the readers, the book had been treated as an object, but once it is read and interpreted by someone in the reading-room, it gains meaning, life and character. It ceases to be an object. However, Resnais seems to have more freedom of expression on a commission for the Sécurité Sociale that he directed with André Heinrich: *Le Mystère de l'atelier quinze* [*The Mystery of the 15th Workshop*] (1957).[34]

The most striking of Alain Resnais's shorts is a film about plastic: *Le Chant du styrène* [*Polystyrene Song*]. It appeared the following year, 1958, commissioned by the firm, Péchinay. It celebrates the material and its manufacture, yet manages to be more about poetry and art than anything else. It begins with a title page of a few verses by Victor Hugo: '*L'homme se fait servir par l'aveugle matière./Il pense, il cherche, il crée./A son souffle vivant les germes dispersés dans la nature entière./Tremblant comme frisson une forêt au vent.*'[35] The very first images of the film that follow the title are like an abstract painting. Different bright plastic particles are assembled with a symmetry resembling a Mondrian. The whole film has a futuristic feel to it, on the bright optimistic side. Alain Resnais asked Raymond Queneau to write the text. It is like a modernist hymn, and Resnais wrote that he would have even preferred for it to be sung.[36] '*O temps suspends ton bôl./O matière plastique d'où viens tu?*' ['O time hold up your bowl./O plastic stuff, whence have you come?'] are opening lines. The very modern process of manufacturing plastic is made to sound archaic, and brings to mind Blake's *Jerusalem*, as it is used, again, by Humphrey Jennings. Art and industry in *Le Chant du styrène* have fused into one. At first Péchinay was unhappy about the commentary being in verse and asked for a second version with a didactic scientific commentary. But, finally, it was the original version which found commercial success.[37]

Each Resnais short film has a relationship, not necessarily in theme, but in form with its preceding and succeeding one, developing or contrasting the previous film. For example, in *Nuit et brouillard* Resnais wanted the colours to be as close to reality as possible, while in *Le Chant du styrène* the colours are deliberately striking and contrasting. From one short to the next there is a progression. But it is easy to get carried away with Alain Resnais because anyone familiar with his films today can see how, over sixty years later, he is still exploring and developing aspects in sound, colour and editing that he began with *Van Gogh* in 1947.

As I have indicated, I feel that there is a relationship in his shorts with Humphrey Jennings, the most poetic and impressionistic of the Griersonians – a man, significantly, himself very much in tune with French modernist culture. The two film-makers made the most original and moving documentaries on World War II. If their other short films beg to differ in their Britishness or Frenchness, they are nevertheless similar in that they strive to experiment in commentary, sound, colour, as well as style and form in general. It is not purely accidental that their films share so many qualities. Resnais had, in fact, met Jennings, first when Jennings came to a preview of a Nicole Vedrès film, *Paris 1900* (1947) on which Resnais was assistant director. *Paris 1900* is an archival montage film where GPO Film Unit techniques and Jennings's input are obvious. Resnais has said that he was very much struck by Jennings, who had an influence on his short films, although he is not sure how.[38]

An explanation, to my mind, is that when filming a topic, both Jennings and Resnais film not the obvious but the unfamiliar which surrounds it. This is how they reach 'the truth' or 'the real'.

Alain Resnais made only shorts before he moved into features, but this was not a well-worn path as making shorts conferred its own prestige. Jean Grémillon, the senior member of the group, began on shorts, went on to make features only to return, after a series of problems, to short films. He did so with increased creative ardour. He first made documentaries on art exhibitions and astrology, and then founded a small production company making short films on print-making, tapestry-weaving and the painter André Masson. Grémillon put his own skills in the service of making links between art and craftsmanship.

Court métrage suffered something of an *annus mirabilis* in 1949. On the fiction side, Jean Grémillon and Pierre Kast together directed *Les Charmes de l'existence* [*The Charms of Life*], a satire on the bourgeois society, produced by the company Les films de Saint-Germain des Près, which had just been founded by Fréderic Chauvelot and Jean-Pierre Vivet. *Pacific 231*, Jean Mitry's short film, was also produced that year by Tadié Cinéma. The title is the name of the crack French steam locomotive and it was cut to a preexisting soundtrack, a programmatic orchestral piece written by Arthur Honegger, a famous composer. This was the year of *Chaudronnier* by Rouquier, as well as Jacques Baratier's *Désordre* [*Disorder*], a film on the Saint-Germain des Près circle featuring the Vian brothers, Cocteau, Sartre and Simone de Beauvoir.

One of the few women involved in the group, Yannick Bellon (a pseudonym for Marie-Annick Bellon) directed *Goémons* [*The Seaweed Workers*] (1948) for Etienne Lallier films. Her account in *Ciné-Club*[39] explained that she was astonished how the workers lived on the remote island of Beniget off the coast of Brittany, where they extracted iodine from the '*goémons*'. Once they had accepted the job, it was compulsory for them to stay on the island for months or even years without leave. There was only one woman, the wife of the foreman.

The following year, 1950, can be considered one of innovation building on this foundation. Jean Genet directed the avant-garde reverie *Un Chant d'amour* and René Vautier the controversial *Afrique 50*. This was originally commissioned by the government, as was *Les Statues meurent aussi*, but subsequently it too was censored because of its anti-colonial attitude. Both these original films were to remain semi-clandestine for years. The company Trident organised the highly ambitious project of a filmed encyclopaedia, aptly entitled *Encyclopédie filmée*. All in all, twelve entries were completed, but they did not get beyond the letter 'A'. Among these film was *Absence* by Jean Dreville and Collette Audry, *Amazone* by Nicole Vedrès and Alexandre Arnoux, *Atlantique* by René Lucot and Jean

Marin and the legendary *A comme Arithmétique*, an absurdist cod lecture delivered by Raymond Queneau, directed by Pierre Kast.

But some thought all was not well, despite this body of work. On 5 June 1950, the journalist Jean Thévenot wrote 'SOS *court métrage*' for *Le film français*. The threat was what it had always been – the exhibitors' preference for double features. Thévenot made a plea to the French government to establish a policy to save short films. *Court métrage* was, in his view, 'a miracle that constantly renewed itself', but it still needed help. Jeancolas perceives this dramatic reaction as anticipating an ever worsening situation for the *court métrage*, which he refers to as a *'fleur fragile'*.

But, in the meantime, the flower continued to blossom. In 1952 Alexander Astruc directed for Argos Films a short (forty-four-inch) fictional period piece, *Le Rideau cramoisi* [*The Crimson Curtain*] (1953). It received the Louis Delluc Prize. More vexed political history was seen in the documentary *La Commune* (1951) by Robert Menegoz. This got into difficulties with the censors, as did *Ces gens du nord* [*People of the North*] (1951) by Lucot, produced by Les Ecrans modernes. Nevertheless, this last represented France in Cannes in 1953.

For *Le groupe des Trente*, defending quality was the same thing as defending freedom of expression. The group's manifesto outlined the shorts' value in terms of recognition, nationally and internationally. The official secretary of the group, Paul Paviot, asked for 'the right to exercise one's profession without concessions, to take on an interesting subject and to make a quality film'. For this a committed producer is needed. The producer Anatole Dauman had success with Le Prix Louis Delluc for *Le Rideau cramoisi* by Alexander Astruc; and he won the Prix Jean Vigo for Resnais's *Nuit et brouillard*. Resnais's *Van Gogh*, produced by Braunberger, won the Grand Prix in Venice for *film d'art* and was the first French Oscar-winning short. In 1955 *Nuit et brouillard* received the documentary Grand Prix at Karlovy Vary. Chris Marker's *Dimanche à Pekin* [*Sunday in Peking*] (1956) won the gold medal at Moscow in 1957.[40]

The films were also successful domestically. The left bank cinema, Le Panthéon, was owned by Pierre Braunberger and regularly showcased them. A programme of the six documentaries he had produced played for six months in 1951. At the end of that same year six other art films, produced by Anatole Dauman and Philip Lichitz's Argos Films, were presented in two Parisian cinemas. Similar experiments took place at other cinemas: La Pagode, Studio Ursulines and Studio Parnasse. Some producers and directors persisted in putting quality over quantity and did not worry too much about sponsorship.[41] Some other traditional producers, though, put quantity over quality and sold to distributors films which had been sponsored by industrial groups, *syndicats d'initiative* or

public services. Either way, the exhibitors, despite the blossoming of the *court métrage*, still believed that having double features would be more profitable.

And, in 1953, the exhibitors won the argument and double features were allowed.

The 1953 manifesto of *Le groupe des Trente* was the response. It said:

> Our group refuses to believe that it is too late. It is making an appeal to the public, to relevant organisations and to government representatives. The future of French short films depends on how these bodies will respond to our request.[42]

It took until March 1955, but then a law was passed restoring a mandate for the inclusion of a short film at all public commercial screenings.[43] That same year the Tours Film Festival, specifically for shorts, was also created.

But, although the law restored protection and shorts continued to be made, the rules of the game were to change. After 1958–59 film-makers with a reputation in short films, such as Georges Franju and Alain Resnais, moved on to direct features. The critics Godard, Rivette, Rohmer and Truffaut who had originally started out with short films also moved on to features. In his 1962 book *Le cinéma français*, Georges Sadoul wrote a chapter '*Vers une nouvelle vague*', seeing *Le groupe des Trente* as the germ for a revivified French feature cinema and this phase took his term as its own: the *nouvelle vague*. The connection is there.[44] The *nouvelle vague* ushered in a golden age – but it was for a fictional cinema. '*Court métrage* became the "antichamber" of the feature.'[45]

The *groupe des Trente* distinguished itself by bringing poetry – à la Flaherty – to educational films and documentaries. It showed that sponsored films could be artistically creative. Grierson's legacy has obscured the fact that the French tradition of poetic documentary also had cross-border influence in the rest of Europe. Shorts were being made in many countries whose language and smaller populations precluded extensive feature productions. They were even seen in anglophone art cinemas. In the 1950s, in cinephile circles, directors such as Sweden's Arne Sucksdorff and the Dutchman Bert Haanstra ranked with Franju, Resnais and others of the *groupe de Trente*. Haanstra, for example, won the Oscar for *Glas* [*Glass*] (1958), a brilliantly witty wordless picture of glass-blowing cut to a jazz score. But all this was to be drowned – in France by the *nouvelle vague* and in Western Europe by a rising tide of national feature production. Documentary, anyway, was also to undergo a sea-change. In the 60s, cinéma vérité (or cinéma direct) started to take centre stage in France, beginning with Edgar Morin and Jean Rouch's *Chronique d'un été* [*Chronicle of a Summer*] (1961) – a film made, one should not be surprised, for the producer Anatole Dauman.

NOTES

1. Law no. 53-684 entitled 'Loi portant création d'un fonds de développement de l'industrie cinématographique'. This law had three decrees called 'décrets Louvel' after the Minister of Industry and Commerce of Cinema. For details, see Jean-Pierre Jeancolas, 'Structures du court métrage français 1945–1958', in Dominique Bluher and François Thomas (eds), Le court métrage français de 1945 à 1968: de l'âge d'or aux contrebandiers (Rennes: Presses universitaires de Rennes, 2005), p. 41.

2. The popularity of the court métrage can be seen, for instance, in the fact that a festival was inaugurated in the town of Tours devoted solely to short films in 1955.

3. 'A côté du roman ou des œuvres les plus vastes, existent le poème, la nouvelle ou l'essai, qui jouent le plus souvent le rôle de ferment, remplissent une fonction de renouvellement, apportant un sang nouveau. C'est le rôle que le court métrage n'a cessé de jouer. Sa mort serait finalement celle du cinéma, car un art qui ne bouge pas est un art qui meurt,' Déclaration du groupe des Trente, Paris, 20 December 1953, reprinted in Bref no. 20, Spring 1994.

4. Pierre Kast, 'Courte histoire du groupe des Trente', Positif, July–August 1954.

5. Jean-Pierre Jeancolas, 'Toute la mémoire du court', Bref no. 20, 1994, p. 39.

6. François Thomas, 'Avant Propos', in Bluher and Tomas, Le court métrage français de 1945 à 1968, pp. 10–12.

7. Film documentaire ou un documentaire film didactique, présentant des documents authentiques, non elaborés pour l'occasion.

8. It was the official organ of the Fédération Française des Ciné-Clubs (FFCC). Raymond Bardonnet was the director of the journal; Claude Souef, the editor-in-chief.

9. This law was made available to the public when it was issued in the Journal Officiel on 6 December 1940. Jeancolas, 'Structures du court métrage français 1945–1958', p. 29.

10. Ibid.

11. This was controlled by the COIC.

12. René Lucot, 'Acteurs', Bref no. 20, 1994, p. 33.

13. Jeancolas, 'Structures du court métrage français 1945–1958', p. 31.

14. Ibid.

15. Ibid., p. 32.

16. Ibid., p. 33.

17. Thomas, 'Avant Propos', p. 12.

18. Ibid.

19. Jeancolas, 'Structures de court métrage français 1945–1958', p. 35.

20. Ibid.

21. Shot for Vigo by Boris Kaufmann, Dziga Vertov's brother.

22. Lotar also had a connection with Jacques Brunius, another film-maker who was part of the British documentary group and would later work for the BBC. Both had worked for Renoir on Partie de Campagne [Day in the Country] (1936). Brunius was one link in the chain which brought the poet Jacques Prévert and his brother Pierre, who became a director, into film-making (Pierre Prevert, Mon frère Jacques [1961], ed. Catherine Prévert, Doriane Films DVD, 2004, France).

23. Roxane Hamery, Jean Painlevé, Le cinéma au coeur de la vie (Rennes: Press universitaire de Rennes, 2009), pp. 121–2.

24. Georges Rouquier, 'Farrebique', Ciné-Club no. 3, December 1947.

25. Jean Painlevé, 'Une nouvelle bataille d'Hernani, le film qui ne sera pas montré à Cannes: Farrebique', Les Etoiles, 24 September 1946.

26. Georges Rouquier, 'Pasteur', Ciné-Club no. 1, October 1947.

27. Hamery, Jean Painlevé, p. 280.

28. Based on a Hans Christian Anderson story.

29. Jean-Pierre Berthomé, 'Classicisme et héritiers: les musiciens du court métrage français (1945–1960)', in Dominique Bluher and Philippe Pilard (eds), Le court métrage documentaire français de 1945 à 1968, Création et créateurs (Rennes: Presses universitaires de Rennes, 2009), p. 42.

30. Alain Resnais, 'Une Expérience', Ciné-Club no. 3, December 1948.

31. Paul Paviot, 'Acteurs', Bref no. 20, 1993, p. 37.

32. Noel Burch, 'A Conversation with Alain Resnais', Film Quarterly vol. 13 no. 3, Spring 1960, p. 27.

33. Alain Resnais, Cinémonde, interview by Gilbert Guez, 14 March 1961, reprinted in Premier Plan no. 18, October 1961, p. 38.

34. François Porcile, 'Commandes avouées, commandes masquées: la production française de courts métrage de de Gaulle à de Gaulle', in Bluher and Pilard, Le court métrage documentaire français de 1945 à 1968, p. 21.

35. Man is served by an invisible substance./He thinks, he searches, he creates./With one breath everything around him disappears into nature./Trembling and shivering like a forest in the wind.

36. Resnais, Cinémonde, interview by Gilbert Guez, Premier Plan, p. 69.

37. Alain Resnais, interview by Jean Medam and François Porcile, Connaissance du cinéma no. 1, March 1962, reprinted in Porcile, 'Commandes avouées, commandes masquées', p. 21. 'O temps suspends ton bôl ...' is a play on words: 'O temps! Suspends ton vol ...' from Lamartine's poem 'Le lac'.

38. Alain Resnais, interview book by Suzanne Liaudrat-Guiges and Jean-Louis Leutrat, Alain Resnais, Liasons Secrètes, Accords Vagabonds (Paris: Cahiers du cinéma, 2006), p.178.

39. Yannick Bellon, 'Goémons', Ciné-Club no. 5, March 1948. Yannick Bellon also discussed the technical problems encountered in filming on an island with no electricity.

40. Arnaud Chapuy and Jean-François Cornu, 'Les producteurs du groupe des Trente, fondateurs d'une pré-

Nouvelle Vague?', in Bluher and Thomas, *Le court métrage français de 1945 à 1968*, p. 49.

41. Jeancolas, 'Structures du court métrage français, 1945–1958', p. 36.

42. *'Notre groupe refuse d'admettre qu'il soit trop tard. Il en appelle au public, aux organismes responsables, aux parlementaires. De la réponse qui va lui être donnée dépend l'existence des films français du court métrage.' Déclaration du groupe des Trente*, Paris, 20 December 1953, reprinted in *Bref* no. 20, Spring 1994.

43. 'Les structurent meurent aussi', *Bref* no. 20, Spring 1994, p. 26. It was not until then that a controversy was resolved over a law of 6 August 1953 that did away with 'l'aide automatique', based on a percentage of profit, and replaced it with the system 'prime à la qualité'; while on 21 August 1953 the other crucial law was passed which no longer made it compulsory for the exhibitors to include a short film in their programme.

44. Chapuy and Jean-François Cornu, 'Les producteurs du groupe des Trente', pp. 47–58. The authors explore how these two groups are linked by producers and production modes.

45. Thomas, 'Avant Propos', p. 13.

2.10 Cinéma Vérité: Vertov Revisited

GENEVIÈVE VAN CAUWENBERGE

In the 1960s, the French changed direction. Although the turn also made much of synchronous sound, Direct Cinema dogme was not adopted (nor was the older educative, journalistic anglophone documentary tradition). Instead, French documentary, against a background of considerable theoretical debate on the cinema in general, turned back to Vertov and Kino-Pravda.

In the 1960s, documentaries obtained a new lease on life in France, as well as in Canada and the USA. The revival of the genre came about due to a renewed interest in examining people's ordinary lives: hearing their voices, capturing their accents or clumsy syntax and observing their gestures and interactions. Right from the start, this change in documentary practice was connected to the evolution of new recording equipment: the lightweight 16mm, silent, synchronous-sound hand-held camera. In France, this 'new documentary' was called cinéma vérité. Film-maker Jean Rouch and sociologist Edgar Morin (who published *Cinema or the Imaginary Man* and *The Stars*[1] around that time) coined the expression.

Morin, a jury member of the 1959 Florence ethnographic film festival, was an aficionado of Rouch's films, as well as those of Karel Reisz (*We are the Lambeth Boys*, 1958, UK) and Lionel Rogosin (*On the Bowery*, 1956, USA). Morin was particularly struck by the connection established between the film-maker and his subjects in these films. On his return to France in January 1960, he wrote an article for the French journal, *France Observateur*, entitled 'Pour un Nouveau Cinéma-Vérité'.[2] The article described the emergence of a cinematic style based on total immersion of the 'film-maker-diver into real life situations', which was now possible thanks to the portable camera.[3] The cinéma vérité formula was blithely borrowed from Dziga Vertov's *Kino-Pravda*, and was subsequently used at the request of film producer Anatole Dauman as a publicity stunt for the launch at Cannes of Rouch and Morin's *Chronique d'un été*,[4] the first attempt in France at shooting with a lightweight camera. When the film was released, its ambiguity led to misunderstandings and stormy disputes. Some critics took cinéma-vérité literally as claiming to reveal truth on film and were irritated by its pretentiousness, while others understood it more figuratively: cinéma vérité meant 'the truth of cinema' and not 'the cinema of truth'.[5]

The debate made film journal headlines for months and was still a major discussion point at the 1963 MIPE-TV (*Marché International des Programmes et Equipements de Télévision*) meeting in Lyon. The meeting was organised by Pierre Schaeffer, at the time head of the research service of the French television channel RTF. It brought together technical professionals, cameramen, journalists, film-makers and critics from Canada, the USA and France. Participants included the leading French film-makers of the cinema vérité movement, Jean Rouch and Mario Ruspoli, the pioneers of the Canadian *cinéma vécu*, Pierre Perrault and Michel Brault, and the Drew-Leacock associates. The engineers Stefan Kudelski and André Coutant also attended.

To put an end to the arguments about the cinéma vérité label, Ruspoli suggested that the term be dropped and replaced by the name 'cinéma direct' (Direct Cinema), which was less controversial and would adequately express what the new documentary was all about: a cinema that establishes 'direct and authentic contact' with 'lived reality'. This expression, he argued, was an umbrella term that could henceforth be used for the following terms: the Canadian 'candid camera', Pierre Perrault's *cinéma vécu*, the American 'living camera', as well as the French cinéma vérité. Ruspoli's proposal was well received. From then on the term cinéma direct replaced the expression cinéma vérité in France. The life span of this term was therefore very short in its country of origin.

Ruspoli's expression cinéma direct shifted the emphasis from the goal of the new documentary movement to its technology. This accent on technology became even clearer a few months later in a report he wrote in October 1963 at the request of UNESCO and presented at a round table on cinema in Beirut, entitled: 'The Light-Weight Synchronised Cinematographic Unit'.[6] For Ruspoli, Direct Cinema meant three things:

- use of a lightweight and silent-running mobile camera that gave the cameraman greater mobility and established a new relationship between the film-maker and his equipment – that is, the camera became an extension of the film-maker's body, allowing him to relate to the people he filmed in a much more intimate way;

- a reduction in the size of the film crew to three or four people – film-maker, cameraman and sound man, with perhaps an assistant – who could now work on an equal footing and on a friendly basis;
- an understanding of cinema as a means of observing human behaviour, of investigating and revealing the human psyche.

Ruspoli, depicted by French film historians as the theoretical brains behind the movement, attempted to smooth away the differences between the practitioners of new documentary. But it was a failed attempt, according to Louis Marcorelles's account of the 1963 conference.[7] From a strictly technical point of view, the meeting was quite productive: due to the collaborative efforts of film-makers and technicians from different nationalities (Coutant, Ruspoli, Rouch, Brault and Leacock), it led to the improvement of the KMT prototype camera that had been used to shoot the French cinéma vérité film. Specifications for the Éclair 16 camera, known outside France as the Éclair NPR, were written.[8] This collective effort to improve equipment – an example of the international cross-fertilisation of ideas taking place at the time – was based on a shared belief among participants in the revolutionary potential of lightweight synch-sound equipment. The new technology was expected to change not only documentary film practice but cinema as a whole.

During the conference, Raymond Bellour commented in *Artsept*[9] that 'one could witness the progressive endowment of a metaphysical dimension to a mere mechanical object'. Despite the common ground they shared, however, deep disagreements emerged among participants about their film-making methods as they began to discover each other's work. Marcorelles recalls that two men dominated the debates: Richard Leacock, a proponent of the 'observing camera', and Jean Rouch, an advocate of the 'participating camera'. Though both of them claimed Robert Flaherty as a legitimising figure, Leacock and Rouch became rivals. Their exchange of views was harsh, with the crux of their debate revolving around ethics and ideology. Rouch criticised Leacock for his lack of reflexivity, stressing the unavoidable subjectivity of the film-maker's gaze, insisting that Leacock's unobtrusive, observing camera was far from neutral. Taking an ironic stand towards the 'naiveté' of Leacock's attempt to reach a zero level of reality in his films – that is, free from any culturally ingrained idea about what it should be – Rouch said Leacock was in fact 'selling Coca Cola to the world' – that is, reproducing cultural stereotypes while pretending not to.

Leacock's riposte was to condemn French films as too 'talkative'. He claimed that, by using his camera and micro-phone to intervene in filmic situations and provoking his subjects, his opponent was 'forcing meaning and interpretation', imposing preconceived ideas on the viewer instead of showing him the world as he (Leacock) purported to do. 'It is dispiriting to see these twin pioneers of an exciting revolutionary movement in the cinema so at loggerheads,'[10] commented Marcorelles afterwards. In an attempt to restore order to a confusing debate, he attributed Rouch and Leacock's incompatibility to their cultural differences:

Richard Leacock and Jean Rouch gave expression to two chief (and opposed) tendencies of this cinema of immediacy. And in fact the evident hostility between their points of view suggested not merely an incompatibility between two different ways of looking at things, but even in a sense between two rival forms of civilisation, the French and the Anglo-Saxon.[11]

Along with Morin's manifesto and Ruspoli's text, Marcorelles's account of the meeting and the report he subsequently wrote for UNESCO[12] constitute the third major written contribution on cinéma vérité in France. Marcorelles's writings sowed the seeds of the idea that there was a strong division between the American and the French approach to what he called 'the cinema of immediacy'. For him, the French were advocates of the 'provocative camera' and the Americans of the 'non-interventionist, observing camera'.

The idea that practitioners of the 1960s lightweight documentary were divided into two opposite camps – the French and the American – was espoused by Eric Barnouw in his influential history of documentary.[13] Bill Nichols, another influential writer on documentary, also had the same view.[14] For the last thirty years, this has been the conventional wisdom in Anglo-Saxon academic studies on documentary from the 60s. However, in the 90s, when the controversy had died down, some scholars began to challenge that conventional wisdom.[15] If one revisits the films of the period, it becomes clear that a neat division between the American 'observing camera' and the French 'participating camera' does not account for the complexity of the movement. It overlooks points of convergence between the American and French output while denying the differences between film-makers working within the same national context.

Certainly in France, there are obvious differences, for example, in the way Rouch, Morin and Marker used new recording techniques in *Chronique d'un été* and *Le joli mai*,[16] two major cinéma vérité films of the 1960s. The two films also share some common features. Both are social enquiries about French society in the early 60s. Along with Godard's *Masculin féminin* (1966) (which pays explicit homage to both *Chronique* and *Le joli mai*)[17] they form a trilogy, probing the limits of the interview-as-technique to the critique of society through cinema. Moreover, *Chronique d'un été* and *Le joli mai* are both self-reflexive films. Each is regarded as a manifesto on the potential use of the new lightweight equipment. But their positions diverge on this issue, as does their approach to the filmic subjects.

A fourth leading figure of the 60s French cinéma vérité movement, Mario Ruspoli, made two films during this period: *Les inconnus de la terre* [*Stangers of the Earth*] (1961) and *Regard sur la folie* [*Looking at Madness*] (1962).[18] These works explore areas of life shielded from the experience of most humans, such as the exploration of a mental institution in *Regard sur la folie*. Ruspoli's films are also statements about the potentialities of the new equipment. A look at these four film manifestos, made within a time span of just four years, sheds a great deal of light on the way French film-makers in the 60s positioned themselves vis-à-vis the debate over the 'new documentary'.

Chronique d'un été is the first cinéma vérité film. It begins with a travelling shot of the Paris suburbs, another of the city early in the morning, followed by a shot of Parisians coming out of the subway. The image shows viewers that they can expect to be immersed in 'real life' for the duration of the film: 'This film', Rouch explains in voiceover commentary, 'was not played by actors, but lived by men and women who have given a few moments of their lives to a new experiment in cinéma-vérité.' The aim of the film is clearly laid out: *Chronique d'un été* is a piece of contemporary sociology on French society in the early 60s. This period of the twentieth century – remembered today as the country's golden age of prosperity – saw French society go through a period of rapid modernisation. As the purchasing power of French people improved, electronic appliances and cars became part of the average Frenchman's daily life. The population of France was also on the rise due to decolonisation and the return of its colonialists (the '*pieds noirs*' of Algeria and elsewhere), immigration and the post-war baby boom. This led to a housing crisis and huge building projects were set in motion to solve the problem. Emerging from the post-war period, France became a 'leisure society',[19] although it had mixed feelings about progress linked to modernisation and economic growth, and the possibility for individual happiness within a society increasingly structured around materialism.[20]

Chronique d'un été, whose working title was 'How do you live?', reflects these concerns. The film focuses on a group of young men and women, mostly the film-makers' friends and acquaintances, who represent different strata of French society: workers, students, employees and the film-makers themselves. It documents the lives of its subjects during their work but also at home during their leisure time. There are many sequences that rely on observation in *Chronique d'un été*, in the North American fashion, a fact that has too often been ignored. Some of these sequences aimed at capturing what Rouch called 'the poetics of daily life' in a pre-New Wave style, by following people's actions with fluid camera movements in an outdoor environment. Others, shot in factories (with a hidden camera) and focused on workers' movements rather than on those of the machines around them, endeavour to reveal the alienating nature of factory work – thus anticipating what militant cinema would do a few years later.

Yet, the bulk of the film consists of interviews with the subjects by Morin. These are intertwined with scenes of lively group discussions, usually during a meal. In these interviews, Morin broaches various topics such as the housing problem, the increase in leisure time and the importance of work in helping people lead satisfying lives. Behind his questions, he is researching the possibility of personal happiness in an emerging consumer society. Morin was one of the first sociologists to point to a general malaise in contemporary society, which he attributed to a loss of real communication. Like American Direct Cinema film-makers, he showed the gap between people's appearances – the social front they erected – and their true nature. People in social situations use a façade, which prevents them from communicating properly with other people. Moreover, again like the American film-makers, Morin and Rouch placed a humanistic faith in cinema as a means of re-establishing an authenticity in human relations that had been lost in daily life. At the onset of what Guy Debord would a few years later call 'the society of spectacle', cinema was dreaming of recovering a lost innocence.[21]

Chronique d'un été is an experiment in ciné communication. 'Can't cinema be one of the means of breaking the membrane that isolates each of us from others in the metro, on the street, or on the stairway of the apartment building?'[22] wonders Morin. To explore this hypothesis, the film sets up encounters between people who would probably have otherwise never met. For example, it introduces Angelo, the factory worker, to Landru, an African student, and then observes how they relate to one another. They eventually establish a friendship under the gaze of the camera.

'The film is a research project,' Morin says. 'It is not, strictly speaking, a sociological film. Sociological film researches society. It is an ethnological film in the strong sense of the term. It studies mankind.'[23] As a sociologist, Morin has, of course, reflected on the proper conditions for film encounters to take place and devised the idea of what he called 'commensality': bringing people together in a private apartment around excellent meals washed down with good wine is conducive to communication. This is what *Chronique d'un été* did. Technicians, cameramen and film-makers took part in the meals. The film is a collective experience in which everyone concerned – film-makers,

Chronique d'un été (1961): as they take centre stage in the film, Rouch and Morin themselves become the subject and object of the camera's gaze

technicians and subjects – was expected to be intimately involved and placed on an equal footing. By involving people in the process of their representation on film, Rouch and Morin break the divide between the people filmed and the film-makers. As they take centre stage in the film, Rouch and Morin themselves become the subject and object of the camera's gaze. The idea behind the film's collaborative approach is to create a close encounter with the Other in his singularity. *Chronique d'un été*, which Morin describes as a 'cinema of camaraderie', pursues what Maxime Scheinfeigel describes as 'the ambitious project of reinventing the approach of the other'.[24]

In *Chronique d'un été*, Morin and Rouch set up situations and then simply let things happen, thus relying largely on improvisation and chance. There is no script. What induces people to speak on film is not just the specific situations that the film-maker sets up but also the presence of the camera. As film analysts have repeatedly noticed, *Chronique d'un été* makes use of the camera as 'a catalyst, an accelerator' to draw out the personality of the person being filmed. Morin conducts in-depth interviews that he defines as 'an effort towards the elucidation of the inner self'. Indeed, according to Morin,

> people wear a mask not only towards others but also for themselves. The self appears not as an irreducible unit but as a system which can be compared to that of an atom. The core itself is not made of a basic element, but it involves a dualistic structure around which are alternatively displayed and embodied personalities that are more or less crystallised, some more intimate, secret and deeply imbedded, others more socialised. There are conflicts and inconsistencies between inner personalities and between these personalities and outward social appearances.[25]

Thus, Morin yearns for cinema to help the individual cope with his atomised personality by coaxing him towards self-understanding. This clearly lends a psychoanalytical dimension to this type of cinema.

Two sequences in the film are symptomatic of the confessional dimension of speech in *Chronique d'un été*: Marie-Lou Parolini's intensive interview and Marceline Loridan's testimony. In both instances, the characters reveal intimate details about their lives under the stimulating gaze of the camera. The first sequence is shot inside Marie-Lou's room and is symptomatic of the empathetic dialogue that Morin established with his subject. Morin places himself in the shot and, relinquishing the authoritarian posture of the scientist, establishes very intimate contact with the subject. Marie-Lou's self-enquiry brings her near to emotional collapse.

The second confessional sequence is Marceline's testimony, one of the first instances of an on-camera testimonial of the Holocaust. The scene takes place at Place de la Concorde in Paris and is not only an experiment in ciné communication but a technological experiment with the new, light equipment. As Marceline walks through Les Halles – the setting suggestive of her deportation – she begins talking about that grim experience. She is carrying a tape recorder (Kudelski's Nagra), hidden under her raincoat or later in a large handbag.[26] The cameraman, Michel Brault, follows her in Rouch's Citroen 2 CV, shooting through its sunroof with the KMT Coutant prototype camera. Rouch jokingly called this moment 'an experience in pedovision'. Today, we see the technical flaws of the sequence, but at the time it was quite revolutionary. A new filming style came into being then. 'That day, the foundation of cinema changed,' said French film critic, Jean-Louis Comolli.

> For the first time a body in its singularity, an identity, a biography, a mindset, a history, a voice, a speech formed an indivisible whole. Such a subjective dimension had never before been attained in the representative arts. The body, the word, the text, the character – up to that point, separated elements – became joined. It is no longer up to the viewer to mentally establish the connection. The 'other' appears in his subjectivity. The voice can no longer be separated either from the body that carries it or from the space that houses it or from the moment in time that shapes it.[27]

After the film was completed, Rouch and Morin showed a rough cut to the participants, who expressed their views about it. Their reaction is recorded in the film. This experience showed the danger that cinéma vérité represents for filmic subjects, since the participants (and later the general public) did not judge the film but the people in it, and were quite critical: Marie-Lou's behaviour on film was considered as too exhibitionist and her persona was strongly rejected by some of the participants. 'It's not exactly exhibitionism: it's a very strange kind of confession in front of the camera, where the camera is, let's say, a mirror, and

also a window opened to the outside', Rouch replied.[28] As the documentary theorist Michael Renov has observed:

> The camera is for Rouch a kind of two-way glass that retains a double function: it is a window that delivers the profilmic to an absent gaze and, at the same moment, a reflective surface that reintroduces us to ourselves.[29]

This view of the camera both as a window open to the world and as a mirror was embraced by Mario Ruspoli in the films he made in the early 1960s, *Les inconnus de la terre* and *Regard sur la folie*. Similar to *Chronique d'un été*, the films represent a manifesto for Direct Cinema. Ruspoli, author of 'The Light-Weight Synchronised Cinematographic Unit' report, emphasises in his work the potential of lightweight equipment as a means for a film-maker to immerse himself in film, to blend into an environment and establish a close relationship with the subjects. He also indicates some of the problems that the intrusion of a camera into people's lives can create.

Les inconnus de la terre explores, with great sensitivity, the difficulties facing a rural area of France, La Lozère, which Ruspoli knew well. The film exposes the hardships that country folk had to endure just to survive. It shows their destitute situation, of which most French people were unaware at the time. The rural poor had to adjust to new types of land use, buy new and expensive equipment and switch from traditional farming methods to mechanised ones. While the older among them stuck to traditional ways of farming, the younger ones – encouraged by the government – chose to buy equipment collectively or to simply abandon the countryside for work in the cities. This film is one of the first to have explored the lurching transformation of France from rural to modern society and the problems of displacement as people left the countryside in large numbers to live in cities.

The film is structured around the figure of the school teacher, whose mission is to convince the farmers to embrace modernity. It opens with a demonstration showing farmers carrying a banner with the words 'Don't farmers have the right to eat?' and closes with a voiceover commentary stressing how urgent it is for farmers to use more modern techniques of land exploitation in order to survive. The film presents itself as a sociological enquiry and gives a voice to farmers, who comment on their own situation. Their speech is heard against the backdrop of their living environment, the landscape of La Lozère.

As much as it is about the farmers of France's region of Cevennes, *Les inconnus de la terre* is also an example of Direct Cinema. Shot by camera operator Michel Brault with the KMT Coutant camera, the film conveys a sense of excitement about the new lightweight equipment. Brault clearly enjoys exploring the arid landscape of La Lozère by quickly moving his camera across its fields. He thereby created a very distinctive filming style of his own, which he would go on to use in his own *Pour la suite du monde* (1963, Canada) and which became widely used in 1960s documentaries.

Ruspoli expands and clarifies Rouch and Morin's view of the ambivalence of the camera as a self-effacing 'observing tool' and as something which provokes a reaction. The film makes a point of illustrating the unobtrusiveness of the lightweight equipment. As Ruspoli commented on the shooting of the film in his 1963 report,

> during the interviews in *Les inconnus de la terre*, it was hard to tell whether Michel Brault had been filming or not since he was constantly acting as if he was not filming. He seemed to consider that his little KMT was a totally unimportant object that was not operating.[30]

Lightweight equipment, the film suggests, allows for an informality in the exchanges that take place between the film-maker and the subject. With cinéma vérité 'the camera is in the field', Rouch jokingly said. In *Les inconnus de la terre* it literally is.

In one instance, for example, the interviewer and the boom operator are casually sitting in a field talking to a farmer. This is a typical image of the new, friendly mode of interaction between film-makers and subjects that cinéma vérité claims to achieve due to the ease of the recording process. But Ruspoli also acknowledges the effect of the presence of the camera on the interviewees as a stimulant that encourages them to speak. Ruspoli, who is rather self-effacing as an interviewer, was able to capture the texture, syntax and rhythm of the farmers' speech due to the quality of exchanges he had with them. For his part, Brault skilfully captured the gestures and the accompanying facial expressions. As Piault commented, *Les inconnus de la terre* caught 'speech in action', very much as Pierre Perrault did around the same time in his script for *Pour la suite du monde*.[31] Today, the film stands as an archeological document on how French farmers of the 1960s spoke.

Giving a voice to those who are usually silenced is also a driving force behind the *Regard sur la folie* project, the film Ruspoli shot in the psychiatric hospital of Saint Alban in La Lozère. Ruspoli gives a voice to the inmates (at least to one of them who is able to communicate), as well as to the doctors. The camera introduces the viewer into a world which is cut off from the outside. It moves smoothly through the hallways, accompanying and mingling with the patients rather than looking at them from the outside. The film does not attempt to show the failings of the institution, as Wiseman did in *Titicut Follies* (1967), but rather to take a very empathetic approach to the doctors, nurses and inmates, and to challenge the gap that society has created between sanity and insanity. But, like *Les inconnus de la terre*, *Regard sur la folie* is also about cinéma vérité.

Ruspoli encourages the filmic subjects to take a reflexive approach to the film-making process. The members of the institution have the opportunity to talk openly about the impact of the film on their behaviour. A doctor explains the discomfort he feels as he is filmed and how the process affects his behaviour. He performs not only as a doctor towards his patient, but also as filmee for the camera, thinking about the public's reaction: 'I have two ears: a psychiatrist's ear and an ear for the public. You have to accept this inner division of your personality,' he says. The film stresses the idea of an egalitarian connection between the film-maker, the inmates and the doctors, who are part of the same world. It also shows the cameraman's ability to move along with the filmed subjects, which makes this kind of relationship possible.

The final scene of the film is a demonstration of the cameraman's skills, the potential of the equipment as well as Ruspoli's concept of film-making. As two doctors leave the hospital, the cameraman is seen going along with them, first by walking backwards and then at their side, before finally following them – a perfect demonstration of the possibilities of the 'walking camera', a true extension of the cameraman's body. As the people go off screen, the cameraman keeps walking forwards, staring straight at the viewer, who becomes the subject of the film. This reversal of the camera's gaze invites the viewer to engage with the film on its own terms by questioning the divide society establishes between those who are insane and those who are mentally healthy. It also offers a cinematographic equivalent of the Rouch take on cinema, both as a window open to the world and as a mirror that reflects our own image as an invitation to self-enquiry.

Chris Marker and Pierre Lhomme's *Le joli mai* is the last of the filmic manifestos about cinéma vérité from the early 1960s. Shot in May 1962, just after the signing of the Evian agreement, which put an end to the Algerian war, it was one of the first films within the official French distribution network that dared explore the Franco-Algerian conflict and expose the country's widespread political lethargy. As a politically committed film that challenges the French people's indifference to the Algerian war and its aftermath, the film is a landmark in the history of French leftist cinema. At the same time, like *Chronique d'un été*, it is a sociological investigation of Parisian society in the early 60s. Wryly dedicated, in English, to the 'happy many', an oblique reference to *Chronique d'un été* and its collection of rather unhappy people (as well as a twist on Stendahl's cherished elitist address to the 'happy few'), the film portrays ordinary life in Paris, as did the films of Rouch and Morin.

There are many points of contact between *Le joli mai* and *Chronique d'un été*. Both films make use of the lightweight synch-sound camera (the prototype KMT Coutant) and rely on detailed interviews with ordinary citizens to carry out a social enquiry about Paris and its inhabitants. Both films document the rapid changes France underwent in the early 1960s due to modernisation and decolonisation. Like Morin, Marker is wary of the possibilities for happiness in a society based on consumerism and rampant individualism. He places a humanist faith in cinema as a mean of re-establishing a sense of community. Marker said in a public debate on the film:

> what I wanted to come out of Le joli mai is a sort of call to make contact with others, and for both the people in the film and the spectators, it's the possibility of doing something with others that at one extreme creates a society or a civilization ... but can simply provide love, friendship, sympathy.[32]

Like Chronique d'un été, Le joli mai reflects on the relationship between the individual and society, defining itself as 'a cinema of brotherhood'.

Le joli mai is also comparable to Chronique d'un été for its self-reflexivity. But Le joli mai sets itself apart much more strongly than Chronique from the position of Direct Cinema film-makers about the potential of new equipment. The boundary was not as clear as they thought at Lyon, but it was there – somewhat complicated, it must be said, because the French did not present a united front. Marker dissociates himself from Morin and Rouch's self-acclaimed ability to capture raw reality on film – a stance that, despite their film's self-reflexivity, echoed American claims.

As his film's prologue indicates, Marker considers that film-makers inevitably look at the world through the filter of their cultural and personal memories; it is thus impossible to 'discover reality anew' by filming it. Indeed, instead of opening with the Parisian sidewalk on which interviews with ordinary Parisians take place, Le joli mai starts with overhead panoramic views of Paris shot from a rooftop (as a reference to the tradition of classical painting). This is followed by a series of dynamic shots of urban traffic and city noises (referring to the modernist tradition and more precisely to the city symphony documentary feature of the 1920s). Along with its voiceover commentary hinting at the impossibility of discovering Paris 'without memories', the film's references to previous representations of the city are a clear indication to the viewer that Marker's work is to be placed within – and indebted to – an artistic tradition.

To these representations, the film-maker adds his personal vision. Marker asserts the specificity of his own gaze by referring, in the prologue's voiceover commentary, to cats and owls as the subject of his enquiry about Paris. Later in the film, images of cats and owls appear at several points: they are purely self-referential and reminders of Marker's legendary fondness for these animals. The film's emphasis on these tags reveals that Marker's outlook on Parisian life is a subjective one moulded by his imagination and ideological

viewpoint. Even at a subconscious level, Marker suggests, the film-maker sees the world through the deforming prism of his emotions and personal concerns.

Marker also dissociates himself from Direct Cinema's deceptive attempt at conflating temporalities,[33] which gives the viewer the false impression of experiencing an event almost at the very moment of its occurence. He points to the gap between the pro-filmic moment and the actual viewing time. An event is already gone as soon as it is recorded and images can only retain traces, frame memories of it. One caption that immediately follows the film's credits says: 'This scene takes place in the month of May 1962, which some people then called "the first spring of peace".' This is indicative that the film's images are archival and meant to document a passing way of life. The caption also suggests that in 1962 Marker saw his film as being watched in the distant future. Only the people of the future, Marker indicates in the film scenario, will be able to grasp the images' significance and their meaning. Unlike his contemporaries, Marker does not believe that images are transparent, that they are 'a window open to the world'. In his view, their understanding depends upon the viewer's knowledge about the event.

This is an idea to which he will return again and again in his later works. Reflecting on his own films from a distance, he will bring to the fore the differences between what he thought he was seeing when images were recorded and what he would perceive in the very same images years later. A final observation to make about the 1962 caption is that it lays the foundation for a complex juxtaposition of temporal perception: Marker transforms the viewer from his position of contemporary witness (of a film created in 1962) to that of a chronological observer-from-the-future. Marker demands that the 60s viewer regard his contemporaries with a distant, archeological gaze, one requiring a detached point of view about the people he portrays. This is quite different from the viewer's immersion within the pro-filmic space attempted not only by Direct Cinema film-makers, but also by Rouch, Morin and Ruspoli.

In Le joli mai, Marker simultaneously divorces himself from Direct Cinema film-makers and takes his distance from the methods of Rouch and Morin. His mode of approach to the people he films, and the goal he sets for his interviews, is different. 'To track the unspeakable was not what this film is about,' he says in the voiceover commentary, obviously referring to Morin's in-depth interviews. Even if Marker makes use of the camera as 'provocateur' à la Rouch and Morin, he does so in a very different way. Contrary to the sociologist, Marker does not rip away any social masks to expose the truth they may conceal about the people he films. Never does he prod his subjects into losing emotional control in an attempt to uncover a personality radically different from that displayed in the social contacts of daily life. On the contrary, Marker encourages self-control and the individual's awareness of the social dimension of their interaction. He believes that the social mask people choose to wear is not a cover to be lifted but rather a way of expressing their inner personality. If awareness of a film situation has an influence on people, it reinforces the natural theatricality of their gestures.

There is no attempt by Marker to establish an intimate and casual relationship between himself and his subjects. Even with the people he knew well, there are few, if any, friendly exchanges. Speech is pursued in the film as a social act, but a regulated one. Marker did not believe, as his contemporaries did, that the lightweight equipment abolishes the power relationship that the making of a film creates between film-maker and subject. It is an asymmetrical relationship – even when the equipment is light and the crew reduced to a few people. Indeed, there is very little that Marker does to go against this truism. Though he is occasionally seen on screen, he does not share the space on camera on an equal footing with the interviewee by setting up an empathetic dialogue with them as Morin does. On the contrary, Marker remains on the edge of the screen or is off screen, protected from the viewer's gaze. While questioning his interviewees, Marker at times uses biting irony or asks unsettling questions to interviewees. Furthermore, he exercises control over people's speech through montage by 'drawing critical comparisons and contrasts that track the wider social, political and radical fault lines of contemporary France through the life and opinions of individuals'.[34] Marker has often been criticised for his authoritarian approach to the interviewee. Rouch, for example, often regretted the fact that Marker did not turn the camera on himself and give his subjects the chance to challenge him.[35] Others, such as Roger Tailleur, came to the conclusion that *Le joli mai* was not '*cinéma vérité* but *ciné-ma-vérité*': not a cinema of truth but one that expresses a personal view on truth.

But this is going too far. *Le joli mai* is cinéma-vérité. Like Rouch and Ruspoli's films, *Le joli mai* embraces with enthusiasm the 'slightly heady discovery' of the period's new equipment. As the film's sound engineer Antoine Bonfanti noted, during the shooting of *Le joli mai*, cameraman Pierre Lhomme used headphones that enabled him to frame the images spontaneously in accordance with the sound. 'It was a great breakthrough in the sound/image relationship. It was this which was the very spirit of *Le joli mai*.'[36] Thus, *Le joli mai* also shares with other films of the period the intention of capturing ordinary people's spontaneous speech along with the facial expressions and gestures that accompany their words. Since for Marker and for his contemporaries, as Gilles Deleuze has observed,

the body is no longer the obstacle that separates thought from itself, that which it has to overcome to reach

thinking. It is on the contrary that which it plunges into or must plunge into, in order to reach the unthought, that is life.[37]

NOTES

1. Edgar Morin, *Le cinéma ou l'homme imaginaire* (Paris: Minuit, 1956); Edgar Morin, *Les stars* (Paris: Seuil, 1957).
2. Reprinted in Jean Rouch, *Chronique d'un été* (Paris: Domaine Cinéma 1, Inter-Spectacles, 1962). (English translation Edgar Morin, 'For a New Cinéma-Vérité', in Steven Feld (ed.), *Ciné-ethnography: Jean Rouch* [Minneapolis: University of Minnesota Press, 2003], p. 229.)
3. 'Rouch,' Morin said, 'ridding himself of the customary technical encumbrances and equipped only with a 16mm camera and a tape recorder slung across his shoulders, can then infiltrate a community as a *person* and not as the director of a film crew' and capture 'the truth of human relations in real life'. Morin, 'For a New Cinéma-Vérité', p. 230.
4. Jean Rouch and Edgar Morin, *Chronique d'un été* [*Chronicle of a Summer*], 1961, France.
5. As Rouch recalled many times during interviews, the distinction between truth in cinema and the truth of cinema is due to the historian Georges Sadoul, who introduced the writings of Dziga Vertov in France. See, for example, Jean Rouch, 'Le vrai et le faux', *Traverses* no. 147, 1989 (reprinted in Jean-Paul Colleyn [ed.], *Jean Rouch: Cinéma et anthropologie* [Paris: Cahiers du cinéma, 2009]), p. 113.
6. Mario Ruspoli, 'Le groupe synchrone cinématographique léger', Paris, UNESCO, 11 October 1963.
7. Louis Marcorelles, 'La foire aux vérités', *Cahiers du cinéma* no. 143, May 1963, pp. 26–34. (See also Louis Marcorelles, and Andrew S. Labarthe, 'Nothing But the Truth', trans of 'Entretien avec Robert Drew et Richard Leacock', *Sight & Sound* vol. 32 no. 3, Summer 1963, pp. 114–17.)
8. This camera was quieter and better balanced than the KMT prototype camera. Gilles Marsollais retraces the evolution of the lightweight camera in his seminal book, *L'aventure du cinéma direct* (Paris: Seghers, 1974), pp. 220–2. See also Barry Salt, *Film Style and Technology: History and Analysis* (London: Starword, 2009 [1983]), p. 291.
9. Raymond Bellour, and Jean-Louis Leutrat, 'Préface', *Artsept* no. 2, 'Le cinéma et la vérité', April/June 1963, p. 5.
10. Marcorelles and Labarthe, 'Nothing But the Truth', p. 115.
11. Ibid. Jean-Claude Bringuier shares this view in his account of the Lyon meeting: America, he said, 'is the real author of Leacock's films': 'Libres propos sur le cinéma-vérité', *Cahiers du cinéma* no. 145, July 1963, pp. 14–17.
12. Louis Marcorelles, 'Une esthétique du réel, le cinéma direct', Paris, UNESCO, 12 October 1964.
13. Eric Barnouw, *A History of the Non-fiction Film* (New York: Oxford University Press, 1974), pp. 254–5.

14. Bill Nichols, *Representing Reality: Issues and Concepts in Documentary* (Bloomington: Indiana University Press, 1991), pp. 38–56.

15. See Brian Winston, *Claiming the Real: The Documentary Film Revisited* (London: BFI, 1995), p. 187.

16. Chris Marker and Pierre Lhomme, *Le joli mai* [*Pretty May*], 1963, France.

17. Antoine de Baecque, 'Le sociologue contestataire', in *Godard: Biographie* (Paris: Grasset, 2010), pp. 302–8.

18. Mario Ruspoli, *Les inconnus de la terre* [*Strangers of the Earth*], Paris, Argos-Film, 16mm, 1961; *Regard sur la folie* [*Looking at Madness*] Paris, Argos-Films, 1962. (Ruspoli's cameramen were Michel Brault and Roger Morillère who had shot for Rouch and Morin.)

19. See Joffre Dumazedier and Aline Ripert, *Le loisir et la ville* (Paris: Seuil, 1966) and Joffre Dumazedier, *Vers une civilisation du loisir* (Paris: Seuil, 1972).

20. This now-cliché critique would spread through the decade to a point whereby Jean Baudrillard, in 1970, could assert in his *Consumption Society* that 'Just as medieval society balanced its equilibrium between God and the Devil, ours lies in an opposition between consumption and its denunciation' (in Jean Baudrillard, *La société de consommation* [Paris: Gallimard, 1970], p. 316). Reference works on the period include Edgar Morin, *L'esprit du temps* (Paris: Grasset, 1962); Jean-Pierre Rioux, *La France de la quatrième république*, vol. T.2, *L'expansion et l'impuissance 1952–1958* (Paris: Seuil, 1983); Michel Winock, *Chronique des années soixantes* (Paris: Seuil, 1987).

21. I owe this observation to Jean-Louis Comolli, in 'Lumière éclatante d'un astre mort', *Le cinéma direct, et après?* *Images documentaires* no. 21, Spring 1995, p. 13. Comolli connects 'the emergence and the spreading throughout the world of different types of direct cinema to the 1968 revolutionary constellation and the criticism of the society of spectacle'.

22. Edgar Morin, 'For a New Cinéma-Vérité', p. 231.

23. Ibid.; Edgar Morin, 'Chronicle of a Film', in Feld, *Ciné-ethnography*, p. 232.

24. Maxime Scheinfeigel, *Jean Rouch* (Paris: CNRS, 2008), p. 92.

25. Edgar Morin, *Le vif du sujet* (Paris: Seuil, 1969), p. 153.

26. The tape recorder was connected to a clip-on lavaliere microphone brought by Brault. (Morin, 'For a New Cinéma-Vérité'; see Morin, 'Chronicle of a Film', p. 240.)

27. Jean-Louis Comolli, 'L'oral et l'oracle, séparation du corps et de la voix', *Images documentaires*, *La voix* no. 55–6, Winter 2006, pp. 36–7.

28. Ian Cameron and Mark Shivas, 'Interview with Jean Rouch', *Movie*, no. 8, April 1963 (quoted in Mick Eaton, *Anthropology, Reality, Cinema* [London: BFI, 1979], p. 51).

29. Michael Renov, *The Subject of Documentary* (Minneapolis: University of Minsesota Press, 2004), p. 197.

30. Ruspoli, 'Le groupe synchrone cinématographique léger'.

31. Marc Henri Piault, *Anthropologie et cinéma* (Paris: Nathan, 2000), p. 182.

32. Chris Maker, quoted in Catherine Lupton, *Marker: Memories of the Future* (London: Reaktion, 2005), p. 80.

33. The ultimate achievement of a quasi-immediacy of perception is the direct transmission on TV or video screen (the video of surveillance), which some theoriticians have considered as the abolition of the signifier, the pure display of the referent on screen. See, for instance, René Berger, *La télé-fission, alerte à la télévision* (Paris: Casterman, 1976), p. 25.

34. Lupton, *Marker*, p. 83.

35. 'I regretted the fact that there was no "Edgar Morin" in *Le joli mai*. Many spectators felt he was despicable but in Chronicle he was absolutely necessary, because he is the one that asks questions and the one to which one can ask questions. I would have liked to see the worker-priest turn to Marker and ask him "do you believe in God?"', Jean Rouch said, for example, in Eric Rohmer and Louis Marcorelles, 'Entretien avec Jean Rouch', *Cahiers du cinéma* no. 144, June 1963, p. 12.

36. Antoine Bonfanti, *Positif* no. 143, March 1997, p. 92. Quoted in Min Lee, 'Chris Marker's Work from WWII to May 68 and Beyond: Shifting Realities in Time and Image', PhD dissertation, University of Warwick, July 2004, p. 162.

37. Gilles Deleuze, 'Cinema, Body, Brain and Thought', in *Cinema 2: The Time-Image* (London: Athlone Press, 1989), p. 189.

2.11 Beyond Sobriety: Documentary Diversions

CRAIG HIGHT

The erosion of Direct Cinema dogme and the recovery and exploitation of a Vertovian alternative paradigm comprehensively weakened Grierson's legacy. Among much else, that had ensured that documentary was always what had been called 'a discourse of sobriety'. But now, amid the wreckage of the paradigm, even this fundamental assumption was to be challenged by an emerging range of 'documentary diversions'.

Documentary culture is arguably less coherent in the twenty-first century than it has been at any other time in its history, and to some extent this is the culmination of factors which have also informed the broader (western) visual culture since the 1960s. European intellectuals such as Roland Barthes, Jacques Derrida, Michel Foucault and Julia Kristeva were key figures in the emergence of post-structuralist (and postmodernist) attacks on the 'meta-narratives' that they argued were inherent to western institutional knowledge and discourses. Their detailed deconstructions of the discourses of 'official' voices were an important, if indirect, influence on the emergence of new kinds of documentary practice.

The most significant of a new generation of documentary film-makers to emerge in the 60s were those associated with cinéma vérité and Direct Cinema. Both of these movements shared a fascination with the documentary camera as an instrument of observation, and prioritised this aspect of documentary form above all others. In part, this emphasis was a reaction against the constraints of a dominant documentary practice centred on the rational, seemingly objective presentation of an argument by a presenter or so-called 'voice-of-God' narrator. This expositional mode of documentary representation[1] was suspect from a post-structuralist perspective, for its claims to offer an objectivity that somehow transcended the social-political discourses of dominant institutions.

The distinctions between cinéma vérité and Direct Cinema partly derive from their origins within different national contexts, and especially from the particular concerns of key film-makers. Saunders argues that the Direct Cinema movement could not have emerged outside of the specific intersection of factors operating within the USA

during the 1960s, being 'predicated as much on a philosophical reawakening as on the portability of equipment: roving camera-sound systems, developed at first to assist orthodox journalistic or anthropological endeavour, eventually became totems of a new-found cinematic transcendence'.[2]

Aiming for a more 'direct' relationship between reality and audiences, film-makers within these new documentary movements sought to downplay the role of themselves as mediators of actuality. They insisted that documentary film should instead be a 'window on reality', with their own role reduced to that of capturing and faithfully representing the reality that appeared before their cameras. It is important here to reiterate the key role played by the emergence of new forms of film-making technologies, some developed themselves by the new generation of film-makers. The arrival of portable, hand-held camera and synchronous-sound equipment suddenly allowed for a freedom of movement by small documentary crews, opening access to new kinds of social spaces. This new documentary practice could seemingly capture the rhythms and sounds of life unfolding and directly relay that to audiences.[3]

As with later image-capturing technologies, including video and particularly digital image and sound equipment, the new equipment of the 1960s was associated with somewhat naive rhetoric about its potential for 'democratising' documentary culture itself. Instead of being distorted by a conventional institutional voice, falsely claiming an ahistorical objectivity, documentary could instead become a site for the voices and perspectives of everyday people, transforming it into a genre about and for the masses. Although clearly drawing from post-structuralist influences, these (exclusively male) film-makers did not represent all of the complexity of these emerging political and intellectual traditions. Both cinéma vérité and Direct Cinema sought to re-energise documentary practice by shifting to a more mechanically centred notion of objectivity, drawing on long-established discourses of the indexicality of photographic images. If the documentary film-maker could be seen as suspect because of his traditional role as a voice of authority, these newer generations of practitioners would transcend such biases by relying on the ability of the camera itself to document and record. They would move away from meta-narratives about the world, and aim instead for more 'authentic' and meaningful fragments, captured by the scientific instrument of the camera, at ground level.

These are not quite the politics of feminist post-structuralists. Haraway, for example, has similarly articulated a demand for a knowledge that was not validated by institutional authority, but based on a more decentred and contextualised avenue of insight. Her notion of objectivity, however, builds from the notion of 'situated knowledges', a kind of 'embodied' objectivity that continually highlights partial and critical acts of deconstruction as necessary to practices of knowledge generation.[4] Haraway argues particularly for the importance of deliberately reflexive practices, and, while the documentary movements of cinéma vérité and Direct Cinema incorporated textual reflexivity (particularly with Rouch), such tendencies did not extend to a critique of all forms of documentary practice.

Since the late 1980s and early 90s reflexivity in a number of guises has emerged as a core component of the broader documentary culture, but in tandem with other trends such as the rise of autobiographical documentary and especially the proliferation of television documentary hybrids. Referring to texts within commercial television broadcasting, the term 'documentary hybrids' encompasses reality-based formats which range from those initially tagged 'Reality TV' in the late 80s (Cops [1989–], America's Most Wanted [1988–]), docusoaps (the British Airline [1982] or American The Real World [1992–]), reality game-shows or 'gamedocs' (the prototypical formats being Survivor [2000–] and Big Brother [1999–]), through to reality sitcoms (The Osbournes [2002–05]), situation documentaries (Wife Swap [2003–]) and other fact-fiction formats that may have a tenuous or conflicted relationship with reality.

Corner has argued that these formats represent a new function within documentary culture: 'documentary as diversion'.[5] Rather than suggesting that these television formats represent a complete break from the conventions of the documentary genre, he offers the useful term 'post-documentary' to suggest a broadening of documentary culture. These television formats thus represent one end of the spectrum of documentary and documentary-related media, although their popularity may have profound implications for the future development of the genre.

Neither postmodern skepticism nor the techniques of digital manipulation present documentary with its biggest future challenge. This will undoubtedly come from the requirement to reorient and refashion itself in an audio-visual culture where the dynamics of diversion and the aesthetics of performance dominate a greatly expanded range of popular images of the real.[6]

Although it is possible to trace their development back to the hand-held immediacy of cinéma vérité and Direct Cinema, and the later integration of video aesthetic into television documentary, these formats are more performative and playful in their representations. Their agenda is to entertain by integrating documentary material with the narrative structures and aesthetics of fictional genres such as game-shows and sitcoms. This popularising of documentary media, bringing reality formats back into prime-time television schedules, involves a transformation of many of the fundamental aspects of the genre itself. Their success means that new generations of audiences and film-makers have different expectations towards documentary (expectations that are the subject of intense debate within academia over their significance and longer-term implications).

A core aspect of television documentary hybrids is their naturalisation of reflexivity, particularly as part of the varieties of forms of participation they encourage on the part of audiences. Writing on the archetypal reality game-show Big Brother, for example, Andrejevic notes;

> As a media event, Big Brother assumes its audience to be highly media-literate. It is assumed that viewers know the show is constructed for television, that they are able to engage with it as a hybrid format, and that they are able to acknowledge it as a performance of the real. There are many moments of self-reflexivity built into the event, from the behind the scenes studio tours, through to the insider gossip on the Saturday show, and the on-screen discussions between the housemates about their experiences of being in front of the camera 24 hours a day.[7]

The audience is assumed to be 'sophisticated', at least in terms of their awareness of the constructed, entertainment-centred nature of such formats. They encourage direct forms of participation, auditioning for participants and allowing viewers' voting to decide aspects of their narratives, and assume that audiences are generally engaged with and supportive of broader discourses of surveillance.

The reflexivity evident within such television formats draws from that practised within more avant-garde or auteurist traditions of documentary, but it is naturalised as part of the broader practice and aesthetic of hybrid programming. There is a continual flagging of the presence of a camera crew (particularly through comments by participants, or the movement of the camera itself exaggerating a vérité aesthetic) or techniques such as video diary, which foreground a direct and intimate address to the audience. And there is an emphasis on a narrative simplicity presented through specific editing strategies (fast-paced montages set to music and emphasising spectacle) that continually foregrounds the act of mediation itself. Instead of operating to subversive effect, here self-reflexivity reinforces television's perpetual meta-commentary on itself as a medium. These techniques have informed documentary proper over the last two decades, combining with other forms of documentary practice, such as autobiography.

Autobiographical documentary has been an enduring strand of the documentary, part of a pattern of increasing subjectivity within audiovisual culture[8] sparked initially by the emergence of amateur film cultures with easy access to photographic technology and reinforced and broadened by the rise of interactive (digital) media centred on user-generated content. In a sense, these cultures all contribute to an obvious drift towards self-surveillance, as audiences engage in frenetic practices of capturing, manipulating and circulating images of their everyday lives. Documentary culture has been energised by such trends, as individual film-makers draw upon a sudden wealth of audiovisual material to construct narratives and arguments (see *Capturing the Friedmans* [Andrew Jarecki, 2003, USA] and *Grizzly Man* [Werner Herzog, 2005, USA]) and talented amateurs explore their own autobiographical archives (*Tarnation*, 2003, USA [Jonathan Caouette]).

The most interesting examples of autobiographical documentary, in terms of this discussion, are those Dovey terms 'klutz films'.[9] Here Dovey builds on Arthur's discussion of an 'aesthetics of failure', a distinctive strand of documentary where a film-maker constructs a narrative coherence centred on the failure to achieve a stated objective, such as a key interview, rather than an effort to present an overall social-political argument.[10] Drawing on the aesthetic traditions of cinéma vérité and Direct Cinema, this strand nevertheless questions the ability of the film-maker to escape a subjective perspective. Dovey discusses the work of film-makers such as Ross McElwee, Michael Moore, Alan Berliner and Nick Broomfield, who all develop on-screen personas that offer variations on that of a 'klutz'; 'a failure who makes mistakes and denies any mastery of the communicative process'.[11] It is important to reiterate that these are still extremely skilled professionals, and there is a key distinction to be made between an on-screen performance of disorganisation and naiveté, together with a deliberately non-confrontational and conversational interviewing style, and the evident skill which these film-makers apply to the creation of the final edited texts themselves.[12]

The overall aim of such films is not necessarily to build towards an ultimate revelation, or to engage with aspects of the social-historical world outside of the immediate concerns of their interviewees. The film-makers are instead focusing on their own subjective responses to their encounters, while providing the audience with space to pull these pieces to together, to accumulate information about the worldview and ideologies of subjects and make some (guided) conclusions. There is no less artistry here, but a superficially off-hand approach, saturated with reflexive commentary about the subjectivity of the documentary camera, and crucially often involving inflections of humour. As Dovey notes, it is perhaps not coincidental that all of the exemplars he discusses are male film-makers: 'This popularisation of self-referential reflexivity by male documentarists has occurred at precisely the same time that feminist and Third cinema advocates have championed a radical reflexivity as privileged political discourse.'[13]

One consequence is a veering away from the social and political arguments that have traditionally been the province of documentary (with the exception of Michael Moore). All of these film-makers look to 'create identification not through proclamations of authority but through its opposite: accounts of failure, clumsiness, confusion and ambivalence'.[14] The use of humour is integral to this practice, centred particularly on the actions of the on-screen persona interacting with interviewees. Moore's approach, particularly in the template for his own klutz persona in *Roger and Me* (1989), involves a more explicit use of irony and satire couched within sequences that offer a critique of neo-liberal economics (an approach which has attracted harsh critics).[15] This is a commentary inflected with autobiographical content from Moore, which serves to reinforce the moral authority of his rhetoric.[16]

Dovey positions the emergence of the klutz film-maker within broader cultural trends prompted by post-structuralist and postmodernist paradigms, arguing that:

> the desire for emotional connectivity, for a discourse of sentiment, can also be seen as a response to the confusion of postmodern living. As we experience ourselves as more and more unstable, chaotic and contradictory, as we experience a public sphere that holds no comfort, so our communicative acts depend upon the performance of more and more open, individual, 'authentic' versions of self.[17]

As noted above, such trends have been nurtured by the development of digital means of image gathering. The use of digital video cameras continues the trajectory begun with cinéma vérité and Direct Cinema, eroding distinctions between public and private space by allowing for an expansion of the documentary gaze into increasingly intimate areas of everyday life. The emergence of digital cameras, together with the capability of software packages such as Photoshop to play with commonsense notions of the indexical quality of photographic images, has led many commentators to claim that we have long entered a 'post-photographic' era. The paradox of a post-photographic era, however, is that there is both an increased awareness of the potential for the manipulation of photographic images *and* the desire for more authentic representations of the real. Fetveit, in fact, has argued that the appeal of television hybrids themselves is one response to this paradox, as audiences increasingly search for moments where the ability of the camera to capture reality can transcend any subsequent manipulation.[18]

All of the trends discussed above can be seen to inform the variety of documentary practices that incorporate humour in some form. There are some key patterns here (discussed below), but these are expressions of increasingly incestuous practices within the broader documentary culture, as individual film-makers and television producers experiment with different forms, freely combining modes and techniques from other genres to appeal to audiences who have broad and often contradictory expectations of such media.

KLUTZ DOCUMENTARY AND HYBRIDITY

While the 'klutz' tendency is well established within conventional documentary, *Super Size Me* (Morgan Spurlock, 2004, USA) demonstrates how this approach can be combined with a hybrid sensibility. At the core of *Super Size Me* is a stunt; director Spurlock decides to live for thirty days only on food from the McDonald's chain of restaurants, as part of an investigation into the impact of fast food on the health of Americans. He sets up some nominal conditions for his 'experiment', including enlisting the services of three doctors and his girlfriend to help record the physical and emotional toll on his life. The countdown until his thirty days are complete provides the basic narrative arc for the film, which also uses a variety of familiar aesthetic techniques.

Spurlock relies especially on an expanded video diary approach, using hand-held camcorders to record his everyday activities, often simply by holding the camera at arms length, in his lap, or placing it on a table or the dashboard of his car. The grainy, hand-held look and feel is the same aesthetic that saturates television hybrids. The same approach, but this time with a camera person to allow Spurlock to be more at ease in the frame, is used in the sequences within doctors' offices, domestic scenes with his girlfriend, vox-pops with Americans and occasional interview scenes with medical experts and fast-food spokespersons. Spurlock's personal journey is regularly interrupted by expositional sequences, as he provides basic background information about the size of the American fast-food industry and its assumed causal links to an obesity epidemic among the American population. These sequences use lots of colourful graphics and fast-paced editing, set to rock music and accompanied by Spurlock's sardonic and ironic voiceover commentary.

The film overall, however, is dominated by Spurlock's subjective account of his physical and emotional journey through his self-imposed experiment. The aim is obviously to reach an audience through building an emotional authenticity, rather than constructing a more conventional distanced objectivity towards his topic. The hybrid approach here allows for more everyday forms of humour, as an increasingly anxious Spurlock stumbles towards a threatened personal medical catastrophe, while he maintains an ironic and more reflective tone in voiceover (recorded in post-production). There is a clear underlying argument generated by the film, on the relationship between personal and corporate responsibility, but disguised as Spurlock's emotional journey towards everyday self-knowledge, with the film-maker offering himself as a proxy for the audience.

DOCUMENTARY AS COMEDIC PRACTICE

A contrasting approach comes from the work of Mark Lewis, a director who specialises in nature documentaries that play with audience expectations of this sub-genre. In an online interview with the BBC in 2005,[19] Lewis explained that key to his approach is to look for the banal, taken-for-granted animals and to celebrate their interactions with humans (rather than focus on 'A-list' animals from exotic locations). *Cane Toads: An Unnatural History* (Mark Lewis, 1988, Australia) was his first use of the approach and demonstrates some of the specific techniques that are central to his practice. *Cane Toads* is set in Australia, and documents the devastating impact that the introduction of the cane toad (intended as a form of pest control in the sugarcane industry) has had on the local fauna and flora. Eschewing a conventional voiceover, Lewis constructs his narrative from the voices of his interviewees, framed and countered by the apparent perspective of cane toads themselves. Instead of spectacular footage of a natural world untouched by humans, seamlessly edited into a romanticised anthropomorphic narrative of animal life cycles,[20] in *Cane Toads* we have a mosaic of anecdotes enthusiastically told by a cross-section of Australian society.

Lewis has chosen stories from everyday people who celebrate the oddities of cane toads, or who appear to share an affinity with toads themselves, and from scientific experts whose interest in the amphibians is framed as quirky, subjective or otherwise apparently at odds with a stereotypically scientific detachment. The result is a playful, layered set of perspectives, rather than the conventional intimate voyeurism of nature documentaries or the omnipotent authority of presenter-led texts from exemplars such as David Attenborough. The director emphasises the humour of interviewee's stories partly by framing each interviewee against a background of their social setting – in their own 'habitat' – as they speak directly to the camera. Scientific experts are encouraged to articulate the surprisingly emotive attachments which drive their research,

Cane Toads: The Conquest (2010): a somewhat bemused view of the human world

devotees of the toad relate their favourite anecdotes and an assortment of self-proclaimed nemeses vent their frustrations at the toad's placid but remorseless colonisation of the Australian ecosystem. Their intimate knowledge of cane toads is positioned as a marker of eccentricity and marginalisation within the local population.

To illustrate their stories, Lewis intersperses close-ups of cane toads, low-angle footage seemingly from their point of view, and dramatic reconstructions that are edited to include apparent 'reaction shots' from toads. The effect is to construct a somewhat bemused view of the human world from the perspective of the amphibians themselves.[21] The documentary's comic timing is enhanced through the strategic use of music, which serves to emphasise key points in the human's anecdotes and provide extravagant support for the on-screen 'performances' of the cane toads.

This playful approach captures the ambiguities and contradictions of the complex interrelationship between cane toads and Australians, who are variously curious, hostile, celebratory and exploitative of the invaders. This is a folklore approach to natural history, both educative and tongue-in-cheek. Lewis's achievement is to effectively expand the repertoire available to documentary film-

makers. Designed for an audience which is already overly familiar with the genre's modes of presentation, he has crafted a memorable account of what could easily have remained a minor subject. Here a playful approach to factual discourses broadens the appeal of the genre itself while deliberately engaging with a broader questioning of institutional voices.

American Movie: The Making of Northwestern (Chris Smith, 1999, USA) offers a another demonstration of contemporary humour-inflected documentary practice. Ostensibly a 'making of' documentary, *American Movie* is really the story of struggling Wisconsin film-maker Mark Borchardt, a thirty-three year old trying to realise his own version of the American Dream. Borchardt is a fast-talking optimist whose ambition to have a career as a feature-film director seems unlikely to be realised in the industrial wastelands of his hometown. His life story has pathos and there is a touch here of the focus on life's 'losers' that so strongly characterised the early wave of British docusoaps. This, in fact, provides some of the ambiguity of the film; as viewers we are unsure whether we should be laughing at Borchardt or empathising with his dreams.[22] Part of the humour of the film comes from the offbeat characters who make up his friends and family, all of whom are drafted into Borchardt's low-budget film-making ventures. Romney, in fact, suggests that *American Movie* operates almost as a 'docu-sitcom', or reality sitcom.[23] Especially key is the role played by Mike Schank, a childhood friend who seems quite slow and dependent on Borchardt for imagination. Together they serve almost as *American Movie*'s comedic double-act.

Middleton's discussion of the film focuses on specific editing techniques that are used to emphasise the comedic potential of these characters and their relationships. In particular he discusses a technique he calls 'cutting on the absurd'. Here specific points in a character's dialogue are treated as punchlines, created by a cut to another shot specifically for comedic effect and often highlighted by a shift in musical counterpoint. The effect is typically to construct a satiric perspective on characters in a documentary, by juxtaposing a character's discourse with 'footage that ambiguates, contradicts, undermines or just provides a broader context'.[24] In the case of *American Movie*, Borchardt's ambitions are constantly contrasted with the modesty of his surroundings and limited means to actually become a film-maker. His best friend Schank's acoustic guitar-playing provides a melancholic soundtrack, in playful juxtaposition with Borchardt's talkative energy.

MOCKUMENTARY

Comedic documentary practice can be difficult to distinguish from mockumentary, although mockumentary is a much broader and more established counter to discourses of sobriety. Mockumentary is closely referenced to the development of a broader fact-fiction continuum that encompasses documentary, television news and current affairs together with more explicitly hybrid forms. In simple terms, mockumentaries are fictional texts (from a range of different media) which employ a sustained appropriation of codes and conventions from this fact-fiction continuum. There is an inherent reflexivity to this appropriation through mockumentary's demonstration of how easy it is to fake non-fictional (and related) modes of representation.[25] Most examples of mockumentary, however, do not develop an explicit critique or commentary of such forms, and tend to be easily labelled by audiences as 'playful' rather than subversive.

It is a measure of the complexity of mockumentary discourse that it has been able to be employed to a variety of ends by different media producers, across different media. One strong pattern, for example, within cinematic mockumentary is a range of non-comedic mockumentaries, or those which employ the mockumentary form for dramatic purposes. This tendency has been used to particular effect to revitalise horror (*The Blair Witch Project* [Daniel Myrick and Eduardo Sanchez, 1999]), science fiction (*Cloverfield* [Matt Reeves, 2008]) and even superhero (*Chronicle* [Josh Trank, 2012]) storytelling conventions.

The bulk of mockumentary practice has clearly emerged from within parodic and satiric traditions, producing a broad range of mockumentaries reflective of the complexity of parodic discourse itself. Parody typically exhibits an ambivalence towards its target, offering both a mocking of the text that it references and an effective reinforcement of its authority; what Hutcheon refers to as the 'paradox' of parody.[26] This, however, does not necessarily suggest that parody is only ever parasitic, nor that it does not have the potential to be subversive or transgressive – in the sense of directly challenging or transcending the codes and conventions that it references. *David Holzman's Diary* (Jim McBride, 1967), for example, anticipates the practices of autobiographical and cinéma vérité documentary, which were still emerging at the time, while *C'est arrivé près de chez vous* [*Man Bites Dog*] (Rémy Belvaux, André Bonzel and Benoît Poelvoorde, 1992) endures as a devastating critique of the ethics of documentary film-making.

Mockumentary texts can range from a superficial referencing of non-fiction and related forms to densely layered and innovative textual constructions looking to engage with audiences in a multitude of ways. Exemplars of the discourse typically construct a complex set of potential engagements for audiences, drawing upon a range of intertextual references and seeking to engage with viewers' knowledge of wider visual culture and key social-political discourses. They establish characters with which the audience can identify, and develop narratives which do not depend purely upon knowledge of other texts in order to be successful. In general, mockumentary provides for audiences a number of specific forms of play, encouraging viewers to engage with their own detailed expectations of a continuum of fact-fiction forms. Mockumentary discourse deliberately engages in particular with documentary's rhetorical address to its audience, transforming documentary's call to action into a *call to play*.

Among the more interesting mockumentary texts are those that blur the line between obviously fictional sequences and those that closely reference the social-historical, where audiences can find it difficult to separate the performed from the actual. *Borat: Cultural Learnings of America for Make Benefit Glorious Nation of Kazakhstan* (Larry Charles, 2006) offers a useful demonstration of how a fluidity of modes can be central to the manner in which a mockumentary creates humour, by presenting scenes which are playfully ambiguous in their relationship to reality.

Borat takes its cue from klutz films, pretending to be a 'documentary' by inept Kazakh film-maker 'Borat Sagdiyev' (Sacha Baron Cohen). Sagdiyev's film begins as an exploration of American culture, and eventually turns into a romantic quest for Pamela Anderson. The bulk of the film, in-between these scripted elements, presents a series of encounters between Cohen (in character as Sagdiyev) and Americans who do not appear to realise that he is performing. At its heart the film involves an innovative blending of mockumentary performance and a documenting of these encounters. Drawing upon the conventions of television stunt comedy, as well as longer traditions of the 'trickster',[27] Cohen's Borat persona tests the patience of the Americans he meets by appearing as a bricolage of Eastern European traits and characteristics. Apparently ignorant of American cultural norms, socially inept and somewhat 'primitive' in his morals and attitudes,[28] Borat forces everyday Americans to respond by patiently explaining the inconsistencies and contradictions of American culture. In the process, they often reveal their own prejudices and questionable attitudes towards the European Other.[29] The tension between modes of documentary and mockumentary defines the film's distinctive approach to humour, often creating deliberately ambiguous scenes that mesh these modes in expected ways. The audience is often left confused about which scenes are completely scripted, and which involve people who are not complicit with Cohen's performance.

THE PRICE OF 'FLUIDITY'

All of the above examples suggest how the documentary project, partly codified by John Grierson in the 1930s and 40s, has become increasingly fluid. Film-makers and television producers have an expanded fact-fiction continuum to draw upon, a palette that includes documentary hybrids, documentary comedy and even mockumentary. Despite their distinctions, these forms share an openness to more playful modes of representing reality, strategies which in turn often require more from their audiences. In particular, such examples of contemporary documentary culture perhaps demand a more critical form of reading and interpretation from viewers (there remains much research to be done in this area).

The trend towards incorporating humour within the broad continuum of fact-fiction forms thus also involves a challenge to, and potential drift away from, established documentary ethical practice. Borat has been criticised by many of its participants for what they perceive to be exploitation of their gullibility.[30] Likewise Mark Lewis's approach walks a fine line between providing a space for people to reveal their enthusiasms and presenting interviewees as eccentrics allowing viewers to confirm themselves as more sane and normal in their own attitudes towards the animal kingdom. American Movie, in turn, could easily have lapsed into open ridicule of its subject, following the worst traditions of television documentary hybrids, but for the efforts of director Chris Smith and producer Sarah Price to construct a complexity of perspectives towards Mark Borchardt's ambitions. They closely involved Borchardt in the editing process for the film (and he responded by actively participating in its promotion). The

challenge faced by all of the directors discussed here is how to strategically use humour in ways that prompt the audience to rethink their own attitudes, rather than the more conservative response of simply laughing at subjects. As Brian Winston acknowledges, in his call for the exploration of post-Griersonian, irreverent and satiric documentary forms of expression: 'Once the film-maker is liberated from implications of actuality and creativity, then ethical behaviour becomes even more crucial than it was previously.'[31]

NOTES

1. Bill Nichols, *Representing Reality: Issues and Concepts in Documentary* (Bloomington: Indiana University Press, 1991).

2. Dave Saunders, *Direct Cinema: Observational Documentary and the Politics of the Sixties* (London: Wallflower Press, 2007), p. 189.

3. See Chapter 2.6; Chapter 2.10.

4. Donna Haraway, *Simians, Cyborgs and Women: The Reinvention of Nature* (London: Routledge, 1991), pp. 188–96.

5. John Corner, 'Performing the Real: Documentary Diversions', *Television & New Media* vol. 3 no. 3, August 2002.

6. Ibid., p. 267.

7. Mark Andrejevic, *Reality TV: The Work of Being Watched* (Lanham, MD: Rowman & Littlefield, 2004), p. 485.

8. Michael Renov, *The Subject of Documentary* (Minneapolis: University of Minnesota Press, 2004).

9. Jon Dovey, *Freakshow: First Person Media and Factual Television* (London: Pluto Press, 2000).

10. Renov, *The Subject of Documentary*.

11. Dovey, *Freakshow*, p. 27.

12. Stella Bruzzi, *New Documentary: A Critical Introduction* (London: Routledge, 2000), p. 172.

13. Dovey, *Freakshow*, p. 54.

14. Ibid., p. 36.

15. David Hardy and Jason Clarke, *Michael Moore is a Big Fat Stupid White Man* (New York: HarperCollins, 2005).

16. J. Lane, *The Autobiographical Documentary in America* (Madison: University of Wisconsin Press, 2002).

17. Dovey, *Freakshow*, pp. 53–4.

18. A. Fetveit, 'Reality TV in the Digital Era: A Paradox in Visual Culture?', *Media Culture Society* no. 21, p. 6.

19. BBC, *Storyville – Animal Magic: The Films of Mark Lewis*, 2005, http://www.bbc.co.uk/bbcfour/documentaries/storyville/animalmagic.shtml. Accessed January 2009.

20. Derek Bousé, *Wildlife Films* (Philadelphia: University of Pennsylvania Press, 2000).

21. Mark Taussig, 'Cane Toads: An Unnatural History', *American Anthropologist* vol. 92 no. 4, December 1990, pp. 1110–11.

22. Paul Arthur, 'American Movie', *Film Comment* vol. 35 no. 6, November/December 1999, pp. 78–9; Jason Middleton,

'Documentary Comedy', *Media International Australia incorporating Culture and Policy* no. 104, August 2002, pp. 55–66.

23. J. Romney, 'American Nightmare', *New Statesman*, 3 July 2000.

24. Middleton, 'Documentary Comedy', p. 61.

25. J. Roscoe and C. Hight, *Faking It: Mock-Documentary and the Subversion of Factuality* (Manchester: Manchester University Press, 2001); C. Hight, *Television Mockumentary: Reflexivity, Satire and a Call to Play* (Manchester: Manchester University Press, 2010).

26. Linda Hutcheon, *A Theory of Parody: The Teachings of Twentieth-Century Art Form* (Chicago: University of Illinois Press, 2000), p. 68.

27. N. Kononenko and S. Kukharenko, 'Borat the Trickster: Folklore and the Media', *Slavic Review* vol. 67 no. 1, 2008.

28. D. Wallace, 'Hyperrealizing *Borat* with the Map of the European "Other"', *Slavic Review* vol. 67 no. 1, 2008, pp. 35–49.

29. J. Muravchiti, 'Borat!', *Commentary* no. 123, 2007, p. 1; L. Torchin, 'Cultural Learnings of Borat Make for Benefit of Glorious Study of Documentary', *Film & History* no. 38, p. 1.

30. Mark Cenite, 'Ethical Learnings from Borat on Informed Consent for Make Benefit Film and Television Producers', *Journal of Mass Media Ethics* vol. 24 no. 1, March 2009.

31. Brian Winston, *Claiming the Real: The Griersonian Documentary and its Legitimations* (London: BFI, 1995), p. 258.

PART THREE:
Documentary Horizons

3.1 Eastwards

ABÉ MARK NORNES

The western urban social necessity that engendered the cinema in the late nineteenth century was felt everywhere as an integral element of the West's overal cultural presence. It needed to be negotiated and absorbed; and absorbed it quickly was to the point where it cannot be said to have a western 'heartland', however much Europe is imagined as the centre point whence is measured the rest of the world. And this is as true of documentary as it is of all else.

In December 1896, François-Constant Girel journeyed to Asia lugging the newly invented Lumière brothers camera, accompanied by August Lumière's acquaintance Inabata Katsutaro. After a brief visit to South-east Asia, he made his way to Japan. Girel was followed by Lumière camera-man Gabriel Veyre, who backtracked Girel's journey; he spent 1898–99 in Japan, before hopping to French Indo-China. Over in India, Marius Sestier conducted the first Indian screening in a hotel in June 1896. And then, in the Philippines, Spaniard Antonio Ramos showed the first films in Manila before moving to Shanghai when the Americans took power. He was preceded by James Ricalton, who probably showed the first film in China at a teahouse using the Edison projector. By the turn of the century or shortly thereafter, the first Asian film-makers took up the cameras themselves. Such is the dawn of cinema in Asia – first by Europeans, with Asians waiting.

This chapter takes on the impracticable task of representing 'The East' in this hefty *tour d'horizon*, so where else to start but at the horizon with that cinematic sun peeking out from behind the curvature of the Earth? Yet the original positioning of the chapter itself, in the larger context of the book-in-hand, was going to be towards the end of the volume – the editor being seized with a vision of 'documentary's heartlands', which he firmly saw as being Britain and its white colonies, North America and France. Had he not been persuaded otherwise, documentary was going to be represented by a tree – its roots ontological questions leading to a canopy of branches and eventually arriving at the other horizon: 'beyond documentary's heartlands'. This overtly Darwinian structure would have clearly reflected what has been called the ur-text for enquiries into colonial and neo-colonial representations of non-western cultures,[1] Hegel's *Introduction to the Philosophy of History*. A quote sets us on our way:

> World history goes from East to West: as Asia is the beginning of world history, so Europe is simply its end. In world history there is an absolute East, *par excellence* (whereas the geographical term 'east' is in itself entirely relative); for although the earth is a sphere, history makes no circle around that sphere. On the contrary, it has a definite East which is Asia. It is here that the external physical sun comes up, to sink in the West: and for that same reason it is in the West that the inner Sun of self-consciousness rises, shedding a higher brilliance.[2]

Thus, a similar philosophy was initially shaping this volume's *tour d'horizon*, ranging over an imaginary geography. That passage from Hegel is preceded by the strong image of a blind person that suddenly gains sight, and is dumbfounded at the dawn's brilliant light; he then begins to take up the objects he finds about him to construct a building (perhaps a movie theatre) by the use of his own 'inner sun' – and when he contemplates it in the evening, he values it higher than that first external sun. However, we must reject a vision of Asian spectators being dazzled by the light coming from those first cameras, that product of European genius, and then being inspired to pick up the machine themselves (or sometimes reverse engineer it!) to build their own indigenous film cultures, local cinemas they inevitably compare unfavourably to the shining example of Europe. In such an account they lag behind European progress, technologically and aesthetically, because geographical distance from the heartlands is both spatial *and temporal*. This yields an historical narrative for the dawn of Asian documentary, repeated in every single country across the region. It is paradigmatic of the situation of Asian documentary film-makers (and their historians): they are always relegated to the waiting room of history, as Dipesh Chakrabarty has so eloquently put it.[3]

In fact, Chakrabarty's book, entitled *Provincializing Europe*, informs my own (alternative) tour of Asian documentary.

It would be easy to move from country to country and chart out the historical sequence starting with the Lumière/Edison arrival scene, followed by the colonial propaganda, then liberation and the subsequent Griersonian documentary of the nation-state (first on celluloid, then on television), ending with the liberatory videos of independent video artists. This, however, would be yet another account tied to the historicism that 'made modernity or capitalism look not simply global but rather as something that became global *over time*, by originating in one place (Europe) and then spreading outside it'.[4] Nationalist historians in Asia are clearly bothered by the implications of the conventional historiography. This is why, for example, the post-revolutionary histories of Vietnamese documentary ignore the early films Girel and Gabriel Veyre shot for the Lumières (such a perfectly Hegelian name!), or all the imperial propaganda produced by the French, or the USIS documentaries made under the Americans in collaboration with Filipino tutors. Thus, all this history is elided to celebrate 'the birth of documentary' marked by *Resolve to Fight, Resolve to Win: Dien Bien Phu* [*Quyet chien, Quyet than Dien Bien Phu*] (1954–55). Of course, they fail to mention that the Vietnamese directors Nguyen Tien Loi, Nguyen Hong Nghi and Nguyen Phu Can collaborated with Roman Karmen (and, of course, only the Karmen-produced compilation *Vietnam on the Road to Victory* [1955] made it to the West).

In their revolutionary situation, it was easy for Vietnamese historians to erase the colonial-era documentary simply by ignoring it. However, their conundrum is felt across across the region. The typical strategy of Asia film histories starts with the arrival of cinema (almost invariably in the luggage of European businessmen) and the (subsequent) first film created at the hands of an Asian entrepreneur. This initiates an unforgiving temporality marked by the turn-of-the-century arrival scene, one in which Asian film-makers can only be seen to be perpetually trying to keep up with the West.

Needless to say, such nationalist historiographies must be critiqued and avoided at all costs. These historians have internalised the historicism of progressive history. My goal here is to map out the contours of Asian documentary, tour around its vastness and provide some sense for alternative ways of thinking about the 'now' of Asian documentary (as opposed to its 'not yet'[5]) and perhaps rethink our understanding of documentary itself in the course of things – drawing a new map of the documentary world where Europe has been provincialised.

The first strategy we might try is to disjoint the usual time-line. Looking across the breadth of the globe, the various national documentary histories do seem marked by the same progression: from actualities to newsfilm to Griersonian approaches to Direct Cinema and cinéma vérité, to a baffling heterogeneity of approaches spread across a variety of formats. This roughly echoes the previous structure of this book and, indeed, we seem to find this sequencing everywhere we look. However, a look at the time-line in Japan roots up some surprises. Auguste Lumière's good friend, the Japanese businessman Inabata Katsutaro actually showed the first film; it's easy enough to see Girel as a collaborator – or perhaps little more than a tourist. Two decades later in February 1927, a group of leftwing activists established the Proletarian Film League of Japan (or Prokino), nearly two years before the renowned Worker's Film and Photo League.[6] Furthermore, the subversive found-footage montage we identify with de Antonio was the foundation of Kamei Fumio's remarkable films of the China War (1937–41), as well as the basis for Kamei's imprisonment just before Pearl Harbor.[7] And the principles of observational cinema were explored by Hani Susumu five years before *Primary* (1960) in his *E o kaku kodomotachi* [*Children Who Draw*] (1955), along with assorted articles and books.[8]

I could go on, but it wouldn't prove much. This kind of 'search for firsts' remains trapped in the logic of historicism. And it is refreshing to see writers like Winston and Musser challenging it in this book. However, inserting the East into the mix highlights the ideological and political stakes of the search. There is the further danger of concluding from such firsts that they indicate some pure indigenous modes of documentary, when, in fact, those Japanese film-makers from Prokino on were all driven by notions of social justice rooted in western philosophy. It is safe to say that no Asian documentarist has been untouched by the Enlightenment. Searching for 'firsts' is, basically, pointless.

At the same time, Chakrabarty argues that these categories of political modernity are braided with 'other ways of worlding' which interrupt the totalising thrusts of historicism. Redrawing the map of documentary, we might look to Asian films that bring these two into a tension

Children Who Draw (1955): the principles of observational cinema were explored by Hani Susumu five years before *Primary*

through innovative aesthetic strategies or experimentation in embodying temporalities that are anything but empty and homogeneous, to use Benjamin's terms. One thinks of the films of Ogawa Productions in Japan (especially *Heta buraku* [Heta Village, 1973] and *Sennen kizami no hidokei* [*Sundial Carved with a Thousand Years of Notches*, 1986]), Filipino film-maker Kidlat Tahimik (*Why is Yellow Middle of Rainbow?*, 1981–94), Takamine Go from Okinawa (*Okinawa Chirudai*, 1976) or China's Mao Chenyu (*Shenyan xiang* [*Ximaojia Universe*, 2009]). Rather than the search for untouched Otherness that is clearly the desire driving Sol Worth and John Adair's *Through Navajo Eyes*,[9] this kind of analysis would concentrate on films that self-consciously embody that braiding of temporalities, that make it their main theme. The problem is that it too easily slips into facile nativisms or orientalisms – on the part of the film-makers or the historians.[10] This avenue must be chosen with great care.

Alternatively, we could try to remap the documentary by highlighting the work of sojourners. True, there are figures like the eminent director Lester James Peries, who consciously helped import Griersonian documentary to Sri Lanka, returning from England in 1952 for a job in the newly established Government Film Unit of Ceylon. (He swiftly quit the documentary for an impressive career in feature film-making because, according to his wife, he felt it had 'more truth, more freedom and more reality'.[11]) However, there are plenty of film-makers that confound the clean borders between Europe and Asia, their practice ranging across the Earth. Kidlat Tahimik made his contribution to Third Cinema by documenting his travel to far-flung places like Germany and Monument Valley. There are film-makers who enjoyed profound study-abroad experiences and returned home to change the course of documentary in their home countries, such as Kamei Fumio (Leningrad/Japan), Nick Deocampo (New York/Philippines), Apichatpong Weerasethakul (Chicago/Thailand). We must not forget exiled film-makers that live between worlds, such as Rithy Panh, who left the killing fields of Cambodia for Paris (S-21, *la machine de mort Kmhère rouge* [S-21: *The Khmer Rouge Killing Machine*, 2003]) and Soda Kazuhiro (*Campaign*, 2003), who moved from Japan to New York.

We should also note Asian documentary sojourners who chose routes that avoided Europe altogether. For example, there was a productive circulation between the proletarian film-makers of Tokyo, Shanghai and Seoul in the 1930s. And in the post-war era, Adachi Masao and Wakamatsu Koji produced one of the most extreme guerrilla films ever made in a circuit between Lebanon and Japan; the opening intertitles of their *Sekigun/PFLP: Sekai senso sengen* [*Red Army/PFLP: Declaration of World War*] (1971) loudly declare 'The best form of propaganda is armed struggle.' This was their attempt to bring their home-grown materialist theory of 'landscape' (*fukei*) into practice.[12] More

recently, film-makers like Kidlat Tahimik (Philippines), Fen Yan (China), Wu Wenguang (China), Kim Dong-won (Korea), Byun Youngju (Korea) and Wu Yii-feng (Taiwan) had life-changing, career-making encounters with Japan's Ogawa Shinsuke just before his early death of cancer.

In contrast, there are those Asian film-makers who made prominent contributions to western documentary history. The works of figures like Ono Yoko, Iimura Takahiko or Oe Masanori are often claimed for American film history. As for Oe, he was one of the founders of Newsreel and collaborated with Marvin Fishman on films like *No Game* (1968). Historians' default treatment of these film-makers is to identify them with American film, or sometimes simply New York cinema. For example, Wheeler Dixon discusses Iimura and Ken Jacobs in the same breath in *Exploding Eye: A Re-visionary History of 1960s American Experimental Cinema*.[13] We should foreground their presence at the heart of western film culture, avoid folding them into the historicism that erases their sojourn and, rather, highlight this geographic circulation to blur boundaries and redraw the map that emphasises the geographic distance and supposed temporal lag between the West and the rest.

Clearly, a major obstacle to redrawing the map is translation. Achieving a more nuanced history of all the film-makers and films gestured to above is exceedingly difficult absent the translation of both films and writings. Language acts as a bottleneck in the traffic of the film world. The English-language 'heartlands' of documentary are notoriously monoglotal, and those who do know foreign languages speak only European tongues. This turns Europe into a linguistic echo chamber, where the historicist narratives of documentary reverberate, replicating themselves ad infinitum and breeding an indifference to other histories that would complicate their world.

How else to explain the missed opportunity of the precious multi-volume *Encyclopedia of the Documentary Film*,[14] which – despite plenty of information in English and multilingual formats – misses nearly all the major pioneers in Asian documentary, including the likes of Kidlat Tahimik (Philippines), Wu Wenguang (China), Byun Young-ju (Korea) and Anand Patwardan (India). This is a book that projects the comprehensiveness of the moniker 'encyclopedia' yet eschews an entry on India, one of the largest producers of documentary in the world, for a single biography of feature film-maker Satyajit Ray (which doesn't even mention Ray's documentaries)! On the other hand, there are several pages of information on Louis Malle's *Phantom India* (1969) and Robert Gardner's *Forest of Bliss* (1986). Disengaged from the issue of translation, *Encyclopedia of Documentary Film* is reminiscent of the brilliant building Hegel's blind man constructs through his 'inner Sun of self-consciousness'. It is a magnificent work on a very flawed foundation.

Moreover, as I argued in *Cinema Babel: Translating Global Cinema*,[15] a close look at actual translation practices reveals a lot about the inequality of languages in translation flows. From the perspective of much of the world, the documentary scenes of Europe and North America appear hermetically sealed – put another way, provincial. While film-makers around the globe are deeply familiar with the history of European and North American documentary, the typically parochial film-makers from those regions are remarkably disinterested in learning about their colleagues. A side-effect of historicism is that an enormous amount of information is translated, films subtitled and then transported to other parts of the world from Europe, but the barest of trickles flows towards that bright inner light illuminating the 'heartlands' of documentary.

This would be the perfect time to stop and ask what to do with Grierson. It is probably no exaggeration to say that most documentary in Asia has, historically speaking, been 'Griersonian'. But it would also be rather wrong to say this – historically inaccurate, if you will. It is true that most documentaries from the 1930s to recent memory have used voiceover narration, incorporated fictional strategies, served governments (foreign or domestic – who else in Asia could afford film-making in the age of celluloid?), concentrated on victims and assumed films could change the world, while – as Brian Winston puts it – fleeing from social meaning. These are, indeed, the hallmarks of the cinema we associate with the British producer, but to subsume all such film-making practices under the sign 'Grierson' is a prototypically historicist move. It positions the British documentary movement as a 'dawn' whose light enflames the hearts of documentary film-makers across the empire, and then the world. Alternatively, it is a root sending up a sturdy tree trunk from which branches spread across the sky … or the root of a particularly aggressive weed that swiftly blankets the Earth; take your pick.

True, the Griersonian method was translated to different parts of the world. While most readers might take this in the metaphorical sense, I believe it behooves us to constantly turn to the actual translations of these ideas. Doing so will bring out the full complexity of these interactions. Consider the Japanese case, which I unpack and analyse at great length in an entire chapter of *Cinema Babel*.[16]

As in most countries in the world, Japan started with actualities and newsreels, before longer and more complex forms of non-fiction appeared on the scene in the 1920s and 30s. There were early experimental documentaries, shot both by amateurs and famous intellectuals like philosopher Nakai Masakazu. The first feature-length documentaries were hybrid speech films, produced at the coming of sound, called montage films, but these were joined by expedition films, war records, science films and PR films for Japan's imperial adventures on the continent. Then, as the war in China escalated at the end of the 30s, film-makers turned to a more expository mode with synch sound and a mingling of scripted action, interview and

documentary footage. Kamei Fumio made his city trilogy: the strongly observational *Shanghai* (1938), the city symphony *Peking* (1938) and the subversively edited (and ultimately suppressed) *Tatakau heitai* [*Fighting Soldiers*] (1939). Kamei and other film-makers swiftly elaborated non-fiction cinema into what appears to be Griersonian documentary just as Paul Rotha's *Documentary Film* took the film scene by storm.[17] Within a short while, four competing translations appeared and spawned debates in the pages of journals and on the film studio lots. Before this flurry of translation activity he was, basically, unknown.

On the face of it, the Rotha translation evidences Grierson's influence. However, the story is far more complicated. First, it is significant that the Japanese film-makers began making their 'Griersonian' documentaries *before* the British Embassy screened the British movement's work. When Kamei finally read Rotha (to this day, no one ever talks about Grierson in Japan), he was mainly happy to see that people thought like they did over on the other side of the world.

There might be another reason for this consonance. Looking closely at the Japanese translations, one sees that – thanks to both intense censorship of Rotha's more political ideas and also to remarkably bad translation – Japanese film-makers were reading a Rotha cut to the measure of their desires. Every sentence had problems, and many of these problems involved projecting local understandings of documentary into Rotha's text. But these impoverished, competing versions were also remarkably productive, though not exactly the book read in Great Britain. This demonstrates how the translation of words can only imperfectly overcome the barriers that language difference throws up to the supposedly free circulation of ideas and the films they inform. It calls for a renovation in the way we think of western 'influence'.

That Japanese film-makers produced Griersonian documentary without knowing Grierson suggests some provocative implications for anyone interested in the non-fiction form and its histories, whether in Asia or beyond. 'Griersonian documentary' should be dropped for neutral terms like 'expository' for much of the world. Should we do so, we will stop seeing an idea take root in Europe and branch across the world through direct influence, and see figures like Kamei and Grierson as contemporaries living in very different temporalities. The decisive difference is that Grierson had (and has) the British Empire at his back, so his blinding sun rose and never set, at least in the West. And as for Kamei, he's left in the waiting room of history. It is stunning, though unsurprising, that so few western experts of documentary know this incredible film-maker.

This brings me to the issue of 'The East' *as a region* – which, as Hegel reminds us, is a direction and not a territory. In asking for a chapter that accounts for Asia, the editor of this volume admitted that, 'putting these areas together only makes sense geographically'. Indeed, geographically speaking this chapter purports to 'cover' three-fifths of the world's land mass where half the human race resides. As Prasanjit Duara writes in his recent essay 'Asia Redux',[18] this means that any idea of Asia must be marked by 'flexibility and pluralism'. So let us loosen 'Asia' from its cartographic moorings and consider what Asian documentary is, and has been, and what it is now becoming.

Duara's essay argues for a new emerging conception of Asia in this post-Cold War moment. He quotes Henri Lefebvre to set a basic premise: that 'powerful systems such as capitalism create the space they require'.[19] Capitalism itself drives energies across national borders and it easily traverses regions. It is a de-territorialising force, particularly in its present neo-liberal incarnation. Documentary tends to have an ambivalent relationship to capital, as it clearly does not lend itself to capitalism's hunger for profit, while proving to be a ubiquitous tool of centripetal nationalist aspirations. Wherever one looks across the Asian region, from the 1910s on, documentary has served as a key mechanism to solicit identification and integration, whether it is with an empire, a nation, or a supra-national body like the 'proletariat'.

Documentary cinema was left untouched by these intellectual currents. Quite the contrary, it served colonial masters almost exclusively and there probably was no conception of 'Asian documentary' per se. However, as Japan's ambitions grew and its territories expanded, so too did an intensifying rhetoric around the idea of Asian cinema. In the early to mid-1930s, the map was directional: Japanese critics and bureaucrats spoke of 'nanpo' (southward) and 'hokuho' (northward) films. The former conceived of cinema sweeping across Taiwan, then a colony, and to its protectorates in the South Pacific; the latter projected across Korea and Sakhalin, deep into the continent. As Japan barrelled towards world war, the rhetoric transformed into a broadly inclusive vision of Asia – most of which would belong to Japan. At this point, and I can only speak to the Japanese context, the first significant conceptualisation of an 'Asian cinema' appeared in a book called *Ajia Eiga no Sozo oyobi Kensetsu* (*The Creation and Construction of Asian Cinema*, 1940), which was published months before Pearl Harbor. A book like Ichikawa's was inevitable at this point in time, precisely because it had become possible to imagine such a thing as 'Asian cinema'. The proof was in the films which, aside from their host of pleasures, documented the emergence of a heady Asian modernity of bustling urban spaces filled with cafés, smoky cabarets, smart fashion, crime and money. Movie theatres were a key part of this newly built environment, significant for the buildings themselves as well as the celebratory documents they featured inside. These documents – both fictive and documentary – were projected across the Asian region in every which direction. Naturally, this has an ugly edge as

well, as Japan actively took up the task of creating and constructing Asian cinema as it colonised most of the region.

Under Japanese imperialism's modernisation of institutions, cinema benefited greatly. Documentary film achieved uncommon prestige in Japan and its territories throughout the 1930s and early 40s, precisely because it served imperial projects in such a spectacular fashion. Wherever the Japanese military or settlers went, standing studios were appropriated and new ones built. The industry was infused with capital and, when the war dragged on, the industrial structures were nationalised and rationalised, but the flow of film stock and finished prints was relatively protected until the very end. The prestige of documentary even infected the feature film. If a global characteristic of documentary in this era was fictionalisation and re-enactment, a local variation was the widespread incorporation of documentary convention by feature film-makers. And because of this prestige, the Japanese-language writings on documentary from this era are incomparably richer than the English-language archive in both size and depth. There are many specialised journals and books, but the topic was also broached in the popular press and by major writers and philosophers. This was all brought to a close shortly before the atomic bomb laid waste to Nagasaki.

In the rubble of the various film industries, the old colonial powers reinserted themselves and busied themselves with the resurrection of film units and bureaus in places like Saigon, Manila, Seoul, Taipei and Jakarta (although the only episode in this important story known in the West is the last one, and then only because Joris Ivens's name is attached to it). This all sorted out, with varying degrees of violence, as the post-war, post-colonial flux gave way to the certainties of Cold War nationalisms. With few exceptions (mainly rabble-rousing communists and avant-garde artists in Japan), the documentary served the nation-state, capitalist industrial expansion, or, typically, both. In fact, one of the largest producers across the region became the USIS, the propaganda wing of the United States State Department.

A renewed idea of 'Asian cinema' emerged in the mid-1950s, when studio heads Nagata (from Daiei in Japan) and the Shaw brothers (Hong Kong) spearheaded the Motion Picture Producers Association of South-east Asia and its yearly event, the South-east Asian Film Festival (which was shortly thereafter changed to Asia Film Festival).[20] This was a self-consciously Cold War initiative, as countries like the newly formed North Korea and the People's Republic of China were excluded. Their goal was to promote distribution and exchange of personnel within 'free Asia'.

Ironically, the supra-regional interchange between the West and its Cold War allies hardly helped Asian filmmakers, as only a handful of auteurs like Kurosawa and Ray managed any success at cracking those markets. In the era of Bandung and ASEAN, this indifference enabled film-makers in Asia to think and act regionally. However, if we may speak of an emergent 'Asian cinema', the idea of 'Asian documentary' is another problem. The Asia Film Festival was all about the fiction film, which rode capitalism's de-territorialising energies wherever it could. Non-fiction film, tied as it was to national projects, never enjoyed this intra-regional circulation. It was a cinema, after all, for captive audiences. Thus, there was no 'Asian documentary' during the second half of the twentieth century.

Thankfully, the situation changed drastically with the end of the Cold War and we are seeing Asian documentary coalesce before our very eyes. In the post-Cold War situation, writes Duara, 'Regionalism has clearly strengthened, emerging as an intermediate zone between the deterritori-alizing impulses of capitalism and the territorial limits of nationalism.'[21] While neo-liberalism is inventing novel forms of exploitation across Asia (which documentarists are dutifully documenting), it is no doubt an exciting era that leaves absorption or rejection for 'interconnection and encounter'.[22]

I want to conclude by looking closely at one such encounter, or rather series of encounters, that vastly influenced the current situation while providing a barometer of its steady development. It took place in the northern mountains of Japan in 1989: the Yamagata International Documentary Film Festival, the first of its kind in Asia.

As organisers planned the festival, they watched the Berlin Wall fall and the massacre in Tiananmen Square take place. Huge changes were afoot, and the implications for documentary were tantalising but obscure. The festival was organised by the local city with the help of Ogawa Shinsuke, whose collective had been living and filming in a nearby village for over fifteen years. This was the most unlikely of locations for a documentary film festival, but with a healthy budget they were able to invite Jon Jost

(USA), Robert Kramer (France/USA), Marceline Loridan (France), Nestor Almendros (Cuba/USA), Johan van der Keuken (The Netherlands), Monica Flaherty (USA) and many others. Joris Ivens was to come, but he passed away several months before the festival.

Most of those film-makers were represented in the international competition, but not a single Asian film-maker made the cut. This was distressing to the organisers, so they held a panel discussion to enquire into the state of documentary in Asia. The panelists included Tsuchimoto Noriaki (Japan), Stephen Teo (Malaysia), Nick Deocampo (Philippines), Teddie Co (Philippines), Zarul Albakri (Malaysia), (Peggy) Chiao Hsiung-ping (Taiwan), Kong Su-Chang (South Korea), Manop Udomdej (Thailand) and Kidlat Tahimik (Philippines), with Hong Ki-Seong (South Korea) and Tian Zhuangzhuang (mainland China) unable to attend for political reasons. Posing the question, 'Why are there no Asian films in the competition?' Ogawa asked all the representatives to talk about the situation in their respective countries. It lasted more than a day, with story after story about the political and economic obstacles confronting documentary film-makers. At the end of a long day, people boiled with both frustration and the determination to work together somehow and do something about their situation. At the same time, the historical nature of their gathering became clear and, near the end, Kidlat Tahimik invoked the Oberhausen Manifesto and proposed a declaration of their own. At the end of the festival, they had a press conference where they signed it. Here is an excerpt of the Yamagata Manifesto:

> We, the Asian Film-makers present here, at the Yamagata International Documentary Film Festival '89, call attention to the sad absence of any Asia film in the competition ... We ask then in earnest ... why are the documentaries 'of quality and of interest' that enter the international exchange of information mainly in the hands of those countries who have the material resources to realize these films? We note, with regret, that there exist many obstacles to the opportunities for our film visions to be produced and disseminated in the real world dominated by political and market motivations. We acknowledge, with sadness, that these institutional roadblocks originate from a complex mix of third-world realities as well as international imbalances. We accept, with concern, that these cannot be eradicated overnight. But we believe that these obstacles can be overcome only with concerted efforts by ourselves, the Asian filmmakers, for a start ... with support from the energies generated at international gatherings like YIDFF, committed to the belief that independent social and personal documentaries are invaluable to present and future generations. Therefore, we the Asian filmmakers present here, declare our commitment to maintain a network of

Yamagata International Documentary Festival: not a single Asian film-maker made the cut. This was distressing to the organisers, so they held a panel discussion to enquire into the state of documentary in Asia

Asian Filmmakers sharing of our visions, as well as our problems and solutions. We dramatize here, our desire to plant the seeds for the renaissance of independent documentary filmmaking in our region. We affirm here with optimism, our determination to seek, develop and implement approaches to deal with the obstacles, so that future international events like YIDFF will not be short of good Asian films. We declare here, the SPIRIT of the independent Asian documentary filmmakers is alive! And will one day, soar with the wind![23]

The following year, Yamagata established its Asia Programme, now called New Asian Currents. The consonant Japanese name is actually far more evocative: *Ajia Senpa Banpa*, or, literally, 'The Countless Onrushing Waves of Asia'. The biennial event quickly became the hub of documentary film-making across the region. Every year, it became larger and larger. The films became more powerful and finely produced. Within years they were not only in the international competition, but winning the grand prize. The festival became a site where waves of Asian film-makers arrived every other year. They showed their new works, and saw the variety of documentary being shot around Asia and the world. Furthermore, Yamagata's large retrospectives provided Asian film-makers the rare opportunity to view the canonical documentaries of Europe they had been reading about (this was still before documentaries were readily available on video or the internet). In no time, the far-flung network the manifesto signers envisioned became a palpable reality. Some of these encounters were fateful; for example, Chinese documentary would look completely different today had not Wu Wenguang and Duan Jinchuan encountered Ogawa Shinsuke in 1991 and Fredrick Wiseman in 1993. New documentary film festivals, from low-key queer events to major government-sponsored festivals, appeared in steady succession; they explicitly modelled themselves on Yamagata and its regional focus. Thus, the 'countless onrushing waves' bounced off Japanese shores, spread across Asia only to bounce once again in every direction. Here's the evidence: twelve years after the Yamagata Manifesto, the 2011 New Asian Currents programme was crafted from 705 entries from sixty-three countries.

This statistic is impressive. It indicates vast changes in the conditions for documentary. These include the invention of digital video (DV), which brought images captured on camcorders in competition with 16mm (which was almost exclusively the medium of industry and government). Editing became increasingly easier with its migration to PCs. These personal computers came into the reach of a rising middle class of artists across Asia, just as dictatorships fell and censorship loosened. Whereas most Asian video documentary in the 1980s and 90s was being shot by political collectives (for example, Green Team in

Taiwan and PURN in Korea), by the turn of the century there were independent documentaries of every variety being produced in nearly every country, while government documentary migrated to national television networks or simply stopped altogether. In other words, government and capital lost its totalising grip on the form just as a vast network of independent artists, schools and events emerged. A century after François-Constant Girel stepped off a boat in Singapore, we can finally say that there is, beyond a doubt, something called 'Asian documentary' and it calls for a remapping of the roads to that province called 'Europe'.

NOTES

1. Arvind-Pal Mandair, *Religion and the Spectre of the West* (New York: Columbia University Press, 2009), p. 394.
2. G. W. F. Hegel, *Introduction to the Philosophy of History*, trans. Leo Rauch (Indianapolis, IN: Hackett, 1988), p. 92.
3. Dipesh Chakrabarty, *Provincializing Europe* (Princeton, NJ: Princeton University Press, 2000), p. 8.
4. Ibid., p. 7.
5. Ibid., p. 8.
6. What's more, the WFPL itself was inspired by a Japanese Worker's Camera Club in New York City according to Fred Sweet, Eugener Roscow and Allan Francovich, 'Pioneers: An Interview with Tom Brandon', *Film Quarterly* vol. 26 no. 5, February 1931, pp. 26–7. Significantly, German left-wing film-makers found inspiration in Prokino through an article by playwright Senda Koreya, who was living in Europe at the time: Senda Koreya, 'Proletarische Film-Bewegung in Japan', *Arbeiterbuehne und Film* vol. 18 no. 2, February 1931, pp. 26–7. Prokino's efforts were far more ambitious than its western counterparts, having established seven branches across Japan, forty-eight films and more than six books and five film journals. These and more are reprinted, along with several films, in the historiography of the proletarian film movements (English): Makino Makino Mamoru, 'Rethinking the Emergence of the Proletarian Film League of Japan', in Abé Mark Nornes and Aaron Gerow (eds), *In Praise of Film Studies: Essays in Honor to Makino Mamoru* (Victoria: Trafford/Kinema Club, 2001), https://www.cjspubs.lsa.umich.edu/electronic/facultyseries/list/series/prewar/journals.php. Accessed 5 October 2012.
7. For more information, see my *Japanese Documentary Film: The Meiji Era to Hiroshima* (Minneapolis: University of Minnesota Press, 2003).
8. Analysis of these films may be found in my *Forest of Pressure: Ogawa Shinsuke and Postwar Japanese Film* (Minneapolis: University of Minnesota Press, 2007).
9. Sol Worth and John Adair, *Through Navajo Eyes* (Bloomington: Indiana University Press, 1972). Worth and Adair distriubuted 8mm film cameras to Navajo colloborators. Adair explained: 'We wanted to fulfil Malinowski, the famous anthropologist of the twenties,

who said that the first duty of the ethnographer is to see the culture through the eyes of the natives themselves, to see their world through their own eyes' (Peter D'Agostino, 'Visual Anthropology: An Interview with John Adair', *Wide Angle* vol. 4 no. 3, 1980, p. 61). Worth and Adair believed that the films showed they had achieved this ambition (Larry Gross, 'Sol Worth and the Study of Visual Communications', *Studies in Visual Communications* vol. 6 no. 3, Autumn 1980, pp. 3ff.). However, this can be disputed (Brian Winston, *Claiming the Real II* [London: BFI, 2005], pp. 179–80).

10. I explore this problem at length in *Forest of Pressure*, see especially pp. 113–27, 197–216, 228–30.

11. Ken Erikawa, Stephen Teo and Yano Kazuyuki (eds), *Asia Symposium 1989* (Tokyo: YIDFF, 2007), p. 38.

12. See Yuriko Furuhata, 'Returning to Actuality: Fukeiron and the Landscape Film', *Screen* vol. 48 no. 3, Autumn 2007. Adachi eventually spent nearly two decades in exile in Lebanon. Jasper Sharp, 'Interview: Adachi Masao', *Midnight Eye* 21 August 2007, http://www.midnighteye.com/interviews/masao_adachi.shtml. Accessed 5 October 2012.

13. Wheeler W. Dixon, *Exploding Eye: A Re-visionary History of 1960s American Experimental Cinema* (New York: SUNY Press, 1997), p. 84.

14. Ian Aitken, *Encyclopedia of the Documentay Film* (New York: Routledge, 2006).

15. See my *Cinema Babel: Translating Global Cinema* (Minneapolis: University of Minnesota Press, 2007).

16. An earlier, but more readily accessible version of this chapter may be found online in *Screening the Past 7* (July 1999): http://www.latrobe.edu.au/screeningthepast/firstrelease/fr0799/MNfr7c.htm. Accessed 5 October 2012. It originally appeared as '*Pôru Rûta* and the Politics of Translation', *Cinema Journal* vol. 38 no. 3, Spring 1999, but was reprinted in John Izod and Richard Kilborn, with Matthew Hibberd (eds), *Breaking Boundaries: From Grierson to Docu-Soap* (Luton: University of Luton Press, 1999); Mona Baker (ed.), *Critical Readings in Translation Studies* (London: Routledge, 2009); and Mona Baker (ed.), *Translation Studies: Critical Concepts in Linguistics*, Vol. 1 (London: Routledge, 2009).

17. Paul Rotha, *Documentary Film* (London: Faber, 1935).

18. Prasanjit Duara, 'Asia Redux', *The Journal of Asian Studies* vol. 69 no. 4, November 2010.

19. Ibid., p. 963.

20. A forthcoming book by SangJoon Lee explores the role of the Asian Film Festival in rich detail.

21. Duara, 'Asia Redux', p. 974.

22. Ibid., p. 978.

23. The Asian Filmmakers at Yamagata YIDFF, 'The Yamagata Manifesto', in Erikawa, Teo and Kazuyuki, *Asia Symposium 1989*, p. 63.

3.2 Mapping Africa

N. FRANK UKADIKE

The cinema, after its long incubation as a technology, was quickly everywhere – but in Africa the conditions of colonialism ensured that it was not in indigenous hands, so that its capacity to reflect local subjectivities was repressed. The colonial had to recede before an African documentary voice could be heard. To contextualise this development, all Africa can be delineated on two different, overlapping maps. The first reflects the spacial linguistic legacy of anglophone, francophone and lusophone spheres of control; the second, a temporal sequence of colonial, post-colonial and contemporary eras.

MAPS

The story of cinema in Africa offers a lesson in commonalities, reflecting the far-reaching consequences of the economic and bureaucratic predicaments that began in colonial times and continue into the present. I would suggest that the patterns of film production in the anglophone, francophone and lusophone regions are essentially consequences of the ideological assumptions of the colonial British, French and Portuguese governments. While the latter two were relentless in their promotion of the so-called assimilationist policy, the former's policy of indirect rule emphasised pragmatic politics intertwined with pure business affairs. Similarly, it has been pointed out that while the French 'brought' fiction film to its colonies, the British 'gave' theirs the documentary. (Though the Portuguese left no infrastructure in the lusophone, the revolutionary documentary film practice born out of oppression and resistance there followed the Cuban model.) In essence, my purpose here is to offer insights into the policies that have determined the development of the documentary tradition across, essentially, sub-Saharan Africa.[1]

The practice of documentary film-making in Africa can be virtually said to date back to the 'invention' of cinema. Numerous studies have pointed out that, although Africa was left out of the Euro-American coalition that led to the creation of the cinematic apparatus, cinema itself reached Africa shortly after 1895, the year when the first projected motion picture images were shown to paying audiences. In the sub-Saharan and Maghreb regions, not only were films projected as early as 1896, but also an Algerian, Felix Mesquich – one of the Lumières' cameramen – was then sent to several countries, including those in North Africa. He was not only to demonstrate *cinematographé* by screening films, but also to use the camera when there to capture the moving images of 'far-away' people.

However, because of colonialism, Africa-as-producer came late into the film business. For the cinema's first half-century and more, the continent's image was to be imagined, reproduced and interpreted by non-Africans. Thus, Africa was relegated to the background, serving but as exotic decor for the fiction and documentary films made there. Herein I will reveal how this vacuum provoked challenges, eventually leading to the emergence of African film-makers. However late this was, nevertheless it opened up a vast opportunity for future contestation of the representation of Africa; for questions of ideology; and for the interrogation of western aesthetic precepts. More than that, this late development occasioned a repostulation of the very notion of cinema and African film-makers' role in such a transformative agenda.

It is easy to understand why, during the colonial period, fiction (imaginary tale) would take precedence over reality (documentary veracity). Along with colonialist tendencies, film in its original 'pure' form (in, say the Lumière programme of those short, funny movies designated documentary, *actualité*, 'interests', educational or travelogue) was anyway then propounded as brief exhibitions of observable life. Soon this notion of 'pure cinema' dissipated as successive film techniques began to be suffused with ideology, or 'contaminated' by an increased divergence from reality via (in Erik Barnouw's terminology) 'trickery' and 'fakery'. Because Africans lacked the basic skill or technical know-how to make films that would positively define them, the colonisers set forth their own often bigoted agenda in all areas of the film business – production, exhibition and distribution. Needless to say, the titles they made or brought into the continent were alien – or were deceitful about Africa. Either way, these films were the very ones that made the initial impact on Africans.[2]

The cinema came to Africa as an integral partner of colonialism, so the diverse types of films that the colonisers made or brought to show to the African people served to ensure the ideological prerogatives of the colonial agenda. As to when and how cinema first entered sub-Saharan Africa, conflicting accounts abound. However, it appears that it was introduced into South Africa by a vaudeville magician with a stolen 'theatregraph' projector in 1896; in Senegal mobile cinemas showed animated cartoons as early as 1905, the same year that a French circus group and film-makers exhibited the Lumière brothers films *L'arrivée d'un train en gare de Ciotat* and *L'arroseur arrosé* (both 1895) in Dakar. Some studies have also pointed out that Méliès' *La marche de Dakar* and *Le cake-walk des negres du nouveau cirque* (both 1905, still available at the Cinémathèque Française) were made in that region at that time.[3]

So, apart from the spatial colonial cultural and linguistic map, a second temporal 'map' can also be imposed. The history of film-making in Africa can be sub-divided into three major eras: the colonial, the post-colonial and the contemporary (e.g., post-1980s). Film-making in each era is therefore distinguished by the different colonial arrangements under which it initially occurred. The consequences of this are still being reflected in today's African cinema. This, I would suggest, means that politics, ideology and cultural affirmation/transformation have played crucial roles in the underdevelopment, and subsequent contemporary development, of documentary film-making in Africa.

COLONIAL FILM: 'INSTRUCTION'/ETHNOGRAPHY/PROPAGANDA

Given the significance of Africa to the British Empire, it is not surprising that the continent would become the focus of cinematic enquiry dating back to the early days of British film-making. This starts in the nineteenth century: the Warwick Trading Company made *Savage South Africa – Savage Attack and Repulse* in 1899. Just over a minute long, this film, which was actually filmed in London with African performers from South Africa, was said by a reviewer to have been 'genuine enough, ... a dramatic re-enactment of a real-life event from the Matabele wars between African natives and British infantry'.[4] Both the title and the faked setting, suggest that it is not hard to establish *Savage South Africa* as the template for the questionable treatment of the African subject in subsequent films. It exemplifies the role that the motion picture was to play in the British colonial process.

As both Rosalyn Smyth and Jeffery Richards have stated, as early as the 1920s through the Colonial Office, the British had started exploring 'the possibilities of using the cinema as a medium of instruction'.[5] Since the colonisers believed that complicated narratives were harmful to Africans' underdeveloped, childlike minds, the structure of such instructional films oozed overt simplicity, The resultant colonial film style produced amateurish and uncinematic or, as Burns puts it, 'dull, unconvincing, and ultimately ineffective' films;[6] nevertheless, the British claimed that their impact was successful. Colonial film units (CFUs) were established in virtually all of Britain's African colonies.

Perhaps the best-known film by the CFU in Nigeria is *Daybreak in Udi* (1949), which won the Academic Award for documentary the year of its release. Produced by the (London-based) Crown Film Unit in Nigeria, it was praised for portraying the progress made by colonial officials implementing community projects in eastern Nigeria. However, the truth of the matter, which the film obfuscates, is that communal self-help projects had sustained the people of Igbo land long before the arrival of the British. Through such efforts, the natives built roads, houses, schools, community halls, churches and organised marriage, birth and death ceremonies. Yet this film gives the impression that such things would not be happening but for the presence of the colonial officers.

Unlike the British (and the Belgians, who also established colonial film units in their African territories), the French had no such policy for making films solely intended for their African subjects' consumption. However, in 1934, in order to control film-making activities in the colonies, the French promulgated a law (*La Décret Laval*/'Laval decree') named for Pierre Laval, the then French minister for the colonies. Its dual purpose was to control the content of films shot in francophone Africa and to curtail the roles played by Africans in the film-making process. In effect, the French systematically deprived Africans of the ability to attain technical know-how and, in effect, stifled the development of cinema in Africa by the natives. Film-making was essentially the province of independent ethnographic film-makers whose work can be seen as constituting a veritable 'explorer-anthropological' genre.

Like the films produced by the British colonial film units, these films are also credited with influencing the development of cinema in Africa. Functioning as a major tool for propaganda, perhaps the most influential film in this category made in Africa is *La croisière noire* [*The Black Cruise*] (1926), directed by Lèon Poirier of France. By documenting the Citroën car expedition of 1924–25, the film did a good job of advertising the ruggedness of Citroën vehicles under adverse African road conditions, but it ignored the reality of the welfare of Africans under colonialism. Similarly, the ethnographic film-making of Jean Rouch in Africa has led people to question, not only his methodology, but the whole concept of ethnographic film practice. Indicative of their tactics and ideology, these ethnographic film-makers represent a phase in the development of colonial cinema. Rouch's method has continued to raise disturbing questions about what critics have called his wrongful portrayal of Africa and Africans ever since. His surreal 'ciné-transe' documentary, *Les maîtres fous* [*The Mad Masters*] (1955) remains the most offensive to Africans and the most controversial of his African films. African critics and film-makers have attacked it as 'making Africans look like "scientific specimen" and "laboratory subjects"', or as Sembène puts it: 'treating Africans like insects'.[7] Long a major voice in French cinema, Rouch made over sixty films, the majority focusing on Africa. Yet Africans and other critics hold his films partly responsible for perpetuating the exoticism and exploitation originating under colonialism.[8]

POST-COLONIAL VOICES

Nevertheless, there is no denying these colonial filmmaking activities initiated Africans in the techniques of film production – not only, as in the British case, as assistants in the CFUs. More formal training centres were established by the Catholic church in Belgian-ruled Africa where basic film-making instruction was given with a view to producing African film-makers who would make films extolling religious virtues. But the apprenticeship model (as it were) was to have profounder impact on the development of African cinema as the continent, post-World War II, began to throw off colonial control and achieve independence.

Even in the francophone sphere, where no official film units had been established, it must be admitted that among Rouch's helpers, whom he habitually involved in filming as technicians or actors, were some of the first post-colonial African auteurs: the late Oumarou Ganda of Niger, for example, who starred in Rouch's documentary 'psychodrama' *Moi, un noir* [*I, A Black Man*] (1958); or Safi Faye of Senegal, who appeared in *Petit à petit ou Les Lettres Persanes 1968* [*Little by Little or the Persian Letters*, 1968] (1971).

In the post-independence period France saw the need to help its newly independent former colonies develop their own audiovisual media. Hence, in 1961 the Consortium Audio-visuel International (CAI) was created in Paris to assist these newly independent countries to produce their own newsreels and documentaries for government departments. This was also seen as a way of inspiring the development of national cinema industries in the ex-colonies. The CAI was responsible for providing filmmaking equipment, and through its subsidiary the Bureau du Cinema an arrangement was set up to co-share production costs with participating African governments. It allowed aspiring independent African film-makers to make their own films and encouraged African government involvement in financing. From 1961–75, some visible evidence of success was noticed, with the CAI, in conjunction

with African production units, releasing 416 newsreels and documentaries a year.[9]

Senegal became the first nation to sign the CAI agreement, and one of its own sons, Paulin Soumanou Vieyra, a pioneer of African documentary film practice, was an early beneficiary of this arrangement. In 1961, he made *Une Nation est née* [*A Nation is Born*], a government-funded documentary that the French disliked because of its critique of colonialism; but it was embraced by the Senegalese. Even before his acclaimed *Borom Sarret* [*The Cart Driver*] (1963) and *La Noire de ...* [*Black Girl*] (1966), Ousmane Sembène had also made an obscure documentary called *L'Empire Songhai* [*Songhai Empire*] (1963). Set in pre-colonial Africa, it attempted to recapture the history of the old Songhai state, a history implicitly at odds with colonial assumptions of African primitiveness. This particular history, for example, was not exactly prominent in the many ethnographic Songhai films made by Jean Rouch.[10] In fact, in the 1960s, film-makers such as Sembène, citizens of newly independent states, felt compelled to narrate African issues long distorted by western film-makers, explorers and colonisers, and to present to them like a history lesson. Thus, films were not only unabashedly political but also extremely didactic.

Aside from Sembène, others – Moustapha Alassane, Jean-Pierre Dikongue-Pipa, Souleymane Cissé, Henri Duparc, Kramo-Lancine Fadika – can also be named as film-makers with a desire to reassert Africa's lost cultural heritage. The inscription of identity becomes central, channelled through the auspices of providing 'useful information';[11] or, as Jude Akudinobi puts it, 'defining certain "realities" in relationship to specific representational strictures'.[12] From the francophone regions, a number of documentary films have pursued similar objectives showing concern for culture and identity: *Lamb* (about Senegalese wrestling, 1963) by Paulin Vieyra, chosen for the 1964 Cannes Film Festival; *Ganvié, mon village* (1967) by Benin's Pascal Abikanlou, about life in a village built on stilts over a lagoon; the series *Fêtes et traditions populaires au Niger* (1977) by Inoussa Ousseini.

In 1965, after graduating from a Parisian film school, Jean-Pierre Dikongue-Pipa of Cameroon made three documentary films that Françoise Pfaff felt, 'appear as trial runs in his formative years as a filmmaker',[13] leading to the debut of his acclaimed masterpiece *Muna Moto* (1975). They are: *Un Simple* [*Down to Earth*] (1965), *Rendez-moi mon père* [*Give Me Back My Father*] (1966) and *Les Cornes* [*The Horns*] (1966). Moustapha Alassane, the pioneer of Niger's cinema, whose nickname is the 'Méliès of African film' for his creative/imaginative advances, filmed *L'Arachide de Santchira* [*Santchira Peanuts*] (1966), an educational documentary about the commercialisation of peanut crops. This was followed by two others: *Jamya* (1971), about a farmers' cooperative, and *Soubane* (1975), about family planning.

National sovereignty and the quest to present its post-independence progress is the focus of Timité Bassori, the first Ivorian to attend the Institut de Hauntes Etudes Cinematographiques (IDHEC) film school in Paris. He also began in the 1960s, with documentaries for Ivory Coast television, including: *Les Forestiers* [*The Foresters*] (1963), on forest conservation; *L'Abidjan-Niger* (1963) about the Ivorian train system; and *Feux de brousse* [*Bush Fires*] (1968), portraying the destructive effects of bush burning. Bassori's Ivory Coast counterpart is Henri Duparc, better known for his raucous comedies and explicit sexual content, as in *Bal poussière* [*Dancing in the Dust*] (1988). He too first made documentary films that promoted national development projects. From 1968–70, he filmed seven documentaries that highlighted economic issues, tourism and the history of Côte d'Ivoire: *Récolte du Coton* [*Growing Cotton*] (parts 1 and 2), *Profil ivorien* [*Ivorian Profile*], *Achetez ivorien* [*Buy Ivorian Products*] and so on.

There is a common pattern of overseas film-school experience followed by official government or television documentary production leading to features. Because of this, the documentary work of film-makers such as Ousmane Sembène, Med Hondo and Souleymane Cissé, is largely overlooked. In 1969, Sembène made two documentary films, *Traumatisme de la Femme Face à la Polygame* [*Women and the Trauma of Polygamy*] and *Les Dérives du chômage* [*Unemployment Problems*] and, in 1972, *Basket Africain aux Jeux Olympiades*, followed in 1973 by *L'Afrique Aux Olympiades*. When, in 1969, Souleymane Cissé returned to Mali from the Soviet Union, where he had studied film production, he was recruited as a film director by the Service Cinématographique du Ministère de l'Information du Mali (SCINFOMA) and, in the period from 1970–72, he made thirty newsreels and five documentaries on Malian issues.[14] After leaving the ministry to form his own independent directing company, Cissé directed two further documentaries, *Dixième anniversaire de l'OUA* (1973) and *Chanteurs traditionnels des îles Seychelles* (1978).

It is little wonder, then, that when these directors made features documentary technique loomed large. Many of the first African-made African fiction films, although of course structured as fictional narratives, also exhibit a pronounced documentary/fictional synthesis. In this they echo contemporary Latin American documentary film practice (see Chapter 3.3). For example, *Xala* (also by Sembène, 1974); *Soleil O* (Med Hondo, 1969, Mauritania); *Cabascado* (Omarou Ganda, 1969, Niger); *Sambizanga* (Sarah Maldoror, 1972, Angola) and *Mirt Sost Shi Amit* [*Harvest: 3,000 Years*] (Haile Gerima, 1976, Ethiopia) are all suffused by a documentary mode of address. This juxtaposing of fictional and documentary images reflects a certain counter-hegemonic impulse, but it is one that heightens emotional impact and audience involvement.

Soleil O depicts the vicious racism and discrimination that blacks and Arabs have often felt in France. It is an anti-colonialist film that demands immediate, extreme action from its audience as it presents colonial and neo-colonial injustices (as well as ideological contradiction – France's concept of assimilation in particular) in a striking, stylistically shocking way. Not merely observational, as are many fiction and documentaries of this pioneering period, this film is a strong proponent of the combination of the political with both the avant-garde and oral traditions. As Archer Winsten claimed: *Soleil O*,

> is not an indictment that can be shrugged off. There is much truth and a corroding bitterness in the picture. Essentially it is documentary rather than fiction. It is an argument by one who has been hurt deeply and is hitting back. It is a picture with something to say, and Med Hondo says it with plain, hard power.[15]

Between 1974 and 1978, after making *Soleil O* and before releasing the acclaimed *West Indies* (1979) and *Sarraounia* (1986), Med Hondo made two feature-length documentaries: *Nous aurons toute la mort pour dormir* [*We'll Have All Death to Sleep*] (1977) and *Polisario, Un Peuple en armes* [*Polisario, a People in Arms*] (1979). Both are important historical documents depicting the Polisario movement's struggles for an independent western Sahara. They belong in the category of African films made for posterity in the interest of preserving what Captain Thomas Sankara termed: 'the cry from the heart … the nobility and the necessity for struggle in Africa'.[16]

Such *engagé* work is rarer in the ex-anglophone sphere. Unlike the French, the British had come to encourage the production of official documentaries and basic educational films by Africans who had acquired film-making skills in the colonial film units. This continued as the CFUs were taken over by the new states. The colonial legacy was reflected not only in these official film units, but was also seen when, with independence, came television. As on the small screen in Britain, documentary found a welcome in ex-'British' Africa. In the early years of Nigerian television, production departments included a film division (just as did the BBC). However, the CFUs' successors remain significant for the future. In independent Nigeria, for example, a Federal Film Unit emerged, with an expanded remit that included full-scale formal training of Nigerian technicians to take charge of production. Some of the films then made, such as *Lagos* (1965) and *Nigeria* (1968), both directed by Bayo Imeovbere, are noteworthy, displaying 'fine technical ability and great sensitivity'.[17]

Since the late 1960s, Ola Balogun has made a series of documentaries in the same spirit. Upon his return home after his education at IDHEC, he held various posts in the Nigerian civil service, making short Griersonian documentaries. He formed his own production company in 1973 and has made more than a dozen feature-length fiction films;

but he also continued to make documentaries: *Destination Barbados* (1997); *The Magic of Nigeria* (1998) and *River Niger: Black Mother* (1998). Since 2001, though, this versatile artist, one of the pioneers of Nigerian cinema, has been more satisfied utilising his talent elsewhere – leading his band, Iroko.

The continued existence of the Federal Film Unit ensured that Nigerian documentaries tended to be educational in focus, touching upon many aspects of life. This certainly includes, for example, even longer-form epic documentaries such as *Shaihu Umar* (1976) by Adamu Halilu on the influence of Islam on Nigerian life.

In comparison to other British African countries, Ghana was exceptional in upgrading and maintaining its own infrastructure stemming from the legacy of the Colonial Film Unit there. In 1957, with the advent of independence under Nkrumah, the new president gave the country structures that were unique to all of Africa. He nationalised film production and distribution and injected enormous funds into the building of the Ghana Film Industry Corporation (GFIC), the first of its kind in Africa with ultramodern facilities that enabled the production of films from conception to completion. But the presence of Europeans also continued and, although many documentaries emerged, some still reflected older upbeat political propaganda agendas. Nevertheless, over forty-six years, until it was sold off in 1996, the GFIC made over 220 documentaries, approximately 400 newsreels and, albeit only a few, fiction films.[18]

The absence of sanctioned film-making activity during the colonial period did not necessarily mean that film, and the possibilities of documentary primarily as a political tool, were unknown. Unlike the anglophone and francophone states, which had remnants of film production facilities prior to independence, the lusophone countries had virtually none, and the people there – anyway largely kept from literacy – had no opportunity to acquire technical training in the area of film production until after independence came in 1975. According to Ron Hallis, the Portuguese film-makers who worked in Mozambique had no interest in developing African cinema or allowing the African workers employed by them to learn the process of film-making.[19]

Nevertheless, prior to independence, film played a vital role in the lives of the lusophone African peoples. Because of the guerrilla warfare being waged against the Portuguese, who refused to grant them independence, media coverage was deemed imperative for the explanation of their cause. Foreign film-makers and news organisations were invited to cover their activities and, with that, reliance on the documentary format became inevitable. The first films made about the liberation movements and the wars in lusophone Africa include mainstream western coverage (e.g., *Angola: Journey to a War* [1961], produced by NBC news); coverage from the communist perspective (e.g., the Cuban newsreel compilation *Medina Boe* [1969] on the struggles in Portuguese Guinea-Bissau; or independent radical documentary (e.g., *A luta continua* [*The Struggle Continues*, 1972] and *O povo organizado* [*The People Organise*, 1975] made by the African American documentarist, Robert Van Lierop).

Apart from explaining the war, the significance of these films lies in their also having contributed to consciousness-raising, something that the freedom fighters badly needed in order to sustain the revolution. To this end, the struggle for self-determination is what led the liberation movements in the lusophone world to discover the importance of cinema as a weapon for revolution The product of this insight proved very beneficial to Angola, Guinea-Bissau and Mozambique. In contrast the 'instructional' and the 'ethnographic' legacies left by the British and the French, despite (or, better, a consequence of) Portuguese oppression, the lusophone sphere embraced a documentary film-making practice rooted in the tradition of socialist ideology and Marxist dialectics – in effect, a Cuban rather than a British or French template.

Just five months after independence, the Mozambique Film Institute (Instituto Nacional de Cinema, INC) was launched. As in Ghana, the institute began operation with help of foreign directors, necessary because the country had no fully educated film-makers. But these workers, brought in from Britain, Brazil and Canada in order to teach film production, reflected the radical agenda of the new government. The courses they gave led to the graduation of Mozambican film-makers such as Camillo de Sousa, Luis Simoa, and João Costa. Such an infrastructure as was provided by the institute also helped Pedro Pimete and others who were receiving their film education in Cuba and France when they returned, as well as exiled film-makers like Ruy Guerra, an IDHEC graduate who became the director of the institute in 1978.

To solidify its quest to put cinema at the service of the people in the spirit of Third Cinema, *cinema Novo* or Cuban revolutionary documentary film practice, the Mozambican National Film Institute launched the production of a monthly documentary film series *Kuxa Kanema* [*The Birth of Cinema*].[20] In addition, two feature-length films were made. *Mueda: Memória e massacre* [*Mueda: Memory and Massacre*] (1979) is Guerra's documentation of the annual re-enactment of the 1960 massacre of 600 Mozambicans by Portuguese troops in Mueda. *Estas são as armas* [*These are the Weapons*] (1978), a compilation documentary dealing with the struggle against Portuguese colonialism and Rhodesian aggression, was directed by the Brazilian Murillo Salles. It was the first Mozambican film to win a major award: the first prize, the Silver Dove, at the Leipzig International Film Festival in 1978. These were followed by Camillo de Sousa's *Offensiva* [*The Offensive*] (1980), an extraordinary Direct Cinema film which actually shows the late president of Mozambique, Samora Machel, acting as an investigative reporter and uncovering the coordinated effort of saboteurs undermining the nation's development projects in order to throw a bad light on the socialist policies of his government. *Borders of Blood* (Mario Borgneth, 1985), is a colour documentary itemising the numerous ways used by South Africa to destabilise Mozambique's reconstruction efforts.

Kuxa Kanema was truly prolific, but, after 395 weekly editions, 119 short documentaries, thirteen feature-length documentaries and dramas, political instability and a horrific fire led to the institute's collapse in 1990. As a filmed epitaph *Kuxa Kanema: The Birth of Cinema*, documenting the impact of the series, was made in 2003 by Margarida Cardoso. This film also brings us to the present phase.[21]

CONTEMPORARY AFRICAN DOCUMENTARY

Kuxa Kanema: The Birth of Cinema, was directed by a woman, thus effectively crystallising one of many important characteristics of the current diversity of African documentary production.

Ingrid Sinclair, a versatile white Zimbabwean director, has been making films for more than twenty years throughout this contemporary era. Sinclair's acclaimed feature film, *Flame* (1998), winner of numerous awards, is about women's roles in Zimbabwe's liberation war. She now works in both fiction and documentary. *Biopiracy: Who Owns Life?* (2009) is her ground-breaking work, offering a shocking revelation about how powerful multinational corporations steal genetic resources from poor Third World countries.

'Newcomer' Florence Ayisi, together with Kim Longinotto, directed the award-winning documentary film *Sisters in Law* (2005). Shot in Longinotto's classic Direct Cinema style, this may be the most powerful film directed by women to emerge from Africa in recent years. Set in a small courthouse in Cameroon, where a 'tough-minded state prosecutor and court president are serving up justice by helping women in their village fight abuse in the face of societal pressure – and helping to change the world'.[22] The film certainly speaks to that agenda. For example, the female prosecuting attorney is shown aiding one plaintiff escape from an abusive relationship – the first (of only two) cases in which a Muslim woman successfully divorced a husband in Cameroon.

In a similar vein, the works of the renowned novelist Assia Djebar, specifically *La Nouba des femmes du Mont Chenoua* [*Nouba*] (1977) and *La Zerda ou les chants de l'oubli* [*The Zerda and Songs of Forgetting*] (1979) also impacts on women film-makers. These can be found across the continent, from Anne Mungai (Kenya) to Osvalde Lewat (Cameroon), from Franceline Oubda (Burkina Faso) to Monique Mbeka Phoba (Congo).

In fact, since 1963, a number of African women have ventured into the profession of film-making and have been at the forefront of the social and cultural dynamics of gender and feminist perspectives in [re]writing history. Like their male counterparts, they work in fiction and documentary formats, as well as in television, and they use the medium to address the challenges and contradictions of colonial and post-colonial Africa, often focusing more deeply on women's issues. Notable pioneers the already mentioned include Safi Faye (who acted for Rouch) and Sarah Maldoror; but there are a number of significant film-makers who also started work in the early post-colonial period – for example, Cameroonian journalist, Thérèse Sita Bella (*Tam Tam à Paris*, 1963) and Ghana's Efua Sutherland (*Araba: The Village Story*, 1967).

Safi Faye, who has doctorate in ethnology and went to film school in France, remains the most accomplished among them and is the first sub-Saharan African woman to make a feature-length film, *Kaddu Beykat* (1975). Apart from fiction, since her first short, *La Passante* (1972) she has made more than ten documentaries about African cultural, economic and political experiences, some for international agencies, the UN or UNESCO. Others were commissioned by German and French television. For the latter, *Ambassades nourriciers* [*Nurturing Embassies*] (1984) was, significantly, not focused on African experience.

In my studies of African cinema, I have noted the significant impact of the younger generation of African film-makers and the diverse ways that they have transformed the aesthetics of African films. This clearly applies to African women directors' relentless and engaging films; what we are witnessing attests to the innovative ways that thematic and aesthetic prerogatives are determined by specific social, political and gender objectives. Consider *Deluge* (1995), by Ethiopia's Salem Mekuria, a tapestry of memory and historical specificity concerning the loss of her brother to the power struggle which culminated in Ethiopia's civil war. Described on Mekuria's website as a

Deluge (1995): 'personal visual meditation on history' – Salem Mekuria

'personal visual meditation on history', the director sees this introspective essay as a 'tool for looking back to get a sense of how we can look forward to a future in which responsibility and choice inform our conduct'.[23] Or take *Femmes aux yeux ouverts* [*Women with Open Eyes*] (1994), by the Togolese film-maker Anne-Laure Folly. This paints a compelling portrait of African women in four West African nations: Burkina Faso, Mali, Senegal and Benin. What shocks in such a work – at least for the non-African audience – is observing how African women can now organise and participate fully in the era of post-colonialism and so-called globalisation. So, a health worker demonstrates condom use in a marketplace, explaining how diseases are sexually transmitted, but this does not register as taboo; nor do portrayals of a woman activist speaking in support of marital rights and campaigning against female excision; nor are we shocked when the economic power of highly successful women traders, 'Mercedes Madams', is highlighted.

There is now enough of such work to warrant a festival: Women of the Sun was the first, held in Johannesburg, South Africa, in September 2010. It featured '25 films by 23 talented women film-makers from 15 African Countries' and showcased 'some of the best examples of the film-making [comprising] a diverse range of genres and styles, from family drama to social justice documentaries to experimental films'.[24] Eve Rantseli, the festival director, was far from controversial when she claimed: 'Women in film have much to say and are saying it with unique vision and flair.' Such film is produced, not for the almighty dollar, but to fulfil the human soul's need for justice, equality and worldwide grasp of one's culture. Included were eleven feature-length documentaries in all and one short. The organisers believe that the festival has helped to reverse the notion that 'only certain people make films and that only certain places/countries have a film industry'. Instead, it has affirmed the reality of the 'distinct female voices from far flung places across the continent and highlight emerging industry and talent', while also pointing to the fact that 'the time is ripe to change the widely held belief that filmmaking is a male domain'.[25]

Technology has also worked to reduce exclusivity by removing prohibitively expensive celuloid. The Kenyan Institute of Mass Communication has facilities for 16mm production, sound transfer, editing and dubbing, as well as a laboratory mainly geared towards the production of tourist-attraction films, educational and informational documentary films.[26] But here, as is happening also in Nigeria and Ghana, Kenyans are now also following the trend for the proliferation of video use, finding it to be completely viable for local productions: a basis on which an entire self-sustaining indigenous film industry can be built. The film production unit of the government-owned parastatal, the Voice of Kenya, has produced numerous video documentary films for itself and other government agencies.

In Nigeria, while important documentaries continue to role out of the Federal Film Unit, traditional channels of exhibition remain elusive since there are no well-organised distribution and exhibition outlets other than showings at the Nigerian embassies and, occasionally, on school premises within Nigeria. Nevertheless, with the advent of the video phenomenon, Nollywood film-makers are now breathing fresh air into Nigerian documentary film practices. Miguel Enwerem directed *Lagos Hot* (2009), an exhilarating documentary that explores the phenomenal recent growth of Nigeria's entertainment industry, focusing on the impact of Nollywood as well as fashion, music and art.

African documentary cinema has successfully evolved from the early practices of its pioneers' sociopolitical goals by giving greater attention to aesthetics. Interestingly, in this contemporary era, which can be dated from the late 1980s to the present, innovative documentary films have reflected the diversity of African cinema and the willingness of film-makers, including those considered to be hardline pioneers such as Haile Gerima, to keep exploring more audacious and innovative styles of presentation, while 'at the same time looking at African societies today through new eyes'.[27] With his usual panache for depicting diasporic issues with utmost intensity, Gerima's *Adwa: An African Victory* (Ethiopia, 1999), shows the gallantry of the Ethiopian forces who defeated formidable Italian forces in the Battle of Adwa in 1896. The film illuminates 'one of the hidden sources of African empowerment' propelling its audience to acknowledge what Gerima feels is a 'transforming rite of passage linking contemporary Africans in Africa and the Diaspora with the early founders of the Pan-African movement'.[28]

The questions of politics and culture continue to be addressed in contemporary African documentary, which explores the past, showing how it invades and defines the present. *Asientos* (Françoise Woukoache, 1992, Cameroon) jolts one's conscience in its audacious representation of slavery. History, memory and culture also play important roles in *Rostov–Luanda* by Abdelrahman Sissako (Mauritannia, 1997). The film starts in Sissako's birth-place in Mauritannia and follows the director to Luanda in Angola in search of his friend, Baribanga, whom he met as a student in Moscow. *Rostov–Luanda* 'is a film about disillusionment and the recovery of a kind of hope',[29] in the same manner that *Asientos* juxtaposes questions of memory/amnesia and past/present.[30]

Aesthetics aside, as with the issues I highlighted above in the fight for women's liberation depicted in *Sisters in Law*, African film-makers have also been increasingly focusing on other contemporary issues. There are now numerous documentaries, for example, about the genocide in Darfur. One of them, *All About Darfur* (2005), was made by Taghreed Elsanhour, a British-based, Sudanese-born woman. Another example would be *Afro@Digital* (Congo, 2002) by Balufu Bakupa-Kanyinda of the Democratic Republic of Congo, a documentary on the digital revolution in Africa. This film dispels the idea that Africa is again fading to the historical margins in the face of this newest factor of human progress. It is especially informative and creative in how it delineates the proliferation of internet, mobile telephones and digital video camera usage in everyday milieus. Before making this film, Balufu directed the short called *Thomas Sankara* (1991), a biographical documentary on the life of the former charismatic leader of Burkina Faso who was assassinated.

In typical Third Cinema fashion, deriving from the concept of putting the film medium at the service of the people, *Arlit: deuxième Paris* (2004, Benin) by Idrissou Mora Kpaï is one of the most powerful exposé documentaries made in Africa. It focuses on a man-made disaster, and one of the worst atrocities ever committed against mankind. It is set in Arlit, a city in the West African country of Niger where uranium mining has totally devastated the environment. The film is, per California Newsreel's description, 'a case study in environmental racism'.[31] Having made away with huge profits from the extraction of uranium for nuclear power at the cost of unleashing an horrific ecological disaster, the European corporations who owned these mines abandoned them. Arlit has been left to face abject poverty, unemployment, contamination and death from radiation-related illnesses. The story might not be new, but emotional intensity here stems from hearing the voices of the people narrating their own story, rather than the use of the traditional voiceover, voice-of-God narration. *Arlit* forces one to rethink the dichotomy between the colonised and the coloniser.

In general, the African documentaries, among other things, reflect the fact that the legacy of the 'mother countries' has not changed over time. Now the influences are more subtle than one hundred years ago, but in some ways more powerful. Even communities that are able to sustain their traditions are inevitably alienated by dominant European behaviour. Though the colonial powers are no longer in place, the structures that they established still have a strong-hold on the countries they colonised. They imposed their neo-colonial ways of thinking upon the Africans, changing the ways that Africans had thought of themselves, their neighbours and their land. More than anywhere, this struggle against the colonial legacy is most specifically explored in the films of Jean-Marie Teno.

Cameroon's Jean-Marie Teno is Africa's pre-eminent documentary film-maker. Unlike many of his peers, since the 1980s he has consistently produced one or more documentaries a year. Even in the video age, this is remarkable considering the perennial funding problems that still

prevent African film-makers' ability to regularly make films. Teno's view of documentary is at odds with most assumptions which rank it below fiction film-making. According to him, it is from 'the process of experimenting with making short films [fiction] that I learned about making real films [documentaries]'.[32] Today, he stands out as one who has not only advanced and popularised the African documentary tradition, but who has also made the medium an ideal communicative and educational tool for scrutinising African developmental, social and political issues. His 1993 feature-length documentary, *Afrique, je te plumerai* [I will Fleece You, Africa], whose structure deliberately mixes modes of address, is a powerful example of unconventional narrative patterns. The film's construction perfectly embodies a political manifesto. Its mode of interrogation stems from the juxtaposition of documentary with fictional images, and from narrative discontinuity as well as oral tradition. Most astounding in this mix of cinematic and indigenous narrative codes is how what seems to be a mélange of film styles (documentary, experimental and narrative; montage editing, lighting, alternation of silence and sound), coheres to strongly express key, deep-rooted issues.[33]

Afrique, je te plumerai dynamically focuses on how the process of cultural assimilation imposed upon the Cameroonians by the colonising powers slowly engulfed native culture. Teno intentionally strays from common storytelling approaches. Instead he utilises this montage of vivid imagery and historically significant archival footage to narrate Cameroon's history. It is remarkable that (as did Esfir Shub) he reverses the meaning of archival footage. Films produced during colonial times to show the Europeans in a good light and to mock the Africans illustrate instead the negative effects of colonisation on the African people. By interspersing the film's structure with such images, Teno works to demonstrate on screen the complexity of recollecting one's history by 'peeling away layer[s] … of cultural forgetting' (California Newsreel). He uses these multiple layers to suggest that no single experiential understanding or representation can exist in such a diverse country with so intricate a history. The result is not unlike that ascribed, by Teshome Gabriel, to Sembène's feature *Xala*: it produces 'a cinema of wax and gold', the filmic equivalent of the *cire per due* ('lost wax') method of metal casting.[34]

Aside from *Afrique*, Teno has directed over twelve other politically charged informative documentaries, including *Malentendu Colonial* [Colonial Misunderstanding] (2004). In this, Teno explores Germany's colonial African past (which was curtailed by the loss of its holdings to the British after World War I). Teno highlights how Namibia was colonised and the role that missionaries played in laying the groundwork for colonialism. But this story also functions as an indictment of Africa's own ineptness and complicity in the colonising process. More specifically, *Colonial Misunderstanding* successfully reveals how colonialism and early Christian missionaries in Africa destroyed African beliefs and social systems, replacing them with European ones in the name of modernity, civilisation and evangelism. Like *Afrique*, the film's captivating power resonates. Teno appropriates traditional representational codes, blending them with 'dominant' conventions in unique and critical ways as to address current trends in post-colonialism and debilitating modernism.[35]

Modernity, on the other hand, has never been fixed in a particular time and location, as the colonial mentality would make one believe. As Stuart Hall observes:

> the world is absolutely littered by modernities. It is littered by artists, practicing artists, who do not regard modernism as the secure possession of the West, never regarded it as such but always regarded it as a language which was both open to them but which they would have to transform.[36]

Hence, the numerous kinds of representation in Teno's films diversify the authoritative voice. These forms evoke the multiple voices of Africa's oral tradition, which offers many forms of representation in its abundant use of culturally established iconographic codes of explication. This blend of methodology, I would argue, is a classic example of technique acting as a catalyst for creative process. Teno's oeuvre defined a new era for African documentary film aesthetics that echoes the rich reservoir of creative leitmotif. This is so significant that Teno's combining or merging of styles might well be termed the 'height of convergence', a defining bricolage of avant-garde styles, documentary film practice and an underlying militancy typical of African cinema.

FLIP FLOTSAM: THE JOURNEY OF AFRICAN FILM

Flip Flotsam (2003, Kenya), directed by Etienne Oliff and Lucy Bateman, is a light-hearted film about the life/death/resurrection of flip-flop shoes on the coast of Africa. From the manufacturing plant in Mombasa, Kenya, the flip-flops make their way to the soles of their owners. After being discarded, some are seen to wash ashore onto Kiwaiyu island's beaches on the Lamu archipelago. There they are transformed into artwork and toys by the dexterous hands of the beachcombing Kenyan islanders. While the overall feel of the film is one of an interesting and fun journey, upon closer examination this film can be seen as a metaphor for the spirit of African films.

At first, I wondered why anyone would waste his or her time watching a documentary about flip-flops, but, as a member of the 1994 Zanzibar International Film Festival jury, I had to. This was fortunate as, since discovering this film, I have come to see it as a beautiful work of art, its relevance surpassing that of festival's glamour and gripping me to the point of shaping the ways that I reflect on the African cinematic journey anew.

As examined in this chapter, since its inception African cinema has had specific intentions with its films, reflecting the emerging styles and energy of its documentary film tradition. The story of the flip-flop exemplifies the dynamic struggles that African cinema has had to overcome, from the burden of colonialism to neo-colonialism, and the immanent continued restrictions over production, distribution and exhibition. The transformation of such flip-flops into art work and toys is not unlike how African film has developed as, along the way, it created a special, touching feel and a style all its own despite the political and economic constraints.

At the beginning of *Flip Flotsam* the shoes are seen to roll off the production line by the thousands, at an estimated 20 million pairs produced annually. The African market is flooded, just as it is with mainstream alien movies. This flow started during the colonial period but has continued and remains one of the main tools of neo-colonialism. Mass-produced Hollywood excess, along with Chinese and Indian films of similar ilk, has squeezed the distribution within Africa to where it is a struggle to show films made by Africans, especially documentaries. The film *Flip Flotsam* reminds us that every African foot wears a flip-flop, just as a foreign movie is in every African cinema.

While this film may be whimsical, it has profound meaning, capturing the resilience and strength of the African people. For, like the flip-flops in the movie, the African people adapt to their changing environments and stay afloat while riding the many waves of life. As the flip-flops become worn and run down beyond repair they are discarded and may find their way into the ocean; just as, during decolonisation, African countries were left to run themselves, or rather to be run by a puppet government, and the world turned its back on the continent. The film has a positive ending, demonstrating the cycle of life, death and rebirth, much as that colonialism forced the continent of Africa to undergo. African cinema mirrors the culture of recycling and reappropriation documented in *Flip Flotsam*. The themes found in African films express this feeling of a search for a place and purpose in a world that seems as contradictory as it is intractable. African documentary serves as an indispensable pedagogical tool for sustaining, (re)imaging and (re)contextualising the continent's prerogatives. A strong stance was taken in the early post-colonial African films which continues, expressed in a variety of innovative modes all directed towards reawakening the consciousness of the people.

NOTES

1. This chapter is but a survey, essentially of sub-Saharan African documentary. It deliberately avoids dwelling on documentary film practices in Arab North Africa; furthermore, it does not emphasise South Africa and the immense archive of documentary film works on Apartheid which numerous studies have addressed (e.g., Jacqueline Maingard 'To Change Reels: Film and Film Culture in South Africa', in Isabel Balseiro and Ntongela Masilela (eds), *Framing South African National Cinema and Television* [Detroit: Wayne State University Press, 2003]. See also Keyan Tomasseli, Martin Botha, Rosaleen Smyth etc.). It can also be noted that, although works from the ex-Belgian Congo are referred to, Belgian colonial practices do not quite match the proposed map. Belgian colonising policy involved, perforce, the French language, but otherwise denied the French assimilationist approach and Belgian film policy also echoed the British.

2. For a fuller discussion of this issue see my article 'African Cinematic Reality: The Documentary as an Emerging Trend', *Research in African Literatures* vol. 26 no. 3, Autumn 1995.

3. Jean-René Debrix, 'Le cinémaafricain', *Afrique Contemporaine* no. 38/39, July–October 1968, p. 7.

4. BFI ScreenonLine (2003), http://www.screenonline.org.uk/film/id/725486/. Accessed 15 September 2012.

5. Rosaleen Smyth, 'Movies and Mandarins, the Official Film and British Colonial Africa', in James Curran and Vincent Porter (eds), *British Cinema History* (London: Weidenfeld and Nicholson, 1983).

6. J. M. Burns, *Flickering Shadows: Cinema and Identity in Colonial Zimbabwe* (Athens, OH: Ohio University Press, 2002), p. xvi.

7. Quoted in Nwachukwu Frank Ukadike, *Black African Cinema* (Berkeley: University of California Press, 1994), p. 51.

8. For further discussion of *La croisiere noire* and other ethnographic films about Africa, see Ukadike, *Black African Cinema*, pp. 21–58.

9. Guy Hennebelle, 'Entretien avec Jean-René Débrix', *Afrique littéraire et artistique* no. 43, 1975, p. 82.

10. Notwithstanding Jean Rouch's great reputation as the 'father' of cinéma vérité (see Chapter 2.10 and Chapter 6.1), nevertheless, it must be said that Rouch's treatment of Africans in his films has raised numerous questions regarding ethnography, reality and cinema (see my critique of Rouch's African ethnographic films in Ukadike, *Black African Cinema*, pp. 49–52).

11. Clement Tapsoba, 'The African Documentary', *Ecrans d'Afrique* no. 16, April 1996.

12. See Jude Akudinobi's provocative article on this topic 'Reco(r)ding Reality: Representation and Paradigms in Nonfiction African Cinema', *Social Identities* vol. 6 no. 3, 2000.

13. Françoise Pfaff, *Twenty-five Black African Filmmakers* (New York: Greenwood Press, 1988), p. 72.

14. Ibid., p. 53.

15. Archer Winsten, *New York Post*, 15 March 1973, p. 50 (in Pfaff, *Twenty-five Black African Filmmakers*, p. 165).

16. Ukadike, *Black African Cinema*, p. 252.

17. Françoise Balogun, *The Cinema in Nigeria* (Enugu: Delta [Nigeria Limited], 1978), p. 22.

18. For a study of the GFIC, see Kwamina Kakyi, 'The Problems and Achievements of the Ghana Film Industry Corporation in the Growth and Development of the Film Industry in Ghana', MA thesis, School of Communication Studies, University of Ghana, Legon, July 1996.

19. Ron Hallis, 'Movie Magic in Mozambique', *Cinema Canada* no. 62, February 1980.

20. Since, at the time of independence, there was no national television in Mozambique, the only way the government could disseminate news to its people was via visual media – that is, the *Kuxa Kanema*, a weekly newsreel programme. The newsreels were shown in the 35mm format in the few available cinema halls.

21. For an in-depth discussion of *Sidet* and women's films of the black diaspora, see N. Frank Ukadike, 'Reclaiming Images of Women in Films from Africa and the African Diaspora', *Frontiers: Journal of Women Studies* vol. 15 no. 1, Spring/Summer 1994.

22. As described at http://www.pbs.org/independentlens/sistersinlaw/. Accessed 15 September 2012.

23. *Ye Wonz Maibel: Deluge*, http://www.salemmkuria.com/films/deluge.htm. Accessed 15 September 2012.

24. From the brochure promoting the Women of the Sun Film Festival held in Johannesburg South African, September 2010.

25. Ibid.

26. See World Story Organization's Kenya Film Industry Report: Justin Edwards, 'Building a Self-sustaining, Indegenous Film Industry in Kenya', January 2009. http://worldstoryorganization.org/documents. Accessed 15 September 2012.

27. Tapsoba, 'The African Documentary'.

28. See the description/synopsis of *Adwa* at http://www.sankofa.com (Haile Gerima's website). Accessed 15 September 2012.

29. Anon., 'Rostov–Luanda: Notes for Viewing the Film', California Newsreel (US distributors, n. d.) newsreel.org/guides/rostov.htm. Accessed 15 September 2012.

30. Jude Akudinobi, 'Reco(r)ding Reality: Representation and Paradigms in Nonfiction African Cinema', p. 347.

31. Anon., 'Arlit: Deuxieme Paris', California Newsreel (n. d.), http://newsreel.org/video/ARLIT-DEUXIEME-PARIS. Accessed 15 September 2012. All quotes relating to this film are from this source.

32. For Jean-Marie Teno's conversation with the author, see Nwachukwu Frank Ukadike 'Jean-Marie Teno (Cameroon)', *Questioning African Cinema: Conversations with Filmmakers* (Minneapolis: University of Minnesota Press, 2002).

33. For an expanded discussion of *Afrique je te plumerai*, see: N. Frank Ukadike, 'African Cinematic Reality: The Documentary as an Emerging Trend', *Research in African Literatures* vol. 26 no. 3, Autumn 1995.

34. Teshome Gabriel, '*Xala*: The Cinema of Wax and Gold', *Monthly Film Bulletin* vol. 33 no. 515, 1976.

35. For an extended discussion of *Maletendu Colonial*, see: Nwachukwu Frank Ukadike, 'Critical Dialogues: Transcultural Modernities and Modes of Narrating Africa in Documentary Films', *Matatu: Journal for African Culture and Society* vol. 36 no. 1, 2009.

36. Stuart Hall, as quoted in Institute of International Visual Arts brochure, July 2000.

3.3 Images from the South: Contemporary Documentary in Argentina and Brazil

ANA AMADO AND MARIA DORA MOURÃO

For Grierson, claiming that the documentary was a 'pulpit' was a mere rhetorical ploy. That this lacked substance was arguably not his fault; rather it was a consequence of his society's broad tolerance for debate which easily absorbs all criticism. In other places and at other times, more repressive circumstances conspire to give documentary a salience in the public sphere which has greater impact. In Latin America, later twentieth-century militarism having faded, documentary has become not so much a pulpit for proselytising, more a psychiatrist's couch for healing social trauma.

A POSSIBLE MAP

'Latin American' implies many things, including a continental imaginary. It is a concept – a thought which ties together policies, cultures, languages and literatures to build an imagined community and establishes a present based on common foundations. It is not easy, however, to think of images and experiences that actually synthesise this continent. The attempt to pull Latin America together under a single label had a *raison d'être* in the 1960s and 70s, when there was a common ground – a common search for utopias. Today, that common ground still exists, but within heterogeneous modes of positioning the symbolic construction of a community and of conceiving – or naming – such an integration.

Latin America, as is known, is also Ibero-America. The 'Ibero-American' contains – among many other issues – a linguistic asymmetry originated from the two great imperial powers that a couple of centuries ago divided the territory of the New World: Spain and Portugal. Current integration processes have set shared parameters where cultures touch closely so that it is impossible to think about a Latin American community that excludes Brazil.

Our intention, therefore, is to demarcate, in this extensive continental map, primarily the area that Brazil and Argentina share in geographic and cultural terms.[1] However, there are differences which make this task difficult.

A first difference lies, precisely, in the amount of documentary production in Brazil. The genre has been strengthened, though, in the last two decades – named, in consequence, the 'Documentary Spring'. This is the result of a number of institutional measures which gave a boost to production, as well being encouraged by the existence of É Tudo Verdade – Festival Internacional de Documentários [It's All True – International Documentary Film Festival]. Since its first edition in 1996 in São Paulo, the É Tudo Verdade Festival has continued, taking place every year both in São Paulo and Rio de Janeiro and also in other Brazilian states. There is no doubt that this event has had a great impact in recovering the historical importance of the documentary, which can be clearly seen in the emergence of new trends and new screening spaces. In 2001, the festival added the activities of the Conferencia Internacional do Documentário [International Documentary Conference], at which the documentary, in all its forms and variations, is considered as a fundamental audiovisual form. The effect has been that documentary film has become a main topic of debate and reflections, opening up spaces for more, and more generalised and systematised, research. The particular characteristic of this Brazilian documentary movement is that a continuous flow of documentaries is now seen in a meaningful number of screenings in cinemas. This is a Brazilian phenomenon that is clearly part of an international context, but with its own characteristics, particularly within the continent.[2]

The cultural diversity of Brazil is expressed in the diversity of topics and aesthetics from each of its regions. Argentina does not have such defined regional productions. However, repeating the 'eccentric' movement of the continent – 'eccentricity' nowadays being central – and especially because of a recent Audiovisual Media Law,[3] the production of films throughout the whole country has expanded significantly, providing local television with significant independent production. The opening up of media and the provision of alternative exhibition spaces has allowed for the circulation of voices and themes which are remarkably diverse. This has fuelled a constant search for new forms of documentary expression.

A STARTING POINT AND TWO AXES

To establish necessary limits on the scope of our study of this diversity and experimentation, we have identified certain axes. These are not to enable us to canonise works or authors. Rather, we will examine those films that, taken as a whole, allow us to sketch a preliminary map of the issues raised in general by the encounter (or clash) of the subjective and the public – after all a common articulation in contemporary documentary production worldwide. Such an articulation is clearly crossed on our map by a particularly salient pair of axes, thematic and at the same time conceptual: that is, history and memory.

We understand history not only as a narrow agenda connecting the collective institutionally, but also in a broader sense. We are interested in that history which is built from the quotidian experience of those who live it at different stages of their lives and turn it into their own stories. Precisely in the crossing between private and public lives, in how individual subjectivities relate to the world, lies a bridge between past and present. This, then, allows memory to attempt to organise the chaos of history within the limits of a documentary biography or autobiography.

The questions that serve as a starting point to guide us through this terrain embrace not only these issues as topics, but also include the formal devices that the documentaries we have selected use to address these issues. How are images, sounds, photos, documents, oral and written statements organised to touch the past when such history is recalled in the present? What is the appropriate treatment for audiovisual and textual materials in order into bring to the present its true historical content?

The trend in traditional terms is to propose documentary cinema as a tool for illustration and reflection on this or that period of history. The object of illustration or reflection is understood as an 'event' (a term that we believe triggers as many definitions as there are interpreters). But we prefer to reduce 'event' to its most immediate meaning: facts that bring up often unpredictable processes which have a strong collective impact. These 'facts' about 'events' are capable, for that reason, of producing substantive changes in understanding. Repeatedly, the tool deployed to do this with documentary is the use of archival images with a distinctive inscription of the authorial role (e.g., in editing). This defines the formal structure of Ibero-American documentary when it comes to collective history.[4]

In Brazil, Silvio Tendler's documentaries review the pre-dictatorial period of its twentieth-century history through filmic biographies of a series of failing democratic leaders. *Os Anos JK – uma trajetória política* [*The JK Years: A Political Trajectory*] (1980, Brazil) tells the story of the political rise of Juscelino Kubitschek. To illustrate his presidential years (1955–60), Tendler emphasises the audacity of building Brasilia, the new capital right in the geographical heart of the country and the man's tragic end. Kubitschek's political rights were eventually removed by the military government and he then died in a car accident. In 1981, director Luis Alberto Pereira directed the documentary

Jânio a 24 quadros [*Jânio at 24 Frames*] about the short-lived presidency of Jânio Quadros, who succeeded Kubitschek and resigned in August 1961 after serving only eight months. He was succeeded by Jango Goulart, the subject of the next documentary in Tendler's filmography: *Jango* (1984, Brazil). Goulart was the last democratic president, overthrown by the military coup of 1964. In *Tancredo, a travessia* [*Tancredo, the Crossing*] (2010, Brazil), Tendler continues the filmed documentation of Brazil's presidency with the study of the political career of Tancredo-Neves, the first civilian president after the two decades of military dictatorship. Tancredo was appointed in 1985 as a result of an agreement among military and the political parties at the transition from dictatorship back to democracy, but he passed away suddenly, without ever assuming office.

Documentary was also the vehicle chosen more and more during the 1990s in Argentina to study events of the historical past and social present, eventually becoming one of the main cinematographic genres in Argentinian film production by the beginning of the current century.

A substantial part of Argentina's current cinema uses documentary with different and complex poetic expressions to build accounts of individual and collective memory, as well as giving testimony to the consequences of the crimes of genocide of the dictatorship in that country, which, between 1976 and 1983, destroyed thousands of lives, a generation of young people. The review of these crimes had an aspect of research and denunciation during the first period of the recovery of democracy. For example, in *Juan, como si nada hubiera sucedido* [*Juan: As if Nothing Ever Happened*] (1987, Argentina), Carlos Echeverría, the film-maker, documented, in both formalistic and thematic terms, the investigation of the kidnapping and disappearance of a university student and activist of the Peronist left in the town of Bariloche during the military dictatorship.

Among other visual and narrative resources used by Echeverría, the story is told in the first person with an actor representing the director and the narrative illustrates each stage of his investigation. This approach provided a model which had a remarkable influence on the later work in the genre.

During the 1990s, the focus was also on documentaries about revolutionary organisations. Again, the technique of testimony predominates. In *Montoneros, una historia* [*A History of Montoneros*] (1994, Argentina), directed by Andrés Di Tella, the actions of the militant activists that belonged to the armed group *Montoneros*, and the repressive violence that was unleashed against them, are reported by different political groups. The film is structured around the memories of one protagonist, a survivor of a clandestine detention centre. A year after this film, *Cazadores de utopias* [*Hunters of Utopia*] (1995, Argentina), directed by David Blaustein, presented other testimonies of former *Montonero* militants. These are related in a highly subjective manner, the individual stories edited to give a choral account of historical and political memory.

Since the beginning of this millennium notably there has been a significant documentary production by the children of the victims of this 1970s generation. Each film exhibits different direct or indirect ways of reviewing the actions and political discourse of their parents. *Papá Iván* (2000, Argentina–Mexico), directed by María Inés Roqué, and *Los rubios* [*The Blondes*] (2003, Argentina) are films canonised because of the power of their search for parental truth. They vividly demonstrate the use of the documentary as an instrument for memory and personal identity, as well as also paying respect to the political victims of extreme oppression. In the contemporary context, they affirm generational difference but, at the same time, respect it. There have been many such films – for example, more recently, *(H) Historias cotidianas* [*(H) Everyday Stories*], Andrés Habegger's first documentary (2001, Argentina) and *M* (2008, Argentina) by Nicolás Prividera, among others.

In Brazil this trope is also a recent twenty-first-century development. Even though there are some earlier fiction movies which deal with the period of the dictatorship, it is not until the 2000s that a concentration of documentary feature films dealing directly with the military period emerged. Without a doubt, this movement is a consequence of the creation of the Special Commission in 1995 – within the Brazilian Human Rights Secretariat, which was given, in 2003, the status of a Ministry – to investigate the 'disappeared' of Brazil during the military period.[5]

In this group of movies we have *Cidadão Boilesen* [*Citizen Boilesen*] (2005, Brazil), directed by Chaim Litewski, about the execution by an armed guerrilla of a businessman – Boilesen, the citizen of the title – whom they accused of financing the clandestine 'Bandeirantes Operation' (OBAN). He was held to be guilty of direct complicity in the savage tortures practised by this organisation. Silvio Da Rin's *Hércules 56* (2006, Brazil) tells the story of one of the tensest periods during the dictatorship: the kidnapping in 1969 of American ambassador Charles Elbrick as a hostage to be exchanged for fifteen political prisoners. These were released and flown to Mexico on a Hercules 56 plane – hence the film's title. Five of the kidnappers are filmed seated at a round table remembering details of the event and the political context which motivated them. Their comments are alternated with the testimonies of other people and with archive images. In *Caparaó* (2007, Brazil), Flávio Frederico focuses on the first attempt of armed struggle against the military regime. It tells the story of an uprising against the government in August 1966 by a group of former soldiers cashiered from army units stationed in the Sierra de Caparaó. *Operação Condor* [*Operation Condor*] (2007, Brazil), directed by Roberto Mader, investigates transborder cooperation between the intelligence agencies of the different military governments in South America and their practices of kidnapping and murdering militants and political activists.

Excess of testimony – talking heads as main source of information – which makes the word the foundation for meaning and conditions narratives, is repeatedly deployed in the documentaries we have mentioned. This can be seen as being at the expense of more creative techniques in which more relevance could be given to, for instance, text – writing – and its relation, reconciled or not, with the image. But not everybody would agree in condemning extensive 'talking head' witness as being filmically of limited effectiveness. Agnès Varda, for example, believes that 'the academic prejudice that a documentary can't just be a mere succession of testimonies, [caused] it to be dressed up and inflated with a profusion of irrelevant devices'.[6]

It is essential to mention here the Chilean Patricio Guzmán, whose documentaries perfectly demonstrate the passage between memory and history. The canonical *La Batalla de Chile* [*The Battle of Chile*] (1972–79, Chile–France) offers an exceptional account of the political, social and cultural alternatives being implemented by the government of Salvador Allende. These unfold in a present tense, creating a narrative arc which leads, inexorably, to the military coup and Allende's downfall in 1973. In *La memoria obstinada* [*Chile, the Obstinate Memory*] (1997, Chile), Guzmán returns to these events using the testimonies of many of the people involved. The role of voices and images of survivors and other witnesses is equally central in his *Pinochet* (Chile, 2001) and in *Allende* (Chile, 2004). His recent *Nostalgia de la Luz* [*Nostalgia for the Light*] (2010, Chile) brilliantly explores multiple levels of metaphor for absence. It is a philosophical observation on memory, time and the cosmos under the clear sky of the Atacama desert, where the ancients left thousands of geoglyphes (their meanings largely lost), while modern astronomers now search the heavens as relatives of the disappeared excavate mass graves in which the remains of the dictatorship's victims lie.

The representations of death and massacres are not only signified in the documentaries by oral testimony although this predominates; sometimes, techniques exploring the relationship between texts and visible forms are used also to illustrate what otherwise cannot be represented. *Trelew. La fuga que fue masacre* [*Trelew: The Runaway that was a Massacre*] (2004, Argentina), directed by Mariana Arruti, presents a thorough reconstruction through survivors' testimony. The atrocity, the cold-blooded murder of nineteen guerrillas imprisoned in naval base at Trelew, on the shores of Patagonia, is recalled without any images as only oral (or verbal) narrative describes the execution scene.

In Andrés Habegger's *Imagen Final* [*Final Image*] (2008, Argentina) the missing image is that of the death of

Nostalgia de la Luz (2010): a philosophical observation on memory, time and the cosmos under the clear sky of Atacama desert

cameraman Leonardo Henriksen. Henriksen filmed his killer, the soldier we see shooting at him during the assault on the Palacio de la Moneda in 1973.

In *El predio* [*The Space*] (2010, Argentina), by Jonathan Perel, what is missing is the reverse: words – testimony. For that reason the power of the visual is the only way left to pass on the memory of the horror of the Navy School for Mechanics (ESMA), the largest centre of torture and disappearance during the dictatorship. In *Pacto de silencio* [*Pact of Silence*] (2005, Argentina), Carlos Echeverría establishes truth about the present through the remorseless display of files which visually evidence the complicity of the people of Bariloche in the defence of a Nazi killer, Erich Priebke, who was hiding happily in their midst for decades.

THE PERIOD OF 'IMAGES-VÉRITÉ'/ 'IMÁGENES-VERDAD'

During the 1960s, both in Brazil and Argentina there was a desire to understand 'the people': through the documentary, social history enters the scene. Fernando Birri, with *Tire Dié* [*Throw us a Dime*] (1960, Argentina) and *Los inundados* [*Flood Victims*] (1962, Argentina), had a profound influence across the continent with his neo-realist aesthetic. Using this precedent (and with topics also tackled by the fictions of *Cinema Novo*), Brazilian documentary approached contemporary social and political themes. *Viramundo* (1965, Brazil) by Geraldo Sarno, considered by Brazilian critic Jean Claude Bernardet a 'classic of Brazilian sociological documentary', follows peasants in north-east Brazil fleeing drought only to suffer proletarisation in São Paulo. The narration emphasises in this displacement the role of mysticism and religiosity to relieve the conditions of poverty, social inadequacy and difficulties of integration for the migrants.

The urban environment of heterogeneous classes in São Paulo is also the setting for *Liberdade de Imprensa*

[*Freedom of the Press*] (1967, Brazil), by João Batista de Andrade, a provocative documentary in the cinéma vérité style, made in the middle of the dictatorship. Andrade starts discussions on the streets of downtown São Paolo about the authorities' gagging of the press. With this film, the 'Street Cinema' movement begins, characterised by a strategy of direct intervention by the film-maker. It gives importance to excluded voices, correcting the denial of public debate. In *Opinião Pública* [*Public Opinion*] (1967, Brazil), by Arnaldo Jabor, the focus of the documentary, also in the cinéma vérité style, is the Brazilian middle class, mostly the conservative groups in Rio de Janeiro and their complicity in the military coup of 1964.

Films from the Liberation Film Group (e.g., *El camino hacia la muerte del viejo Reales* [*Viejo Reales Long Road to Death*] [1968, Argentina]) directed by Gerardo Vallejo), stress the human and material symbols of poverty as a call to action in an overtly political sense. *La hora de los hornos* [*The Hour of the Furnaces*], by Fernando Solanas and Octavio Getino (1968–70, Argentina), also of the Liberation Film Group, is a documentary that formally unites the artistic and political avant-gardes, to the extent that it is preceded and accompanied by declarations that highlight the intention of using the film as a tool of intervention and direct political agitation. Through its fraught (because prohibited) national and international distribution, this canonical movie is the greatest example of *engagé* political cinema produced in Latin America (or some would say, anywhere) during the 1970s.

Following an international trend, production in the 70s in Brazil became more diversified. A broader range of topics was dealt with. Experimental and reflexive documentaries were produced, such as *Congo* (Brazil, 1972), in which Arthur Omar documents a folk ritual using visual procedures that break the tradition of ethnographic documentary. *Di* (1977) by Glauber Rocha can be referred to as a documentary recording of an event (the funeral of one of the most important Brazilian painters, Di Cavalcanti); but it also involves direct intervention in the action. This mix of cinéma vérité and the aesthetic of live television reporting promote a style that Glauber would later develop in his television show *Abertura*, between 1979 and 1980.

During this period, film-makers in Brazil began to produce films that explore the border between documentary and fiction, anticipating a most obvious feature of realism as it is now seen in current cinema. Jorge Bodanzky and Orlando Senna had already made us confront the documentary/fiction divide with *Iracema, uma transa amazônica* [*Iracema: An Amazonic Fuck*] finished (and censored) in 1975. The military leaders then in power had developed a national integration and development policy which included building a highway across Amazonia. The film attacks the project by documenting the destruction of the region, the use of slave labour and the spread of

Iracema, uma transa amazônica (1975): the border between documentary and fiction

prostitution. It does so in the context of a fictional story of Iracema, a girl from the area. (Iracema is deceived by a truck driver, Tião Brasil Grande, and ends up becoming a prostitute, working along the Transamazonic road.)

The contemporary movie that echoes *Iracema* is *Serras da Desordem* (2006, Brazil) directed by Andrea Tonacci. This documentary also focuses on a main character, an indigenous man called Carapiru, but introduces a fictional aspect when Tonacci invites Carapiru to reconstruct his own story. Carapiru himself then re-enacts, as an actor, his history of forced acculturation that, as in the case of 'Iracema', reflects the civilising policy of the nation of Brazil. He returned to the forest in which he lived and he retraces his life there; but when Carapiru remembers and reconstructs his story, he approaches fictional narrative. So, the environment is real, the story is real, the topic is the same as in *Iracema* – deforestation problems due to the advance of 'civilisation' causing drastic social and cultural transformations. The film moves forward with fragments and oppositions (individual and society, nature and civilisation, 'reality' and fiction), making it difficult for the audience to feel comfortable. This is exacerbated by a notable formal experimentation with language.

During the 1980s there is a move towards the essayistic with documentaries that were very critical, ironic and conceptual. Sergio Bianchi's *Mato Eles?* (1982, Brazil) denounces the illegal appropriation of indigenous land in the south of Brazil while *Ilha das Flores* [*Isle of Flowers*] (1985, Brazil) by Jorge Furtado condemns poverty, hunger and social exclusion. These are examples of documentaries dealing with social problems, but they subvert the hegemony of the classic approach in that they reject the presentation of a thesis (sociological, philosophical or simply poetic) as the determinant of the film's structure.

ICONOGRAPHY, ALLEGORY, MYTHS AND HISTORY

In order to cut across the dark history and drama of Argentina in the second half of the twentieth century, the language of myth appeared to be a good ally. In both its narrative and visual aspects, the documentary *Pulqui, Un instante en la patria de la felicidad* [*Pulqui: A Moment in the Native Land of Happiness*] (2006, Argentina), directed by Alejandro Fernandez Moujan, incorporates this mythical aspect of history. The inexhaustible iconography from the first period of Peronism inspired visual artist Daniel Santoro to recreate on his canvas key moments of the collective imaginary, synthesised in the figures of Peron and Evita; scenes of domestic well being, public architecture and the ruins of that happy past. Among those images he paints is that of a small plane, the 'Pulqui', an emblematic engineering feat representing Peronism's technical prowess. A scale reproduction being built in the present inspires Moujan, who documents the reconstruction's stages through to its fleeting attempt at flight.

Julián d'Angiolillo, in *Hacerme Feriante* [*Becoming a Stallholder*] (2010, Argentina) deals with another myth, that of the happy leisure times of the people during the first Peronist period. The film focuses on *La Salada* – originally built in the 1950s as a park and resort in the suburbs of Buenos Aires – taking as a starting point the emblematic space's transformation into a gigantic, informal, densely crowded, nocturnal flea-market. With the use of freeze-frames, d'Angiolillo spotlights moments of the past, bringing them to the present, searching those languages and images for some intensity of original moments for which records no longer exist. This is one positive way to work with myths, creating a strong dialectic necessary to understanding the present. In his documentary notes, Pasolini said that no present could be built without appealing to mythical history, a sort of collective unconsciousness as indispensable cement for the contemporary.[7]

Leonardo Favio followed this principle, turning the language of the myth into the basis of visual and narrative articulation in his long documentary *Perón, sinfonía del sentimiento* [*Peron, Symphony of a Feeling*] (1996–2000). In it he gives a fictional treatment to archives and other documentary sources (stills and audio files) by interrelating them to the history. The film announces itself as a documentary and indeed Favio does provide a documentary history of Peronism. The most important feature of the narrative structure, however, is the use of the language of myth; that is, the complex account which emerges from the melding of past and present (a 'back/forward' time). This creates a mythic imagining of the historical facts. Favio makes use of various resources to manipulate images and sound, such as the reconstitution of archival files and, to strengthen the visual representation, the utilisation of actors who are doubles of Peron and Eva, as well as other doubles for the politicians and labour leaders who were around them. All of this material is linked (again) to Daniel Santoro's drawings and paintings that focus on Peronist themes and characters. The result is an almost 'sacramental' vision of the

Peronist past narrated in a plausible and believable way to perpetuate the history.

This transforms myth into a narrative engine of history; but there are those who associate the technique with propagandising, creating exaggerated feelings by replaying 'populist' scenes. Paradoxically, the fact that attention is drawn to this ends up highlighting a mark (or a sort of expressive peculiarity) which is ascribed to our cinema, to Latin America in general and, by extension, to all those countries considered 'Third World'. Artists in this realm are somehow condemned to narrating history always as crisis, catastrophes and misery. In the 1980s, Frederic Jameson coined the concept 'national allegory' – which has had a long life despite the criticisms it has received – to define cinema and literature from these countries that, unlike the hegemonic representation systems, tend to tell private individual stories as an allegory for public situations. Jameson exemplifies this with his interpretation of the movies of Solanas and Ousmane Sembène, among others.[8]

A documentary that must be considered when it comes to the revision of the historical past is *Cándido López. Los campos de batalla* [*Candido Lopez: The Battlefields*] (2005, Argentina), directed by José Luis García. The film does not turn to myth or allegory but rather to the visual arts, since the visual and conceptual guide for his narrative is a series of oil paintings by Cándido López (1840–1902). Cándido López was both soldier and journalist during the War of the Triple Alliance (1865–70) declared by Brazil, Uruguay and Argentina against Paraguay. The director, who also becomes the narrator of the film, starts his journey through Argentinian and Brazilian Mesopotamia, walking around the battlefields (where remains of shrapnel can still be found) and reproducing with his camera the famous 'higher viewpoint' which Cándido López used. This was a very cinematographic technique, portraying battle scenes as if in a high-angle establishing shot showing multiple, simultaneous actions. On the road, the director discovers personal stories and, at the same time, the reasons why these states have hidden this war of extermination unleashed against Paraguay.

Gilles Deleuze analysed the work of 'marginal' authors, perhaps with more subtlety than Jameson, by assimilating an idea postulated by Kafka about the potential but subversive strength of 'minor literature' produced in small central European countries. Such strength can be ascribed to myths which cross the border dividing private issues from politics – for instance, in the films of Glauber Rocha.[9] The slant that guarantees a bridge would be subjectivity – the assumption of the individual's right to interrogate the world in an exercise invoking memories which are neither entirely personally psychological nor completely collective, but rather a two-way street between the personal and the public.

POETICS OF EXPERIENCE AND DOCUMENTS OF MEMORY

The documentary genre broadened and made room for new forms of expression that, in a panoramic and circular movement, open up new ways of representation and enunciation. The classical tradition of observing and/or reflecting the Other was broken and there was an incorporation of the 'I' for the first time. Latin American documentary started seeking a place for the subject in the representation of the world. A new way of constructing subjectivity in contemporary documentary emerged, operating mainly through the creation of sentimental connections between the film-maker and the audience, connections on which a subjective cinema always tries to build.

Subjective narration and personal documentary images allow the exploration of the relationship between watching and memory. And it is in that relationship that an inner discourse is configured to reveal the truth of the artist; and at the same time, images also show some truth about the world, or a stage of history. This search for identity in the world tends towards globalisation. It is a movement that seeks to transform inner discourse into manifest discourse, in which the personal/the subjective are predominant. The first person acquired an expressive cultural and political importance during recent decades, so it becomes important to ascertain where the 'place of the subject' falls in the representation of the world undertaken by the documentary.

João Moreira Salles, in *Santiago* (2006, Brazil), wants to tell the story of Santiago, his family's butler. However, his personal performance as director and interviewer restructures the discourse so much that the film – which should be about the fascinating personality of Santiago, an obsessive and almost delirious researcher of dynasties and aristocracies from the past all over the world – turns more into the story of the relationship between him and Salles, between butler and boss, transforming the focus of the film. Instead of a portrait of the servant, it becomes the unveiling of a power relationship, exposing the identity of the boss, the film's director. This occurs largely because of the different stages of the film's production dynamic; Salles started filming Santiago in 1992 but abandoned the project at the editing stage. By 2005, when he took it up again, Santiago had died. Processing those images thirteen years later, Salles noticed how they tell more of a story about him and his family (the traditions of the upper class, the diplomat father, the mother, siblings, luxurious environments, the business dinners, big parties, etc.) than about Santiago. The narrator is one of his brothers, who, reading the text written by João, superimposes the first person of both of them. The film becomes a shared memory of a house and a world that no longer exists.

Eduardo Coutinho's *Cabra marcado para morrer* [*Twenty Years Later*] (1964–84, Brazil), also tracks through its production processes different time periods. Filming began in 1964 with the reconstruction of the story of a murdered peasant leader, using actors who are themselves peasants. The military coup interrupted the production, which was taken up again in 1981 when Coutinho returned to the locale and found his lead actors from the past. Coutinho is one of the most noteworthy contemporary documentarists in his exploration of the limits of truthfulness exposed by gaps and differences between testimonies, memories. In *Cabra marcado para morrer*, the conflicts of different testimonial 'I's reveal a truly shocking story in which the personal is inexorably bound into the political and social history of the country.

Jogo de Cena [*Playing*] (2006, Brazil) may be the film in which he plays with these issues the most. He solicited life stories from women via a newspaper advertisement as the basis of his script, which he then filmed using actresses recounting on the stage of a theatre in Rio. Coutinho thereby creates a relationship among the informants, the actresses sitting on the stage and himself. The theatrical scene includes Coutinho, his crew and the equipment. He makes himself present, becoming, it could be said, the narrator of his own self.

Among the later films of Andrés Di Tella, those he has made this century, are many in the register that gives literal resonance to the voice by dissecting first-person subjectivity. Di Tella investigates both conscious and unconscious intimacy and memory. Starting with *La televisión y yo* [*Television and Me*] (2003, Argentina), where this is stressed in the very title, Di Tella uses a style which is different from that of the Brazilians. This first film turns on the historical fact that his family owned the company that produced everything from refrigerators to cars for the prosperous Argentina of the first period of Peronism. In this film, with the mediation of a paternal figure, he revives family memory and a lineage both historical and political. In *Fotografías* [*Photograph*] (2007, Argentina), the evocation of his dead mother – an Indian psychoanalyst who had a

remarkable career in Argentina in the 1960s – again creates a narrative flow between the private and the collective. In the drifting of this line, some notions that are upheld by institutional and official history end up being altered by the documentary's unexpected findings.

Voice, language, the archive (the material of history), along with sequences contingent upon memory, all form part of the repertoire used by those that share the condition of being professional film-makers with the condition of being children of the disappeared (Albertina Carri, María Inés Roqué, Nicolás Prividera, among others). They use in their work the formal relationships between document and fiction, intimacy and character. The voice of the 'I' as the bridge between personal and historical time is most meaningfully displayed in Albertina Carri's *Los rubios*, which documents the way in which private mourning and personal exercise of memory come into contact with Argentinian history at its most violent.

Alternatively, the disassociation of voice and image can be seen in *Apuntes para una biografía imaginaria* [*Notes from an Imaginary Biography*] (Edgardo Cozarinsky, 2010, Argentina). Cozarinsky creates a formal and visual tension between subjective and objective, the factual and the recreated – in short, between 'what has been lived and what has been filmed'. This can, therefore, be described (echoing Cozarinsky's title) as an 'imaginary documentary'. His practice justifies the oxymoron because the 'realist' character of the film's materials – archival footage covering various episodes of the second European war, or various historic milestones in Argentina – are subjectively marked by adding personal references to the image and in the voiceover. The 'truth' of these facts of personal or collective history are thus illustrated in the abundance of archive material.

In this and the other documentaries mentioned, speech and subjectivity express memory as an imaginary. They are the tools in which body, voice and the archive of images create a politics of meaning. An element of indecision follows which somehow defines a new mode of realism, one worthy of the comment by Deleuze, who distinguishes it as a quality of 'peripheral' cinema:

> The opposite of fiction is not what is real, it's not the truth, which is always that of masters or colonizers; but rather the fable-making of the poor, in that it gives to the false the power that turns it into a memory, a legend, a monster.[10]

La televisión y yo (2003): family memory and a lineage both historical and political

In *Apuntes*, Cozarinsky's archive of images and the archives of others are the instruments with which, in his editing, he highlights anachronism. He did not do this when following the chronological path of his previous biographical essays (*La guerra de un solo hombre* [*The War of the Lonely Man*, 1981]; *Scarlatti On Sevilla* [1990]; *Bulevares del crepúsculo* [*Bulevares*

of the *Twilight*, 1992]; *Citizen Langlois* [1994]; *Fantasma de Tánger* [*Ghost of Tanger*, 1997]). However, in *Apuntes*, Cozarinksy is the object of his own enquiries; he autobiographically follows the whimsical thread of images that testify – through verbal or just visual complicity – to memories and experiences in which the self and the Other have the Deleuzian power of that which is false to push the memory or the legend.

From one generation of film-makers to another, a common memory unleashes complementary imaginaries. In *Apuntes* and in Albertina Carri's short film *Restos* (2010), a second-degree disappearance is experienced when the images are recorded by film-makers and others who have themselves disappeared in the violent years of the dictatorship. The films they have left behind constitute a sort of ghost archive. Films too 'disappeared'. Originally clandestine, they were seized by the authorities and have left no trace – even of their absence. Memory 'of what is left' is how Cozarinsky describes the fate of celluloid material which 'disappears' in this way to be recycled at an industrial level in clothes, combs, hair, shoe polish (objects that are all metonyms for the body). A memorable shot of *Restos* tells us that there is no turning back; celluloid is not recycled but is dissolved with a literalism that is almost organic, in acid: metonymy of bodies and their disappearance.

FROM MYTH TO CONTEMPORARY FABLES
Before, the idea behind the dramaturgy of documentaries was synthesis, the capacity of a character to symbolise a group, a class. This context had a big impact on the New Latin American Cinema in the 1960s and 70s. Now, it is more important to think about singular characters who pose a particular question to their world or allow for a questioning of the world and its ways through their experiences, sharing a common idea of understanding and living in the world as a representation. This, to a large extent, now cuts through reality and the investigation of history. The documentary in general and the documentaries we mentioned here in particular build and/or evoke the present and past with an accumulation of references; but these references and perspectives, both individual and collective, respond to specific situations in time and space: to ways of living, of occupying a place and a geographic environment, of cutting across history. In short, the documentaries of the south of the American continent intensify the power of the fabulist function of recorded experience.

NOTES
1. Since 1991, Argentina and Brazil have been part of the Mercosur (Common Southern Market), along with Paraguay, Uruguay and, still undergoing the process for incorporation, Venezuela. Bolivia, Chile, Colombia, Ecuador and Peru are associate nations. Its creation implied a number of economic, social, political, cultural and symbolic innovations for the member nations. A key year was 2003, the coalition being relaunched by the governments of Lula in Brazil and Kirchner in Argentina. Since then, a process of strengthening regional integration has taken place over merely commercial issues, but with a broadening of the agenda to different groups and with novel initiatives in diverse areas. Some areas that at first were not considered key for early integration, such as cinematography (the movie industry), entered the agenda. The revamping of the Mercosur is seen through the creation of a specific organisation created to discuss cinema and audiovisual industry issues. The RECAM (Specialised Meeting of Cinematographic and Audiovisual Authorities of the Southern Market), with its central offices in Montevideo, Uruguay, since 2003, is the advisory body of representatives from the highest cinematographic authorities of each participant nation. Between 2003 and 2009, when Mercosur's Audiovisual Programme was launched, thirty-seven movies were completed as co-productions that included at least two member nations of Mercosur, in most cases Brazil and Argentina. For a more exhaustive analysis of the transformations of Mercosur in regards to cinema, see Marina Moguillansky, 'Pantallas del sur. La integración cinematográfica en el Mercosur', unpublished PhD thesis, Social Sciences, University of Buenos Aires, 2011.

2. In 1996, there was only one full-length documentary shown in the cinemas – *Todos os Corações do Mundo* [*Two Billion Hearts*] (Murilo Salles, 1995). By 2006, there were twenty-six and, in 2010, twenty-four. Another interesting detail is that in 2011, in Brazil, the number of documentaries produced was sixty, versus fifty-nine narrative fiction films.

3. Law 26.522 of the Audiovisual Communication Services governs the operation of television and radio media in Argentina. Enacted in October 2009 by President Cristina Kirchner, it replaced the rule enacted during the military dictatorship in 1980, which limited freedom of expression as well as ownership of media to certain companies. Allowing for more permits/licences and spaces, this law encouraged intense audiovisual production with a strong emphasis on the use of the documentary from a number of educational, social and other similar organisations throughout the whole country.

4. In Brazil, the military dictatorship governed from 1964–85. It was the longest period for such a regime and the model spread throughout Latin America during the decade of the 70s. In Chile, the military dictatorship governed from 1973–84 and in Argentina from 1976–83. The relationship between cinema and memory was one of the most explored themes in Latin American documentary cinema, although the issue took different formal perspectives and historical precedents, since

Argentina and Brazil – as well as Chile – followed
different paths and styles in returning to democracy.

5. In 2011, under the presidency of Dilma Rousseff, the
National Truth Commission was created to investigate
the violation of human rights during the period 1946–88.

6. Gonzalo De Pedro, 'Agnès Varda "Es un mal debate el
del cine femenino"', *El Mundo*, 13 April 2012,
www.elcultural.es/version_papel/CINE/30890/Agnes_Varda.
Accessed 11 September 2012.

7. Pasolini, in one of the most interesting sequences of his
documentary *Appunti per un'Orestiade Africana [Notes for an
African Orestides]* (1970), emphatically stated that: 'The

myths of the ancestors must co-exist with your recovered
democracy.' African students, listening to him at a Roman
university, rejected his arguments with the same strength.

8. Frederic Jameson, 'Transformaciones en la imagen en la
postmodernidad' [Transformations in the Image in
Postmodernity], *Revista de Crítica Cultural* no. 6, ed. Cuarto
Propio (Santiago de Chile: Marzo, 1993). Translation of
'Third World Literature in the Era of Multinational
Capitalism', *Social Text* no. 5, Autumn 1998.

9. *L'image-temps. Cinéma 2* (Paris: Les Éditions de Minuit,
1985), p. 202.

10. Ibid.

3.4 'Roadblock' Films, 'Children's Resistance' Films and 'Blood Relations' Films: Israeli and Palestinian Documentary Post-*Intifada* II

RAYA MORAG

Outside of the West, documentary has long been a platform for the ongoing search to uncover and establish national identities. The more vexed the realpolitik, the more significant is this work. Nowhere is this better seen than in the Middle East and in its longest-running conflict. The struggle to possess the documentary screen has become as real as the struggle for land, legitimacy and statehood.

> The colonial situation, by its own internal inevitability, brings on revolt. For the colonial condition cannot be adjusted to; like an iron collar, it can only be broken.
>
> Albert Memmi[1]

Any analysis of the regional documentary cinema of Israel and Palestine must take several factors into consideration. The fact that 130 years have passed since the Zionist movement's return to, and settlement in Palestine during the 1880s makes the Israeli–Palestinian conflict one of the longest in modern history; it is a conflict that is constantly intensifying, escalating through the course of seven wars, two *Intifadas*[2] and a series of short-term armed confrontations. Since the establishment of the state of Israel in 1948 and the War of Independence/Palestinian *Naqba*,[3] an average of one war or armed conflict has occurred every six years.[4] The Israeli occupation (of 1948, but particularly of 1967) has enforced colonial and neo-colonial dependency and subjugating relations on Palestinian society. This has been evidenced by the eruption of two *Intifadas*, Palestinian suicide terrorism and Israeli state terror; it has contributed to the sharp polarisation of Israeli society into left and right camps and led to major political-religious upheavals, specifically the rise of the settlement movement and the growth of Jewish, as well as of Hamas and Islamic, fundamentalism. Since 1910, when the first documentary film was produced by the Jewish community in Palestine, and 1935, when the first was made by Palestinian Arabs, the ongoing endeavour of both sides of the conflict has been to cinematically constitute national identity and document their nations' coming-into-being as a 'community of

memory' deeply attached to the region.[5] Both corpora simultaneously – although in different ways and to various degrees – are concerned with issues of identity (trans)formation and negotiation of the 'I-Other' in a condition of incessant conflictual and traumatic relations.

This chapter aims to analyse both corpora as cinema of conflict by focusing on the second *Intifada*, a major turning point in the Israeli–Palestinian conflict, and thus also in its representation.[6] Since the second *Intifada*, due to the dismantling of traditional contrasts (terror–war, sovereign state–legitimate authority, front–home, civilian–soldier, defence–offence, beginning–end, victory–defeat, moral–immoral), and particularly the 'deliberate targeting of non-combatants', the war has been conducted as a twenty-first-century, 'new' war.[7] This drastic change in the style of war and the very fact of the second eruption of an *Intifada* have dramatically changed the nature of the conflict,[8] creating, on the Israeli part, a major moral breakdown and, therefore, various processes of humanisation of the Palestinian Other (both in public discourse and on television), and intensified, on the Palestinian part, the Palestinian claim to justice and endorsement of the culture of *shahidism*, 'martyrdom'.

It is my contention that during the course of their evolution the corpora shared many characteristics: the dominance of collective, constitutive trauma (the Holocaust [*Shoah*] and the *Naqba*); an ethos of 'return' to one's homeland; the binary conceptualisation of the subject positions of victim and perpetrator; claims to (post-traumatic) victimhood; the denial of perpetration; dialectic tension between the image of the refugee and that of the fighter/soldier; and the deliberate silencing of the Other's master narrative. As the second *Intifada*'s documentary cinema demonstrates, it is despite, or rather because of this conspicuous similitude that their ideological and aesthetic routes as cinemas of conflict are totally different. Israeli cinema's most notable emerging trends relate to the loss of the moral high ground in what I describe henceforth as the 'good Israeli' films and perpetrator trauma films (relating, respectively to the Palestinian civilian and the Israeli soldier). Palestinian cinema relentlessly deals with the conflict's escalation in terms of films depicting the hardship of colonialism, as in the new sub-genre of road-block movie, and with the continuation of the struggle for liberation, as in the new sub-genre of the 'children's resistance' film. However, analysis of both corpora, based on the evolution of I–Other cinematic relations, also reveals a progression towards (at least) a cinematic reconciliation. Both corpora strive to be reality-shaping, offering a new version – conflict-driven but also conflict-mediating – of docu-activism, a version which challenges both peoples' violent histories and their current fundamentalism.

The chapter outlines the disparate ideological and aesthetic routes taken by the two corpora and, concomitantly, the new, regional sub-genres that emerged during the second Intifada. Proposing a taxonomy of conflict cinema is discussed in the conclusion as an evolution that triggers important positive cinematic change, attesting to the complex, fluctuating role of documentary cinema in crisis-ridden zones of protracted conflict.

'ROADBLOCK' FILMS

From its inception, Israeli documentary cinema, similarly to that of its Palestinian counterpart, was revolutionary, propagandistic and nationalist. For almost eight decades between 1910 and 1987 it supported the Zionist project, reproduced its ideology and endorsed the heroism and morality of the Israeli soldier who fights 'just wars'.[9] The few critical documentaries that appeared during this period were mostly made after 1967[10] and only retrospectively attained the status of ideologically pioneering, subversive works. However, over the course of its development, Israeli documentary cinema evinces major ideological transformations with respect to Zionism, occupation and terror, and the ethnic-religious Other: the Palestinian.

While attempting to cope with the psycho-political-moral crisis exposed by the first and, particularly, the second Intifada, left-wing documentary cinema – influenced by the shift towards the Other at the beginning of the 1980s known as the Palestinian Wave films[11] and post-Zionist trends denying Zionism as a revolutionary movement of Jewish renewal[12] – ruptured the Zionist ethos and shifted the 'collective voice' to an 'anti-collective' voice. Negotiating the power of prevailing binarisms – Zionism–post-Zionism, victim–perpetrator, state violence–terror, recognition–disavowal and even left–right – becomes critical in light of the changing nature of the war, emphasising the unbearable transition from Zionism's New Jew to the 'new (war) soldier', a soldier who encounters a civilian population on a daily basis. Through self-critical, un-hegemonic and ideologically fractured films, documentary cinema criticises the occupation, portrays the Palestinian as the ultimate

victim and expresses a heartfelt sense of soldierly and civil (un-cathartic) guilt.[13] Two major trends on the left that emerged during the second Intifada embody these ideological transformations, creating what I consider two sub-genres that I call the 'good Israeli' films and perpetrator trauma films. Both trends negotiate Israel's post-Holocaust claim to victimhood, and thus the binarism of victim–perpetrator that is at the heart of cinematic representations of the Israeli–Palestinian conflict. The deepening of the inherent splits inside Israeli society in terms of right–left, secular–religious and Zionist–anti/a-Zionist is further enhanced by the emergence of a reactionary, religious, national-Zionist trend, mainly on the right.

Unlike the major trends of the first decade of twenty-first-century docu-activism in world cinema – mainly in Michael Moore's post-9/11 work – in post-second Intifada 'good Israeli' docu-activism it is not the director-celebrity who is the hero, but rather the ordinary Israeli assisted by the director, who is often a political-social activist. At centre stage are their relentless efforts to lend visibility to the emblematic Palestinian experience – subjugation to an 'intolerable, illegitimate exercise of power',[14] which is rendered invisible and repressed by many sectors of Israeli society and public discourse – and to promote an improvement in Palestinian daily routine. Therefore, the unavoidable blurring of distinction between docu-activism and social activism defines the 'good Israeli' films.[15]

The activism of the 'good Israeli' trend reveals a spectrum on one side of which films like 9 Stars Hotel (Ido Haar, 2006) lend visibility to Palestinian misery and entail the director's cooperation with Palestinians who are transgressing Israeli law. 9 Stars Hotel depicts the lives of Palestinian labourers building the new city of Mod'in, who are forbidden to stay in Israel. Summer and winter, they live in inhuman conditions in the hills surrounding the city and engage, with the director, in a constant game of cat and mouse with the army and border police. In the middle of the spectrum are films whose directors, as political activists, document their own active participation with, and contribution to the Palestinian political struggle. Bil'in My Love (Shai Carmeli-Pollack, 2007), for instance, depicts in a harsh, direct style a year of participating in, and documenting, the weekly demonstrations against the separation wall and the expropriation of land in the West Bank village of Bil'in. The director occasionally interviews the leaders of Bil'in's 'Popular Committee Against the Fence', tries to mediate with the Israeli commander before the riot escalates and, finally, dedicates the film to the victims of the struggle. At the other end of the spectrum, the films depict Israeli political-social intervention on behalf of the Palestinians. The director documents other social activists, as in The Human Turbine (Danny [Nokio] Varta, 2009). Moving beyond the 'permanent emergency' cliché to deal with the specificity of living conditions, this documentary details three years of Israeli activism: in joint meetings between local residents and group members, four Israelis have created a renewable energy project at the Hebron village of Susia, supplying electricity to residents living in tents and caves. The film follows the project's development up until the activists manage to make another way of life possible for the residents, who are shepherds, by providing them with the option of selling refrigerated milk to make a living and, finally, supplying the entire village with electricity.

Although this form of docu-/social activism is driven by a profound humanistic attitude of 'doing', it is paradoxically limited. The paradox derives from the 'good Israeli' trend's grounding in Israeli long-time coloniser complex: the Israeli left's harsh condemnation of the occupation, while practically and/or symbolically retaining the coloniser's subject position. As the 'good Israeli' films demonstrate, the 'good Israeli' identity is articulated as a movement caught between defying and belonging to the Israeli colonial regime, between Antigone-esque aspirations and preconstituted Creon-like sovereignty. In other words, although this docu-activism is critical-affective, it is subjected, through preconstituted colonial power relations, to a system that reasserts itself through both humanitarian pseudo-humanitarian and de-humanitarian acts.

The roadblock movie, which emerged during the second *Intifada* as a unique, regional sub-genre, encapsulates this long-time coloniser complex and, because of the spatial regime of the occupation, the paradox of socio-cinematic intervention it entails is extreme. Expressing the 'good Israeli' syndrome, roadblock movies, such as Ram Levy's *Close, Closed, Closure* (2002), Yoav Shamir's *Checkpoint* (2003) and Simone Bitton's *Wall* (2004) are highly critical, yet prove the spatial and, thus, symbolic and ethical limitations of this criticism. Depicting a situation where the map becomes a crucial signifier of control over place, which is not 'simply there', but is in a continual process of being 'written' – that is, presenting arbitrariness as a major characteristic of the Palestinian experience – these films are a testament to the roadblock's power over the inscription of being. In other words, the roadblock movie exposes to Israeli spectators the checkpoint as a major signifier of ethnocentricity and homogeneity, assumed and/or imposed by colonialist cartography and routines. Thus, these documentaries became part of the 'spatial turn' in Israeli discourse on the occupation, which helps extend Israelis' political understanding of the conflict to a physical, geographical reality.

Assuming the 'good Israeli' subject position depends, thus, 'upon establishing an interstitial space of identification',[16] which involves the irresolvable tension between personhood – doing good deeds – and the historical and geographical colonised locations in which they occur. Only in the few 'good Israeli' films employing a self-reflexive mode is the camera able to document the over-complexity

Checkpoint (2003): the camera in *Checkpoint* ... seems unaware of its highly ambivalent 'good Israeli' attitude

of the politics of separation in this 'Escher-like territorial arrangement'[17] in a way that clearly demonstrates its own limitations.

The camera in *Checkpoints*, for instance, seems unaware of its highly ambivalent 'good Israeli' attitude. Its omnipresence and all-encompassing movement stands in ironic juxtaposition with the life it strives to document. In contrast, *Close, Closed, Closure*, for instance, detailing endless lines of people from a distance, offers a subversive look at Gaza checkpoints; by keeping the camera at a distance, and limiting its movement and ability to trespass, it demonstrates an awareness, rare in the roadblock sub-genre, of its own helplessness, stuck as it is in the territorial design. In other words, in (un-reflexive) roadblock movies the ability of the camera, symbolising the privileged status of the Israeli subject, to surmount walls and borders, police surveillance and army orders, and to traverse the 'land of checkpoints',[18] makes the ethical encounter at the checkpoint an experience of being-in-difference.

Whenever the 'good Israeli' films do more than scratch the surface by articulating or addressing the conditions that produce or foment violations of human rights and by exposing the treacherous means through which subordination is achieved and regulated through the description of a spectrum of causes, decisions, fallacies and consequences, they rupture the possibility of being simultaneously politically essential and politically regressive. In these cases, they therefore subvert the 'good Israeli' 'humanitarian paradox'. This is clearly discernible, for instance, in Eli Cohen's television mini-series *Fence, Wall, Border* (2006), which analyses the human rights violations caused by the three-year construction of the separation wall.

Furthermore, Israeli intimacy with, and proximity to Palestinian life in 'good Israeli' films might be perceived as a somehow reversed position of Bhabha's paradoxical strategy of mimicry (the colonised ambivalent replication of the coloniser). It is not only the mimicry, as Bhabha suggests, but also this 'reversed mimicry', apparently a de-authorisation, that signifies both intimacy and menace because those Palestinians accepting Israeli assistance might be accused by their fellow Palestinians of collaborating with the Israeli regime and also since, as a moral project, the films' absurd ad hoc limitation re-enhances colonial dependency and discriminatory power. Thus, the 'good Israeli' film in fact creates another authorised version of Otherness. By their very proximity to the Palestinians' daily hardship, the 'good Israeli' embodies a resemblance, based on alleged shared humanity, to the Palestinian; however, it is – to cite Bhabha's famous phrase – 'almost total but not quite'.[19] Staged around temporary proximity, the films, despite their docu-activist nature, unwillingly reveal not only an encounter of 'symbolic sameness', but also of 'practical difference'.

I claim that the 'good Israeli' trend, inevitably dependent on a particular ambivalent and contingent double consciousness, involves a certain degree of misrecognition of sociopolitical differences, which makes its exceptional – ideological and spatial – status as a trend irresolvable. On the other hand, by presenting the everydayness of physical violence and human rights violations, these documentaries fracture the ongoing denial and repression of the occupation prevalent in narrative, mainstream cinema. Moreover, the films (and actions) create a new 'imagined community' of 'good Israelis', as opposed to the settlers and right-wing directors, and thus they play a significant role in terms of social responsibility. However, as Žižek contends,

> [it] is not so much identification with the Law that regulates the community's normal everyday circuit, but rather identification with a specific form of transgression of the Law, of the Law's suspension (in psychoanalytic terms) with a specific form of enjoyment.[20]

The fantasy of the coloniser that she/he has managed to free himself/herself from the most dominant aspects of colonial legacy and practice is embodied in the documentarist's fantasmatic *jouissance* over his/her unique actions of transgression of the law.

The irresolvable tensions embodied in various layers of the paradox that define the 'good Israeli' trend (celebrity/ordinary, docu-/social activism, coloniser/colonised, symbolic sameness/practical difference, imagined community/transgressive *jouissance*) confirms the suggestion, 'paradox appears endlessly self-canceling, as a political condition of achievements perpetually undercut ... and hence a state in which political strategizing itself is paralyzed'.[21] By focusing on, and assisting, the Palestinian as

the ultimate victim of the occupation, the 'good Israeli' film shifts the Israeli post-Holocaust claim to victimhood, but, paradoxically, also maintains the binarism of victim–perpetrator. However, this period, as suggested above, also witnesses a new development in regard to this binarism: the perpetrator trauma film. This new sub-genre, a pioneer in world cinema, neither focuses on the trauma of the victimised Palestinian, nor the Israeli victim of suicide terrorism, but rather on that of the Israeli soldier (male or female) who has become a perpetrator. Films such as Ari Folman's *Waltz with Bashir* (2008), Avi Mograbi's *Z32* (2008), Tamar Yarom's *To See If I'm Smiling* (2007) and Nurit Kedar's *Concrete* (2011) depict the post-traumatic subject position of the perpetrator of atrocities. I regard these films – as I have claimed in other forums[22] – as neither absolving Israeli soldiers from wrongdoing, nor as offering the Israeli audience a spectatorial experience based on a cathartic guilt-freeing, but rather as displaying a mature cinematic-social phase. Unprotected by a moral environment, they give 'a causal or functional account of the mechanism of evil'[23] they participated in, either directly or indirectly. Thus, these ex-soldiers' accounts pave the way for Israelis to assume moral responsibility for the deeds carried out in their name in the occupied territories.

This genre caused the major ideological transformation undergone by documentary cinema, a schizoid cinematic reality exacerbated by the emergence of a new religious wave following Yitzhak Rabin's assassination in 1995. It was only after the assassination that, for the first time in forty years, Israeli documentary and religious cinema began to address the drastic sociopolitical shift rightward. The new religious wave embraced the Haredim (ultra-Orthodox, anti- or a-Zionist Jews) to a degree never before witnessed. Although still far from the dominance of left, secular film production, mainly due to the fact that most of the directors in the Israeli film industry belong to the left-secular camp, and despite the fact that 'inside' critical voices are heard from within the religious community[24] – right-wing film Zionist-national production is expanding both within and without the settler community.[25]

'CHILDREN'S RESISTANCE' FILMS

In contrast to Israeli cinema's deep ideological split between documentary and narrative, and between left- and right-wing films, Palestinian documentary (and narrative) cinema, as cinema of the colonised, has, since its inception[26] and up to the second *Intifada* period, been exclusively devoted to the Palestinian cause and to mediating international attitudes towards Palestinian national goals through film. As a post-'Third Worldist' cinema[27] devoid of affiliation with an independent state and trapped in a colonial situation and blocked space, Palestinian cinema expresses a unified and collective voice that addresses a large, international community. This voice is derived from a profound claim to justice, which overcomes any internal (spatial, social, cultural, or other) difference, and in fact pre-destined the cinematic constitution of Palestinian subjectivity. Be it a first- or fourth-*Naqba* generation, a town or refugee camp resident, modern-secular or religious-fundamentalist, the Palestinian subject's claim to justice, resting on victimhood, becomes the major characteristic of his/her subjectivity, and the films' rationale for representing persistent struggle.

The films display this subjectivity at their core as a sort of substantiation of the nation. The performance of subjectivity on display is rendered solely as a first step towards future liberation, to be enacted on a national scale. In this sense, the director/social actor's performance is a suspended one, a micro coming-into-being of subjectivity in the service of larger powers that have not yet emerged. Acknowledging in advance the power of the camera to induce the display of subjectivity, this version of 'suspended subjectivity', attached to a demand for international recognition, is unique. The tension between constituting a unified self and collective memory and affecting international audiences characterises many films. Inner differences; a lack of home audiences, both in the occupied territories and in Gaza; the existence of diasporic audiences; the difficulty of distributing films in Arab countries; and the acclaimed presence of leading (mostly narrative) film directors in international film festivals all intensify this tension.

Moreover, and unlike its Israeli counterpart, Palestinian documentary cinema has no film industry. Suffering from periods of complete lack of production (1948–67 and 1982–87) and an ever-present struggle to survive, the lack of national institutions, television support, production companies, film laboratories, skilled film crews and movie theatres[28] have made internal and external exile more prominent. Being 'structurally exilic',[29] Palestinian documentary cinema has the option of obtaining either international or Israeli film industry assistance. However, directors who were beneficiaries of Israeli aid, such as Hany Abu Assad, Tawfik Abu Wael, Nizar Hassan, Michel Khleifi and Elia Suleiman were later accused of betrayal and collaboration with the enemy.[30] At a later stage, some rejected any 'normalisation' with Israelis in the post-second *Intifada* period.

The complex conditions that construct this 'cinema of displacement', as Hamid Naficy defines it, exert their influence on the films, especially those produced during the two *Intifadas*. This influence is conspicuous on six levels. First, the vast majority of Palestinian directors, 'caught in historical discontinuities during times of movement toward political self-determination', and involved in a 'passionate search for national culture',[31] have indeed remained committed to producing highly realistic documentaries. Though the films have already begun shifting

from the essentialist rhetoric of the early propaganda videos produced from the 1940s to the 70s into a post-revolutionary stage of artistic production from the 80s into the twenty-first century, they are still firmly embedded in a manifesto-like rhetoric. Second, the films portray narratives of victimhood in harsh settings of despair and violence. They defy the Israeli occupation, denounce the humiliating and brutal behaviour of Israeli settlers, police and soldiers towards Palestinian civilians, and generally dehumanise the Jewish Israeli. Third, the desire for social usefulness and popular impact link specific devices of portrayal to feeling rather than to knowing, while compelling the spectator to explore the ethics of dramatisation or the nature of the documentary effect itself creates a deep tension within the text. Fourth, the corpus emphasises the factual-ontological status of the image, which is depicted more than epistemological preconceptions. This inclination makes the chronicle of events and personal diary forms highly popular. Fifth, the representation of the *Naqba* is connected to the urge to make it a lived and visible memory. Retrieving repressed histories, many films use the iconography of the *Naqba* to represent the *Intifada*. Sixth, linking images and (past) imagination indicates a new conception of the director's voice that is not based on his/her authority as a documentarist, but, rather, on a profound claim to justice.

The dominance of victimhood as a national subject position, torn between passivity and active resistance, is also manifested in representations of the suicide bomber as heroic freedom fighter, a *shahid* (martyr) in the service of the Palestinian liberation struggle. Shot entirely in Dheisheh refugee camp, Dahna Abourahme's *Until When* (2004), for instance, portrays a group of four boys who discuss their desire for martyrdom. In contrast, Azza El-Hassan's *3 Cm Less* (2003) demonstrates an unusual, ambivalent attitude towards this issue. The director describes how she accompanies her protagonist, Ra'eda, in search of information about Ra'eda's father, killed during the attempted hijack of a Sabena plane in 1972. In order to assist her, the director casts Juliano Mer-Khamis, an actor, in the role of her late father's friend to enable Ra'eda to ask the questions that have been tormenting her and thereby derive some comfort. Mer-Khamis and Ra'eda, who is unaware that he is an actor, are seen arguing over the question of terrorism with Mer-Khamis claiming that her father was a terrorist and Ra'eda insisting that he was a freedom fighter who sacrificed his life – and family – for the Palestinian cause. However, we hear only a few sentences from the heated discussion because the director intervenes to inform us that the quarrel raged for hours. The casting of Mer-Khamis, an Israeli-Arab actor and director, is ambivalent, as is the director's decision not to show the entire dispute.[32]

Although internal critical voices are heard, especially women's voices speaking out against their oppression by

Palestinian, male-dominated, traditional society, Palestinian documentary cinema for the most part remains committed to representing external oppression. Even though some narrative film directors, in particular Elia Suleiman, paved the way for internal criticism,[33] documentary cinema silences Palestinian society's acute internal problems, such as *shahidism* as a culture of death, the corruption of the Palestinian Authority and Hamas, Fatah–Hamas relations and the growing power of religious fundamentalism.

During the second *Intifada*, the women's film becomes a two-fold genre: portraying women's lives and protesting their double (internal and external) repression, and foregrounding the 'children's resistance' film. Sobhi Al-Zobaidi's *Women in the Sun* (1998), for instance, tackles issues relating to gender, violence against women, fundamentalism and women's rights; Alia Arasoughly's *This is Not Living* (2001) describes eight Palestinian women and their struggle to live normal lives amid the degrading drama of war, terror and military occupation. Similarly, Mai Masri and Jean Chamoun's *Wild Flowers: Women of Southern Lebanon* (1986) and Ibtisam Mara'ana's *Badal* (2006), *Three Time Divorced* (2007) and *Lady Kul El Arab* (2009) depict various facets of women's desperate struggle for personal liberation under highly repressive familial and social laws.

By foregrounding children, the women's film has created what I consider a new sub-genre – the 'children's resistance' film. Some films portray children working to support their poor families. In Abdel Salam Shehadeh's *Little Hands* (1996), for instance, filmed in Gaza, the camera follows four boys between the ages of eleven and fifteen from early morning until late in the evening. They work in low-income jobs, such as delivering gas balloons and picking oranges. The mother, crying over the hopeless future of her sons, emphasises the tragic irresolvable condition of refugee life.

The narrative of the second- or third-generation child-refugee turned freedom fighter is central in most of the films. This sub-genre attests to the importance assigned to the third- and fourth-generation children of the *Naqba* who, in many films, such as Mai Masri's *Children of Shatila* (1998), express their intergenerational ties and commitment to the right of return. Masri's camera films the children using small video cameras to interview their actual or symbolic grandparents about the past, thus participating in the role of documentation and remembrance ('When you return to Palestine, what is the first thing you will do?' 'The first thing is rebuilding my home'). Importance is also assigned to the pivotal role the 'stone-throwing children' play in the current Palestinian struggle, as in Hanna Musleh's *I Am a Little Angel* (2000) and *Dignified Life* (2002). Depicting the daily lives of refugee children in the West Bank 'ghost town' of Ramallah, Azza El-Hassan's *News Time* (2001) is unique. As a resistance film immersed in manifesto-like rhetoric, it tells the story of a child killed during

a riot and culminates with the representation of a huge demonstration in which the other children participate. But *News Time* is also a meta-reflection on the journalistic function of the documentary, and on news and film industry discourses. Combining the genres of resistance film, chronicle, personal diary and women's autobiography film, it manages to feature the hybridism endorsed by Said as the preferred form with which to describe the Palestinian experience.[34]

In many respects, the 'children's resistance' film draws its strength from the symbolic mother figure, the director, who epitomises both the untraditional Palestinian woman figure and the mythic role of 'mother of the revolution'. Expressing anger, violence and the will to resist power, the children's film becomes a radical extension of the women's film. Mai Masri's *Frontiers of Dreams and Fear* (2001), for instance, traces the friendship between Mona, a resident of Beirut's Shatila refugee camp, and Manar, who lives in Jerusalem's Dheisheh refugee camp, contrasting the experiences of exile and life under occupation. In many scenes, the children perform adult roles, indicating the inseparateness of the first and second *Naqba* generations and their own inevitable and untimely, rapid transition to adulthood. The film portrays the children as victimised heroes through the aesthetics of a plethora of close-ups, intensified sentimentality and emotion-driven encounters.[35] When, for instance, Manar's grandfather takes her on a trip to the site of the village of his birth, destroyed in 1948, she gazes upon the ruins and tells the camera, 'I felt that my land calls me: Come. Take a tent and stay!'

The verbal and visual *J'accuse* format is typical of the 'children's resistance' film. Ghada Terawi's *Staying Alive* (2001), for instance, examines the motives of Palestinian youths who risk their lives to throw stones at Israeli soldiers. The questions the director asks – 'Why don't they fear death or injury? What political thoughts drive them to

Staying Alive (2001): 'Why don't they fear death or injury?'

go and possibly fight to their deaths?' – are meant, above all, to reproduce the mythicisation of the children. This mythicisation becomes particularly pervasive throughout, and after, the media dispute over Mohammad al-Dura's case (2000–05).[36] In many films shot in the West Bank, the camera reveals from time to time walls covered in graffiti where the huge portrait of Mohammad al-Dura, seen everywhere – in the street, in the schoolyard – symbolises the necessity of violent resistance, reflects on the children's heroism and justifies it in advance.

Apart from the 'stone-throwing children' imagery, the military checkpoint became an expressive icon of the occupation. Perhaps more than any other symbol of the occupation, the Palestinian roadblock sub-genre reflects the destruction of what Jacques Derrida calls 'national ontopology' – that is, the sense of naturalness and givenness of territorialised 'national belonging'.[37] Disconnected from a defined territory, on the one hand, and embodying the 'hollow land' on the other, the Palestinian roadblock movie documents the psychological-social-political aspects of the checkpoint experience. As Hagar, one of the protagonists of 3 Cm Less puts it: 'We pretend that we do not see them [the soldiers at the checkpoint]. The problem is that they see us.' The Israeli panoptical gaze, directed at the 'invisible' nameless Palestinian, is felt by Hagar as an extremely objectifying experience that she seeks to defy, ignoring the onlookers by turning herself into an un-seeable person. The doomed-to-defeat, unbearable dynamic described by Hagar represents the checkpoint experience, even though, or rather because, the films are emblematic not only of unstable boundaries and partitions, but, symbolically, also of the rejection of the right of return. This is rendered, for example, in Sobhi al-Zobaidi's Crossing Kalandia (2002), Hany Abu-Assad's Ford Transit (2002) and Hanna Elias's Roadblocks (2002).

Depicting daily and detailed checkpoint routines the roadblock genre exposes the contradictory characteristics of this place/non-place/space experience: a constant state of transition versus closure, order versus chaos, inside versus outside, observation and control versus partition, rationality versus idiosyncrasy, temporariness versus permanent-ness, permeability versus impermeability, connection versus disconnection, and distinction versus contamination.

The emphasis on the representation of the 'ugly (soldier/policeman/settler) Israeli' and the absence of the left-wing activist figure (who is a major part of the Israeli roadblock genre) is meant to cinematically break the 'dependency complex'[38] between the coloniser and the colonised, as well as any normalisation of the occupation machine. In this regard, the major contribution of this new genre is its definition of the space as a category of difference that refuses to adhere to normalising forms, such as the interpellation of shared interests. Under the forced

elasticity of the space, the genre insists on understanding national consciousness not only in terms of acting out and/or working through past traumas (that is, in terms of temporality), but also as a spatial consciousness. In other words, the documentary film's performative mode (as defined by Bill Nichols) means, in this context, an incessant representation of the space, with its complex, contradictory checkpoint system, and the constant movement along separate shards, fragments and discontinuous vectors of the separation wall. Rendering the struggle in spatial, not merely temporal, relations has become the major characteristic of this kind of (docu)activism. Making the checkpoint a symbolic difference staged across disjunctive boundaries confers the docu-activist with agential action and leads the roadblock film towards affective immediacy.

'BLOOD RELATIONS' FILMS: TOWARDS A CINEMATIC RECONCILIATION?

Undoubtedly, in its reframing of the Israeli–Palestinian conflict, documentary cinema's new set of representations, which emerged during the second Intifada, elevates the urgent ethical aspects of the new war. Incessantly representing the new war paradigmatic encounter, the major new forms of Israeli and Palestinian docu-activism ('good Israeli' and perpetrator trauma; roadblock and 'children's resistance', respectively), are centred on the ordinary, daily-based performance of coping with the occupation's evils. Thus, notwithstanding the differences, both corpora offer an ethical concretisation of the 'action-able'. Addressing its audience's ethical stand, the docu-/social activism formed in these years inhabits an in-between, hybrid position of practice and negotiation.

On one hand, as described above, the corpora indeed take dissimilar routes: the Palestinian films represent resistance to the occupation and claim victimhood; Israeli films are critical of the occupation and in the first decade of the twenty-first century also break the binarism of victim–perpetrator (although, as mentioned, right-wing documentary cinema is gradually developing as well). On the other hand, tracing how the new trends/sub-genres are informed by the epistemological and psychic orientations that shifted with the changing of the nature of war – that is, the undermining of binary subject positions (I–Other, 'us'–'them', victim–perpetrator) – reveals an evolution. The horrific dismantling of these binarisms, typical of the new war, becomes in the post-second Intifada period a positive cinematic imagining of an extension of family relations. I consider this a humanistic orientation un-immersed in the systematically ambiguous humanitarian paradox of colonial relations described earlier. Concerned as it is with shared personal evil and tragedy, it proposes a shared ethical stand.

Analysing conflict cinema from the perspective of 'wounded attachments', to use Wendy Brown's vivid metaphor, shows an evolution from ethnonational-centric films, which depict a one-sided perspective of the conflict and exclude that of the other, via confrontation films – usually armed confrontation – using competing images and narratives, to cooperation films, whereby co-producing a film becomes a means for both Israeli and Palestinian directors to share their mutual perspectives on the conflict, and, finally, to 'blood relations' films, which describe real or symbolic blood relations between the two nations. These categories are not exclusive of one another and, in fact, indicate the simultaneous co-existence of a multitude of attitudes towards the other and the conflict; however, as a taxonomy they also reveal a progression towards at least a cinematic-symbolic interrogation of possible reconciliation. This phenomenon has become conspicuous, since in recent years the amount of films that tell the story of blood relations continues to grow, thus, the taxonomy might be applicable to any documentary corpus that represents protracted, ethno-religious armed conflict in world cinema.

In order to reflect on the ethical imperative embodied in this evolution, I briefly outline the pervasive themes that dominate each category and indicate typical, prominent films. The ethnonational-centric category includes Israeli films concerned with terror or war casualties, such as *One Widow, Twice Bereavement* (Orna Ben-Dor Niv, 2005), portraying a group of women who have lost two close relatives – a husband and a child – in the same terror attack; and *Red Dawn* (Jasmine Kainy, 2005), which depicts the lives of Israeli children in the southern city of Sderot under Kassam rocket attacks. It also includes Palestinian films that describe extradition, displacement and the occupation's wrongdoings, like *Legend* (Nizzar Hassan, 1998), which recounts the history of three generations of *Naqba* refugees and their relentless efforts during the past five decades to reunite; and *My Name is Achlam* (Rima Essa, 2010), in which the director accompanies the mother of a child who has cancer in her struggle against both her patriarchal family and the checkpoints.

The confrontation films represent competing narratives and images. The most heightened cinematic confrontation during these years was performed by the films that represented Operation Defensive Shield in the West Bank refugee camp of Jenin in 2002 and the battle in Jenin. The Palestinian film *Jenin, Jenin* (Mohammad Bakri, 2002) describes the battle as genocide;[39] *Invasion* (Nizzar Hassan, 2003) focuses both on the heroism of 2,000 refugee camp residents who participated in the battle with minimal, low-tech, means and on the ruins.[40] The Israeli film *Jenin Diary* (Gil Mezuman, 2003), also shot during the operation, tells the story of the director's reserve unit that lost thirteen soldiers during the battle. All three narratives – a massacre, a heroic resistance, a tragedy of defeat – claim to perform an ethical testimony of the battle.[41]

The cooperation films foster a common political-cinematic identity that transcends the separate ethnic identity of each director. This category includes films such as *Route 181: Fragments of a Journey in Palestine-Israel* (Eyal Sivan and George Khleifi, 2004), a four-and-a-half-hour film, which travels the length of the proposed 1947 border that would have divided Israel into Jewish and Arab states. The route is named for the UN resolution that established the state of Israel. In two languages the directors interview Palestinians and Israelis living near the route about their homes, about the history of the place, the *Naqba* and their view on the conflict and the Other; *Gaza-Sderot* (Arik Bernstein, Osnat Trabelsy, Serge Gordey, Alexander Brashe and Yousef Atwa, 2008) brings testimonies from the two sides of the same border; and *Jerusalem Moments* (artistic producer: Yael Perlov, 2009), a joint project of Palestinian and Israeli cinema students, reflects different facets of life in Jerusalem.

The ethnonational-centric and confrontation films, and even the cooperation films, which are few and relatively rare, reveal the huge rift between these corpora as cinemas of conflict. In contrast, the blood relations films which, by definition, transcend ethnic-conflictual boundaries, offer the extension of imagined communities. This is not based solely on a traditional representation of inter-ethnic marriages, but rather on inter-ethnic caring. Based on an autobiographical story or a highly personal relationship that develops between two people, caring becomes in these films indeed 'the cement of an ethical community'.[42] The blood relations, caring films have three major themes: reconciliation with, and support for, a convicted terrorist (*My Terrorist* [Yuli Gerstel-Cohen, 2002] and *One Day after the Peace* [Erez Laufer, 2012]), or a family who believes in *shahidism* (*Precious Life* [Shlomi Eldar, 2009]); shared meetings and/or activism for peace between Palestinian and Israeli mothers and fathers who lost their children during the *Intifada* (*Lullaby* [Adi Arbel, 2004] and *To Die in Jerusalem* [Hilla Medalia, 2007]); and real or symbolic kinship stories (*Arna's Children* [Juliano Mer-Khamis and Danniel Danniel, 2004], *Citizen Nawi* [Nissim Mosek, 2007], *Blood Relation* [Noa Ben Hagai, 2009] and *77 Steps* [Ibtisam Mara'ana, 2010]).

In the blood relations films forgiveness becomes a performative act, '[a] case of overcoming resentment and vengefulness, of mastering anger and humiliation. ... a result of a long effort'.[43] In these films, this long process, which finally becomes an achievement, re-enacts the dynamics of difference and sameness. Making difference into sameness and sameness into (another, ethical-based) difference, the blood relations films acknowledge their own hybridity as an epistemology that rejects essentialism. Mer-Khamis's presentation of the Jewish origins of his mother simultaneously with the portrait of the Palestinian children whom she taught at the Palestinian theatre in Jenin, one of whom became a suicide terrorist, another of

Blood Relation (2009): in the blood relations films forgiveness becomes a performative act

whom was killed in a battle with Israeli soldiers; Mosek's detailed documentation of his constant efforts to protect his Palestinian lover from the police and to live a normal family life together in Jerusalem; Ben Hagai's rendering of her troubled journey to Nablus, where she meets and tries to assist her recently found Jewish-born Muslim relatives (the children of her grandmother's aunt, who was banished from her Jewish family, married a Muslim and became a refugee in Nablus in 1948); Mara'ana's humorous depiction of her (eventually failed) love affair with a Jewish American-Israeli – all assume multiple identities, and are engaged with fluid, fundamentally ambiguous and modifiable practices, which affirm an imaginary post-colonial subject position. Instead of an economy of complicity and guilt or ghostly colonial powers, the blood relations films break internalised authoritarian epistemology that reproduces power relations, and thus make these powers contestable.[44]

The blood relations films and the evolution towards reconciliation suggested by this taxonomy reflect the maturity of documentary cinema made in the post-second *Intifada* period. As Edward W. Said contends:

No one can deny the persisting continuities of long traditions, sustained habitations, national languages, and cultural geographies, but there seems no reason except reason and prejudice to keep insisting on their separation and distinctiveness, as if that was all human life was about.[45]

NOTES

1. Albert Memmi, *The Colonizer and the Colonized*, Introduction by Jean-Paul Sartre (Boston: Beacon Press, 1957 [1991]), p. 172.
2. Palestinian uprisings.
3. The Palestinian term for the war meaning disaster.
4. See http://en.wikipedia.org/wiki/Military_operations_conducted_by_the_Israel_Defense_Forces#

Additional_Israeli_military_operations_3. Accessed 31 August 2012.
5. Avishai Margalit, *The Ethics of Memory* (Cambridge, MA: Harvard University Press, 2002), p. 69.
6. During the second *Intifada* there were eleven times more Israeli casualties than in the first *Intifada* (eighty-seven Israelis were killed between 1987 and 1991, compared to 996 Israelis killed between 2000 and 2005).
7. See Mary Kaldor, *New and Old Wars: Organized Violence in a Global Era* (Paolo Alto, CA: Stanford University Press, 2001).
8. See Raya Morag, 'The Living Body and the Corpse: Israeli Documentary Cinema and the *Intifadah*', *Journal of Film & Video* vol. 60 no. 3–4, Autumn/Winter 2008.
9. See, for instance, two major television documentary series: *Pillar of Fire* (1981) and *Tkuma: The First Fifty Years* (1998).
10. For example, Ram Levy's *Barricades* (1969), a portrait of an encounter between two families, Israeli and Palestinian, who lost their sons in 1948.
11. See Ella Shohat, *Israeli Cinema: East/West and the Politics of Representation* (Austin: University of Texas Press, 1989; rev. edn, London: I.B.Tauris, 2010).
12. See Elhanan Yakira, *Post Zionism Post Holocaust* (Cambridge: Cambridge University Press, 2010).
13. For a differentiation between cathartic and un-cathartic forms of guilt embodied in soldiers' accounts, see Raya Morag, 'Perpetrator Trauma and Current Israeli Documentary Cinema', *Camera Obscura* vol. 27.2 no. 80, 2012, pp. 93–133; and Raya Morag, *Waltzing with Bashir: Perpetrator Trauma and Cinema* (London and New York: I.B.Tauris, 2013).
14. Homi Bhabha, 'On Mimicry and Man: The Ambivalence of Colonial Discourse', *October* no. 28, 1984, p. 319.
15. In its fervent support of Palestinians and of Israelis who devote their time and efforts to the Other, it is no wonder that this kind of intimate documentation completely vanished at the height of second *Intifada* suicide terrorism (2000–04).
16. Homi Bhabha, 'Editor's Introduction: Minority Maneuvers and Unsettled Negotiations', *Critical Inquiry* vol. 23 no. 3, Spring 1997, p. 438.
17. Eyal Weizman, *Hollow Land Israel's Architecture of Occupation* (London: Verso, 2007), p. 182.
18. See Azmi Bishara, *Checkpoints: Fragments of a Story (Resis'ai Sipur: Kisufim b'Eretz Hamachsomim)* (Tel-Aviv: Babel Press, 2004), p. 100.
19. Bhabha, 'On Mimicry and Man', p. 324.
20. Slavoj Žižek, *Metastases of Enjoyment: Six Essays on Women and Causality* (London: Verso, 1994), p. 55.
21. Wendy Brown, 'Suffering the Paradoxes of Rights', in Wendy Brown and Janet Halley (eds), *Left Legalism/Left Critique* (Durham, NC, and London: Duke University Press, 2002), p. 432.
22. See Morag, *Waltzing with Bashir*.

23. Margalit, *The Ethics of Memory*, p. 170.

24. This is exemplified, for instance, by the rise of the religious-queer film.

25. See, for instance, *The Skies Are Closer in Homesh* (Manora Hazani-Katzover, 2003).

26. The starting point of Palestinian cinema occurred in 1935. See Nurith Gertz and George Khleifi, *Palestinian Cinema: Landscape, Trauma, and Memory* (Bloomington: Indiana University Press, 2008), pp. 11, 13.

27. See Ella Shohat, 'Post-Third-Worldist Culture: Gender, Nation, and the Cinema', in Elizabeth Ezra and Terry Rowden (eds), *Transnational Cinema: The Film Reader* (New York: Routledge, 2006).

28. See Gertz and Khleifi, *Palestinian Cinema*, pp. 33–7.

29. See Hamid Naficy, 'Palestinian Exilic Cinema and Film Letters', in Hamid Dabashi (ed.), *Dreams of a Nation: On Palestinian Cinema* (London: Verso, 2006), p. 91.

30. On the accusations against *Chronicle of Disappearance* (1996), for instance, see Anne Bourlond, 'A Cinema of Nowhere: Interview with Elia Suleiman', *Journal of Palestine Studies* vol. 29 no. 2, Winter 2000.

31. See Franz Fanon, *The Wretched of the Earth*, Preface by Jean-Paul Sartre, trans. Constance Farrington (New York: Grove Press, 1968), p. 209.

32. Juliano Mer-Khamis, the son of a Jewish mother who converted to Islam and a Muslim father, followed in the footsteps of his mother and after her death became the artistic director of the Freedom Theatre in Jenin. He was shot dead in Jenin on 4 April 2011.

33. Elia Suleiman's narrative film *Divine Intervention* (2002) is unique in sketching some of Nazareth's internal problems.

34. See Edward W. Said, *After the Last Sky: Palestinian Lives* (New York: Pantheon, 1986), p. 6.

35. On the tradition of the victim, see Brian Winston's pioneering work 'The Tradition of the Victim in Griersonian Documentary', in Larry Gross, John Stuart Katz and Jay Ruby (eds), *Image Ethics: The Moral Rights of Subjects in Photographs, Film and Television* (New York: Oxford University Press, 1988).

36. See http://en.wikipedia.org/wiki/Muhammad_al-Durrah_incident. Accessed 7 September 2012.

37. See Jacques Derrida, *Spectres of Marx* (London: Routledge, 1994).

38. Memmi, *The Colonizer and the Colonized*, p. 88.

39. *Jenin, Jenin* fuelled a furious controversy and a demand for censorship. Bakri appealed to the Supreme Court to reverse the decision not to screen the film. On March 2003, the Supreme Court ruled that the film could be screened. See http://www.the7eye.org.il:80/Verdicts/freedom_of_speech/Pages/bakri_movie_jenin.aspx [Hebrew].

40. It is noteworthy that an old man (Ali Yoseph Faid) appears in both Bakri and Hassan's films; however, in Bakri's film he recounts that he was wounded by an Israeli sniper, while in an unedited scene in Hassan's film he makes a full account, including a description of the Israeli soldier who bandaged his leg and the tank which brought him to hospital.

41. Pierre Rehov, a French-Algerian film director, made *The Road to Jenin* (2003) as a response to *Jenin, Jenin*.

42. Margalit, *The Ethics of Memory*, p. 75.

43. Ibid., p. 204.

44. See also Abuelaish Izzeldin's famous autobiographical novel *I Shall Not Hate* (New York: Walker & Co, 2011).

45. Edward W. Said, 'Resistance, Opposition and Representation', in Bill Ashcroft, Gareth Griffiths and Helen Tiffin (eds), *The Post-Colonial Studies Reader*, 2nd edn (London: Routledge, 2006), p. 98. The quote is taken from Helen Tiffin, 'Post-Colonial Literatures and Counter-Discourse', *Kunapipi* vol. 9 no. 3, 1987.

3.5 Sacred, Mundane and Absurd Revelations of the Everyday: Poetic Vérité in the Eastern European Tradition

SUSANNA HELKE

Anglophone documentary studies' narrowness of focus not only long excluded (almost entirely) the world beyond the West; it also failed until recently to take much notice of the 'rest' of Europe either. Inattention to Vertov in the West set a pattern which persisted for half a century. However, since the collapse of the Soviet hegemony, documentary production in Europe's east has flourished. And it has found its own way round the Griersonian/Direct Cinema paradigm.

One of the most fundamental distinguishing characteristics of the Eastern European documentary film tradition, when compared to the Anglo-American tradition, is the strong and unwavering perception of the documentary as part of a wider cinematic culture. East European filmmakers have combined social sensibilities with the conception of documentary film as an art form rather than a mere information commodity. Practitioners of the Eastern European documentary have not entirely accepted the Griersonian mission of social education and enlightenment, which continues to exert a strong influence on Western European production culture and is largely regulated by television distribution.

This essential characteristic of documentary cinema in Eastern Europe I shall call poetic vérité. Common to the documentary film tradition in the region is a philosophical lyricism, which often is associated with a black-and-white aesthetic. Poetical, however, is not the same as lyrical. Poetic vérité refers to documentary cinema in which everyday observations are given a heightened relevance. This could mean ambivalent, absurd, or allegorical narration. It is an observational documentary style in which the observational gaze is not harnessed in the service of witnessing and explaining. The aesthetics of slowness represent one of the central devices with which the filmmaker may take banal observations of the everyday and give them new significance.

In poetical narration, the emphasis is not on storytelling, or on furthering a given argumentation. Rather poetic strategies are comparable to the cinema of poetry, to which Gilles Deleuze – quoting the words of Pier Paolo Pasolini – refers in the context of fictional cinema. The primary concern of the cinema of poetry is not to tell a story based around a plot structure but to create a fabric of visions and visual observations. 'In the cinema of poetry, as opposed to what is called the cinema of prose ... the distinction between what characters see subjectively and what the camera sees objectively disappears.'[1]

In this chapter I will approach the subject of Eastern European documentary film thematically, using poetic vérité as something of an umbrella concept. I do not attempt to provide an all-encompassing overview of the documentary production of individual countries, nor, indeed, of the region as a whole, but give particular mention to those practitioners whose films concretise and exemplify the central characteristics and distinctive features of the Eastern European tradition. In many instances it would have been possible to select countless other examples of practitioners and films. I also have chosen to sideline practitioners and stylistic tendencies that fall under other umbrellas, notably from the spheres of the historical documentary, autobiographical and experimental film.

Eastern Europe, which on the political map redrawn after the Cold War is often given the paradoxical epithet 'New Europe', is an entity open to interpretation. This is a group of countries which all share common historical links to Russia and a cultural link to the notion of a pan-Slavic identity, regardless of the fact that most residents of the countries in question do not even speak a Slavic language. These countries shared an allegiance, albeit often forced, to the Communist system throughout the Cold War era. Since *glasnost*, the euphoria that first broke out after the fall of the Berlin Wall and the opening of doors to the West descended, in many of these societies, into the realities of the sudden affluence as well as the sudden poverty brought about by the introduction of brutal capitalism. The dawn of the twenty-first century brought with it the promise of affluence as members of the EU family, but, despite the promises of a market economy, the fate of the work-force in the region has often been to provide low-paid labour to bolster the EU economic machine. The links to western economic systems have proven very inconstant, a phenomenon which has become even more evident during the recent Great Recession.

All this has created a tangle of historical experiences that has contributed to the formation of a 'more Eastern' European identity. I must reiterate that the epithet 'Eastern' is both historically arbitrary and, in many respects, inaccurate. For instance, the Czech Republic is, in both geographical and historical terms, part of Central Europe. The Baltic countries and many of the Balkan countries are linguistically and culturally independent members of the European family, while historically many of them have enjoyed ties variously to Central Europe, Russia and, in the case of the Baltic countries, to Scandinavia or, as in the Balkans, to Islamic cultures.

In the cinematic culture of the countries of Soviet-era Eastern Europe, documentary films enjoyed a special position and the support of national cinematic institutions, most notably in Poland, the former Czechoslovakia and the Soviet Union. Many countries operated film studios that received state funding, such as those in Warsaw, Łódź and Kraków in Poland, Barrandov and Krátký Film in Prague, Koliba in the former Yugoslavia and Mafilm in Budapest. In many of these studios the focus was very firmly on documentary films. The St Petersburg (Leningrad) Documentary Film Studio, founded in 1918, is the oldest documentary production house in Russia and was home to many of the central practitioners of the day. The region also has played host to a number of significant festivals dedicated to documentary cinema, including the Jihlava IDFF in Prague and the DOK Leipzig in former East Germany. These festivals continue to this day and are important 'display windows' where regional films can be shown to the rest of the world. National schools of documentary cinema in Poland, the former Czechoslovakia (modern Czech Republic and Slovakia), Hungary, the Baltic countries and the countries of the Balkans have a long history and have continued significance. These schools or movements often have arisen in conjunction with film schools.

Contemporary documentary production in the countries of Eastern Europe is vital and traces its aesthetic roots to idiosyncratic regional traditions, despite the fact that many practitioners are being funded by western television channels and are working in a production environment largely dominated by the forces of the market economy. For the generation of practitioners that graduated in the twenty-first century, realities of the Cold War, *glasnost*, the Velvet Revolution and the history of the opening up of borders in Eastern Europe seem distant and abstract. These film-makers have matured in the political landscape of the 1990s and 2000s during which the conditions for people's lives have been shaped more by the realities of unrestrained capitalism than by the shadow of socialism. Many of these contemporary practitioners have turned their gaze from the realities of social circumstances to dealing with the more eternal questions of human existence. The political and economic conditions for people's existence are present in these films, though the cinematic language used to refer to these conditions may not necessarily be overtly and explicitly political.

The emergence of the 'direct' documentary film, which occurred at the turn of the 1950s and 60s, is a significant milestone in the international history of the documentary film. From one survey of film history to the next, the cornerstones of this genre are presented as a British, French, American and Canadian continuum – free cinema, cinéma vérité and the tradition of Direct Cinema or cinéma direct. Meanwhile, behind the Iron Curtain, a generation of film-makers was developing, in whose work the observational, vérité and the direct manifested themselves in a manner philosophically and aesthetically very different from western documentary cinema. The tradition of poetic vérité in Eastern Europe, reflections of which are discernable in Eastern European documentaries of the twenty-first century, has remained somewhat marginalised in the canonised history of documentary cinema.

I consider Russian practitioners to be a central part of a continuum of Eastern European documentary cinema. For instance, Viktor Kossakovsky and Sergei Dvortsevoy are internationally acclaimed directors, in whose working methods the ideals of poetic vérité can be recognised. Though I recognise the dangers of pan-Slavism – indeed, the cinematic cultures of the smaller countries understandably have worked to distance themselves from their historical forced link with Russia – I contend that the influence of Russian practitioners on film-makers in smaller countries in the birth of aesthetic ideals and genres is undeniable. Throughout the Soviet era and thereafter, the central directors and founders of cinematic schools in many countries have received their education at VGIK in Moscow. Thus, the traditions of the oldest cinema school in the world have played an intrinsic role in the cinematic culture of Eastern Europe.

Of course, Russia's relation to the cinematic production of the Eastern European countries is also complex and carries the burden of history. In many countries, national documentary film production was, in the years after the war, harnessed to serve the didactic needs of Soviet propaganda and socialist realism. The breakthrough of national cinemas represented a step away from the sphere of Russian influence. In the same manner as in the West, where the breakthrough of direct documentary cinema represented a distancing from the tradition of the didactic documentary, the reforms of the 1960s in Eastern European countries challenged the requirement for socialist realism of the educational films promoted by the Soviet Empire.[2]

THE HIDDEN AND THE UNEXPLAINED

At the heart of the Anglo-American documentary project is the exploration of social wrongs, typically in cinematic works that espouse a largely progressive political agenda. This agenda was shaped during the Great Depression of the 1930s, when the word 'documentary' was first used in association with photography. The photographs of Jacob A. Riis and Lewis W. Hine were essentially pieces of evidence pointing to social problems and were used to effect social change.

Arising from John Grierson's principles of didactic, 'enlightenment' cinema, the contemporary social documentaries explore problems, conflicts and social change. Film-makers' creative and artistic aspirations are downplayed in favour of an agenda of change. The films are based on a problem-solving model: the practitioner observes a problem, understands what is wrong and knows what 'we' should do about it. The practitioner is like a lawyer, who uses the lives and destinies of his/her subjects like pieces of evidence to substantiate his/her arguments. The notion of what is ethical becomes associated with sentimentality – speaking up for people, representing them, or promoting an agenda of the necessity for change as 'we' know it.

In *Na trerjey ot Solntza planete* [*On the Third Planet from the Sun*] (2006), Russian film-maker Pavel Medvedev (born 1963) does not offer the spectator the comfort of precise facts, dates, or statistics. A vast stretch of wetland disappears into the endless horizon. Two men are pulling up ragged pieces of carbon fibre and steel from the resilient bog. As viewers, we wander and lose our way in the wetlands where people are struggling to survive. Collecting scraps left over after tests for the H-bomb and the space programme is a source of income for people living in the Archangel area of northern Russia. At the beginning of the film, we see a series of explosions in archival footage from Soviet-era space programmes, but in the untouched Arctic, the presence of environmental hazards is abstract and immaterial.

One of the central elements of *On the Third Planet from the Sun* and *Otpusk v Nojabre* [*Vacation in November*] (2002), also by Medvedev, are the destinies of people living at the mercy of environmental circumstances and on the wastelands of history. Medvedev, a member of the documentary film studio in St Petersburg, does not examine people living in material poverty, harsh life situations and with only limited possibilities merely as a way of pointing out social problems. At the heart of his films is the existential question of human beings' ability to survive. His protagonists are not victims. He represents people's experience of their own lives as far more complex than what can be expressed in standard-of-living indices or through the material gross domestic product.

Similarly, Lithuanian director Arūnas Matelis (born 1961) belongs – along with his colleagues Audrius Stonys, Valdas Navasaitis and Vytautas Landsbergis – to the generation of Lithuanian directors who have used their work to manifest the metaphorical language of cinema and surrealist poetic realism. Matelis's short film *Sekmadienis. Evangelija pagal liftininką Albertą* [*Sunday: The Gospel According to the Lift-Operator Albertas*] (2003) is a Tarkovskian portrayal of Albertas, a lift-operator at a Lithuanian hospital. In Matelis's narration, observations of reality are like revelations, references both to a transcendental world and to history and the here-and-now. Everyday life is portrayed as surreal and dreamlike.

In contrast to Matelis's short films, *Prieš parskrendant į žemę* [*Before Flying Back to the Earth*] (2005) is a more classical documentary depiction of leukemia patients in a children's hospital in Vilnius. Through his harsh and intense 'observing' use of the camera, he highlights the paradox inherent in the equation of the children's carefree vivacity, their serious illness and the possibility of their death. Hooked up to a drip – and eerily resembling creatures from outer space with their shaved heads – these children are ensconced in the world of childhood. Despite the gravity of the subject matter, the director does not descend into the agenda of the sentimental depiction of victimhood and pity. The metaphorical elements of the film – including its title – lead the viewer towards something invisible and immaterial beyond the painful realities of the material world. With this film, the director is campaigning for a politics of hope rather than of pity.

ABSURDIST REALISM

The films of new-generation Czech director Karel Žalud (born 1971) are satirical, absurdist allegories, imbued with the imagery of the sacred and the profane and of the relation of modern people to the technocratic world they themselves have created. *Gou! Nebo-li pojd'!* [*Go*] (2003) is a

On the Third Planet from the Sun (2006) does not offer the spectator the comfort of precise facts, dates, or statistics

Go (2003): a film 'about mobile phones in a godless world'

film 'about mobile phones in a godless world', as the film's synopsis puts it. It is the portrayal of a village that is waiting for the installation of a new mobile-phone transmitter as though it were a temple. The mobile-phone signal can only be received at the highest point in the village and the villagers making the journey up the hill are portrayed as if they were modern-day pilgrims.

Žalud's *Přízrak svobody II* [*Phantom of Liberty II*] (2009) is an allusion to Luis Buñuel's film of the same name, cast in the tradition of surrealism. The film is a depiction of modern people's relation to the notion of time. It is a chain of anecdotes that occur as if by chance and within the same time-frame. The film's director meets people to whom he tries to tell an anecdote about the clock hand on top of the town hall falling right into the market square at Litoměřice.

Directed by the Bulgarian film-maker Andrey Paounov (born 1974), *Problemat s komarite i drugi istorii* [*The Mosquito Problem and Other Stories*] (2007) is a portrayal of the small town of Belene, situated on the banks of the River Danube, a town whose inhabitants are suffering from a surreal problem. 'Zanzar' is the Bulgarian word for enormous mosquitoes, swarms of which plague the people in the town. In the film we meet a series of local townspeople: a local pianist, who believes his piano once belonged to Lenin's secretary; the town's tourism agent, who, despite the mosquito problem, believes the town, with its boggy surrounding landscapes, could be an attractive tourist destination for travellers; a group of natural scientists, who believe they have the answer to the mosquito problem; and a Cuban refugee, who sings folksy songs in the poppy fields and collects interestingly shaped pieces of wood.

Often filmed against static backgrounds, Paounov's film places these comical characters plagued by the local mosquitoes in a surreal small town in which a new nuclear plant is being built. This colossal project, one that has been incomplete throughout the post-Soviet era, is an allegory

of the past in the present. The black humour and light-hearted satire in this film, and the encounters that link the townspeople to one another by association, conceal the darker currents of recent history. Towards the end of the film we meet the daughter of a woman officer who worked in a local prison during the Soviet period. In archival footage from a trial, we see her mother convicted of murder and sent to the same prison in which she once guarded other political prisoners. The film grows into a fable of the layers of Bulgarian history in a town abandoned by God and left to the mosquitoes.

Of Viktor Kossakovsky's (born 1961) films, the one most well known in the West, which has acquired the reputation of a classic, is *Belovy* (1993). The film is a depiction of two elderly people in a small, run-down Russian village: Anna Belova and her drink-sodden brother. These characters are the antithesis of idealised portrayals of the people common in Soviet-era 'village prose' films.[3] Kossakovsky's minimalist film *Tishe!* [*Quiet!*] (2002) satirises the structural problems facing contemporary Russian society. Kossakovsky filmed the work from the window of his St Petersburg apartment during a visit to his home city. Beneath his window, the city is carrying out endless road-works, year-round, in preparation for the city's 300th anniversary celebrations. A digger appears and cuts a hole in the ground that is then filled in, yet the exertions of the workmen, trying to fill the black hole from one month to the next, seems utterly aimless. At times the director switches laconic observation for slapstick comedy by speeding up the footage and accentuating the images with frantic piano music.

The cinematic language of Žalud, Pauonov and Kossakovsky reveals echoes of the tradition of the absurdism in Russian and Eastern European literature and theatre that is prominently featured in the works of Nikolai Gogol, Daniil Kharms and Eugène Ionesco, or contemporary

The Mosquito Problem and Other Stories (2007): a fable of the layers of Bulgarian history in a town abandoned by God and left to the mosquitos

writers and dramatists like Yevgeni Popov, Viktor Pelevin, Sławomir Mrożek, or Václav Havel. This tradition is grounded in a world of crazy, eccentric characters and incredible coincidences, a world for which the logic of enlightenment is foreign. The human lot is seen as more banal and haphazard than noble and rational. Carnivalistic laughter releases familiar, conformist, bureaucratic reality from its pretentions of seriousness.

'Poems are not pies, and we are not herrings!': The serious yet playful manifesto of the Association of Real Art, which was influential in the years immediately following the Russian Revolution, concisely sums up the function of poetic language. Poetic imagery is not a utilitarian commodity; it does not bend to the needs of marketing or teaching, to guiding or advising the masses. Indeed, poetic imagery is largely useless, and it is this fact that reveals its radical core. It cannot be effectively used to guide or satisfy the masses. Totalitarian power requires a rational people, a hierarchy and structures in which people and their meanings remain in check. Humour, both absurd and abstract as well as poetic, causes disorder, as safe and simplistic answers to the question 'What does this mean?' are absent.

During the Soviet era, the absurdism born in reaction to the totalitarian grip on power was cunning and playful, and societal irony and jesting laughter existed behind a multi-layered wall of hidden meanings. Artists were forced to hide their social satire skilfully. In a paradoxical manner, the ability to construct allegories balancing the serious and the light-hearted, using the devices of black humour and absurd realism, is also a fundamental part of the cinematic grammar of the younger generation of film-makers. Though the political and economic systems have changed, the material for satire about the role of small people within the machinery of economic life and the structures of power has not disappeared.

DURATION AS MEANING

The aesthetics of duration is one of the classic devices of observational documentary cinema. The observational style demands the patience of the viewer's gaze. In the 1990s Sergei Dvortsevoy established his reputation on the documentary cinema map with his films Stšastje [Paradise] (1995), Hlebnyi den [Bread Day] (1998) and Trassa [Highway] (1999). One of the central stylistic strategies of his films is the excessive duration of each shot and almost an 'anti-montage' quality of his editing style.

Paradise tells the story of a family of herders living in the steppes of Kazakhstan. The film consists of individual shots, each lasting approximately a minute, in each of which something small and rather meaningless occurs. These simple events are at once comical and noble, small and universal. A child sits on the floor drinking soured cream from a plate; the cream runs out and the child rolls over and falls asleep. A calf is standing on the steppes drinking from a trough. The calf's head becomes stuck in the trough and people run to help it. The director observes these events through the camera without commenting upon them or highlighting them. The viewer is not guided to empathise with the inner worlds of the protagonists. The images remain mysterious; they do not further the plot or any other rhetorical argumentation. Although his subjects may lead viewers to see his films as ethnographic, Dvortsevoy's observational gaze does not strive towards scientific observation.

In a similar style, Bread Day depicts the arrival of a German bread train in a remote village in the countryside. For the elderly people left in isolation in the village, this bread delivery is of vital importance. A sequence showing the resilient elderly folk pushing a carriage separated from the bread train sums up the premise of the whole film. Dvortsevoy shows the action from behind, in a sequence lasting over ten minutes, consisting of two uninterrupted takes.

Direct Cinema was the counter-cinema of its day, challenging not only the didactic, voiced-over tradition of the documentary genre, but also the emotionally loaded Hollywood narratives based on predetermined plot structure and psychologically predestined characters. That being said, many of the classics of Direct Cinema make extensive use of the linear, protagonist-based structures common to mainstream Hollywood narration.

Dvortsevoy does not strive towards linear storytelling. The poetic element of the narration is born out of the duration of the individual shots. The director stretches the length of a scene far beyond what would be necessary to depict the action of that scene. He breaks the rules to which we as viewers are accustomed in watching mainstream films based on the notion of economic editing. Excessive duration is a stylistic strategy through which Dvortsevoy fosters the inner meaning of the episodes he portrays. The viewer has time to meditate on the event and, layer by layer, the meaningless grows to become meaningful.

CATALYSING THE OTHER

Poland is one of the powerhouses of European documentary film-making. The documentary film has enjoyed a respected position in Polish cinematic culture, and many directors renowned for their fictional films in fact began their careers as documentary film directors. Among these are Krzysztof Kieślowski, Andrzej Wajda and Wojciech Has. In the history of Polish documentary cinema, the role of schools established around individual practitioners and cinema institutes has been very important. In the 1960s directors Kazimierz Karabasz (born 1930) and Jerzy Bossak (1910–1989) founded an aesthetic current often referred to as the 'Karabasz School', which was a unifying trend at the

Łódź Film School. Kazimierz Karabasz's most famous work from this period is *Muzykanci* [*Musicians*] (1960). Central to this aesthetic was the principle of 'par pro toto' – that is, that the phenomena of the world are revealed in fragments. This also was seen as a Polish response to the principles of pure observational style and unadulterated realities common to Direct Cinema.[4]

Marcel Łoziński (born 1940) belongs to the Kieślowski generation of directors who sought to distance themselves from the focus on objectivity and the purity of realism espoused by the Karabasz School. Documentary films of the 1970s and 80s tended to comment upon political and societal reality, though practitioners had to disguise their social criticism in metaphors. The films from this era were studies of the relationship of the individual to structures of power, collective mentalities and the influence of political indoctrination on the worldview of the people. Their methods were socially reflective, rather in the same manner as the French tradition of cinéma vérité.[5]

Łoziński's career forms a cross-section of the central political phases of Poland's recent history and the shifts in its cinematic aesthetics. He has been a key figure in establishing the tradition of political cinema in Poland, and also has been forced by political circumstance at times to hold his silence – for instance, when he refused to direct films during the period of martial law in Poland in the early 1980s. During the 90s, his films shifted perspective to focus more on universal, humanitarian and existential depictions of his subjects. The film *89mm od Europy* [*89mm from Europe*] (1993) is a metaphor for the border between East and West in the era of the 'New Europe'. The title refers to the difference in the width of train tracks in Russia and the rest of Europe. As its point of transition between the two worlds, the film focuses on a border town in Belarus, where trains arriving from the West must have their wheels changed to fit the tracks of former Soviet Russia. The film

89mm from Europe (1993): a metaphor for the border between East and West in the era of the 'New Europe'

displays a tendency to examine wider phenomena through the prism of small metaphorical details. In stylistic terms – Łoziński employs black-and-white aesthetics and the techniques of plastic composition – the film is representative of the classical tradition common in many of the countries of Eastern Europe. Łoziński's young son Tomaszek has a short conversation with one of the Belarusian track workers in the film, and the moment they share encapsulates the theme of encountering the Other, familiar from Levinasian ethical philosophy.

Of particular interest in Łoziński's oeuvre is his use of staged situations and catalysing characters who carry the film's theme forward and get situations moving. Łoziński connects the constructed with that which occurs spontaneously. A puritanical, anti-interventionist ideal of Direct Cinema is foreign to him. He has commented on his working processes thus:

> I am interested neither in pure documentaries nor in features. When making a 'pure documentary', you just watch. In features you use preconceived outlines. I try to benefit from both genres. ... Someone said that to make a film is to find the moment of balance between your own idea and what the reality suggests.[6]

In *Wszystko może się przytrafić* [*Anything Can Happen*] (1995) the catalysing character is once again the director's six-year-old son, Tomaszek, who is shown walking through a park in Warsaw and talking to the elderly people sitting there. With his frank questions, the child coaxes people to open up to him for the camera, observing events further off. The film develops into a depiction of loneliness, the fear of death and the choices one makes in life. Łoziński employed preconstructed elements and catalysing characters in a similar way in his political films from the 1970s and 80s. At the heart of his working method is the notion that everyday reality and the experience of political history do not reveal themselves to the camera automatically; rather, they require a catalyst to bring them out.

HUMANIST REALISM

Alongside documentaries imbued with absurdist, carnivalistic laughter and characterised by the reflection of political history through the use of metaphor, another central feature common to the cinematic schools of Eastern Europe has been their focus on humanist realism. These films demonstrate a respectful and sensitive relation to their protagonists, a lyrical and quiet presence and a certain element of seriousness that beatifies humanity. The conditions of deprivation, hard work and faith of individuals in godforsaken places are depicted almost heroically, with shades of nostalgia, often employing a black-and-white aesthetic.

Even with colour footage, the gaze of the director seems to have looked away first from the actual realities of socialist societies, then from the modern, urban milieus and conflicts of consumer capitalism, and turned instead towards a pastoral, timeless landscape that, though materially poor, is interpreted by the director's gaze as almost picturesque. These films often take their subject matter from the countryside, from small villages and the world of 'happy' but 'simple' people abandoned on the periphery of the modern age.

There is an element of romanticism in the humanism of this approach. Even when depicting an urban environment, the portrayal of humans is always ennobling. One might critically posit that this represents the kind of aesthetics and imagery that western commissioning editors and audiences wished to see of Eastern European realities. There has been something sufficiently different and, therefore, exotic about the memorabilia and run-down milieus of the Soviet era, particularly in comparison to a cityscape filled with Starbucks cafés and designer clothes shops, the reality which brings almost a touristic disappointment: the East already looks just like the West.

Many of the poetic cinematic schools in the region have underlined a humanist ethos. One important example, and one very little known in the West, is the Riga School of Poetic Documentary, which began operating in Latvia in the 1960s. The practitioners who worked at this school expounded the notion of the documentary as an art form, highlighting its formal, visual and rhythmic possibilities while respecting the tradition of Dziga Vertov, the Russian pioneer film-maker of the silent film era. Among the most influential directors involved with the school are Herz Frank, Uldis Braun and Ansis Epners. The film Baltie zvaniņi [White Bluebird] (1961) by Ivars Kraulītis can be considered one of the movement's pioneering works. Many of the practitioners involved with this school received their instruction at the VGIK cinematic school in Moscow.

In the course of his career, Herz Frank (born 1926)[7] has directed dozens of films, written about the art of documentary film-making (in, for instance, The Map of Ptolemy, published in Moscow in 1975)[8] and has worked as a teacher and mentor to generations of Latvian practitioners. Making extensive use of the methods of plastic composition, his films are studies of the fundamental, eternal questions of humanity. They are sculptures in time, portraits grafted on to 35mm film in which humanity is cropped out of its surrounding environment.[9]

For instance, Par desmit minutem vecaks [Ten Minutes Older] (1978), filmed in black and white, is a lyrical study of the nature of childhood that makes extensive use of the Russian tradition of montage. Throughout this short film, the director shows us a close-up shot of the face of a child sitting watching a theatre performance. Augstā dziesma [Song of Songs] (1989) depicts a birth by showing the viewer a close-up of the woman's face. The surrounding world and the birth itself are not shown at all. The surging classical music in the background comments upon the dramatic trajectory of events, from pain to joy and the tender presence of the child's father. At the moment of the birth, the film moves from black and white into colour footage. Augstākā tiesa [The Last Judgment] (1987) is a portrayal of a young man convicted of murder and sentenced to death. Finally, Mūžs [The Trace of the Soul] (1972) is a humanist show of respect to Soviet kolkhoz leader Jēkabs Kūlis, who, in defiance of the Soviet authorities, assumed personal responsibility for the political obedience of the members of his kolkhoz and, in doing so, probably saved many people from deportation.

Of contemporary Latvian directors, the films of Laila Pakalniņa (born 1962) also display the ideals of humanist realism. Par dzimteniti [Three Men and a Fish Pond] (2008) is a portrayal of three bachelors living together in a small Latvian village at the mercy of nature and the seasons. The short documentary films of the Russian director Sergei Loznitza, including Fabrika [Factory] (2004), Artel (2006) and Portret [Portrait] (2002), are products of the so-called 'manifesto of silence', focusing upon lyrical depictions of 'the people' – peasants and working men – and the black-and-white aesthetic of classical photographic documentary.

Many practitioners of the new generation make extensive use of the ideals of humanist documentary realism characteristic of Eastern European cinema. The fate of the individual in the world is depicted lyrically and respectfully. Humanity appears as something sacred and beautiful despite the harshness of living conditions. A protégé of the Warsaw School in Poland, Marcin Krawczyk's film Sześć tygodni [Six Weeks] (2009), which was awarded the Silver Wolf Award at the International Documentary Film Festival Amsterdam (IDFA), is a depiction of the first six weeks in the life of a child born to a poor single mother – the time the Polish authorities allow mothers to decide whether to keep their children or to give them up and send them to a children's home for good. Similarly humanistic and respectful, almost nostalgic in its tone, is the film Sanja i Worobei [Sanya and Sparrow] (2009) by young Russian director Andrei Grjasew, which depicts an encounter between two people moving between construction jobs and the grimness of life in the construction-site cabins. The film's protagonist is a Dostoyevskian character: simple, yet, in his innocence, blessed by God.

THE RADICAL CORE OF THE POETIC

From the very outset, the history of Anglo-American documentary film has been characterised by dualism: the poetic and the political have persistently been regarded as the antithesis of one another. The first rupture occurred when the film-makers of the 1920s avant-garde abandoned the impressionism and poetic language of their earlier works, and when the political realities of the 30s inspired them towards overtly political aims both in Europe and the

USA. Cinematic aesthetics still drew from the techniques of poetic cinema and the Russian montage; these ideals were, however, made subservient to the 'mission'. John Grierson declared his faith in what he called 'totalitarianism for good'.[10]

Even at the early stages of reality cinema, the aesthetic – both visual and poetic – was considered passive, ethereal and powerless in the face of social realities. The juxtaposition between formalism and realism, a recurring theme in art history, began to haunt the documentary too. The suspicion concerning formal questions in art became an ingrained part of a debate that had already lasted decades.

The tradition of 'more Eastern' European documentary film has maintained a natural affinity with the poetic possibilities of cinematic narration, while simultaneously reflecting the acute conflicts of political history and the everyday realities of individual people.

I have chosen to concentrate on the characteristic features of poetic documentary film, aspects which are not limited to the attributes routinely and somewhat arbitrarily assigned to the poetic – chiefly their lyrical qualities, the experimental nature of their formal construction and their visual 'beauty'. Essentially, poetry is not about beauty, sentimentality, or the sublime. Similarly, the primary purpose of the poetic image is not to convey metaphor. Particularly since modernism, poetry has been understood first and foremost as radical in relation to language and the world. It represents language stripped down to its essentials, something new that emerges and permeates the habitual meanings of language and thought. A poetic image is a 'free radical', an explosion, a mutation in the genetic code of human language, a deliberate mistake forcing us to see the world anew. It is an image and a perception that does not yet have a meaning.

> Don't film if you want to say something – just say it or write it. Film only if you want to *show* something, or you want people to *see* something. Don't film, if you already knew your message before filming – just become a teacher. Don't try to save the world.[11]

NOTES

1. Gilles Deleuze, *Cinema 2: The Time-Image* (London: Athlone Press, 1989), p. 148.
2. Maruta Zane Vitols, 'From the Personal to the Public: Juris Podnieks and Latvian Documentary Cinema', dissertation, Ohio State University, 2008, pp. 13–16.
3. Tadeusz Lubelski, 'Współczesny polski film dokumentalny' ['Polish Contemporary Documentary Film'] *Culture PL* (Warsaw: Instytut Adama Mickiewicza, 2001), http://www.culture.pl/en/culture/artykuly/es_film_dokumentalny. Accessed 6 September 2012.
4. Jan Strękowski, 'Marcel Łoziński', *Culture PL* (Warsaw: Instytut Adama Mickiewicza, 2004), http://www.culture.pl/en/culture/artykuly/os_lozinski_marcel. Accessed 6 September 2012.
5. Lubelski, 'Współczesny polski film dokumentalny'.
6. Marcel Łoziński, 'Opening the Reality', *Play-doc*, 30 March–3 April 2011, special edition.
7. Abrams Kleckins, 'Herz Frank Dialogue with Epoch, People, and Oneself', *Films in Latvia* website, n. d., http://www.latfilma.lv/history/9rig03.html http://www.latfilma.lv/history/9rig03.html. Accessed 6 September 2012.
8. Herz Frank, *Ptolemy's Map. A Documentary Film Maker's Sketches* (Moscow: Art. Lebedev Studio, 2011 [1975]) [in Russian].
9. Vitols, 'From the Personal to the Public, p. 12.
10. John Grierson, *Grierson on Documentary*, ed. Forsyth Hardy (London: Faber, 1979), p. 130.
11. Anon., 'Viktor Kossakovsky's Rules for Documentary Filmmaking', 2006, http://www.daily.idfa.nl/index.php?76&PHPSESSID=dffa8b89c2425b92501dbb3a950c9d75, emphasis original. Accessed 6 September 2012.

PART FOUR:
Documentary Voices

4.1 First Person Political

ALISA LEBOW

As much as the nation and the groups within it can find voice in the documentary, so too can the individual – and not just as a film's subject. For the film-maker, documentary can be a medium for autobiography. First person films now speak for a generation who might previously have adopted more collectivist third-person positions as documentarists.

THE PERSONAL REVOLUTIONARY VOICE

There is an anxiety lurking behind much of the scholarly work on first person film, including my own, that deserves to be addressed head on: it prompts the positive assertions that first person film is inevitably political; it propels the position that first person film is inherently relational; it informs decisions to seek first person films outside of the predictable contexts of the self-absorbed, individualistically minded West. This anxiety can be posed in the form of a question: are first person films simply a by-product of the failure of the revolutionary movements and the rise of identity politics in the 1970s, only to gain momentum in the neo-liberal 80s and beyond? To break it down further, what remains of politics once the communist and socialist collective aims seem to have collapsed with no viable liberatory alternative to replace them? The concern is that identity politics surged in to fill the ideological vacuum left in the wake of this collapse and with it came the fragmentation and individualisation of political claims, with, at best, reformist aims. Is the proliferation of first person documentary simply a consequence of this development?

Michael Chanan, in his book *The Politics of Documentary*, responds to these questions in the affirmative, when he asserts with some conviction that,

> what unfolded in the heartlands of capitalism was a passage from the politics of class to the identity politics and social movements which followed the feminist turn of the 70s, in which conventional boundaries of social identity were dissolved and subjective selfhood was asserted in forms which challenged old certainties.[1]

With this passage – from one politics to the next – Chanan believes, comes the emergence of first person film. Yet despite his apparent easy acceptance of this transition, the political left has in various ways expressed concern – or anxiety – over this very matter, which is often regarded as a shift from the certainties provided by the notion of the universal subject to the much less unified question of subjectivities. Indeed, this shift has provoked much hand-wringing on the left, with the fear that the Political, with a capital 'P' would necessarily be dispersed and diluted into a series of competing sectarian concerns.[2] What basis for mass movement lies in this individualist dead end? What neo-liberal divide-and-rule policy subtends such factionalisation? Can the left ultimately sustain itself on a diet of particularism? It was with some of these concerns in mind that an esteemed scholarly journal of aesthetics convened a high-level academic symposium in November of 1991 in New York, assembling some of the best minds of the day, to address this 'question of identity' specifically as it relates to the political.[3] I go back to this moment as it signals the time when critical theory had to recognise the shift and makes sense of it. It is essentially the same moment when first person films began to gain currency in North America, and were soon, within a decade, to proliferate elsewhere around the world as well.

With few exceptions (and quite a number of caveats), it seems these scholars were willing and prepared to accept this shift and to find the politically relevant dimensions to it. Ernesto Laclau, for instance, saw the shift towards particularism as an important corrective against the arrogant universalism of the European left, and a crucial step towards undermining the hegemony of Eurocentrism with its 'privileged agent of history'.[4] Chantal Mouffe was inclined to integrate claims arising from identity-based political movements into notions of the new citizen of radical democracy.[5] Stanley Aronowitz claimed that the emergence of identity politics was a 'breath of fresh air compared to the stifling environments of liberal and Marxist hegemonies'.[6]

Importantly, Laclau posits that already inherent in the particular is some notion of the universal or what we might call 'the collective' wherein any appeal to individual identities always had to imply some belief or adherence to a set of generally held principles, 'such as the right to self determination'.[7] Thus, for Laclau and the other participants, the ultimate conclusion was that there was no need to insist on reading identity politics as necessarily apolitical and non-revolutionary. I reference Laclau here to suggest by implication that the perceived individualism (i.e., particularism) of first person films also depends upon an appeal to more general, and even at times universal, principles of identification. In other words, in the best of cases, when a first person film-maker makes a film about his mother, her lover, her neighbourhood, his sexuality, s/he is at once speaking for and about him/herself, while speaking to and with much larger and indeed politically relevant and resonant collectivities. Moreover, s/he can be said to be addressing an even broader audience with the potential for identification that transcends such particularisms. This is obviously the case with first person films that take as their object directly political aims, however it is not my intention here to confuse the political content of a film (first person or otherwise) with the constitutive political and ideological implications of the modality or mode of address itself. In this chapter, when speaking of 'the political' in first person film, I am not speaking of the political themes it treats, but of the ways in which it enacts – in the sense of putting into practice – a politics.

There are other, somewhat contradictory, political and ideological objections to the first person impulse in film, which suggest that rather than seeing it as a by-product of the demise of the left, it can be seen, just as problematically, as a retrograde form which is insensible to the deconstruction of subjectivity, unaware of the cries declaring the death of the author issued from Barthes onward. This is a point raised by Laura Rascaroli in her impressive study on the essay film.[8] While this remains a concern, it does not account for those first person films which complicate authorship by initiating shared authorship strategies or by simply refusing to perpetuate the illusion of the unified subject.[9] In other words, not all first person films are stuck in an auteurist bubble, a throwback to days heralding the authority of the author, but can be patently and determinedly ensconced in, and constituted by, the discourses of the day. Thus, first person films are neither reducible to narcissistic monologues, nor to authorial indulgences, but, as Rascaroli also notes, may go some distance in undermining certainty (anti-objectivist as they are) and relativising truth. They also always imply an address, even a dialogue, with the spectator 'within a shared space of embodied subjectivity',[10] which creates the ground for an engagement with, if not a participation in, a collectivity much larger than the self.

Admittedly, this 'dialogue' can sometimes remain within a narrow frame. There is nothing that says that an anti-objectivist stance or a shared space of embodied subjectivity per se are implicitly destabilising and thus political,

in the sense I intend it, which is, as you will note, very much in the vein in which Rancière proposes. To be sure, the vast majority of first person films pouring out of especially anglophone western countries only serve to reaffirm hegemonic values by positing a liberal humanist subject who can afford to assume a commonality with his (and it is usually a he) audience based on notions of individual liberties and rights assumed to be shared by all, wilfully ignoring systemic inequities and their own implicit parochial and exclusionary positionalities. Think only of the patriotic pandering of Michael Moore's *Fahrenheit 9/11* (2004, USA), as he assumes a shared pride in 'American values' and uses melodramatic gestures to play on the sympathies of his audience (always posited as American) for a mother who lost her son in Iraq while completely ignoring the (then) hundreds of thousands of Iraqis who lost theirs. Or the film *My Kidnapper* (Mark Henderson and Kate Horne, 2010, UK) that attempts to portray the Marxist Rebels of Columbia as a band of thugs willing to hypocritically snatch individuals' freedoms away when they claim to be fighting for Freedom. Such an inversion, while logical within the rhetorics of western liberalism, simply reveals the ways in which individualist ideology is utterly uncomprehending in the face of collective revolutionary struggles, and shows precisely how first person film can work to sustain hegemonic systems of belief. In Rancière's terms, these would be examples of 'consensus'.[11] So, to be clear, I am not arguing that all first person films, or the first person modality, is always and inevitably politically and ideologically subversive. I am simply attempting to advance the argument that the first person modality is not inherently apolitical or politically retrograde (in spite of the undeniable fact that at times it can be), and can, in fact, entail a radical critique of subjectivity, while also, as I hope to show, enacting the political by 'refram[ing] the given ... [and] inventing new ways of making sense of the sensible'.[12]

This set of film-making practices we are calling first-person films, while not easily or reasonably definable in terms of any necessary aesthetic or generic elements, seem nonetheless to raise the spectre of a tendency towards atomised and individualist (and thus ideologically conservative) modes of self-expression. Yet they, like any other artistic practice, have the potential to create – in Rancière's words, 'new forms of perception of the given'. As he says, 'similar to political action, [they effectuate] a change in the distribution of the sensible'.[13] Of course, he rightly notes that there is no straight path from the viewing of a spectacle to an understanding of the 'state of the world', but at its best, first person film can produce 'a conflict between sensory presentation and a way of making sense of it ... [redrawing] the frame within which common objects are determined'.[14] So it is as *dissensus*, as laid out by Rancière here, that I contend first person film can enact the political.

I have, in my own explorations of this mode of address, found it extremely illuminating to look further afield, beyond the immediately obvious examples of first person film-making available to a western audience[15] to films benefiting from cultural, philosophical, ideological and political assumptions less overwhelming steeped in the liberal humanist rhetorics of individualist rights and liberties. It is here where we may be more likely find the first-person modality at its most fiercely destabilising. This is not to say that, in this era of so-called globalisation, mass migration and worldwide webs of information circulation, that there is any sphere left untouched or unaffected by the ideologies mobilised by western capitalism, but that, despite concern over (undue) influence, there is nonetheless the consideration of diverse cultural and political contexts that necessarily refract the meanings and implications of the individual's articulation on film through different prisms. So my enquiry here will take two turns: one into the past to look at what could be considered two 'ur'-texts of the first person filmic mode of address, each from very different moments and geopolitical vantage points, that may tell us something about drives other than narcissism and ideologies other than neo-liberalism motivating such an articulation; and the second is an exploration of more contemporary work, from a context in which first person films do not frequently arise and have few historical precedents – in this case, a trilogy of films by the Lebanese film-maker Mohamed Soueid. Both turns allow us to consider the ways in which first person film enacts 'the political'.

Let me begin by referencing one of the best-known and most frequently cited masterpieces of the early 'City Symphony' vein: Dziga Vertov's *Man with a Movie Camera* (1929, USSR). We know it as a classic of early cinema, an innovation in style and aesthetics, a harbinger of a range of contemporary movements in documentary from cinéma vérité (the name itself a homage to Vertov's *kino pravda*) and the political documentaries of Jean-Luc Godard and Jean-Pierre Gorin (made under the collective name the Dziga Vertov Group), to the observation of the everyday, generally associated with the North American documentary movement Direct Cinema. The film is, of course, a paean to the collectivist values of the Russian Revolution and a veritable explosion of creative energy, all harnessed in the service of awakening the masses to the truth of their new revolutionary condition. It was also, and this part is less frequently noted, one of the very first 'family affairs' on film (after the Lumière's *Feeding the Baby*, 1895, France). Surely it would not do to claim *Man with a Movie Camera* strictly as a first person film since it is that and so much more; much less would we want reduce it to the status of home movie, but it is important to note for our purposes that the members of Vertov's inner circle of 'kinoks' – the man standing in as the film-maker is Vertov's brother,

Mikhail Kaufman, and the woman behind the editing table is his wife Elizaveta Svilova – are, for this film, surrogates of the film-maker, a trope not at all unfamiliar in later expressions of the filmic first person.[16] Vertov's personal mode of expression passionately conveyed a commitment to the principles that the film professes, as if the film-maker and the above mentioned team of *kinoks* could stand in metonymically for the apotheosis of revolutionary values and lessons. Indeed, we can see in the film a series of substitutions, beginning with Kaufman as Vertov's surrogate, the proverbial man behind the 'man with the movie camera'. There is also the visual rhyming which analogises film editing as a form of spinning, weaving together meaning from strands and spools of film; and then the editor, Svilova, as image-weaver, who becomes an exemplary 'worker' in the factory of meaning-making. Of course, the steady and constitutive repetition of the idea of the cycle (from the spinning of the factory and the film spools or the rotation of train wheels, to the grand themes of the life cycle, and that of the Earth rotating around the sun from dawn to dusk), even the meaning of Vertov's assumed name, which translates as 'spinning top' (his real name was Dennis Arkadievich Kaufman), all allude to or indeed stand in for, the inexorability of political 'revolution'. In effect, Vertov puts himself and his immediate family directly in the service of the revolution, not only by making films for the revolution, but by example. A more thorough-going alignment of the particular and the universal, the individual and the collective, could hardly be made.

Fast forward forty-five years to another place and time entirely and we find with Hara Kazuo's *Extreme Private Eros: A Love Story* (1974, Japan) another, considerably more intimate, enactment of the political in first person film. While in the West at this time, outside of the practices of a handful of experimental film-makers like Jonas Mekas and Stan Brakhage, documentary had yet to

Extreme Private Eros: A Love Story (1974): another, considerably more intimate, enactment of the political in first person film

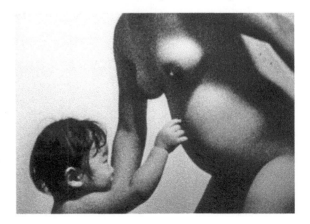

fully articulate its first person address, Hara Kazuo, along with other Japanese film-makers, began exploring the limits of the first person mode in unflinching detail. According to one of the very few sources on the topic available in English, the movement, known as the 'self-documentary' (serufu dokyumentarii) or I-film in Japan, began in the late 1960s with a focus on 'ordinary events'.[17] It is argued by Nada Hisashi, that the release of Mekas's *Reminiscences of a Journey to Lithuania* in Japan in 1973 made a very strong impression on Japanese 'amateur' film-makers, suggesting to them that the events that happen to ordinary people are worthy of representation in film.[18] In a general sense it can be said, as indeed Nada does, that *Extreme Private Eros* had no direct connection to any social incident or politics.[19] This, however, seems to entirely miss the point of the film, which while in part is surely a personal indulgence – as the film-maker undertakes to obsessively track the whereabouts of his lover who left him – is also an aesthetically challenging film that stands as a remarkable record of the zeitgeist of the times, embodying and enacting changing worldviews that certainly have political implications and ramifications.[20]

In the film, Hara's ex-lover leaves him, first to get involved with another woman, and later with an African American GI in Okinawa, with the intention, it seems, to have an interracial baby. The nascent feminist movement, the recent reintegration of Okinawa back to Japan, race politics in Japan, are all issues brought to the fore in this deceptively self-absorbed film. At first glance, in a case of life imitating art, this film-maker appears to be the real-life incarnation, albeit the Japanese doppelgänger, of the narcissistic protagonist of the 1967 mockumentary *David Holzman's Diary* (Jim McBride). McBride imagined that the lightweight, portable equipment developed in the early 1960s and put into the service of

David Holzman's Diary (1967): the spoof proleptically comes before the genre or the form

outwardly oriented observational techniques would inevitably take film-makers beyond their fascination with observing the life of others, only to turn their cameras upon themselves, with the same driving passion and tenacity. McBride's dystopic vision, wherein the eponymous title character essentially films the mundane aspects of his life ad infinitum and to no good end, is a leftist cautionary tale: down this road lies the infinite regress of meaningless, apolitical self-absorption. And thus with Hara's film too, we might want to contend that in its indulgence of the personal it is an indictment of that very mode, a kind of self-reflexive exercise in excess that forces us to recognise the degraded state of political commitment in documentary.

Although I can think of no other case where the spoof proleptically comes before the genre or the form, we can say, with some relief, that McBride's dystopic vision has never been entirely realised (YouTube diary videos notwithstanding). Even with Hara's admittedly extreme excursions into the private realm of intimate relations, the film as a whole, and the characters within it, all have something important to 'say' about a host of political, ethical and cultural concerns. And, beyond this, the film's form itself poses a direct challenge to received political, social and representational norms at its core.

We can begin by analysing the taboos broken within the film. Hara's ex, Miyuki Takeda, transgresses more than sexual and racial miscegenation taboos, when she chooses to live first with her female lover, then among sex workers in Okinawa, later with her African American lover and eventually in a commune, all the while offering her highly idiosyncratic theories about child-rearing and, most startlingly, when she insists on being filmed while giving birth unassisted to her second child. There seems to be no limit beyond which Miyuki – and her co-conspirator, Hara – will not go, and absolutely no sense of a 'private' sphere that should be kept from view. With a title like *Extreme Private Eros*, I suppose it should come as no surprise that after one particularly tense scene between Miyuki and Hara's current girlfriend, we find our vision undulating rhythmically, perilously near Miyuki's face which periodically contorts in unmistakable sexual pleasure. But it is nonetheless slightly alarming, as one finds oneself virtually making love to this woman, the camera following the movements of the film-maker as he thrusts into his lover, filming all the while. I can think of no other documentary scene shot from the perspective of a male lover as he has intercourse with a woman. Even pornographic films tend not to take such a view, fixated as they are on the sexual anatomy and the money shot. But here the viewer is given the precise point of view of the male lover, caught right in the middle of the act, as it were.[21]

Beyond the explicitness and forthrightness of the representation in this scene, and also surely in the unassisted birthing scene (where, despite the fact that the film-maker in later interviews said he simply retreated behind the camera and thought only of film-making,[22] he shoots the entire scene out of focus in an obvious indication of his absolutely freaked-out state of mind), it is the anarchic desire to smash prevailing norms and conventions, both formally and thematically, that is so telling about this film. Through its formal method as much as its subject, it exposes a post-war generational movement in Japan intent on shattering traditional values and carving its own path. Whether it could ever succeed in doing so based on the reactive rebelliousness displayed by Miyuki is questionable, but to only read the film based on the characters within it, wild as they may be, would not do justice to the real power and political implications of this film.[23] It is a film that intervenes in the age-old divide, radically rupturing the split between private and public, breaking all received social norms and arguably laying the ground for radical change. I do not merely want to situate these characters as social signifiers – signs of the times – but to suggest that the forthright, in-your-face, iconoclastic character of the film itself along with its first person mode of address should be read as a radically destabilising political gesture: a sign or symptom of dissensus. It can be seen as a prelude to radical change – the first step being the destruction of traditional (bourgeois) norms.

As you can see, I do not simply hope to assert that these first person iterations, and those to which I will refer shortly, are political in that they are either directly tied to political or social movements or that they take as their direct subject the structures and processes of the political. What I am attempting to argue for is an embodied and integrated politics, where the filmic strategy itself – of placing the film-maker at the centre of the revolutionary metaphor (Vertov) or breaking down the fabric of the social, redistributing the sensible, to paraphrase Rancière, through the film-maker's personal/political incursions (Hara) – is a way of enacting the political.

As John Corner rightly notes, 'there is a sense in which all documentaries are political',[24] and yet to say this is to say only that it is within the 'horizon of expectation'[25] to be so. In fact, it is this very expectation that leads to the concern about the possible apoliticality of first person film, since they also represent a departure from some of documentary's traditionally identifying characteristics – most pronouncedly, its adherence to a posture of objectivity. The objective stance has stood as a guarantor of what Bill Nichols has famously called a 'discourse of sobriety'.[26] It is what authorises documentary to tread into the consequential realm of the political. And it is precisely this intrusion of the personal, subjective, particular, that seems to threaten this authority, hence prompting the anxiety upon which this chapter uneasily rests. As if it needs to be stated, more than thirty years after its first articulation, the

personal is indeed and must be seen as political. I mean this not only in the sense that the feminists famously sloganised, but also in the sense that Simon Critchley reads Jean-Luc Nancy, where the personal, or shall we say, subjectivity, is always intersubjective. Critchley argues that Nancy insists on seeing subjectivity as intersubjectivity precisely to be able to retain a notion of collectivity necessary for political action. It is the condition upon which we can make political claims in the wake of communism and socialism, in that it allows for 'the exigency to say "we"'.[27] Here we must combine Nancy's notion of intersubjectivity with Rancière's concept of dissensus, allowing us to register the first person plural of this filmic modality as it intervenes in the distribution of the sensible. We must do it if we are to grasp that which is – or can be – political in first person film.

IN VERTOV'S WAKE

If earlier I used the example of Vertov to exemplify an artist whose first person address was intended to signal a thoroughgoing integration with the revolutionary spirit, then I wish to close with an example of an artist's work that emerges out of the cinders of the failure of revolution. Where Vertov availed himself of the first person modality in the wake of a successful revolution, Lebanese film-maker Mohamed Soueid takes recourse to it in the wake of extinguished hopes.[28]

First person film-making in the Arabic-speaking world has so far, generally, emerged only in those regions where the incessant over-mediation associated with war and violent conflict has created the conditions into which the intrepid first person film-maker seems compelled to find his or her voice. We see this most explicitly in the case of Lebanon and Palestine, though increasingly also in Iraq. As space is too limited here for a thorough investigation of the entire range of first person film-making in the region, I will focus the remainder of my remarks on the work of a Lebanese film-maker for whom the conditions of political engagement – in armed struggle, civil war, resistance against occupation, defeat, disenchantment and disengagement from an ideological commitment/affiliation, disenfranchisement, alienation from home and polity – all provide ripe circumstances for the development of his idiosyncratic first person films.

Mohamed Soueid was a revolutionary student activist in the 1970s, turned film critic in the 80s and, eventually, film-maker in the 90s. In the years leading up to and immediately following the turn of this century, he directed a series of extended filmic meditations on the destiny of his dismantled student brigade after the civil war[29] that loosely fall into the tradition of the poetic essay. His *Tango of Yearning* (1998), *Nightfall* (2000) and *Civil War* (2002) draw portraits of his fellow fighters – defeated, scarred, disenfranchised – the forgotten soldiers of a revolution that failed in its promise. He tracks their destiny, how they reconstituted their lives in Beirut, itself emerging battered and bereft after a series of devastating wars.[30]

In his films, Beirut appears paradoxically as a city where nothing is as it seems while, at the same time, everything beckons to be read at face value. The car mechanic is a refined cook, the disillusioned alcoholic a heartbreaking poet, the brash woman a broken widow and the family dentist a highly attuned philosopher. The face value of things is nonetheless to be read on the sides of bullet-pocked buildings and in the endless stock of vacant lots. The demoralisation of the people in the films can be read on the surface of the street, which, despite its bustling traffic and gaudy advertisements, continues to unwittingly display, as if one of its many wares, the desolation of war.

Soueid's own obsessions take the fore in all three films: in *Tango of Yearning*, the fixation is with cinema itself (the industry of fiction-making, in a country tirelessly captive to its history and whose history has no official chronicle); in *Nightfall*, with the defeat of the political movement to which he was affiliated; and in *Civil War*, again cinema, dentistry and the ineffability of life. Ultimately, though, each film of the three, in its way, thematises the film-maker's hollow struggle to find meaning in post-war Beirut.

One feels throughout the trilogy (which belatedly transformed into a quartet with *My Heart Beats Only for Her* [2009]), not entirely unlike the experience of being on the streets of Beirut, that the war could resume at any moment. But in the interval that could last a lifetime (or a split second), life goes on and a sign of that ongoing-ness is the struggle to find oneself and the shattered remains of one's own and one's comrades' beliefs. But belief requires certainty whether in relation to the chronology of events, the guiding principles of political commitment, or even the concrete facts on the ground, all of which shift before us like some admixture of phantasmagoria and quicksand. That is to say, one can easily lose the grip of actuality in Soueid's films, where his imaginative flights of fancy intertwine so seamlessly with the rhythms of the street that one can never be sure when the life of the street transitions into the life of the film-maker's mind. There is a cock-eyed logic to these impressions that parallels the illogic of the war: in Lebanon, to date, there has been no official version of the conflict proffered by the ruling powers and people are indeed left to sort out their impressions and experiences independently.

The desire to reconstruct a record of the war, to propose a narrative for a lived experience fraught with failures and ruptures, the chronicles of lives told in seemingly incoherent fragments whose coherence can only be pieced from the collective memory of individuals, drives this series. One has the impression from Soueid's work that this story needs and deserves the space to be as erratic,

impressionistic and as impossible to make sense of as the war itself was. Remember, despite the seeming interminability of that war, there were numerous lulls in fighting and innumerable shifts in allegiances, so that who was fighting whom at any given time was subject to change, as were the loyalties of any given faction.

Mohamed Soueid fought with the Palestine Student Brigade in his youth, a group of young, leftist, pan-Arabists, trained by the PLO, fighting alongside a constellation of secular, progressive multi-confessional coalition of parties and forces (the 'National Front'), and against a coalition of right-wing, Lebanese nationalist, overwhelmingly Christian militias and forces (the 'Lebanese Front'). This group of young idealists were crushed by the sectarian struggle for power in Lebanon, and the films find their circuitous method to treat the effects of defeat. In a series of oblique first person articulations that can't be anything but political, Soueid has the opposite struggle: how to insert the personal, subjective, jaundiced view into the scene, of one who is in effect 'a loser' of the war, of the struggle and of his not-inconsiderable ideals. How, in a word, can he articulate the personal experience of this devastating political reality?[31]

I will refer here to the third film in this series, *Civil War*. The first half-hour of *Civil War* is a speculative search for a character called Mohamed, beginning with a voiceover that tells us 'He was called Mohamed. I'm also called Mohamed. There are too many Mohamed's in this country.' If one watches this film without reading about it beforehand, it is unclear for the first half-hour who, precisely, this film is about. It appears to be about Mohamed, which would be expected from a first person film by a film-maker named Mohamed, except that he interviews several people who speak about Mohamed in the third person, past tense, as if he is not only absent, but perhaps no longer with us. So at once, and from the very beginning of the quest, the film-maker ties his destiny and his subjectivity to the masses of Mohameds who, like him, suffered terrible and even unspeakable losses in the none-too-distant past. The film both is and is not about himself. And indeed, even if the film were just about the film-maker, Mohamed Soueid, the inference would be that some part of him had died during the war and that it would not be inappropriate to speak about at least some significant part of himself in the third person, past tense.

It turns out that at least one of the Mohameds in the text is Mohamed Doaybess, a film line-producer who disappeared mysteriously in the year 2000, only to have been found on the rooftop of a nine-storey building, his body so utterly decomposed that he could only be identified by his teeth. Doaybess had worked with some of Lebanon's most well-known film-makers in the 1970s and 80s. In the minuscule film world of Lebanon, he was apparently quite a figure. This second Mohamed stands in not only as a clear surrogate for the evacuated soul of the film-maker, but for the decomposing landscape of a city, once the 'Paris of the Middle East', now only identifiable by the bombed out structures that litter the skyline like so many rotten teeth.

This series, like other first person films from the region, emerges out of the ruins of the war, like a return gaze of a revenant that has been photographed practically to death. As previously mentioned, the Middle East generally is not a hotbed of first person film-making. The places where it seems to take hold are all zones of overmediation due to violent conflict (war, occupation). The impulse to represent, to be true to one's own perceptions, to admit only for one's own distortions and flights of fancy, rather than those imposed by a relentless and rapacious media, seems a more than reasonable response. What is impressive, however, is the inventiveness and free acknowledgment of the shifting ground of the self that arises, certainly in the case of Mohamed Soueid's work, out of the ruins of the political, but also clearly constituted by the political. His work would make no sense understood otherwise and it would be the height of absurdity to claim that the work was nothing other than the effects of post-political neo-liberal discourses of the individual. I chose this film-maker's work to end on to allow for the full resonance of the claim I want to make, which is that the first person filmic modality, while surely, at times and in certain contexts, prone to the temptations of individualism and particularism, does not necessarily abandon the political potential of documentary as a form, but rather can be a radically destabilising force in and of itself. At times it can instantiate the integration and interpenetration of the particular and the universal, the subjective as intersubjective, intervening in the distribution of the sensible in unsettling ways, and thus, as we see in the work of Mohamed Soueid, can go some way to enact a politics in what appeared in my formulation at the start of this chapter as the post-revolutionary era. Now, as I conclude, a new popular revolutionary potential has begun to express itself across North Africa and the Levant that may well set the terms for a redistribution of what can be sensed politically for all of us. Where and how first person film will find its expression there is as yet to be seen, but it is clear to me that it may well have a place in this new revolutionary era.

ACKNOWLEDGMENTS

I would like to thank Nicole Wolf, Rasha Salti, Tianqi Yu and Başak Ertür for their brilliance as well as the time and attention they gave to help me sort out the thornier aspects of my argument. Any thorns that remain are due to my own negligence or shortcomings. But I am gratified to say the work benefited from our collective efforts.

NOTES

1. Michael Chanan, *The Politics of Documentary* (London: BFI, 2007), p. 242. It is important to note here that this claim may have little currency in places like the Arabic-speaking countries of the Levant, where first person film has been thought to have emerged much more as a response to trauma and to what could be called 'a world coming undone', such as in the aftermath of the Lebanese Civil War, or the first and second *Intifadas* in Palestine, rather than in some newly found (or worse, borrowed) identity politics.

2. Of course, this is not the first or only time the left could be said to be bedeviled by sectarianism, the difference here being that the various groups did not even share a commitment to revolutionary struggle, and the danger was, and remains, that what was once a radical revolutionary platform can too quickly transform into a liberal reformist one where moderate legal change within the existing power structures could easily become the limit of the claims.

3. I refer, of course, to the famous *October* symposium, 'The Identity in Question', held on 16 November 1991, the proceedings of which were published as a special issue (*October* no. 61, Summer 1992). Participants of the symposium included John Rajchman, Joan Scott, Cornel West, Chantal Mouffe, Homi Bhabha, Jacques Rancière, Judith Butler (though her contribution was not included in the printed version), Andreas Huyssen, Ernesto Laclau, Stanley Aronowitz and E. E. Smith.

4. Ernesto Laclau, 'Universalism, Particularism, and the Question of Identity', *October* no. 61, Summer 1992, p. 85.

5. Chantal Mouffe, 'Citizenship and Political Identity', *October* no. 61, Summer 1992, pp. 28–32.

6. Stanley Aronowitz, 'Reflections on Identity', *October* no. 61, Summer 1992, p. 102.

7. Laclau, 'Universalism, Particularism, and the Question of Identity', p. 87.

8. Laura Rascaroli, *The Personal Camera: Subjective Cinema and the Essay Film* (London: Wallflower, 2009).

9. I write about several such films in my book *First Person Jewish* (Minneapolis: University of Minnesota Press, 2008), including Jan Oxenberg's *Thank you and Goodnight* (1991), Gregg Bordowitz's *Fast Trip, Long Drop* (1993) and Jonathan Caouette's *Tarnation* (2004).

10. Rascaroli, *The Personal Camera*, p. 191.

11. In the film, the film-maker and some of the others with whom he was held hostage (a German and two Israelis) go back to the site of their abduction to work through their trauma. As Mark and his German fellow abductee confront two of their former kidnappers (who had initiated contact not long after Mark's repatriation) with stories of personal distress, essentially wrangling an apology out of the now repentant former

guerrilleros, they evoke the discourse of individual human rights, arguing that there was a gross contradiction between the guerrilleros' fight for freedom and depriving these individuals of theirs. The film itself attempts to return the hegemonic power relations back to their global order, with the Europeans and Israelis taking ther 'rightful' place as moral arbiters while holding all of the economic (not to mention cultural) power in their hands. At the same time it neatly transforms characters from former colonial and/or perpetrator cultures, infamous for their human rights infringements, into the victims at the hands of their brutal, inhumane hosts.

12. Jacques Rancière, *The Politics of Aesthetics* (London: Continuum, 2008 [2000]), p. 139.

13. Ibid., p. 141.

14. Ibid., p. 139.

15. A cursory list of such film-making would range from the films of Jonas Mekas, Michael Moore, Nick Broomfield, Alan Berliner, Ross McElwee or the later Agnès Varda, to personal films that specifically ally themselves with identity politics such as Joyce Chopra and Claudia Weill's *Joyce at 34* (1972, USA), Marlon Riggs's *Tongues Untied* (1989, USA) or Gregg Bordowitz's *Fast Trip, Long Drop*.

16. Think only of Agnès Varda's *The Gleaners and I* (2001, France).

17. Jacques Rancière, *Dissensus: The Politics of Aesthetics* (London: Continuum, 2010).

18. It has also been suggested that 'self films' emerged out of the Japanese tradition of '*shishosetsu*' ('I-novel' or 'private novel'), a modern literary form which is premised upon the belief that realism must be 'founded upon authenticated personal experience'. (Aaron Gerow, 'Shishosetsu', 1997, http://www.yidff.jp/97/cat107/97c108-2-e.html. Accessed 30 October 2012.) I want to thank Seio Nakajima for directing me towards this connection.

19. He says this specifically to contrast these films with some of the hard-hitting agitational films that were being made at the time, such as the well-known *Minamata: The Victims and their World* (Tsuchimoto Noriaki, 1972, Japan), which directly takes the corporate giant Chisso to account for polluting the waters with methyl mercury, not only making it impossible for the local fishing economy to continue, but also creating horrific long-term health problems for the local population. And also, of course, the films of Ogawa Shinsuke, about the youth movement (*Sea of Youth*, 1966, and *The Oppressed Students*, 1967), or his *Sanrizuka* series (1971–77) detailing the violent struggles of a population against forced relocation by the government in order to build Narita Airport. See Abé Mark Nornes's fascinating study (*Forest of Pressure: Ogawa Shinsuke*

and Postwar Japanese Documentary [Minneapolis: University of Minnesota Press, 2007]) for more on this topic.

20. In an interview with Hara Kazuo during the 2009 Sheffield Film Festival, the interviewer John Berra, begins thus: 'Although the Japanese director Kazuo Hara has insisted that he is anything but a political film-maker, his 1974 documentary *Extreme Private Eros* (*Gokushiteki erosu: Renka*, 1974, Japan) remains a fascinating snapshot of Japanese society at a time of transition.' I am in agreement with this statement, though I think it does not go far enough.

21. Remember, this documentary came out two years before Nagisa Oshima's then controversially explicit *In the Realm of the Senses* (1976, Japan). Hara notes in his book *Camera Obstrusa* that it was no simple thing to shoot that scene – he feared his back would go out! Hara Kazuo, *Camera Obtrusa: The Action Documentaries of Hara Kazuo*, trans. Pat Noonan and Takuo Yasouda (New York: Kaya Press, 2009 [1987]), p. 106.

22. John Berra, '"Extreme Private Eros": Interview with Kazuo Hara', *Electric Sheep*, 2010, http://www.electricsheep magazine.co.uk/features/2010/01/10/extreme-private-eros-interview-with-kazuo-hara/. Accessed 24 November 2010.

23. Neither should we imagine the characters in the film as somehow standing outside of their social context, two deviants (or one deviant and one obsessive) who represent no one but themselves. Hara Kazuo (in Berra, 'Extreme Private Eros') tells us that he believes Miyuki 'was very representative of Japanese women at that time, especially those who were involved in student activities. But she had more charisma than other women, she was stranger, you could not say she was "normal", although she does represent a time of change for Japanese women.' And although he doesn't say as much explicitly in that one interview, it is fair to suspect that the same goes for him.

24. John Corner, 'Documentary and the Political', *Studies in Documentary Film* vol. 3 no. 2, November 2009, p. 114.

25. Steve Neale, 'Questions of Genre', *Screen* vol. 31 no. 1, Spring 1990, p. 57.

26. Bill Nichols, *Representing Reality: Issues and Concepts in Documentary* (Bloomington: University of Indiana Press, 1991).

27. Simon Critchley, *Ethics-Politics-Subjectivity* (London: Verso, 1999), p. 241. I discuss Nancy's relevance to conceptualising the subject-in-relation in more depth in the introduction to *Cinema of Me: Self, Subjectivity in First Person Documentary Film* (London: Wallflower, 2012).

28. I am indebted to Rasha Salti, not only for introducing me to Mohamed Soueid's work, but also for her invaluable

analysis of the emergence of first person film in the Levant, which has informed much of the reading to follow.

29. The brigade was actually dismantled after the withdrawal of the PLO from Lebanon in 1982, but the films concern themselves with the time period commencing after the wars' end in 1991.

30. For a brilliantly evocative exploration of this theme see Rasha Salti, *Beirut Bereft* (Sharjah, UAW: Sharjah Biennal, 2009).

31. Another extraordinary example of a first person film that struggles to assert a personal perspective as distinct from overdetermined political identifications is Raed Andoni's *Fix Me* (2009, Palestine/France).

4.2 Feminist Documentaries: Finding, Seeing and Using Them

JULIA LESAGE

Film culture's tripartite division of production, distribution and exhibition is taken far too much as read, with the system's distribution and exhibition largely uninterrogated. This failure significantly contributes to obfuscating its ideological underpinnings; but, for normally excluded or marginalised voices (women, for example), consideration of the totality of the system is utterly crucial. A voice without listeners might as well be silent.

Recently I have begun to mix criticism with autobiography. Certainly the topic of this chapter refers to a trajectory in film studies in which I have been a participant, since I have critically defended feminist realist documentary as well as written about more modernist work, often focusing on stylistically innovative documentary.[1] As Diane Waldman and Janet Walker note, in the field of film studies in the 1980s and 90s, debates around realism led many feminist scholars to neglect documentary studies in general.[2] Also in the 80s and 90s, especially with the increasing accessibility of VHS cameras, more and more women began making video, myself included, and often chose to make both documentaries for social activism and autobiographical work.

As with many of my peers, the 70s and 80s were a ferment of activism for me. In those years I taught at the University of Illinois at Chicago, where with other women – faculty and staff and undergraduates – we fought for, founded and collectively taught first a women's studies introductory course and then a women's studies programme with a socialist feminist orientation.[3] In later years, for over a decade I taught video production as well as film theory and criticism at the University of Oregon, where I also made activist documentaries, both in experimental and realist modes.[4] And across all these decades, from 1976 on, I worked with Chuck Kleinhans and John Hess to bring the sensibility of the alternative press to film scholarship with the founding and ongoing publication of *Jump Cut: A Review of Contemporary Media*, which for a number of years now I have managed as its webmistress online. My enduring critical interest has been in alternative media and political sub-cultures. So it is with all these 'hats' that I come to reflect on what's happened to feminist documentary in the last few decades.

One of the things that has changed in terms of women's film-making is that in the 1970s and 80s many more women's works were seen at feminist conferences or women's film festivals than were available anywhere else. In 1974, at the first women's film festival in Chicago, the planning committee, which included B. Ruby Rich and Laura Mulvey, had to work hard to collectively generate a list of women directors of documentary, fiction and experimental work. We found so few. For several decades after that, a grassroots organisation, Women in the Director's Chair, put on an annual Women's Film and Video Festival with assistance from two other Chicago alternative media institutions, the Center for New Television and Chicago Filmmakers.[5] It was at these events that I saw many works that later would be the foundation for my courses on women and film: for example, Carolee Schneeman's *Fuses* (1965), Cecelia Condit's *Possibly in Michigan* (1983) and Ayoka Chenzira's *Secret Sounds Screaming: The Sexual Abuse of Children* (1985). Film screenings played a big role in the early years of 'second wave' feminism in that they gave viewers, often in mainly women's gatherings, a common basis on which to discuss social issues and also to explore women artists' aesthetics, sometimes phrased then as searching for 'new languages' in video and film. In such festivals, the experimental, the documentary and the autobiographical converged.

Of particular importance for my understanding of women's documentary film-making was attending an international feminist film and video conference held in Amsterdam in 1981.[6] The invited international participants began with lengthy introductions. I found out then how widely the parameters of women's media-making and issues of social concern varied from country to country and region to region. Some of the film-makers spoke of trying to get into national film schools and then get women-oriented thesis projects approved; others, especially in Europe, customarily had their films funded by national television, usually in advance of production. Film-makers from francophone Africa told us how they had to send all footage back to France for processing. In some countries there were lively feminist sub-cultures; in others, little outlet for feminist scholarship and teaching, indeed for teaching about film or popular culture at all. What became clear to me was the relation between political activism, money and cultural possibilities, and how unique that constellation is from country to country. In addition, as this conference gave evidence to, I saw how international gatherings could promote border crossings and exchange: among film-makers, scholars, aesthetics and ideas. Participants expanded their professional and personal identities as well as forging new relations that shaped their future media-making and critical work.[7] Because of the insights I gained there, I focus my discussion here mainly on developments and institutions in the USA, where a specific combination of social and economic circumstances has shaped the development of both feminist film theory and feminist film-making and distribution.

In the 1980s and 90s, film festivals, even the expanding circuit of women's film festivals, took on a different function and attracted a different audience than they did at those early women's film events. For many, going to a festival indicates what Pierre Bourdieu would call 'distinction': it marks the viewer as someone who can afford the tickets, perhaps even travelling to see the event; it also marks him/her as someone with elite taste. Currently, cinephiles who can afford it make it a point to attend festivals; distributors send representatives to see new work, as do television producers, especially from PBS or cable TV. At the same time, and with much more anxiety, directors go to festivals with newly completed films to find an outlet for their work. When they do, they find out that getting into a festival is the funnel to an even narrower bottleneck. Few will net a distributor or a spot on TV.

Thus, my concerns in this chapter are not just about feminism and documentary but also about some problems that alternative media generally face, especially in terms of distribution, reception and use. In a parallel way, both feminism and documentary have undergone developments and dispersals. In the USA, both have relied on educational institutions and, now, on the internet to remain visible and to flourish. In each case, that of feminism and that of documentary, the issue arises of how something comes to 'count', of making sure it does not disappear shortly after entering its public life. One of the main reasons that some feminist documentaries have had prolonged use is that they fit feminist or media scholars' concerns and have had academic essays explicating them that makes them ideal for college classroom use.

Feminist film criticism, like other critical tendencies in literature and the arts, has favoured certain kinds of women's media and theoretical approaches in order to promote new frames of knowledge, new ways of theorising gender in film and the discovery of new or lost women artists. In the 1980s film theory needed a more Brechtian style of documentary. Certain women's documentaries,

then, were the right film at the right time. Earlier, in the women's movement in the 70s in the USA, often-seen films included realist documentaries such as *Growing Up Female*, *The Woman's Film, Janie's Janie, Mother of Many Children* and *I Am Somebody*,[8] which served a consciousness-raising function. In the 80s, in the midst of debates around key critical issues framed within terms drawn from Marxism, feminism, psychoanalysis and semiotics, more favour was granted modernist, mixed-genre documentaries such as *Daughter Rite, Reassemblage* and *Thriller*,[9] films which Women Make Movies distributor Debra Zimmerman calls 'evergreens', because they still produce substantial revenue from sales and rentals. In the 90s changes in feminist theory across all academic fields drew from developments in queer, post-colonial and critical race theory. And more media production and criticism by women of colour has led to an expanded canon of media works regularly seen and taught in classes dealing with women's issues. In particular, the prolific and artistically challenging work of Trinh T. Minh-ha, in films and books, has made her a feminist auteur embodying post-colonial media criticism and production from the 80s on. Nevertheless, few women's documentaries have had the distribution success of those select 80s modernist feminist works. In that sense, a small number of film texts became a kind of feminist documentary canon.

In an essay reprinted in an anthology of feminist criticism, Janet Staiger assesses canon formation:

> In film criticism, whether popular or academic, some films will be chosen for extensive discussion and analysis; others will be ignored. In theoretical writing, arguments are buttressed by films cited as examples of points. In histories, films are marked as worth mentioning for one reason or another (e.g., influence, aesthetic significance, typicality). This occurs not only for historiographical reasons (every causal explanation invariably privileges particular linkages or conjunctions), but for practical reasons as well: a history including every film would be trapped by the *Tristram Shandy* contradiction of constantly losing ground to the increasing number of films added daily to the list of those to be covered. Even film-makers are involved in canon formation. Those films chosen to be reworked, alluded to, satirized, become privileged points of reference, pulled out from the rest of cinema's predecessors. As ideal fathers, these select films are given homage or rebelled against.[10]

Scholars of documentary and the avant-garde, as well as feminist film scholars (these are overlapping categories), have reason to celebrate works they admire so as to keep the works in circulation. So do people writing on films outside the mainstream European and US channels of distribution, on art that needs publicity to reach a broader

Films which Women Make Movies distributor Debra Zimmerman calls 'evergreens': *Daughter Rite* (1979), *Reassemblage* (1982) and *Thriller* (1979)

common practice in film studies pedagogy in general is to teach a film along with an accompanying essay or book chapter; perhaps this is also a way of 'credentialling' film studies to sceptical administrators or of giving students a crutch to hang on to, something they can study before the exam. And if a teacher uses a textbook along with a course pack of readings, then she often picks films that reinforce or illustrate concepts in the text. The mixed-genre or reflexive feminist documentary, one that challenges stylistic and epistemological boundaries, finds a home in many academic departments: for example, women's studies, psychology, film studies, or the fine arts.

What is important to understand is that the writer is also a gatekeeper. Films without essays written about them languish at the distributor's. Since the advent of inexpensive HD video production and digital streaming distribution – a phenomenon just beginning to realise its potential – gatekeepers, including festivals, distributors, critics, bloggers and scholars, are playing a more important role than ever in bringing a plethora of available work to our attention. In addition, media artists have the option of publishing their own work on the internet. There is an excessive amount of film and video available to be seen, much less written about, and documentaries compete for our attention along with television and fiction film, now coming to us in a digital form from all over the world. I would argue that both scholars and media-makers will rely even more on gatekeepers, much as they may bemoan the elitism and restrictiveness that those figures seem to embody.

We write and teach about the things that we can see, that we know enough about to choose to see. Earlier in my career, I mostly saw contemporary documentaries in an activist context that I sought out apart from the classrooms: for example, films against the Vietnam War, feminist documentaries and Latin American solidarity films. The ones I taught were the ones the university owned or a few feminist films that I and several other women could persuade the university audiovisual centre to buy, promising to teach them often. For years teaching film studies classes within financially beleaguered institutions, my colleagues and I taught using VHS tapes of feature films rented from the local video store and documentaries taped off of television, lucky to get a budget of $50 for the rentals and tape. When in New York, I would visit Women Make Movies to watch stacks of their tapes, and in Chicago would do so once every few years at the Video Data Bank. From that viewing, I would make recommendations to the department or the university library for purchase of a few titles.

For a decade or so now, I have wondered how many films/videos and what kind of films a film scholar should see, and under what circumstances? The same for television viewing. Does it matter if we see things on a small

audience. In my conversations with women scholars, a number of them indicated that they regularly write about a film because they want it to be used more broadly, and they take pleasure in keeping some film or tape in active circulation for a longer time. But I would not attribute too much power to the scholar and her ability to give a film a big viewership, if only among feminist teachers. The most or big screen, with a TiVo skipping ads, with streaming content over the internet, or via mail order DVD. What orchestrates our narrative attention, our desire to watch? My own experience is that my personal media viewing now has a generally global reach, expanded by mail order video and the use of a digital video recorder, Netflix internet streaming and a multi-regional DVD player. The DVDs and streaming Netflix give me a certain kind of control in selecting what I will watch, but they have also clearly led to a levelling and flattening out of my seeming 'choices', universalising the works because of the way they get to my living room and on to my HDTV. Especially when I am alone, picking a documentary from the TiVo seems like just a high-culture viewing option among a myriad of other entertainment offerings on TV. In addition, as a peculiarity of the neighbourhood where I live, my high-speed internet service is so dreadfully slow that using a wi-fi household computer connection to watch YouTube video leaves me frustrated because even a short video keeps stopping and restarting. I think it important to keep up with internet video as a cultural phenomenon but cannot easily do so. What is important to note about all these media platforms is that far fewer artistic and socially committed productions by women come to me by these means than those by and about men. Gatekeepers impose an implicit, politically inflected point of view, and here those gatekeepers are the competing players in the entertainment industry.

Both now, when we have a plethora of media that might potentially interest us to write about or to teach, and earlier, when a far narrower range of documentaries were available, documentary films have been profitably distributed in the USA through the educational film market, which typically has sold a VHS tape or a DVD to a school audiovisual library for $200–$500. Many educational distributors have come and gone since the 1970s, but some have persisted throughout these years and maintain an active catalogue of many progressive social-issue films, works by people of colour, documentaries around international perspectives, queer and feminist documentaries and experimental works.[11] The distributors vary in the degree to which they actively promote and market the works they carry, across platforms and to targeted audiences. And they function in parallel, if not in competition, with streaming digital media platforms aiming to go directly to the computer or TV. In particular, feminist film criticism has flourished in the USA partly because a feminist distribution company, Women Make Movies, has flourished along with it.

Founded in 1972 mainly as an organisation dedicated to teaching media-making skills to women in New York City, by the 1980s Women Make Movies changed its mission to be a market-driven, non-profit distributor carrying films by and about women. To a certain degree, such a focus – seen in the company's name – grows out of identity politics.[12]

But in another way it is a very smart marketing move, branding Women Make Movies as the place to turn to first for documentaries about women's issues, especially for teaching or for organising campaigns in such arenas as rape prevention or health. Women Make Movies, like the other educational distributors, defends the high 'institutional pricing' charged for its collection, saying that many people get to see each work and that this kind of pricing allows more money to be returned to the filmmakers. In fact, it is the educational market that has kept these distributors in business. Of all the educational distributors in the USA, however, Women Make Movies is also the smartest about marketing. It has got its holdings onto television and into festivals, and it has developed strategies to help each work find the potentially most interested users. In particular, its website frequently gives links under a film's listing, not only to the maker's site, but also to other sites that deal with the issue at hand or to essays that analyse the film, thus reinforcing the tie between written critique and film screening so important in distribution.

Beyond that, the organisation and its holdings bear the stamp of director Debra Zimmerman's curatorial savvy. As Patricia White notes, if early holdings built up the canon of 'evergreens', of critically hailed modernist works, 'acquisitions throughout the 1980s and 1990s followed shifts in cultural thinking about identity toward issues of exile, displacement and hybridity – the works of Tracey Moffat, Ngozi Onwurah, Pratibha Parmar, Mona Hatoum'.[13] The collection has been broadened in this way because Zimmerman travels to many women's and documentary film festivals around the world, so that now almost half the catalogue comes from outside the USA. And these films follow the international spread of feminist activism around specific women's issues – especially around culture, health, globalisation and violence – so that an attentive viewer can trace the historical trajectory of how an issue has been dealt with: in film, in feminist theory and in public policy.

Let me trace a specific example through the Women Make Movie holdings on the topic of female genital cutting (FGC) or clitoridectomy and infibulation. Alice Walker and Pratibha Parmar's film on the subject, *Warrior Marks*, came out in 1993 (earlier Walker had taken up the subject of FGC in her novel *Possessing the Secret of Joy* and also discussed the issue on the *Today Show*). The film was vehemently denounced by Selbe Dawit and Salem Mekuria in the *New York Times* and also by critics Inderpal Grewal and Caren Kaplan in the feminist film journal, *Camera Obscura*.[14] Despite the critique, the film circulated widely. Later, in 2002, Kim Longinotto released *The Day I Will Never Forget*, following women and girls involved in circumcision in Kenya; this film raises issues about voice, authority and voyeurism, in addition to being a striking work of activist

The Day I Will Never Forget (2002): a striking work of activist media

media. Longinotto herself is one of the foremost women documentarists today.[15] The 2009 film *Mrs Goundo's Daughter* (Barbara Attie and Janet Goldwater) approaches the issue another way, focusing on the legal struggles of a woman who fights to remain in the USA because her two-year-old daughter would be subject to FGC if she were deported to Mali. And, finally, in 2010, Women Make Movies added to its collection *Africa Rising: The Grassroots Movement to End Female Genital Mutilation* (Paula Heridia, 2009), filmed in Burkina Faso, Kenya, Mali, Somalia and Tanzania. Significantly, the links on the Women Make Movies web page for the film lead to activist websites; information from the World Health Organisation; personal accounts, news, and an online documentary from the UN around this issue; and grassroots websites from the countries where the film was shot.

I mention this collection of films and links to show a shift in the relation between feminist film scholarship and films of potential interest to women. Walker's film provoked an in-depth response and rejection of the way an African American novelist and a South Asian British film-maker framed and dealt with this topic, but the trajectory of the films, still directed by 'outsiders', traces the rise of African women's activism around this issue. It is that latter aspect, how films on FGC might contribute to activism and changes in civil policy and 'tradition', that remains to be analysed by those interested in the relation between feminism and documentary. The group of films itself demonstrates the increasing number of films one might write about or teach, films that add complexity to debates within transnational feminism, but still films most of us have never heard of. The links are also worth teaching, since they demonstrate the kind of branching out that activist media can and should generate. And the degree to which we know, or more likely do not know about this small collection, to which one might add Ousmane Sembène's fictional feature *Moolaadé*[16] on the topic of FGC, leads to the issue of how we, in fact, learn about new work that we might like to see.

Currently, in this age of digital film-making and distribution, most documentaries will garner a viewership of no

more than a few hundred people. It's become inexpensive to make documentaries, somewhat more costly to ship them out to festivals – especially to get film prints made for that purpose. But at that point, if the works do get into festivals, even fewer films get a distributor, and only a miniscule number achieve theatrical release or purchase by TV. The alternative, do-it-yourself (DIY) route is to try to use the internet to build an audience and prolong a film's life. The internet can reach a potentially large viewership and can be targeted to specific communities with like interests, but it takes money to build and maintain an effective website, and not many film-makers want to limit themselves to just one issue, to which they devote all their efforts. Many a film-maker makes a work and then wants to move on to another planned project. In the USA, film-makers or distributors sometimes get a grant to build a website. And public television, PBS, maintains excellent websites for the films it buys rights to, with extended interviews, sometimes online screening and links to many kinds of social outreach.[17]

At the same time as DIY film-makers are trying to learn how to build an audience via the internet, other media artists are choosing to use the internet either to distribute their work for free or to do a whole new kind of documentary production for online viewing – sometimes interactive narrative, sometimes a cumulative collection of oral history and contextual material, or sometimes audiovisual material incorporated into blogging, arguably often an incarnation of autobiographical media in a new guise. The educational media distributors are also learning how to go digital, with left-feminist distribution collective New Day Films leading the way in selling streaming rights both to home viewers and educational institutions, using digital rights management (DRM) to put its entire catalogue in a streaming format online.[18] Following from the New Day model, a distributors' consortium that carries left/feminist works – Bullfrog Films, Icarus Films, California Newsreel and Women Make Movies – has indicated that it plans to do a similar kind of streaming, especially to school audiovisual centres. Its educational media pricing structure will remain intact and is enforceable because of the strict copyright liability that school libraries face.[19] Distributors still have to do intense marketing campaigns to make viewers aware of their films. And this is increasingly done via the internet.

Internet marketing and distribution, or the use of the internet itself as an exhibition platform, depends on a whole new kind of media and business savvy. As I prowl around the internet looking for things I might like to see, including for download or purchase, I particularly assess the 'quality' of the website, the attractiveness and emphasis of the site design, what tools it contains that would be useful to potential users/viewers, what kinds of communities it becomes a part of (e.g., women's studies, film lovers, activists around x issue, healthcare workers, avant-garde film/video, online narratives, etc.). As I mentioned, teachers often want an essay to teach with a film, so it is especially useful to have PDFs available, including essays written about a work or interviews with the film-maker. One of the foremost avant-garde lesbian film-makers in the USA, Su Friedrich, has a website that is exemplary in this regard, with a long section, 'Reviews', that provides PDFs of essays written about her work. Her site also is a promotional vehicle for a six-DVD set of her work, remastered from film negatives, which she sells at a relatively modest home-viewing price of $109 (educational $495).[20] Distributors' sites are more or less useful in terms of links, address to potential groups of users, or incorporating PDFs. Third World Newsreel, for example, which carries the frequently taught videos of Camille Billops and James Hatch, and Frameline, a major distributor of LGBT work, have scanty internet outreach.

What is significant about internet outreach by documentary film-makers is that it crosses national boundaries and opens up exposure and sales to a worldwide marketplace and potential communities of viewers and users. Understanding this, Canadian Filmmakers Distribution Center of Canada and V Tape, two major Canadian distributors of independent media, have received funding from the Canada Council of the Arts to create 'Fringe Online',[21] a collection of distinct websites by both film-makers and web artists. Found here is the unique internet artwork of Midi Onodera, who has available on her site her 2009 video collections as *Movie of the Week*, as well as PDFs of essays and interviews and an excellent study guide, written by Sylvia Chong and Ann Gronau, to accompany Onodera's experimental narrative, *I Have No Memory of My Direction*, about her relation to Japan and Japanese culture as a Japanese Canadian woman. Much of Onodera's work is also available as DVD.[22]

Multimedia artists expect to communicate with viewers throughout the world. A widely seen, pioneering feminist interactive narrative on the internet is Australian Debra Beattie's autobiographical *The Wrong Crowd* (2008), dealing with police brutality in Queensland and its traumatic impact on Beattie's family and her own growing up. As with many successful large-scale interactive projects, the work had outside funding, here Screen Australia, and it now has its permanent home on the Australian Broadcasting Corporation's website.[23] Of particular interest to teachers who might like to use such a work with a class is the fact that the creative work is part of Beattie's doctoral thesis, the entirety of which is also available as a PDF for download.[24] Her study theorises both 'buried' national/family history and the structure and functioning of online documentary, which makes the thesis useful for both women's studies and media classes and potentiates the value of the site for classroom use.

If Debra Beattie and Midi Onodera have been pioneers in using the internet as an outlet for extensive individual artistic production, established feminist film and video-makers in the USA are also developing internet sites to present and expand the scope of their work. Video-maker Lynn Hershman's ground-breaking documentary *!Women Art Revolution* traces relations between the US feminist art movement and 1970s anti-Vietnam War activism, the civil rights movement and the women's movement; the film features images of artwork, video clips of performances and protests, and interviews with many of the feminist art movement's participants. Over many years, Hershman collected hundreds of hours of interviews with many connected with that movement, and all of these historically important materials are now archived and available online from Stanford University.[25] In addition, and perhaps even more innovative, in conjunction with her installations using this collected material, Hershman has launched an interactive website, RAW/WAR, 'built on user contributions, with the goal of creating a community' around the history and ongoing practice of feminist art. There are not many posts on this site yet, but the film has had an enthusiastic early reception, and the collective participation that the film elicits might build in momentum, especially if students are also encouraged to submit responses to the site. Hershman's work in general stands as an example of how many feminist works by women known in the *experimental* film/video community did not make their way into the feminist film canon described above. Partly, there is a kind of academic ghettoisation of what gets shown in what kind of classes, and certainly a frequent exclusion of avant-garde media in the educational film/video market, but there is also an insularity of the avant-garde media world itself, which maintains its own canon of frequently seen, and taught, works.[26]

Working in a way more attuned to popular culture, Alex Juhasz has both taught from and written about YouTube; her book, *Learning from YouTube*, is published by MIT Press as an online-only academic book with many video clips, one of the first of its kind.[27] With her online book publication, her activist stance and her blog, Media Praxis,[28] in which she theorises her own media work and teaching, Juhasz thoughtfully combines multimedia feminist media production and criticism. In terms of her own work, Juhasz has put up much of her documentary production on the site SnagFilms, which carries documentaries that can be viewed for free.[29]

And, finally, Michelle Citron, director of *Daughter Rite*, has moved across media and over the last few years has created a complex interactive narrative site on the web. Interestingly, she has also faced the economic and technical issues of moving away from documentary film production marketed to a well-established niche. Her autobiographical book, *Home Movies and Other Necessary*

Fictions,[30] won a number of major literary prizes; it clarifies events suggested in *Daughter Rite* but has never been used as frequently as her film, perhaps because the original essays about the film, written by feminist scholars, are so often photocopied and reproduced in course packets. Over the last decade, she has worked on a major multimedia project, a series of CD-roms and DVDs, now put online collectively as *Queer Feast*, also largely in an autobiographical mode. In these works, Citron mixes production platforms – including Polaroids, video with an old DV camera, fake home movies shot with 16mm Bolex, super 8 film from her and other lesbians' lives, photographs, documentary archive footage – and this work also mixes documentary and fiction. Her aesthetic and political goal in making *Queer Feast*, perhaps, is to use her own family history and social context to trace the kinds of complex intersections of identity and social history that might characterise many queer lives, a phenomenology of identity, as it were. However, Citron has been plagued by technical problems that result from competition between platforms among media giants and have led to the rapid disappearance of artists' multimedia works. She began using the software program Macromedia Director, resulting in CD-roms that now can only be played on PCs and not Macs; she then worked with the software Flash, but now Flash video is increasingly unplayable on Apple platforms such as the iPad. Overcoming these challenges was the first step in creating the large online narrative; now comes the problem, as she puts it, of drawing viewers to her site.[31]

I mention these specific feminist multimedia artists because I esteem their work and the scope of their production, both actual and planned. But they all face a number of similar problems. One is the issue of platform. The other is the issue of visibility. Some forms of putting media on the internet will be successful; some artists will build a viewership; some sites or platforms will endure. Others will not. I myself, as editor of *Jump Cut*, wonder about this as I get older. We bought the domain name ejumpcut.org for a hundred years in a grand gesture of hope, but what platforms will *Jump Cut* migrate to after we can no longer tend to it? Film-makers had to decide what to do about video, then about DVD and now about the web. So did distributors. Lots has been lost. Right now, the DVD endures, perhaps a cinephile platform, cheap to reproduce, perhaps as an aide memoire for scholars and an item to be checked out of libraries or taught in class.

With more use of streaming media platforms and with the branching out of feminisms and feminist activism, how is current and future feminist media to be found? Once we move past the canonised feminist works, it is hard to keep up with feminist works we might like to see. We are in the same position as most viewers in the way we find out about the film and television programmes we plan to watch. Feminist documentaries come to our attention via

reviews, festival roundups, the screening schedules we find on cable or satellite TV, the kinds of film information we choose to pursue on the internet, or word of mouth. In neoliberal culture democracy goes hand in hand with marketing, as do most aspects of the public sphere. We rely on gatekeeping practices, often restrictive ones, to select from an over-abundance of potential viewing material. After that, our own writing makes us curators of the work we hope others will see.

RESEARCH NOTE
In preparing for this chapter, I had lengthy conversations with the following people, who helped me better understand the state of feminist documentary, especially in terms of distribution and reception. Some sent me copies of their scholarly and creative work. In this sense, this chapter has been a collaborative effort. Thanks to Jacqueline Bobo, Michelle Citron, Gary Crowdus, Mary Erickson, Christine Holmlund, Chuck Kleinhans, Alex Juhasz, Lynn Hershman Leeson, Janet Staiger, Diane Waldman, Janet Walker, Janet Wasko, Patricia White, Linda Williams and Debra Zimmerman.

NOTES
1. Julia Lesage, 'The Political Aesthetics of the Feminist Documentary Film', *Quarterly Review of Film Studies* vol. 3 no. 4, 1978; JoAnn Elam, 'Rape: Disarming Film Rape', *Jump Cut* no. 19, December 1978, pp. 14–16.
2. Diane Waldman and Janet Walker give an excellent overview of this history in their introduction to *Feminism and Documentary* (Minneapolis: University of Minnesota, 1999). See also Shilyh Warren, 'By, For, and About: The "Real" Problem in the Feminist Film Movement', *Mediascape*: UCLA's Journal of Cinema and Media Studies, Autumn 2008, http://www.tft.ucla.edu/mediascape/Fall08_Warren.html. Accessed 14 September 2012.
3. Judith Kegan Gardiner offers a case history of that programme in 'What Happened to Socialist Feminist Women's Studies Programs? A Case History and Some Speculations', *Feminist Studies* vol. 34 no. 3, Autumn 2008.
4. My documentary video production includes two works made with minority students at the University of Oregon: *Getting Around* (1995) and *In Plain English: Students of Color Speak Out* (1992). Earlier documentaries, made in both realist and experimental styles, where shot within Sandinista Nicaragua: *Mensajeros [Troubadours]* (1987 and 1989); *El Crucero* (1987); *Lamento* (1985); *Parque Wilfredo Valenzuela [Wilfred's Park]* and *La Escuela [The School]* (1985); *Home Life* (1984); and *Las Nicas* (1984 and 1986). These tapes are distributed by Facets Multimedia.
5. Chicago media organisations, past and present, were valuable resources for feminist media-makers: Women in the Directors Chair, Film Center of the Art Institute, Center for New Television and Chicago Filmmakers.

6. This conference was put on by the feminist film organisation Cinemien and, as I recall, other US attendees included Barbara Hammer, Frances Reid and Michelle Citron.

7. Barbara Hammer, *HAMMER! Making Movies Out of Sex and Life* (New York: Feminist Press, CUNY, 2010), p. 112.

8. *Growing Up Female* (Julia Reichert and James Klein, 1971, USA); *The Woman's Film* (Judy Smith, Louise Alaimo and Ellen Sorin, 1971, USA); *Janie's Janie* (Geri Ashur and Peter Barton, 1971, USA); *Mother of Many Children* (Alanis Obamsawin, 1977, Canada); *I Am Somebody* (Madeline Anderson, 1970, USA).

9. *Reassemblage* (Trinh T. Minh-ha, 1982, USA); *Daughter Rite* (Michelle Citron, 1979, USA); *Thriller* (Sally Potter, 1979, UK).

10. Janet Staiger, 'The Politics of Film Canons', *Cinema Journal* vol. 24 no. 3, Spring 1985, p. 4; reprinted in Diane Carson, Linda Dittmar and Janice R. Welsch (eds), *Multiple Voices in Feminist Film Criticism* (Minneapolis: University of Minnesota Press, 1994).

11. Major US distributors of educational media who carry feminist documentaries include Women Make Movies, Cambridge Documentary Films, Third World Newsreel, California Newsreel, Frameline, Icarus, Cinema Guild and Zeitgeist. Video Data Bank and Canyon Cinema distribute independent experimental work.

12. 'Women Make Movies is devoted exclusively to films that are by and about women, which to this day continues to irk, confuse, confound, puzzle, and make men mad'. Debra Zimmerman in a lengthy interview with Pat Aufderheide, 'From A to Z: A Conversation on Women's Filmmaking', *Signs: Journal of Women in Culture and Society* no. 30, 2004, p. 1455.

13. Patricia White, 'Feminist Independents', unpublished conference paper, Console-ing Passions, 2000.

14. Grewal Inderpal and Kaplan Caren, '*Warrior Marks*: Global Womanism's Neo-Colonial Discourse in a Multicultural Context', *Camera Obscura* vol. 13 no. 3; Selbe Dawit and Salem Mekuria (1973) 'The West Just Doesn't Get It', *New York Times*, 7 December 1973, p. A27.

15. Patricia White, 'Cinema Solidarity: The Documentary Practice of Kim Longinotto', *Cinema Journal* vol. 46 no. 1, Autumn 2006; Belinda Smaill, 'Women, Pain and the Documentaries of Kim Longinotto', *The Documentary: Politics, Emotion, Culture* (New York: Palgrave Macmillan, 2010).

16. Amy Borden, 'At the Global Market: Ousmane Sembène's *Moolaadé* and the Economics of Women's Rights', *Jump Cut: A Review of Contemporary Media* no. 52, 2011. Also of interest, with a section on FGC, is an earlier film about women's political organising in Africa, *Femmes aux yeux ouverts* [Women with Open Eyes] (1994), by the Togolese film-maker Anne-Laure Folly (see Chapter 3.2).

17. For example, see the range of activist links on the PBS website for *The Education of Shelby Knox* around contesting abstinence-only education in the USA: http://www.pbs. org/pov/shelbyknox/. In other countries, the BBC is notable for showing whole films online, as is the National Film Board of Canada.

18. New Day Digital, http://www.newdaydigital.com/. Accessed 14 September 2012.

19. Thus, I could teach in class from my own videotape collection or a commercially rented DVD, protected by free speech and fair use, but could not put that material on reserve in the library for students to do make-up screenings or re-view for writing a paper or studying for an exam.

20. Su Friedrich, http://www.sufriedrich.com. Accessed 14 September 2012.

21. From the site: 'Fringe Online is the largest online publication project in the Canadian media arts. It features a wide range of writings, stills and clips from sixteen Canadian media artists. Hundreds of never seen before documents have been made available for the first time, assembled into a suite of virtual libraries which we invite you to explore', http://www.fringeonline.ca/. Accessed 14 September 2012.

22. http://midionodera.com. Accessed 14 September 2012.

23. *The Wrong Crowd*, http://www.abc.net.au/wrongcrowd. Accessed 14 September 2012.

24. Debra Beattie, '*The Wrong Crowd*: An Online Documentary and Analytical Contextualization', thesis, Faculty of Creative Industries, University of Queensland, 3 December 2008, http://eprints.qut.edu.au/15874/. Accessed 14 September 2012.

25. The complete interviews are available at Stanford's Art and Special Collection Libraries: !WAR: Voices of a Movement, http://lib.stanford.edu/women-art-revolution. The film's website is http://www.womenartrevolution. com/. Accessed 14 September 2012. An open history of art based on the film, RAW/WAR is built on user contributions, with the goal of creating a history defined by the community: http://www.rawwar.org/. Accessed 14 September 2012.

26. Michael Zryd, 'The Academy and the Avant-Garde: A Relationship of Dependence and Resistance', *Cinema Journal* vol. 45 no. 2, February 2006, pp. 17–42.

27. Alex Juhasz, *Learning from YouTube* (Cambridge, MA: MIT Press, 2011), http://vectors.usc.edu/projects/learningfrom youtube/.

28. Juhasz's blog is Media Praxis at http://aljean.wordpress. com. Accessed 14 September 2012. Juhasz has placed her *Women of Vision* series and the documentary *Scale* to be viewed for free on SnagFilms at http://www. snagfilms.com. Accessed 14 September 2012. SnagFilms has an app on the iTunes store, as do PBS, BBC, NFB and Netflix. Documentary viewing, free or inexpensive, is

becoming more available on small-screen devices. I suspect that the social-issues documentary, with its strong argumentation, might appeal to small-screen viewers because it is compelling and easy to follow and does not generally rely on spectacle for its appeal as much as fiction film does. Here, too, as with most exhibition platforms, smart-phone and tablet viewers

have access to more works directed by men than by women.

29. At SnagFilms the maker gets paid on a click-through basis.

30. Michelle Citron, *Home Movies and Other Necessary Fictions* (Minneapolis: University of Minnesota Press, 1998).

31. Interview with Michelle Citron, 16 December 2011.

4.3 Pioneers of Black Documentary Film[1]

PEARL BOWSER

The history of black documentary film perfectly illustrates the truth that whatever the problems of mounting and executing a production, actually accomplishing this does not mean dissemination and impact will ensue. African American productions, even when they were brought to completion, remained as marginalised as the community that made them.

FIRST BLACK DOCUMENTARY

The silent era produced a host of newsreels and short subjects, but none was as widely seen or as influential as *A Day at Tuskegee*. The moving force behind this project was Booker T. Washington, the first president of Tuskegee Institute in Alabama. A passionate advocate of industrial education for blacks, and a fiery orator, Washington attracted the support of many wealthy and powerful white businessmen and politicians, including former president Theodore Roosevelt. Welcoming his accommodationist views, many of these individuals provided the financial support that helped Washington to pursue his long-range goal of an economically self-reliant and independent black workforce. In 1900, he established the National Negro Business League (NNBL) to foster his programme and to encourage, by example and shared information, the growth of black enterprises. Annual meetings, located in a different region each year, encouraged new black enterprises around the country. Indeed, one such meeting held during an NNBL convention was filmed and screened for the general public at a nearby theatre. This experiment proved successful, and was repeated at other NNBL conventions. While informational, such films were also objects of race pride; they permitted the general audience to take part in events at the NNBL convention meeting that was taking place in their town. At the same time, they promoted participants' individual businesses by associating them with the larger national organisation wherever the film was screened.

Recognising the persuasive power of film, Booker T. Washington commissioned George W. Broome to make a short film about Tuskegee Institute that would help to promote his industrial education programme. This project resulted in *A Day at Tuskegee*. Broome and a group of NNBL businessmen in Boston formed a production company, and shot the film on the Institute's 2,400-acre grounds and in buildings erected with student labour.

In December 1909, a private screening in Boston exhibited some forty-three scenes shot at the Alabama school, depicting the industrial education of young men and women. Emmett J. Scott, Dr Washington's assistant at Tuskegee, attended the screening at the Crescent Theater and commented favourably on the film. A reporter for the *Chicago Defender* promised to make every effort to bring the film to Chicago and noted, 'Booker T. was way ahead of the game. ... [The film] will show our would-be leaders what makes Booker T. so great.'[2]

The film opened at a public meeting in New York's Carnegie Hall on 24 January 1910. The press reported that an audience of 2,000 (black and white) attended the meeting, which was chaired by New York's former mayor, Seth Low. Speakers included President Finley of City College, Dr B. F. Riley of Alabama and Dr Booker T. Washington. Producer George W. Broome had previously spoken at an NNBL meeting about the importance of the motion picture as an instrument of communication capable of delivering information to African American communities 1,000 miles away. The black press reviewing the film reported, 'People could see what the school was doing and what an industrial education, as Booker T. Washington conceives it, means.' The *New York Age* maintained that critics of Tuskegee have usually been 'those who know the least about it'.[3] The Broome company announced its intention to produce similar films showing the progress of blacks along industrial lines for the Shaw Institute in North Carolina, the Hampton Institute in Virginia and the Fisk Institute in Tennessee.

Washington's industrial education programme did not escape criticism, however. Two factions emerged in the debate over the development of trade schools. One group of black intellectuals and educators, including W. E. B. Du Bois, put the education of black professionals at the top of their agenda. Du Bois was the author of *The Souls of Black Folk* (1903) – an essay collection that was to shape the course of the emerging civil rights movement, and one of Washington's staunchest critics.

Du Bois believed that it was essential to develop leadership among young men and women through a college education steeped in the arts, sciences, history and literature; he asserted that the realisation of full citizenship would be hastened through the development of an intellectual elite or 'talented tenth'. On the other side of the debate was the powerful machine built by Washington at Tuskegee with the backing of northern industrialists and southern segregationists. Washington described his critics as 'artificial' men – 'graduates of New England colleges' who did not represent the masses of black people.[4] His comments did not name, but referred to, not only Du Bois, but also Monroe Trotter, publisher of the *Guardian*.

Washington was confident that he not only had the total support of blacks, but would also be listened to by whites in high places. But his access to the White House and his association with white industrialists sparked controversy when President Theodore Roosevelt disastrously mishandled two key events: the Brownsville raid of 1905 and the brutal outbreak of violence against blacks in Atlanta in 1906. In the first case, Roosevelt summarily and unfairly discharged and disgraced the famous black 25th Texas Regiment, which had taken part in the charge up San Juan Hill.[5] In the second, the president belatedly ordered the use of federal troops to quell the mob.

In the aftermath of these events, the rock-solid support Washington had enjoyed showed signs of erosion. He weathered the storm, however, and over the next decade the Tuskegee Institute became the focus of a number of films shown in churches, schools and theatres. These films helped to shape the public discourse of the day concerning Washington's accommodationist views and Du Bois's more progressive stance on education and leadership. Long after his death in 1915, Booker T. Washington's industrial education programme, his bootstrap approach and identification with the greater mass of the working class proved to have seductive power. His image and his influence have pervaded popular culture through portraits, statuary and film; his name has become synonymous with self-reliance (a bootstrap approach to the progress of the race) and African American entrepreneurship.

The images that filled *A Day at Tuskegee* became symbols of what could be achieved: not only the stately buildings that graced the campus, but also the images of students at work in the classroom and in the fields. By 1915 the school was not only a monument to its founder, but also a symbol of progress and race pride. Films about Tuskegee and the controversial educational experiment continued to have an audience as late as 1923.[6]

What role did Washington play in making *A Day at Tuskegee* beyond commissioning the Broome company? Was he in a position to suggest or encourage black camera operators to participate in the project? Press reports indicate only that Washington's assistant, Emmett J. Scott, attended the preview screening of the film prior to the New York public event. There appears to be no mention of anyone else from the Institute staff taking part in the project. Some years earlier, Tuskegee students had participated in a 'parade of 100 wagons' exhibiting the various activities of the school before a reviewing stand occupied by former president Theodore Roosevelt and his party. The documentation on film of the school's vocational studies programme was indeed a novel idea in 1909 – a time when print dominated communication. Washington apparently recognised that film could be not only a powerful educational tool, but also an effective fund-raising instrument, and he used it when he approached white industrialists and educators in the north for support.

On 10 January the *New York Age* provided a detailed description of the film's content and named George Broome as the manager, but provided no other credits. Three years later *A Day at Tuskegee* was picked up by another company, the Anderson Watkins Film Company.

A final word about *A Day at Tuskegee*. While Booker T. Washington launched this project, others deserve credit for the production itself and for the technical quality of the film. But who these individuals were remains a mystery, in spite of the attention the film enjoyed in the black press. Tuskegee certainly had a professional photographer on staff.[7]

'THE MAN BEHIND THE MOVIE SHORTS'

By the mid-1920s, race movies were on the decline. They had always been undercapitalised, but now fewer venues and smaller profits plagued the field's veterans and made the enterprise less attractive for newcomers. In the years that preceded the advent of sound and the collapse of the stock market, Hollywood was actively developing theatre chains and squeezing out the smaller independent movie houses. In that atmosphere there were fewer and fewer new black production companies, and among the veterans in the field only Oscar Micheaux successfully negotiated the transition into the era of sound. As sound took over the next decade, the market for short films focusing on black music was dominated by Hollywood and by white independent film-makers. It was against this backdrop that a talented young cameraman, Edward Lewis, ventured forth with a novel idea – an all-sports African American newsreel.

An article in the *Amsterdam News*, under the headline 'The Man behind the Movie Shorts', profiled twenty-six-year-old Edward Lewis, producer of two popular series that were making the rounds nationally: *The Colored Champions of Sports* and *Colored America on Parade*. The article described Lewis as 'the youngest motion picture producer in America and the only one who does his own camera work and script writing'.[8] In 1938, Lewis purchased his own movie camera and left a promising career as photographer for the *New York Daily News* to start over as an independent film-maker.

As an experienced news photographer Lewis knew how to tell a story with pictures and, in 1938, he set out to create a series of documentary shorts joined by a common theme. This series, *Life in Harlem*, followed a day in the lives of Harlem residents. Working as a one-man production company – scripting, shooting, and editing his own material – Lewis produced twelve documentary shorts in 1939 which were released by Million Dollar Productions.

Lewis followed up with a second series that capitalised on the popularity of African American sports figures. His *Colored Champions of Sports* brought to the screens of neighbourhood theatres the players most viewers had only read about in the entertainment sections of black newspapers. Shown in ten-minute segments along with regular programmes, the series featured World Heavyweight Champion Joe Louis at his training camp or socialising in the community; Josh Gibson of the Grays, the heaviest-hitting catcher in the black league; Smokey Joe Williams, one of the oldest and best pitchers in black baseball; and boxer Henry Armstrong, who held both the lightweight and welterweight titles.[9]

Sitting in their local movie houses, audiences could watch the Black Yankees play, or witness young athletes representing the USA abroad at Olympic competitions. Segments on athletes like track star Jesse Owens or Negro League pitcher Satchel Paige could be seen at the Loew's Theaters in Harlem, for example, and often these short pieces were as big an attraction (if not bigger) than the Hollywood features sharing the marquee.

Despite his substantial accomplishments, Edward Lewis never achieved prominence as a film-maker. While he was well known in Harlem for his documentaries, audiences outside New York City seldom knew his name or realised that he was African American. The expense of producing his documentaries made his operation unprofitable. The value to black audiences of the short films he made far exceeded the small monetary returns the film-maker realised in his all too brief career.

Lewis was not the only journalist to contribute to documentary film-making. For example, veteran reporter St Clair T. Bourne was often called upon to write a script for one of Lewis's *Colored Champion of Sports* reels or for William Alexander's *All American Newsreels*. A versatile writer, Bourne reported on both domestic and international news, sports and entertainment. He contributed film reviews and wrote for the society pages. Bourne says that black reporters had to be ready for anything: they could expect to be sent by an editor to Washington one week to cover the activities of a half-dozen federal agencies, and then to the deep south the next week to report on segregation, jobs, race relations, or other issues of the day. Such broad experience made journalists like Bourne a valuable asset for independent film-makers like Lewis, who were always short-staffed and strapped for funds.[10]

In the years leading up to World War II, a number of other black film-makers were devoting themselves to producing newsreels and documentaries. In the 1930s, Gordon Parks was beginning to shape a career in photography. A high school dropout from Kansas, Parks was a self-taught, multi-talented artist who developed his craft in the field, first as a commercial photographer and then as a cinema photographer. With the advent of war, Gordon Parks and his contemporaries, Carlton Moss and William Alexander, seized the opportunity to broaden their experience as cameramen and journalists in the military, and to bring to public attention black participation in the war effort at every level. They wanted to bring home the sacrifices made by blacks despite the bigotry and oppression they experienced at home.

This goal proved very difficult for Parks to pursue. African American pilots and their segregated units were assigned to escort the big bombers making raids on German strongholds in World War II. The black pilot's job was to divert anti-aircraft guns and enemy fighter planes from the bombers. The government was not eager to publicise this strategy or the success of the African American pilots – this was an issue of racism, not military secrets. When documentaries appeared recently about the 'Tuskegee Airmen', they ended a half-century of suppression of images of these men in combat. For the most part, war correspondents representing the black press had to rely on interviews conducted on the ground and handouts provided by the government. Papers with small circulations had to make use of letters from returning soldiers or interviews that took place stateside.[11] Images of black troops in combat were systematically suppressed, edited out of mainstream media in the USA.

Gordon Parks set out to document the experience of the black airmen. Although he held the rank of first lieutenant in the Office of War Information (OWI), his efforts to carry out an assignment to follow the 332nd fighter pilots into action were thwarted. The experience ended in bitter disappointment, and his formidable skills as a photo-documentarian went unrealised.

Parks went on to become a fashion photographer and photojournalist for *Life* magazine and the first African American producer, director, writer and composer to make his mark in Hollywood. (He filled all of these roles in his first feature film, *The Learning Tree* [1969].) *Diary of a Harlem Family*, a twenty-minute short made for television in 1968, was Parks's first film documentary and sought to give poverty in America a human face. Parks spent the winter months of 1968 getting to know the family and winning their trust by talking to them about what he was trying to do. The project grew out of a photo essay entitled *Flavio* that Parks had previously published in *Life*. *Flavio* depicted poverty in São Paulo, Brazil, by telling the story of a teenage boy who tries to hold his family together in the face of poverty, illiteracy and unemployment. It also showed individuals and communities reaching out to help the boy and his family. The strong emotional impact that *Flavio* had on the magazine's large readership moved Parks to undertake *Diary of a Harlem Family*, this time capturing the family's experience on film. Another documentary made nearly two decades later, *Moments without Proper Names* (1987), brought to the screen a brilliant visualisation of the film-maker's life – his travels, the films he produced and the people he knew. Covering nearly forty years, the film is impressionistic and lyrical, employing Parks's artistry not only as a film-maker, but also as a photographer, writer and musician.

Near the end of World War II, Parks's contemporaries, Carlton Moss and William Alexander, were more successful in their wartime film-making efforts. Moss's *The Negro Soldier* (1944) and Alexander's *A Call to Duty* (1946), depicting blacks in the Navy, were part of the war effort to boost civilian morale and patriotism. Both films resurrected the theme of black soldiers' heroism, as earlier documentaries had done in the World War I era.

THE NEGRO SOLDIER

Carlton Moss (1909–1997)[12] was born in Newark, New Jersey. As a young man he toured with the theatre company of Morgan College, one of the first black colleges to organise a touring drama group. As a member of the Federal Theater Project in Harlem, he wrote, directed and acted on stage. His original play, *Prelude to Swing*, had been performed by the Harlem Federal Theater. Moss also staged plays and pageants at the 135th Street YMCA, and wrote scripts for his own NBC radio show. He made his film debut in two Oscar Micheaux feature films, *The Phantom of Kenwood* (1927) and *Harlem after Midnight* (1934). During World War II, the War Department's Information and Education Division needed a scriptwriter for a special project on black troops. The first script, written by Marc Connelly, the playwright known for *Green Pastures*, was rejected as too stereotypical. An approach that had worked on stage as folksy fable appealing to a white audience would not help stir patriotic passion in black viewers. The War Department realised that they needed a black writer, and Moss's name was put forth by Vincente Minnelli. But to get the assignment, Moss had to be okayed by a white Southerner in the agency. The officer asked him one question: 'Where you from boy?' Moss replied, 'North Carolina – Sir.' He was bending the truth a bit, but it worked; by the code of southern paternalism, he was 'one of our Negroes', which meant he would know his place.

Moss was designated a special consultant to the Office of War Information. He was neither a draftee nor a volunteer, yet he was on the front lines of battle in France, attached to the film unit assigned to shoot *The Negro Soldier* on location. On one occasion Moss was spotted by Ollie Stewart, war correspondent for the *Afro-American*, accompanying Brigadeer General Benjamin O. Davis, the military's highest-ranking black officer and the first African American to hold that position. The General was in France to observe the action, and spent part of his time with the special pictorial unit that was filming black troops.[13]

As a civilian on the front, Moss proved something of an embarrassment for the Army. It was customary, during the war, to induct whites in the entertainment industry and the media (actors, photographers and journalists) into the special services, where they would automatically be awarded the rank of officer. Moss remained a civilian because the military simply did not know what to do with him. They had already filled their quota of black officers. Chaplains, doctors and dentists could hold the rank of first lieutenant but Carlton was none of the above. Officials in Harlem's local draft board tried to pressure the Army into giving Moss the rank he was due as an artist, but to no avail.

Moss's final script was accepted by the War Department – except for the title. Moss had taken his title, *Colored Men to Arms!*, from a Frederick Douglass speech. Lest it be interpreted as a call to arms against white people, the title was changed to *The Negro Soldier*. Although the new title sounded more bland, the film's narrative and images offered a strong, historically accurate account of black soldiers' participation in every conflict that involved American soldiers, including the Civil War. After a selected panel of viewers backed Moss's contention that the film should be seen by white audiences as well as black, a national public relations campaign was organised. General Davis was flown to Hollywood for a round of social functions to help gather support from the Hollywood community. The result was endorsements, personal appearances by movie stars such as Judy Garland and expressions of support from other public-spirited individuals. The press and radio were effectively used to publicise the film's premiere. All of this brought national attention to Moss's personal mission – offering a lesson in history by telling the story of black Americans' courage and contributions, and making it available to large audiences on the silver screen. The film toured the country and travelled abroad.

Moss returned to Europe to produce a sequel to *The Negro Soldier* entitled *Teamwork* (1946). He subsequently produced a number of other documentaries based on historical figures and events, including *Two Centuries of Black American Art* (1976), *Frederick Douglass: The House on Cedar Hill* (1953) and *The Gift of Black Folk* (1978). Moss also taught film production for eight years at Fisk, and cinema studies at the University of California at Irvine.

The Negro Soldier (1944): a strong, historically accurate account of black soldiers' participation

THE FILMS OF WILLIAM ALEXANDER

The early pioneers of the black documentary, like George Broome and Peter P. Jones, were dedicated men with a mission. They were motivated by the desire to break new ground, to burst through the colour line, and in the process to make names for themselves. Others continued in their footsteps in the decades that followed. Oscar Micheaux (1884–1951) certainly had their pioneering spirit and commitment to individualism. A producer, writer and director, Micheaux was determined to go it alone right up to the end of his thirty-year career. While Micheaux is credited with being the most prolific black feature film-maker of his time, William H. Alexander has an equally strong claim as producer of documentaries. Compared with Micheaux, Alexander kept a lower profile. He tended to be a team player who surrounded himself with top professionals – the best talent he could find.

For example, Alexander engaged working journalists to write scripts for some of his projects. Veteran reporter St

Clair T. Bourne wrote and narrated scripts for a number of his documentaries. Alexander was always on the lookout for ways to improve the quality of his productions and would seize any opportunity that would help meet his goals. In 1973 a Paramount Pictures press biography described Alexander as the 'consummate producer' and offered this account of his career:

> For more than a quarter of a century, Colorado-born William Alexander has been roaming the world performing minor miracles of communication through filmmaking. ... A man of boundless energy, close associates have known him as a daring self starter, full of original ideas, with the aggressiveness to set the domino theory in motion and effect its ultimate results.[14]

Alexander grew up in Colorado, where he attended Greeley High School and Colorado State College of Education before spending several years studying at Chicago State

University. He moved to Washington, DC, where he ran a radio show interviewing blacks in government and generally covering the social life of the African American middle class in the nation's capital.

Like Moss, Alexander's career was deeply affected by his work with the Office of War Information during World War II. Headed by Elmer Davis, OWI played a key role in boosting Negro morale around the country through press releases sent out to black newspapers. Planning and carrying out this effort was the work of a group of men sometimes known as the 'Black Brain Trust' who fed the black press with stories and pictures. In addition to Alexander, information specialist and chief of the black press section, the group included William Bryant, an organisation analyst attached to the Bureau of Intelligence, and Charles Austen, staff cartoonist.

Recognising the power of film, Alexander's group at OWI went beyond the print media and formed a production company. In an interview given after the war, Alexander explained it this way:

> We were very concerned about the morale of 'minority groups' – whatever that meant. They worked in war industries, but when people went to the cinema, it looked like a white man's war. We formed the All American Newsreel Company and used to take OSS film crews and shoot stuff all over the world. One of the most interesting stories was on Willa Brown Coffee, the second black woman aviator (Bessie Coleman was the first). She trained all the instructors for the black 99th Pursuit Squadron at her Coffee School of Aeronautics outside Chicago. Although the releases were made in a government agency, the documentaries were privately filmed. Two of our shorts were on blacks in the Army and Navy: *The Highest Tradition*, narrated by Fredric March, and *Call to Duty*, narrated by Walter Huston.[15]

The All American Newsreel Company, under Alexander's direction, produced more than 250 newsreels.

After the war, in 1945, Alexander moved to New York taking with him a wealth of experience and contacts acquired in his work for OWI. There he established the Associated Film Producers of Negro Motion Pictures Inc., and started producing short musical films and features for theatrical release. Like Edward Lewis, Alexander leased these shorts to theatres. He then found a new market for his work, taking three- to five-minute performance segments from the shorts and selling them as soundies that played in coin-operated jukeboxes in restaurants, bars and cafés.

These short performance pieces had very simple stories or plot lines. They were cheap to produce and easy to sell, according to Haryette Miller Barton, Alexander's production assistant and one of the few African American

women working in the film industry behind the camera. She explains:

> Mr Alexander's shorts were sometimes made just to give a group of musicians work, making up the story as they went along or using the lyrics of a song for plot. Sometimes we shot in donated spaces – a barber shop after hours or on a Sunday. But for top performers like Billy Eckstine and his band, the Sweet Hearts of Rhythm, and Dizzy Gillespie's band, we worked with larger budgets, in a studio with a hired union (usually white) crew. Soundies and shorts were quick, easy to set up, and required little or no costuming. The plus was … they helped to pay the rent and salaries.[16]

In 1950 Alexander moved to London and established the Blue Nile Production Company. With London as his base, he travelled to Africa, where he produced a series of documentaries for and about the newly independent countries of the sub-Sahara. These films, many commissioned by individual states, reflected life after independence and were used for public relations purposes and to record the historic changes that were taking place.

Alexander's films reflected life in the newly emerging African nations. The documentaries were used by individual states for public relations purposes and to record the historic changes that were taking place. He often worked with heads of state and, in two cases, took on an official capacity: Alexander became the official film producer for the Republic of Liberia, and subsequently served in the same post for the government of Ethiopia. The documentaries produced by Alexander in these capacities received critical acclaim around the world. *The Village of Hope*, about a leper colony in Liberia, won a prize for the Best Short Film at the 1964 Cannes Film Festival. At the Venice Film Festival the following year, Alexander won a prize for his *Portrait of Ethiopia*, and in 1967 he received the United Nations Award at the International Festival in Madrid for *Wealth in Wood*.

Alexander spent nearly eighteen years working in Africa and Europe. Relatively little of the work he produced during the African period has surfaced so far. The scope of his work is well documented, however.

Alexander filmed some of the first conferences of the Organisation of African States. He helped bring television equipment to Liberia and Ethiopia, and assisted in developing TV programming in those countries. He received awards or decorations from heads of states in all of the twenty-two countries where he worked, including Liberia, Ethiopia, the Sudan, Morocco, the United Arab Republic, Zaire, Kenya, Senegal, Ghana, Algeria, Malagasy, Dahomey, Togo, Malawi, Sierra Leone, Tanzania, Zambia, French Congo, the Ivory Coast, Guinea and the General African Republic. (His work was also recognised by the government of Singapore.)[17]

The films Alexander produced between the mid-1950s and 1973 constitute a sizable body of work. Despite the awards he received abroad, his contribution as film-maker and visionary at a critical juncture in Africa's history has yet to be fully acknowledged at home. Scholars have yet to address key questions about his work. What contributions did his documentaries make to each nation's development? How was his perspective and approach influenced by the heads of state who hired him, including such leaders and thinkers as Sekou Touri, Julius Nyerere, Jomo Kenyatta, Gamal Abdul Nasser and Leopold Senghor?

BRIDGING THE GENERATIONS

Alexander remained active into the early 1970s, when he undertook an ambitious project to produce a film version of William Bradford Huie's novel, *The Klansman*. He acquired the screen rights to the novel and then, according to the Paramount Pictures press biography, travelled more than 300,000 miles to acquire financial backing ($4.5 million), engage a top director and crew, and attract a cast that included Richard Burton, Lee Marvin, O. J. Simpson and Lola Falana. His expansive film-making career bridged a gap between the first generation of black documentary film-makers that had all but disappeared by the 1950s, and a new generation of more strident, independent voices that emerged in the 60s and helped to shape and record the civil rights struggle. In the tradition of Peter P. Jones, Jennie Toussaint Welcome, Addison N. Scurlock and other pioneers of black documentary film-making, these new chroniclers of African American history and culture used film to capture events as they were happening, and to empower their community by offering a deeper, stronger sense of its own identity and history, and ultimately to effect change. Their call to action helped to break the iron circle of segregation, racism and containment, and to bring about a new era of race consciousness and renewal. While the media brought film clips and sound bites of the revolution in the streets to a national audience, African American film-makers challenged viewers with a fuller, more textured sense of black culture and history, providing a context for the scenes of protest that were appearing more and more often on the evening news.

Today, as one generation reaches out to the next, the list of African American film-makers is steadily growing. Foremost among them is William Greaves, who became executive producer of the public affairs programme *Black Journal* in 1969. Greaves's work in network television created crucial new outlets for black documentarians. He helped to usher in a new era of film-making not only through his own work, but also through his efforts to mentor and support other film-makers. William Miles, Louis Massiah, St Clair Bourne, Julie Dash, Stan Lathan, Michelle Parkerson, Yvonne Smith, Stanley Nelson, Carroll Parrott Blue, Gil Noble, Henry Hampton, Charles Hobson,

Black Journal (1969–): Greave's work in network television created crucial new outlets for black documentarians

S. Pearl Sharp, Carol Munday Lawrence, Orlando Bagwell, Ayoka Chenzira and (the late) Jackie Shearer and Toni Cade Bambara – these documentarians, and many others, are helping to light our way.

To be sure, current documentary techniques and approaches are light years away from those of the early pioneers, but, for the most part, today's black film-makers share the commitments of their forerunners: recording the highs and lows of ordinary folk, as well as extraordinary moments in black history and culture as seen from within. From the 1910 Tuskegee footage to Jones's marching bands and regiments to Alexander's newsreels, to today's commentaries – each has contributed to bringing to life the great canvas of African American experience.[18]

NOTES

1. Taken from Pearl Bowser, 'Pioneers of Black Document', in Phyllis Klotman and Janet Culter (eds), *Struggles for Representation: African American Documentary Film & Video* (Bloomington: Indiana University Press, 1999).

2. *Chicago Defender*, 31 December 1910.

3. Ibid.

4. David Levering Lewis, *W. E. B. Du Bois: Biography of a Race, 1868–1919* (New York: Henry Holt and Company, 1993), p. 301.

5. The Brownsville raid occurred in 1905, when a group of black soldiers was accused of starting a gunfight and 'shooting up' the town. Soldiers in the famous black 25th Texas Regiment, though innocent, were summarily discharged by order of President Theodore Roosevelt, without a trial or court martial. This was the same regiment that had fought with Roosevelt in Cuba in the taking of San Juan Hill. Now, by his order, its members were disgraced and discharged from the military without pay or benefits. The President, who had claimed to be a friend of the Negro and Washington, refused to rescind the order even though he knew the regiment was innocent. Roosevelt's popularity among African American voters was further eroded after the bloody riot in Atlanta in 1906. Federal troops had been sent in by Roosevelt's order.

6. Booker T. Washington's *Great Industrial School at Tuskegee, Alabama*, shown on 3 February 1910 (*New York Age*); *A Trip to Tuskegee* (*New York Age*, 11 August 1910); *A Tuskegee Pilgrimage* (Reel Productions, 1922); *Tuskegee Finds a Way Out* (Crusader Films, 1923).

7. Following this account of this pioneering effort, Bowser notes a number of other production companies making 'race films', especially noting the screen presence of black soldiers in battle after World War I (Pearl Bowser, 'Pioneers of Black Documentary Film', pp. 15–19).

8. *Afro-American*, March 1939.

9. Handbill for Loew's Victoria and Loew's 116th Street theatre, 5–9 January 1938.

10. St Clair T. Bourne telephone interview, conducted by Pearl Bowser, 11 September 1997.

11. *This Is Our War: Selected Stories of Six War Correspondents – Six Who Were Sent Overseas by the Afro-American Newspapers* (Baltimore: The Afro-American Company, 1945), p. 7.

12. Carlton Moss interview, conducted by Pearl Bowser, May 1987.

13. *This Is Our War*, p. 28.

14. *By Line*, biography of William Alexander.

15. Newspaper article provided by Harryette Miller Barton, undated.

16. Harryette Miller Barton interview, conducted by Pearl Bowser, 1990.

17. Based on an interview, conducted by William Greaves, with William Alexander a week before Alexander's death on 20 November 1991. William Greaves starred in Alexander's *The Fight Never Ends* (1947) and *Souls of Sin* (1949).

18. Since Pearl Bowser wrote this account, her wish has, with difficulty, been in part fulfilled by film-makers such as Marlon Riggs (see Chapter 1.1).

4.4 Documentary Identity

CHRISTOPHER PULLEN

For the excluded, the search for a voice points up the potential force of the documentary to capture, and re-present, lived experience (and its sometimes tragic consequences), both to the excluded community itself and to the majority. In such a context the social value of documentary expression becomes glaringly obvious.

THE WORLD

In the month of September 2010, in the USA, two thirteen-year-old victims of homophobic abuse killed themselves. Asher Brown, severely bullied at school, shot himself in the head, while Seth Walsh hanged himself, remaining in a coma for nine days before he eventually died. In that same month, gay-identified Raymond Chase, aged nineteen, also hanged himself in his dorm, and Billy Lucas, aged fifteen, who was told by fellow students to kill himself, then hanged himself in a barn later that day. Also that September, Tyler Clementi, a freshman student of Rutgers University, was secretly filmed (with a male sexual partner) on a webcam by his room-mate in service of humiliation, and this was streamed on the web. On discovering the news, Tyler allegedly left a note on Facebook that he would end his life. His death appears as a suicide (e.g., on ABC News, 2010). I dedicate this chapter to their memory and to all who were (and are) the victims of homophobic abuse.

DOCUMENTING THE WORLD

For LGBT (lesbian, gay, bisexual and transgender) identity, documentary representation extends from the cinematic to televisual and online new media documentary forms. Through varying documentary phases/modes, which should be considered in relation to cultural, political and social expression, and oppression, LGBTs are involved in new processes of 'self-production' and 'becoming'.

Exploring the evidence of US and UK documentaries,[1] I argue that not only have LGBTs shifted from invisibility and subjugation towards affirmation and celebration, but that in this progress issues of commoditisation, usefulness and self-production have become central. Although historically within media, and notably within Hollywood cinema, LGBTs have largely been constructed as an Other,[2] in recent times they have taken control of their identities

to manage more 'positive' discourses. This is particularly evident within New Queer Cinema;[3] moreover, LGBTs' authorial production within contemporary documentary reconstructs notions of diverse sexuality in productive ways both for them and for their audiences.[4]

Although subaltern 'fictional' cinema engenders heightened senses of subjectivity, citizenship potential is more easily stimulated for mainstream, and niche, audiences by documentary than by fiction. Possibly, this may be because documentary offers the iconic signifiers of actuality and ethnography, and such 'authentic' documentation potentially leads to social enfranchisement. Historically, gay men and lesbians have employed the documentary form to render new opportunities for citizenship. The concept of social worth has become central in this, from the presentations of 'normality' evident in the production of 'everyday' civic representations, to the responses to the advent of AIDS which revealed (for gay men) the personal, the caring and the family oriented. Later yet, a foundation established within Reality TV allowed issues of commodity and 'self-production' to also become central. It could be, I argue, that this programming translated social worth into social usefulness. At the same time, a continuous political strand of documentary production highlighted the agency of LGBT individuals, rather than the workings of a coalescent LGBT community.

The historical and foundational representation of gay and lesbian identity is found within the cinematic documentary in *Word is Out: Stories of Some of Our Lives* (Mariposa Film Group, 1977, USA). The film gave voice to the individual, expressing citizenship and deeper senses of emotion, rather than directly offering countercultural politics. Although the collective was headed by a celebrated documentary-maker (Peter Adair), in essence *Word is Out* is the anthropological product.[5] The 'talking head' interviews, which make up the bulk of the film, express the community but through the personal voice. David Gillon, for example, tells us in the film:

> I thought I was one of those cold people who could never love anyone, and when I fell in love with [Henry] … it

Word is Out (1977): the 'talking head' interviews express the community but through the personal voice

meant so much to me. It meant I was a real person. I wasn't just a machine. I had really incredibly deep emotions. It was beautiful. I'll never forget it. I was using part of me – feeling part of me – that I'd never felt before, and the best part too: my capacity to love somebody.

Through affirmation of the positive potential of gay social/sexual life, David's personal testament can be said to mark the beginning of a theme in documentary which, for gay identity, rejects subjugation and oppression. Instead intimacy and aspiration through personal performance is foregrounded. Such agency extends ultimately from the personal potential of self-reflexivity in documentary offering 'new storytelling' in the service of changing the world.[6] At the same time, such personal potential is framed within shifting historical, contextual and political circumstances, varying documentary form. Consequently, this chapter not only explores the notion of subjectivity and the significance of self-reflexivity within cinematic, televisual and online documentary expression, but also it establishes a framework of key documentary eras/modes for LGBTs, which reveal these shifting cultural, social and political contexts.

A key point of concern may be the tension between assimilationist discussions and the context of 'queer' identity.[7] This might broadly be termed as either defining 'similarity' or 'difference' to the mainstream. In both instances, subjectivity is produced, advocating either 'fitting in' with, or being 'oppositional to' heteronormativity. This cannot be explored in depth here, but a wider concern is suggested by the Foucaultian potential of discourse and the idea that it affords the opportunity of power resistance, allowing for the formation of new identity. In just this way, documentary production often involves a response to subjugation, and offers opportunities to produce new identity. At the same time, we should consider the Deleuzian ideal of shifting from 'being' to 'becoming'. Ultimately, although LGBTs respond to a certain subjectivity, new documentary works are more concerned with the potential beyond a

mainstream-imposed subjectivity. For David Ruffolo, in 'post queer politics' such 'becoming' can offer new expressions of identity, no longer anchored within the 'limitation' of subjectivity.[8] Hence, personal self-reflexive documentary subjectivity may provide the discursive context of community. However, illuminating contemporary visions hold that subjectivity is nevertheless limiting as it may compartmentalise LGBT identity as being simply oppositional to heteronormativity.

Furthermore, while LGBT identity is a useful acronym representing varying socially constructed sexual diversity, at the same time it is problematic. Significantly, in defining LGBT, the primacy of gay and lesbian discourses should be acknowledged as foundational even though contentious.[9] Although identity politics and issues of sexual citizenship are important, these concepts are founded on the gay and lesbian civil rights movement, which potentially subordinates bisexual and transgender voices.[10] Additionally, issues of race and ethnicity also need to be considered in attempting to form any critical discussion of LGBT identity, which challenges the primacy of white western-oriented discourses inherent in LGBT. This is exactly why Marlon Riggs's focus on sexuality *and* race in *Tongues Untied* (1989, USA) is so foundational. It critically illuminates the exclusivity of a white civil rights discourse in LGBT identity, one which might well itself subjugate or ignore non-white identities.[11]

However, through the contemporary idea of post-queer becoming, documentary producers and participants potentially challenge universal notions of identity. This includes questioning the primacy of a western LGBT model, and offering a way forward for diverse LGBTs involved in documentary production.

LGBT DOCUMENTARY PHASES/MODES

I propose that LGBT identity within documentary may largely be considered within these historical phases and modes:[12]

- Pre-1960s: Invisibility and Covert Identity phase. This was before the open acknowledgment of sexual diversity. Documentaries might allude to difference and homo-sociality, but there were no direct references to a coherent social identity.
- 60s/early 70s: Pathology and Criminalisation phase. Attempts were made by documentary producers to explore the problem of diverse sexuality, including consideration of the appropriate punishments for transgression.
- Late 70s: Self-affirmation and Consciousness-raising phase. Innovative documentaries appear which involved openly gay men and lesbians announcing their sexual identity, with a sense of 'normality' attempting to explore the 'everydayness' of gay and lesbian experience – for example, *Word is Out*.

- Mid-80s to the present: Epic and Historiographic phase. This offers historical and citizen-oriented discussion, focusing on the endurance and resolve of the LGBT insistence on identity. These documentaries build foundations for new ways of viewing history, reframing citizenship discussions and exploring key political moments, primarily stimulated by *The Times of Harvey Milk* (Rob Epstein, 1984, USA).

This last contemporary period also reflects a number of different modes:

- The late 80s: Victimhood Rejection and Caring mode. In specific response to the AIDS crisis, key documentaries focused on the subjectivity of gay men dealing with AIDS. In these films, the notion of caring and family became central.
- The late 90s/early 2000s: Citizen and Family Orientation mode. This is found largely within Reality TV (aka 'formatted documentary'). This starts with *The Real World* (Bunim Murray for MTV, 1992–, USA). Gay people were represented as members of family and community, with, moreover, a prioritisation of their narratives.
- The 2000s on: Public Commodity Asset mode. Now the prioritisation becomes central. This development can be traced to the success of *Queer Eye for the Straight Guy* (Scout Productions for NBC/Bravo, 2003–07, USA). Gay men were increasingly represented to heterosexual audiences as self-evidently socially worthy individuals.
- Mid-2000s on: Political and Reflective Self mode. Capitalising on the increasing profile of gay men in Reality TV, various other documentary forms (including online new media, such as YouTube) centred on 'self-production'. Produced by openly gay men, lesbians and transgender people, these texts offered self-reflexive visions of the self, addressing key political and social concerns.

PHASES

To deal with these in turn:

The Invisibility and Covert Identity phase requires subliminal readings to decode the sexual identities being represented in situations where bonding and intimacy may be considered as homo-social. For example the documentaries *Tunisian Victory* (Frank Capra, 1944, USA) and *Merchant Seamen* (J. B. Holmes, 1941, UK) reveal instances of homoeroticism – for example, in the former, images of semi-clad men working in the heat of North Africa as part of the war effort; and in the latter the camaraderie of seamen isolated by their situation. Also, the Nazi Leni Riefensthal, notably in the documentaries *Triumph of the Will* (1935, Germany) and *Olympiad* (1936, Germany), foregrounded the cult of the physical form and *Kameradschaft* (camaraderie between

men), with homoerotic visions of the male (and female) physical form.[13]

Later, in the Pathology and Criminalisation phase, this trope was deployed to reveal the sexual dissident's 'condition' as a 'problem' for society, and for themselves. For example, a focus was often placed upon the threat of the adult male homosexual preying upon emerging heterosexual youth. *Boys Beware* (Sid Davis, 1961, USA) is an archetypical educational 'docudrama' produced in association with the Inglewood (CA) Police Department and the town's School District. It directly focuses on the need for vigilance on the part of teenage boys if homosexual predators, men whom we are told are suffering from 'a disease of the mind', are to be apprehended.[14] In 'The Homosexuals' (Harry Morgan, 1967, USA), an episode in the highly regarded, long-running *CBS Reports* series, interviews with experts and homosexuals (many with shadowed faces) are cross-cut with repeated noir images of a 'seedy' underworld. Presenter Mike Wallace's voiceover informs us:

> The average homosexual, if there be such, is promiscuous. He is not interested, nor capable of, a lasting relationship, like that of a heterosexual marriage. His sex life, his 'love life', consists of a series of chance encounters at the clubs and bars he inhabits. And even on the streets of the city, the quick one-night stand, these are characteristic of the homosexual relationship.[15]

An opposition is made between the normative (heterosexual) world and peripheral, dysfunctional (homosexual) existence. A central focus is the insistence that homosexual lives are inferior, and ultimately shameful, offering no social satisfaction, or value (in normative terms).

Despite this basic media frame, the first instance of a more contented, and self-sufficient vision of homosexuality, would eventually also occur on television – in a 1973 US PBS proto-Reality TV series. *An American Family* was a long-form, intimate Direct Cinema look at the lives of the wealthy. It was produced by Craig Gilbert, and filmed by Alan and Susan Raymond. Lance Loud, the precocious son of the Santa Barbara family being portrayed, would become the first gay male in a documentary to be seen as being unconcerned about the 'problem' of their 'condition'. Although Lance is not blatantly identified as gay, in a pivotal sequence he announces his 'difference' to his mother on camera. This was widely reported and discussed in the media at the time and can only be read as Lance's 'coming out', confident in his gay identity.[16]

Lance's screen appearance may be considered as a precursor to the phase of Self-affirmation and Consciousness-raising, which was first seen in the landmark film *Word is Out* and in *Gay USA* (Arthur Bressan, 1978, USA).[17] Through the representation of an 'everyday' gay and lesbian presence in both domestic and public spaces, these documentaries offer new contexts for sexual diversity. *Gay USA*, in a similar vein to *Word is Out*, was a large-scale collaborative project. However, rather than focusing on intimate narratives filmed in domestic settings, Bressan compiled footage of protest marches from San Francisco, San Diego, Los Angeles, Chicago and New York. This archive brings into focus a particular political moment. The film airs public comments on gay identity (mostly in response to anti-gay bigots such as Anita Bryant and John Briggs[18]) and public outrage at the murder of gay youth Robert Hillsborough in San Francisco.[19] Therefore, unlike *Word is Out*, which possesses both a cinematic/documentary and developed anthropological/psychological quality, *Gay USA* generally exhibits an ephemeral, snapshot/vox pop journalistic approach to present a 'passing glimpse' of public opinion. Nevertheless, both offered a similar sense of citizen affirmation.

A deeper sense of 'political' identity was developed within the Epic and Historiographic phase. Robert Epstein and Richard Schmiechen's *The Times of Harvey Milk* explored the impact of openly gay elected political icon Harvey Milk. The classification of his assassination as a hate crime, and the community protest it engendered, revealed changing notions of citizenship.[20] John Scagliotti's *Before Stonewall* (1985, USA) similarly reflects the sense of citizenship identity as it existed before the emergence of an openly politicised gay and lesbian era.

Furthermore, older aspects of LGBT history were being recovered in print and these too found their way onto the screen. Arthur Dong celebrated the twentieth anniversary of Allan Bérubé's *Coming Out Under Fire*, a study of the contribution of gay men and lesbians to the war effort by turning that text into a documentary of the same name (1994, USA). Robert Epstein and Jeffrey Friedman did likewise with *The Celluloid Closet* (1995, USA), a film adaptation of Vito Russo's 1987 examination of the historical (mis)representation of sexual difference in Hollywood cinema.

Notions of oppression and persecution were also to be found in other documentaries in the Epic and Historiographic phase. Stuart Marshall's *Desire* (1989, UK) and Robert Epstein and Jeffrey Friedman's *Paragraph 175* (2000, USA) deal with the murderous pre-World War II denial of citizenship to gays by the Nazis as Weimarian tolerance gave way to the concentration camps and the gas chambers.[21]

MODES

The emergence of AIDS in the 1980s stimulated new documentary responses. AIDS clearly enflamed bigoted opinion, but most importantly these documentaries rejected the victimhood status imposed on the gay community by liberal opinion.[22] In doing so, these films expressed relatively unexplored narratives previously not associated with gay male identity: caring and social responsibility within the domestic context of same-sex partnerships.

Common Threads: Stories From The Quilt (Rob Epstein and Jeffrey Friedman, 1989, USA) and *Living Proof: HIV and the Pursuit of Happiness* (Kermit Cole, 1993, USA), addressed a wider audience by framing the discourse of gay men with AIDS in normative social terms. These 'victim rejection' documentaries explore the potential of a coalescent community in which gay men are leaders in resistance to the syndrome, and also in combating the societal oppression of all those afflicted with it.

At the same time, apart from victim rejection, smaller-scale documentaries reflected the caring theme. *Absolutely Positive* (Peter Adair, 1990), *Fighting in Southwest Louisiana* (Peter Friedman, 1991, USA) and *Silverlake Life: The View From Here* (Tom Joslin and Peter Friedman, 1993, USA), all offered intimate narrative space to gay men, revealing visions of caring and domesticity. *Silverlake Life* was made by film-maker Tom Joslin with his partner Mark Massi, documenting their own personal experiences living with (and dying of) AIDS. Unforgettable is the image of Mark Massi cradling Tom's recently expired body.[23] *Fighting in Southwest Louisiana* similarly frames a couple coping with AIDS, yet manages to present an everyday vision of gay men simply living together. These texts frame a previously ignored domestic, caring and romantic context. It is not one, though, that arises exclusively in response to oppression. Rather it is that the AIDS narrative is used to reveal responsibility to community, and to the subjects themselves.

The impact of AIDS, I would further argue, also stimulated a Citizen and Family Orientation mode. The Reality TV series *The Real World* from its outset included a gay participant[24] as part of the regular 'cast'. However, it would not be until the appearance of Pedro Zamora, a young Cuban gay man who had AIDS, in the 1994 San Francisco iteration of the show, that significant attention would be given to the contribution of gay participants.[25] Notably, Pedro was an AIDS activist who received high-profile media attention for his work generally,[26] not just for his participation in *The Real World*. He embarked on a romantic relationship, which culminated in an on-camera same sex-marriage ceremony. Pedro Zamora, who died from complications from AIDS just after the series was broadcast, offered a foundational presence within Reality TV forms.

As the formatted Reality TV show proliferated it became quite usual to include gay men or lesbians as cast members. For example, *Castaway 2000* (BBC, 2000–01, UK), which claimed to be establishing an ideal community on a remote Scottish island, featured a gay participant, Ron Copsey. While Ron would be represented in relatively stereotypical terms (as neurotic and aggressive) and he would leave the series midway, his presence obviously built on the foundation laid by *The Real World*. In these settings gays appeared to be part of 'everyday' communities, even if the communities were palpably artificial and the gay participants were at times subjected to stereotypical representations.

This then was no unambiguous good. Copsey is the only reality show participant thus far to have won a legal case for misrepresentation in the UK. The court found that 'creative' editing gave the impression he was mentally unstable.[27] On the other hand, it could be that the danger of such stereotyping is a price worth paying – even if audience research suggested hostility continues.[28] It can be argued that any LGBT presence at all was a positive step. Certainly, the openly gay co-creator of The Real World, Jonathan Murray, announced that the participation of openly gay people was his political purpose. Hence, this mode can be properly designated as embracing the possibility of LGBTs as Citizen and Family: any citizen's house, even one belonging to Big Brother, now could contain an LGBT presence.

The Public Commodity Asset mode builds on the foundations laid by The Real World and the Citizen and Family mode. The formatted series Big Brother and Survivor may be considered as developments of the 'household' environment of The Real World. These shows changed the open access accommodation of The Real World into a contained environment where cast members would compete with each other, and there would be a cash prize for the winner, elected by the participants and/or audience votes. The first series of Survivor (2000) in the USA and the second series of Big Brother (2001) in the UK, were won by openly gay men. While Survivor's winner Richard Hatch and Big Brother's winner Brian Dowling may be considered as conforming to stereotypes, with the former represented as a Machiavellian competitor and the latter represented as a court jester, it was notable that openly gay characters earned popular attention and support as central figures within community environments.

Further evidence of this may be seen in the 'reality' competition series The Amazing Race (CBS, 2001–, USA), which (like The Real World) has consistently included gay and lesbian participants. Notably, the fourth season (in 2003) included a gay couple (Reichen Lehmkuhl and Chip Arndt), who would become the eventual winners, albeit they (like Survivor's Richard Hatch) were represented as ruthless. The attention afforded to gay men would be even more foregrounded in Queer Eye for the Straight Guy. An openly gay cast offered dating advice to 'straight' clients, in terms of knowledge about culture, grooming, cuisine, decor and so on. The always-present underlying ambiguities of this programming mode was again evidenced here. Although placing a focus on gay identity, at the same time the potential of gay social lives was rejected in terms of disavowal.[29] Instead, gay sensibilities and understandings were commoditised as an asset for the mainstream audience – commodity in the service of community.

These ambiguities persisted in some 'reality' formats which even more centrally focused on gay male narratives:

for example, the US and UK versions of Playing it Straight (Fox, 2004, USA, and Channel 4, 2005, UK)[30] and the US show Boy Meets Boy (Evolution for Bravo, 2003, USA). Both series involved challenging stereotypes surrounding gay male identity. However, because format twists involved concealing the straight or gay identity of the participants, an essentially heterocentric narrative framed such discourse. The UK reality television series There's Something About Miriam (Sky, 2004, UK) might seem to offer rather more pathos by foregrounding a transgender person who is looking for romance. Miriam's 'straight' suitors, who were unaware of her gender, were revealed to be thoughtless and cruel on discovering her identity; but again, this did less to expose their prejudice than it stressed her 'difference'. Miriam remained the Other.

So consider Nadia Almada, a transgender person who won the Big Brother contest by the popular vote of the audience (UK series 5, 2004). The cast's uncertain knowledge of her gender/sexuality may be considered as the central narrative device in stimulating such audience engagement. This was achieved in terms of suspense and anticipation, rather than acceptance or understanding. Similarly, on the rare occasion when bisexuality figures in a documentary, as in My Husband is Gay (Sky, 2007, UK), the assumptions are of a dominant morality and the complications of disloyalty provide the central narrative arc. Any imaginative investigation of bisexuality, or diverse sexuality, is totally eschewed.

Despite the commoditisation of LGBT identity in the 'reality' shows, a new Political and Reflective Self mode was also emerging in contemporary LGBT documentary production itself. Recent 'self-production'-oriented documentaries, with directors themselves as central subjects, have built upon the emergence of 'political' self-reflexivity first seen in Word is Out. I have outlined how this has extended through documentary responses to AIDS, and even the few 'positive' opportunities within Reality TV, such as the contribution of Pedro Zamora in The Real World. Examples of this later development include Sandi Simcha Dubowski's Trembling Before G-D (2004, USA) and Parvez Sharma's Jihad for Love (2007, USA). The films deal with adherence to religion (Judaism and Islam, respectively) and both offer deeper insights into LGBT identity within confessional documentary forms. At the same time these texts exemplify the impact and innovation of non-western and non-white LGBTs in stimulating transgressive discourse. Placing a central focus on the film-maker as 'self-producer', and as the central narrative point of emotion and stimulation, illustrates Giddens' concept of a 'transformation in intimacy'.[31] Individuals express their life stories, relating to contemporary social contexts in this process of disclosure and sharing.

The educational documentary work of Debra Chasnoff, may also be considered as such 'transformation in intimacy'. *It's Elementary: Talking About Issues at School* (1996, USA), *That's a Family* (2000, USA) and *Straightlaced* (2009, USA) not only explore LGBT family, but also highlight bullying, gender stereotyping and name calling in school. As a lesbian activist, Chasnoff's work stresses her own identity, exploring diversity as beneficial and LGBTs as integral components of community.

An exemplary instance of the Political and Reflexive-Self documentary mode is Gwen Walker's *She's a Boy I Knew* (2008, Canada). Gwen is personally invested not only as the central subject of the film's narrative, as it documents her sex change, but also as the agent of its production, totally responsible for the representation of identity it presents. Gwen tells the story of her early life as a boy, the later pressures of having to conform to masculine norms, her academic study of psychology and film production (in service of self-examination); and her eventual path to sex change. Added to this is the portrayal of her family (including her ex-wife) as supportive and co-present in sharing her journey. She also documents her later questioning of fully transitioning to a 'heterosexual' identity in her new form (she considers herself as a lesbian). Gwen offers deep insight into her emotional journey, one not necessarily fixed to any specific destination.

THE WORLD REVISITED

She's a Boy I Knew may be the key documentary text in the Political and Reflexive Self mode of contemporary LGTB documentary but it is far from unique. Let me return to the spate of homophobic tragedies with which I began because in the response to those deaths can be seen further evidence of the new mode for which I am arguing.

She's a Boy I Knew (2008) may be the key documentary text in the Political and Reflexive Self mode of contemporary LGTB documentary

Anderson Cooper 360:CNN Live (2010): a moving interview with Asher's parents in a news programme painted a vivid picture of the boy, an outsider ... bullied into despair for allegedly being gay

'Citizen' documentary producers on YouTube may also be considered as extending it.[32]

Asher Brown was the thirteen-year-old school student who was relentlessly bullied at school, and consequently shot himself in the head, his body to be discovered by his stepfather in a house closet. The response to his death may be considered as central in stimulating discourse in this new mode. A moving interview with Asher's parents in a news programme (*Anderson Cooper 360*, 2010, USA)[33] painted a vivid picture of the boy, an outsider, considered as a 'geek', uninterested in fashionable clothes or expensive media technology (such as iPods), who was therefore bullied into despair for allegedly being gay. When the interview was posted through YouTube, a deep emotional audience response was elicited. Such identification and empathy produced engagement in terms of 'therapeutic discourse'[34] in a similar manner to experiencing therapy. The new mode and the new media platform allowed audiences to 'place themselves within the frame'. They became agents.[35]

In this manner, using the social networks and the documentary mode of self-reflexivity, Asher's story (and that of Seth, Billy, Raymond and Tyler) stimulated gay and lesbian youth to offer support to their peers. This is evidenced by a social network stream entitled It Gets Better Project. This was founded by a gay male couple sharing their own difficult times with school and family, but also telling how things improved.[36] Among many other contributions within the It Gets Better Project at this time was a video produced by a gay Muslim male youth, recently arrived at university, filming himself in his dorm.[37] Another youth, admitting that he denied his gay identity at school but eventually came to terms with this, now advocated the general theme of 'it get's better'.[38] [39] These intimate new media discursive interventions stimulated wider and more intertextual responses about the problem of an imposed subjectivity. The subjugation of gay identity was challenged, and punishment for imagined Otherness and deviancy was questioned.

With all these varying contemporary documentary media forms, LGBTs have shifted from being ignored and travestied by others to defining their own agendas within 'self-production', to being integrated, displayed and valued. There is a new confidence in the representation of the LGBT self, which foregrounds the context of the individual, expressing new ideas of self-identity, family and community – all working towards a sense of becoming.

Such a focus on the individual suggests documentary forms which privilege an adherence to subjectivity. However, any potential to frame the personal subject though performance within documentary[40] implicitly recognises the limitations of paradigmatic documentary as 'an ethnographic film tradition that has sought to represent others (such as ethnic and sexual minorities, who have been told they could not represent themselves)'.[41] This foregrounds the centrality of self-representation and subjectivity in all attempts made by minorities to present themselves to the world within documentary form. However, I argue that we should pay less attention towards the imagined stability of hierarchies and norms evident in subjectivity – whether it is attaining new subjectivity or rejecting imposed subjectivity. Instead, an understanding of the immediate, the participatory and the intuitive should be sought. We might consider these documentary moments as components of the Deleuzian and Guattarian 'machine'[42] which is evidenced by stimulating 'self-production', revealing identity and representation as constantly moving processes.

Such constant mobilisation, as David V. Ruffolo suggests (in connection with a 'post-queer' politics), should not involve a 'single subjectivity' evidenced by the reframing of identity ideals. Instead, it should move forward in the strategy of becoming:

> where desire is based on production rather than lack. ... [This is] not defined by subjects and subject capacities [which in Freudian terms connects desire to repression,] but productive flows of desire that are creatively and indefinitely becoming other.[43]

This is enabled through the multiplicity of connections made by politicised LGBTs working within documentary forms. A shift away from 'being', defined by a corporeal framework, towards a state of 'becoming', produced as constant mobility, is thereby revealed.

Contemporary documentary producers such as Debra Chasnoff and Gwen Walker, alongside diverse 'citizen journalist' documentary producers using online new media

express the potential of LGBTs working within 'self-production'. These are social agents oriented in the process of disclosure, reflection and mobilisation. While inevitably affirmative visions of gay men, lesbians, bisexuals and transgender people connect to the everyday psychology of mainstream audiences, the process of 'becoming' may not extend from personal subjectivity, as fitting in the larger world, but be found within a *constantly imagined world* where new possibilities may exist.

NOTES

1. This chapter largely focuses on US documentary, but also places UK texts within context, in offering an Anglo-centric analysis.

2. On Hollywood see V. Russo, *The Celluloid Closet,* rev. edn (New York: Harper & Row, 1987); P. Tyler, *Screening the Sexes: Homosexuality in the Movies* (New York: DaCapo Press, 1993). On the Other, see S. Hall, 'The Spectacle of the "Other"', in Stuart Hall (ed.), *Representation: Cultural Representations and Signifying Practices* (Maidenhead: Open University, 1997), pp. 223–79; M. Pickering, *Stereotyping: The Politics of Representation* (Basingstoke: Palgrave, 2001).

3. See M. Aaron (ed.), *New Queer Cinema: A Critical Reader* (New Brunswick, NJ: Rutgers University Press, 2004).

4. See R. Dyer, *Now You See It: Studies on Lesbian and Gay Film* (London: Routledge, 1990); C. Holmlund and C. Fuchs (eds), *Between the Sheets, In the Streets: Queer, Lesbian, Gay Documentary* (Minneapolis: University of Minnesota Press, 1997); C. Pullen, *Documenting Gay Men: Identity and Performance in Reality Television and Documentary Film* (Jefferson: McFarland, 2007).

5. Pullen, *Documenting Gay Men*; C. Pullen, *Gay Identity, New Storytelling and the Media* (Basingstoke: Palgrave Macmillan, 2009).

6. On self-reflexivity in general see A. Giddens, *Modernity and Self Identity: Self and Society in the late Modern Age*, rep. (Cambridge: Polity Press, 1992); in documentary, see M. Renov, *The Subject of Documentary* (Minneapolis: University of Minnesota Press, 2004); for 'new storytelling', see Pullen, *Gay Identity, New Storytelling and the Media*.

7. On the one hand, see A. Sullivan, *Virtually Normal: An Argument about Homosexuality* (London: Picador, 1995); B. Bawer, *A Place at the Table, The Gay Individual in American Society* (New York: Poseidon Press, 1993); on the other, see S. Seidman (ed.), *Queer Theory/Sociology* (Oxford, Blackwell, 1996); M. Warner (ed.), *Fear of a Queer Planet* (Minneapolis: University of Minnesota Press, 1993).

8. D.V. Ruffolo, *Post-Queer Politics* (Farnham: Ashgate, 2009).

9. C. Pullen, 'Introduction', in C. Pullen and M. Cooper (eds), *LGBT Identity and Online New Media* (New York: Routledge, 2010).

10. C.A. Rimmerman, *From Identity to Politics: The Lesbian and Gay Movements in the United States* (Philadelphia: Temple University Press, 2002); D. Bell and J. Binnie, *The Sexual*

Citizen: Queer Politics and Beyond (Cambridge: Polity, 2000). For those excluded from it, see S. Munro and L. Warren, 'Transgendering Citizenship', *Sexualities* vol. 7 no. 3, 2004, pp. 345–62; N. Tucker, *Bisexual Politics: Theories, Queries and Visions* (New York: Haworth Press, 1985); B. Beemyn and E. Steinman, *Bisexual Men in Culture and Society* (New York: Haworth Press, 2002).

11. C. Cagle, 'Imagining the Queer South: Southern Lesbian and Gay Documentary', in Holmlund and Fuchs, *Between the Sheets, In the Streets*, pp. 30–45; Bill Nichols, *Introduction to Documentary* (Bloomington: Indiana University Press, 2001); Pullen, *Documenting Gay Men*.

12. Although it is possible to make connections with Bill Nichols's modes of documentary performance, this typology is more related to identity concerns than historical and formal progression.

13. H. Oosterhuis and H. Kennedy (eds), *Homosexuality and Male Bonding in Pre-Nazi Germany* (New York: Haworth Press, 1991).

14. See YouTube, Education on Homosexual *'Boys Beware'*, 2010, http://www.youtube.com/watch?v= MmqNiFJyI28&feature=related. Accessed 9 October 2010.

15. See YouTube, *CBS Reports:* 'The Homosexuals', 2010, http://www.youtube.com/watch?v=a-b19wXL0Jk. Accessed 9 October 2010.

16. See Pullen, *Gay Identity, New Storytelling and the Media*; J. Ruoff, *An American Family: A Televised Life* (Minneapolis: University of Minnesota Press, 2002).

17. See R. Dyer, *Now You See It*.

18. D. Clendinen and A. Nagourney, *Out for Good* (New York: Simon and Schuster, 1999); L. Gross, *Up From Visibility: Lesbians, Gay Men, and The Media in America* (New York: Columbia University Press, 2001).

19. Arthur Bresson dedicated *Gay USA* to the memory of Robert Hillsborough.

20. See B. Beemyn (ed.), *Creating a Place For Ourselves: Lesbian, Gay and Bisexual Community Histories* (New York: Routledge, 1997); J. D'Emilio, *Sexual Politics, Sexual Communities: The Making of a Homosexual Minority in the United States 1940–1970* (Chicago: University of Chicago Press, 1983); S. LeVay and E. Nonas, *City of Friends: A Portrait of Gay and Lesbian Community in America* (Cambridge: MIT Press, 1995); D. Herzog (ed.), *Sexuality and German Fascism* (New York: Berghahn, 2005).

21. See Herzog, *Sexuality and German Fascism*; Oosterhuis and Kennedy, *Homosexuality and Male Bonding in Pre-Nazi Germany*.

22. S. Watney, 'The Spectacle of AIDS', in D. Crimp (ed.), *AIDS: Cultural Analysis, Cultural Activism* (Cambridge: MIT Press,

1987); S. Watney, *Imagine Hope: AIDS and Gay Identity* (London: Routledge, 2000).

23. See also Nichols, *Introduction to Documentary*; Pullen, *Documenting Gay Men*; B. Seckinger and J. Jakobsen, 'Love, Death, and Videotape: *Silverlake Life*', in Holmlund and Fuchs, *Between the Sheets*, pp. 144–57.

24. Norman Korpi was the first gay participant in the series, even though discourse suggests that he may be bisexual.

25. Pullen, *Documenting Gay Men*.

26. E. Morgenthaler, 'Pedro's Story: Teen with AIDS Virus Tries to Teach Youths Some Lessons for Life', *Wall Street Journal*, 4 September 1991, p. A2, A4.

27. Ron Copsey, 'How Castaway Made My Life Hell', 2010, http://www.guardian.co.uk/tv-and-radio/2010/aug/11/ castaway. Accessed 15 October 2010.

28. Joshua Gamson, 'Publicity Traps: TV Talks Shows', *Sexualities* vol. 1 no. 1, February 1998.

29. See Hall, 'The Spectacle of the "Other"'.

30. The US version of *Playing it Straight* was cancelled on Fox after three episodes due to poor ratings (Reality TV Planet, 2004).

31. Giddens, *Modernity and Self Identity*.

32. See S. Allan and E. Thorsen (eds.), *Citizen Journalism: Global Perspectives* (New York: Consortium, 2009).

33. YouTube, AC360 – Asher Brown – Bullied To Death, http://www.youtube.com/watch?v=Hk-ERYSi44A. Acccessed 9 October 2010.

34. M. White, *Tele-Advising* (Chapel Hill: University of North Carolina Press, 1992).

35. Pullen, *Gay Identity, New Storytelling and the Media*.

36. YouTube, It Gets Better Project, 2010, http://www.youtube. com/watch?v=7IcVyvg2Qlo. Accessed 9 October 2010.

37. YouTube, It Gets Better – Muslim Gay Teen, 2010, http://www.youtube.com/watch?v=Wj8zBtcgTj. Accessed 9 October 2010.

38. Central within these responses was a need to contact supportive organisations, such as the Trevor Project, 2010, http://www.thetrevorproject.org/. Accessed 15 October 2010.

39. YouTube, It Gets Better – Coming Out and Gay Bullying, 2010, http://www.youtube.com/watch?v=1dxrW94tFI0. Accessed 9 October 2010.

40. See Bill Nichols, *Blurred Boundaries: Questions of Meaning in Contemporary Culture* (Bloomington: Indiana University Press, 1994); Nichols, *Introduction to Documentary*.

41. Nichols, *Blurred Boundaries*, p. 91.

42. G. Deleuze and F. Guattari, *A Thousand Plateaus* (London: Continuum, 2010).

43. Ruffolo, *Post-Queer Politics*, p. 41.

4.5 Docusoaps: The Ordinary Voice as Popular Entertainment

RICHARD KILBORN

The plight of the social victim had been a dominant theme in the Griersonian documentary until the 1990s. Then television in the UK, eschewing much of its inherited public education and adopted journalistic remits, came to embrace the documenting of ordinary subjects who were not 'victims'. Seen as performing quotidian tasks, though, their 'ordinary' lives were rendered automatically, as it were, dramatic, entertaining and extraordinary as everything else on the television.

'THE PERFORMANCE OF INDIVIDUAL INDENTITIES'

In recent times the domain of documentary has been considerably expanded. It now encompasses modes and types of work that would previously have been considered out of bounds by those convinced of the inherent seriousness of the documentary enterprise.[1] While some regard the progressive extension of documentary's bounds as a very welcome development, others express concern that these increasingly diverse attempts to chronicle or document the real are leading to a devaluation of the documentary currency. Some observers have even begun to question whether the term 'documentary' itself may have outlived its useful function.[2] In order to get round some of the problems created by having to operate with such an imprecise descriptor, critics have come up with a number of new terms in the attempt to get some purchase on what is now a bewildering array of factual forms and documentary subgenres. One such sub-genre is the docusoap, a hybrid form that enjoyed what one critic has described as an 'unexpected blip of popularity'[3] when it first came to the fore in the mid-1990s.

THE RISE OF THE DOCUSOAP

In assessing the rise of the docusoap, it would be wise to admit at the outset that docusoaps are essentially a televisual phenomenon.[4] They began to make their mark in the second half of the 90s at a time when UK broadcasters were actively seeking to commission forms of factual programming that could be produced at relatively low cost and would appeal to a wider demographic than some of the more traditional forms of documentary.[5] For the

companies who had begun to specialise in what came to be known as factual entertainment, this meant having to develop forms of factual/documentary programming designed to fulfil a particular function within designated slots in the TV schedule.[6]

The actuality-based product that programme-makers came up with in response to commissioning editors' promptings was a hybrid format that combined certain features of observational documentary with elements borrowed from soap opera. Producers of docusoaps have never sought to disguise the fact that, in the attempt to produce an accessible form of programming, they drew heavily on several existing popular TV modes and formats. The emergence of such a manifestly entertainment-oriented form of factual programming was seen by some observers to be indicative of a lamentable decline in broadcasting standards. As a consequence, docusoaps rapidly became a favoured target of those who delighted in complaining that the barbarians were at the gate and that modern media's obsession with celebrity and entertainment would result in a progressive banalisation of our culture.[7]

DEFINING FEATURES OF DOCUSOAPS

In terms of a set of defining features, docusoaps exhibit many of the traits that we have come to associate with other contemporary factual formats. They place a high premium on audience accessibility and are principally conceived as vehicles for providing a mildly diverting form of entertainment rather than Griersonian enlightenment. Docusoaps do not attempt, in any meaningful way, to engage with serious or pressing issues of the day, but are principally concerned with offering viewers the opportunity to become involved in the lives of a chosen group of characters and to delight in the latter's capacity to indulge in various types of (self-)performance. As Dovey perceptively observes: '[The docusoap] is another new genre that foregrounds the performance of individual identities'.[8]

In view of this performativity requirement, one of a producer's principal concerns when putting together a new docusoap will be to assemble a cast of subjects who are willing to participate in a venture that has many of the features of a real-life soap. One of the main expectations of docusoap subjects is that they will be able to produce the kind of gossipy banter that typifies exchanges between characters in a sitcom or soap opera, the TV genres on which docusoaps are so clearly modelled.

In their quest to come up with raw material that can form the basis of a docusoap narrative, producers have developed a fine nose for the types of situations and the kinds of people that would best suit their purposes. When the docusoap boom was at its height, for instance, producers were able to reel off the required constituents of a good docusoap in the manner of a recipe. Here, for instance, is one programme-maker reflecting on his experience of working on several docusoap projects over the previous two or three years:

> Take any aspect of British life – it could be shopping, parking, travelling, eating, pet care or clubbing. Find a contained location where a manageable cast of characters will engage in these activities, or more importantly, interact with the Great British Public. Keep an eye out for the one or two characters who will become your 'stars'. If all goes well, they will give you a publicity boost by setting the balls rolling on the Lottery or launching a solo recording career. It's not essential, but in the first few episodes you will need at least one shouting match and the commentary line, 'Unfortunately all did not go well for Tracey ...'[9]

While Bethell's set of 'must-have' ingredients perhaps underestimates the amount of post-production work that goes on once the raw material has been collected, it gives a good idea of the level of contrivance and manipulation involved in putting together programmes in which one of the supposed aims is to open viewers' eyes to what is going on behind the scenes in certain well-known institutions.

Even though many critics have derided docusoaps for their persistent blandness, there can be no doubting their popularity with TV audiences. At the height of the docusoap boom in the period 1996–99, programmes like *Airport* (BBC One, 1996–2005) and *Driving School* (BBC One, 1997) were regularly attracting between 8 and 12 million viewers. *Airport* had started out as a six-part series set in London's Heathrow airport, but had had its life extended when broadcasters discovered that audiences had developed a huge appetite for this form of undemanding, character-centred entertainment.[10] *Airport* introduces us to a comparatively large cast of characters, including both airport and airline employees, as well as members of the travelling public. *Driving School*, on the other hand, has a smaller group of participant subjects and – as the title of the series suggests – most of the narrative interest focuses on the

Airport (1996–2005): the gold standard for all the later docusoaps

trials and tribulations of learner drivers as they attempt to acquire basic driving skills. In many ways *Airport* and *Driving School* set the gold standard for all the later docusoap. It is therefore quite instructive to consider some their basic structuring and narrative features.

LARGER-THAN-LIFE CHARACTERS

One of docusoaps' highest priorities is, by common consent, the need to focus attention on the performative contributions of select leading characters. Just as in a popular soap, these characters provide a point of identification for viewers. Thus, in *Driving School*, it is the irrepressible Maureen Rees who becomes the narrative lynchpin for the whole series, while *Airport* features the larger-than-life character of Jeremy Spake, the decidedly camp Aeroflot supervisor, who would not have been out of place in a TV sitcom. Jeremy Mills who was involved in the production of both the above series, has this to say about the pivotal function of characters such as Jeremy and Maureen:

> These series were structured round characters who didn't have big stories to tell. In the past we'd thought you had to have a really big story to hold the attention of an audience, but now we realised quite slight individual stories could be worked into an entertaining narrative mix.[11]

The ratings success of both *Airport* and *Driving School* sent out a clear signal to others working in the factual entertainment field and it was not long before other producers began to jump on the docusoap bandwagon. Series such as *Holiday Reps* (BBC One, 1997), *Airline* (ITV, 1998–) and *Pleasure Beach* (BBC One, 1998) were just three of a whole host of docusoap products commissioned and aired during a period when the nation was seemingly in the grip of docusoap fever. All these series adhere to the same basic formula and many were produced by companies who had begun to specialise in docusoap production.[12]

THE NURTURING ROLE OF THE BBC

One aspect of the docusoap phenomenon that observers have frequently commented on is that the institution most closely associated with fostering this form of factual entertainment was the BBC.[13] Increasingly, voices of disquiet began to be raised that the factual/documentary output of such a revered public service institution should now be so closely identified with what was seen as an essentially lightweight form of programming.[14] Particular fears were expressed that this proliferation of docusoaps would lead to a concomitant reduction in the type of documentary that aimed to provide a more serious engagement with historical or contemporary issues. Concern was also raised that the over-commissioning of docusoaps ran the risk of killing the goose that laid the golden egg. There was certainly increasing evidence that – as producers sought to keep pace with broadcasters' demands – any original generic vigour the docusoap may have once possessed quickly began to drain away. As the decade wore on, widespread cloning of docusoaps became the order of the day.[15] Docusoaps also became the target of an increasing number of satirical jibes, as commentators jokingly began to speculate as to which institution would be the next port-of-call for a docusoap visitation.

DOCUSOAP FOREBEARS

Though docusoaps are now regarded as a televisual sub-genre in their own right, when they first came to the fore, the fact that they had so evidently married together elements of observational documentary with techniques borrowed from TV drama production led many critics to seek after possible docusoap forebears. Since one of the defining features of docusoaps is their attempt, over an extended period of time, to follow a group of individuals as they go about their day-to-day affairs, some observers have homed in on Paul Watson's *The Family* (BBC One, 1974) and *Sylvania Waters* (BBC One, 1993) as obvious antecedents.[16] While it is true that Watson employs a serialised presentational technique and that some of his featured subjects, like docusoap stars, have acquired celebrity status as a result of their media exposure, Watson himself has always gone out of his way to reject any notion that he is the 'father of the docusoap'. In an interview he gave in 2000, he attempts to draw a clear distinction between what he sees as the superficiality and irrelevance of the docusoap and his own more committed and serious type of film-making: 'Docusoaps aren't even funny, they aren't enlightening; they don't even scratch the surface of understanding. They are just cheap, mostly made by middle-class people sneering at ordinary people, and I deeply resent that.'[17]

Though Watson may feel that he has been misrepresented as direct precursor of the docusoap, a series like *Sylvania Waters* nevertheless could be seen as anticipating

a movement away from the more conventional observational modes of documentary and towards what Corner has described as 'a rather stronger authorialism', one which is often connotatively playful and aware of the kind of 'look' which its images are providing for viewers.[18] What mainly attracted the attention of critics at the time, however, was that *Sylvania Waters* seemed to display decidedly soap-like qualities. At the time of its transmission, one journalist, for instance, referred to the series as a 'soapumentary',[19] while another reviewer characterised the series as a 'docusoap'[20] which is – to my knowledge – the first recorded use of the term. Watson's approach in *Sylvania Waters* certainly anticipates the later docusoaps in that – as well as employing a serialised mode of presentation – it also openly acknowledges the presence of the camera and the interventionist, shaping role of the film-maker.[21] The fact that Watson, just like docusoap film-makers, never seeks to disguise the fact that he is actively intervening in the lives of those who have agreed to participate also ensures that the final edited work becomes – in certain important respects – a filmic record of the developing (or in Watson's case disintegrating) relationship between a film-maker and his/her subjects.[22]

While docusoaps can be seen as part of a more general development in factual/documentary film-making as film- and programme-makers began to experiment with more personal forms of documentary, their origins can also be traced back to more specific antecedents in which – both stylistically and thematically – an approach similar to the one later practised in docusoaps had been first attempted. According to Jeremy Mills, for instance, a major impetus for later docusoap series such as *Vets in Practice* (BBC One, 1996–2000) and *Animal Hospital* (BBC One, 1994–2004) was provided by shows developed by the BBC towards the end of 1980s such as *The Vet* (BBC One, 1989) and *The Doctor* (BBC One, 1990). Both these series followed working professionals as they went about their daily business, but also contained scenes where subjects are filmed at home or pursuing leisure-time activities. *The Vet* and *The Doctor* also foreshadow the later docusoaps in the way they interweave story-lines, some of which are carried across the whole series, while others are contained within a single episode.[23]

Another form of television programming that may have provided a spark of inspiration for docusoap is the type of show exemplified by the MTV series *The Real World* (1992–). This show, developed in the USA in the early 1990s, features a group of carefully selected individuals who have agreed to be corralled within a contained environment and to have their conversations and interactions recorded for the purposes of creating a piece of diverting entertainment. *The Real World* and its British counterpart *The Living Soap* (BBC Two, 1993–94) are early examples of what has come to be known as 'formatted reality', the kind of programme in which situations are contrived where aspiring thespians are encouraged to indulge in types of self-performance that can – in suitably edited form – become part of a factual entertainment package. While docusoaps do not carry the contrivance to the same level as in *The Real World* or *The Living Soap*, they still rely on a much higher degree of intervention that would be the case in more traditional forms of documentary.[24]

THE CRITICAL RESPONSE TO DOCUSOAPS

As already suggested, docusoaps were accorded quite a hostile reception when they first burst on the scene in the mid-1990s. One of the particular butts of criticism was that they were so obsessively character-centred and had such little interest in uncovering what John Corner has termed 'serious social knowledge'.[25] Docusoaps constantly gave the impression that one was tuning into, or eavesdropping on the inconsequential banter of individuals who had been willing to sign up for this particular type of media exposure. As Jon Dovey has noted,

> In terms of 'first person media' the docu-soap, like the chat show or Reality TV, portrays 'ordinary people' talking about themselves in the first person. In fact 'talk' is the central activity of the docu-soap. Despite the handheld mobility of the visual design ... it represents a deeply conversationalised documentary form.[26]

As docusoaps proliferated, so it became increasingly obvious that one of the subjects' principal motivations for appearing on these shows was the craving for media celebrity. One of the consequences of this was that, rather than being seen as just 'people like you and me', as was frequently claimed by programme-makers, some of the leading protagonists in these shows were fast becoming 'semi-professional performers', thus losing any claim they may have had to real-life ordinariness.[27] When pressed, most docusoap stars have been ready to acknowledge that there was something of a trade-off as far as their involvement in the project in question was concerned. In exchange for their participation, they were willing to allow themselves to be moulded and manipulated in accordance with the wishes of the docusoap production team. Subjects were also in little doubt that they had been selected not to reflect on the role they played within their workplace environment but more for their potential as personable telegenic performers. Most subjects were happy to agree to such terms of engagement, though not all realised, at the outset, what some of the longer-term consequences of protracted media exposure might be. This is what Trude Mostue had to say about her leading role in the long-running series *Vets in Practice*:

> I've been directed for four years of my life ... I'm always used to having a director, film crew around me.

> Sometimes I feel a bit like a property. I think they would go to great lengths to stop me from leaving *Vets in Practice.*[28]

COLLUSION, COMPLICITY OR JUST A TRADE-OFF?

Trude's recognition that she had, in effect, acquired the status of 'star performer' could also be seen as one more pointer to docusoaps' limited horizons. Docusoaps' overriding concern is to produce a piece of diverting entertainment that can be easily digested by a prime-time audience. A large gulf, therefore, separates them from the work of the investigative documentarist, one of whose aims will be that of attempting to expose any shortcomings in the institutions to which they gain access. While it would, of course, not be impossible for docusoaps to turn a more critical eye on, say, certain institutional malpractices, the fact remains that programme-makers never seem to lose sight of the fact that they have an altogether 'softer' agenda.

In more traditional forms of documentary there is frequently an understanding or agreement between film-makers and subjects that the film-making process will involve a 'quest for knowledge' whereby subjects are exposed to a more or less searching examination in the course of which the investigator – and by extension the audience – may learn more about issues or have their eyes opened to states of affairs which may give cause for disquiet or concern. The production of a docusoap, on the other hand, involves an altogether different set of arrangements between film-makers and their subjects, one in which there is, arguably, a much higher degree of complicity, if not collusion.[29] Docusoap characters are encouraged to express their hopes, fears and aspirations directly to the camera, but seem to have few misgivings about unburdening themselves in this way. Comparing the docusoap approach with other more interrogative modes where the film-maker is a far less assuring presence, one observer has the following comment to make: 'Docusoaps aim for a cosier approach, presenting the camera as a friend to whom subjects [can] open up in confidence.'[30]

In agreeing to participate in any docusoap project, subjects can virtually rest assured that they will hardly ever be put on the spot by a probing investigator. In terms, then, of power relationships, there seems to be a tacit understanding between producers, subjects and the organisations from which the docusoap participants are drawn that the latter can expect a positive pay-off with respect to the free publicity they will garner through this kind of involvement. It is interesting to note in this connection that docusoap producers use the 'promise-of-free-publicity' argument when seeking to persuade organisations to become the subject of a docusoap treatment.[31]

MORE SOAP THAN DOCU?

In most critical analyses of docusoaps undertaken to date, a fair amount of discussion has centred on the relationship between the 'docu' and the 'soap' elements within this hybrid concoction. The following section sets out to examine how techniques and practices largely borrowed from sitcoms and soap opera are employed to construct a form of programming that can be consumed much like any other light entertainment product.[32] Docusoaps may seek to create the impression that they are bringing real-life ordinariness to our screens, but it is always a carefully constructed and heightened form of reality that is on offer.[33]

The simple truth is that, in many key respects, docusoaps are always tilting in the direction of soap opera, though still retaining certain vestigial connections with documentary. This should really come as no surprise since docusoaps' very raison d'être was the broadcaster-led need for an undemanding form of programming with a softer agenda that could be inserted into that part of the early evening schedule traditionally reserved for soaps, sitcoms and lifestyle shows. Because docusoaps were principally designed as vehicles for easy viewing, it was almost inevitable that they would rely so heavily on some of the tried and tested techniques and devices developed by producers working in these genres.

Docusoaps bear a close affinity to sitcoms and soaps in that – like their fictional counterparts – they prefer to focus most of the narrative interest on a single location or setting with which viewers become increasingly familiar as the series develops. Just as in soap opera, the centrality of the setting is signalled in programme titles such as *Paddington Green* (BBC One, 1999), *Airport, Dover* (ITV, 1997) or *Lakesiders* (BBC One, 1998). The importance of the setting is further reinforced by the employment of appetite-whetting credit sequences that act as a visual and auditory reminder for viewers of the familiar world they are about to enter. Thus, *Hotel* (BBC One, 1997) features shots of the façade of the Adelphi hotel while *The Cruise* (BBC One, 1998) starts with helicopter shots of the illuminated cruise ship to which viewers will presently be conveyed. Carefully chosen upbeat signature tunes also play their part in cueing an audience as to the domain they are about to enter and the characters they will encounter there.

Just as with TV soaps, docusoaps operate with a cast of characters who are strategically deployed across a number of different story-lines.[34] Producers are always on the lookout for events and situations that will generate inter-character conflict or disagreement. *Hotel*, for instance, was memorable for some notable spats between the head chef and other hotel employees, while almost every episode of *Clampers* (BBC One, 1998), the series about traffic wardens, would include a scene where patrolling wardens were confronted by one or more angry motorists

protesting their innocence. Other favoured scenarios include ones in which a boss or manager disciplines a junior member of staff or occasions where the featured organisation confronts difficulties that may threaten its very survival. Such situations are all grist to the mill of docusoap producers. Though there is every reason to believe that these crises are genuine, one sometimes gets the impression that the subjects themselves – well aware of what constitutes 'good television' – will use these occasions to act out their roles with half an eye to how they will come across on screen.

Docusoaps are also, of course, indebted to TV soaps as far as their serial mode of presentation is concerned. As I have written elsewhere:

> The serial format enables programme makers to present material and to manipulate characters so as to enhance narrative interest and to inculcate in viewers the desire to return to the scene of the unfolding drama, as characters reveal more of themselves or as new intrigues are unveiled.[35]

The one device that, above all others, betrays docusoaps' structural affinity with soaps is that of interweaving story-lines.[36] Typically, a docusoap will develop a rhythm whereby, in any one episode, the narrative focus is switched back and forth between three or four story-lines. This not only has the effect of quickening the narrative pace but also has the additional benefit of disguising the fact that at least some of the story-lines are relatively lightweight or even threadbare. It is docusoaps' use of what is sometimes called 'narrative segmentation' that might encourage some viewers to apply soap-opera terms of reference when responding to these works.

Though docusoaps are indebted to soaps for many of their structural features, they nevertheless retain at least some kinship with more traditional forms of documentary. This is perhaps most discernible in what has become a defining feature of docusoaps: their heavy use of voiceover narration. Narrators tend to acquire a dual function in docusoaps. First and foremost they provide viewers with orientational guidance as to the identity of participants and to the locations where events are taking place. (Docusoaps' heavy dependence on a narrator figure to cue viewers about locational switches ['Meanwhile in the foyer guests are assembling ...'] has been much parodied, as in the series *People Like Us* [BBC Two, 1999]). It might also be claimed that – given the importance they assume in setting the tone of a docusoap – narrators virtually become characters in their own right. They assume the role of a trusty companion whose light-hearted quips, comments and musings become just as much part of the overall entertainment as the contributions of the foregrounded characters.

FACTUAL ENTERTAINMENT

Having enjoyed unprecedented popularity in the second half of the 1990s, docusoaps gradually began to lose their 'brand-leader' status. Docusoaps still continued to be produced in the first decade of the twenty-first century, but in much smaller numbers than hitherto. It is worth reporting, however, that the two airport-based series, *Airport* (BBC One) and *Airline* (ITV), have proved to be almost as long-lived as some of the most popular TV soaps. In terms of the broader developments of factual entertainment, however, docusoaps were progressively displaced by the new reality formats, including both the so-called reality game-docs (*Big Brother* and *Survivor*) and other strands of factual programming in which volunteer subjects act out roles in specially contrived situations – for example, *The 1900 House* (Channel 4, 1999), *The Trench* (BBC Two, 2002) and *Wife Swap* (Channel 4, 2004).

In spite of being met with a good deal of adverse publicity, docusoaps' success at attracting substantial audiences in peak time also had some positive impacts. In particular, it provided ammunition for those working in the broad area of factual programming to argue the case for factual/documentary material to be given greater prominence in the TV schedule. John Willis, former Director of Programmes at Channel 4, once observed, for instance, that though in some ways docusoaps were a 'symbol of the terrible commodification of factual television', they had at least helped maintain a level of interest in documentary. In his own words: 'For those of us who've seen years of documentary budgets being cut and documentaries pushed to the edges of the television schedule, it's a pleasure to see so much factual programming in peak time.'[37]

What docusoaps also achieved was to promote discussion around the broader topic of the aims and purposes of documentary. Because they were a manifestly hybrid form that combined structuring devices from the world of fiction with techniques and conventions drawn from the domain of observational documentary, docusoaps became the subject of often quite intense debate concerning issues such as the legitimacy of certain types of reconstruction and re-enactment in documentary work as well as the alleged threat they posed to more 'deserving' modes of documentary.[38] It was felt in some quarters, for instance, that not only were docusoaps devaluing the currency of documentary, but also that their very popularity was making it more difficult to campaign for the continuing presence of cutting-edge, consciousness-raising documentaries in the TV schedules.[39] Fears were expressed as to whether acquiring the tools of the documentarist's trade by working on docusoaps offered aspiring young filmmakers the kind of training needed to maintain the tradition of serious documentary film-making. Once or twice, broadcasters such as Paul Hamann, at the time Head of Documentaries at the BBC, had voiced the hope that it might be possible for docusoaps to explore some of the darker areas of human experience.[40] As subsequent events have shown, however, docusoaps have continued to be regarded, by producers and viewers alike, as vehicles the main function of which is to provide a mildly diverting form of entertainment for an undemanding audience. It is as if it is part of docusoaps' generic make-up to cast their eyes towards the sunny uplands.

For all the hostility to which they were often exposed by critics, docusoaps remained quite warmly regarded by viewers. There is some evidence to suggest, in fact, that audiences developed the kind of easy-going relationship with docusoaps that allowed them to be regarded in much the same manner as they would their favourite soap. The results of focus group surveys conducted in 1998 suggest, for instance, that most viewers showed considerable media savviness in perceiving docusoaps for exactly what they were: highly constructed vehicles for factual entertainment.

Space precludes any more detailed examination of docusoap influence in the longer term, but it is certainly worth recording the 'inspiration' they may have provided for other TV genres. There can be no doubt that the high profile that docusoaps had during the period that their star was in the ascendancy encouraged writers and producers working in other TV genres to continue the exploration of the border territory where factual and fictional discourses meet. I have already commented on how docusoaps occupy the same generic space as TV sitcoms and it was possibly inevitable – in the fullness of time – that sitcoms would begin to explore this same territory. Imitation is, after all, the sincerest form of flattery. The creators of the highly rated comedy series *The Office* (BBC Two, 2001) were clearly using docusoaps as a reference point in developing a sitcom series that combined elements of apparently unscripted observational documentary with the comedic artfulness of the traditional sitcom. One should also make mention in this respect of the long-running BBC series *The Royle Family* (1998–), which – with its focus on larger-than-life characters interacting within a contained domestic environment and its emphasis on 'real-life ordinariness' – carries decidedly docusoap overtones.[41]

In the final analysis, it is probably best to regard docusoaps as simply marking an important stage in the overall development of more personalised forms of factual entertainment over the last two or three decades. The late 1980s had seen the rise of the incident-packed shows centred on the work of the accident and emergency (A&E) services, but frequently featuring interviews with A&E personnel. Docusoaps were, by contrast, a kind of antidote to these earlier shows. They were more gently paced and more conversationally based. For some three or four years the docusoaps were in the ascendancy, but their moment quickly passed, as they were supplanted by other types of reality programming, in which the idea of 'real-life performance' quickly took on an entirely new meaning.

NOTES

1. As Paul Ward has noted: 'Factual films and programmes have now reached such a level of hybridity, that it is very difficult to sustain a notion for there being stable categories.' See his *Documentary: The Margins of Reality* (London: Wallflower, 2005), p. 1.

2. John Corner, 'What Can We Say About "Documentary?"', *Media, Culture & Society*, 22 September 2000, pp. 687–8.

3. Brian Winston, *Lies, Damn Lies and Documentaries* (London: BFI, 2000), p. 39.

4. See note 22.

5. See Anita Biressi and Heather Nunn, *Reality TV: Realism and Revelation* (London: Wallflower Press, 2005), p. 16.

6. See Richard Kilborn, *Staging the Real: Factual TV Programming in the Age of Big Brother* (Manchester and New York: Manchester University Press, 2003), p. 89.

7. See Richard Kilborn and John Izod, *An Introduction to Television Documentary: Confronting Reality* (Manchester: Manchester University Press, 1997), pp. 115–16; Winston, *Lies, Damn Lies and Documentaries*, p. 45.

8. Jon Dovey, *Freakshow: First Person Media and Factual Television* (London: Pluto Press, 2000), p. 11.

9. Andrew Bethell, 'A Job, Some Stars and a Big Row', *Sight & Sound: Mediawatch'99* (supplement) vol. 9 no. 3, March 1999, p. 14.

10. There were ten series of *Airport*, each comprising six thirty-minute episodes, which were produced and aired between 1996 and 2005. The first series of *Airport* was aired on BBC Two, but such was its popularity that it was quickly transferred to a prime-time BBC One slot, where it remained until 2005. In 2008, the BBC broadcast an update entitled *Return to* Airport that included interviews with the 'stars' of yesteryear as well as clips from the original series.

11. Interview with author, London, 1998.

12. Producer Andrew Bethell provides details of these companies and a list of the most successful docusoap series in his 1999 article 'A Job, Some Stars and a Big Row'. For further information on docusoaps broadcast during the 1996–99 period, see Dovey, *Freakshow*, pp. 139–40; Kilborn, *Staging the Real*, pp. 96–100.

13. It is perhaps worth reminding readers that, from the early 1990s onwards, BBC executives were faced with the considerable challenge of having to reconcile the Corporation's traditional public service role with its need to compete in an increasingly globalised broadcasting environment.

14. At a specially convened BBC Governors' Seminar held in London in November 1998 the then Head of BBC Documentary was forced to admit that the Corporation had no fewer than twelve docusoaps currently in production.

15. The short-lived series *Dover* (ITV, 1997), for instance, was an unsuccessful imitation of the BBC's *Airport*, while *Chalet Girls* (ITV, 1998) was a virtual carbon copy of the earlier BBC series *Holiday Reps*.

16. Stella Bruzzi, *New Documentary: A Critical Introduction* (London: Routledge, 2000), pp. 78–9; Dovey, *Freakshow*, pp. 134, 137; Kilborn, *Staging the Real*, pp. 91–4; Ben Walters, The Office: *A Critical Reading of the Series* (London: BFI, 2005), p. 63.

17. In François Verster, '"I am like a poacher": Paul Watson Interview', *DOX (Documentary Film Magazine)* no. 31, October 2000, p. 10.

18. John Corner, *The Art of Record: A Critical Introduction to Documentary* (Manchester: Manchester University Press, 1996), pp. 182–3.

19. David Dale, 'The Neighbours from Hell', *Daily Telegraph* (Australia), 21 April 1993, p. 17.

20. Melanie McFadyean, 'Family Entertainment'?', *Guardian* (part 2), 2 December 1993, pp. 4–5.

21. Kilborn and Izod, *An Introduction to Television Documentary*, pp. 70–2.

22. Much of Molly Dineen's work is likewise characterised by its acknowledgment of the participative presence of the film-maker (see Bruzzi, *New Documentary*, pp. 96–7; Kilborn, *Staging the Real*, p. 109).

23. For more on docusoap antecedents, see Bruzzi, *New Documentary*, pp. 80–5; Kilborn, *Staging the Real*, pp. 90–6. Other examples reflecting docusoap practice can be found in the late 1980s. *Jimmy's* (1987–97) was a series of observational films made in a Leeds hospital by Nick Gray. Gray, who had worked on the long-running UK fictional soap opera *Emmerdale Farm* (1972–), began by producing intertitial vignettes of the hospital's life. These became full half-hours with multiple story-lines. Eventually the series ran for ten years (Brian Winston, *Claiming the Real II: Documentary: Grierson and Beyond* [London: BFI, 2008], p. 263).

24. Broadcasters will sometimes attempt to talk up these series by characterising them as some kind of 'social experiment'. The following claim, for instance, is made in the opening title sequences of *The Real World*: '[This show] is a true story of a group of individuals picked to live in a house and have their lives taped to find out what happens when people stop being polite and start getting real.'

25. John Corner, 'Different Documentary Modes: *World in Action, Hotel* and *Wife Swap*', in G. Creeber (ed.), *Tele-Visions: An Introduction to Studying Television* (London: BFI, 2005).

26. Dovey, *Freakshow*, p. 138).

27. Leading docusoap performers such as Jane Mcdonald (*The Cruise*), Ray Brown (*Clampers*) and Trude Mostue (*Vets in Practice*) have indeed gone on to pursue quite lucrative media or show-business careers.

28. R. Kilborn, M. Hibberd and R. Boyle, 'The Rise of the Docu-soap: The Case of *Vets in Practice*', *Screen* vol. 42 no. 4, Winter 2001, p. 388.

29. See also Bruzzi, *New Documentary*, pp. 86–92; Dovey, *Freakshow*, p. 139; Kilborn, *Staging the Real*, pp. 107–8.

30. Walters, The Office, p. 64

31. Andrew Bethell, 'Pleasure Plus Principle', *Guardian* (Part 2), 2 February 1998, p. 5.

32. Docusoaps have certain common attributes with the long-established talk-show, as well as anticipating some of the bolder and brasher reality game-docs that were soon to come on stream. Lively conversational exchanges between participants are one of the basic ingredients of all these different formats.

33. Some observers have expressed concern about the amount of manipulation employed in putting together a docusoap, especially where subjects are called on to re-enact a particular scene or where situations are contrived to fit in with the requirements of a particular story-line. Some of this concern has to be seen in the context of the high-profile fakery scandals that afflicted documentary production during the later 1990s (see Kilborn, *Staging the Real*, pp. 107–8, 122–57, and Winston, *Lies, Damn Lies and Documentaries*, pp. 54–8).

34. Bruzzi, *New Documentary*, p. 78; Dovey, *Freakshow*, p. 152.

35. Kilborn, *Staging the Real*, pp. 114–15.

36. Bruzzi, *New Documentary*, p. 78; Kilborn, *Staging the Real*, pp. 116–17.

37. John Willis, in John Izod and Richard Kilborn (eds), *From Grierson to the Docu-soap: Breaking the Boundaries* (Luton: University of Luton Press, 2000), pp. 100–1.

38. Ward, *Documentary*, p. 25.

39. David Hogarth, *Realer than Reel: Global Directions in Documentary* (Austin: University of Texas Press, 2006), p. 98.

40. Richard Kilborn, 'The Docu-soap: A Critical Assessment' in Izod and Kilborn, *From Grierson to the Docu-soap*, p. 118.

41. Walters, The Office, p. 67.

4.6 Reality TV: A Sign of the Times?

ANITA BIRESSI AND HEATHER NUNN

After the docusoap, TV producers came up with popular, cheap programming wherein individuals were placed in artificial environments (rather than discovered in actual ones). This was branded as 'Reality TV' and classed as 'formatted' documentary. The ethical issues raised were rebutted by claims that the participants had been given a voice; but, because of the inauthenticity of their 'playing' and the interventionism of the producers, some in the documentary community dismiss Reality TV as not being documentary at all.

'A DIME-STORE MIRROR'?

Confronted with the widespread commercial success of reality television in the early 2000s, novelist and cultural critic Salman Rushdie lamented, 'The television set, once so idealistically thought of as our window on the world, has become a dime-store mirror instead.'[1] His widely syndicated article, entitled 'Reality TV: A Dearth of Talent and the Death of Morality', proposed that 'success on this scale insists on being examined, because it tells us things about ourselves, or ought to'.[2] His own examination, which was critical rather than analytical, made two observations: first, that the ideal of television had been degraded by Reality TV (the dime-store mirror) and, second, that Reality TV was both ethically dubious and socially damaging. The connection between these two readings of the Reality TV phenomenon was less than clear except to say that it seemed to be effected through a robust disapproval of the untalented and unremarkable people parading across the screen. Rushdie asked rhetorically, 'Who needs images of the world's rich otherness, when you can watch these half-familiar avatars of yourself – these half-attractive half-persons – enacting ordinary life under weird conditions?'[3] It seemed that the ubiquitous 'tawdry' exhibitionism of the untalented 'half-person', which in Rushdie's terms rendered 'real values' such as modesty, decency and intelligence redundant, not only damaged the ideal function of television to document the richness of real life, but it also undermined the wider values that underpin civil society.

Rushdie was only one of a number of commentators whose evaluation of the significance of Reality TV was formed along these lines, linking Reality TV's dilution of serious television culture to a wider culture of declining public values.[4] As Holmes and Jermyn have noted, definitions of Reality TV, discussions of its forms, content, claims to the 'real', its inclusion of ordinary people and even its economics have all been underpinned and structured, sometimes covertly, by invested cultural values, hierarchies of taste and stratifications of social difference.[5] At the centre of complaint lodges bemusement and the question mockingly posed by Peter Bazalgette: why are 'all these *awful ordinary* people on television'?[6] Bearing in mind this context, this chapter begins with a consideration of Reality TV as an innovative and challenging incursion into the established field of documentary and factual television culture. It then steps back to consider its broader significance as a cultural phenomenon and the values that it appeared to endorse, challenge or contravene. In doing so, it aims to highlight an issue spanning these two areas of debate: that is, the prevalence of the unschooled, ordinary person on popular factual television.

REALITY TV: DOCUMENTARY AS WE KNOW IT?

Since the late 1980s, the proliferation of popular factual television has inspired concern about the marginalisation and devaluation of established 'analytic' documentary genres;[7] their commercial success triggering spiky debates about the degradation of documentary content, formats and functions. These new 'people shows', now more commonly referred to as 'Reality TV', including crime and emergency services, 'docusoap' and 'life-swap' formats ('documentary lite', as it was sometimes dubbed[8]) and social experiment or 'game-docs' all served to stimulate the public appetite for watching non-professionals in a variety of contrived but 'real' scenarios. These shows, mostly featuring ordinary people in *staged* but apparently unscripted situations for the purposes of entertainment, marked a significant shift in the relationship between text and audience, eroding the distance between television subjects and viewers,[9] while, more often than not, drawing attention to their own artifice. Reality TV staging is incredibly varied, including, for example, the domestic space, cultural institutions, hospitals, airports and even, in the case of social observation programming, the tower block, the Mumbai sweatshop or Thai seafood industry. But the emphasis will be quite different from the documentaries they replaced because, in Reality TV, any lessons learned are expected to be inferred via the *experience* of the subjects involved rather than through the deployment of evidential documentary modes.[10] In other words, whereas more conventional public service documentary drew on macro socioeconomic frameworks for understanding the social, Reality TV offered micro frameworks of intimacy, game-playing and the personal journey of self-realisation in order to understand everything from personal relationships, family and small group dynamics to class structures, globalisation and gender roles. As Corner explains it, in the context of his discussion of *Big Brother*, Reality TV builds in the social in order to reveal the personal.[11] For many critics, then, the primary significance of Reality TV continued to lie in the generic consequences of this 'populist imperative' for the more 'serious' documentary forms[12] and its contribution, alongside the forces of tabloidisation, to the weakening of the public sphere and its fields of rational communicative action.

Retrospectively, it's possible to trace at least three notable and to some extent overlapping phases of what might loosely be described as popular factual programming and, in some cases, more specifically as 'Reality TV'. The first phase, dating from the mid-1980s and originating in the USA, was oriented around policing and the emergency services and was notable for importing fast and dramatic editing and surveillance technologies into programme structures in order to produce pacey and action-driven entertainment.[13] In contrast, the second phase from the mid-90s (popularly dubbed the 'docusoap') consisted of observational format series involving intertwining stories driven by strong 'characters' or 'personalities' and taking place in a huge range of settings and scenarios from the intimate (home, marriage) to the public arena (work, public organisations), but all of them with an emphasis on people 'playing themselves' (see Chapter 5.3). Dating from the early 2000s, the third wave featured competition-based factual formats, the most notable being *Big Brother* (launched in 1999 in the Netherlands, 2000 in the UK). These series often required participants to be contained in 'social experiment' situations or 'simulations'[14] often filmed twenty-four hours a day from multiple cameras and isolated from normal social relations; conditions in which they underwent set tasks to remain in the game. Running alongside all of these was an undertow of lifestyle and makeover programmes, which had a far older lineage and arguably refreshed itself by adopting and adapting elements of the docusoap and game-doc formulas.[15]

All of these formats, most of which have been referred to as 'Reality TV' at one time or another, are innovations

Big Brother (1999–): 'social experiment' situations or 'simulations'

resulting partly from genre hybridisation, a process which, as Richard Kilborn explains, itself takes on different 'modes': the 'additive' and the 'integrated'.[16] The former is characterised by the way in which the specific generic features, borrowed from other forms and serving to refresh the genre, remain easily distinguishable, while the latter comes together as a more thoroughly integrated 'amalgam'. It is the integrated or amalgamated formats which come closest to offering a 'new' viewing experience, although whether they mark a clear break or departure from previous factual broadcasting provision continues to be debated. But as Kilborn notes, it is the docusoaps and the game-docs (rather than, say, the reality crime or lifestyle shows) which come closest to presenting as a 'new species' due to their unique blending of structural, narrative and other elements formerly associated with older genres such as the soap opera and the fly-on-the-wall documentary.[17] We would also add that these second- and third-phase formats are also distinguishable by their *exceptional placement of ordinary people centre stage*. For example, in the first phase of reality crime programming ordinary people appeared only to play their parts as victims, villains or public service guardians in narratives frequently assembled and anchored like a magazine programme and dramatised like a fictional prime-time serial. They were necessary to the format but they were very far from being its centre of gravity. The same might be said of the lifestyle formats such as fashion, property, cooking, health and consumer programmes, where presenters, experts and celebrities of all kinds are the key protagonists in episodes and across series. What distinguishes reality programming, then, from these cognate genres is its investment in ordinary people as 'characters' and in situations which seem analogous to everyday life or daily social interactions.

Having established these byways of categorisation and genre formation it is clear that public debate about the production values and ethics of popular factual programming can be fairly securely situated under the umbrella term 'Reality TV'. Taking the long view, Reality TV needs to be understood as only the most recent in a long line of genres and formats to be singled out by critics as emblematic of a decline in ethical, moral and educative standards or by defenders as a platform for popular expression. In many cases, these battle lines are drawn around (reality) television's potential demotic *and* democratic qualities, with each allegedly impacting on the other – although, in fact, there is no established instrumental connection between them. From this perspective Reality TV has become another casualty of either the well-established critical pre-occupation with television as an instrument to be measured against the ideal of the democratically educative public sphere or the ideal of television as a popular and common culture. Reality TV is an easy target in the resurrection of debates about the role of (and feared demise) of television as purveyor of information, a shift or slippage from what Bill Nichols memorably called the 'discourses of sobriety'[18] in which documentary at its best, alongside news and current affairs, symbolised the media's place (together with education, the law and science) in opening up the social world to empirical scrutiny. The concerns aired about Reality TV, then, addressed not only the function of factual and documentary programming on television, but also trepidation about the dissolution of older forms of public service and 'quality' commercial production and the shift in the late twentieth century to an accelerated commodity model in which the formatted documentary would become the ideal output in the contemporary television landscape.

Linked to the feared dissolution of quality output was an unease with Reality TV's capacity to unsettle already wobbly boundaries between factual and fictional content. It mixed factual material (real crimes, emergencies, neighbourhood clashes, people's jobs) with fiction (staged events, reconstructions, behavioural experiments) and unsurprisingly, for media scholars at least, conversation turned to the ethical dilemmas this raised in terms of measuring the veracity of a programme's version of the real. But, as always, context is everything and the reception of Reality TV also needs to be read against a backdrop of growing public scepticism about the authority of official culture. Importantly, as Jon Dovey has noted, the rise of Reality TV in the late 1990s coincided in the UK with a series of public denunciations of fakery that engulfed more conventional documentary practice, culminating with commercial regulator ITC fining Carlton TV £2 million for 'faking' a documentary called *The Connection* (1996).[19] So, while scholars and documentary-makers themselves were never going to be surprised at discovering that actuality is highly constructed or even at times 'faked', in the public mind these stories led to greater doubts about whether documentary might be trusted to sustain and develop public knowledge and discussion – falling, for a while, into an absurd reduction of documentary to 'damn lies'.[20] As

such, then, public debate about Reality TV was arguably formed in a critical arena in which a populist contempt for documentary's hidden practices was counterpointed with the embrace of observational television that brazenly flourished its simulation of real events and social gatherings. The docusoap setting, the *Big Brother* house, the *Castaway* (2000–01) or *Survivor* (2000–) island, the boardroom in *The Apprentice* (2004–) and so on made only modest claims to authenticity because the 'truth' of these scenarios lay in the dynamics of interpersonal relations, with a non-professional cast playing themselves, rather than in the pursuit of actuality as documentary impulse. In fact, the very performance of the 'ordinary' (never wholly bona fide, but nonetheless not faked) became the marker against which one was invited to measure moments of authenticity. Here, these programmes' treatment of the ordinary people-turned-performers (debates already well aired in relation to TV social documentary and drama-doc) was identified by critics, media professionals and scholars as a key feature in the changing topography of the televisual landscape.

From the perspective of popular factual programming this shift into a 'post-documentary culture'[21] was and continues to be engaged in refiguring documentary practices, forms and even functions into something both disarmingly familiar and also new and strange. John Corner importantly argues that the post-documentary culture of television involves not the demise of documentary per se, but rather, alongside tried and tested documentary formulas, new modes of 'documentary as diversion'.[22] Concerned to articulate Reality TV to aspects of the documentary tradition, yet signal new transformations, he has highlighted their 'performative, playful element' and a 'broader range of cognitive and affective investments' on the part of audiences,[23] representing perhaps the kind of narrowing of distance between the subject and the audience that is a consequence of the dramaturgy of emotion played out on screen.

Reflecting on this 'colloquial turn' in TV programming, Corner emphasised the 'greater engagement of the media with everyday terms of living and the varieties of ordinary "private" experience, both pleasant and traumatic'.[24] Factual genres have, in the 2000s, he underlined, demonstrated an 'expanded desire for "emotional knowledge" about events – about what it is like to be "inside" an event, "inside" an experience'.[25] That colloquial turn and its emphasis on sharing experience is, we would argue, one of broader cultural importance, evident in the ways in which reality media (Reality TV, social networking sites, blogs, YouTube, mobile-phone technology) have all become tools for turning oneself into media material and for sharing the consumption of media. Its larger significance lies then in the politics of unprecedented opportunity for the increased visibility of so many non-elite, non-celebrity, non-professional people in an environment where one is invited to 'broadcast yourself'. Admittedly, this politics lies in the promise rather than the evidence of Reality TV (now alongside other digital forms) to change lives by changing the self through the experience of going public. As the predictable opening sequences of many reality programmes establish, those contestants who pass eliminating auditions are assured the chance of a heightened (mediated) self-reflexivity: performance on Reality TV is posited as a therapeutic encounter with a chance to remodel the self. Indeed Graeme Turner[26] has argued that one of the crucial elements of Reality TV is the way that participation in *Idol*, or we might add *Wife Swap* (2004–), *How the Other Half Live* (2009–10), *The X Factor* (2004–), *Big Brother*, *Meet the Natives* (2007–), *Tribal Wives* (2008–) or *The Apprentice*, is inflected as 'a certain kind of recognition of the self' and one which is in keeping with a broader 'demotic turn'.

Here, one recalls Roger Silverstone's[27] prescient consideration of the 'emergence of a more public private self' as the marker of contemporary media culture, outlined in his meditation *Why Study the Media?* For Silverstone the emergent public private self is inaugurated by modernity and sanctioned, facilitated, articulated and complicated by the media. He argues that we know about performance as both practitioners in our daily lives and as audiences accessing the mediated lives of others and, consequently, we move across the boundaries between public and private spaces 'with increasing ease, as a matter of course'.[28] We argue that Reality TV has, for good or ill, become one of the key vehicles for the transportation of private lives into the public realm and as such has helped re-landscape Silverstone's 'mediasphere' into a terrain where the public presentation of formerly private aspects of the self is not only encouraged but strongly encouraged. The social and/or professional pressure to *present* oneself on various digital platforms is increasingly felt and ever more difficult to resist.

As we have noted elsewhere[29] we have taken this broader space of media culture, which is clearly a post-documentary space (refigured through digital media as well as on television), to be a radically altered economic and cultural environment that allows for and promotes entertainment and diversion, the further erosion of the boundaries between the public and private spheres, between the 'ordinary person' and the celebrity and between the media and social space. Indeed, the last few years have seen these erosions further worn away by the rise of web 2.0 and its enabling of social media, user-generated content and other participatory digital cultures. Advances in technology have not only changed dramatically the way documentary media are produced, but also opened up the ways in which conventional documentaries and new media reality-documents can reach wider international audiences. For example, DVD, video on demand, satellite-distributed

collaborative activist projects and YouTube have altered long-established distribution models.[30] We continue to move into a post-documentary era 'as a result of the widespread dispersal ... of documentarist energies and appeals across a much larger area of audio-visual culture' and in which 'electronic mediations of real life' have a growing reach and appeal.[31]

REALITY TV: LIFE AS WE KNOW IT?

In the summer of 2000, a British public debating forum called the Institute of Ideas (IOI) organised a number of salons and debates focused on the key issues of the day. It aimed to offer public platforms for intelligent debate over and above the special-interest enclaves of academia, policy development and government. These issues, which later found their way into the Debating Ideas series published by Hodder and Stoughton, included such controversial and important topics as ethical tourism, the value of contemporary art, abortion, the social and cultural impact of the internet, genetic technologies and 'designer babies' and ... reality television. The inclusion of entertainment-led factual programming in this line-up recalls that, in even in its early days, Reality TV not only attracted the attention of audiences or media scholars but also of cultural pundits and social commentators and was increasingly being read, by the latter at least, as culturally significant, worthy of closer inspection and a cause for concern. Some went so far as to assert that Reality TV was the logical (if disagreeable) extension of a wider cultural embrace of the demotic, the popular and the relentlessly trivial. A frequently cited *Observer* newspaper article written by cultural critic Germaine Greer in 2001 was full of foreboding: 'Almost overnight Reality TV seems to have become the mainstay of popular culture. But it hasn't turned us into voyeurs – it's much worse than that.'[32] Greer, who herself was later destined to take up a short-lived residence in the *Celebrity Big Brother* house, went on to declare that 'Reality TV is not the end of civilisation as we know it: it is civilisation as we know it.'[33] She proposed that the ubiquity of video technology, together with our easy acceptance of media visibility as not only inevitable but desirable, meant that television, finally, has become 'more real than life', functioning as arbitrator of what is truthful ('video is fact'), authentic and real.[34] Greer's comments chimed with many other opinion formers (including journalists, politicians and religious leaders) who spied in Reality TV the signs of a broader cultural shift in the relationship between the public and private realm. It also intersected with strands of early cultural and media studies scholarship which began to make the case for theorising Reality TV as symptomatic of the ongoing transformation of the public sphere, with Reality TV, as Craig Hight put it, being one of the 'more obvious signs of the emergence of a significantly different configuration of individual, state and culture'.[35]

Thus, the ubiquity of Reality TV, its vulgarity, boisterous appeal and shameless promotion of the trivial, the intimate and the ordinary, prompted concerns that it was something worse than an unpleasant interloper on the television scene; it was a sign of the times and a harbinger of a broader decline in both cultural values and public civility. Shows such as *Big Brother* attracted opprobrium on grounds of both morality and taste, inspiring a 'late modern panic'[36] in a variety of national contexts, including in Germany, Britain, Africa and France. In many cases the shows were regarded as both an affront to established cultural values and as evidence of declining standards as played out in youth culture, over consumption, hyper-sexualisation, self-indulgence, narcissism, voyeurism and even abject humiliation.[37] In a few cases, media commentators went so far as anticipating wide-sweeping cultural decline.[38] Meanwhile, its defenders spied a differently informed anxiety: one commentator observing, for example, that the contretemps over the French reality show *Loft Story* (2001–) revealed 'what probably disturbs us most: the innocent, insistent and brutal presence of another generation and another social class'.[39] It seems, then, that Reality TV was to be regarded variously and sometimes simultaneously as the instigator of both a 'crisis in content'[40] and a crisis in culture.

These early debates posited that popular factual entertainment was seizing previously privileged claims to represent social reality and that its subjects had lost the naivety needed to produce the more honest television associated with the documentary project. Now TV's subjects knew from which angle they photographed best and even had ambitions to enter the television industry as professional players. As early as the mid-1990s documentary-maker Bernard Clark spied in this new canniness 'the end of innocence', observing that, '"reality" at least in the documentary sense, wasn't worth the bother'.[41] Attached to this was the additional provocation of popular factual programming presenting ordinary, perhaps 'unqualified' people, as markers of the emotionally and/or culturally credible, as spokespersons and opinion-formers. Reality TV worked for mass audiences because it dragged the ordinary, the familiar and the everyday out of its fictional enclave of the soap opera, the sitcom and the drama and into the realm of the 'real', while retaining the theatricality and emotional power of narrative, plot and timing. Increasingly (sometimes inadvertently), social reality and the possibilities of self-construction or critical reflection were not only played out in popular media but were dependent on the increased participation of non-professional media performers. Subsections of the reality genre could be sold fairly credibly as participatory culture for which ordinary people could audition, perform or cast their vote and which invited viewers to measure themselves and their ideals against those who made it onto the shows. Reality media were inexorably

becoming prime sites of individual and collective exploration, offering apparently appealing models of aspiration, competitiveness, self-presentation, cooperation and sociality. The platform supporting non-actors as they talk, compete, work, play and transform was clearly highly manufactured and unstable, but it became, nonetheless, the scaffold upon which late-modern audiences seemed to measure and re-evaluate their own identities, values and behaviours.[42]

Where critics did step back to evaluate Reality TV's broader cultural significance beyond the television industry, its burgeoning commercial success and devotion to showcasing ordinary people and 'youth'-oriented topics were cited as further evidence of the ongoing vandalism of established culture and civility by the new outriders of demotic 'low-brow' entertainment – the end of civilisation as we know it. It seemed at times that these, sometimes highly vituperative, attacks on Reality TV and its subjects were rooted in an acute discomfort about ordinary people (most often read as non-middle-class subjects) rising above their station. A prominent example would be the news media coverage of the notorious 2007 *Celebrity Big Brother* racism scandal in which the bullying behaviour undertaken by Jade Goody against Bollywood star Shilpa Shetty was interpreted in the context of debates about class, the public sphere and civility via some very direct attacks on Goody as a classed subject. Media coverage dramatised Goody as the bad citizen par excellence and politicians and the press promoted the vote to eject Goody from the *Big Brother* house as a referendum on racism which would restore Britain's reputation as a tolerant society. It was the lead story on BBC Radio 4's *The World Tonight* (18 January 2007), and *Celebrity Big Brother* was the subject of a police investigation and an Office of Communications enquiry.[43] Much of the coverage focused on the alleged influence of televised bad behaviour on children, the citizens of the future. Goody may have been a poor role model and a bad citizen, but much of the coverage also suggested that popular fascination with the event and its aftermath was also fixed in the contest of class versus race and that class difference, fascination and fear (which are arguably already foundational to popular fascination with reality and lifestyle programming) was allowed full rein in reaction to the Shetty affair. Vanessa Feltz, writing in the tabloid *Star* newspaper, observed of Goody and the two women with whom she was aligned, 'These harpies will never be allowed to forget their disgusting behaviour – and, as they stack shelves and shovel shit, it will be delightful to see the punishment fit the crime.'[44]

To conclude, it is perhaps the consistent presence of the 'ordinary person' in Reality TV, and, as already indicated, quite often the 'common' person marked by their classed status, their 'limited' cultural knowledge and the visible markers of their social difference, which has not only been taken as a defining feature of the genre, but also as the element which most often offends. The offence seems to lie not only in the topics addressed and behaviours revealed (sex and sexuality, plastic surgery, aggression, profanity, mawkish sentimentality, retrogressive conservatism and personal trauma), but specifically in the types of people who are increasingly given access to media space and an anxiety that they may be representative of wider cultural change. In fact, the IOI's Reality TV publication, edited by Dolan Cummings, begins with the premise that no matter how diverse the programming labelled as 'reality television' might appear to be its common feature is its preference for 'ordinary people' as its subject.[45] Reality TV then, in theory at least, provides a platform for people from diverse sexual, ethnic and classed backgrounds to gain air-time[46] and promises more inclusive representation. For the lucky few, it also seems to offer an opportunity for social mobility as they become professionalised media celebrities in their own right. But for critics, these new-style celebrities are both garrulous and vacuous; their voluble, often unschooled personas read as emblematic of the vulgarity and shallow values of the newer formats and perhaps also of the declining standards of public behaviour in the social realm. For the defenders of Reality TV, and for those who choose to read it 'against the grain' or with an eye on its democratic possibilities, the centrality of ordinary people represents the potential democratisation of the media, the possibility of a move away from elitist values and towards the inclusion of 'real people and real language'.[47] Cummings closes his collection by suggesting that the consideration of the presence of 'ordinary Joes' in Reality TV is, finally, fundamental because their visibility informs (and we would add dramatises and amplifies) debates about the democratisation of media, the challenge to elitist cultural values and social prejudices and even the threat to broadcasting standards. As he suggests to his readers: 'how you feel about that debate [about ordinary people] is likely to influence your thoughts about the merits of Reality TV' overall.[48]

NOTES

1. Salman Rushdie, 'Reality TV: A Dearth of Talent and the Death of Morality', *Guardian*, 9 June 2001, http://www. guardian.co.uk/books/2001/jun/09/salmanrushdie
2. Ibid.
3. Ibid.
4. For example, Germaine Greer, 'Watch with Brother', *Observer*, 24 June 2001, http://www.guardian.co.uk/ theobserver/2001/jun/24/features.review7; Oliver James, 'Danger: Reality TV Can Rot Your Brain', *The Times*, 20 December 2002, pp. 4–5; Melanie Phillips, 'Degradation TV and a Sinister Flight from Reality', *Daily Mail*, 31 May 2004, http://www.dailymail.co.uk/debate/columnists/ article-304835/Degradation-TV-sinister-flight-reality.html;

Paul Watson, 'Why Sneering Reality TV is as Bad as the Roman Amphitheatre', *Daily Mail*, 22 April 2008, http://www.dailymail.co.uk/tvshowbiz/article-561173/Why-sneering-reality-television-bad-Roman-amphitheatre.html; A. N. Wilson, 'In this Excoriating and Provocative Essay …', *Daily Mail*, 8 April 2009, Nexis UK Online Database.
5. Su Holmes and Deborah Jermyn, 'Introduction: Understanding Reality TV', in Su Holmes and Deborah Jermyn (eds), *Understanding Reality TV* (London: Routledge, 2004), pp. 8–9.
6. Ibid., p. 9, original emphasis.
7. Charlotte Brunsdon, Catherine Johnson, Rachel Moseley, Rachel and Helen Wheatley, 'Factual Entertainment on British Television: The Midland TV Research Group's "8–9 Project"', *European Journal of Cultural Studies* vol. 4 no. 1, February 2001.
8. See John Corner, 'What Can We Say about Documentary?', *Media, Culture and Society* vol. 22 no. 5, September 2000, p. 687.
9. Estella Tincknell and Parvati Raghuram, 'Big Brother: Reconfiguring the "Active" Audience of Cultural Studies?', *European Journal of Cultural Studies* vol. 5 no. 2, May 2002.
10. John Corner, *The Art of the Record: A Critical Introduction to Documentary* (Manchester: Manchester University Press, 1996), pp. 27–9.
11. John Corner, 'Performing the Real: Documentary Diversions',*Television and New Media* vol. 3 no.3, August 2002, p. 257.
12. Richard Kilborn and John Izod, *An Introduction to Television Documentary: Confronting Reality* (Manchester: Manchester University Press, 1997).
13. Richard Kilborn, *Staging the Real: Factual TV Programming in the Age of Big Brother* (Manchester: Manchester University Press, 2003), pp. 55–7.
14. Jon Dovey, 'Simulating the Public Sphere', in Thomas Austin and Wilma de Jong (eds), *Rethinking Documentary: New Perspectives, New Practices* (Maidenhead, Berkshire: Open University Press, 2008).
15. Chronologies such as these are inevitably open to dissent. For alternative accounts of phases or waves of popular factual programming and definitions of Reality TV see, for example, Anita Biressi and Heather Nunn, *Reality TV: Realism and Revelation* (London: Wallflower Press, 2005); Corner, 'What Can We Say about Documentary?', p. 687; Kilborn, *Staging the Real*; Susan Murray and Laurie Ouellette (eds), *Re-making Television Culture* (New York: New York University Press, 2004), pp. 3–7. See Beth Montemurro, 'Toward a Sociology of Reality TV', *Sociology Compass* vol. 2 no. 1, December 2007, for a helpful mapping of the field of Reality TV research.
16. Kilborn, *Staging the Real*, p. 12.
17. Ibid., p. 123.

18. Bill Nichols, *Representing Reality: Issues and Concepts in Documentary* (Bloomington: Indiana University Press, 1991).

19. Dovey, 'Simulating the Public Sphere', pp. 254–5; see also Brian Winston, *Lies, Damn Lies and Documentaries* (London: BFI, 2000), pp. 9–39.

20. Winston, *Lies, Damn Lies and Documentaries*.

21. Corner, 'What Can We Say about Documentary?'; Corner, 'Performing the Real'.

22. Ibid., pp. 263–5.

23. Ibid.

24. John Corner, 'Afterword: Framing the New', in Holmes and Jermyn, *Understanding Reality TV*, p. 291.

25. Ibid.

26. Graeme Turner, *Ordinary People and the Media: The Demotic Turn* (London: Sage, 2010), p. 3.

27. Roger Silverstone, *Why Study the Media?* (London: Sage, 1999), p. 70.

28. Ibid., p. 71.

29. Biressi and Nunn, *Reality TV*, p. 2.

30. Danny Birchall, 'Online Documentary', in Austin and de Jong, *Rethinking Documentary*; Alex Juhasz, 'Documentary on YouTube: The Failure of Direct Cinema of the Slogan', in Austin and de Jong, *Rethinking Documentary*.

31. Corner, 'What Can We Say about Documentary?', p. 688.

32. Greer, 'Watch with Brother'.

33. Ibid.

34. Ibid.

35. Craig Hight, 'Debating Reality-TV', *Continuum: Journal of Media and Cultural Studies* vol. 15 no. 3, May 2001, p. 391.

36. Daniel Biltereyst, '*Big Brother* and its Moral Guardians: Reappraising the Role of Intellectuals in the Big Brother Panic', in Ernest Mathijs and Janet Jones (eds), *Big Brother International: Formats, Critics, Publics* (London: Wallflower, 2004), p. 14.

37. See Christopher Dunkley, 'It's Not New, and It's Not Clever', in Dolan Cummings (ed.), *Reality TV: How Real is Real?* (London: Hodder and Stoughton, 2002); Baris Kiliçbay and Mutlu Binark, 'Media Monkeys: Intertextuality, Fandom and *Big Brother* Turkey', in Mathijs and Jones, *Big Brother International*; Kilborn, *Staging the Real*, pp. 62–4.

38. Ib Bondebjerg, 'The Mediation of Everyday Life: Genre, Discourse and Spectacle in Reality TV', in Ann Jerslev (ed.), *Realism and Reality in Film and Media* (Copenhagen: Museum Tusculanum Press, 2002), p. 186.

39. Ibid.

40. Graham Barnfield, 'From Direct Cinema to Car-wreck Video: Reality TV and the Crisis of Content', in Cummings, *Reality TV*.

41. Bernard Clark, 'The Box of Tricks', in Cummings, *Reality TV*, p. 11.

42. Gay Hawkins, 'The Ethics of Television', *International Journal of Cultural Studies* vol. 4 no. 4, 2001.

43. The Office of Communications (Ofcom) is the independent regulator and competition authority for the UK communications industries.

44. In Peter Preston, 'Just Who is Bullying Whom Here?', *Observer*, 21 January 2007, Nexis UK Online Database.

45. Cummings, *Reality TV*, p. xi.

46. See, for example, June Deery, 'Reality TV as Advertisement', *Popular Communication* vol. 2 no. 1, November 2004; Chris Pullen, 'The Household, the Basement and *The Real World*: Gay Identity in the Constructed Reality Environment', in Holmes and Jermyn, *Understanding Reality TV*; Rebecca Stephens, 'Socially Soothing Stories? Gender, Race and Class in TLC's *A Wedding Story* and *A Baby Story*', in Holmes and Jermyn, *Understanding Reality TV*.

47. Cummings, *Reality TV*, p. 26. See also, for example, Su Holmes, '"All you've got to worry about is the task, having a cup of tea, and doing a bit of sunbathing": Approaching Celebrity in *Big Brother*', in Holmes and Jermyn, *Understanding Reality TV*; Su Holmes and Deborah Jermyn, '"Ask the fastidious woman from Surbiton to hand wash the underpants of the aging Oldham skinhead": Why Not *Wife Swap*?', in Austin and de Jong, *Rethinking Documentary*.

48. Cummings, *Reality TV*, pp. 69–70.

PART FIVE:
Documentary Disciplines

5.1 Anthropology: The Evolution of Ethnographic Film

PAUL HENLEY

All the paradigms established for the documentary film are grounded in the capacity of the camera to furnish evidence of reality. Documentary therefore offered a ready template for making vivid records, especially for a variety of sciences (natural and social). Anthropologists were among the first to exploit this possibility. It is no accident that Nanook of the North (1922), conventionally the film documentary's founding title, also has (as it might be) 'ethnographic value'. Attempts to put documentary at the service of anthropology march in lockstep with documentary itself and evolved equally various forms.

On 24 September 1894, a small group of Sioux performed two short dances before a kinetograph in Thomas Edison's celebrated Black Maria studio in East Orange, New Jersey. One was a 'ghost dance', lasting twenty-two seconds, the other a 'buffalo dance', lasting sixteen seconds. As this seems to have been the first time that moving-image technology was used to film subjects who were culturally exotic relative to the film-makers, these films are considered by some to represent the very first examples of 'ethnographic film'.

But this begs a series of questions about how one should define this genre of film-making. Although they were dressed 'in full war paint and war costumes' according to the Edison catalogues, the Sioux performers were far from home: they were members of Buffalo Bill Cody's Wild West Show, based in Brooklyn, New York, and the whole troupe was due to leave on a European tour the following month. There can be little doubt then that these films were made for promotional purposes. What is certain is that, given that they were of very brief duration and were performed on a cramped stage by no more than a handful of people, these filmed dances would have been very different from the ghost dances and buffalo dances performed back on the Sioux reservation in South Dakota. In fact, these films undoubtedly tell us much more about the entertainment industry in late nineteenth-century America than they do about traditional Sioux culture.[1]

Yet for some authors, particularly those of a post-colonial studies persuasion, *any* film from this early period of film history that deals with culturally exotic subject matter should be considered 'ethnographic'. Within this category, they would include not only the Sioux films and the many others that Edison company made about Native American performers over the coming years, but also the great surge of often racist travelogues that were produced in the early twentieth century by the likes of Martin and Osa Johnson, as well as fictional feature films that touched upon issues of exotic cultural difference such as F. W. Murnau's 1931 Polynesian love story, *Tabu*, and even Cooper and Schoedsack's 1933 tropical adventure fantasy, *King Kong*.[2]

For anthropologists, on the other hand, the term 'ethnography' has been defined, since at least the 1920s, not so much by reference to the cultural exoticism of its subject matter, but rather as a method of research. According to the origin myth, it was the Polish anthropologist, Bronislaw Malinowski, based then in Britain but stranded in Melanesia by World War I, who first developed a method based on what came to be known as 'participant observation'. This involved total immersion in the daily life of the subjects over a prolonged period, learning their language and studying that life from the inside. It depended not just on listening to what the subjects said, but also on closely observing the non-verbal and the performative aspects of their culture as well. It entailed making connections between different spheres of life: what have ideas about the family got to do with ideas about spirits, what have body postures and table manners got to do with ideas about gender, how do rules of inheritance impact on modes of subsistence? Malinowski worked in a culturally exotic location, but by the 1930s, these ethnographic methods were being used for research in US cities. Today, they are used to study elite Californian scientists working on the human genome project and middle management in the UK National Health Service.

'Ethnography', as it is used at the present time, should also be understood as a relative term since there is not a given degree or mode of participant observation at which point a research project suddenly qualifies as 'ethnographic'. In recognition of the fact that a given study can be more or less ethnographic according to the degree to which it conforms with the ideal model, the somewhat awkward but useful term 'ethnographicness' has come into circulation.[3] Moreover, today, it is not only anthropologists who do 'ethnography', nor only academic social scientists, but also, among others, town planners, advertising companies and market researchers – and, in varying degrees, documentary film-makers.

Each of these groups has a different take on what they consider to be 'ethnographic'. All ethnography, one could argue, should minimally involve some form of cultural analysis and a commitment to describing the world accurately as it is in everyday reality. But the profundity of that analysis and the complexity of the description, not to mention the intentions underlying both, may be very variable. So too might be the period or the depth of immersion in a community that is considered necessary for a study to qualify as 'ethnographic': anthropologists conventionally require a year of total immersion, but other practitioners of 'ethnography' may expect very much less both in time and depth of engagement.

By these relativistic modern criteria, one could argue that the ethnographicness of the early Lumière films to be considerably greater than that of *Ghost Dance*. Although they were not academic in intention, the Lumière films were based on acute observation of the non-verbal and the everyday, and they arose from extended participation in the lives of the subjects. Through these methods, the film-makers managed to communicate a substantial amount about the cultural manners of France in the 1890s. Given that the subjects were often members of the Lumière family or were the friends or employees of the film-makers, one might even consider these films to be early examples of what has come to be known as 'auto-ethnography'.

If 'ethnography' is a contentious term whose meaning has varied through time, so too, of course, is 'documentary'. However, at the risk of seeming insensitive to an extended and intricate debate, let us, for present purposes, define this famously disputed term as simply a genre of film-making that involves the manipulation, for narrative purposes, of a literal representation of the world while at the same time being based upon a claim to provide a representation of the world that remains faithful to its everyday social and physical realities.

Films that were both ethnographically complex and, at the same time, as sophisticated as documentary in the sense that I have defined these terms did not really begin to appear until after World War II. That they should first develop around then was due, at least in part, to the great improvement in the quality of sound recording over the 1950s, with the final achievement of synchronous-sound recording outside studio situations around 1960. Sound permitted both film-makers and subjects to provide a more elaborate social and cultural context for what was visible on the screen and in this way to enhance the sophistication of the ethnographic analysis that could be offered through a film. But in *la longue durée* prior to arrival of synchronous sound, between the emergence of moving-image technology in the 1890s and the first ethnographic documentaries fully worthy of the name in the course of the 1950s, there were many films that one could readily consider ethnographic, even if they lacked anything resembling a coherent documentary narrative. Equally, there were many examples within the burgeoning genre of documentary that involved a certain degree of ethnographicness, even if their profundity was variable.

ETHNOGRAPHIC FILM AS SCIENCE

As the first example of ethnographic film actually shot in the course of anthropological fieldwork, most sources point to the 4 minutes of material shot by Alfred Haddon, leader of a multi-disciplinary expedition from the University of Cambridge to the Torres Strait, a small archipelago lying between northern Queensland in Australia and what is today Papua New Guinea. This material was shot in September 1898 on the island of Mer, then known as Murray Island. It consists of a series of dances, with the exception of a brief sequence of three islanders making fire by spinning a stick between their palms into a block of wood, without success, sadly, before the roll of film ran out.[4]

As with most of the material shot by anthropologists during this early period of ethnographic film, the moving-image camera was employed by Haddon as a scientific instrument, gathering visual data for later analysis. He certainly had no ambition to create any documentary narratives. In line with the collecting rationale that underlay the general conception of anthropological fieldwork at the time, Haddon's intention rather was to collect images, both moving and still, much as one might collect material

Torres Strait (1898): the moving-image camera was employed by Haddon as a scientific instrument

objects for a museum. There was also a strong 'salvage' ideology associated with Haddon's film-making – that is, a concern to preserve a record of traditional customs before they disappeared. This powerful idea runs throughout the early period of ethnographic film and indeed continues to be associated with some approaches to ethnographic film-making to this day.

Yet even in this first use of the moving-image camera in the field for the purposes of academic ethnography, its limitations as a scientific data-collecting device become apparent. For not only had all the dances and the fire-making been performed expressly for the camera, thereby compromising the objectivity of the visual data gathered, but the most significant dance filmed by Haddon also had involved a considerable degree of artifice. This dance had once been performed as part of a large male initiation cer-emony, known as the Malo-Bomai after the ancestral spir-its that it invoked, in which all the men of the island had participated. But this ceremony had been abandoned and the masks associated with it destroyed following the arrival of Christian missionaries on the island some twenty-five years previously. So that Haddon might film the dance, three islanders made up some cardboard masks out of his packing cases and briefly recreated it by dancing in a small circle within the visual field of his camera.[5] In fact, although Haddon's intentions may have been entirely academic, it could be argued that the ethnographicness of his film of the Malo-Bomai dance was not so very much greater than that of the dances that the Sioux had performed in Edison's Black Maria exactly four years earlier.

Over the following decades, there were a number of similar attempts by anthropologists and others to use a camera as means of scientific data-collecting. In 1901, Baldwin Spencer, a biologist from Manchester who had taken a professorial chair in Melbourne some fifteen years beforehand, filmed a number of dances performed by Arrernte Aboriginal people in Central Australia. He did rather than better than Haddon, filming about forty min-utes in total, and even changed camera positions in the course of filming one of the dances. But the filmed ver-sions were still a pale shadow of the real events since, although they did not involve the revival of long-aban-doned customs, as Haddon's filming had done, the dances could not be filmed at night, which was when they were normally performed. So that there would be sufficient light, the dances had to be performed in the heat of the day with an inevitable impact on the liveliness and spon-taneity of the performance as well as on the number of people in attendance.[6]

Once he returned to Melbourne, Spencer used the material to give large public screenings of his film in order to raise money for his university department, a practice for which he is now roundly condemned by some authors and which certainly blurs the boundary between those making films for supposedly scientific purposes and those, such as Edison and the Lumières, who had unabashed commercial objectives. Today, a restriction has been placed on most of Spencer's material since it concerns secret-sacred cere-monies that the Arrernte consider should only be seen by initiated men. However, even the small part that is freely available remains fascinating: for example, entirely unbeknownst to Spencer, it turns out that in among the unrestricted material, there is a dance that was part of a then-active millenarian cult aimed at destroying the invading white cattle herders by ritual means.[7]

Another much fêted figure of the early period of eth-nographic film is Rudolf Pöch, an Austrian anthropologist who took a moving-image camera first to Papua New Guinea in 1904–06, then later to the German colony in what is now Namibia and, finally, to South Africa in 1907–09. During this latter expedition, Pöch made a sixty-nine-second film of a San 'bushman' speaking into the horn of a wax-cylinder phonograph. Many years later, probably in the 60s, aided no doubt by the fact that the man's mouth is partially obscured by the horn, the image and the recording were synchronised, thus making this the first synch-sound ethnographic film, albeit retrospectively.

But for all his celebrity on this account, Pöch is a very sinister figure in the history of ethnographic film since he held the most radical raciological views, believing that cul-ture was primarily determined by racial biology. Although there has been much comment on the synchronicity of Pöch's film of the San bushman, virtually no attention has been paid to the actual content of what the subject is saying. In fact, in the YouTube version of the film, a com-mentator's voice comes in just as he begins to speak, obscuring his words.[8] The man is speaking with a passion-ate intensity and gesturing extravagantly with his arms, seemingly outraged. In considering what he might be saying, it may well be relevant that the principal purpose of Pöch's expedition to southern Africa was to collect anthro-pological 'specimens', that is, skeletons of the San. In total, he gathered up 150 of these, mostly buying them from white farmers, though he was not above digging them up himself. It could also be relevant that Pöch arrived in Namibia just at the end of a three-year conflict in which it has been estimated that some 80 per cent of the indige-nous inhabitants had perished directly or indirectly as result of the actions of German colonial troops. Could it be to protest about these outrages that the San allowed him-self to be recorded? No doubt, Pöch would have felt that the scientific value of the material that he was collecting over-rode any concerns about how it was acquired. Later, during World War I, Pöch went into the prisoner-of-war camps and filmed Africans and members of Russian ethnic minorities who had been captured on the battlefield. After his rela-tively premature death in 1921, his ideas were warmly embraced by the Nazis.[9]

From the 1920s, as anthropology became less of a museum-based discipline, particularly in the English-speaking world, interest in visual images of all kinds declined, along with the collection of objects. However, there were still some anthropologists prepared to confront the costs and technical difficulties associated with making films. The most celebrated are surely Margaret Mead and Gregory Bateson, then husband and wife, who shot twenty-four hours of 16mm footage during the fieldwork that they carried out in Bali and New Guinea in 1936–39. But although this material was very much more extensive than anything that had ever been produced by anthropologists before, it was still not shot with the intention of developing a documentary film narrative. Rather, the moving-image camera was used by Bateson in alternation, for reasons of cost, with a still camera, and in conjunction with highly detailed written notes taken by Mead and a Balinese assistant, I Madé Kalér, in order to generate as comprehensive as possible a record of certain events that were of interest to them scientifically.[10]

These events were mainly related to parent–child interactions, though Bateson also filmed a traditional Balinese theatrical event that culminates dramatically with many of participants entering a state of trance and threatening to stab themselves with daggers. In making this film, Bateson was assisted by Jane Belo, an expatriate American artist who was living in Bali. Indeed, it was Belo who shot the culminating moments of the film when the dancers threaten to stab themselves – in slow motion, interestingly – since Bateson's magazine happened to have run out at that point.[11]

Many years later, in the early 1950s, by which time Mead and Bateson had gone their separate ways, both pro-fessionally and personally, Mead edited some of this material into a series of short films. These mostly deal with various situations in which parents and children are interacting, though probably the most screened film in the series is *Trance and Dance in Bali* (1952), which presents the material filmed by Bateson and Belo at the theatrical event. In all these films, the literal account of the world captured by the camera has certainly been manipulated for narrative purposes, particularly so in the case of *Trance and Dance*. This film not only combines two different events and presents them as if they were one but it also features a soundtrack of gamelan orchestra music arranged by Jane Belo's sometime husband, the modernist composer Colin McPhee, probably on the basis of some studio recordings made by two German record companies in the 20s.[12] But, taken as a whole, these films are primar-ily akin to illustrated lectures or moving-image slide shows, with Mead's voiceover commentary directing attention to what is happening on screen as empirical con-firmation of the argument that she is making verbally. In short, although they might be considered documentaries

Trance and Dance in Bali (1952): the literal account of the world captured by the camera has certainly been manipulated for narrative purposes

of a sort, the Mead–Bateson films are, at best, documen-taries after the fact.

DOCUMENTARY FILM AS ETHNOGRAPHY

Left to their own devices, then, what anthropologist film-makers primarily produced prior to the 1950s were what one might call 'documentation films' rather than docu-mentaries. The inspiration for applying documentary nar-ratives to ethnographic subject matter came from entirely outside academic anthropology. The figure of Robert Flaherty looms large here since he is often referred to as both the 'father of documentary' and the 'father of ethno-graphic film' on account of various early works that com-bined documentary techniques and ethnographic subject matter, beginning, of course, with *Nanook of the North*, the celebrated two-days-in-the-life story of an Inuit man and his family, released in 1922. But, contrary to the claims often made regarding Flaherty's inspired originality by his admirers, if not actually by Flaherty himself, there were a number of films that could be said to have preceded *Nanook* in combining a certain degree of ethnographicness with documentary narrative techniques.

A little-known example from outside the English-speaking world is *Rituaes e Festas Borôro* (1917). With a dura-tion of twenty minutes, this film concerns the famously elaborate funeral ceremony of the Bororo of the Mato Grosso, one of the most well known of Brazilian indigenous groups.[13] It was both shot and directed by Luiz Thomaz Reis, who was the official film-maker on a major pro-gramme to colonise the interior of the country that was rolled out over several decades of the early twentieth cen-tury. This programme was headed by a certain General Cândido Rondon, who was himself of part-Bororo descent, so the protection and valuation of indigenous Brazilian communities became an important element in this nation-building enterprise.

For the period, *Rituaes e Festas Borôro* is a highly accom-plished example of a documentary. The quality of both the cinematography and the editing is remarkable. The camera is invariably very well placed and the framing well chosen, allowing the dancers to move through the frame elegantly. There is a judicious mixture of wide and mid-shots, and very few jump cuts. The ceremonial events are given ethnographic context both by a preliminary sequence covering the preparations and a well-placed set of informative intertitles. After its release, the film was shown throughout Brazil and even in New York, and everywhere it was screened, it was received with acclaim.[14]

There is, however, a major problem with this film from an ethnographic point of view. In common with many indigenous peoples, the Bororo practise secondary burial: that is, immediately after death, the body is buried in the centre of the village plaza and the elaborate ceremonial dancing begins. After about a month, by which time the flesh will have decomposed, particularly when aided by regular dousing of the grave with water – as shown in the film – the body is exhumed and the skeleton is taken apart. The bones are then decorated with feathers and placed in a small basket before finally being immersed in a nearby lagoon.[15] Probably due to the propaganda purpose of the film, if not the express instructions of his patron General Rondon, Reis appears to have concluded that there was a limit to the degree of ethnographic accuracy that it was necessary to inflict upon his audiences. For, in cutting the film, he has placed the burial of the corpse right at the end, as if it followed the dancing, whereas in reality the sequence of events was the other way round. As for the challenging scenes of exhumation and secondary burial of the bones, these do not appear in the film at all.

A film that is more often identified as a possible predecessor to *Nanook* as an example of ethnographic documentary is *In the Land of the Head Hunters*, released in 1914.

Rituaes e Festas Borôro (1917): as for the challenging scenes of exhumation and secondary burial of the bones, these do not appear in the film at all

The producer and director was Edward S. Curtis, already famous for his romantic photographs of Native Americans in traditional costumes and poses, from which all evidence of their contemporary situation as subjugated peoples had been carefully excluded. *Head Hunters* represented an attempt, with explicitly commercial objectives, to employ the same methods in producing a moving-image film. At the time, fiction films on Native American themes, but with white actors playing the leading roles, were enjoying some commercial success in the nascent US film industry. Curtis hoped to tap into this market while at the same time aiming at a higher degree of cultural authenticity by using only Native American actors and by ensuring that the props were based on careful reconstructions of traditional forms of dress, technology and architectural styles.[16]

Head Hunters was shot on Vancouver Island, off the Pacific coast of Canada, among the people who were known for many years in the anthropological literature as the Kwakiutl, but who are now more commonly referred to as the Kwakwaka'wakw. Although the leading roles were played by actors from other indigenous groups or by people of mixed descent, most of the cast were Kwakwaka'wakw. However, notwithstanding Curtis's concerns about cultural authenticity, in order to ensure the commercial viability of the project, the narrative of the film was constructed around a melodramatic 'love-triangle' story, involving the young warrior Motana, the beautiful Naida, whom he sees in a dream while on a vision quest, and the Evil Sorcerer to whom Naida is engaged to be married.

This film contains some truly spectacular ceremonial performances. Perhaps the most impressive is when three great war canoes approach the camera and, on their prows, the three masked and costumed figures of the Wasp, the Thunderbird and the Grizzly Bear are seen dancing ecstatically, arms outstretched. Yet, despite the care lavished on these reconstructions and the melodramatic story-line, the film was a failure, certainly commercially and, more debatably, ethnographically as well. Although it received highly positive reviews when it first appeared, in cinemas across the USA it generally closed after a very short run. Meanwhile, among the many ethnographic criticisms that have been made of the film is that neither the vision quest, nor head-hunting, both of which underpin key plot points in the narrative, were of such central importance to the Kwakwaka'wakw as the film implies.

After its box-office failure, the film was lost for many years until it was reconstructed from fragments in the 1970s and rechristened *In the Land of the War Canoes*. However, this first reconstruction has subsequently been criticised for presenting the film as if it were some flawed attempt to make an ethnographic documentary rather than as Curtis originally intended it to be, namely, as a fictional 'motion-picture drama' aimed at popular audiences. A second reconstruction has now been produced which aims to present the film in this spirit, with the original melodramatic intertitles restored, colour tinting of the images and with a soundtrack based on the recently rediscovered musical score commissioned by Curtis from John Braham, an English musician best known for his work with the US branch of the D'Oyly Carte light opera company.[17]

It was out of this cinematic environment that *Nanook of the North* emerged. Flaherty knew Curtis and even sought his patronage to get funding for his own film-making ventures. There can be little doubt then that he would have been highly familiar with *Head Hunters*. Indeed, there are a number of parallels between the two films. Both involved the romantic reconstruction of an idealised version of a Native American past from which the present-day troubled circumstances arising from contact with non-Native people have been eliminated. For, as is well known, apart from the cute sequence in which the eponymous hero visits the trade-store of Revillon Frères, the French fur-traders who sponsored the film, *Nanook* does not refer to contact with the non-Native world: there are no references to the schools, the missions or the mining camps, let alone to the alcoholism and the prostitution associated with the latter, nor to the steel traps, shotguns and blankets, all of which were already rapidly transforming Inuit life.[18]

These absences clearly raise a question over the status of *Nanook* both as ethnography and as documentary. Much has also been made of the fact that Flaherty required his protagonists to become, in effect, actors, changing their names and their relationships, dressing in costumes that he himself supplied, performing scenes of going to bed and getting up in an open-sided igloo in the midst of winter, not using shotguns when hunting walrus, in itself a practice in which Nanook's particular group of Inuit had not engaged for a generation and so on. But from an anthropologist's point of view, perhaps the greatest weakness of *Nanook* considered as an ethnographic film, and one that also characterises Flaherty's writing about the Inuit, is the complete lack of interest in any social life beyond the nuclear family. Indeed there is hardly any reference at all, in either film or text, to this broader social world within which the family lives, let alone any attempt to establish the connectedness between the individual and the collective that is one of the hallmarks of the ethnographic method. For, contrary to what one might think from watching *Nanook* or reading *My Eskimo Friends* (1924), Inuit families do not live in complete isolation from any kind of social network but are in regular contact with one another, be it for collaborating on subsistence tasks, for intermarriage or for religious and ceremonial activities. This neglect of the broader social environment in favour of an exclusive emphasis on an individual family is also a feature of Flaherty's later films on what might be considered ethnographic subjects, such as *Moana* (1926), *Man of Aran* (1934) and *Louisiana Story* (1948).

In many ways, it could be argued that *Nanook* has more in common with the genre of early twentieth-century Native American historical romance films exemplified by *In the Land of the Head Hunters* than it has with what we now understand to be ethnographic documentary. But what is distinctive about *Nanook* in comparison with *Head Hunters*, and which may be considered Flaherty's particular achievement, is not only the sheer technical virtuosity of the camerawork, but, more importantly still, the nature of the narrative around which it is constructed. Rather than a melodrama of the kind that Curtis had employed, Flaherty came up with the idea of telling a story about an Inuit man and his family, and their daily struggle against the elements. 'What biography of any man', he asked rhetorically, 'could be more interesting?' Rather than being built on a series of fanciful dramatic events, as *Head Hunters* had been, Flaherty's narrative strategy consisted of following a series of everyday events structured according to an imaginary but naturalistic chronology. The audiences of *Nanook* knew that the film had come to an end and that they could therefore go home satisfied, not because the hero had won the maiden's hand and cut off the head of the Evil Sorcerer, but rather because he had settled down to sleep, snug within his igloo, while outside in the gathering gloom, his dogs endured the Arctic blasts.[19]

What is also very significant is that the narrative of *Nanook* was built upon an intimacy and engagement with the protagonists of a kind that is completely absent from *Head Hunters*. While Motana and Naida are no more than shallow archetypes, Nanook and his family, despite the absence of synch sound, are sympathetic flesh-and-blood characters, with whom the audience can readily identify despite the cultural difference. Yet this was not some lucky accident: rather it was a direct consequence of Flaherty's film-making methods. These revolved around a commitment – despite the technical challenges that this entailed in a small cabin on the shores of Hudson Bay in the midst of winter – to screening back the rushes to his protagonists as the film-making proceeded and, equally importantly, to seeking their advice about how it should continue thereafter. By this means, the protagonists came to understand what Flaherty was trying to do, with the result that they became no longer mere subjects, but rather his accomplices. Indeed, so great was their identification with the project that they literally risked their lives in order that Flaherty could get the sequences that he wanted. Nor was this the only time, since the same would happen later when Flaherty came to film *Man of Aran* on an island of the west coast of Ireland in the early 1930s.

The status of *Nanook*, and indeed all of Flaherty's later films, be it as ethnography or as documentary is certainly highly contestable by present-day criteria. But Flaherty's participatory film-making methodology, deployed in combination with a narrative based upon the experiences of a sympathetic group of central characters and structured according to an artificial but naturalistic chronology, has had a profound impact upon future generations of ethnographic film-makers. For Jean Rouch, the French anthropologist who is surely the best known of all ethnographic film-makers, Flaherty was 'without doubt the most gifted and most modest of film-makers … an ethnographer without knowing it'. Writing in 1975, Rouch declared that, through his working methods, Flaherty 'did not know that, with absurdly inadequate means, he had just invented both "participant observation" … and "feedback" with which we are still so clumsily experimenting'.[20]

THE EMERGENCE OF ETHNOGRAPHIC DOCUMENTARY

It was only in the 1950s that anthropologists themselves began to use the documentary methods pioneered by Flaherty and others. Yet, notwithstanding the enthusiastic endorsement of these methods by Jean Rouch, the tension inherent in Flaherty's approach between, on the one hand, the rhetorical claim to show the world as it really is and, on the other, authorial manipulations for narrative purposes, has continued to haunt the practice of those who have subsequently attempted to present ethnographic subject matter through the language of documentary film.

Even Jean Rouch himself never fully reconciled himself to the demands of what he once called 'that devil, editing'. Over the course of the 50s, he cut his ethnographic films shot in West Africa with some of the leading French editors of the day, including Renée Lichtig (later to work with Jean Renoir), who cut *Bataille sur le grand fleuve* (1951), a film about traditional hippopotamus-hunting on the Niger river; Suzanne Baron (who worked with Jacques Tati and Louis Malle), who cut *Les Maîtres fous* (1955), Rouch's celebrated film about spirit possession among migrant workers to colonial Accra in what was then the Gold Coast (and now is Ghana); and Marie-Josèphe Yoyotte (later to work with François Truffaut), who cut *Moi, un noir* (1958), about the life of a migrant labourer in Abidjan on the Ivory Coast, a semi-fictionalised film that was awarded the Prix Louis-Delluc, the French equivalent of an Oscar.[21] Through these exemplary practitioners, Rouch discovered, despite his initial scepticism, that his films could be greatly improved through skilful editing. So much so that in his manifesto-essay, 'The Camera and Man', first published in the mid-1970s, he declared that the participation of an editor was essential to the success of any ethnographic film.[22]

And yet, at the same time, it was only with great reluctance that Rouch would accept the excision of any his rushes. The dialogue between editor and director was often, he conceded, 'harsh and difficult', while the cuts that he was required to make in editing *Chronique d'un été* [*Chronicle of a Summer*] (1961), he compared to the 'amputation of a limb'.[23] Inspired in part by his youthful engagement with Surrealism and its emphasis on the importance of spontaneity, Rouch's response to the challenges posed by editing was to advocate what was in effect the removal of editing from the edit suite to the location. Here, he recommended that the film-maker, working in complicity with the subjects, should aim to deliver an inspired performance, editing in the camera.[24]

Over the 1960s, as 16mm technology developed and synchronous sound became more established, one can detect a certain bifurcation in Rouch's works, but, in both cases, the role of editing in the edit suite became increasingly subsidiary to editing in the camera. On the one hand, Rouch made a series of conventional ethnographic documentaries based on 'sequence-shots', whereby a whole sequence or even a whole film would be covered in a single unbroken take lasting, ideally, for the full eleven-minute duration of a 16mm magazine. The subject matter of these films was most commonly traditional religious ceremonies, particularly those involving spirit possession, though the most elaborate examples from this period are the series of films that he made between 1966 and 1974 among the Dogon of eastern Mali. These mostly concerned the Sigui, a world-renewal ceremony held each year over the course of seven years, but only at sixty-year intervals, the period which, in the Dogon view, corresponds to the interlude between successive human generations.[25]

Over the same period, Rouch also made a series of semi-fictionalised films in the manner of *Moi, un noir* – that is, featuring a small group of collaborators, sometimes African, at other times Parisian, who, working without a script, would improvise scenes from their lives while he would seek to cover these improvisations with sequence shots. Typical of this manner of working was *Petit à Petit* (1971), a film featuring a group of his closest West African collaborators, whom he had first followed in the 1950s on their migration from their homes on the edge Sahara to the cities of the Gold Coast. This earlier work had resulted in *Jaguar*, one of Rouch's most accomplished films, though one that was not released until 1967, for budgetary reasons. *Petit à Petit* represented a reprise of *Jaguar*, though this time the protagonists are shown engaged in an expedition of 'reverse anthropology' to Paris, the citadel of their former colonial masters.[26]

Meanwhile, Rouch's ethnographic film-making contemporaries in the English-speaking world were also seeking to reconcile objective documentation with the requirements of documentary authorship. A leading figure of this period was John Marshall, who, in the early 1950s, as a late teenager, went on an ethnographic expedition to study the Ju/'hoansi bushmen in southern Africa. The expedition was led and largely funded by his father, Laurence, a retired electronics engineer, whose ideas about ethnographic film-making had been influenced by

Margaret Mead, whom he happened to know. Laurence gave his son a simple Kodak camera with a clockwork mechanism and told him to produce 'a record, not a movie'.[27]

Having taught himself how to use the camera from the instruction booklet, John went about shooting a series of documentation films about hunting. But he then joined these together to produce *The Hunters* (1957), a classic 'movie' in the Flaherty mould (though John always insisted that he had never seen any of Flaherty's works prior to this point). This film follows four Ju/'hoansi hunters as they track a female giraffe for five days across the salt pans of the Kalahari Desert before they finally dispatch her with their seemingly puny poison-tipped spears and then return home to tell their story.

The Hunters soon became one of the most celebrated ethnographic films in the English-speaking world. But, gradually, various details emerged about just how constructed it had been. It transpired that the hunt shown in the film as a single event had actually been made up of a number of different hunts, involving several unidentified hunters in addition to the four principals. Instead of tramping through the scorching desert for five days, in reality the hunters had travelled around in Marshall's Jeep. Although the principal giraffe had indeed been finished off by the hunters with their spears, it had already been wounded by a rifle shot some time beforehand, and it was this wounding that had slowed her up and had allowed the hunters to catch her.[28] Within a paradigm in which an ethnographic film was supposed to provide an objective record, this degree of manipulation was regarded by many as a source of scandal. But any experienced documentary film-maker would have been able to surmise most of the constructions simply by looking at the film. They would certainly not have been either surprised or offended, since such strategies are commonplace among documentarists, even to this day.

Nevertheless, in making *The Hunters*, John had clearly strayed a long way from his father's injunction to make a 'record, not a movie'. As if in expiation, he then went on to make a number of shorter films that conformed more closely to the original brief. In doing so, he employed a method that allowed him to give a narrative shape to his films while at the same time remaining close to the actual chronology of the events filmed. He developed this method in conjunction with Timothy Asch, who was then working as as his editorial assistant though he would later go on to become a leading ethnographic film-maker in his own right. Marshall and Asch used various terms to describe this way of working, but here I shall refer to it as the 'event-sequence' method.

The principles underlying the method were very simple. It was presumed that on the basis of prior ethnographic knowledge, the film-maker would be able to

The Hunters (1957): John had clearly strayed a long way from his father's injunction to make a 'record, not a movie'

identify significant events with a clear beginning and a clear end. Given that such an event would also necessarily have a 'middle', a film that followed it chronologically would automatically have a 'beginning-middle-end' structure without recourse to any further manipulations. Over the 1960s, with Asch's assistance, Marshall cut a number of short event-sequence films about the Ju/'hoansi. Since he was by now shooting with some degree of synchronous sound, these films proved that even the simplest event, such as a few minutes of innuendo-laden banter between a young woman and her great-uncle – a so-called 'joking relationship' in southern Africa – could be deeply infused with both drama and ethnographic meaning. This method did not entail making an entirely literal copy of an event since it did allow cuts to eliminate redundancy and irrelevance. But otherwise it represented an attempt to have the best of both worlds, offering a way of making films with the structured narrative characteristic of a 'movie' while simultaneously providing a minimally authored 'record'.

Later, Asch would further develop the method while making over forty films among the Yanomami of southern Venezuela in the period 1968–71, in collaboration with the anthropologist Napoleon Chagnon. Most of these films lasted only a few minutes and also showed simple single-cell events such as a senior man telling a myth or children playing in the rain. But Asch then applied the method to more complex events covered in a series of chronologically consecutive sequences. A well-known example is *The Feast* (1970), which concerns the celebration of an alliance between two villages that had recently been at war. This begins with a lengthy series of stills over which the social context of the event is explained in narration before it is then allowed to play itself out in full without further comment.

But as the 1970s progressed, Asch became increasingly troubled by the limitations of the event-sequence method. This was exemplified particularly in *The Ax Fight* (1975), which concerns a dispute between some Yanomami villagers and visitors who had overstayed their welcome. After an initial skirmishing between a few men armed with clubs, a more general scuffle ensues, culminating in one man being felled by a blow from the blunt side of an axe-head. But, after a few moments, the victim gets up, staggers groggily away and the crowd disperses. In the by-then standard pattern of event-sequence films, there is a montage of shots summarising this central event, accompanied by explanatory narration. This is then followed by an edited version of the event, with subtitles, but without commentary.

But what makes *Ax Fight* distinctive is that these two sequences are *preceded* by the original rushes. This enables one to identify what has been excluded from the other two versions of the event presented in the film. One discovers, for example, that various shots revealing the presence of Chagnon and the sound recordist have been eliminated and the chronology has been manipulated, albeit modestly. The latter mainly consists of moving two shots from the end of the rushes to a point near the beginning so as to cover certain camerawork deficiencies. As these two shots feature women shouting insults across the village plaza, this has the effect of giving greater emphasis to the role of women in the dispute.[29]

There is a tendency in the visual anthropology literature to hail *The Ax Fight* as some kind of masterwork. But it is arguably more significant as a landmark example of a particular methodological strategy than as an ethnographic film in itself. By the simple device of allowing one to compare the original footage with the two edited versions, it reveals the processes of authorship involved in its construction. Significantly, however, these authorial processes are not revealed in their entirety. It is only from the CD-rom released many years later that we discover that although the duration of the rushes presented in the film is eleven minutes, the event actually took place over a period of about thirty minutes.[30] One might ask, therefore, what authorial decisions resulted in most of the event *not* being filmed. It also seems very likely that that the reason why the guests had overstayed their welcome, thereby giving rise to the dispute in the first place, was that they were hoping to get a share of the trade goods that Chagnon and Asch had brought with them.

Yet these evidences of authorial influence on the event would only be disturbing to those still holding on to the illusion that an ethnographic film could deliver some entirely objective account of the world. Some years later, Asch would comment that, as he was cutting this film, he had the feeling that the whole field of ethnographic film was beginning to fall apart before his eyes.[31] We should perhaps allow him a little poetic licence here, since there were other ethnographic film-makers at that time who had already abandoned any hope that film could rescue anthropologists from the subjectivity of their fieldnotes, as one astute contemporary commentator put it.[32] But, by revealing its own internal contradictions, what *The Ax Fight* did do was signal the end of the road for the event-sequence method and, with it, an end to the whole tradition of event-based documentation film-making that stemmed not just from Margaret Mead, but from Haddon and Spencer in the earliest days of ethnographic film-making.

THE LEGACY OF ETHNOGRAPHIC DOCUMENTARY

Since 1975, ethnographic film-making has diversified greatly. As it has spread across the world, particularly in Eastern Europe, China, Japan and Latin America, many different traditions of ethnography have combined with a similar diversity of documentary film-making traditions. In the West, the character-based, stylistically realist approach known as Observational Cinema, which first arose from a collaboration between anthropologists and film-makers at the University of California at Los Angeles (UCLA) in the 1960s, has been particularly influential.[33]

During this period, there have also been significant changes in both methodology and technology, though the issues posed by authorship have not gone away. In the 80s, there was a reaction against the supposedly 'objectifying' gaze' of earlier periods when the film-makers mostly came from powerful imperial metropoli while the subjects were 'subaltern' Others in the global South. Ethnographic films became more 'participatory' in the sense that the subjects played a much greater part in their realisation. In some cases, they took over the technology completely and effectively became the authors of their own films.[34] In the 1990s, the arrival of the web was seen by some as an opportunity to allow the viewer-reader to become the author, the role of the film-maker being merely to put their material up on the web, along with any relevant textual materials, so that the viewer-reader, as an audience of one, could navigate at will across these materials, using the links between them offered by the film-maker but unconstrained by any authorial narrative devices.[35]

In the last decade, as film-making has become technically easier and cheaper than ever before, the number of ethnographic film festivals and training courses has multiplied. Within this profusion of activity, there are no clearly dominant paradigms, though there is a tendency for the films that win prizes at international festivals to owe something to the Observational Cinema approach. Also, despite the increased activity, and the strong demand from students, ethnographic film-making remains something of a specialist interest within academia, even though it has achieved much greater acceptance than it enjoyed in earlier periods.

NOTES

1. Charles Musser, Film notes. Text published as accompaniment to *Edison: The Invention of the Movies*, a four-disc DVD set from the collections of the Museum of Modern Art and the Library of Congress. Curated by Steven Higgins. Kino International Corporation.

2. See, for example, Fatimah Tobing Rony, *The Third Eye: Race, Cinema and Ethnographic Spectacle* (Durham, NC: Duke University Press, 1996); Alison Griffiths, *Wondrous Difference: Cinema, Anthropology and Turn-of-the-century Culture* (New York: Columbia University Press, 2002).

3. The first to use the term 'ethnographicness' was probably Karl Heider in his influential early book *Ethnographic Film* (Austin: University of Texas Press, 1975), though his criteria for determining this quality were somewhat different to those proposed here.

4. See Chris Long and Pat Laughren, 'Australia's First Films: Facts and Fables. Part Six: Surprising Survivals from Colonial Queensland', *Cinema Papers* no. 96, pp. 32–6.

5. Alfred C. Haddon, *Head-hunters: Black, White and Brown* (London: Methuen, 1901), p. 47; Anita Herle, 'The Life-histories of Objects: Collections of the Cambridge Expedition to the Torres Straits', in Anita Herle and Sandra Rouse (eds), *Cambridge and the Torres Strait: Centenary Essays on the 1898 Anthropological Expedition* (Cambridge: Cambridge University Press, 1998), pp. 87–96.

6. Baldwin Spencer, *Wanderings in Wild Australia* (London: Macmillan, 1928), pp. 230–8.

7. Tony Swain, *A Place for Strangers: Towards a History of Australian Aboriginal Being* (Cambridge: Cambridge University Press, 1993), pp. 224–33.

8. See http://www.dailymotion.com/video/x1hr8x_rudolf-poch-audio-phonograph-1908_shortfilms. Accessed 5 August 2012.

9. Alan G. Morris, 'The Reflections of the Collector: San and Khoi Skeletons in Museum Collections', *South African Archaeology Bulletin* vol. 42 no. 1, pp. 15–16; Margit Berner, 'From "Prisoners of War" to Proof of Paternity: Racial Anthropologists and the Meaning of "Others" in Austria', in Marius Turda and Paul Weindling (eds), *Blood and Homeland': Eugenics and Racial Nationalism in Central and Southeast Europe 1900–1940* (Budapest: Central European University Press, 2006).

10. See Paul Henley, 'From Documentation to Representation: Recovering the Films of Margaret Mead and Gregory Bateson', *Visual Anthropology* vol. 26 no. 2, 2013, pp. 1–34.

11. Fatimah Tobing Rony, 'The Photogenic Cannot be Tamed: Margaret Mead and Gregory Bateson's *Trance and Dance in Bali*', *Discourse* vol. 28 no. 1, Winter 2006, p. 26, n. 47.

12. Colin McPhee, *A House in Bali* (London: Victor Gollancz, 1947), pp. 71–2.

13. Largely on account of the visit made to them by Claude Lévi-Strauss in the 1930s. See Claude Lévi-Strauss, *Tristes Tropiques* (Harmondsworth: Penguin, 1992), pp. 259–320.

14. See Fernando De Tacca, 'Rituaes e festas Bororo'. A construção da imagem do índio como 'selvagem' na Comissão Rondon', *Revista de Antropologia* vol. 45 no. 1, 2002. See http://www.scielo.br/scielo.php?script=sci_arttext&pid=S0034-77012002000100006

15. See Sylvia Caiuby Novaes, 'Bororo Funerals: Images of the Refacement of the World', *Tipití, Journal of the Society for the Anthropology of Lowland South America* vol. 4 no. 1–2, 2006, pp. 177–98.

16. The discussion of this film draws on a number of sources, including Edward S. Curtis, *In the Land of the Head Hunters: Indian Life and Lore Series* (Yonker, NY: World Book Company, 1915 [1992]); Bill Holm and Quimby George Irving, *Edward S. Curtis in the Land of the War Canoes: A Pioneer Cinematographer in the Pacific Northwest* (Seattle: University of Washington Press, 1980); Brian Winston, 'Before Flaherty, Before Grierson: The Documentary Film in 1914', *Sight & Sound* vol. 57 no. 4, 1988, pp. 277–9; Rony, *The Third Eye*, pp. 90–8; Catherine Russell, *Experimental Ethnography: The Work of Film in the Age of Video* (Durham, NC: Duke University Press, 1999), pp. 98–115; and Griffiths, *Wondrous Difference*, pp. 238–51.

17. See the website prepared in connection with this newly restored version by Aaron Glass, Brad Evans and Andrea Sanborn at http://www.curtisfilm.rutgers.edu/. See also Brad Evans, 'Catherine Russell's Recovery of the *Head-Hunters*', *Visual Anthropology* vol. 11 no. 3, pp. 221–41; Pauline Wakeham, 'Becoming Documentary: Edward Curtis's *In the Land of the Headhunters* and the Politics of Archival Reconstruction', *Canadian Review of American Studies* vol. 36 no. 3, 2006, pp. 293–309.

18. This discussion of *Nanook* draws on various sources, including Paul Rotha with Basil Wright, 'Nanook and the North', *Studies in Visual Communication* vol. 6 no. 2, 1980, pp. 33–60; Brian Winston, 'The White Man's Burden: The Rxample of Robert Flaherty', *Sight & Sound* vol. 54 no. 1, Winter 1984–85, pp. 58–60; Jay Ruby, *Picturing Culture: Explorations in Film and Anthropology* (Chicago: University of Chicago Press, 2000), pp. 67–93; and Alan Marcus, 'Nanook of the North as Primal Drama', *Visual Anthropology* vol. 19 no. 3–4, May–September 2006, pp. 201–21.

19. This passage concerning the 'chronologic' of the narrative of *Nanook* is strongly influenced by the arguments of Winston (particularly *Claiming the Real: The Documentary Film Revisited* [London: BFI, 1995], pp. 99–102).

20. See Jean Rouch, 'Le film ethnographique', in Jean Poirier (ed.), *Encyclopédie de la Pléiade: Ethnologie générale* (Paris: Gallimard, 1968), pp. 447–55; Rouch, 'The Camera and Man', in Paul Hockings (ed.), *Principles of Visual Anthropology* (Berlin and New York: Mouton de Gruyter, 1995 [1975]), p. 82.

21. Paul Henley, *The Adventure of the Real: Jean Rouch and the Craft of Ethnographic Cinema* (Chicago: University of Chicago Press, 2009), pp. 61–2, 82–91, 101–34.

22. Rouch, 'The Camera and Man'; Henley, *The Adventure of the Real*, pp. 278–309.

23. Edgar Morin, 'Chronicle of a Film', in Steven Feld (ed. and trans.), *Ciné-Ethnography* (Minneapolis and London: University of Minnesota Press, 2003), p. 264, n. 16.

24. Henley, *The Adventure of the Real*, pp. 255–7.

25. See ibid., pp. 218–34.

26. See ibid., pp. 70–81, 210–17.

27. John Marshall, 'Filming and Learning', in Jay Ruby (ed.), *The Cinema of John Marshall* (Amsterdam: Harwood Academic, 1993), p. 19.

28. Ibid., pp. 36–7.

29. Bill Nichols, 'What Really Aappened: A Reassessment of *The Ax Fight*', in E. D. Lewis (ed.), *Timothy Asch and Ethnographic Film* (London and New York: Routledge, 2004), pp. 231–2. Nichols suggests that this narrative reordering 'flirts' with the ethnocentric suggestion that women are the cause of all trouble; but see also Patsy Asch and Linda Connor, 'Subjects, Images, Voices: Representations of Gender in the Films of Timothy Asch', in Lewis, *Timothy Asch and Ethnographic Film*, pp. 176–7). They argue that, more generally, the film neglects the role of women in provoking the dispute.

30. Peter Biella, Napoleon A. Chagnon and Gary Seaman (eds), *Yanomamö Interactive: The Ax Fight*. CD-rom, Case Studies in Cultural Anthropology Multimedia Series (Fort Worth, TX: Harcourt Brace College, 1997).

31. Quoted in Jay Ruby, 'Out of Synch: The Cinema of Tim Asch', *Visual Anthropology Review* vol. 11 no. 1, 1995, p. 28.

32. Colin Young, 'Observational Cinema', in Hockings, *Principles of Visual Anthropology*, p.100. Young, the original theorist of Observational Cinema, was influenced by (and deeply involved with) the Direct Cinema pioneers.

33. Anna Grimshaw and Amanda Ravetz, *Observational Cinema: Anthropology, Film and the Exploration of Social Life* (Bloomington: Indiana University Press, 2009).

34. See Faye Ginsburg, 'Native Intelligence: A Short History of Debates on Indigenous Media and Ethnographic Film' in Marcus Banks and Jay Ruby (eds), *Made to be Seen: Perspectives on the History of Visual Anthropology* (Chicago: University of Chicago Press, 2011).

35. See Sarah Pink, 'Digital Visual Anthropology: Potentials and Challenges', in Banks and Ruby, *Made to be Seen*.

5.2 Science, Society and Documentary

TIM BOON

Because the camera's 'record' function is distinct from documentary's narrative imperative, the one does not necessitate the other. However, the usefulness of cinematography to science has not simply been limited to making records of experiments and other data, although the limitations of its evidentiary capacity have, as with social sciences such as anthropology, undercut its viability as a technique of scientific record.

Science documentaries have never been an independent genre. But subjects which contemporaries have defined as 'scientific' – science, nature, technology and medicine – have been key concerns of non-fiction film-making since its earliest days, and they persist in the schedules of television documentary today.[1] It is generally recognised that the origins of cinema lie partially in the new experimental scientific tradition of the nineteenth century, especially in the work of French physiologist Etienne-Jules Marey. Then, after the Lumière brothers' first showings, the kinematograph continued to be employed in scientific visualisation. But this instrumental use of the cameras is not the subject of this chapter, which is concerned with films – and latterly programmes – made to be shown to general audiences.[2] In

exploring this subject, the core questions relate to how scientists and film-makers or television producers have perceived the benefits of representing science to the public in the past. The evidence shows that different genres of scientific film-making embody not just different representations of science, but also different relationships between scientists and film-makers.

To simplify, we may speak of four major categories of scientific documentary film and television programme. Nature films, initially with a direct observational approach, were first shown in public in 1903. Technology also became the subject of similar films in the Edwardian period, taking on a specifically modernist tenor from the 30s. That decade also saw the emergence of documentaries that advanced arguments about the social role of science. Television science absorbed some of these older genres, but also, in the context of the Cold War, developed new genres more concerned with the culture and method of science than with its social role. Each of these genres also marks a different relationship between scientists and film or television producers. Furthermore, although each of these broad genres was the product of specific social, cinematic and scientific circumstances, once established, they became the rubric for later films and programmes. Sometimes the fate of these genres – such as those on the social role of science – was to fluctuate in popularity. Other genres, notably the nature films, have never ceased to be popular.

NATURAL HISTORY FILM-MAKING

The first scientific films made for lay consumption were shown to the public at the Alhambra Music Hall, Leicester Square, in August 1903. Attendees saw, in the midst of novelty acts including Servais Le Roy and his famous illusion 'Asrah, the Floating Princess', a programme of new kinematograph films introduced by their author, Francis Martin Duncan, produced using a device with the imposing Edwardian title the 'Urban-Duncan Micro-Bioscope'. The novelty of the one-minute film *Cheese Mites*, which was the sensation of the programme, was in attaching a kinematograph camera to a microscope and thus producing giant moving pictures of microscopic creatures. This was typical

L'Hippocampe (1934): the kinematograph continued to be employed in scientific visualisation

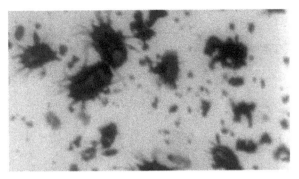

Cheese Mites (1903): the sensation of the programme ... giant moving pictures of microscopic creatures

of late nineteenth- and early twentieth-century popular entertainments, which featured sensational performances, playing to what Tom Gunning has called the 'aesthetic of astonishment'. The programme, masterminded by the entrepreneur Charles Urban, included three other microcinematographic studies, some moralising animal films, such as *The Greedy American Toad*, and a suite of bee films made by C. T. Overton of Crawley.[3] We may generalise about the origins of nature film-making, which became established as a fixture in the cinema of the inter-war period, by looking at Duncan together with Percy Smith, the doyen of the popular 1920s and 30s series, *Secrets of Nature*. Duncan, before he worked for Urban, was an amateur naturalist, who had also developed substantial skill in taking microscopical photographs. He published 'how to' manuals and also in magazines such as *Amateur Photographer*, explaining, for example, how to build the apparatus to photograph worms. Smith, initially working as a clerk at the Board of Education, devoted his spare time to amateur natural history, with a detailed knowledge of the genera and species of British spiders and a collection to match. But he was also a member of that other amateur tradition, the garden-shed inventor, improvising apparatus to make his beautiful films from domestic items such as clocks and Meccano. From 1925 he joined other nature film-makers, including Oliver Pike and Charles Head, making *Secrets of Nature* for Bruce Woolfe's company, Gaumont-British Instructional.[4] Smith produced both microcinematographic studies of plants and micro-organisms, for example *Magic Myxies* (on slime mould, 1931), and observational wildlife films such as *Romance in a Pond* (on newts, 1932).

For Duncan and Smith the amateur naturalists, making kinematograph films was not the popularisation of science, but the doing of amateur science in a new medium, enabled by the commercial nous of the businessmen Charles Urban and Bruce Woolfe. Amateur activity had a long and honourable history in the natural historical sciences, dating back to the period when the

term 'amateur', following its etymology, denoted someone who loved what they did, a connoisseur rather than a hobbyist. But at this point at the turn of the twentieth century, such amateur science was beginning to be elbowed out by a more laboratory-based professionalised experimental form of biology. Duncan's and Smith's allegiance is signalled by their membership of the Quekett Microscopical Club which, from its foundation in 1865, was established with the aim of 'affording to microscopists ... opportunities for meeting and exchanging ideas without that diffidence and constraint which an amateur naturally feels when discussing scientific subjects in the presence of professional men'.[5]

These nature films, then, were no popularisation of elite science because there was no pure professional science that was being rendered more popular here, but real lay science, already partially in the public sphere. They were amateur natural history films with a mode of address that sought a larger audience of potential amateur naturalists. The film *World in a Wine Glass* (1931), for example, suggests that the viewers could repeat the experiment using their own microscopes. The independence of these films from professional science is also indicated by the use of comic effects and anthropomorphic and moralising tendencies, which had been found in the earliest animal films, but which became a prominent feature of the mature 1930s versions.

Nature and wildlife films have continued to be an important staple of non-fiction film and television. From 1952 to 1961, Countryman Films produced several dozen films for showing in cinemas in the series *The World of Life: A Journal of the Outdoors*, covering a range of animal and zoo-based stories. Oxford Scientific Films, established in 1968 by the entomologist Gerald Thompson, has probably been the most significant non-BBC centre for natural history film-making. Many of Thompson's films were shown on the BBC series *Look*, which ran for over a decade from 1955. This series may be seen as a transitional form of screen-based natural history, specialising as it initially did in presenting wildlife footage and its amateur film-makers in discussion with the presenter, the ornithologist Peter Scott. It later became more thematic, treating subjects such as extinction, and including live animals in the studio. David Attenborough, the figure who has dominated television natural history, first appeared on screens in *Zoo Quest*, a programme that, between 1955 and 1961, presented stories on the collecting of animals for London Zoo, with Attenborough on location in the habitats of the target species. With the foundation in 1957 of the BBC's Natural History Unit at Bristol, formalising an existing specialism there, the popularity of films on plants and animals was institutionally recognised. As Gail Davies and Jean-Baptiste Gouyon have both argued, the unit at Bristol not only represented but, in its programme-making, also claimed to do

The Private Life of Plants (1995): technological revelation of living nature

scientific work in natural history. Guoyon calls the proponents of this kind of programming 'telenaturalists'.[6] Nature television, like the earlier films of Francis Martin Duncan and Percy Smith, subsists on the technological revelation of living nature. This is as true of Attenborough's *Life on Earth* (1979) or *The Private Life of Plants* (1995), as it is with *Battle of the Plants* (1926) from the *Secrets of Nature* series. In a sense, even the claim to the Bristol unit's film-making *being* as well as *representing* science is of a piece with how Percy Smith and his collaborators represented their films, in the books *Secrets of Nature* (1934) and *Cinebiology* (1941).[7]

TECHNOLOGY DOCUMENTARIES

Marshall Berman suggests in *All that is Solid Melts into Air* (1988) that, confronted with modernity in all its bureaucratic and technological facets, citizens have the choice to reject or to embrace it. We can see that Percy Smith was inclined to turn away from modernity; as he stated,

> the world now sacrifices everything to speed; quiet seems to be regarded as a detestable condition to be expurgated by any means which applied science can devise; and this state of affairs does not encourage the production of the type of individual who can satisfy himself in an investigation of the hidden beauties of Nature.[8]

In technology documentaries, by contrast, we find gleeful modernists at work. Early film-makers' cameras were not only aimed at nature; they were very soon turned on the human world, including technology, with films such as Urban's *The Motor Climbing Contest at Crystal Palace* (1904), which simply shows people driving cars up flights of steps. These were films with the same kind of amused eye on the wondrous that we saw with *Cheese Mites*. In the fifteen years before Grierson annexed the term 'documentary',

there were significant numbers of these films, some of which, including Pathé's *Imperial Airway* (1924), contained significant detail. But, starting in the early 1930s, in the context of British documentary, these celebrations of technology took on a decisively modernist aesthetic.

It's an often-told story how, in the 30s, British documentary started within government departments at the British Empire Marketing Board and developed at the General Post Office. Less often noted is how this provided the institutional and ideological base for new representations of science, technology and medicine. British documentaries, I argue, should be seen as modernist celebrations of modernity, and especially of technological modernity. The subjects of the films were often those modernistic touchstones – electricity, telecommunications, air travel, express trains and ocean liners – which might otherwise be found, for example, in Corbusier's *Towards an Architecture*. It may well be that the sponsors called the tunes on the subjects of many of these films, but that fact merely reinforces the centrality of these themes to the period, and the typicality of the film-makers as members of their society and culture.

The treatment of these subjects in the documentarists' films also followed the aesthetic prescriptions of the modernist masters of Soviet cinema, Eisenstein and Pudovkin. The use of composed camera angles and shot-framing, movement within frames and, especially, editing learned from Soviet examples, all contributed to the effect. In films including Stuart Legg's *The Coming of the Dial* (1933), Paul Rotha's *Face of Britain* (1935) and Cavalcanti's J. B. Priestley vehicle, *We Live in Two Worlds* (1937), technology and applied science are hymned as the route to a more rational world. But, it should be noted, the scientists shown in films such as *The Coming of the Dial* are not named laboratory scientists, but Weberian creatures of the

The Coming of the Dial (1933): celebrations of technology took on a decisively modernist aesthetic

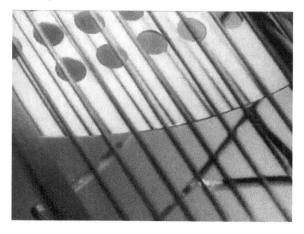

early twentieth century, technologists employed by state bureaucracies, in this case the Post Office. What we see here is not elite university science, but applied science and technology, peopled by technicians, who are the subjects of the documentarists' cameras, not active participants in their own representation.[9]

Technology has been a potent subject for documentarists ever since the 1930s. For example, in 1963, Geoffrey Bell, who had cut his teeth at the Shell Film Unit with films such as *Transfer of Power* (1939, on the evolution of gear wheels), in identifying some of the best recent documentaries, singled out two technological examples. *The Peaceful Revolution*, directed by Atma Ram for Associated Electrical Industries, was a paean to the transformative power of electricity in India. *A Hundred Years Underground* (1963, directed by John Rowdon for British Transport Films) told the story of London's Underground railway system. Looking wider, *Today in Britain* (1964, Peter Hopkinson for the Foreign Office) is typical of many national portraits in stressing science and technology. Befittingly for the era of Wilson's 'white heat' speech, this film starts with a sequence praising Britain's nuclear power stations. As the new wave of scholarship on post-war documentary is beginning to make clear, applied science and technology were enduring and ubiquitous themes for sponsored filmmaking in the post-war period.[10] In 1964 also, Britain's third television channel, BBC Two, began to broadcast. The producers of its flagship science documentary strand *Horizon* frequently chose to report on new technologies, including, in the first series, computing and new forms of energy. Similarly, *Tomorrow's World*, its BBC One sibling a year junior, also concentrated on technology, in live reportage style. The trend has continued: when Channel 4 commissioned the documentary series *Equinox* from the *Horizon* veteran Patrick Uden (1986–2001), different technologies were once again the main subjects.

DOCUMENTARY AS AN INSTRUMENT OF THE SOCIAL RELATIONS OF SCIENCE

Established histories of British documentary note a mid-decade shift to social concern, stressing *Housing Problems* (1935) as the emblematic film.[11] But, with our concern focused on science, technology and medicine, we may periodise slightly differently and take the 1936 nutrition film *Enough to Eat?* as the emblem of the new documentary film-making. Here, a new power of basic science – to diagnose and cure social problems – was added to the existing model of scientific benefit, that of its application in new technologies. *Enough to Eat?* also indicated a new relationship between film-makers and scientists. At the tail end of 1935, the documentarist Paul Rotha formed an organisation named Associated Realist Film Producers to broker contacts between documentarists and potential clients.[12] In addition to film-makers, this organisation had a panel of advisors, including the biologists Julian Huxley, J. B. S. Haldane and Lancelot Hogben, who were all active in the so-called 'social relations of science movement'. Formally bringing these scientists into the orbit of film-making had a significant impact on how science could be represented in documentary. Hogben expressed the point clearly in 1936:

> Money and effort spent in diffusing political propaganda might be far more usefully employed in promoting *ad hoc* societies to finance the production of documentary films dealing with specific social issues of national importance. … The willing co-operation of men of science, the financial support of persons belonging to different political parties (or to none at all) and the creative work of film directors with the outlook of Grierson and Rotha could be enlisted to quicken the social imagination of England.[13]

Enough to Eat?, released in October 1936, was effectively the product of one of these 'ad hoc societies'. It reiterated arguments that had been raging throughout the 1930s, but with particular intensity that summer, about the social class dimensions of effective nutrition. In a sense it is a popularisation of John Boyd Orr's book *Food, Health and Income*, a meta-analysis of dietary surveys that argued that less than half the British population could afford a properly nutritious diet.[14] To represent this contentious subject matter, its director Edgar Anstey introduced, or used in combination for the first time, several techniques that established it as the model for documentaries. Although to our eyes it may look rather conventional, it was revolutionary in 1936: it has its commentator – the biologist and popular scientists Julian Huxley – present on screen; it features several expert points of view; it uses statistical diagrams; and it includes interviews with the dispossessed. Here, Huxley was appearing *as a scientist*, using this novel position to assert the appropriateness of science as the appropriate approach to understanding social problems and to guiding policy to solve them. Anstey later described *Enough to Eat?* as 'a scientific argument deployed by scientists' and there is a strong sense of this in the presence in the film not just of Huxley, a scientist with a highly active portfolio of public activities, but the work of a series of scientists, including Orr, Frederick Gowland Hopkins and Robert McCarrison, who variously worked on biochemical micronutrients – minerals and vitamins – or the differential effects of various diets.[15]

This model of scientific documentary-making, allied to films promoting other forms of rationality such as architectural and town planning, flourished in the decade up to 1947, especially in the films of Paul Rotha with Orr as a major ally. Of the larger-scale films, particular mention should be made of *World of Plenty* (1943) and its successor

The World is Rich (1947). In highly wrought works of impressionistic dialectical montage, using Rotha's trademark multi-voice commentary, these films forcefully promoted Boyd Orr's world food plan, designed to banish world hunger. There is a moment in *World of Plenty* where one of the commentary voices exclaims of Orr's world food plan that it is 'revolutionary'. But it is important to remember that, for all that Rotha was a socialist, Orr was a political conservative; the 'revolutionary' potential revealed in these films is the actualisation of the potential of science, not of a Marxist class transformation of society.

In many ways, Rotha's 'world' films were products of the idealism that grew in circles of planners and their fellow travellers under the cover of the war. Both could be made because they were envisaged as prestige films funded by the British state to show the superiority of democratic values in an age of totalitarianism. When Rotha went to the BBC to run their documentary department between 1953 and 1955, he infused the same kind of idealism into the United Nations-supported series, *The World is Ours*. Here, once again, were scientists, doctors and rationalists of every hue, making a better world. But, already in these programmes, the science is more instrumental and less revolutionary. This too is the tone of Stuart Legg's *Food – Or Famine?*, the 1961 film he made for Shell from a script by Michael Orrom, Rotha's assistant on *The World is Rich*. Increasingly in the 1960s and 70s, other kinds of moral link were made between science and society in television documentaries, and these were often counter-cultural and environmentalist voices. In the second ever *Horizon*, *Pesticides and Posterity* (1964), for example, the spirit of Rachel Carson's *Silent Spring*[16] was abroad. In this more journalistically influenced model of science film-making, the unreservedly benign view of science held by the apostles of the pre-war social relations of science movement was open to respectful question.

THE ESTABLISHMENT OF NEW TELEVISUAL GENRES FOR SCIENCE

The 1950s was the decade in which television began to seem the natural medium for scientific documentaries because of the audience that could be reached. By 1955 4.5 million homes in the UK had TVs, and by 1964 there were 16 million homes with sets.[17] Across the period from the early 50s, BBC executives were pressing the production staff to develop specifically televisual modes of programming, using the virtues of live broadcast to its full. Several departments competed to create effective televisual genres for science and technology using the different techniques specific to each. Alongside the continuation of the genres already noted, the crucible of television generated new ways of representing science in new ways that suited the spirit of the Cold War.

Science television followed the pattern that Paddy Scannell has found with politics. He has argued that BBC television made a division between social concern and party politics, which were treated separately and in different televisual modes.[18] Like party politics, as television developed, scientific subjects were increasingly treated separately from the generality of non-fiction broadcasting. They became the province of a very small number of programme-makers who specialised in science, who mainly worked in the Talks Department, separate from the producers responsible for the social reportage and documentary drama styles, who worked in the Documentary Department, which was the main place where medicine and public health were covered until its closure in 1955. From 1957, a third department, Outside Broadcast (OB), began seriously to produce science programmes. The key series, *Eye on Research*, produced by Aubrey Singer, took outside broadcast cameras into scientific laboratories. The emphasis was on 'the many years of thought and experiment in laboratories all round the world [and] the long periods of painstaking exploration that lie between the bold announcements' on subjects such as satellites, atomic energy and automation.[19] What is notable about this significant series was that it turned its back on the older social-benefit model. It embodied a narrower Cold War view that stressed experiment, and the excitement of doing science. The emphasis was on society revolutionised by the applied science of technology and not by the quasi-moral and political goal of the alleviation of human social problems as the earlier model had emphasised.

During this same period, scientists were waking up to the power of broadcasting. Since the early 1930s, individual scientists and science-watchers such as Gerald Crowther had sought to influence the representation of science on radio. Approaches were stepped up in the late 40s, initially from within the newly reconstituted BBC General Advisory Council. Further delegations from the Royal Society and British Association for the Advancement of Science were seen by the Corporation from 1958, and again in 1961 in the context of the Pilkington Committee on the Future of Broadcasting. Initially these approaches focused on radio, but, as television became a more influential medium, so the scientists' demands embraced it too. Consistently, these representatives of elite science sought control in one way or another over how television represented science and technology. They made demands that included putting senior scientists in charge of science broadcasting, establishing a separate science department and employing more scientists as producers. The BBC consistently rebuffed these approaches on the grounds, essentially, of resisting the ceding of control of production. In the interactions between scientists and the BBC we see contrary attempts at enrolment: of broadcasters seeking to retain the upper hand in control of their medium, and of scientific bodies seeking to control the public relations of science. The currency traded in the discussions in each case was expertise. As Harold Perkin explains, expertise is a type of property traded by the professional classes: 'most professional expertise does not enjoy a natural scarcity, and its value has to be protected and raised, first by persuading the public of the vital importance of the service and then by controlling the market for it'.[20] In the case of the clashes between scientists and broadcasters, different types of expertise may be seen being contested *between* professional groups.

Despite the BBC's retention of control, the output of television science came very much to reflect the view of science that scientists wanted. The keynote had been struck in 1949, when Marcus Oliphant, Professor of Physics at Birmingham and a member of the BBC's General Advisory Council, initiated a discussion on the broadcasting of science. He saw himself as a standard-bearer for basic, as against applied, science. The contrast with the Rotha model could not have been greater. Oliphant wrote:

I would like to see ... some break away from the perpetual theme of 'science and society', with the inevitable excursion of the scientist into fields of politics where he does not shine ... Cannot we sometimes forget war and atomic weapons, industrial advance or productivity, medicine and food production or science and religion and say something more of the great revolution wrought by the introduction of the experimental method, of the intellectual satisfaction and fun of science.[21]

That emphasis on 'the experimental method, of the intellectual satisfaction and fun of science' and, latterly – with *Horizon* – on the culture of science, was the way that science television went. The seeming paradox – of producers' dominance over scientists being maintained while reproducing a view of science that elite scientists approved of – can be explained by looking at how the most important science producers worked. Both James McCloy from Talks and Aubrey Singer from OB emphasised their access to senior scientists. McCloy asserted that,

whatever the showmanship involved in presentation, the programme aims at being entirely responsible in its treatment of science. It must be responsible not only in question of fact but also in selection and emphasis, and *earn the good will of the scientific profession*.[22]

Singer stressed elite contacts:

we generally start by visiting a group of scientists who are in touch with a wide field of research; people like Professor Thompson at Oxford, Sir Charles Harrington at the Medical Research Council and Dr David Martin at the Royal Society.[23]

These tendencies continued. Aubrey Singer, by 1966 Head of Features and Science, articulated the BBC's view of science broadcasting in a public lecture. He maintained that,

the televising of science is a *process of television*, subject to the principles of programme structure, and the demands of dramatic form. Therefore, in taking programme decisions, priority must be given to the medium rather than scientific pedantry.[24]

He asserted that 'the aim of scientific programming ... is not necessarily the propagation of science, rather its aim is common with all broadcasting, an enrichment of the audience experience'.[25] In the deferential world of the BBC's flagship cultural channel in the mid-1960s, fidelity to the values of the scientific establishment would have been expected. But, seen from close to the fiftieth anniversary of *Horizon*, this emphasis on the audience experience may look like the root of later problems for science television, which has been blown in many different stylistic directions. *Horizon* has tried many televisual approaches, including biopics such as the 1987 DNA drama, *Life Story*, and 'reality show'-style investigations such as *Battle of the Brains* from 2007. All the same, scientists have tended to escape the kinds of critical scrutiny routinely aimed by television journalists at other communities. Exceptional and isolated examples of more critical or authored kinds of science television were Bob Young's ill-fated series *Crucible* (1982–83) from the early days of Channel 4 and Adam Curtis's one-off series *Pandora's Box: Six Fables from the Age of Science* from 1992. The latter presented a critique of six aspects of science and technology using Curtis's now familiar style that combines his own voiceover with visually literate montages of archive film. *Crucible* was one series in the original short-lived roster of radical Channel 4 programming that sought to provide an alternative to the output of the other three channels. Young, a highly respected left historian of science sought to make the series a critique of the scientific establishment; the programme's commission was not renewed; he reviewed the production process as being intrinsically compromised.[26]

SCIENCE, SOCIETY AND DOCUMENTARY

Overall, we may see science documentary film-making as following the broader picture of the social and public relations of science, but with some delay. The sciences were growing in size and influence across the twentieth century and, as they did, they pressed upon the rest of the culture and economy. But the majority of professional scientists remained aloof from the power of the screen until after World War II. This is one reason for the diversity of styles of science documentary; the differing values placed on scientific film-making by film-makers and scientists have, from different circumstances, produced remarkably different representations of science. In the first case, especially with the microscopic examples, there was no gap between the amateur science and the films. These observational films embodied a kind of science remote from professional university- and laboratory-based biology. In the case of the 1930s technology documentaries, we see not elite university science, but applied science and technology, peopled by technicians, who are the subjects of the documentarists' cameras, not active participants in their own representation. In the socially inflected science films, the representation of scientists as socially conscious and also socially powerful was a product of the close ideological agreement and collaboration between them and film-makers. In the last case, the representation of science as a culture all of its own was the fruit of an elaborately negotiated relationship between the BBC and organised science in the shape of the Royal Society and British Association.

The majority of the science television that we have today is generally most like the nature and technology films: either it parallels science by revealing the natural world in quasi-scientific terms or else it represents the technological promise of scientific research. It has neither the focus on the culture of science typical of 1960s television, nor the passionate commitment to social improvement of the social relations of science model, nor yet the sceptical overview of *Crucible* or *Pandora's Box*.

NOTES

1. This chapter reprises the major themes of my book, *Films of Fact: A History of Science in Documentary Films and Television* (London: Wallflower Press, 2008); where I give no specific reference in the current chapter, sources and an expansion of the argument can be found in that work. For the sake of space, there is also limited coverage of medical films here, but they are covered in another summary: Timothy Boon, 'On the Varieties of Medical Filmmaking: An Alternative Path to the Cultures of Bio-Medicine', in M. Jackson (ed.), *Oxford Handbook of the History of Medicine* (Oxford: Oxford University Press, 2011), pp. 617–34.

2. Equally, the making of films for instructional classroom purposes represents a different type of engagement; these would be a separate subject of study. See Devin Orgeron, Devin, Marsha Orgeron and Dan Streible (eds), *Learning with the Lights Off: Educational Film in the United States* (New York: Oxford University Press, 2012).

3. Oliver Gaycken, 'Devices of Curiosity: Cinema in the Field of Scientific Visuality', unpublished PhD thesis, University of Chicago, 2005.

4. A selection of these films can be seen on the BFI DVD of the same title.

5. Arthur Morley Jones, 'President's Address: History and Reminiscences of the Quekett Microscopical Club', *Journal of the Quekett Microscopical Club* vol. 4 no. 3, 1949, p. 10.

6. Jean-Baptiste Gouyon, 'Experts in the Wild: Natural History Film-Making as a Culture of Knowledge-Production', unpublished PhD thesis, University of York, 2009, p. 99. See also Jean-Baptiste Gouyon, 'The BBC Natural History Unit: Instituting Natural History Film-making in Britain', *History of Science* vol. 49, 2011, pp. 425–51 and Jean-Baptiste Gouyon, 'From Kearton to Attenborough: Fashioning the Telenaturalist's Identity', *History of Science* vol. 49, 2011, pp. 25–60.

7. For general accounts of nature and wildlife film-making, see Derek Bousé, *Wildlife Films* (Philadelphia: University of Pennsylvania Press, 2000); Gregg Mitman, *Reel Nature: America's Romance with Wildlife on Film* (Cambridge, MA: Harvard University Press, 1999).

8. Mary Field and Percy Smith, *Secrets of Nature* (London: Faber and Faber, 1934), p. 111.

9. See Timothy Boon, 'Old Industry, New Science? The GPO Film Unit between Palaeotechnology and Neotechnology' in Scott Anthony and James Mansell (eds), *The Projection of Britain: A History of the GPO Film Unit* (London: BFI, 2011).

10. See Patrick Russell and James Taylor (eds), *Shadows of Progress: Britain's Forgotten Post-War Documentaries* (London: BFI, 2010).

11. Brian Winston describes this shift to social concern as embodying a 'problem moment' structure, in which real social problems are politically neutralised by being represented as transitory and soluble by technocratic intervention (Brian Winston, *Claiming the Real: The Documentary Film Revisited* [London: BFI, 1995], pp. 42–3.

12. Boon, *Films of Fact*, pp. 81–3.

13. Lancelot Hogben, 'The New Visual Culture', *Sight & Sound* no. 5, Spring, 1936–37, pp. 6–9.

14. John Boyd Orr, *Food, Health and Income: Report on a Survey of Diet in Relation to Income* (London: Macmillan, 1936).

15. Anstey, interviewed in *On the March*, a series on the history of the *March of Time* Newsreel, Flashbacks production, 30 October 1985. Winston notes that the film 'pulls its punches' in its approach to social problems (Winston, *Claiming the Real*, p. 45). More surprising within my interpretation – that the radicalism of the film is scientific, not political – is the failure to decide between the dominant explanations for malnutrition, namely ignorance or poverty; an earlier script had been more hard-hitting (see Boon, *Films of Fact*, p. 100).

16. Rachel Carson, *Silent Spring* (London: Penguin, 2000 [1962]).

17. Asa Briggs, *Sound and Vision: The History of Broadcasting in the United Kingdom vol IV* (Oxford: Oxford University Press, 1979) Asa Briggs, *Competition: The History of Broadcasting in the United Kingdom vol V* (Oxford: Oxford University Press, 1995), p. 1005.

18. Paddy Scannell, 'The Social Eye of Television, 1946–1955', *Media, Culture & Society* vol. 1 no. 1, January 1979.

19. Aubrey Singer, 'Keeping an Eye on Research', *Radio Times*, 15 November 1957, p. 7.

20. Harold Perkin, *The Rise of Professional Society* (London: Routledge, 1989), p. 378.

21. M. L. Oliphant, 'The Broadcasting of Science', 16 May 1949, BBC Written Archives Centre Caversham (BBCWAC), R6/34.

22. McCloy to Adam, 'Presentation of Science by Television', 7 October 1958, BBCWAC, T16/623, emphasis added.

23. Singer to Kenneth Adam, '*Eye on Research*: Planning, Preparations and Policy Considerations', 17 October 1958, BBCWAC, T14/1502/1.

24. Aubrey Singer, 'Science Broadcasting', *BBC Lunch-Time Lectures*, Series 4 no. 1–6 (London: BBC, 1966), p. 9, emphasis added.

25. Ibid.

26. R. M. Young, *What I Learned at Summer Camp: Experiences in Television*, 1995, http://human-nature.com/rmyoung/papers/paper29h.html. Accessed 7 August 2012.

5.3 History Documentaries for Television

ANN GRAY

Of all the humanities disciplines, none provides more material for documentary films than does history. In Britain, the past looms particularly large and so is well reflected on television. History films, though, are a different case from those made in the service of the natural and social sciences. There is little cultural presupposition that the authenticity of the filmed accounts of the past will be at all superior (in terms of evidence) to accounts of it in other, older media.

TELEVISION AND 'PUBLIC HISTORY'

I will begin by contrasting two accounts of the commissioning of history programmes for television. The first takes place around a now legendary lunch table at the BBC's then new Television Centre in White City some time in 1966 and the second in a lift between floors at the UK History Channel some time in 2008. Members of the lunch party were Sir Kenneth Clark, former director of the National Gallery, art historian and the first chairman of the Independent Television Authority, David Attenborough and Stephen Hearst, then heads of BBC Two and BBC Two Arts Department, respectively, and, with the timely arrival of Huw Weldon, Controller of Programmes, for coffee, the result was a done deal for a series of thirteen presenter-led programmes about European art and architecture. Travelling in the lift, forty years on, are a hopeful TV history producer and the MD of the UK History Channel, who insists on pitches for the relatively small number of programmes he commissions. He told me:

> If you can't sell it in the lift between the first and the second floor the audience aren't going to get it. I get 187 characters, including spaces, to explain to the audience what the show is about – if you can't do it in 187 characters you're not making the right programme for us.

These events provide insights into very different worlds of television. In the one, a newly born third channel (BBC Two) was keen to demonstrate 'quality' colour transmission; in the other, hundreds of channels are fighting for endlessly distracted 'eye-balls' (especially when scanning the electronic programming guides [EPG]). Lest we mistakenly imagine that these worlds have nothing at all in common, Kenneth Clark's title preference of 'What is Civilisation? A Personal View by Kenneth Clark' was simplified by the BBC to *Civilisation: A Personal View* which rapidly became known simply as *Civilisation*. Good for the EPG, I think.

John Ellis usefully charts these changes which British television has undergone in the last fifty years in terms of 'eras': 'scarcity' (1950–80), 'availability' (1980–95) and 'plenty' (1995–2005).[1] These, of course, can be mapped onto the technological, social and cultural changes of each period. The first era, 'scarcity', saw the establishment of public broadcasting and the development of mass market consumerism. In terms of product, this is the 'one size fits all' model. The second, 'availability', is coterminous with the increasing diversity of consumer markets. In these two eras television is a time-based medium; it assumes a domestic audience and its dominant mode of address is intimate. Its scheduling patterns and developing forms of programming reflected and assumed an audience distracted by the rhythms and

Civilisation (1966): a personal view

chaos of everyday domestic life.[2] The third era, 'plenty', registers the introduction of digital technologies enabling increased numbers of channels and an increasing freedom from time-based media.

Ellis's analysis stops at 2000 and, to a great extent, echoes Amanda Lotz's characterisation of changes in US television as: 'network era', 'multi-channel transistion' and 'post-network era'.[3] The decade since has clearly evolved into what we might call 'the digital era', as multi-platform delivery potential increases and where the felt need of commissioners and producers is to grab hold of the viewer's eye-balls and to retain their attention. This is evidenced in the enticing and punchy 'opening tease', 'story so far' and 'coming up next' sequences in documentaries produced for commercial networks – what Discovery Channel terms the 'bumps in and out' of each of the six 'acts' which are determined by commercial breaks. The non-commercial networks, such as the BBC, also insist that documentaries include 'the story so far' summary at the halfway point. This structure can be seen in even the most serious-minded history documentaries.

Although these developments are far reaching and do not always fit neatly into the periods, the changes to styles of history programming can be understood, to a certain extent, with reference to them. It is interesting to note, however, that, as in our understanding of all historical development, especially that which seeks to identify and explain change, what happens on the ground often contradicts the neatness of periodisation. As an example, in 2000 on British television, Simon Schama's thirteen-part series *A History of Britain*, which shares many characteristics of the period of austerity, was running alongside *1900* and *1940 House*, a format which attempted to widen the audience for history through the use of 'reality television', a genre more associated with popular forms of entertainment, and locatable in Ellis's period of 'plenty' (see below).

Thus, if we dig more deeply into the differences reflected within the periods and keep our focus on the history documentary, then we have a good starting point from which to pose the question: 'What does television do to the history documentary?' By putting this into an historical context we can go beyond recognising that television is a powerful mediator of the past and, indeed, history (for those two are not the same thing) to considering how developments within the television industry itself influence and shape that very mediation and, by extension, what television offers to the circulation of public knowledge about the past. These changes encompass regulation, technological development, market competition and audiences, elements which are often defined, in analytical terms, as 'structural'. Yet these certainly have consequences for what we actually see on television: that is, the forms, the genres, the modes of address of programming and how these are presented for the viewer

(i.e., via marketing and scheduling). Although histories which seek to explore the effects of these changes on programming, could be plotted for all television genres – news, entertainment, drama, for example – the documentary has received the most consistent attention in this respect.[4] This is in part because the documentary had a history prior to television but, as Winston reminds us, British 'documentaries went to television'.[5]

Television, then, in spite of huge change, is still a major site for the production of documentary, albeit in an ever-expanding range of generic forms, many of which, as we shall see, are the creative product of television itself. Television is also the medium through which most of the population gets to know about the past and, to a certain extent, history. Although history programming has been a staple of British television since its inception, in the increasingly competitive markets from the mid-1990s onwards, history as content has proved to be the surprising success story of that period through to the present. This chapter will chart this development and along the way raise some issues in relation to what happens when television documentaries 'do' history, how the imperatives of television lead to the development of genres, styles and modes of doing history with consequent differences in audience engagement. It will also argue that the overall development in ways of doing television history reflect debates in historiographical practice, reminding us of the important relationship between 'professional' history and television as a form of 'public history'.

WHAT DOES TELEVISION DO TO HISTORY?

I want to begin by stating the fairly obvious. That is, that the documentary form of history on television is not a unified entity, but, like all television, is diverse and multiple. It now finds its place across a number of channels, terrestrial and satellite; it inhabits a range of 'popular' and 'serious' documentary genres; and it has a complex production base. Currently, in addition to the BBC, many independent companies specialise in history television, most notably and with indicative productions: Wall to Wall (*Who Do You Think You Are?*, BBC Two, 2004–06, BBC One, 2006–; *The1900 House,* Channel 4, 1999; *The 1940s House,* Channel 4, 2001; *The Edwardian Country House,* Channel 4, 2002), Lion TV (*Days that Shook the World*, BBC Four, History Channel, 2003; *Tales from the Green Valley*, BBC Two, 2005; *Victorian Farm*, BBC Two, 2009), Flashback (*Auschwitz: The Forgotten Evidence,* Channel 4 and History Channel, 2005; *1983: The Brink of Apocalypse*, Channel 4 and Discovery, 2008; *50 Things You Need to Know About British History*, History Channel, 2009), Juniper (*The Great Plague*, Channel 4 and TLC, 2001; *Brief Histories*, Discovery, 2004; *Edwardian Winners and Losers*, BBC Four, 2007), Brook-Lapping (*Death of Yugoslavia*, BBC Two, 1995; *Israel and the Arabs: Elusive Peace*, BBC Two, 2005; *Iran and the West*, BBC Two, 2009) and Testimony Films (*A Secret*

World of Sex, BBC Two, 1991; *Green and Pleasant Land*, Channel 4 1999). Many programmes made for television have an extended shelf-life via DVD, websites and popular books, as well as stimulating interest in heritage sites and local 'historical attractions'. This fluid and complex production environment is reflected in the range and multiplication of genres. Television has a great capacity to endlessly produce and reproduce programme forms, to combine and articulate genres at what Wayne Garvie[6] describes as a rapid 'churn rate' and, in the words of the now BBC Two Programme Controller, Janice Hadlow, this demonstrates 'television's power to reinvent itself'.[7] Arguably history programming is evidence of this self-proliferation.

I want to pose the question 'What does television do to history?' and propose some sites of investigation. One place to look in order to begin an exploration involves the encounters between two of the major stakeholders: professional historians and television producers. These occasionally appear in the press and other media, but also at the relatively few gatherings which bring these two professions together. Analysis of the statements and discussions reveals that each group is driven by what are the often conflicting notions of what makes 'good history' and what is 'good television'.

Taylor Downing, history programme-maker and managing director of Flashback Television, is clear that, while history on television today takes many forms, styles, formats and techniques, for him successful history programmes share the following characteristics:

> Firstly, television is a visual medium: I earn my living by finding visually compelling ways to express ideas, which means I need a strong visual core to my programmes. It can come from archive film or photographs, it can come from people recalling events, it can come from reconstructions, it can come from a talented expert capable of telling stories well. But equally important, it must be good *narrative*.[8]

Many historians, however, consider the emphasis on narrative, on character and the necessity to engage the audience immediately as elements more usually associated with 'entertainment', which oversimplify and potentially compromise their work.

It is clear that the framing of debates about history on television needs to go beyond 'good' versus 'bad' history and should be replaced by an investigation into how images and the particular language of television work in terms of representing the past. More recently, television and media scholars have entered the dialogue and encouraged historians to acknowledge the ways in which both professional history and television history mediate the past. Thus, by analysing television history *as television*, rather than simply dismissing it as 'bad history', we can look at how television does history and ask questions of the different forms, genres and formats which are employed. Furthermore, as I shall attempt to do here, we can map these developments onto the history of British television itself.

Taking Ellis's schema of the development of British television, the mapping of styles of history documentaries might be: 'scarcity' – grand narratives and national unity; 'availability' – innovation, histories from below; 'plenty' – reviving history, formats, identity, empathy.

'SCARCITY': GRAND NARRATIVES AND NATIONAL UNITY

History has been a constant staple of television output.[9] According to Taylor Downing, television's first history programme was a series, *Victory at Sea*, produced in the USA by NBC in 1951.[10] The films consisted of newsreel and official film from World War II with a 'voice-of-God' commentary. The superior editing produced visually exciting scenes and lavish music (by Richard Rogers) added to the generally triumphalist and celebratory mood. Downing argues that this was an important vehicle for restoring confidence in the post-Korean USA, which, following its success on NBC, was reformatted as a feature for cinema exhibition and sold to forty countries. This was the first 'compilation' history programme on television[11] – a mix of newsreel, archive and narrator, many examples of which are still being made today.

In 1964, the BBC commemorated the fiftieth anniversary of the outbreak of the 1914–18 war with its transmission of its twenty-six-episode series, *The Great War*. In addition to newsreel, archive and narration, the producers added eye-witness accounts to the mix, a convention well suited to the domestic and intimate address of television and described by Steve Humphries of Testimony Films as the beginning of oral history on television.[12] This series, Downing argues, proved that television history could be 'serious, powerful and popular'.[13] History, documenting the past, which aimed to reflect the nation to itself, was, therefore, an early and potent mix to emerge from the early 'scarcity' days of television.

In the UK this commitment to remembering and commemorating the nation's past did more than mark key historical events. It formed a large part of the public service ethos for both BBC and ITV. The 'compilation' form of *The Great War* was by no means the only history genre employed in this period. A notable example was Peter Watkins's 1964 experimental film *Culloden*, scripted by John Prebble, in which local people performed dramatic reconstructions of the 1746 defeat of the Jacobite rebellion by the English army, filmed in the then fresh hand-held observational news documentary style with an historical interpreter commenting on the events. It was shown on BBC One at 8 pm. If *Victory at Sea* and *The Great War* established a particular genre of television history programming, then the strategies used by Watkins in *Culloden* are arguably the precursor of 'living history' programme formats, which have some of their origins in the re-enactment movement.

While commemoration and national unity (albeit challenged by Watkins) was clearly the impetus behind the commissioning of series such as *The Great War*, there are often other explanations for programme commissioning. A demonstration of this takes us back to the lunch party at the BBC and the origination of *Civilisation*, which more accurately should be described as an arts programme, however, is important to include here. David Attenborough provides testimony to his role as the first controller of BBC Two in the establishment of this style of documentary.

The intrinsic element, according to Attenborough, was the fact that the newly launched channel, with 625 lines, was to be the first in the UK to transmit in colour. He describes the general disdain for and suspicion of colour television held by senior staff at the BBC. This was in the main because of the US experience with a colour television system which was widely held to be seriously inadequate. According to Attenborough, the colours were 'garish, appalling, really' and the concomitant US programming exploited colour in a 'crude' way. The BBC, however, had opted for a superior German system, PAL, and it fell to Attenborough to find a way of convincing the 'opinion formers' inside and outside the BBC that this delivered a colour image worth having. To avoid the 'crude', his idea was to 'create a series which would look at all the most beautiful art and buildings which human beings in Europe had created and to set the images to equally sublime music'.[14]

It is useful to excavate the roots of this particular style of authored documentary and especially to acknowledge the particular institutional-technological environment from which it emerged. Attenborough's anxious obsession with the quality of the pictures and his lack of confidence in 16mm led to his decision to shoot on 35mm, which effectively doubled the budget. But, as Jonathan Conlin points out, *Civilisation* was significantly important beyond British television and its audiences. It was first seen by American audiences as part of a series of highly successful screenings at the National Gallery in Washington before being shown on the newly established Public Broadcasting Service (PBS). Conlin suggests that we should consider *Civilisation* an important stalking horse which paved the way for other series developed (and partly US funded) by Attenborough – for example, Alastair Cooke's *America* (UK, 1972; USA, 1973) and Jacob Bronowski's *The Ascent of Man* (UK, 1973; USA, 1975).[15]

The account of the birth of this kind of scholarly authored, picturesque historical narrative form of television is revealing of its patrician roots in its fusion of high culture, quality and refined comportment and taste. It is also a testament to the way in which institutional pressures can shape the form and style of programming and, by extension, an understanding of the past. These examples of history documentaries fall into the category of what Bill Nichols describes as 'documentaries of sobriety' – serious, measured and, above all, authoritative. This form of history documentary arguably renders the audience passive. History, often presented as a closed narrative, is knowledge to be imparted by the professional historian. The audience is kept at a distance, occupying the position offered of receiver.

'AVAILABILITY': INNOVATION – HISTORIES FROM BELOW

My starting point for this section is from a historiographical perspective: some university history departments, and especially those in the post-1960s universities, began to interrogate and question the 'great men' mode of history and, inspired by historians such as E. P. Thompson, changed their perspective to that of 'history from below'. The leaders of this trend came from the History Workshop movement established in 1967 at Ruskin College, Oxford (the trade union college for mature students). Raphael Samuels, a member of staff, developed the notion that 'history is too important to be left just to professional historians' and that history should be seen from a non-elitist perspective. The historiographic mood of the times has a bearing on the developing forms of history documentary.

The World at War is the emblematic case. In 1971 Jeremy Isaacs, then Controller of Features at Thames, began the three-year project with a team of fifty people which was to become the twenty-six-episode series (Thames, UK, 1973–74). Isaacs had produced a programme about Irish history *The Troubles 1912–20s* (ITV, 1962) and the series *All Our Yesterdays* (ITV, 1960–73) for Granada. *The World at War* was remarkable for many things and is well documented,[16] but perhaps particularly in its involvement of eye-witnesses who were not confined to politicians and commanders or even soldiers and airmen but which included civilians. Isaacs felt that the time was right to approach such witnesses as the thirty-year period since the start of World War II would provide sufficient distance from the often traumatic events which were recalled and recounted for the camera.[17] It is also notable for the fact that it was made by an ITV company, albeit financed by a tax windfall granted to all the ITV companies.

Although *The World at War* painted a large canvas of the conflict, there is no doubt that the testimony of 'ordinary people' caught up in total war echoed the democratic mood of the period. The History Workshops became very well established at Ruskin and one outcome was the founding of the *History Workshop Journal* (1977), whose manifesto was the democratisation of history, its de-professionalisation and its politicisation. The emphasis was on working-class

The World at War (1973–74): the emblematic case

history, but later, after fierce debate, feminist history also. This movement is reflected in a tendency in television history programme-making and, especially, in the oral history method and the significance of the eye-witness account, although not necessarily with the political and critical edge of *History Workshop Journal*.

The producer Stephen Peet pioneered this form for television in his series *Yesterday's Witness* (BBC, 1969–81) based on 'ordinary people telling extraordinary stories',[18] which resonated with broader social events. By using oral history methods, history and an understanding of the past could be gleaned from those who lived through events which, if not directly challenging the dominant narratives of the past, could certainly furnish them with more everyday detail. Significantly, those whose lives and stories were not usually heard were encouraged to tell their story including their everyday and ordinary experiences. But perhaps two of the most remarkable 'history from below' programmes of the time, commissioned by the BBC, were the social histories of working-class life and feminist histories represented in Peter Pagnamenta's *All Our Working Lives* (BBC Two, 1984) and Angela Holdsworth's *Out of the Doll's House* (BBC Two, 1988).

The strong relationship between the dominant mode of television, that of the talking head and the oral history method cannot be over-emphasised. According to Humphries this is because it has 'emotional power: the power of people telling their stories directly to camera'.[19] However, it does raise questions – now interrogated within historical studies, anthropology and sociology – about the veracity of the eye-witness account and the tendency of television producers, holding faith with their contributors, to rely on compelling testimony as the origin of authenticity and historical truth.[20]

The Broadcasting Act 1982 established Channel 4 with a remit to innovate and to cater to minority interests and groups hitherto neglected by the terrestrial mainstream broadcasters. There was also a requirement on broadcasters in general to commission more programming from the independent sector. The Act fuelled great hope in the hearts of those eager to produce more exciting and challenging history programmes. One of these was Colin Thomas, who produced *The Dragon has Two Tongues: A History of the Welsh* (Channel 4, 1985) which set two opposing historians in, as it were, the ring to fight out and demonstrate their particular versions of Welsh history.

In an attempt to challenge the BBC's dominance in public service history programming, in addition to producing individual history programmes Channel 4 also responded to the BBC's archeological series *Timewatch* (1982–), established by Tim Gardam, with their series, *Today's History* (1982–84). Both series were in part influenced by the 'history from below' movement in that many items dealt with ignored or marginalised histories and challenged received wisdom. In each attempts were made to produce more challenging and less conventional programming. The 'magazine' format allowed for a number of stories, or 'features' to be included. Academic historians presented self-contained items. In 1991 Channel 4 established the *Secret History* series, a sort of historical detective work, which ran until 2004 and which continued challenging and sometimes radical versions of history.

Although comparisons between UK and USA television must be approached with caution, it is worth noting that the 1980s saw the rise to popularity in the USA of Ken Burns's documentaries. Burns, a self-defined popular historian with his own television production company, Florentine Films, was commissioned by PBS to make a number of history documentaries. These covered well-known aspects or events in US life, such as *The Statue of Liberty* (PBS, 1985), *The Congress* (PBS, 1989) and, perhaps the best-known example, the eleven-hour *The Civil War* transmitted in 1990 across five nights between 23 and 27 September of that year to great acclaim and enormous popularity. The programme averaged 12 million viewers at any given moment.[21] Burns's style is organised around his belief in 'the need to restate the old heroes ... [and] the old dramas ... in a new visual way'.[22] Clearly there are differences between the US broadcasting context and that in the UK, including their much more developed notions of the public historian, but, arguably, the great success of Burns's documentaries confirmed the appetite for these popular, or populist, programmes which would have been important evidence for commissioners and TV executives on both sides of the Atlantic.

'PLENTY': REVIVING HISTORY – FORMATS, IDENTITY, EMPATHY

The structures and working practices in the UK television industry have undergone major change since the 1990 Communications Bill. This de/re-regulation of broadcasting includes changes to ITV franchise arrangements, decimation of the unions and new technological developments which have resulted in increased competition for programming commissions, the expansion of niche satellite channels and the consequent decrease in available funding for programmes. Hence the regulatory and technological possibilities for Ellis's period of 'plenty'.

For many commentators there has been a 'dumbing down' of television output. In relation to documentary, the epitome of so-called 'serious programming', 'dumbing down' is evidenced by the growth of 'reality television'. It should be said, however, that some television producers take the opposite view and argue that documentary programming is alive and well, and not only in Reality TV formats.[23] Certainly, it is clear that the renaissance of history programming which took place in the mid-1990s gave 'factual' programming a large boost. This provided newly formed independents the opportunity to pitch commissioning editors their ideas for new ways of doing history.

In the 90s history programming came into its own and became extremely popular – this can be charted in the UK, the USA and in other parts of Europe. The year 1995 saw the birth of the History Channel, the establishment of the BBC TV History Unit and the approaching millennium appeared to give rise to certain important developments in the BBC's engagement with history. The BBC launched its now well-established *History Magazine* and broadcast Simon Schama's *A History of Britain*. Channel 4 responded with David Starkey's *Elizabeth* (Channel 4, 2000) and *Monarchy* (Channel 4, 2004–06). This saw the 'reinvention' of the historian presenter and the success of these programmes gave confidence to the commissioners that audiences were still attracted to the authoritative presenter of earlier times. The historian presenters became household names and history was referred to variously as 'the new rock and roll' and 'the new gardening' in terms of television programming.

I have argued elsewhere that this flourishing of the television history documentary at this particular point in time can be understood as the consequences of a formation of creative television professionals working together whose interests lay in history.[24] For example, Janice Hadlow, the present controller of BBC Two, was involved in the setting up of the BBC History Unit but then moved to Channel 4; Tim Gardam, originator of *Timewatch*, moved to Channel 4 in 1997. The establishment of a number of independent television companies – many by individuals previously employed by the BBC and ITV – especially in the 1990s, was part of this dynamic mix. Their 'signature' was history programming, and a highly competitive and dynamically creative environment was established for its development.[25]

The director and producer Laurence Rees was a key mover in the BBC TV History Unit. He notably collaborated with Professor Ian Kershaw on three series: *Nazis: A Warning from History* (1997), *War of the Century* (1999) and *Auschwitz* (2005). These were 'compilation' films but were informed by the 'history from below' movement in Germany – for example, the 'Bavarian project' and the *Alltagsgeschichte* (history of everyday life). This marked an important shift from the existing institutional and structural histories of this period to an examination of everyday life. It broke with the dualism of 'motive' vs structural explanations for the Nazis, which had dominated historical interpretation. Bringing these shifts in thinking about the past to the screen was a considerable achievement, but one which was arguably only possible within this broadcasting climate.

Perhaps the most telling indication of the significance of history programming in this period was the establishment of a separate category of the Grierson Awards sponsored by *History Today* in 2000–01.[26] It is given to the best 'single documentary or an episode from a strand or series on a historical subject'.

The 'television history documentary' had arrived. Increased competition and the drive for attracting audiences for history television within an increasingly international context, led the programme producers, networks and channels to search for easily reproducible formats. One of the earliest and most successful examples of this was what became the *House* format, which was developed originally as a 'science' programme by Wall to Wall Television, an independent production company. The production of *The 1900 House* utilised elements of the format which came to be known as 'reality television' or, to give it a more specific term for our purposes here, 'living history'. Its transmission in 1999 pre-dated the BBC's *Castaway* (2000–01) and Channel 4's *Big Brother* (1999–). *The 1900 House* was followed in 2001 by *The 1940s House* (Channel 4) and demonstrates the commitment of that channel to the continuation of innovative programming. The power of the format is further demonstrated by the take-up of what became an international *House* franchise, with national examples in the USA, Canada and Australia.

The 1900 House (1999): the impact of, usually, the privations of the past on individuals

These programmes adopt some techniques of observational documentary in evidencing the impact of, usually, the privations of the past on individuals, most often families. They have been variously criticised for further examples of the 'emotionalising of the documentary project'.[27] Simon Schama complained that these programmes allowed the viewer to stay in the comfort zone of a present in which people inhabiting the past are 'just like us'.[28] However, as Jerome de Groot points out, the roots of 'reality history' can be traced back to the re-enactment movement[29] and, in historiographical terms, to the history philosopher R. G. Collingwood, who saw value in attempting to understand the past as a 'living past' through a mental re-enactment of events and conditions. Arguably, reality history, as developed through hybrid documentary forms, invites this empathetic identification of 'being there' – a transaction with which television and its audience are entirely familiar.

Vanessa Agnew has noted history's 'affective turn' and relates this to the rise in popularity of the historical re-enactment with its 'emphasis on affect, individual experience and daily life rather than historical events, structures and processes'.[30] This shift within historical studies (which can also be seen in other disciplines within the humanities and social sciences) has echoes in the increasing focus on the personal and the intimate in contemporary everyday life, which is, in turn, reflected in television documentary genres.

It is true, however, that it is 'reality history' which has attracted the strongest critics and seems to be, for some, the epitome of 'bad history' and, indeed, of 'bad television'. Tristram Hunt, himself a historian who has presented a number of history programmes based on his own research, sums it up thus: 'The transition from Corelli Barnett's *The Great War* with its incisive, questioning, if patrician, commentary (delivered by Sir Michael Redgrave) to the facile "experience" of *The Trench* is itself a micro-history of broadcasting.'[31]

The 'facile' programme to which Hunt refers, *The Trench* (BBC, 2002), was a re-enactment of the Battle of Ancre in 1916. Twenty-five young male volunteer participants from Hull, several of whom were descendents of veterans who had fought in the war, were recruited. The series 'followed' participants as they relived some of the 10th Battalion East Yorkshire Regiment (the 'Hull Pals') experiences before the battle.

In spite of Hunt's earlier insistence that we should understand history on television as a diverse and multiple beast, he falls into the trap here of failing to engage with the specifics of this 'reality-experiential' genre as a form of history documentary.[32] It was claimed that *The Trench* did not set out to be military or even cultural history but rather was an attempt to represent 'life on the Western Front' through what John Corner has described as the 'physicality of history'.[33] According to Hanna, *The Trench* challenged what has become the dominant image of the Great War, that which has been and continues to be mediated through the World War I poets or through an understanding of 'military history' experts. The day-to-day horrors of trench warfare experienced by their great grandfathers' generation had a profound effect on the participants. *The Trench* also included 'talking head' testimony from survivors, as well as a narrator voiceover. In addition, the series drew on war diaries and army manuals as its source, through which elements of the narrative were structured. Throughout the series, the pull of the logics of television can be seen as the narrative was structured through the 'reality television' tropes of 'tasks', of personal challenges and of the cliff-hanger climax.

There are numerous examples of this genre of history documentary and new ones being commissioned. These are evidence of the more general shift to the personal, the intimate, the individual and the emotional in a broader culture. The historian Jurgen Kocka suggests:

> Nowadays, many people deal with history in order to find out where they come from and who they are ... a quest for identity and empathy is at work with TV producers ... explanation has become less obvious, less self-evident, less desirable, or less manageable for many historians. Understanding has regained centre stage.[34]

Possibly the most successful history format is the genealogy show *Who Do You Think You Are?* (BBC, 2004–). Here, celebrities or well-known people, usually from television, are taken on an 'emotional journey' to discover their own family history, in the course of which they discover their own identity. This is another popular format which is in the main, but not exclusively, treated with disdain by historians. Hunt again argues that this is 'warm bath' history.[35] However, while the celebrities are an undoubted draw for the audiences, *Who Do You Think You Are?* intersperses the individual stories with social and historical context, often dealing with topics which are untouched by other history programmes.

THE DIGITAL ERA (AND BEYOND)

As we noted earlier, periodisations can never be distinctly drawn. Within Ellis's period of 'plenty' there were innovations in UK history television to be noted briefly here. One such was marked by internal changes within the broadcasting organisations, the BBC in particular, and with technological developments which have had and will continue to have enormous impact on the ways in which historical data and representation can be made available and constructed. The digitisation of archives and the increasing sophistication of computer-generated imagery (CGI) shaped the continuing expansion of the history documentary. In October 2000 the BBC established its new Factual and Learning Division, which incorporated science, natural history, arts, business, religion and ethics and history under one controller, Glenwyn Benson. Benson was keen to develop 'cross-disciplinary' projects to produce what she described as 'event' or 'immersion' television. Thus, big-scale productions such as *Pompeii: The Last Day* (BBC One, 2002), *Pyramid* (BBC One, 2002) and *Coliseum: Rome's Arena of Death* (BBC One, 2003) pulled in personnel from different areas of production and CGI special effects. This we might describe as 'history as spectacle'.

Following these productions, commemorative 'historical event' programming once more provided the BBC with a national platform in 2004 with their productions of *D-Day 6.6.1944* (BBC Two, 2004) and *Dunkirk* (BBC Two, 2004). These programmes broke new ground as 360 degree projects which combined dramatic reconstructions, archive footage, eye-witness testimony for the television screen with an interactive facility 'press the red button' which linked to a special website with access to digital sources as well as the 'Peoples' War' chat room which invited recollections from viewers. According to James Bennett,[36] these programmes and their digital facilities were demonstrations of the BBC's role in 'building digital Britain' and re-emphasised the BBC's remit to public service broadcasting in a period of difficulty.[37] *D-Day* was a co-production with, among others, the Discovery Channel, a relationship which has now been extended to 2014 which will, according to Jana Bennett (formerly of BBC Worldwide), enable the BBC to continue to produce the 'most ambitious and creative landmark factual programming for viewers until 2014'.[38]

The BBC, Channel 4 and ITV have established digital channels all of which have a brand identity. This works through into history programming, which responds to the requirements of schedulers and target markets. Presenters have become even more important in this respect, with broadcasters nurturing 'on-screen talent' to arrest viewers

and guide them through the delights of history. Co-production deals and joint ventures such as the BBC and Discovery look towards history 'content' for their big-budget projects and the BBC and Open University partnership continues to develop increasingly sophisticated online support to which broadcast television acts as a portal.

The history documentary has survived the vicissitudes of British television and is alive and well, if, admittedly, a more hybrid beast than could have been imagined by the guests at the lunch table in 1966.

RESEARCH NOTE

The research for this chapter was carried out for the AHRC-funded project 'Televising History: 1995–2010' based at the University of Lincoln.

NOTES

1. John Ellis, *Seeing Things: Television in the Age of Uncertainty* (London: I.B.Tauris, 2000).
2. John Ellis, *Visible Fictions. Cinema, Television and Video* (London: Routledge, 1982).
3. Amanda Lotz, *The Television Will Be Revolutionized* (New York and London: New York University Press, 2007).
4. Brian Winston, *Claiming the Real II: Documentary: Grierson and Beyond* (London: BFI, 2008 [2000]).
5. Brian Winston, 'Not a Lot of Laughs: Documentary as a Popular Form', in M. Wayne (ed.), *Dissident Voices: The Politics of Television and Cultural Change* (London: Pluto Press, 1998), p. 147.
6. Wayne Garvie, Head of Entertainment, BBC, addressing the MeCCSA Conference, January 2005, University of Lincoln.
7. 'History and the Media', Institute of Historical Research conference, London, December 2002.
8. Taylor Downing, 'Bringing the Past to the Small Screen', in David Cannadine (ed.), *History and the Media* (London: Palgrave Macmillan, 2007), p. 9, original emphasis.
9. Robert Dillon, *History on British Television: Constructing Nation, Nationality and Collective Memory* (Manchester: Manchester University Press, 2010).
10. Taylor Downing, 'Screen Saviours', *History Today* vol. 59 no. 8, 2009, pp. 40–2.
11. The earliest archival film compilation in the canon, though, is Esfir Shub's *Fall of the Romanov Dynasty*, 1927, USSR.
12. Steve Humphries, 'Oral History on Television: A Retrospective', *Oral History* vol. 36 no. 2, 2008, p. 100.
13. Downing, 'Screen Saviours'.
14. David Attenborough, *Life on Air: Memoirs of a Broadcaster* (London: BBC, 2003), pp. 213–14.
15. Jonathan Conlin, *Civilisation* (London. BFI, 2009), p. 102.
16. See James Chapman, 'The World at War: Television, Documentary, History', in Graham Roberts and Philip

Taylor (eds), *The Historian, Television and Television History* (Luton: University of Luton Press, 2001); Jeremy Isaacs, *Look Me in the Eye: A Life in Television* (London: Little, Brown, 2006).

17. Isaacs notes the role of television researchers in finding sources, such as film archive and tracing people willing to speak to the camera about their experiences. Much of this archive still exists. Norma Percy's films based on recent political events – for example, *Death of Yugoslavia* (BBC, 1995) and *The Fall of Milosevic* (BBC, 2003) – also have provided the Kings College archive with a mass of material which will be useful to future researchers.

18. Humphries, 'Oral History on Television', pp. 99–108.

19. Ibid.

20. This dimension of 'good television' and its relationship to the politics of knowledge and historiography has been the subject of little debate but is discussed in a recent publication (Ann Gray and Erin Bell, *History on Television* [London: Routledge, 2012]).

21. Gary Edgerton, 'Mediating *Thomas Jefferson*: Ken Burns as Popular Historian', in Gary Edgerton and Peter Rollins (eds), *Television Histories: Shaping Collective Memory in the Media Age* (Kentucky: University Press of Kentucky, 2001), p.170.

22. Burns's programmes attracted much criticism from historians for his problematic portrayal of African Americans and women. See, for example, *Ken Burns's The Civil War: Historians Respond*, http://www.amazon.com/exec/obidos/ ASIN/0195093305, and Jeanne Attie, 'Illusions of History: A Review of *The Civil War*', *Radical History Review*, Winter 1992, pp. 95–104.

23. C. Dover, '"Crisis" in British Documentary Television: The End of a Genre?', *Journal of British Cinema and Television* vol. 1 no. 2, 2004.

24. Ann Gray, 'Contexts of Production', in Erin Bell and Ann Gray (eds), *Televising History: Mediating the Past in Postwar Europe* (London: Palgrave, 2010).

25. Ibid.

26. The Grierson award is the UK's premiere award specifically for documentary. It is organised by the trust established in Grierson's memory in 1974.

27. Gareth Palmer, '*Big Brother*: An Experiment in Governance', *Television and New Media* vol. 3 no. 3, August 2002, p. 297.

28. S. Schama, 'Television and the Trouble with History', in Canadine, *History and the Media*, p. 9.

29. Jerome deGroot, *Consuming History: Historians and Heritage in Contemporary Popular Culture* (London: Routledge, 2009).

30. Vanessa Agnew, 'History's Affective Turn', *Rethinking History* vol. 11 no. 3, July 2007.

31. Tim Hunt, 'Reality, Identity and Empathy: The Changing Face of Social History on Television', *Journal of Social History* vol. 39 no. 3, Spring 2006, p. 856.

32. Emma Hanna, 'Reality-Experiential History Documentaries: *The Trench* (BBC, 2002) and Britain's Modern Memory of the First World War', *Historical Journal of Film, Radio and Television* vol. 27 no. 4, October 2007.

33. John Corner, 'Performing the Real', *Television and New Media* vol. 3. no. 3, August 2002, pp. 255–70.

34. J. Kocka, quoted in Hunt, 'Reality, Identity and Empathy'.

35. Tristram Hunt, 'The Time Bandits', *Media Guardian* 10 September 2007, p. 3.

36. James Bennett, 'Interfacing the Nation: Remediating Public Service Broadcasting in the Digital Television Age', *Convergence: The International Journal of Research into New Media Technologies* vol. 14 no. 3, August 2008, p. 213.

37. This refers to the controversy over aspects of the BBC's coverage of the Iraq war, which led to the replacement of the BBC Board of Governors by the BBC Trust and, following the report of the Inquiry into the Circumstances Surrounding the Death of Dr David Kelly conducted by Lord Hutton, the resignation of both the governor of the board of directors, Gavyn Davies, and the director general, Greg Dyke.

38. Jana Bennett, quoted in 'BBC and Discovery Communications Announce New Partnership', 15 November 2010, http://www.bbc.o.uk/pressoffice/bbcworldwide/worldwidestories/pressreleases/2010/11_november/discovery_bbc.shtml

5.4 Music, Documentary, Music Documentary

MICHAEL CHANAN

Perhaps the least vexed and richest interaction between docu-
mentary and an art is to be found in the films made about music
and musicians. At one level, here is deployed – potentially at least
– documentary's 'record' capacity, its ability to preserve evidence
in a vividly iconic form, at its best.

THE PROMISCUOUS FLOW OF DIFFERENT MUSICS

The music documentary is a paradoxical genre. Films
about music and musicians have been a major strand of
documentary since the 1960s, but you wouldn't know it
from the attention they've received in documentary
studies – all the more odd given the huge predominance of
music in popular culture. There is no ready explanation for
this omission, but a pioneering conference on the subject
recently threw up an interesting suggestion: that music
documentary tends to operate according to an unwritten
law in which the film-maker looks at the musician with
the eyes of the fan, which results in the film being seen as
essentially promotional and therefore unworthy of serious
attention.[1] It is certainly true that many music documentaries are made at the bidding of the musicians (or their
managers), but, even so, this should not become an excuse
for ignoring their filmic qualities, which are not only
many and varied, but in some cases paradigmatic for
documentary as such.

At all events, many films from back then have disappeared from view, buried in more or less inaccessible television archives, awaiting digital rebirth, except for a few
celebrated titles like D. A. Pennebaker's famous Bob Dylan
film, *Dont Look Back* [sic] (1965). Yet public service television in
Europe in the 60s saw a steady stream of variegated music
programming. As well as the classical concerts that had
already featured as prestige shows on US television in the
50s, you could see a whole range of documentary sub-
genres: biographies of composers (dead and alive), portraits of famous artists, eavesdropping on rehearsals and
masterclasses, magazine items and even panel games, all
produced under the aegis of the public service remit. (The
present writer appeared in a musical panel game on BBC
television as a student in around 1967; then made his first

music documentary for the same organisation three years
later.) Although the output was strictly divided between
'serious' and 'light' (or 'popular'), in line with the old established patrician view of the functions of public broadcasting, this is less important than the promiscuous flow of
different musics in the expanding acousmatic world, and
film-makers drew inspiration wherever they found it, independent of genre, as a good proportion of their viewers
would increasingly also do.

Music documentaries have contributed to a breakdown
of musical – and cultural – barriers by introducing new
publics to musics to which they might not otherwise have
paid attention (though their interest might have been
piqued by hearing it in a movie, or featured in a commercial). Perhaps this very confusion is one of the problems:
despite the growing fluidity of contemporary musical culture, it remains split between camps, indeed camps within
camps. It would be relevant here to look at T. W. Adorno's
typology of the listener in his *Introduction to the Sociology of*
Music[2] where he addresses the contradictory and contrasting traits to be found in contemporary listening habits not
in terms of empirical analysis but the subjective relationship between listener and music. There is no type of listener, he believes – even the so-called 'tone deaf' – who
escapes the social construction of music, and on this reading the music documentary becomes one of the prominent
means through which this social construction has come to
be conducted. Adorno's first category, the 'expert listener',
comprises the very people – musicians, academics and
critics – who are likely to be in front of the camera,
although many amateur musicians of all social classes also
fall into this category, while there's also a large public
comprising his second category, the 'good listener'.

Demographically, however, the television audience is
probably to be found mostly among his middle categories:
the 'culture consumer', the 'emotional listener' and the
'entertainment listener', which overlap and share many of
the same susceptibilities and predilections. These layers
are differentiated by a kind of caste system, in which the
culture consumer is up-market, the emotional listener is
middle-brow and the entertainment listener is the hoi

Sounds and Silence (2009): an ideal image of today's perfect listener

polloi. It is virtually impossible to address them all at the same time. Not to mention the interference of Adorno's most curious category, the 'resentment listener', who chooses to listen to one thing in order to express disapproval of something else.

A notable recent documentary by Peter Guyer and Norbert Wiedmer, *Sounds and Silence* (2009), offers an ideal image of today's perfect listener in the shape of the priestly figure of the independent record producer Manfred Eicher, founder of the ECM record label, as he moves around from city to city and continent to continent, recording musicians regardless of genre – be it classical, jazz, funk or folk – such as Arvo Pärt, Dino Saluzzi, Jan Garbarek, Eleni Karaindrou, Anouar Brahem, Gian Luigi Trovesi, Kim Kashkashian, Nik Bärtsch and Marilyn Mazur, lending them the benefit of his acutely discriminating ears. For their part, professional musicians frequently welcome frontier clashes and many move across the boundaries with ease. Journalists, commentators and pundits do so rather more rarely; the highly compartmentalised media apparatus generally refuses them authority. Unfortunately, the same often applies in academia, especially in the study of popular culture. Consequently, since there's been no systematic study of the music documentary that this writer is aware of, these lines are meant only as preliminary thoughts.

TRANSFORMATION OF THE MUSICAL OBJECT

My contention is that, over the space of a dozen years or so, all the major sub-genres of the music documentary made their appearance one by one. In the process, the musical object began to undergo a transformation strongly related to the changing functions of music within contemporary culture. The gramophone had separated music from the moment of its performance and spread it far afield. Sound cinema gave performance a new visibility in the musical, but in a form where musical numbers were wrapped up in narrative envelopes and filmed (generally to playback) in the studio, for which the new recording systems were primarily designed. As long as location sound filming

remained a cumbersome and awkward process, music was of little interest to documentary (with rare exceptions like Humphrey Jennings) before the 1960s, when the key factor in promoting innovation was the introduction of portable synchronous-sound filming. This amounted to a breakthrough: the ample illusion of live music-making in its rightful place and for its own sake which would restore the musical object to the social reality of its practice – and then go on to reveal new aspects. This is not meant as an argument for technological determinism: I see the introduction of new technical means of film production as akin to that of new scientific instruments, which open up new areas of experimentation (and the new questions that they raise). Indeed, the new gear immediately stimulated two rather different approaches on opposite sides of the Atlantic, with Direct Cinema in New York developing a new form of observational reportage, while cinéma vérité in Paris adopted a more reflexive mode which took account of the effect of the camera on its subjects.

The first intimations of a filmic revaluation of music date from the preceding decade, when the first portable tape recorders appeared, not yet capable of synchronisation, but allowing direct recording of musical performance in situ. Documentary always sooner or later raises the question of authenticity, and the anthropologist Jean Rouch, recoiling from the orchestral score added to a film of his by the distributor, took a prototype portable tape recorder on location to West Africa as early as 1951. *Cimetière dans la falaise* [*Cemetery in the Cliffs*] is the first time in a film of Africa that we hear – as we're told in a title at the start of the film – the actual music of the people we are seeing. This is not a music documentary, but the same editing technique of laying continuous location-recorded music over (or under) a succession of short individual shots in continuity with the rhythm – already a standard trope in narrative cinema – could also be used for musical subject matter. Two examples appear in 1954 and 1956, respectively: Roger Tilton's *Jazz Dance* and *Momma Don't Allow* by Karel Reisz and Tony Richardson. Both sessions were mounted for the camera, the former in a New York dance hall, the latter at a jazz club attached to a pub in north London. Both films dispense with commentary. According to Richard Leacock, one of Tilton's cameramen, he shot hand-held with a wind-up Eymo camera, darting around all over the place, while a second cameraman using a rudimentary synch system attached to his camera (and therefore less mobile) filmed the musicians. By means of clever and painstaking editing, it was possible to create a sustained illusion of synch.[3] The same technique (without any synch footage at all) was used by the Free Cinema pioneers in England. *Momma Don't Allow* isn't usually thought of as a music documentary, but it's that and more: an emblematic film of the time, the candid portrayal of a contemporary sub-culture.

The problem of synchronisation was overcome by the photographer-cum-director Bert Stern in *Jazz on a Summer's Day* (1960), a landmark film of the 1958 Newport Jazz Festival (held in the exclusive ambience of Rhode Island's summer resort for the East Coast elite) and incorporating a soundtrack for which Columbia Records provided the master tape-recording. Shot by five cameras (three fixed and two hand-held, moving among the audience), Stern anticipates multi-camera concert films of the late 60s such as Pennebaker's *Monterey Pop* (1968) and Michael Wadleigh's *Woodstock* (1970), and, like those films, *Jazz on a Summer's Day* is already more than a transcription of concert performances, but an almost ethnographic portrait of the audience in its natural habitat.

In short, what we see is an image of music as a form of social activity that corresponds to what Christopher Small has called 'musicking', which is not just making music but also participating in a musical activity in some way.[4] Both musicians and audience are often seen in close-ups, which have two effects: first, they help the viewer to concentrate on listening to the music and, second, they emphasise the physicality of musicking, as we cut between the sweat on the players' foreheads and the tapping feet of the listeners, with which in all likelihood we join in while watching. Small believes the conventional emphasis on pieces and performances is too restrictive, and we should think of music as a site of encounter that takes place through the medium of sound organised in various certain ways. Musicking, in other words, is an activity always located in particular social settings and involving certain relationships – among the musicians; between musician and listener; between individual and group; and beyond the group, within society ... wider still, between society and the natural world; perhaps even, if you like, the supernatural, or at any rate the sense of transcendence. All of these

Jazz on a Summer's Day (1960): an almost ethnographic portrait of the audience in its natural habitat

relationships, culminating with the redemptive gospel singing of Mahalia Jackson, are present in this film, which records a moment when jazz, in all its varieties, had been accepted within the cultural mainstream of the American upper classes, just before it was overtaken by rock and youth culture and the divisiveness of the social and political turmoil of the coming decade. At all events, this film serves as a lasting model, and the portrayal of musicking becomes a touchstone of the music documentary as a genre.

If the real breakthrough came with mobile synch location filming, the result, in the felicitous phrase of Mario Ruspoli, one of the new breed of film-makers who first filmed this way, was that for the first time 'sound and picture stroll along arm-in-arm with the characters in motion', or in Leacock's more prosaic description, 'For the first time we were able to walk in and out of buildings, up and down stairs, film in taxi cabs, all over the place, and get synchronous sound.'[5] The hallmark of the new documentary thus became unrehearsed synchronous speech, overheard or addressed to the camera, and live musical execution, private as well as public. Leacock himself used 16mm film sound equipment for the first time in 1957, on *Bernstein in Israel*, when he accompanied the American conductor on a trip to Tel-Aviv for the inaugural concert of the Mann Auditorium, the new home of the Israel Philharmonic. But the gear was still cumbersome, and I remember Leacock once talking about his frustration at missing scenes in the hotel room. Nevertheless, another innovation, Bernstein's first-person narration, gives the film an intimate diaristic feel.

There were also moves in new directions in the third centre of direct documentary, which was found in Canada, where it was supported by the National Film Board. Many of the typical elements of the emergent sub-genre of the rock documentary are already present in *Lonely Boy* (1962), a portrait of the Canadian pop singer Paul Anka by Wolf Koenig and Roman Kroiter – the hand-held camera, the backstage scenes, the screaming girls, the vox pops in the street, the conversations in the car, the interviews. It also shares the Canadian predilection for unforced self-reflexivity, moments when subjects spontaneously acknowledge the presence of the camera – for example, when the camera finds Anka in his dressing room where he tells his entourage to 'just forget they're even there', addressing the words to himself as much as them, as he strips to his underpants in order to don his stage costume. Indeed, as the camera enters the intimacy of backstage space, the scene is emblematic of the great promise of the new documentary to show what's real: what you see when the camera takes you into private spaces, with the hint of voyeurism as a metaphor for the forbidden view. This is documentary as the breaking of taboos.

While there's a lot in this film about the singer, there is nothing, except for one brief scene when Anka runs through a new tune on the piano for his manager, about the song. What we generally hear is the same musical object that was sold over the counter, the carefully controlled, properly mixed and balanced product of a process of creation and production which remains invisible, like a hidden mystique. But, considered as a document of cultural history, the film is a snapshot of a transitional moment: while Anka's manager is grooming him for the cabaret circuit, the razzmatazz which engulfs him belongs to the new sphere of rock 'n' roll.

Meanwhile, if the natural and legitimate instinct of the new documentary is to turn to the proximate world of contemporary society for subject matter, a rather different trend emerges from the marriage of the new gear with the instincts of ethnomusicology. Rouch himself made several such films, sometimes working with the ethnomusicologist Gilbert Rouget, where he developed the art of the synchronous long take. *Yenendi de Ganghel* [*Rain Dance at Ganghel*] (1968), for example, employs long takes with a mobile hand-held camera moving smoothly between musicians and participants in the ceremonial, with no cutaways. Recorded by a directional gun-mic which moves with the camera, this means that the sound perspective – the balance between the different groups of drummers, or between drums and voices – changes, but in retaining the camera's perspective, the viewer hardly notices. This is completely the opposite of the self-reflexive concept of cinéma vérité with which Rouch is indelibly associated. It is practically the purest form of ethnographic record-footage you can get.

The ethnomusicological documentary of the 1960s, notwithstanding its tiny audiences, lies at the origins of a major trend which emerged a decade later, with films that help succour the popularisation of non-western musics, like Jeremy Marre's *Roots Rock Reggae* of 1977. The first of a series shot on location in different continents, this is the domain that comes to be known as 'world music', a designation borrowed from the ethnomusicologist Japp Kunst and applied by a group of record producers in the late 80s as a marketing label, to be used on shelf dividers in the record stores: a catch-all to exploit the proliferation of musics from different parts of the world brought into play by factors like mass economic migration and globalisation. These films are not ethnomusicological documentaries as such, but include valuable ethnographic episodes, which they typically combine with the full range of documentary techniques in an orthodox and televisually acceptable style. Neglected by the critical literature about documentary artistry, films like these are nevertheless significant interventions in the process of cultural change and its representation, not merely the symptom of a commercial phenomenon but the expression of an authentic cultural undercurrent; not just another form of cultural exploitation but part of a growing awareness of other musics and cultures, a process of cultural exchange that produces a transformation of both musical and social consciousness that later comes to the surface in various forms of fusion music.

THE MUSIC DOCUMENTARY COMES OF AGE

The same year as *Lonely Boy* came another innovative film but in a completely different vein: Ken Russell's *Elgar* (1962). Russell persuaded the BBC bosses to wave the paternalistic prohibition on the use of actors to portray historical personages, allowing Edward Elgar – played here at different ages by different (non-professional) actors – to be seen in the appropriate locations, although not heard. These acted scenes are combined, under a stylish narration, with photographs of Elgar and his family, and a good deal of archive footage, edited to substantial chunks of music with the voiceover narration mixed in. Visually, the film is highly striking. The image of Elgar riding across the Malvern Hills to the strains of the *Introduction and Allegro for Strings* created a fresh new icon for the established patriarchal figure that Elgar had become. The masterly editing is entirely consonant with the music without 'mickey-mousing': in other words, sympathetic, without the music being slavishly tied to the image (or vice versa). This is hardly to disturb the integrity of the musical object, but there is also one sequence which works differently, by introducing a contradiction between the music and the image content which it would be appropriate to call dissonant: the extraordinary juxtaposition of 'Land of Hope and Glory' with archive shots of the carnage of World War I, where music and image are both so strong that neither overwhelms the other, but both become imbued with an intense poignancy.

This ability of the film medium to both expand and contradict the connotations of the musical object with new visual intertexts is not new, and not exclusive to documentary. Russell's evolving style is taken not from the new documentary but classical models crossed with European New Wave cinema, bringing the latter into television in a new context and new combinations. I am put in mind of Dai Vaughan, one of television's best documentary film editors, writing about *Television Documentary Usage* in 1976, where he mentions the ironic remark of a fellow film editor about the exciting innovations of the 60s: 'In those days we were developing the conventions. Now we merely apply them.'[6] Russell invented his own form of excess, and *The Debussy Film* (1965) is the first time he indulges in the kind of visual provocation for which he later became notorious. This is not only Russell as iconoclast, but also at his most experimental, including his pioneering use of direct sound in the dialogue scenes. What is ostensibly an acted documentary with a self-reflexive narrative schema allows him to fantasise freely, abandoning any kind of documentary truth in the image, but in a manner that transforms the

The Debussy Film (1965): Russell invented his own form of excess

musical object quite radically. When the fantasy is consonant, then it calls on images of the kind we associate with
chocolate boxes and television commercials. When it's dissonant, however, it becomes an exercise in visual travesty
and intemperance. Debussy is reinterpreted, but in a form
that doesn't gel. The affects produced by the imagery
refuse to combine with those produced by the music. No
wonder that later commentators on the film describe it as
a piece of postmodernism ahead of the game.

The music documentary comes of age when it begins
to work on the musical object itself, not only by foregrounding performance and inviting the viewer to listen,
but also capturing music in its social context, breaking
down the musical commodity, historicising it or opening it
up to interpretation. In the field of popular music, two paradigmatic films where this turn first occurs are Peter
Whitehead's *Charlie is My Darling* (1965), the first documentary of the Rolling Stones, and Don Pennebaker's Bob Dylan
film, *Dont Look Back*. Both are musical travelogues:
Whitehead accompanies the Stones on a two-day two-gig
trip to Dublin and Belfast, Pennebaker follows Dylan on a
week-long tour of England. This gives both films a simple
trajectory to follow in their narrative design, in which
musical numbers are interspersed by travelogue observation and other verbal sequences. *Dont Look Back* is the
more strictly observational, conforming to the non-interventionist credo of Direct Cinema. *Charlie is My Darling*
includes interviews to camera and montage sequences of
musical tracks over observational shots. Both films include
sequences of informal music-making where music escapes
the commodity form, such as a hotel room sing-song,
which returns us to the simplest form of musicking by an
ordinary bunch of people in an intimate setting, where the
musical object is immediate and carries no trace of commercial values. In Whitehead's film, the rawness of the
unmixed and unbalanced sound, always following the

camera's point of view, has much to do with the scene's
impact. This is also true in the theatre, the camera being on
stage with the group, running continuously but darting
around restlessly, when audience members invade the
stage and, amid the fracas, the direct sound takes on a distorted, almost surreal effect. This is probably the first time
a camera has captured a moment such as this, the frenzy
at a rock concert when the bacchanal explodes. It is a
moment that perhaps anticipates the more sinister violence which we witness a few years later in *Gimme Shelter*
(1970) by the Maysles brothers and Charlotte Zwerin.

Dont Look Back is particularly rich in sequences of
informal music-making which not only transform the
musical object but simultaneously work on the image of
the musician. These scenes run counter to one of the
major criticisms launched against Direct Cinema: that its
claim to truth was flawed because the camera didn't
simply record what was there, but affected people's behaviour and induced them to perform. When Pennebaker was
criticised for this over his portrayal of Dylan, he replied (if
memory serves) that of course Dylan was performing, 'he
was playing himself, and doing it very well'. But something
else is going on in these moments of musical making,
because here the subject is already performing, and the
camera doesn't necessarily affect their behaviour.
Whether there's an audience to whom the performance is
directed, or the camera is part of a private gathering where
people are playing for each other, someone making music
is already performing a role which the camera, in
favourable circumstances, can observe without affecting,
because making music is a form of behaviour that already
involves the whole person in an act of expressive communication. This doesn't mean the subject is unaware of
the camera's presence, any more than the classical pianist
on stage is unaware of the audience; but when someone is
making music, the camera can adopt the same role as any
other listener.

In films like *Monterey Pop*, *Woodstock* and *Gimme Shelter*,
performance is centre stage, but as the focus of a portrayal
of musicking which makes them more than simply concert
films. In the case of *Gimme Shelter* there is the added
element of self-reflexivity as the Stones watch the rushes
in the cutting room. These films, by mythologising the
events, entered into a wider circuit of musicking, not
simply a surrogate for the live experience but an integral
component of the social form of musical experience within
contemporary mass culture.

Entering the 1970s, there was a wide range of models
and techniques available for music documentarists; a
thriving music industry with operators both large and
small; and cinema and television both eager and open to
experiment. One of the results was a stream of films in the
UK which Kevin Donnelly calls 'the visualised live album'.[7]
Basically consisting of live concert films, often paired with

a live LP release, they included The Beatles in *Let It Be* (1970), Emerson, Lake and Palmer's *Pictures at an Exhibition* (1971), T. Rex's *Born to Boogie* (1973), Yes's *Yessongs* (1973) and Led Zeppelin's *The Song Remains the Same* (1975). According to Donnelly: '[C]oncept albums led to rock operas and live albums became concert documentaries, a subset of the "rockumentary" format.'[8] The rockumentary was made by film-makers who were less drawn to the mainstream than to experiments on the periphery – and to the interplay of personalities and clashes of will backstage. The concert film, on the other hand, was not produced by the film industry but by record labels; they were generally made by technicians, and focused on the stage in a visual style unerringly subordinated to the primacy of the soundtrack, which was 'heavily sweetened' in the rerecording studio; these indeed were essentially a fan product.

AGAINST THE GRAIN

There were also counter-currents. It was against those emergent conventions mentioned by Vaughan that two avant-garde films of 1968 were made – *The Chronicle of Anna Magdalena Bach*, by Danièle Huillet and Jean-Marie Straub, and Jean-Luc Godard's *Sympathy for the Devil*. Further contributions to this tendency include Maurizio Kagel's *Ludwig Van* (1970) and Nam June Paik's video *A Tribute to John Cage* (1974). These are all, so to speak, anti-music documentaries, which reject the conventions and, in the process, exhibit one of the characteristic modes of all avant-garde cinema in which the normal cinematic ordering of time is discarded. They each do it differently. Straub and Huillet suspend camera motion and cutting, handing duration over entirely to the music; Godard imposes the arbitrary duration of the camera tracking around the musicians in the studio. Kagel, a composer who also made experimental films of his theatrical concert pieces, celebrated the bicentenary of Beethoven's birth with a surreal spoof of the television documentary biopic, a little à la Godard: a pianist wearing nothing more than a pair of shorts, playing a Beethoven sonata, while the camera pulls back to reveal wires which link him to a machine that records every movement of his muscles. A mock-up of the music room in the Beethoven House is guarded by life-size cardboard cutouts of Beethoven, Mozart and Haydn, where every available surface is covered by sheets of his music; for ten minutes the camera pans around the room, while the soundtrack is the result of instructing the musicians in the recording studio to play whatever their eyes alight upon. Being top-notch musicians, they cannot help but obey this instruction musically, and produce what Kagel called 'a contribution by Beethoven to the music of our time'. This is a musically composed made-for-television musical document. Paik, in a piece shown on WGBH Boston, takes his cue from Cage himself, emulating the composer's use of chance operations to destroy any sense of purposeful

authorial progression. In all four of these films, their temporal deconstruction lies at the opposite extreme to commercial culture's imposition of time regulation on commercial entertainment, in which music provides segmented periods of escape from daily chores.

There are other departures on the independent scene in the USA. The subject of Jill Godmilow's film of 1974, *Antonia: Portrait of a Woman*, is Antonia Brico, who in 1930, at the age of twenty-eight, became the first woman to conduct the Berlin Philharmonic Orchestra and, at the time of Godmilow's film, in her early seventies, conducted a semiprofessional orchestra in Denver just a few times a year. The film, in which Brico is interviewed by the singer Judy Collins, traces her struggles to survive in a male profession. The result, said one New York critic, was 'a film that is both a testament and a tribute' and 'much the best example so far of a new feminist consciousness' on the screen, while another called it a 'truly subversive and revolutionary' film about 'one woman's resistance against public prejudice'.[9] Music here is seen as a sociopolitical battleground more than a utopian realm of transcendence, and a field of contestation rather than aesthetic consumption.

In England, again away from the main centre of activity, Philip Donnellan, working at the BBC in Birmingham, came up with a music documentary of an entirely different kind. *The Big Hewer* (1973), a portrait of coal miners, was one of a number of adaptations of the 'radio ballads' produced for the BBC in 1958–64 by Charles Parker, working with the singers Ewan McColl and Peggy Seeger, which presented subjects in working-class history in what Parker described as a form of narrative documentary told in the words of the participants, spoken and sung.[10] Donnellan recreates the radio format's magical mixture of song and speech, keeping the singers off screen, weaving the soundtrack over and under a rich visual montage of new and old footage. Replacing the disembodied and impersonal commentary with song is to displace the voice of authority in favour of musical utterances that directly embody social experience through what Roland Barthes famously called the 'grain of the voice'.[11]

The same device occurs to delightfully teasing effect in Octavio Cortazár's *Hablando de punto cubano* [*Speaking of Typical Cuban Music*] (1974), one of the many music documentaries for the cinema produced by Cuba's state film institute (the ICAIC), many of them celebrating popular artists and traditions of pre-revolutionary years. Here Cortazár gives the commentary to a singer, the incomparable Joseito Fernández, who in the 1930s used to improvise a popular commentary on politics and current events in a weekly radio programme with the world-famous *Guantanamera* as theme tune. The result is one of the most playful documentaries this writer has ever had the fortune to see.

In another of the Cuban examples, Juan Carlos Tabío's *Miriam Makeba* (1973), the African singer and her band on tour in Cuba meet up with a group of Cuban musicians to learn about each other's music. The language gap between them proves no obstacle, and the camera witnesses a spontaneous exchange of purely musical communication. The same capacity of music to leap across language – and cultural – barriers, the same focus on visualising ways of listening, is demonstrated when Isaac Stern visits China in *From Mao to Mozart* (Murray Lerner, 1980), which again suggests the possibility of an encounter of cultures through the non-verbal language of music, but here music is portrayed as a form of international diplomacy: as China was opening up after Nixon's famous visit of 1972, here is the western patrician teaching teenage violinists emerging from the Cultural Revolution, when everything western was vilified, how to play Mozart. And why not?

THE WELLSPRINGS OF MUSICKING

In all these examples, the musical object undergoes multiple transformations as the pursuit of music is located in different sites of musicking across society and continents. The various strands of television documentary include the exotic, but also show a marked preference for portraits and biopics of celebrity musicians, with which the subjects happily collude, along with their managers and entourage, pretending to remain oblivious to the cultural effects of the process of mediatisation which marginalises the music but sexes up the musician. Tony Palmer, widely considered the primary practitioner of the celebrity sub-genre, escapes these strictures, but his films, while often musically absorbing, remain thoroughly conventional as portrayals of genius. The 1990s and the innovations of digital video countered this with the return of a renovated observational style, now in series form and minimally narrated, offering a new look at ordinary musicians at work. The risk here is that of turning the world of musicking into soap opera, as in the case of Michael Waldman's riveting six-parter on the management of the Royal Opera House, *The House* (1996). A decade or so later, when every corner of every channel succumbed to the most shameless populism, television discovered the musical 'reality show', like *Maestro* (2008), where famous entertainers compete to see which one of them might make the best orchestral conductor. It sounds crass, but was actually both entertaining and instructive.

None of these trends ever challenges, except by accident, what Adorno meant by the 'ideological' use of music, the use of music in favour of the ruling order, not just in obvious jingoistic forms, but more insidiously by uncritically reproducing the norms and values of traditional musical language (a practice generally followed by Hollywood film composers). However, an alternative take can be found in the art house, in occasional forays such as

François Girard's *Thirty-two Short Films About Glenn Gould* (1993), which uses a novel and fragmented narrative structure not only to portray the famous eccentric, but also to induce the viewer to open their ears to what he meant. There are also films where the voice which claims our attention is not individual but collective. A prime example is *A Great Day in Harlem* (Jean Bach, 1994), which tells the story of a day in 1958 when Thelonius Monk, Dizzy Gillespie, Roy Eldridge, Count Basie and dozens more top jazz musicians assembled in a street in Harlem for a legendary photograph. Although they do little more than reminisce, with the aid of personal photos snapped by participants and even some 8mm footage, the result is a rare self-portrait of a whole artistic community. In Heddy Honigmann's *The Underground Orchestra* (1997), a kind of ethnographic enquiry into the variety of nationalities working as buskers on the Paris metro, the music comes in the widest variety of styles, and the film becomes a poignant reflection on music and exile. Here the voice is both collective and subaltern. The same is true of a couple of films which push at the conventional boundaries of documentary to create new forms of musical narrative. *Latcho Drom* (Tony Gatlif, 1993) is a documentary song cycle in which gypsy musicians in different countries recount the history of the migration over the centuries of the Roma from India through the Middle East to Europe. *Poligono Sur* (Dominique Abel, 2003), the musical portrait of a gypsy community in Seville who have been rehoused in a bleak new public housing project, is a novel kind of documentary concert film. These are perhaps the music documentaries we need most, because they bring our musical world back into alignment with the real wellsprings of musicking in the contemporary world. They are also, in this writer's view, among the very finest examples of documentary art of the past couple of decades.

NOTES

1. Frank Meyer, 'No "Hall of Fame": Music Documentaries between Social Awareness and High Gloss Journalism?', Sights and Sounds: Interrogating the Music Documentary Conference, University of Salford, 3–4 June 2010.

2. T. W. Adorno, *Introduction to the Sociology of Music* (New York: Seabury, 1972).

3. www.richardleacock.com/#14880/Jazz-Dance. Accessed 6 August 2012.

4. Christopher Small, *Musicking: Meanings of Performing and Listening* (Middletown, CT: Wesleyan University Press, 1998).

5. Michael Chanan, *Politics of Documentary* (London: BFI, 1977), pp. 166, 177.

6. Dai Vaughan, *Television Documentary Usage* (London: BFI, 1976), p. 19.

7. K. J. Donnelly, 'British Cinema and the Visualized Live Album', Sights and Sounds: Interrogating the Music

Documentary Conference, University of Salford, 3–4 June 2010.

8. Ibid.

9. Jay Cocks, 'A Fine Romance', *Time*, 10 March 1975; Tom Allen, 'XXXX', *New York Magazine*, 22 September 1974.

10. Charles Parker, article reprinted in booklet accompanying *The Ballad of John Axon* (London: Topic Records, TSCO 801, 1999).

11. Roland Barthes, 'The Grain of the Voice', *Image, Music, Text* (New York: Farrar, Straus and Giroux, 1978).

5.5 Art, Documentary as Art

MICHAEL RENOV

Cinema is, of course, a twentieth-century addition to the six Hegelian Arts and, in its documentary voice, it has served not only to document these other modes but also to essay artistic expression on its own behalf. The current embrace of experimentalism in documentary practice and the increased presence of documentary material in museums and galleries harks back to the non-anglophone pioneers. (And is thus nothing new. Whether with Ivens, Vigo or Vertov, aesthetics were always important. The expressive power of the piece was seen to be the necessary and essential support of the ideological agenda.)

The increasing convergence of documentary film and contemporary art practices has come more and more into focus over these past decades. A conference entitled Truth or Dare: Art and Documentary, for example, held in London at the Whitechapel Gallery in February 2006, provided a forum for exchange between members of the documentary community and their counterparts from the contemporary art world. The title of the colloquium, Truth or Dare, was meant to be ironic. For, despite the presumed distance between the two spheres – with the documentary practitioner devoted to 'authenticity' or 'realism', on the one hand, and the contemporary artist providing the experimentation or daring, on the other – the conference organisers intuited a decidedly less oppositional relationship. They wrote,

> We noticed how increasingly the boundaries between artists using moving image to explore 'documentary' themes, and documentary makers experimenting with structure, form and content, as well as exhibition possibilities, had brought some film-makers from both disciplines closer together. We also suspected both groups knew little about each other as the two worlds could be hermetic.[1]

The conference was notable for the degree of local participation from makers, curators, teachers, scholars and enthusiasts from both sides of the putative art/documentary divide.

At an international colloquium held in conjunction with the 2006 Sydney Biennale of Art, whose theme was Zones of Contact, the consensus view was that film and video installations have become more and more prevalent in galleries and museums – fully one-quarter of the 2006 Sydney Biennale works were film or video-based – and that these works frequently tend to display a decidedly documentary character. These single- or more often multi-channelled installations often are composed of material captured from everyday life: landscapes, interviews or first-person (artist) testimonies. All of these formats are familiar from the documentary vernacular (the nature or landscape film, the city symphony, the talking head, auto-biography). Again, the speakers at the colloquium approached their topics from across gaps that spoke to their respective placement within the art or documentary worlds. Differences of political economy and institutional infrastructures were the easiest to identify across the two discursive regimes. The hegemonic status of Australian television as an outlet for locally produced documentaries (few theatrical outlets for 'Aussie docos' exist) helped to sharpen the divide between non-fiction film and work that circulated in the more globalised, better capitalised circuit of museums and galleries. Yet it could be argued that such differences are far from intrinsic ones.

Some of the dissimilarities between the art and documentary contexts are not difficult to anticipate. One very broad arena of difference, formal in character, is related to shot duration, editing style or pacing – in short, temporality. Artists' installations face a set of audience expectations and reception conditions quite unlike those associated with the work of the documentary film-maker. For the gallery artist, there are no commissioning editors, broadcasters or exhibitors whose concerns for expository style or brevity of expression respond to perceived institutional needs (e.g., preordained time slots) or imagined revenues. In fact, the documentary material found in gallery or museum settings is often displayed on a loop or is reprojected at frequent intervals rather than screened discretely in a theatre or to home audiences. To speak briefly of just one component of spectatorship, one need only recall the old debates within film and television studies in which the filmic gaze (immobilised and in the dark) was opposed to the more distracted televisual glance. In the gallery, one confronts a fully mobilised or flaneurist gaze of the sort discussed by Anne Friedberg and others, perhaps even an aesthetic of boredom. The work is there to be encountered at one's own pace and with an unpredictable level of attentiveness.

For a variety of reasons, the documentary film has long been associated with a sense of urgency, indeed a mission. It was understood to be a vehicle for social change and a potentially powerful educative tool. For John Grierson, founding father of the British Documentary Movement during the late 1920s and 30s, film was 'an instrument much more suited to the specific purposes of education than any other of the arts'; documentary film-making under his tutelage was developed with specifically pedagogical goals in mind.[2] In the years leading up to World War II, a radically disparate group of makers, including Leni Riefenstahl, Pare Lorentz, Dziga Vertov and Humphrey Jennings, showed the documentary film to be a formidable nation-building tool.

In the early 90s, Bill Nichols famously characterised documentary as one of the discourses of sobriety, grouping it with other sorts of 'serious business' such as economics, politics, religion and foreign policy. All of these non-fictional systems, as he called them, 'can and should alter the world itself, they can effect action and entail consequences'.[3] Nichols described the documentary as essentially argument-driven (argument is to non-fiction, he wrote, as story is to fiction), while philosopher Trevor Ponech suggested that non-fiction film is best understood as a special condition of language, one rooted in assertion or claim-making; it is thus defined by its locutionary force.[4] Such assertiveness – consistent with documentary's historical role – is an occasional rather than a core value of contemporary art. By contrast, and again I stress the provisionality of my observations, I would propose that the moving image-based contemporary art works found in today's galleries and museums tend towards a greater rhetorical *obliquity*, *partiality* and textual *openness* than their conventional documentary cousins.

Yet I also want to argue for some important commonalities between the non-fiction film and its gallery or museum-based counterpart. In doing so, I propose that we consider the explicitly *documentative* dimension of the work as a kind of functionality that may be present no matter the setting or context. Some elaboration is required. I have elsewhere characterised documentary discourse as responsive to four general but historicised functions or modalities of desire, 'impulses which fuel documentary discourse'.[5] These are the urge to record, reveal or preserve; the drive to persuade or promote; the need to analyse or interpret; and the will to express. Any moving image-based contemporary art practice that engages in an act of historical witnessing or testimony is perforce preservational in character just as artists' interventionist or advocacy-

oriented works (quite common in recent years) are efforts at persuasion.

Nonetheless, important art/documentary distinctions remain. With regard to preservation and persuasion, what may strike us as possible or even familiar traits for moving image-based contemporary art approaches defining conditions for the documentary film. Grierson's helpful thumbnail definition of the documentary – the creative treatment of actuality – speaks to this filmic form's anchorage in yet reorchestration of the real. Over the decades, documentary-makers have consistently felt the need to resurrect the past or re-present some facet of social life, typically, as I've said, to construct an argument about it, to interrogate it or even intervene in it. Not surprisingly, documentary has been repeatedly linked to movements for social change; media activists who once wielded 16mm cameras now stream their digital images on the internet or post them to YouTube. Contemporary gallery-based artists frequently share such engagements and are increasingly drawn to the landscapes of social memory, experience or historical trauma for their raw material.

The third function, the analytical impulse, is what I've termed 'the cerebral reflex of the record/reveal/preserve modality ... it is revelation interrogated'.[6] This reflexive turn in documentary film-making places it in parallel with much contemporary art and springs, I would argue, from the same modernist sources. As for the expressive register, here the documentary tradition has, at times, lagged behind its art cousin. For this function, the inverse of what I've posed above appears to obtain: what for the commercially produced documentary could be termed a special circumstance (the 'experimental documentary') is for moving image-based contemporary art a defining condition.

To review then: the documentary 'project' (as we may call the culture of non-fiction film-making that has arisen since the 1930s) has been notable for its rhetorical urgency and frontal attack on social problems, state repression or public complacency. These are values enforced by decades of media activism and cultural resistance. The makers have, on occasion, attempted to interrogate their impulses or source materials, to engage in analytics. At certain historical moments, documentarists have, in producing their creative treatments of actuality, chosen to put the emphasis on the 'creative' side of the equation. It is this expressive component or functionality of the documentary drive that builds the strongest bridge between non-fiction film and its counterparts in the gallery.

What I will argue here is that the seemingly novel convergence between art and documentary now being touted at events held at Whitechapel Gallery or at Sydney's or Barcelona's Museums of Contemporary Art has a lengthy and controversial genealogy. As it happens, documentary has long shared historical and conceptual roots with various strands of twentieth-century art or avant-gardism. In parallel with the surrealist movement which, in the 1930s, refocused its concerns from the purely aesthetic domain to the political, documentary put aside much of its formal experimentation for the duration. I will conclude my remarks by proposing a fifth documentary function, one that I hope will suggest what the art world may have to gain from its current encounter with documentary culture.

Up until the past decade or two and despite the influence of the 1920s documentary innovators, the expressive or aesthetic function had been consistently undervalued within the non-fiction domain. Quite often and particularly in the anglophone world, the central task of the documentary had been to mobilise mass opinion, to draw attention to an injustice or to offer to public view a previously unknown corner of the world. (One might want to modify this account in light of the post-war French documentary tradition of Franju, Resnais, Marker and Varda, but the Griersonians held sway in Britain, the USA, Canada and Australia. See Chapter 2.9.) Yet it is important to note that expressivity is always the support of the other discursive goals. The greater the expressive power of the piece – that is, the more vividly the film communicates – the more likely an audience is to feel persuasion, educative value or revelation. The camera that follows John F. Kennedy into that Milwaukee auditorium in *Primary* (1960) allows us to gauge the man's charismatic power, to witness the laying on of hands as Kennedy winds his way to the stage, in a manner that no other camera placement could have done. The strength of the cinematic gesture heightens the film's power to persuade us of the candidate's extraordinary personal appeal.

The centrality of the expressive domain is a crucial point to make for documentary studies in light of a tradition of disparagement towards Formalism, meant to be an unyielding focus on the beautiful rather than the true. Dziga Vertov suffered from such an indictment even from comrade Sergei Eisenstein himself, who chastised the monumental *Chelovek s kinoapparatom* [*Man with a Movie Camera*] (USSR, 1929) as 'formalist jackstraws and unmotivated camera mischief'. Vertov, one of documentary's totemic ancestors, voiced certain modernist ambitions which constitute, for the documentary tradition, the road less travelled. Vertov, pseudonym of Denis Kaufman – newsreel producer, manifesto writer and creator of the landmark film *Man with a Movie Camera* – celebrated the cinema's unparalleled possibilities. In Vertov's view, these possibilities had nothing to do with film-drama, deemed to be 'the opiate of the people'.[7] Vertov wrote, the main and essential thing is:

> The sensory exploration of the world through film. We therefore take as the point of departure the use of the camera as a kino-eye, more perfect than the human eye, for the exploration of the chaos of visual phenomena that fills space.[8]

The camera – freed from the physical limitations of human perception, capable of contracting or expanding time, of plunging and soaring through the heavens, of linking and combining disparate spaces and bodies – could do far more than merely copy the eye. 'Starting today,' wrote Vertov in 1923, 'we are liberating the camera and making it work in the opposite direction – away from copying.'[9]

A decade later, altered circumstances and new ideological pressures led documentary to become a tool for struggle, one that happily embraced its mimetic potential. In the 1930s, the Griersonian tradition sought to show the face of industrial Britain to the world, to valorise the state's best efforts and the common courage of its citizenry. The same held true in the USA, evidenced by the work of Pare Lorentz, Willard Van Dyke and, from a more radical perspective, the Workers Film and Photo League. During more than a decade of worldwide depression and war, aesthetics tended to be seen as a luxury ill-suited to the urgency of the times.

Perhaps Joris Ivens offers the clearest instance of an anti-aesthetic that emerged within the documentary tradition during the 30s and 40s. While filming his monumental *Misère au Borinage* [*Misery in the Borinage*] (1933, Belgium), Ivens, whose earlier film *Regen* [*Rain*] (1929, Netherlands) had celebrated the camera's power to evoke the subtleties of atmosphere and sensory memory, decided that beautiful images could sabotage his goal of alerting the world to the dire conditions faced by striking coal miners in the Borinage region of Belgium.

> During the filming of *Borinage* we sometimes had to destroy a certain unwelcome superficial beauty that would occur when we did not want it. When the clear-cut shadow of the barracks window fell on the dirty rags and dishes of a table the pleasant effect of the shadow actually destroyed the effect of dirtiness we wanted, so we broke the edges of the shadow. Our aim was to prevent agreeable photographic effects distracting the audience from the unpleasant truths we were showing.[10]

Far from moving away from copying as Vertov had wished, documentary-makers of the period embraced the documentary cinema's mimetic capacities wholeheartedly as a way to move an audience to grim recognition and social mobilisation.

I would, nonetheless, argue that it is the clickity-clack rhythm of W. H. Auden's narration in Wright and Watt's *Night Mail* (1936, UK) or the flawless editing of people and machines toiling as one to defeat the Germans in Jennings and McAllister's *Listen to Britain* (1942, UK) that burn these films into the world's memory. They do their work to persuade and promote all the better for their ability to engage our senses and induce our pleasures. In *Claiming the Real*, Brian Winston has argued that the Griersonians were more interested in 'prettifying aesthetics' and the search for the picturesque than in investigating the social ills which their films appeared to address.[11] I don't deny the shortcomings of these films' social reformist politics, but I must oppose the terms of the critique. The formal construction of a work is far from an add-on or surface feature that the 'prettifying' label would suggest (aesthetics as the icing on the cake). Rather the formal domain is about the work of construction, the play of the signifier, the vehicle of meaning for every instance of human communication. The formal regime is the very portal of sense-making; it determines the viewer's access to the expression of ideas, its power to move and transform an audience.

Thus far I have argued for the centrality of formal or expressive concerns for documentary film-making at both the conceptual and historical levels. I have also suggested that a sort of documentary anti-aesthetic emerged in the 1930s and early 40s which has marked this cinematic mode ever since. I would argue that it was the dire necessity of that moment that has cut documentary off from its avant-garde roots. Here I'm thinking of the city symphonies of Walter Ruttmann, Jean Vigo and Alberto Cavalcanti, Luis Buñuel's *Las Hurdes* [*Land without Bread*]

(1932, Spain) or later works such as Georges Franju's *Le Sang des bêtes* [*The Blood of Beasts*] (1949, France) or Alain Resnais's *Nuit et brouillard* [*Night and Fog*] (1955, France).

Now, in my view, the last two decades have been a very good, indeed a revitalising time for documentary aesthetics. This work has developed, I would argue, largely outside the mainstream documentary tradition yet, through its vibrancy and increasing popularity, has begun to reinvent that tradition, leaving it forever transformed. The innovations that have moved non-fiction media 'away from copying' have emerged in quite different contexts by practitioners who once may not have considered themselves documentarists.

CONVERGENCE

> I think of my films as documentaries. I never fantasize. I have never invented something just for the sake of making an interesting image. I am always struggling to get an equivalent on film to what I actually see.
>
> Stan Brakhage[12]

The late Stan Brakhage is considered by many to have been America's premiere avant-garde film-maker with a career spanning fifty years and more than a hundred films. One of his first films, *The Wonder Ring* (1955), was a short work commissioned by artist Joseph Cornell, who wished to

The Wonder Ring (1955): a luminous work, silent, filled with shimmering images that play at the edges of abstraction

have a filmic memento made of New York's Third Avenue El before its destruction. It is a luminous work, silent, filled with shimmering images that play at the edges of abstraction. Some of these dancing images are reflections captured from the imperfect window glass of the moving car, rippling distortions attracting the eye of the film-maker, neither graphically produced nor optically printed. These images are the product of Brakhage's visual fascination, offered up to the viewer as the equivalent of what he sees. It is what we ourselves might have seen had we been there and had we been so attentive.

Critic P. Adams Sitney has called such works as *The Wonder Ring* 'lyrical films':

> The lyrical film postulates the film-maker behind the camera as the first-person protagonist of the film. The images of the film are what he sees, filmed in such a way that we never forget his presence and we know how he is reacting to his vision.[13]

The subject matter of such a film as *The Wonder Ring* is the visible world – the stuff of documentary – enlivened by the eye and mind of the film-maker, a dialectical play of subject and object. Although the documentary tradition has tended to repress the emphasis on the subjectivity of the maker in favour of the world on the other side of the lens, the non-fiction film is always the result of an encounter between the two.

Much the same could be said of photography, which demonstrated its capacity for the literal transcription of reality as early as 1839. A gesture, a landscape, an event could now be rescued from time's passage; the photograph delivered an incontestable existential warrant, bearing the physical traces of the light beams that once touched the object itself. The photograph, like its progeny the documentary film, bears witness. But witness to what? To history, no doubt, so long as we trust the image's indexicality, its physical connectedness to the referent, not so easy to do in this digital age. But Roland Barthes for one has argued otherwise. 'I would … say that the photographer bears witness essentially to his own subjectivity, the way in which he establishes himself as a subject faced with an object.'[14] For Barthes, every photograph is a fabulous relic of pastness but it is, even before that, a physical expression of a perceiving self. Subject trumps object.

As a paradigm for documentary film-maker and historical world, I prefer the notion of the encounter, a dialogue between seer and seen, the subjectivity of the maker facing the objecthood of the world. Most often in the documentary tradition, the world rather than the filtering sensibility has taken precedence. But there is nothing inherent to the documentary endeavour that requires that this be so.

In tracing some of the important new directions that have evolved within the realm of documentary film-making in the past decade or two, it seems to me crucial to begin by establishing both a conceptual grounding for such innovation and a sense of its historical antecedents. I would argue that there has been an explosion of recent work in which film- and video-makers have explored the historical world from diverse perspectives, employing a range of methods and approaches which, through their innovations, have drawn the documentary film ever closer to the realm of contemporary art. The work of these artist-practitioners is drawn to the world 'out there', as has been the work of documentarists since the Lumière brothers in the late nineteenth century, but shaped and informed by the world 'in here', by personal experience, cultural and sexual identities, political and aesthetic engagements.

There is a new balance being struck between subject and object and the result is a reinvention of documentary practice. In this regard, one might include the uses of personal voice and performance in Marlon Riggs's *Tongues Untied* (1989, USA) or Sadie Benning's *It Wasn't Love* (1992, USA), the adaptation of animation to documentary ends in Jonathan Hodgson's *Feeling My Way* (1997, UK), Dennis Tupicoff's *His Mother's Voice* (1997, Australia) or Andy Glynne's *Animated Minds* (2004, UK) with Len Lye as precursor, the reinscription of home movies or found footage in Alan Berliner's *Nobody's Business* (1997, USA) or Peter Forgacs's *The Maelstrom* (1997, Hungary), the latter-day revision of the city symphony (as perfected in the 1920s by such cineastes as Flaherty, Cavalcanti, Vigo and Ruttmann) in Jem Cohen's *Lost Book Found* (1996), Harun Farocki's profoundly analytical gaze in *Images of the World and the Inscription of War* (1989), the melding of ethnographic subject matter and an aestheticising gaze in Leandro Katz's *Paradox* (2004) or the movement beyond narrative form towards seriality in Jay Rosenblatt's *Phantom Limb* (2005). While these works are in powerful dialogue with a century of documentary film practice, they are also reworking the syntax of documentary film-making and reconfiguring its

The Maelstrom (1997): powerful dialogue with a century of documentary film practice

boundaries, indications of a remarkable vitality within the realm of contemporary non-fiction media.

As a case in point, consider *Paradox*, a work by the long-time photographer and film-maker Leandro Katz. Shooting on a Guatemalan banana plantation of the southern lowlands, very near the Dragon of Quirigua, a 1,300-year-old Mayan stone altar to which Katz repeatedly returns for shots that linger well beyond our comfort or expectation, Katz offers us brief access to a world of famously alienated labour. It is the world of the banana republic, a country whose domestic economy has been wholly sacrificed to the demands of the global marketplace. And yet, while showing us the grinding labour and the gender segregation of this tropical, outdoor factory (shirtless men cut the hands of bananas and load them on a primitive conveyor belt while long lines of women wash and pack the fruit), Katz also shows us the unexpected. How surprising to confront the beauty of bodies in motion in this place (far from Vertov's socialist utopia), the grace and economy of the repetitive gesture or the pleasant tension between abstraction and representationalism as Katz pulls in tight or softens the edges of the image through his play with focal depth. While never entirely departing from the realm of ethnography or advocacy, we are shown this world in unexpected ways, ways that cause us to reflect upon our preconceptions and move us towards new imaginings. This is the province of art. But I would also want to pose the ethical question. Are Katz's banana plantation workers plastic material rendered dynamic through their movements or do they, despite their seeming servitude, emerge as partners in an ethical encounter?

It is perhaps worth mentioning, moreover, that many of the contemporary film- and video-makers whose works have helped transform documentary culture received their training in art schools around the world in the 1970s, 80s and 90s: Isaac Julien (*Derek*, 2008, UK) and others of the Black British workshop movement; Peter Forgacs in Hungary; Rea Tajiri (*History and Memory*, 1991) in the USA;

Paradox (2004): how surprising to confront the beauty of bodies in motion in this place

Canadian Richard Fung (*Sea in the Blood*, 2001); Sandra Kogut (*A Hungarian Passport*, 2001) and Cao Guimaraes (*The Soul of the Bone*, 2003) in Brazil. All of these artists have produced works that have circulated and made an impact in the documentary world (at festivals, via broadcast, in museums and universities) and have won awards at important international documentary festivals. In doing so, they have helped to reconfigure documentary discourse. Moreover, most of the above-named practitioners also produce installation-based work for museums and galleries that extends or challenges their documentary engagements.

The expressive function which I am stressing here can often be linked to and supported by what I would now call documentary's fifth function, the ethical function, its attentiveness to the mutuality and commensurability of self and Other despite the differences of power, status and access to the means of representation. A 'you' and an 'I' placed in delicate balance. It is the zone of what Emmanuel Levinas has termed 'non-indifference to the Other' arising from the founding obligation self owes Other prior to being. Here too – in the realm of ethics – can be discovered traces of the art of documentary practice.

Are Katz's banana plantation workers mere plastic elements rendered dynamic through their movements or do they, despite their servitude to the inexorable logic of the conveyor belt, emerge as partners in an ethical encounter? I sense in *Paradox* a projected *kinship of bodies*. Katz, shooting alone and under wraps for a single day, is himself engaged in a rigorous physicality linking self and Other. It is a film that recalls Barthes's belief in the photographer's intrinsic act of self-disclosure, the way in which his every framing of and attitude towards his object gives him away. The artist's encounter with the human form, with a corporeality that Levinas has called 'a knot or denouement of being ... a knot that cannot be undone'[15] becomes a vehicle for self-expression that is equally an act of testimony. Why testimony? Judith Butler has recently written: 'to take responsibility for oneself is to avow the limits of any self-understanding, and to establish these limits not only as a condition for the subject but as the predicament of the human community'.[16] Self and Other are irreducibly entwined. Katz bears witness to the labours of those workers – exploited, quotidian, to be sure, but also virtuosic and vividly gestural. A Marxist critique reducing workers to an exploited class is displaced by a portraiture that depicts bodies in motion, the artist's own and others', powerful in their productivity and thrilling to the eye. The ethical function is here linked to the expressive, the aesthetic value of the depiction rooted in an ethos of responsibility, an enactment of intersubjectivity.

My interest in tracing the ethical in relation to other documentary functions is inspired by non-fiction's recent migration into the gallery and museum and my impression that film and video artists have often chosen to focus on the human figure, that most highly charged instance of pro-filmic material. There is an innate fascination that attaches to the visual encounter with our like, a special sort of epistephilia that is fed if we sense the spontaneity of a documentary encounter, a face-to-face exchange between artist and subject. That encounter, ethical by its nature, bears with it an intrinsic risk or perhaps, better, a challenge. The responsibility to which Butler alludes ('I find that my very formation implicates the other in me, that my own foreignness to myself is, paradoxically, the source of my ethical connection with others'[17]) is the glue that binds artist and subject. It constitutes the core of documentary ethics, the domain of the fifth and still too-little regarded function of documentary film discourse. If, at the outset, I posed the question, 'What does contemporary art have to gain from its engagement with the documentary tradition?', it is surely not by way of lessons learned about formal innovation, intellectual stringency or cultural critique. It is, I would argue, the ethical realm in which the documentary tradition may take the lead.

For nearly a century, as makers pointed their cameras at factory workers, smiling Inuits and feckless political campaigners, debates raged over the obligations owed the documentary subject. The documentary films that have left the most indelible impressions are often those that have posed the most intractable ethical dilemmas. A case in point might be the Maysles brothers' *Grey Gardens* (1975, USA) which offers a view of the lives of an aging mother and daughter locked in co-dependency and advancing age. My students never tire of arguing about who is exploiting whom in that film, of trying to untangle voyeurism from exhibitionism or find a comfortable angle of reception for themselves. Student responses have been heightened recently by the success of the Broadway version of the film, its presence on the web via countless fan sites and the promise of an upcoming feature version. What does one say when Angelo gets fired from his factory job in Jean Rouch and Edgar Morin's trail-blazing *Chronique d'un été* [*Chronicle of a Summer*] (1961, France)? How does one calibrate the good and right in the representation of Angelo, memorialised as the worker/activist but reduced to joblessness? When Fred Wiseman filmed at the Massachusetts Institution for the Criminally Insane at Bridgewater for *Titicut Follies* (1967, USA), did those inmates ridiculed and demeaned on camera for all eternity really exercise informed consent? Is informed consent even possible in such circumstances and how much does that matter? Should the public's right to know or the film-maker's will to point a finger at social injustice trump privacy or a steady pay cheque for his subjects? In the case of *Paradox*, are Katz's factory workers being valorised or objectified?

What these films and our responses to them have in common is a tendency to jam the moral compass, to jostle us out of our comfort zone as we strive to decide the 'rightness' of the representation. Questions such as these resonate deeply in the documentary community and have done so for decades. Perhaps, by contagion, such ethical debates and the heightening of moral sensitivities will be generated in the galleries and museums where documentary art now flourishes. Such an activation, like the exercise of any muscle, can only be salutary for our collective health.

NOTES

1. Gail Pearce and Cahal McLaughlin, 'Introduction', in Gail Pearce and Cahal McLaughlin (eds), *Truth or Dare: Art and Documentary* (Bristol: Intellect, 2007), p. 9.

2. John Grierson, 'Films and the Community', *Grierson on Documentary*, ed. Forsyth Hardy (Berkeley: University of California, 1966 [1932]), p. 194.

3. Bill Nichols, *Representing Reality: Issues and Concepts in Documentary* (Bloomington: Indiana University Press, 1991), p. 3.

4. Trevor Ponech, *What is Non-fiction Cinema?: On the Very Idea of Motion Picture Communication* (Boulder, CO: Westview Press, 1999).

5. Michael Renov, 'Toward a Poetics of Documentary', in Michael Renov (ed.), *Theorizing Documentary* (New York: Routledge, 1993), p. 22.

6. Ibid., p. 30.

7. Dziga Vertov, *Kino-Eye: The Writings of Dziga Vertov*, ed. Annette Michelson (Berkeley: University of California Press, 1984), p. 71.

8. Ibid., pp. 14–15.

9. Ibid., p. 16.

10. Joris Ivens, *The Camera and I* (New York: International, 1969), p. 88.

11. Brian Winston, *Claiming the Real: The Griersonian Documentary and Its Legitimations* (London: BFI, 1995), pp. 38–9.

12. Stan Brakhage, 'The Independent Filmmaker: Stan Brakhage', in Joseph McBride (ed.), *Filmmakers on Filmmaking: The American Film Institute Seminars on Motion Pictures and Television* (Los Angeles: J. P. Tarcher, 1983), p. 203.

13. P. Adams Sitney, *Visionary Film: The American Avant-Garde 1943–1978* (New York: Oxford University Press, 1979), p. 142.

14. Roland Barthes, 'On Photography', *The Grain of the Voice*, trans. Linda Coverdale (New York: Hill and Wang, 1985), p. 356.

15. In Judith Butler, *Giving an Account of Oneself* (New York: Fordham University Press, 2005), p. 83.

16. Ibid.

17. Ibid., p. 84.

PART SIX:
Documentary Futures

6.1 Documentary as an Open Space

HELEN DE MICHIEL AND PATRICIA R. ZIMMERMANN

By the first decade of the twenty-first century documentary, it can be argued, was undergoing a profound change in its direction of travel. The rhetoric surrounding the use of moving images as a tool of social action was acquiring a fresh lease of life. The notion of the socially engaged documentary was not, of itself, new, but now, in the post-Griersonian era, the very idea of the 'documentarist' as a species of professional communicator was being called into question more comprehensively than ever before.

NEXT

The coordinates and practices of documentary have shifted dramatically in the last decade – and now require our critical attention to rethink how we consider and reframe the documentary project for the twenty-first century.

This chapter provides some initial theorisations and case studies mapping an approach to emergent documentary forms across the analogue, the digital and the embodied we call 'open space' documentary. To open more dialogue and debate, this chapter threads through speculations on open space documentary, invoking and continuing the legacy of Dziga Vertov, an early theorist and practitioner who also probed the nexus of new technologies, new political configurations and new ways of considering the audience and spectatorship.[1] In homage to Vertov, our exploration and argument for open space documentary is organised in sections, mixing theory, case studies and speculations.

From the static, fixed objects of analogue film and video, documentary is now redefining itself as a fluid, collaborative, shape-shifting, responsive environment for encounters we call open space documentary.[2] The spaces invoked in these works are open to many iterations, communities and engagements, rather than closed deductive arguments. These significant changes in the documentary ecology require a reconsideration of documentary theory and practice, a shift from a text-centred criticality towards a nexus of technology, form, histories, community, politics, convenings, collaborations, mobilities, movements and strategies that have developed in performance art and community arts practices of the last decade and have

migrated into documentary.[3] The emergence of new media and new platforms, such as Web 2.0, social media, Wikis, remix technologies and amateurisation of media tools have contributed *partially* and *incrementally* to these changes and recalibrations of the documentary project.[4]

But technology can account for only part of these quite significant shifts – and does not sustain sufficient explanatory models. In the current era, a perfect storm of social, cultural, aesthetic and economic recalibrations has also mobilised the emergence of new forms of open space documentary. Resources to support long-form documentaries across the globe have either been expunged or diminished.[5] Interrogations into documentary ethics in relation to the active agency of subjects have accelerated in the context of social media virality in Iran and Eqypt, China and Indonesia.[6] Documentary forms that foreclose space for community engagement and collaboration have been critiqued as remnants of one-way communication and control not only by international activist organisations and non-governmental social media organisations, but also by communications scholars seeking to remap the connection between technologies, representation and politics.[7] Transnational political restructurings insist on the importance and urgency of the micro-local and its multiple mappings.[8] All have functioned as key drivers – beyond new technologies – of this shift to a more open and fluid form that holds the possibilities of opening space for convenings and dialogue.

These emerging documentary forms are developing beyond the status quo of long-form feature-length documentary – with their characters, narrative arcs and resolutions – designed for festivals and public television. These open space documentary projects move in more mobile, flexible, public spaces characterised by indeterminacy, community and risk. New possibilities for combinatory storytelling are proliferating in spaces now enabled by disruptive broadband, new media and mobile technologies.[9] Community needs to map specific histories and stories into spaces colonised by the state, corporate interests or environmental destruction also propel these new forms of documentary.

The range of works this chapter groups as open space documentaries includes analogue short form, digital interfaces for mosaic projects, user-generated projects, web archives and locative media. Open space documentaries deploy combinatory storytelling strategies embracing the local through community engagement, participatory media and user-produced histories across multiple platforms that intermingle the digital and analogue with lived social relations and places.[10] Open space conceptions and mobilisations of community, collaboration, place and migration across digital interfaces undergird the projects described in the case studies below. These works – whether video projects, websites, performances, or social media – open up with participation by people, places, ideas, change.[11] The social is as important as the technological – a key distinction of open space documentaries that separates these works from the euphoria encircling many discussions of the relationships between the social/political and new technologies.

Open space documentaries move among analogue and digital platforms, constantly adapting to engagement with participants and locales while migrating across transmedia formations – from videos, to websites, to media events, to dialogues, to archives, to performance. These open space documentaries extend documentary's legacy of collaborative models into the present and the future. Although much of documentary history and theory heroicises individual authorship, an equally long tradition of collaborative work exists, starting from Flaherty's *Nanook of the North* (1922) and moving through the Workers Film and Photo Leagues of the 1930s, to George Stoney's *All My Babies* (1953) and his Canadian Film Board work on *You Are On Indian Land* (1969), to community media operations that started in the 70s and early 80s like Appalshop, Kartemquin, Third World Newsreel, Paper Tiger Television and the entire cable access movement in the USA since the late 70s.

Open space documentary forms extend these legacies and then explore these newly emerging spaces where technologies are meeting places and people in new and unpredictable ways. Not simply one form or mode, open space documentaries chart a new, highly diverse, ecologically complex documentary space and landscape. Open space documentary practice is reciprocal, human-scaled and localised, reflective and multi-voiced: it is structured not as a deductive, expository argument but as a shifting mosaic of ways to consider a concept or a place.

The coordinates of documentary have shifted from a quest for meaning, construing the text as a mysterious puzzle to be deciphered, into a more mobile and flexible environment of many technologies and vectors that open up to indeterminacy, community and risk. Documentary is not so reductively, in this open space model, about changing lives or establishing deductive rhetorical arguments, but about opening up complex dialogues that reject

binaries through polyphonies and which creates mosaics of multiple lenses on issues.[12] Open space documentary is where technologies meet places meet people.

Documentary now assumes many forms and occupies many locations in the transnational media landscape. It moves across many platforms. It engages and builds publics in myriad ways. It operates in fixed analogue forms as well as in open, fluid, endlessly transforming digital forms and social-media iterations. If the documentary triangle of subject, film-maker and audience formed a central image for documentary studies, open space documentary conceptualisations shift towards the documentary circle, where vectors are no longer straight lines of contact but endless circular engagements that change and open up discourse and spaces for action.[13]

Although many open space projects work within the participatory promises of Web 2.0 interfaces, the works discussed in this chapter reject the idea that these different platforms are simply ways to trap the user/spectator within a story-world conceived by the director or a corporate media entity. Web 2.0 social media and networked technologies such as Wikis, blogs, user-generated content, gaming, viral media, Facebook, Twitter, Second Life have, of course, been effectively deployed for increasing awareness of social justice issues, advocacy campaigns and critique.[14]

In these virtual worlds of utopian democratic fantasies, images and ideas are easily captured, easily consumed, easily circulated, easily erased in endless loops of record, process, delete. As Douglas Rushkoff has argued in *Life Inc*, social-media production is the new camouflaged face of consumption, with this quasi-participatory mode part of the corporate chain creating marketing webs to advance global capital.[15] However, all of these more corporatised, commodity-chain modalities function within a similar structural model of pushing out an idea and controlling its usage and circulation through the institution of hierarchies of control, either in the form of argumentation, positionality, or campaigns with predetermined actions and outcomes.[16] Story-worlds, then, function as a form of enclosure and linearity that is highly problematic politically: they propel consumption and colonisation.

We propose another form of documentary practice that we argue is equally significant, salient and powerful. We have identified this form as the open space model of documentary, where ideas of collaboration, microterritories, contingency, horizontality, bottom up, multiple agency, decentralisation, migration across media platforms and through different communities, permeability and mutability are key. These different registers layer on each other, forming what we identify as a strategy of conceptual compost that creates new ways of thinking about documentary and engaging the social, the political and the community.

FROM KINO-PILOT TO KINO-COLLABORATOR

From director to convener and designer
From confrontation to collaboration
From characters to communities
From one to many
From argument to exploration
From story to stories
From incantation to invitation
From fixed to permeable
From closure to open
From pushing out to pulling in
From expository argument to mosaic constructions
From the documentary triangle to the documentary circle

RELATIONAL AESTHETICS

Our theoretical model of open space documentary invokes collaboration, multiple iterations, decentralisation and migration across media platforms and through distinct communities. This theoretical framework – a way to understand and locate how open space documentaries differ from traditional fixed analogue forms and present some new possibilities for rethinking documentary theory – engages relational aesthetics, collaborative public art theory and landscape design theory.

Open space documentary presents a different routing through representation of the real and trauma than more traditional, analogue forms of documentary practice. In place of the politics of representation, it offers the politics of convenings. In place of artistic vision and hierarchies, it offers collaboration and horizontality. In place of argument, it offers dialogical conversation and contingencies. In place of positions, it offers encounters. In place of the global and the national, it offers provisional microterritories. In place of separations between analogue and digital, it offers a wide palette of technologies, platforms, performances. In place of a fixed image as object, it offers fluidity, permeability, intersubjective exchanges, processes.

Open space documentary has a long lineage in twentieth-century experimental arts, from Dada and futurist performances, to Fluxus happenings, conceptual art, minimalism, feminist art, art practices that required the audience to activate the work. In his book *Conversation Pieces*, Grant Kester argues that a new form of practice has emerged that refutes individual artistry, shock-value, abstractions, ambiguities, privileged subject, specularity of modernism and postmodernism with an emphasis on the everyday, accessibility and conviviality. Kester identifies these newly emerging, performative practices as a 'collaborative and dialogical model' that catalyses the viewer into creative encounters and conversations where the outcome is not predictable. These creative encounters, he explains, produce multiple, complex, knowledges in a generative way that establishes a 'collective identity through a shared experience'.[17]

French theorist and art curator Nicolas Bourriaud, in his important book *Relational Aesthetics*, has also charted these new forms of participatory art based on encounters, contingency and collaboration that produce microcommunities. He contends that each art work in this genre is 'a proposal to live in a shared world ... giving rise to other relations'.[18] Intersubjectivity and conviviality join together to form the machine provoking new encounters that create micro-utopias. Proximity rather than distance is operative in this move from the visual to the tactile and the interactive. Bourriaud contends that works produced in this way produce a space of openness, a social interstice for possibilities. 'Art ... is no longer seeking to represent utopias; rather it is attempting to construct concrete spaces,' claims Bourriaud.[19] A relational aesthetics introduces the networks of plurality into a work that extend beyond families, institutions and technologies; the emphasis here is on new arrangements of agency, ideas and space. A relational aesthetics restores polyphony and 'binds heterogeneous arenas together'.[20]

These ideas of relational convenings, performative encounters, polyphony and engagement have also emerged in the World Social Forum and its debates about open space politics and praxis. Indian architect Jai Sen has forcefully argued that open space can be defined through its horizontality, uncertainty, transparency, networking, autonomy and emergence. As Sen explains in his essay 'On Open Space', open space is non-centralised, open-ended, indeterminate and adaptive, where simple convenings across difference lead to complexity.[21] Interaction, exchange and reflexive practice reconfigure existing networks through encounters with multiple subjects with diverse interests.

Open space serves as central organising concept in urban planning, landscape design and architecture. Sen shows how international feminist movements, radical Indian politics in the 1970s, Latin American liberation theology, Latin American magical realism, improvisational jazz and 90s direct action have fused into open space practices. In open space, uncertainty, indeterminacy, agency and chaos challenge enclosure. For Sen, open space does not exist a priori, but must be constructed by people in face-to-face interactions in real spaces. Open space is always a 'struggle against enclosure' and, thus, open space 'moves from being a noun to being a verb'.[22] In this sense, open space is always about possibility and change in specific places, and will look and feel different in different locations, whether in the global north or the global south.

In the open space documentary project, we conceptualise open space as that juncture where complexity and ambiguity meet participatory media through dialogue and community in a provisional node. Media, then, are not objects or arguments, but instead are places for people to wander around in, a landscape of ideas, actions, networks, histories. It is a place where producers and subjects and audiences work together through dialogue in grounded production, deploying a wide variety of tools and moving across many versions and iterations of a work that are endlessly adapting.

OPEN SPACE DOCUMENTARY: A JUSTIFICATION

1. It restores human-scaled, localised, social agency in new and unimagined ways. It invites new conversations and connects people.
2. It is a practice that drives people to convene in and pay attention to real places, and to understand together how to reclaim the pervasive social-media environment from global corporatism.
3. By reaching out to contributors across disciplines and generations, a media project, in multiple versions, can live and evolve through expansive networks, communities and clusters beyond traditional distribution channels.
4. It is a practice whereby media practitioners and exhibitors become *context providers* rather than *content providers*, creating scenarios that facilitate dialogue, participation, collaboration, shared experience and interconnections across boundaries.
5. It is a practice grounded in micro-territories.
6. It is a practice of continual engagement between convener and participant. Practices of collaboration, contingency, horizontality, multiple agency, adaptability, decentralisation, migration across media platforms and through different communities, permeability and mutability are central.

CASE STUDY: *PRECIOUS PLACES*

Scribe Video Center's community media and oral history project, *Precious Places*, an ongoing collaborative video anthology of short documentaries inaugurated in 2005 to explore the historical memories imbedded in public spaces, buildings, parks, street corners, churches and monuments, constitutes an imaginative and empowering example of open space documentary. Scribe Video Center, started in 1982 and based in Philadelphia, is a non-profit media arts centre providing instruction in film, video, audio and digital media to residents of Philadelphia, Camden and Chester. The short pieces produced in *Precious Places* over the years employ a realist documentary style of interviews and cutaways to places, with editing structures advancing storytelling as a collective and active historical enterprise. Taken as a whole, the project sizzles with polyvocal vitality that counters touristic propaganda promoting cities as places for high-end hotels, symphonies, theatre and expensive restaurants.

As a unique kind of Philadelphia neighbourhood advocacy project, *Precious Places* has developed an open space documentary model where everyone on the creative team is generating content from a very special point of view that only emerges when something – like your home place – is at stake and where retrieval of public memory is urgent. This slow, local and democratic creative investigation offers an example of how to reroot new technologies in history, ethics, ordinary people and communities at risk of violence, poverty and social isolation from the mainstream.

Precious Places reconfigures the documentary triangle between film-maker, subject and audience as an open space circle of mutual concern and collaboration. *To Badlands and Back Again* (2005), a short community video produced by the Fair Hill Cemetery activist group as part this project, shows how a working partnership between Philadelphia Quakers and concerned local African American and Latino residents transformed an historic cemetery from a dumping ground for garbage into a safe green space for the community.

In this short video, sustainability and environmental issues are not white, middle-class greenwashing, but multicultural, engaged political activism that produces visible and usable changes in real places where people live and work. Although important early feminist and anti-slavery activists are buried there, this knowledge was lost; Fair Hill had disintegrated into a haven for drug pushers and an eyesore in the community. The Quakers and community groups worked together to clean up the cemetery, disposing of the refuse as well as the drugs and drug-dealers. In the project, community members explain the landscape and drug-dealing clean-up process, and how they reclaimed the latent histories of the cemetery.

Precious Places shorts are produced by a wide, diverse range of organisations such as the African Cultural Art Forum, the Community Leadership Institute, Mt Moriah Preservation Society, Germantown Historical Society, Odunde and West Girard Community Council. The pieces focus on specific places that have significant historical, cultural, religious or political meaning for the residents who live there. Although aided by professional historians from Philadelphia colleges and universities and with experienced video-makers as consultants, *Precious Places* was conceived to document a particular place – a micro-territory – through oral histories of residents as a response to a wide range of development initiatives that can potentially destroy communities and their histories.

The *Precious Places* project, a mosaic of community interaction and places, moves documentary towards networked, collaborative interactions between neighbourhoods, places, film-makers and scholars who create new histories in an open space design. As a result, *Precious Places* embodies polyvocalities and micro-histories as a way to reclaim and revitalise ideas about the archive, history and memory, a creation of open space at the micro-level.

Precious Places is not conceived along the lines of a more traditional long-form documentary project, where a director researches an idea and then searches for archival material, informants and images to advance an argument, position or point of view. Rather than this top-down model of single authorial vision, *Precious Places* advances a collaborative ethnographic and historical open space model, where community participants become the authors and not simply the subjects of community history.

In *Precious Places*, development and sustainability are rethought from the perspective of communities, eminent domain, reclaiming parks and restoring lost histories to particular buildings or blocks. It provides a micro-history that zeroes in on public places, individuals as part of the fabric of a community who remake and rejuvenate these places and spaces. For example, in *Putting the 'Nice' Back in 'the Town'* (2005) the Neighborhood Advisory Committee works to restore the area.

Precious Places extends the important legacies of collaborative community media by retelling the history of Philadelphia from very specific locations, such as churches that were part of the Underground Railroad, the Friends Housing Cooperative, a community garden call Las Parcelas, Mt Zion Baptist Church, or the Uptown Theatre.

Precious Places materialises a powerful, eye-opening and collaborative open space response to diverse neighbourhoods and the press of development that completely alters how one might think about cities, their inhabitants and the links between sustainable development and history.

CASE STUDY: *LUNCH LOVE COMMUNITY*

In 1999, the Berkeley Unified School District created its ground-breaking and influential food policy mandating a goal to 'provide nutritious, fresh, tasty, locally grown food that reflects Berkeley's cultural diversity ... and ensure that the food served [in the schools] be organic to the maximum extent possible'. It took ten years for the School Lunch Initiative in Berkeley, California, to realise that dream. And now, this Bay Area city is leading the national movement to eliminate childhood obesity and change the way children eat.

Helen de Michiel[23] produced documentary project *Lunch Love Community*.[24] It is designed as an open space documentary continual work-in-progress. It presents a multi-layered story of how this determined community of cooks, educators, parents, health advocates, politicians and food purveyors created a programme that offers fresh, homemade, organic breakfast and lunch to all children in the public schools.

Lunch Love Community started as a story of how the Berkeley, California, community pioneered school lunch transformation. The short, five- to seven-minute-long films in the project deal with issues of food reform, health, community sustainability and citizen-based democracy.

Lunch Love Community started as a story of how the Berkeley, California, community pioneered school lunch transformation

Lunch Love Community demonstrates how an open space documentary model can create dialogue across divisions, bring communities together and help build citizen action. It elaborates the traditions of well-crafted analogue documentary, yet also innovates with new digital and software applications. *Lunch Love Community* constitutes a mosaic of films about schools and food explicitly designed to be shown and discussed in a variety of venues. The project depends on a continuous process of paying attention to, and engaging with, all the different communities coalescing around the subject of food reform. This endlessly fluid and responsive approach connects and engages an ever-expanding sphere of participants involved with schools and food.

Lunch Love Community is mounted on a simple, user-friendly, inviting website. It features luscious and bold imagery, clear descriptors and a minimum of visual clutter. The storytelling approach invites viewers to open up to the subject, engage with it and form their own conclusions. The short films can be watched both on the *Lunch Love Community* website and on a designated YouTube channel for download and embedding. The short films on school gardens, cooking and parent advocacy for healthy food were designed to be viewed on phones, tablets, laptops and in larger, more public exhibition venues.

In the *Lunch Love Community* project, the films are not the singular attraction. Instead, the films inhabit a context beyond their own textuality – the social web that is fluid, impermanent and unstable but marked by connectivity and engagement with online visitors, users and live audiences. *Lunch Love Community* weaves together media social events and online activities to reach new users and engage larger issues. By committing to flexibility, adaptability and attention to viewers/users responses and requests, the project operates within a process-orientation that moves outward from traditional documentary approaches. To balance the ephemeral and virtual nature of social media, *Lunch Love Community* designs public programmes called 'media socials'. These events connect the town hall to interactive performance. While eating and taking away table literature, audiences become involved in the conversations and connections about food policy and schools that the films open up.

In this project, media socials emerge from relationships built with individuals and organisations involved with food, nutrition and health. *Lunch Love Community* designers contact community organisations, universities, parent groups and arts exhibitors to collaborate with them on presenting a ninety-minute public event. The format is customised in collaboration with these local groups to activate public gatherings around food, nutrition and health issues. Local experts frame a ten- to fifteen-minute discussion following one of the short films. Discussions have dealt with the process, politics, educational impact or systemic issues of school lunch reform. Speakers and audience participation adds depth to and extends the film stories. Audiences comment, question, argue and offer solutions, while the hosting organisations hand out printed resource materials from groups such as the Center for EcoLiteracy or other local nutrition-related organisations.

The *Lunch Love Community* films, online distribution process and live public events integrate work as open space documentary. In this transmedia model, the film-maker is a convener, creating stimulating encounters among people and places, ideas and new technologies. For food system reform advocates, parent groups, health educators, school administrators and community food policy councils, the *Lunch Love Community* films are 'media tools' to be spread around the internet and screened in public settings.

A key open space strategy, *Lunch Love Community* has established connections with potential partners to host and hold community-based media socials, training individuals how to use the films in a variety of educational environments, educating them around the innovative use of media to support their objectives, and how to host convenings where participants leave inspired for future actions. The media social events not only serve to locate food issues within communities, but also refresh and boost the social-media components of *Lunch Love Community*.

Since *Lunch Love Community* inhabits a dynamic, always moving online stream, these short films work with different constituencies. While one film might connect with those working on food policy issues, another might be reposted on a nutrition website. Some of the shorts have been posted on Twitter feeds and Facebook pages advocating for children's health and diet issues, food justice and the economy, or local citizen calls-to-action. The *Lunch Love Community* monthly e-newsletter connects readers to current events in the news cycle like health and education news, and to updates on op-eds about legislation like the Farm Bill and the Child Nutrition Reauthorization Act. For example, school garden advocates have used *The Whole World in a Small Seed* (2010). *Flamin' Hot* (2010) has been posted and discussed across the country and internationally. *The Parent Factor* and *Feeding the Body Politic* (both 2010) are used with Parent Teacher Association groups motivated to go to Board of Education meetings and ask the tough questions about school food.

The school lunch reform movement has expanded into multiple directions – from the relationship to local agriculture and procurement infrastructure, to the youth-driven food justice movement, to changing community food systems in a climate-changing world. The *Lunch Love Community* transmedia project demonstrates how open space documentary models link issues with communities through strategic use of dynamic transmedia platforms.

CASE STUDY: *SAVING THE SIERRA: VOICES OF CONSERVATION IN ACTION*

Saving the Sierra is an ambitious three-year multi-media project created and developed by public radio producer Catherine Stifter and community organiser jesikah maria ross.[25] Its purpose has been to co-create, along with people living in the communities of the Sierra Mountain Range in California, a set of communication platforms where residents could talk to each other about the issues that affect them. It was also designed to reach out to urban people outside the region to deepen understanding of what is happening across this extraordinary biosphere – from water issues to rural poverty, land pressures and development, conservation and agriculture, history and cultural memory.

The Sierra mountain range area is 400 miles long and eighty miles wide with only 2 million residents. How could this team pull together a project that would represent this immense place and give voice to its inhabitants that would be authentic to their experiences and influence policy outside the region? It started with conversations, storytelling and building relationships first, before any media products were developed or created.

Stifter and ross started their own collaboration by understanding what their different skills could contribute to the project. Then, during this first year, came the process of social networking, both through old-fashioned face-to-face community organising and through internet-based outreach. They found and invited local non-profit conservation organisations to become partners in the project. They held meetings with people across the region to understand what the issues were and what the stories were that people had to tell. When they secured initial funding, they created mobile audio 'story-booth' vehicles, manned by volunteers, that travelled the length of the Sierras and collected the personal stories of people across the mountains, starting off by inviting people to talk about the Sierra places they love. With more than a hundred stories recorded, they created this website that collected and organised the audio stories into a database-driven mapping interface. It was designed to include user-generated content, from news of the area to ways for community members to get involved and participate in this and other Sierra-related environmental projects. The team built the interface so all the material could be shared and repurposed by visitors and users. All of this groundwork and public engagement took place before they began producing their centrepiece national radio documentary.

It was a challenging project for the producers. They were committed to trusting an open space technique of documentary engagement. It started with a wide-ranging participatory process before any media was produced. People's stories were freely posted online as contributions to a multi-faceted dialogue, spurring and opening up conservation in the Sierras. The producers' intention was to bridge people and the dynamic new media forms, while co-existing in this newly emerging public media sphere. By opening up the media-making process to citizens in the Sierra communities, Catherine and jesikah were able to build identity and engagement around the project, draw in more participants and, most importantly, develop the capacity of organisations and individuals to integrate this media for their own purposes: on their own websites, in meetings, in newsletters, at events and share the media through their own social networking platforms.

When they were ready to produce the national radio documentary in the second year of the project, they knew their subject would be the hyper-local, rural responses to the urban development pressures being placed on the mountain range. How were local people working to conserve their environment at the dirt level? By the time the documentary was created, Stifter and ross had established a mosaic of voices giving a rich and detailed portrait of the issues. They created a living archive for activists and researchers to return to and reuse. And they awakened individuals and organisations throughout California about the possibilities to reclaim social media as a way to open up new forms of social dialogue and engagement around the issues among people who might never otherwise find ways to talk to and interact with one another.

CASE STUDY: *TRIANGLE FIRE OPEN ARCHIVE*

The *Triangle Fire Open Archive* expands in multiple directions and reaches across decades as a living documentary collaboration: it offers participants a contemplative encounter with this seminal event in American labour history.[26] The website's design invites the visitor to engage, reflect and speculate, a prismatic story rediscovered and revivified through contributed artefacts. This project exemplifies an open space strategy of designing an archive that engages and amplifies a specific history through user engagement.

This open archive conceives history as a network of associations, rather than a linear story. It is built as a horizontal internet-based open space that invites citizen historians to contribute images of ephemera, mementoes, photographs, film clips or writings directly or tangentially related to the 1911 Triangle Shirtwaist Factory Fire in Lower Manhattan in New York City. It widens the pathways between the past and the present.

A photograph or a news clip can trigger a question that expands into a narrative travelling across decades. From a group photo: why does Triangle Fire survivor and anarchist Mary Domsky live in exile in Mexico in the 1930s? From a staged portrait and family commentary: how do the living descendants of teenage factory seamstress and Triangle Fire victim Rosie Weiner keep her memory alive as a real girl with hopes and dreams? From multiple video clips, art works and news items: what can this 1911 labour tragedy signify a hundred years later in the global struggle to protect worker and immigrant rights – especially those of the most vulnerable in the workplace – women?

The project developed from a collaboration between the Remember the Triangle Fire Coalition and Buscada for the hundredth-year memorial of the fire. The *Triangle Fire Open Archive* is simple and straightforward – a visitor can easily click through an expanding collection of digital entries that project creators call 'objects', and explore new patterns and entry points towards understanding history through ancestral, political, cultural and emotional associations. Gabrielle Bendiner-Viani and Kaushik Panchal formed their interdisciplinary creative practice, Buscada, to bring together 'place and dialogue' across communities and disciplines, through a variety of place-based and online public projects. They call the *Triangle Fire Open Archive* a 'people's archive' because it encourages anyone who might want to contribute – a text, an image, media or physical pieces – to copy it digitally and upload it, along with a comment or personal note about its significance.

This archive is not locked up: it is always open for access and activity by participants, peers and users. By generating a mosaic-like history through artefacts, anyone can share in deepening the impact of the Triangle Fire event across the generations. History is a living entity in this open space interface, where the story begins on a Saturday in 1911 in the Brown-Asch building in New York City, and continues today across the global labour map.

When individuals and communities (families, neighbourhoods, labour organisers, artists, students and professional historians) make a contribution to the *Triangle Fire Open Archive*, they can choose from four thematic areas: people, politics and activism, cultural response and memorial. The pieces are also cross-tagged for ease of navigation, with a list of thirty sub-categories where the visitor can move deeper and more specifically around topics. Even in the choosing of sub-categories, the donor decides how to interpret the meaning of their object contribution – from fatality to Italian, from protest to legislation and occupational safety. The contributor becomes enmeshed in a dialogue with the past, with the official records of history and with an actual tragedy that called people to act and make change. From the extreme close-up (a piece of jewellery saved by a descendant) to a landscape view (a recorded lecture by a feminist labour historian), participants are anchored in the specifics of a real event.

A visitor can comment on the objects that are being shared, and is invited to submit contributions. The archive's visual simplicity and friendliness invites user participation, while promising a transparent interactive environment that invites returning to contemplate and review new connections among the materials. An archive object can take the user back to the era. Contributor Edward Mullen writes about his photo of a chalking on the sidewalk outside a building in Hoboken, New Jersey, for fire victim Vincenza Bilota, age sixteen:

> I couldn't help but think how we're only separated by time. Vincenza, who I don't know, am not related to, walked down that same street 100 years ago on the way to work. My brother-in-law, who lives a couple blocks from here, is 16. He's skateboarded by that spot many times, I'm sure. But also, that 100 years can make the fire seem artificially far away.[27]

These entries suggest a history that is necessarily incomplete, always changing and presenting multiple stories simultaneously and across time.

The *Triangle Fire Open Archive* interface functions like a deck of cards that stimulates associations – a model for documentary quite distinct and different from a film or live exhibition. The archive tethers the user and participant to events, geography and people in a deeply immersive way, facilitating an historical narrative enlivened through the user's associations. Gabrielle Bendiner-Viani explains the process:

> We created the Open Archive as an ongoing participatory online archive to understand the Triangle Fire not only through historical narrative but also through contemporary human connection, inspired by the variety of perspectives represented by the Coalition. To tell the story, we sought out 'objects' (rather than oral histories or images alone) for their power both to ground us in the present and to form links across lifetimes.[28]

The *Triangle Fire Open Archive* models a documentary storytelling practice that is neither fixed nor permanent. It refrains from a top-down hierarchical intrepretation of history in favour of one that is constantly assembled and reinterpreted through encounters in the intervals of daily life across eras, places and people.

CASE STUDY: PREEMPTIVE MEDIA COLLECTIVE AND LOCATIVE MEDIA

Locative media represents another form of open space documentary interested in the convergence between digital domains and geographic spaces. It anchors the digital, often viewed as ambling around in a place-less realm, in geographic space. Artists marshal portable, networked computing devices like GPS, mobile phones and radio frequency identification devices (RFID), as well as wearable technologies, to map space and intervene into data streams. Locative media is horizontal and user-led, and conjures up convenings. The Preemptive Media Collective (PM) re-engineers thinking about mobile digital technologies imbedded in everyday environments.[29] In live performances and real-time actions, the PM art, technology and activist collective disturbs, dislodges and redesigns new media technologies that we often ignore, like the bar codes on drivers' licences or radio frequency information devices used for EZ pass on highways. PM empowers participants to feel like they can actually understand wireless and RFIDs.

Preemptive Media repositions highly specialised technologies within the democratic discourse of low-tech amateurism. The emerging locative media movement has gathered steam and attention since 9/11 and the 2001 Patriot Act, which authorises unprecedented data mining, invasions of privacy, wiretapping and internet surveillance. In *SWIPE* (2001), Preemptive Media investigated how bar codes on the backs of drivers' licences activate data collection most people are oblivious to. Bars and convenience stores use licence scanners to determine age – and to build free-of-charge but enormously valuable databases on their clients. Last autumn in Irvine, California, PM set up a bar at an arts event and swiped the drivers' licences of every drinker. A monitor over the bar visualised the scanned information with computer-matching to census data, demographics and voter information. Customers received a data receipt detailing their buying preferences, philanthropy, income, profession, housing.

SWIPE foregrounds issues of privacy in data streams, demonstrating the invisible and discreet nature of automated identification data collection (AIDC). AIDC not only lacks prior notification and consent, but is also largely unregulated. Although the mainstream press highlights individual criminals who pirate cyber-identities, *SWIPE* suggests that the real issue of data mining resides in the increasing interdependence between corporations and the government. Data-mining companies are now more efficient than the FBI. Preemptive Media reverses and makes visible how data mining and surveillance technologies create a new ecology of consumer social control – not simply privacy invasions. Their tactics resonate with the war on terror where cyber-warfare, information gathering, tracking and networked technologies have been mobilised by the Patriot Act, the military and retail outlets. Comprised of artists Brooke Singer, Beatriz da Costa and Jamie Schulte, Preemptive Media rethinks a wide range of mobile technologies. It veers away from a fascination with the aesthetically constructed image to a collaborative interrogation of the mobile interface. The collective's skill set includes an alchemy of programming, graphic design, robotics, photography, electronics, video, carpentry, data visualisation and data mining.

WORKING PRINCIPLES OF OPEN SPACE DOCUMENTARY

1. Open space documentary is intentional creative enquiry into how we create dialogues.
2. Open space documentary is multiple voices in dialogue.
3. New interfaces open up new ways to frame community activities as creative practice rather than avenues for consumption.
4. Open space documentary organises projects around concepts, contradictions and communities. These projects open to a horizontal process with inputs from a variety of different participants.
5. Open space documentary can help build and strengthen local infrastructures. It can capture significant public memories and histories not controlled by consumer/corporate agendas.
6. Open space documentary engages a strategy of amplitude: to see a given topic from every possible perspective, to provoke curiosity about and compassion for the thinking of other people, to encourage reciprocal and open-ended collaborations and interactions.
7. Open space documentary advances and makes space for co-creation among people.
8. Open space = networks, redefined away from corporatist story-worlds. Networks are digital systems, but also social systems of people, places and technologies.
9. Open space documentary can offer environments for ongoing dialogue that lead participants to connect, communicate and collaborate on human-scaled, local actions.
10. Open space documentary practice reclaims technologies from their hyper-utopianism and rethreads them within social and political relationships.

THE TEN Cs OF OPEN SPACE DOCUMENTARY AS THE NEW KINO-EYES

Complexity
Connections
Community
Collaboration
Continuum
Conversation
Context
Circular
Cost
Composting methods, ideas, practices into something new

NOTES

1. Yuri Tsivian (ed.), *Lines of Resistance: Dziga Vertov and the Twenties*, trans. Julian Graffy (Gemona: Udine [Le Giornate del Cinema Muto], 2004); Jeremy Hicks, *Dziga Vertov: Defining Documentary Film* (New York: Palgrave Macmillan, 2007); Dziga Vertov, *Kino Eye: The Writings of Dziga Vertov*, trans. Kevin O'Brien (Berkeley: University of California Press, 1985).

2. For additional writing from this chapter's authors on the concept of open space documentary, see Patricia R. Zimmermann's blog, Open Spaces, at http://www.ithaca.edu/fleff/blogs/open_spaces/ and Helen De Michiel's website, http://www.thirtyleaves.org. For an expanded version of De Michiel's thinking on open space documentary, see her essay, 'Open Space Documentary', http://animatingdemocracy.org/sites/default/files/documents/reading_room/HDeMichiel_TrendPaper.pdf

3. For an excellent review of recent socially engaged arts practices that engage audiences in public performance and convenings to sustain new, aleatory publics in the face of globalisation, see Nato Thompson (ed.), *Living as Form: Socially Engaged Art from 1991–2011* (Cambridge, MA: MIT Press, 2012); and Shannon Jackson, *Social Works: Performing Art, Supporting Publics* (New York: Routledge, 2011).

4. For a good overview of the heterogeneous dimensions of new media practices emerging across many different platforms in the late 1990s and early 2000s, see Martin Reiser and Andrea Zapp (eds), *New Screen Media: Cinema/Art/Narrative* (London: BFI, 2002). For an excellent introductory overview of the multiplicity of new media forms emerging and their geneaologies in older technologies and media forms, see Martin Lister, Jon Dovey, Seth Giddings and Ian Grant, *New Media: A Critical Introduction* (London: Routledge, 2009). For an international analysis of the rise of mobile media, see Maunel Castells, Mireial Fernandez-Ardevol, Jack Linchuan Qui and Araba Sey Sey, *Mobile Communciation and Society: A Global Perspective* (Cambridge, MA: MIT Press, 2007). For a thorough and systematic analyses of how networks are reorganising political structures, legal systems and technologies, see Yochai Benkler, *The Wealth of Networks: How Social Production Transforms Markets and Freedom* (New Haven: Yale University Press, 2006). For a review of the affordance of miniaturised and amateur new technologies, see: Byron Hawk, David Rieder and Ollie Oviedo (eds), *Small Tech: The Culture of Digital Tools* (Minneapolis: University of Minnesota Press, 2008).

5. For example, see the recent concerns of the entertainment industry about arts defunding limiting the nurturance of new talent, in Ted Johnson, 'Arts Orgs Seek GOP Champions', *Daily Variety*, 29 August 2012, p. 5; Ted Johnson, 'Election Year Fuels Clash over Art Coin', *Daily Variety*, 27 March 2012, p. 1; see also Americans for the Arts, a national arts advocacy organisation that engages in significant lobbying and public education on the issues of the arts and economic sustainability, that posts position papers, http://www.artsusa.org

6. For a critique of the techno-euphoria surrounding social media and the Arab Spring, see Ulises Mejias, 'Liberation Technology and the Arab Spring: From Utopia to Atopia and Beyond', *Fibreculture* (n. d.), http://twenty.fibreculture journal.org/2012/06/20/fcj-147-liberation-technology-and-the-arab-spring-from-utopia-to-atopia-and-beyond/. Accessed 1 November 2012. For a discussion of internet issues in China, see Guobin Yang, *The Power of the Internet in China: Citizen Activism Online* (New York: Columbia University Press, 2011). For user-generated videos and discussions of the importance of new technologies in post-Reformasi Indonesia, see KUNCI Cultural Studies Center and EngageMedia, *Videochronic: Video Activism and Video Distribution in Indonesia* (Collingwood, Australia: EngageMedia, 2009).

7. For an example of the movements emerging around participatory media practices and reconsiderations of the nexus of documentary, technology, politics and social change, see Meg McLagan and Yates McKee (eds), *Sensible Politics: The Visual Culture of Nongovernmental Activism* (Brooklyn: Zone, 2012).

8. Tim Cresswell, *Place: A Short Introduction* (Malden, MA: Blackwell, 2004); Merlin Coverley, *Psychogeography* (London: Pocket Essentials, 2006); Pierre Bourdieu, *Acts of Resistance: Against the Tyranny of the Market* (New York: New Press, 1998); Janet Abrams and Peter Hall (eds), *Else/Where: Mapping New Cartographies of Networks and Territories* (Minneapolis: University of Minnesota Press, 2006).

9. For a vibrant discussion of the dialectics of control and possibility in the intersection of mobile technologies, place and social relations, see Adriana de Sousa e Silva and Jordan Frith, *Mobile Interfaces in Public Spaces: Locational Privacy, Control, and Urban Sociability* (London: Routledge, 2010). For an explanation of the concept of combinatory storytelling forms, see Maria Popova, 'Networked Knowledge and Combinatorial Creativity' (n. d.), http://www.brainpickings.org/index.php/2011/08/01/networked-knowledge-combinatorial-creativity/. Accessed 1 November 2012.

10. For an analysis of this shift from producer-centric forms to user-generated practices, see Axel Bruns, *Blogs, Wikipedia, Second Life and Beyond: From Production to Produsage* (New York: Peter Lange, 2008).

11. For an exploration of the historical legacies of participatory modes in modernist as well as contemporary arts practices, see Clair Bishop (ed.), *Participation* (Cambridge, MA: MIT Press, 2006).

12. The question of polyphonic historiographies has been productively explored in Dipesh Chakrabarty, *Provincializing Europe: Postcolonial Thought and Historical Difference* (Princeton, NJ: Princeton University Press, 2000). A key book arguing for a polyvocal and dialogic documentary ethics is David MacDougal, *Transcultural Cinema* (Princeton, NJ: Princeton University Press, 1998).

13. This concept of documentary practice moving from the documentary triangle to the documentary circle was first formulated at the workshop Open Space Documentary, at the 2012 National Alliance for Media Arts and Culture Conference in Minneapolis. The workshop featured theorist Patricia R. Zimmermann and new media artists/conveners Helen De Michiel, Laura Kissel and jesikah maria ross.

14. A primer on using social media in advocacy campaigns is Jessica Clark and Tracy Van Slyke, *Beyond the Echo Chamber: Reshaping Politics through Networked Progressive Media* (New York: Free Press, 2010). For a scholarly assessment of social media and participatory practices in a variety of social and political milieus and formations, see Aaron Delwich and Jennifer Jacobs Henderson (eds), *The Participatory Cultures Handbook* (New York: Routledge, 2013).

15. Douglas Rushkoff, *Life Inc: How the World Became a Corporation and How to Take it Back* (New York: Random House, 2009), pp. 84–158.

16. For examples of the entertainment industry's interest in the development of story-worlds as expanding control over consumers, see David Cohen, 'Delux gets into Clipping', *Variety* 23 February 2010, p. 5. For a discussion how the independent sector is mimicking this strategy by promoting independent films engaging a transmedia component, see David McNary, 'Sundance sets Screenwriters Lab', *Variety*, 14 December 2009, p. 3. The 2011 The Future of Entertainment Conference at MIT in November 2011 assembled industry representatives to discuss how to extend story-worlds on properties to increase brand recognition and engagement.

17. Grant Kester, *Conversation Pieces: Community and Communication in Modern Art* (Berkeley: University of California Press, 2004), pp. 51–119.

18. Nicolas Bourriaud, *Relational Aesthetics* (Paris: Les presses du reel, 2002), p. 22.

19. Ibid., p. 46.

20. Ibid., p. 294.

21. Jai Sen, 'On Open Space: Explorations Towards a Vocabulary of a More Open Politics', *Antipode* vol. 42 no. 4, September 2010, pp. 1000–6.

22. Ibid., p. 1016.
23. Full disclosure: Helen is also the co-author of this chapter.
24. *The Lunch Love Community Project,* http://www.lunchlovecommunity.org
25. *Saving the Sierra* http://www.savingthesierra.org
26. *The Triangle Fire Open Archive,* http://urbanomnibus.net/2012/09/making-meaning-together-the-triangle-fire-open-archive-and-open-museum/
27. Ibid.
28. Ibid.
29. *Preemptive Media Collective,* http://www.preemptivemedia.nt

6.2 'This Great Mapping of Ourselves': New Documentary Forms Online

JON DOVEY AND MANDY ROSE

Documentary has always been prone to the seductions of technology. From Vertov's kino-eye, through the search for portable synch to video's changing formats, its promise has often been seen as being dependent on technological capacities. But throughout moving-image history no technological changes have impacted so deeply on the film-makers and their controlling role as digital technology is promising to do

WEB 2.0

Distinctive documentary forms are emerging in the Web 2.0 online environment. There are some features that online affords that merely continue or intensify already existing cultural forms and practices. But there are also some forms emerging that point to major new developments for documentary as the new century gets into its stride. Media production *platforms* have different affordances that offer different possible processes of production, different cultural forms and genres, and different audience or user experience. As a platform, online is a new site where all kinds of media material including documentary can be uploaded and potentially seen. In this straightforward sense online offers documentary more distribution possibilities. However, the seemingly revolutionary fact that every documentary producer can now run his or her *own* Vimeo or YouTube channel is only the start of what we argue is significant for documentary form in the affordances of online. Our contention is that the *processes* of documentary production can change through new forms of collaboration, and that, in fact, the *forms* of documentary are changing through software design and interactivity, and the *user experience* of documentary can change through the new facility for participation offered by the online environment. These developments can be seen in the growth of vernacular media cultures, leading to the recruitment of increasingly interactive audiences co-producing meaning in new modes of participatory documentary production. Although our interest here is in what is distinctively novel, we will have recourse to history to emphasise the ways in which new technologies often re-energise previously marginal cultural practices.

THE RISE AND RISE OF VERNACULAR VIDEO

The new potentials for documentary referred to above are all evolving in the context of the unprecedented increase of vernacular video. For most of its history documentary has been produced by a privileged cadre of artists, technicians and producers who have used their access to the means of media production to observe and interpret the world on our behalf. However, the very category of documentary as a distinct form with distinct traditions (however much we might argue over them) is surely under question when the media ecosystem which constituted this distinction is itself mutating so wildly. In short when the rise of vernacular video is characterised by more hours of 'actuality' footage than we can either measure or imagine, then surely the forms of its 'creative treatment' will also change. Online documentary finds its traditions of evidence, argument and rhetoric intermingling with the burgeoning practices of the newly video literate.

Vernacular video is demotic, promiscuous, amateur, fluid and haptically convenient, technology at hand and in the hand. These material qualities and affordances are important. It's also a set of practices that have come to be characterised by naive attachments to indexicality, or 'zero degree simulation'.[1]

We derive the idea of vernacular video from Jean Burgess's 2007 doctoral work and subsequent work with Joshua Green on YouTube, where she defines vernacular creativity as 'the wide range of everyday creative practices (from scrapbooking to family photography to the storytelling that forms part of casual chat) practised outside the cultural value systems of either high culture or commercial creative practice'.[2]

This idea of a 'vernacular' form of moving-image expression has at least three historical tributaries. As Sorenssen points out, it was an avant-garde dream as long ago as 1948, when Alexandre Astruc published his essay calling for the 'camera-stylo', a system of cinema that would have the flexibility of the written word bringing about 'several cinemas just as today there are several literatures, for the cinema, like literature, is not so much a particular art as a language which can express any sphere of thought'.[3] These visions of a film and video culture available to everyone also underpinned radical media access movements in North America, Europe and Australia in the 1970s and 80s.

The second history concerns that of the amateur. The category of the vernacular also has something in common with the practice of amateur film, where the amateur signifies an everyday cultural activity for which one is not paid. Taking up Zimmerman's work on the history of amateur film and using Bourdieu to frame the investigation Buckingham, Willet and Pini have undertaken recent research into amateur video production. Their detailed work concludes that, during their survey period (2002–08), categories of the amateur were losing whatever stability they may formerly have evolved and that 'amateur media production is likely to play an increasingly significant role in the future cultural landscape. Studying this phenomenon as it evolves will raise significant new questions about creativity, identity and culture.'[4] This seems to us a drastic understatement in the face of the development of so-called 'user-generated content' in the 2005–10 period. The category of amateur rested upon a set of settled notions about what constituted the professional. Astruc's 1948 essay was a utopian call for the dissolution of boundaries between amateur and professional. Now that media literacy in the crude sense of basic reading and writing has become so very widespread in the developed West, his prescription is being lived out. However, given that very little online media of any kind actually makes money, the vast majority of it must by previous definitions be understood as in some way amateur. In reality, of course, we find a whole range of ways that allows online users to move along a ramp from viewer, to posting comments, to exchanging material, to uploading material, to shooting, editing and producing actuality-based video works as part of an extended online social network which the producer learns to manipulate in order to draw attention to the work.

Finally, the online forms of vernacular video also develop from what one of the current authors defined as 'camcorder cultures' of the 1990s[5] and display many of the same characteristics. The grammar of this vernacular is characterised by affect, intimacy, desire and display. Like any demotic it is mercurial, endlessly inventive, driven by the self-replicating memes of web culture. The ubiquity of the video camera in everyday life ensures a fluidity of subject position that film cameras could never sustain: the sense that the video camera can simply be handed back and forth and turned on by whomever facilitates this intimacy.

Camcorder cultures facilitated the rise of artists' first-person documentaries such as Sophie Calle's *No Sex Last Night* (1992), Robert Gibson's *Video Fool for Love* (1996) and Jonathan Caouette's not dissimilar *Tarnation* (2003). In the case of vernacular video practices, miniaturisation and mobility appear to have the effect not of effacing the presence of the film-maker (as in the dominant late twentieth-century aesthetic of Direct Cinema), but of emphasising it. The vernacular video document is often nothing but an inscription of presence within the text. It announces 'I was here' , 'I experienced this', 'I saw that'. Camcorder culture paved the way for this documentation of embodied presence, which has taken on precisely structured forms in its own online grammar.

So, over the period 1995–2005, camcorder culture became part of many people's 'everyday creative practices',[6] part of a cultural vernacular and, indeed, became a part of mainstream televisual and art-house documentary film practice. More space would allow us to trace the ways in which these forms infiltrated the web during this period,[7] but it is clear that since the launch of YouTube and the penetrations of broadband we have experienced a sudden, awesome growth of moving-image culture online. In the subsequent period, we have seen the vernacular forms of video that had developed as part of camcorder culture turbo-charged, digitised and uploaded as phone cams, webcams and high-definition. Flip cams are added to the already highly dispersed tools of image generation and cheap, easy-to-use editing programmes become part of domestic data apparatus. Among US adults, 52 per cent have watched video online, with 14 per cent of net users uploading video in 2009 compared to only 8 per cent in 2007.[8]

We argue that this new context for documentary challenges its traditional epistemologies. Where twentieth-century documentary depended for its functionality on an idea of the observer fixing the world with his [sic] camera, this new epistemology is entirely relational. It accepts that all knowledge is situated in particular embodied perspectives, the 'actualities' of online are the symbolic expression of this multi-perspectival, relational knowledge. One hundred years ago documentary did not exist – just the beginnings of the distribution of single-reel actuality films bringing the wonders of creation to your nearest travelling show or nickelodeon. These fragments were then worked and reworked until, in Bill Nichols's words, documentary invited us to share the film's interpretation of our shared world, 'Look, the world is like *this*, isn't it?'[9] The documentary enjoined us to see things as they were as if there was one way of seeing them that would capture the totality once and for all. Though many documentary film-makers and theorists have challenged the common sense of such a claim, the world of vernacular video online may finally, and perhaps regrettably, have put paid to the idea that the documentary can be anything but relational, situational and personal. As Michael Renov has put it, 'the VERY IDEA of autobiography reinvents the VERY IDEA of documentary'.[10]

NAVIGATION AND INTERACTION

One of the problems brought about by such a superabundance of actuality-based material is navigation, just finding a way to what the viewer wants to see is a problem in itself. The user finds herself increasingly subject to the human machine assemblage of search engines, meta tags and databases, where programme choices are filtered by algorithms and user recommendation. The online media consumer is likely to develop a very high tolerance to fragmented and aleatory media experiences. Thomas Elsaesser has written a wonderful account of navigating YouTube, asking how the traditional forms of narrative organisation hold up in the 'boiling sea of magma'[11] that is YouTube, where our journeys are dominated by 'the workings of contiguity, combinatory and chance'.[12] In the essay he chooses to investigate one video and is led on a 'rhizomatic' journey circling round sources, forking off into new territories and returning to the same names and themes. This experience, he concludes, 'is to find oneself in the presence of strange organisms, pulsing, moving and mutating, depending on the tags one enters or encounters, as YouTube sorts, filters and aggregates the choices I am not even aware of making'.[13]

This beguiling post-human description somewhat under-emphasises our role in navigation – after all, our choices are determined by a powerful mix of affect and epistephilia. We want to know something or we want to feel something; joy, desire, connection. So our search and navigation experience begins with a goal-oriented desire, but we must be willing to digress and to wander in the hope of a serendipitous encounter. These dynamics are at play in the development of the interactive documentary.

The click-driven experience of online media navigation has spawned its own form of documentary based on the user interacting with documentary materials which have been shot and edited by a documentary team following many of the traditional demands of documentary (e.g., information, education, or poetry). In the interactive documentary, however, the material is then assembled in short clips held in a database. The viewer is offered the choice of what order to view the clips in; this choice is made available to the viewer through links. Each clip can be linked to another by its tags, the descriptive words that the database uses to classify the material. So, having watched a particular clip, the viewer is offered a choice of what to see next based on links between the just-viewed segment and others in the database. These links can be structured through content, colour, space, time, character: any number of values. In this emergent form of the documentary, the nature of the links programmed into the clip collection and the nature of the interface design become significant new determinants of the documentary experience. The art of documentary rhetoric is being retooled with the techniques of database design.

Miami/Havana: Times Are Changing (2010), for example, is a well-funded, Arte (France/Germany)-backed project designed by Upian (Alexandre Brachet), which ran 'live' online from February–June 2010. The project follows the lives and aspirations of twelve young aspirational subjects, six in Havana and six in Miami, of Cuban heritage. Divided by only ninety miles of sea, the project seeks to portray the common hopes and fears of younger generation of Cubans and their Miami counterparts. The user can choose to navigate the two-minute clips by time-line, people or topic. The Upian design is brilliantly elegant, making for an easy and attractive user experience. The screen is divided into thumbnail shots with the Miami material above and the Havana material below. The innovation of the time-line creates the sense that the viewer is comparing lives in a diary-like chronology across the divide. We are also able to navigate up, down and sideways in the media player adapted by Upian for the project in ways that create a very fluid experience. The format here is adapted from a previous Arte/Upian project *Gaza Sderot: Life in Spite of Everything* (2008), which consists in eighty clips uploaded over a three-month period from towns just three kilometres apart on either side of the Gaza/Israel border. *Miami/Havana* will also become a full-length conventional documentary. The overall effects of watching *Miami/Havana* are complex; first of all, we are definitely *not* in Elsaesser's 'boiling sea of magma' dependent on contiguity, combination and chance. It is more as if the linear documentary has been reconstructed in space, like a gallery piece where we are free to wander about inside the film, discovering links and resonances. (In this sense the metaphor recalls, of course, *Welcome to Kuba* [2004] the documentary installation by Kutlug Ataman which did just that – recording the testimonies of residents of the Istanbul district and then mounting them on individual monitors for the viewer to wander through and experience the area as a kind of semi-autonomous zone.) *Miami/Havana* is certainly a diverting twenty-minute experience, but, in terms of documentary traditions, it's a curiously static one; that is to say, we are impressed by the shared aspirational yearnings and desires of the subjects on both sides of the divide, which delivers a very simplistic humanist solidarity message; we all share common hopes and fears, whether capitalist or communist (like the Jew and the Arab of *Gaza Sderot*). However, beyond that the viewer would look in vain for argument or analysis. The astonishing difference in setting between third-world Havana and first-world Miami is unaddressed, the abstractions of history or policy left untroubled by the documentation of ordinary life. In this, *Miami/Havana* merely replicates the absence of analysis in most reality-based TV forms. However, the appeal to essentalist humanism of these new 'post-human' documentary forms is a theme to which we will return below.

Works produced using the Korsakow system for interactive documentary represent a slightly different form and aesthetic. The Korsakow system is an open-source software written by Florian Thalhofer. Nina Simoes used it to make *Rehearsing Reality* (2008) as part of her doctoral work at the University of London; the project is an account of the use of Augusto Boal's Theatre of the Oppressed techniques with the MST (Movimento dos Trabalhadores Rurais Sem Terra), Brazil's landless peasant movement. The piece opens with an introductory homepage explaining what she calls the 'docufragmentary' project, then a movie window opens, giving the context of the MST; at the end of this sequence three windows open beneath the viewer window; we choose. Following Act 1 shows the viewer a group of workers re-enacting land seizure, the landlord's agents (as performers) intervene, they hold guns to the heads of the actors. The watching crowd is chilled, some women start to cry. The frame freezes – we are offered another set of choices. These include reflections on Boal's method by academics and activists as well as in interview with Boal himself. Each section, once chosen, runs for its own length, during which we are not offered the choice to stop or skip. The strands of the work follow the peasant group working through a Boal-based exercise, other parts reflect on this process. The experience is moving, interesting, satisfying; though fragmentary, it feels thorough and complete. The project succeeds due to the 'meaningfulness' of the associative links offered to the viewer combined with the power of each individual clip. We are offered a combination of linearity and interactivity that balances. Although we are not sure what kind of choices are being offered to the viewer there is still satisfaction to be found in the intriguing journey that we discover for ourselves.

The Korsakow software allows the author/producer to programme links into video clips, so that at the end of each clip thumbnail choices are offered that are called up by the relationship between their tags and the tags of the previous clip. The user follows a variety of navigational paths which are determined through the associative links programmed into the database by the author. Clips are tagged with text strings of words; while viewing one clip the system searches for associated key words. So the art in the overall construction is in writing the key words and tags that provide interesting, useful, pleasing juxtapositions. The art of montage becomes the art of database authoring.[14]

Presenting at the Documentary Now conference in London in January 2010, Korsakow's designer Florian Thalhofer was confronted by a familiar set of critical responses from documentarians. Wasn't he just abdicating control? What did he really have to say about his subjects? Why wouldn't he let the audience just sit back and relax, what is this compulsion to make us interact? His defence is primarily aesthetic rather than theoretical or critical,

The world is a cloud that is constantly changing. One cannot fully grasp it, because as long as one is part of this world one cannot view its exterior to understand its shape. Theoretically you could examine all of the cloud's molecules. However, this would require a lot of time. Time during which the world would change again. One would have to freeze the world to watch the molecules in peace in order to understand the world this way. But that is not possible either. The whole world is much, much too large. One could try to freeze and understand smaller sections. And I think this is what we are doing here. We are trying to freeze small sections of the world in order to understand it.[15]

The aesthetic of the network has been the object of critical attention and excitement ever since hypertext methods of writing first made their appearance twenty years ago. Thalhofer's critics are essentially responding to the challenge at the heart of hypertext studies – *how can we evaluate a text that never reads the same way twice?* This is a fundamental question that haunts the relationship between the linear media forms (e.g., the nineteenth-century novel or the classical Hollywood film) and the database. On one hand, it produces anxiety about the disappearance of authority and meaning, and, on the other, a celebration of the *same* qualities as answering the post-structuralist prescription for textual liberation and the death of the author. In this sense the documentary field is absorbing the lessons of New Media Studies apparent in, for example, Landow, Moulthrop, Aarseth, Reiser and Zapp. At the outset of these studies great excitement was generated at the apparent homologies between post-structural literary theory, especially Foucault and Derrida, and their apparent literary correlatives in hypertext experiment. We now find some similar kinds of writing in critical responses to the interactive documentary:

digitality, then, implies an opening to ways of conceiving one's place in the world that is not constrained to the linearity of most analogue formats and has the potential to challenge the historical legacies that have deployed such technologies as they have intersected with colonialism, racism, ethnocentricsm, sexism, class oppression, homophobia, religious fundamentalism and war.[16]

While, as we have argued above, polyvocality and relationality do seem to us be important features of the Web 2.0 ecosystem for documentary, this kind of hyperbolic enthusiasm for the political potential of technology is questionable, to say the least. New media practices are about experience design, where creating coherence from technologically afforded fragmentation is the key challenge. From the point of view of the producer of interactive documentaries, the challenge is to design interfaces and databases that offer a meaningful user journey for viewers. This is certainly a different mode of authorship, where the production team have to work with their imagined users in order for the text to become meaningful; to a degree, therefore, authorship can be said to be distributed and meaning co-produced. However, this is more often than not a process of programming constraint and direction into the database rather than infinite polyvocality. As ever, this is an editorial process in which some voices/ideas get silenced while others are given a platform. The examples discussed above really point up that, yes, the interactive documentary may afford polyvocality, but it is still editorial control, rigorous work with meta data, imagination and a grasp of database aesthetics that creates meaningful documentary experiences. Without these qualities, far from challenging 'racism, ethnocentricsm, sexism, class oppression, homophobia' we are merely left back in Elsaesser's magma.

THE POETICS OF COLLABORATION AND PARTICIPATION

The generation of web technology known as Web 2.0 is sometimes called the 'social web' for its characteristics of participation, dialogue and sharing. As documentary producers begin to take advantage of these affordances of the network, we are beginning to see the emergence of a new poetics of collaboration and participation.

As in the case of vernacular video, discussed earlier, the cultural practices we see emerging within so-called 'new media' are not without precedent. Typically, 'new media' reconfigure media histories, giving sudden prominence to forms previously considered marginal. There has always been the potential for collaboration and participation within social documentary. After all, the documentary project is based on a relationship between the documentary-maker and the human subject (or perhaps, object). While making *Nanook of the North* (1922) Robert Flaherty went to great lengths so that the rushes could be processed on location. 'It has always been most important for me to see the rushes,' he said in an interview in 1950, 'but another reason for developing the film in the North was to project it to the Eskimos so that they would accept and understand what I was doing and work together with me as partners.'[17] Flaherty's partnership, however, ended with the shoot, and conventional documentary practice has generally followed this pattern. The producer's need for access leads to a carefully negotiated arrangement around filming, but the human subjects have no involvement or leverage on what meaning is made from the content after the rushes have been *captured*. 'This is the world as *I* see it,' says the documentary-maker, and that auteur position has been strictly guarded, with some noteworthy exceptions.

The French ethnographic film-maker Jean Rouch saw documentary as a collaborative undertaking between producer and subjects and, from the 1950s, expressed a post-colonial attitude by working in collaboration with participants in a series of films in West Africa, following a process he called 'shared anthropology'.[18] The pioneering American artist Wendy Clarke has been exploring the therapeutic potential of video since the 1970s, creating contexts for people to express themselves to camera. As well as her epic *Love Tapes* project for which, since the late 70s, over 800 people have now recorded short video statements, other key projects have been within disenfranchised communities – prisoners, teens, AIDS patients. In the UK, precedents derive from Community Media and Access TV, which sought to bring unheard voices into media – in the co-creative practices of the BBC's camcorder projects *Video Diaries* (1990–99) and *Video Nation* (1993–2001), for instance. The latter was itself inspired by and to an extent modelled on an earlier collaborative 'documentary' experiment – *Mass Observation*, the 'anthropology of ourselves' for which diary writers around Britain recorded everyday life from 1937.[19] Now the architecture and culture of the web bring the potentialities of participation and collaboration for documentary centre stage.

In the celebrated 2009 YouTube hit *ThruYOU*, for instance, the Israeli musician and composer known as Kutiman worked with eclectic samples of videos made by YouTube musicians. By layering and interweaving the music tracks and picture cutting playfully and rhythmically, he created unique afro-beat, funk and reggae mixes. While YouTube recordings are not, formally speaking, offered for reuse under a Creative Commons licence, Kutiman treated them as if they were, with the interface design on his website displaying the YouTube link and credit for each recording as the clip plays.[20] *ThruYOU* thus expresses an open-source aesthetic, and enacts a collaborative relationship between Kutiman and his co-creators, despite the absence of an overt participatory interaction. 'I had a great time searching for you and working with you,' says Kutiman in a piece to camera on the final track of *ThruYOU*, thanking the musicians who 'took part' in this virtual creative community conjured out of search terms.

At the meeting of participatory culture and documentary we are, thus, seeing the emergence of new arrangements within the production process and innovation in documentary form. Projects offer participants varying degrees and modes of editorial influence and control. Where participation is part of the process we can see the networking of aspects of linear production, as in open research processes where editorial is developed with a community of interest and forms of distributed authorship whereby participants produce modules within a non-linear project. Where the documentary experience is reconfigured as a user journey through non-linear content, we would argue that the computer becomes a further non-human participant in the production of meaning. These emerging practices can all be seen as forms of co-creation in which documentary storytelling is shaped not by an auteur or by a collective, but within a network of relationships.

Clay Shirky provided one of the first popular commentaries on the collaborative culture of the web in his 2008 book *Here Comes Everybody*. His account covered major emerging social-media platforms Wikipedia and Flickr, small, short-lived groups like flash mobs and large, long-term involvements like the story of the development of Linux open-source software. As Shirky describes it, there is no recipe for success in a collaborative project,

> every working system is a mix of social and technological factors, yet each project must have a successful fusion of a plausible promise, an effective tool, and an acceptable bargain with the users. The promise is the basic 'why?' for anyone to join or contribute to a group. The tool helps with the 'how' – how will the difficulties of coordination be overcome ... And the bargain sets the rules of the road: if you are interested in the promise ... what can you expect, and what can be expected from you?[21]

While the documentary projects under discussion here are not necessarily collaborative ventures across the whole production process, the 'promise, tool, bargain' model is relevant to particular aspects of production. In a participatory interaction, Shirky notes, the terms of the bargain will differ widely, but what matters is the transparency of the arrangement. This can be a challenge for the conventionally closed world of documentary production, where the opening up of video content production within the online network is a significant and growing trend. Participants can be seen playing a variety of roles in what becomes a process of co-creation. In the case of the *Global Lives* project (2010) this was an effective means to crowd-source production effort in distributed locations. This American initiative set out to, 'collaboratively build a video library of human life experience that reshapes how we as both producers and viewers conceive of cultures, nations and people outside of our own communities'.[22] To make this happen the producers recruited more than 500 volunteers who, between them, followed an agreed template to record twenty-four hours in the everyday life of ten individuals selected to reflect global demographics, so that six out of the ten are Asian, for example; most of them earn less than $9 a day. Through this major distributed collective effort, ten twenty-four-hour films were successfully co-created and then brought together as an immersive installation in a San Francisco gallery in Spring/Summer 2010, with an online content archive planned. The documentary material, as described by the producers, is in the tradition of Direct Cinema, with, 'no narrative other than that which is found in the composition of everyday life ... we invite audiences to confer

close attention onto other worlds, and simultaneously reflect upon their own'.

While the volunteer film-makers who made *Global Lives* worked in a Direct Cinema style that effaced their individual perspectives, the call to action for *The Message*, the first YouTube collaborative piece to gain substantial attention and homepage promotion, invited participants to express a strong point of view. The anonymous creator of *The Message*, MadV, was, significantly, already a star on YouTube, popular for illusions performed in a Guy Fawkes mask. Then he saw the montage video *Youtubers* by Mike B, which 'triggered the thought that maybe a deliberate collaboration (as opposed to an edit of pre-existing clips) could be possible – with moving effect'.[23]

In autumn 2006, MadV posted a brief video showing the words 'One World' written on his hand, and offered an invitation: 'to make a stand, make a statement, make a difference. Be part of something. Post your response now.' He received over 2,000 replies – the highest number registered on YouTube at that time. The piece he created from those vernacular video responses, *The Message*, is a four-minute montage of webcam recordings of mostly teens and twenty-somethings, showing their own written notes and slogans, accompanied by a track by Mugwai. 'Respect, Compassion, Integrity, Honor, Altruism ...' they read, in an outpouring of yearning for positive values which culminates in ideas around human connectedness – 'Together as One, United as One, We're all in this Together ... One World'.[24]

The Message can be seen as a breakthrough in the development of the 'collab' form on YouTube. It was described in *Wired* magazine as a 'curious mongrel form ... a new language of video',[25] and inspired a host of imitators. Most recently, in 2010, the collab has made a decisive move from cultural margins to mainstream. Film-makers Ridley Scott and Kevin Macdonald have partnered with YouTube and the Sundance Institute for a 'historic global experiment to create a user-generated feature shot in a single day'.[26]

Through a multi-versioned promo available in twenty languages they invited YouTubers around the world to record on 24 July 2010 for *Life in a Day*, a portrait of twenty-four hours on earth. Macdonald cut selected contributions into a feature documentary released in June 2011. The promise to participants was that those featured would receive a credit, with twenty selected to fly to the USA to join Macdonald at the Sundance premiere.

Life in a Day is the latest in a spate of projects aspiring to capture life on Earth which have been shaped by the affordances of digital video and participation. These include the *Global Lives* project discussed above, Yann Arthus-Bertrand's *6 milliards d'autres* [6 Billion Others] (2003), for which he and his team travelled the world shooting over 5,000 interviews, with gallery visitors invited to add

Life in a Day (2011): the latest in a spate of projects aspiring to capture life on earth

their contribution at the touring exhibition. In what is fast becoming a cliché of online documentary, the web interface of *6 Billion Others* presents its myriad of micro-portraits as a mosaic, a screen full of faces which seems to attempt a literal reflection of the multitude, the diversity of human life.

Like the work of Upian discussed earlier, the projects above (*The Message*, *Global Lives*, *6 Billion Others*) have a thoroughgoing humanism at their heart. They recruit the potential viewer to understand him or herself as a common part of a common humanity 'Together as One, United as One, We're all in this Together ... One World'. The affordances of the web have made a different and exciting kind of global consciousness available as *those with broadband access* are able to create everyday symbolic resources with others from around the world. However, the claims implicit in this mode of production and reception should remind the documentary scholar of an earlier debate about documentary photography occasioned by the great *Family of Man* documentary photography exhibition held in Paris in 1955. Where then photography was being celebrated as

the medium that could capture humanity and reveal universality, now it is 'new media' technologies that are being cast in that role. But the critique of the humanistic project, articulated by Roland Barthes at the time of the Paris exhibition, is pertinent for these contemporary projects:

> This myth of the human 'condition' rests on a very old mystification, which always consists in placing Nature at the bottom of History. Any classic humanism postulates that in scratching the history of men a little, the relativity of their institutions or the superficial diversity of their skins (but why not ask the parents of Emmet Till, the young Negro assassinated by the Whites what they think of *The Great Family of Man?*), one very quickly reaches the solid rock of a universal human nature. Progressive humanism, on the contrary, must always remember to reverse the terms of this very old imposture, constantly to scour nature, its 'laws' and its 'limits' in order to discover History there, and at last to establish Nature itself as historical.[27]

Barthes's insight should offer us some critical purchase on these Borgesian attempts to map all of humanity. His critique reminds us that common humanity (as 'nature') is an historical construct determined through discursive assemblages and, therefore, through power. In celebrating our connectedness we should also remember the massive inequalities of wealth, gender and race that celebrations of 'one world-ism' ignore. It is not too hard to go one step further and understand this upsurge in globalising documentary projects as the inevitable corollary of a globalised economy driven by the web.

While sitting on non-linear platforms, in formal terms, *Global Lives*, *The Message*, *Life in a Day* and even *ThuYOU* provide types of linear viewing experience, with beginnings, middles and ends. But producers are increasingly looking to non-linear forms to express the polyvocal nature of participatory content, exploring curatorial strategies that allow the viewer to navigate their own documentary experience through databased content, like the interactive documentaries discussed earlier.

An attitude to database as a creative opportunity for participatory documentary is core to the realisation of *Mapping Main Street*, a collaborative project developed as a response to American politicians invoking Main Street to stand for 'ordinary America' during the 2009 election campaign. Main Street has long been a contested space, 'a shifting metaphor for what constitutes traditional American values and the "average" American experience'.[28] *Mapping Main Street* was designed to reflect the diverse realities of Main Street America, unsettle assumptions and foster dialogue in and about community life. In other words, the work is not intended to present or investigate a particular view but to provide a stage for debate around the idea of Main Street.

Jesse Shapins, an artist and theorist in the Main Street team, articulates the role of the producer in these projects as 'leading and designing frameworks that do have very specific constraints and that have very specific thematic and geographic focuses that then create a context for many different voices to come in'.[29]

Mapping Main Street kicked off in May 2009 with the team taking a 12,000-mile journey across the country to visit main streets and gather material. The project was then promoted to the team's networks and, through a National Public Radio series, to the wider public. Audio stories with stills made by the team act as seed content to inspire and encourage contributions to be posted on Flickr or Vimeo. These take the form of micro-documentaries or slide shows with music or voiceover. These are drawn into the *Mapping Main Street* website using public data feeds often known as Application Programming Interfaces (APIs). The website is structured to allow content to be experienced as a lean-back experience, on-demand, through generative paths offered as journeys across a map, or through alliterative themes – in an approach the producers have called 'algorithmic curation'. Thus, a search for the city of Buffalo brings up a brief documentary about a drag club on Main Street which prompts another short film about the micro-brewery tradition in the city, followed by another on public art on Buffalo's Main Street. Alternatively, the 'Path' option takes one on a content journey away from the city. As options are taken, 'related routes' are generated based on meta data in the content currently on view – for example, Architecture, Children, Night.

The user experience is one of shifting frames, modalities and identifications, as one makes a unique journey through modules of content by diverse authors. (There are around 500 items of content at the time of writing, with new contributions still coming in.) For the producers of *Mapping Main Street*, the affordances of the digital space assist the realisation of a polyvocal aesthetic, 'What the database enables in the context of public media arts is open-ended, indeterminacy. Instead of simply representing a singular thesis, the database allows for multiplicity ... a framework that brings together multiple voices and multiple media formats.'[30]

As information architecture meets participatory content we can, thus, begin to see the emergence of twenty-first-century documentary forms which are founded in a poetics of the database. This creative territory is one which is being explored by a number of digital media artists interested in factual storytelling, among them the celebrated American information architect, Jonathan Harris. Harris has said:

One thing we have in common is the desire to express ourselves ... in the last few years a lot of those individual acts of self-expression have been moving onto the

internet, as that happens people have been leaving behind footprints ... I write computer programs that study very large sets of these footprints.[31]

Harris became well known for works including *We Feel Fine* (2006), *I Want you to Want Me* (2008) (both created with Sep Kamvar) and *Universe* (2007), projects which apply a generative treatment to the participatory content contained in public datasets. In the case of *We Feel Fine* he created a live portrait of human emotion by searching newly posted blog entries for the words 'I feel' or 'I am feeling', offering these for exploration by visualising data feeds based on these terms through a series of playful interfaces. *I Want You To Want Me* took a similar approach to the content people posted on dating websites. These engaging, innovative works fuse art and documentary, micro and macro perspectives, spectacle and intimacy, offering a twenty-first-century reinterpretation of what the 'creative treatment of actuality' might entail.[32]

More recently Harris has been moving into creative territory and working with types of content (stills, video) that can be identified more easily in relation to histories of documentary practice. For *The Whale Hunt* (2007) he explored a classic documentary theme. During nine days living with an Inupiat Eskimo family in Barrow, Alaska, he documented the hunt, from preparation to the kill, in a sequence of 3,214 photographs, taken at five-minute intervals – more often in moments of intensity. His purpose was 'to experiment with a new interface for human storytelling', and he used the stills to create an open interactive work that each viewer would experience and understand uniquely. Harris also describes the project as an opportunity for him to reflect on the role of the computer as co-creator in his creative output,

Much effort is spent making computers understand what it's like to be human (through data mining and artificial intelligence), but rarely do humans try to see things from a computer's perspective. I was interested in reaching some degree of empathy with the computer, a constant thankless helper in my work.[33]

In *The Sputnik Observatory* (2009) Harris has applied 'algorithmic curation' to a substantial video archive of interviews with leading thinkers on,

topics and ideas that may seem fringe and even heretical to the mainstream world ... Sputnik is dedicated to bringing these crucial ideas from the fringes of thought out into the limelight, so that the world can begin to understand them.[34]

In *The Sputnik Observatory* Harris locates the participatory involvement as an activity in response to the archive, which he allows the user to experience through an interactive browsing experience or through curated paths. In addition to taking these offered routes, the committed user/viewer can, by becoming a project member, add their own paths through the content as well as leaving comments or contributions in the form of text, audio or video. He thus invites the user into a collaborative relationship which opens up the curatorial perspective.

In these projects we can see the emergence of a variety of participatory and collaborative forms that draw upon histories of documentary and documentary arts practices, as well as upon the affordances of networked social media. In *Mapping Main Street*, *The Whale Hunt* and *The Sputnik Observatory* the producers employ non-linear structures designed to reflect polyvocal content and provide a satisfying though open-ended interactive experience.

In these co-creative practices the documentary project is not an expedition into the field to capture and bring back content/data; instead it becomes a co-creative venture in the emergence of meaning. This collaborative practice presents a challenge to the observational with its social scientific perspective, and to the totalising vision of the auteur. It offers instead forms of insight created by participant observers and an open text. The role of the artist/producer in these collaborations remains central – but shifts towards a curatorial position, a role of setting up rule sets, boundaried digital processes that establish the conditions of emergence. The intervention of the artist/producer in making something meaningful remains central, while the post-human contribution of the computer injects a dimension which is truly new for documentary. Models like these suggest ways in which everyday life as well as excessive experiences can be represented through polyvocal hypertexts.

THE REAL SURPRISED BY VIRTUALITY

We have tried to map what seem to us to be the significant new opportunities emerging from documentary's integration into the Web 2.0 online environment. These developments raise a number of significant critical debates for twenty-first-century documentary studies which researchers will develop in the future.

The field has had a stubborn attachment to questions of the real and its representation. As documentary practice becomes absorbed in the fields of media virtuality our critical understandings will change. Clearly the evidence above suggests we will have to spend a lot more time thinking about what constitutes an open text as documentary develops through the affordances of Web 2.0 which facilitate linking, association, user-generated content and mash-up. Furthermore, documentary studies will be forced into a shift towards the post-human. From the point at which the chemistry of film became the electronic signal of video we have been moving towards the point where all

media becomes data. All our data experiences are now subject to the agency of the human machine assemblage, or, as Elsaesser has it, 'strange organisms, pulsing, moving and mutating, depending on the tags one enters or encounters'[35] and as Jonathan Harris acknowledges determined in part by 'the computer, a constant thankless helper in my work'.[36] Not only does this context shift documentary epistemology, the new conditions of networked media also reconfigure our understandings of documentary's public and political purpose.

Against this general critical background there are at least two sets of new and specific ideas that emerge from our thinking in this chapter. The first is that in beginning to define a poetics of the database that works for documentary we will need to consider the polarities that we have identified between the highly specific and everyday utterance of the vernacular, on one hand, and the totalising map on the other. We have observed the profusion of autobiographic and everyday particularity in the rise of vernacular video. One of the things that appears to occur when documentary-makers enter this domain is the revival of global humanism in the idea that somehow it is possible to represent *everyone and everything* through the infinite network architecture of the web. This is an understandable response to the potential of the network in affording distributed authorship. However, in terms of documentary traditions we would argue that this is a redundant move. Attempts to say everything about everyone finish up saying nothing about anything. Borges's map ends up tattered and useless in the desert.

The key for us is in the idea of 'staging a conversation'; the documentary producer working online with Web 2.0 is called upon to 'stage a conversation', with a user community, with research subjects, with participants, co-producers and audiences. The question for the documentary producer is how do we stage that conversation? How do we design the stage? Do our co-producers even know the stage is there in the massively long tail of online media abundance? Do they understand its terms of entry? What are the pre-existing discursive formations that determine a public's attitude to the stage in the first place? What are the constraints on our action once on this stage? What kinds of utterance and linkage does the stage afford? These are all questions of structure and rhetoric: questions that return responsibility to the authorship team and in turn reconfer the possibility of intervention and argument.

NOTES

1. Jon Dovey, *Freakshow: First Person Media and Factual Television* (London: Pluto, 2000), p. 62.
2. Jean Burgess and Joshua Green, *YouTube* (Cambridge: Polity, 2009), p. 25.

3. Bjorn Sorenssen, 'Digital Video and Alexandre Astruc's Camera-stylo: The New Avant Garde in Documentary Realized?', *Studies in Documentary Film* vol. 2 no. 1, February 2008, p. 47.

4. David Buckingham, Maria Pini and Rebekah Willett, '"Take Back the Tube!": The Discursive Construction of Amateur Film and Video-Making', in David Buckingham and Rebekah Willett (eds), *Video Cultures: Media Technology and Everyday Creativity* (Basingstoke: Palgrave Macmillan, 2009).

5. Dovey, *Freakshow*.

6. Sorenssen, 'Digital Video and Alexandre Astruc's Camera-stylo'.

7. M. Lister, J. Dovey, S. Giddings, I. Grant and K. Kelly, *New Media: A Critical Introduction* (London: Routledge, 2009), pp. 225–31.

8. Pew Internet and American Life Project, http://www.pewinternet.org/Reports/2010/State-of-Online-Video.aspx. Accessed 3 August 2010.

9. Bill Nichols, *Representing Reality: Issues and Concepts in Documentary* (Bloomington: Indiana University Press, 1991), emphasis original.

10. Michael Renov, 'First Person Films: Some Theses on Self Inscription', in T. Austin and E. de Jong (eds), *Rethinking Documentary New Perspectives, New Practices* (Maidenhead: McGraw Hill, 2008), p. 42, capitals original.

11. Thomas Elsaesser, 'Tales of Epiphany and Entropy: Around the Worlds in Eighty Clicks', in Pelle Snickers and Patrick Vondereau (eds), *The YouTube Reader* (Stockholm: National Library of Sweden, 2009), p. 181.

12. Ibid., p. 167.

13. Ibid., p. 183.

14. Lev Manovich, *The Language of New Media* (Cambridge, MA: MIT Press, 2001).

15. Florian Thalhofer (n. d.), http://www.cloudx.eu/. Accessed 5 November 2012.

16. Hudson Dale, 'Undisclosed Recipients: Database Documentaries and the Internet', *Studies in Documentary Film* vol. 2 no. 1, February 2008, p. 90.

17. Robert Flaherty, 'Going to Extremes', in Kevin Macdonald and Mark Cousins (eds), *Imagining Reality: The Faber Book of Documentary* (London: Faber and Faber, 1996), p. 41.

18. Jean Rouch, 'The Camera and Man', in Steven Feld (ed.), *Cine-Ethnography* (Minneapolis: University of Minnesota Press, 2003), p. 44.

19. Humphrey Jennings, Charles Madge and Tom Harrisson, 'Letter', *New Statesman*, 1937, http://www.massobs.org.uk/original_massobservation_project.htm. Accessed 3 August 2010.

20. *ThruYOU* (n. d.), http://thru-you.com/#/videos/. Accessed 3 August 2010.

21. Clay Shirky, *Here Comes Everybody* (London: Penguin, 2008), p. 262.

22. *The Global Lives Project*, http://globallives.org/about/. Accessed 3 August 2010.

23. *Interview 2 – MadV* (n. d.), http://collabdocs.wordpress.com/about/on-collaborative-creativity-interviews/interview-2-madv/. Accessed 3 August 2010.

24. *The Message* (n. d.), http://www.youtube.com/watch?v=Z-BzXpOch-E. Accessed 3 August 2010.

25. Clive Thompson, 'How YouTube Changes the Way We Think', *Wired* 22 December, 2008, http://www.wired.com/techbiz/people/magazine/17-01/st_thompson. Accessed 3 August 2010.

26. *Life in a Day* (n. d.), http://www.youtube.com/user/lifeinaday. Accessed 3 August 2010.

27. Roland Barthes, 'The Great Family of Man', *Mythologies*, trans. Annette Lavers (New York: Hill & Wang, 1972).

28. Jesse Shapins, 'Mapping Main Street: Tracing an American Political Mythology, Urban Imaginary and Built Environment', *Writing Cities*, May 2009, p. 2.

29. Jesse Shapins and Kara Oehler, 'Interview' (n. d.), http://collabdocs.wordpress.com/about/interview-4-kara-oehler-jesse-shapins-on-mapping-main-street/. Accessed 3 August 2010.

30. Jesse Shapins and Kara Oehler, unpublished presentation to the Northeastern School of Architecture, February 2010.

31. J. Harris, 'The Web's Secret Stories', *TED: Ideas Worth Spreading*, July 2007, http://www.ted.com/talks/lang/eng/jonathan_harris_tells_the_web_s_secret_stories.html. Accessed 3 August 2010.

32. Ibid.

33. Thomas Elsaesser, 'Tales of Epiphany and Entropy: Paranarrative Worlds on YouTube', *Film Theory and Contemporary Hollywood Movies* (New York: Routledge, 2009), p. 169.

34. J. Harris, 'Statement: The Sputnik Observatory' (n. d.), http://www.number27.org/sputnik.html. Accessed 3 August 2010.

6.3 New Platforms for Docmedia: 'Varient of a Manifesto'

PETER WINTONICK

In 1926, Vertov, faced with the technology of the cinema, wrote that: 'The movie camera was invented, in order to penetrate deeper into the visible world so that we do not forget what happens and what the future must take into account.' Why then, in our day, have new digital platforms been 'invented'? Vertov's answer, for documentary, was a 'basic, programmatic objective … to aid each oppressed individual and the proletariat as a whole in their effort to understand the phenomenon of life around them'.[1] So what then is our 'basic programmatic objective' for documentary in the age of digital platforms?

UTOPIA

> Utopia (Uto´-pia) noun.
> A visionary, imaginary state with perfect political and social conditions.
> A paradise.[2]

To begin with, I have no idea what everyone else in this book [except for the contributors to this last section, ed.] is on about … documentary cinema this, and documentary cinema that … For now, and forever, I am banishing the word documentary from our lexicon. I am replacing it with a contemporary word, one which reflects the future and the now. My new word is: *docmedia*. We all used to believe that documentary was hot media, as fellow Canadian McLuhan defined it. However, new silicon-based technology is transforming documentary expression and non-fiction media, allowing for a full spectrum of possibilities. Our brave, new and complicated world is filled with change and choice. What we once called 'new media', and then 'next media' has now been transformed, transplatformed and transformated into what I call 'Now Media'. Docmedia is Now Media. Now and then, now and Zen.

Utopian thinking is the belief that individuals, micro-societies and states have the possibilities to create a better, perfect world. Such thinking is essential to the creative imagination. Utopias are about how we wish to visualise an ideal world, and how we reconcile and manage that vision against the irrational impulses of the real world. This is my definition of utopia. Utopias are about images

and visions. Utopias place pictures of possible worlds in our minds. By building utopias, we define our collective and individual stories. For some of us who create for the screen, caught by the spark of the ideal, utopias are possible. They can be forged and created.

I am very interested in utopias. In fact, I am now shooting a major documentary about the subject, in more than a dozen countries. Actually, it's neither a film nor a documentary. More accurately, it's a web-intended reality-based game-show mega-digital information base, a meta-linear webnet experience. I am making it because I want to offer hope to a sad world in the form of what we formerly called documentary cinema and what I now call docmedia.

So, in terms of 'documentary cinema', I will here imagine those characteristics which we will need to rebuild documentary into a digital utopia, or a 'digitopia'. As a 'way' of facing reality in this digital age.

All utopias need platforms – and plat*forums* – upon which to exist. These days, all docmedia culture must be nourished and grow within a petri dish of an enabling platform. However, for me, the word 'platform' is much too horizontal. While I am at the task of banishing words like 'documentary' to the dustbins of film history, I am also going to blow up the word 'platform'. To explode it. To make it four-dimensional. In this chapter of what used to be called a book, I will journey through a pentagram of ideas about new platforms for documentary cinema. Once upon a time, platforms were things you stood upon while waiting for a commuter train; or platforms were statements of a political party's programmes, issues and objectives; or a scaffold where window-cleaners worked; or they were ungodly, unwieldy high-heeled shoes that beautiful tall people wore to discotheques; and stages in theatres where one enacted scenes from a play. And, finally, platforms were places in public parks where one set up a speaker's soap-box, upon which he or she could proselytise, predict, or harangue. I'll adopt this latter definition for platform.

Docmedia is the hot Now Media. Documentary-makers are adapting to a mediascape rapidly shifting beneath their reality-based feet. Technology is transforming documentary expression and non-fiction media into a full spectrum of docmedia possibilities. In this international zeitgeist, the very definition of documentary itself is morphing into something wider, more exciting and challenging. Profound changes are transforming the creation and distribution of classic theatrical, educational and broadcast documentary.

These days, documentary cinema has morphed into non-fiction 'faction' – which is what I call fact-based fiction. New narrative devices are being devised. New forms of storytelling. 3D graphics have led us to animate documations. Hybrids are now viral. Reality-infused computer games, many with an ethical twist, surface as docugames. Mobile docs and webdocs are everywhere, everyplace. But also they appear as cross-media, trans-platform digital documentary in all its incarnations: cyber-docs, netcasting, interactive docs. Online all the time. Media have become more democratic. There is a new lexicon for documentary. The words 'documentary' and 'democracy' have fused into – documocracy.

Like world music before it, new platform documentary practice is alive and well and being forged in every corner of the planet: from Indonesia to Argentina; from Guangzhou, China, to Cape Town to Bangalore; the user-generated generation is uploading its own docs.

What does this all mean for documentary cinema? New doc-makers must investigate and ingest all new forms of docmedia: documentary tools, expressions, forms, platforms, formats and new ways of financing creative documentary media. The old doc priesthood has retreated into their Plato's cave retirement homes – or their linear television offices. New ways of financing films are being devised. 'Third Sector' foundations and non-governmental organisations (NGOs) are back in the game. Educational markets are opening up again.

Nowadays, platforms are Earth-friendly vehicles that we construct in docollective factories for documentary cinema. We use them to propel docmedia into the world; to rocket screen-based imagination towards a new moon of documentary cinema. These days, making documentary cinema is about the synthesis of methods, production tools, monetising schemes, delivery systems, multi-screens and virtual marketing systems. Oh, and it's also still about reality. I am naming all of this *Gestalt* – a platform. A way of seeing, a 'documentary way of life' – as Lao Tzu would have called it. Documentary platforms are as all pervasive as the sound of a temple bell ringing out over a place called Docmedia.

Let us pretend, for a minute, that a generation in documentary now only lasts six months. Let us admit that since those first screenings of Lumière's films in the salon of the Grand Café of the Hotel Scribe in Paris in 1895 that everything has changed and nothing has changed; that since the brothers Kaufman-Vertov's manifest dreams took them to the streets with unwieldy cameras – nothing but everything has changed; that since Rouch, Leacock, Maysles,

Filgate, Pennebaker, Koenig and dozens of other 'kinoks' (as Vertov called them) liberated documentary cinema from itself and went portable in the Direct Free/cinéma vérité revolution, minds and world have changed; that land-based cinematic dogma was completely overthrown in 1995 when I first launched the Virtual Film Festival on a thing we now call the netweb; or that change has been with us since the first docs for mobile devices went online. In other words, for the enterprise of this idea we call documentary cinema, there has always been flux and rejection and growth, that across time and technologies, an umbilical chord/cord has joined together a documentary-maker's intentions with the latest machines of his or her era with the viewer's ever-developing understanding of how to consume images. In other words, every succeeding doc-generation always builds for itself and works upon a new platform. There have always been new platforms for documentary. A fusion of creator, technology and audience. This is the legacy of the documentary ethic, which is a hard-wired genetic code which never changes across the cinematic ages. This is the new platform I am considering here. I will now take you through a few conceptual frameworks, cite a case study example, rant and roll, and move us all to the future of documentary cinema.

These days, it's essential that documentary-makers adapt to this new lexicon, or they will get drowned out in the digital tsunami. I think I can help. If I wanted to promote collective progress in the understanding of what lays ahead for documentary cinema, I would call together ten docmedia creators and thinkers from all points on the planet to an open virtual space and have them interface with half-score more traditional, classical documentary film-makers. I would welcome our whole community to contribute to the rebranding process: new and established doc-makers, producers, distributors, funders, niche-casters, web-makers, creatives, exhibitors, foundations, NGOs, non-profits, marketeers, institutions, educators, students, viewers and the new docitizens who I term 'produsers' – that is, a producer-users. We would brainstorm and debate together, seeking new definitions and standards for best practices, without regard to dogma, the past, to preconceptions or boundaries.

I would showcase and celebrate transplatform digital documentary in all its docmedia incarnations: cyber-docs, digidocs, transmedia docs, cross-docs, cross-media, 360 degree docs, netcast docs, interactive docs, 3D-docs, made-for-mobile docs, docomedies, real-life docugames and animated documations. Long form and short form. Broadcast, Broadband-cast or hypercast. Multi-media. Multi-platform. The documentary dictionary is expanding. Factual TV is transmuting into factivism. Our simulated focus group would find that consensus would be impossible. That a thousand definitions of new platforms for docmedia are blooming now. But they would also find that the very act of considering new platform possibilities for docmedia allows us all migrate to the future – to live in harmony as digital natives.

DOCAGORA

One of the initiatives I co-created with others in the last decade, was DocAgora. DocAgora was an open netspace to consider new forms, new platforms, new tools and new ways of financing creative and socially engaged docmedia. It was a non-profit public web portal to help the documentary media community to navigate through the information overflow around Now Media: a tool to aid the understanding and use of these new possibilities for docmedia; a freely accessed, public information service about our new platform world. In ancient Athens, the Agora was a meeting place, a marketplace and a public place, a site of spirit and commerce, community and renewal. The DocAgora organisation co-organised real-world events that touch down as conferences, development labs, debates, new pitch systems, discussion circles and funding opportunities at leading documentary film festivals and media markets throughout the year. Beyond its real-world iterations, DocAgora's main goal was to operate as an internet interchange based at the DocAgora Webplex.[3]

Services like DocAgora function as honest brokers, offering the docmedia community an unbiased review of funding and distribution opportunities, events, partners and tools currently available in the ever-changing docscape. They point to new models and useful resources for sustainable documentary financing. DocAgora's WebPlex database was populated with content by its users and partners. Access to the system was open, collaboratively filtered and allows the docommunity to contribute feedback on the various elements of the database. DocAgora and other similar non-profit initiatives allow us all to make sense of the new possibilities for shape-shifting reality.

DocAgora: an open netspace to consider new forms, new platforms, new tools and new ways of financing

Because, we all acknowledge, as sci-fi novelist Philip K. Dick once wrote, that: 'Reality is that which, when you stop believing in it, doesn't go away.'[4]

The internet offers documentarians opportunities for essential face-to-multi-face networking. It brings together a pervasive grid of emerging, technologically adept docmedia-makers who create their own visions with their own voices. They build web destinations that facilitate creation. They forge new strategic alliances, enabling practical plans and model working systems in order to sow the seeds for future ones.

New platforms embrace open-source ideas, input, musings and social-media meta-links from a community of produsers. To build a better documentary webworld with our own ideas, examples and critique. New platforms can facilitate information interchange. To point at, and share, case studies, emulata and new modes for sustainable documedia financing. In new platform-speak, such social-media tools optimise what was once called distribution and marketing, but which we now term 'outreach'.

CASE STUDY: SUBMARINE

At this point, instead of theorising, I offer you an example. I know there are now thousands of docmedia platforms, however defined, and web-intended docmedia projects, either already existing out there or now in progress and process. Instead of listing them here in a linear book with unclickable links, we will save that kind of notation for any future Now Media iteration of these mutterings and a docmedia webnet incarnation of this paperback. But I will offer, by way of example, one case study that embodies, practically, what I am going on about here.

In my experience, there is one company responding to the new zeitgeist in documentary platforms in exemplary ways. They are leading us all out of the desert of old media – in a submarine, no less. Submarine[5] is an Amsterdam-based transmedia multi-tasking production company. They do award-winning documentaries, games, online sites and animation. They have their own showcase webchannel[6] and DVD label.

They do installations for museums, work for hire and commissions. They work in Holland, across Europe and around the globe. They synthesise new realities and wild ideas, which in the new parlance we now call memes, into digital forms. Submarine serves as a template for the new production models I think we all must follow.

Bruno Felix and Femke Wolting co-founded Submarine in the shadow of Y2K in 2000. It's fitting that one of their earliest films was called *It's the End of TV As We Know It* (2000), a long-form doc and website about the future of digital media starring Jeff Bezos of Amazon.com and James Murdoch of Newscorp. Previously, Felix was responsible for developing new media strategy and output for the Dutch public broadcaster VPRO. By forming Submarine, he says:

We wanted to move beyond the talk of the new media gurus of the 1990s, and the dogmatic divisions between theory and practice. We just wanted to do it. We were not afraid of commerce. We work with companies and artists. We are idealists trying to be part of all, and at the same time, fighting for innovative factual media.[7]

Femke Wolting also worked in the 1990s at VPRO Digital. When not piloting Submarine, she has also directed such cross-media documentaries as *Sneakers* (2004), about the rise of the sports shoe, and *Another Perfect World* (2009), a doc about online worlds as places for work, play, friendship and love.

When I asked her what had made her so enamoured with docmedia, she said:

After graduating from university in 1994, I started to work for the Rotterdam International Film Festival and initiated a new section there called Exploding Cinema. It was a programme about how cinema is changing in new directions through digital technologies. I was fascinated by the fact that digital culture was changing film, and that everything seemed possible. Many people – scientists, designers and programmers – were inventing new kinds of storytelling, in games, on the internet and in computer-generated film. There were no rules established yet about how to make a successful project. The industry was also very young, so there was lots of room for young people to be revolutionary and start new companies. That was, and is, still very inspiring about digital culture.

At the same time, I still love cinema. I love making and producing films. The fact that there is an audience and an industry with established structures for financing films and for distributing is also great, although film financing and distributing is quickly changing, too. So, I think that's why at Submarine we started out with our love for the combination of film and digital media.

Submarine's projects are challenging in content, artistic vision and technology. It works with renowned directors on original documentaries and stories that expand the lexicon of non-fiction film-making. Douglas Gayeton's *Molotov Alva and His Search for the Creator: A Second Life Odyssey* (2008) is the first machinima documentary made in a virtual world, 'second life'. Bregtje van der Haak's *Satellite Queens* (2007) takes us behind the scenes of *Kalam Nawaem*, a prime-time Arab talk-show for women.

Submarine also joined with the infamous Peter Greenaway on *Rembrandt's J'Accuse* (2008), a masterpiece in essay form multi-screen documentary, which has the illustrious director making the case for conspiracy and murder by closely examining Rembrandt's great *Night Watch* painting. As well, Submarine produced Greenaway's film trilogy *The Tulse Luper Suitcases* (2003) which crossed genres,

becoming docmedia-maker Christiaan de Rooij's award-winning online multi-player community game, *The Tulse Luper Journey*.

Submarine's core staff collaborates with, if you allow me to neologise, a term I'll call createams (creative teams): a network of freelance directors, digital artists, film crews, programmers, interactive designers, writers, illustrators, co-producer partners, funders and commissioning editors, creating what Submarine calls 'contemporary stories that take a critical, dynamic and often playful look at modern society'.

For Wolting

Right now people tend to think of themselves as either a film-maker or game designer or an animator. I think platforms and genres will blend into a new hybrid and that people won't think of themselves as these specialised craftsmen (or craftswomen). The ubiquity of technology is forcing people to shed these ideas and get back to the roots of storytelling while using these tools in new and exciting combinations.

Submarine sails under, through and over the seven seas of docmedia and meta-media, all made for the digital age. They work in diverse forms, from web comedy to online video art, from grassroots journalism to hardcore propaganda, on frameworks for artistic game production, interactive roadtrips, autobio novels, online experiences and mini-movies. They also produce animation for TV and the web, and everything from animated graphic novels and hybrid flash games to rotoscoped documentaries and an interactive animated series for kids.

Wolting was energised about developing *Energy Risk* (2011),

a documentary combined with an online alternate reality game about economic and political scenarios. Through the game and the documentary, we attempt to provide a deeper insight into the complex issues surrounding global energy politics, by forcing the player to make choices that leave their mark on a national and international scale.

The back-story is a scenario by Coby van der Linde, a renowned professor in climate change at the Clingendael Institute (Netherlands Institute of International Relations).

Submarine also has its own dedicated net-based SubmarineChannel, which is both a distribution and a production platform for film-makers and interactive artists who are exploring the potential of the web. As a showcase and a test-bed for digital culture, it's a place for digital artists to create new, interactive, cross-media formats that use the qualities of the internet that can also migrate to other media, like television, mobile devices and film.

So the future of the documentary dictionary looks promising. Moving old words – and subjects – into new work, formerly submerging doc-makers can, with a few new added skill-sets, emerge again. For Wolting:

> Five years from now will come much faster than I suspect, but I feel we can look at what we are doing now and project out to what we will be doing. Submarine is really an experiment that has been challenging, interesting and rewarding in ways we never imagined. As a complete cross-media production company, we look at all platforms, but, in the end, we just try to tell good stories. Until now, people have specialised in one platform or genre. We are committed to storytelling as a cross-platform medium. Whatever new and interesting ways we can tell a story, in emotionally engaging ways, we will do it. It is easy to get caught up in technology, but technology comes and goes, [while] good storytelling is much more enduring.

A PLACE CALLED DOCMEDIA

How can we work together to build a dynamic docmedia digitopia? What are the futures for digital documentary film-making and all these new platforms for documentary?

Seven years ago, I visited the brilliant labs in the Architecture Department at the University of South Australia (UniSA), which use unreel software to envision three-dimensional documentary spaces based on software engines for computer games. At UniSA's wearable computer lab, Bruce Thomas and his team were developing virtual and interactive wearable computers. These have many applications, only limited by one's imagination. Bruce's cyborgian, utopian devices use GPS, silicon, IP and all manner of chips, bells and whistles. You can build your own real-yet-virtual world in front of your very own eyes. You can build your own reality-based utopias. You can be your own movie. You can both be the camera and the cameraperson. The object and the subject. The documenter and the documenteur (a word I just coined which fuses documentary with the French word for liar).

These cyberdoc devices extend the skin, as fellow Canadian, Marshall McLuhan would say. Eventually nano-media machines could be woven into cloth, or fashioned into a contact lens. You could become your own documentary. You could wear your documentary, media-making machine as fashion. I can see myself as a living, talking, walking, breathing documentary machine. I am my own platform. I will become my camera and my distribution machine all rolled up into one.

In the here and now of this digitopia, I can enter reality without altering it a bit, which has been the Holy Grail for documentarians since the beginning of time. Truth and illusion will then become one. It's the unified film theory all rolled up into one inspired, wearable media machine. This new vision is about personally interpreting, filtering, converting and sculpting reality into a three-dimensional, time-based audiovisual art, destined for any screen and all screens. Any media and all media. This kind of vision is called docmedia.

To peer twenty years into documentary's future, you should use your own looking glass. You can follow the paths and rivers and roads of what I term the 'great river of documentary history', to see what might come to pass as trendancies. That's a neologism which fuses the words 'trends' and 'tendencies'. I want you to extrapolate out to a point where you might be able to predict where docmedia platforms will be two decades from now. (That is, if there is to be a humanely habitable Earth two decades from now.)

Many things have changed since Hermann Snellen first measured 20/20 vision using his famous eyesight letter chart in the mid-nineteenth century. For one thing, documentary, as an art form and as a sociophilosophical approach to understanding reality, was born. Documentary, as a formula for generating commerce at the expense of real people, was born. Since documentary's first 'lie' – created, as the Lumières' workers emerged from their factory in Lyon – the many ways of documenting, picturing, imaging and imagining the real world have mutated. Our real-vision has been transmogrified.

HYPERDOCS

Let me put on a vaudevillian magic cape, buff up my crystal ball and backcast a few predictions. Looking directly into the sun and the future, where will new platforms for documentary be? Eclipsed by neo-media moons? Blanked out by a hydrocarbon blanket? In dire need of sunglasses to disguise itself?

To be sure, what has always been important to documentary will always be. What's important is image history and image future. Transferred values. Subject lessons and object lessons. Looking at real media as ethical active agents and powers of persuasion, as montage, passion, philosophy, poetics and pedantics. As a theory of understanding reality. As parallel and converging tracks of interest for both the film-makers and their audiences.

Since the days before time, the Native Inuit of northern Canada have always installed large, monumental stone structures upon the hills, all along the frozen river valleys. These 'sculptures' resemble the human form. They are called Inukshuk. Their origin is mysterious. They hold stories. In practical terms, they are used to channel the caribou hunt. Some say that these cairns are spiritual icons, some say they are geographic signposts that help in northern navigation. They are similar to the Aboriginal Australian's cosmology of dreamtime and songlines.

The new documentary platform is our meeting place, our Inukshuk. Our signpost. The documentary form is a language system. One that always changes and that never changes. As social solidarity media-workers, let us all help to rebuild a new documentary cinema, as a locus-point in the struggle against mega-media myths filled with apoca-lyptic lies and locusts; old Hollywood; old fictive fantasy; old reality; old news; old world; old vision; old inhuman-media; old disembodied, corporate media dreams.

Docmedia's new platform is web-intended, or multi-platform. Now Media. Filled with ideas about documocracy. Interactive screens and proactive screams. So, take what we know about the language and history and qualities and complexities of traditional documentary, and fuse it to what's great about the Now Media. The playing with time. The responsibility to audience and subjects. The documen-tary as database. Interactivity. Access. Point of view. Truth at 1,000 frames a second. Innovation. Incubation. Creativity. Our own voice. Our own vision. Our own stories. All are fundamental for the docmedia project. All are build-ing stones for new platforms for a new screen culture.

A COUNTDOWN TO THE FUTURE OF DOCTOPIAN PLATFORMS

In this little rant about the future of documentary cinema's new platforms, we know the invisible elephant in the room, and in this book, is that, despite the canon of all the great documentary works in the past, documentary as we knew it, as an earnest, boring, linear experience, is drown-ing in the digital water. And the infrastructure to support such old-form documentaries is on its deathwatch. Its life support system will soon be unplugged.

So I will be McLuhanesque about this and look to the future, not to the inevitable future of inundated post-carbon cities, but to the future of docmedia, through a rear-view mirror.

One hundred years ago, in 1909, the Italian poet Filippo T. Marinetti, published his *Futurist Manifesto*. He stated:

> We want to sing the love of danger, the habit of energy and rashness. ... The essential elements of our poetry will be courage, audacity and revolt. ... We are on the extreme promontory of the centuries! What is the use of looking behind at the moment when we must open the mysterious shutters of the impossible? Time and Space died yesterday. We are already living in the absolute, since we have already created eternal, omnipresent speed.[8]

In a California debate in 1981, critic Pauline Kael once said about Jean-Luc Godard's fiction films that he was actually making documentaries of the future, but set in the present, because capturing the moment before it passed was more important to Godard than presenting a 'finished' work.

I agree with the future of futurism. Each of us has to write our own docmedia manifesto, or what I call a mani-fiesta – that other media-makers may well take to heart. Where will docmedia be twenty years from now? Here are twenty stimulating possibilities, my top twenty idea-memes, in a countdown to the future.

20. Fiction will cease to exist. People will extract all the drama, characters, stories and pleasure from non-fiction documentary media – docmedia – that they used to enjoy with fiction.

19. Every docitizen will have eye-camera implants. As a third, intuitive eye, or I.

18. Closed-circuit surveillance cameras will become the next TV channels. The next theatres. The next opera houses.

17. The motion pix and docmedia industry will become a green industry and adopt greencode standards and initiatives.

16. By using biochips, the internet will turn into a living biological, or illogical organism. We will communicate with the grid, and with each other, just by thinking or dreaming about it.

15. Wars will be fought in virtual dystopian gridspace. With journalistic doc-coverage by its participants. No one will get hurt. Hunger, disease, famine will cease to exist. Peace will break out. Thanks, in part, to doc-media-makers. And an active, educated docitizenry.

14. Everyone will be docmedia literate.

13. Documentaries will have saved the world. There will no longer be a need for documentaries. But we will make them anyway, out of habit.

12. As islands of sanity, docmedia platforms will have pointed to positive solutions to cure the world's ills, and will convince people to create a sustainable future.

11. Documocracy will replace ideology, religion and poli-tics. Direct documentary democracy will rule. Communities, tribes, doc-diversity, one-world.

10. Pacifist documentary freedom fighters will feed the world with doctopian ideas.

9. Illusion factories and mind-numbing mega-media corps/corpse will shut down. Voluntarily.

8. Television, like nations and profit, will cease to exist.

7. Happiness will rule, and there will be no more need for sad docs. We will put ourselves out of work.

6. Non-fiction data-gathering, creation and distribution will be accomplished through a kind of expansive pro-jection of the individual's doc persona. Docu-souls. Docmedia, as well as our body/minds, will be able to fly anywhere, like Malaysian dreamtimers, without the need for aeroplanes. Or wings.

5. Documentaries will never replace real sex. Mind melds might do in a pinch.

4. Work and slave wage slaves will be replaced. Everyone will be a documentary-maker.

3. The non-proprietary open-source movement will flourish. Free will be the basis of the new economy. As well as tenderness. Although gossip might become the new currency.

2. Documakers will no longer need to take the vow of poverty. They will be appreciated and well paid.

1. Five-dimensional holograms will replace reality as we know it. Documations will come down off the screen to become people. Artificial intelligence will replace the need for most human needs. Docintelligence will have such capabilities as natural language processing, lip-reading, mind-reading, planning picnics and common-sense reasoning. Second life will become first life. HAL 9000, the fictional computer in Arthur C. Clarke's/ Kubrick's 2001, a Space Odyssey (1968), will direct all documentaries, thus freeing the rest of us to rest.

And those, ladies and gentlemen, and others, are my predictions for the future of new platforms for documentary cinema. The future is yet to come, and yet the future is here, now, in all the little things that we do, now. Indeed, capturing documentary's future is an unfinished work. However, it is up to all of us to create it. Now. It's up to you.

NOTES

1. Quoted in Annette Michelson (ed.), *Kino-Eye: The Writings of Dziga Vertov* (Berkeley and Los Angeles: University of California Press, 1984), p. 49.
2. From Sir Thomas More's book about an imaginary island nation, *Utopia*, 1516: etymology: from the Greek *ou* (not) and *topos* (a place). In other words, nowhere.
3. You can visit the legacy site at www.docagora.org.
4. Philip K. Dick, 'How To Build A Universe That Doesn't Fall Apart Two Days Later', in Philip K. Dick, *I Hope I Shall Arrive Soon* (New York: Doubleday, 1985 [1978]).
5. http://www.submarine.nl/ www.submarine.nl)
6. http://www.submarinechannel.com/www.submarine channel.com
7. All quotes are from personal statements unless otherwise stated.
8. F. T. Marinetti, *The Futurist Manifesto*, 1909,vserver1.cscs. lsa.umich.edu/~crshalizi/T4PM/futurist-manifesto.html

Afterword: 'What Must We Film Now?'

BRIAN WINSTON

The current direction of documentary film, as analysed in the last section of this book, and elsewhere throughout it, can be questioned, interrogated and doubted: but, however McLuhanesque and technicist, it cannot be dismissed. The direction of travel is clear: the post-Griersonian documentary owes more to Vertov than to Grierson. It accommodates a broad reflexive heterogeneity rather than constraining documentary to a narrow observationalist orthodoxy. That this profound change seems thus far to have been largely unnoticed by the public (including journalists) and is, indeed, still rejected in some traditionalist professional documentary circles as well is of little moment. Travel is underway and perhaps nothing better illustrates it than Dziga Vertov's own changed status in the cinema pantheon.

In 2012, the *Sight & Sound* decadal international poll of film critics to discover their collective notion of 'The Ten Greatest Films of All Time' produced a documentary in eighth position. The magazine has been doing this exercise since 1952 and perhaps no more sustained an application exists of a bourgeois positivist social science methodology to create an art form's canon.[1] Nevertheless, however much a 'boy's list' caper, the results do interestingly illuminate the collective *mentalité* of an ad hoc group of cinema 'experts'. That a documentary appeared in it was entirely unexpected and is as good an omen of the form's current fashionability as anything. Only once before had such a thing happened: in the very first poll, *Louisiana Story* (1948, USA), Robert Flaherty's romantic paean of praise to the beneficence of oil exploration in the Louisiana bayous (paid for by Esso), came fifth. But what is more interesting – startling even – than that is that the film which came eighth in 2012 was *Man with a Movie Camera* (1929). Clearly, the observationalist hegemony no longer holds unquestioned sway.

In no way, though, does this render the issues annually discussed at the Visible Evidence conferences and laid out in this volume moot. All the questions remain and, for the documentary, the central difficulty of definition is now further complicated by the liberal hetereogenity that marks the post-Griersonian documentary.

Peter Wintonick, though, is right to pour scorn on the sterilities of 'documentary cinema this, and documentary cinema that ...' discussions.[2] What indeed have we all been, as he puts it above, 'on about' in this book? I would argue, not for the first time, that the answer to this was given – succinctly, comprehensively – by Esfir Shub as the rows swirled around what Vertov was 'on about' nine decades ago. I can do no more than repeat it here. However documentary is defined, whatever hardware is deployed for making it on whatever 'platforms' to whatever purpose, the 'whole question' is surely unchanging: 'what we must film now?'[3]

That's what we have been on about.

NOTES

1. The survey seeks to transform personal opinion into a species of fact by aggregation. In this it resembles the so-called Delphi Method of 'futurologists', whose predictive opinions are similarly enhanced by surveying large numbers of 'experts'.
2. See above, p. 376.
3. Esfir Shub, 'Symposium on Soviet Documentary', with Sergey Tretyakov, Viktor Shklovsky and Osip Brik, in Graham Robert, *Forward Soviet!: History and Non-Fiction Film in the USSR* (London: I.B.Tauris, 1999 [1927]), p. 34. See also Osip Brik, Viktor Shklovskii, Esfir Shub and Sergei Tretiakov, 'LEF i Kino' [LEF and Cinema], *Novy LEF* vol. 11 no. 12, 1927, in '*Novy Lef* with an Introduction', *Screen*, trans. Ben Brewster, vol. 12 no. 4, Winter 1971.

Index

Note: Page numbers in **bold** indicate detailed analysis. Those in *italic* refer to illustrations. *n* = endnote; *t* = table/diagram.

LIST OF ILLUSTRATIONS

While considerable effort has been made to correctly identify the copyright holders, this has not been possible in all cases. We apologise for any apparent negligence and any omissions or corrections brought to our attention will be remedied in any future editions.

Hoop Dreams, © Kartemquin Educational Films; *L'arrivée d'un train en gare de La Ciotat*, Pathé Frères; *Nanook of the North*, Robert Flaherty; *Housing Problems*, British Commercial Gas Association; *Primary*, Time-Life Broadcasting/Drew Associates; *South*, Imperial Trans-Antarctic Film Syndicate; *Komsomol, Pioneer of Electrification*, Mezhrabpom-Russ; *Les Raquetteurs*, National Film Board of Canada; *La Sortie de l'Usine Lumière à Lyon*, Lumière; *A Married Couple*, Allan King Associates; *Titicut Follies*, © Bridgewater Film Co. Inc.; *Thin Blue Line*, © Third Floor Productions; *The Man with a Movie Camera*, VUFKU; *Chronique d'un été*, Argos-Films; *Roger and Me*, Dog Eat Dog Gilms; *Société nouvelle*, La Société Nouvelle Pathé-Cinéma; *Surname Viet Given Name Nam*, Idera Films; *Tongues Untied*, MTR Productions; *An Injury to One*, Travis Wilkerson; *Grizzly Man*, © Lions Gate Films; *The Cove*, © Oceanic Preservation Society; *Biggie and Tupac*, Lafayette Films/Channel Four; *Bowling for Columbine*, © Iconolatry Productions Inc./© Babelsberger Filmproduktion GmbH; *The Lost Evidence*, Flashback Television; *Animated Minds* (2004), Documentary Film Group; *Invasion*, Granada Television/Nederlandse Omroep Stichting/Belgische Radio en Televisie; *Words for Battle*, Crown Film Unit; *Catfish*, © Supermarché/© Hit the Ground Running LLC; *The Battle of the Somme*, British Topical Committee for War Films; *Drifters*, New Era Films; *School in the Mailbox*, Australian National Film Board; *The Coaster*, New Zealand National Film Unit; *The River*, United States Department of Agriculture; *Dont Look Back*, © Leacock Pennebaker; *The Fall of the Romanov Dynasty*, Sovkino; *Misère au borinage*, Education par l'Image; *Farrebique*, Ecran Français/Les Films Etienne Lallier; *Cane Toads: The Conquest*, © Screen Australia/© Radio Pictures; *Children Who Draw*, Teizo Otuchi; *Deluge*, © Salem Mekuria; *Nostalgia de la Luz*, © Atacama Productions/© Blinker Filmproduktion GmbH/© Cronomedia; *Iracema, uma transa amazônica*, Stop Film/Zweites Deutsches Fernsehen; *La television y yo*, Andrés di Tella; *Checkpoint*, AmythOS Films/Eden Productions Ltd/New Israel Foundation for Cinema and TV/Noga Communications/Noga Channel 8; *Staying Alive*, BBC Science/The Learning Channel; *Blood Relation*, Eden Productions; *On the Third Planet from the Sun*, Documentary Film Studio; *Go* (2003), Karel Žalud; *The Mosquito Problem and Other Stories*, Independent Television Service/Filmtank Hamburg; *89mm from Europe*, Studio Filmowe Kalejdoskop/Telewizja Polska; *Extreme Private Eros: a Love Story*, Shisso Production; *David Holzman's Diary*, Jim McBride; *Daughter Rite*, Michelle Citron; *Reassemblage*, Trinh T. Minh-ha; *Thriller*, Sally Potter/Arts Council of Great Britain; *The Day I Will Never Forget*, Channel Four; *The Negro Soldier*, Special Service Division War Department/The Army Service Forces; *Black Journal*, NET-TV; *Word is Out*, Mariposa Film Group; *She's a Boy I Knew*, © Shapeshifter Films; *Anderson Cooper 360:CNN Live*, CNN; *Airport*, BBC; *Big Brother*, Endemol Entertainment; *Torres Strait*, A. C. Haddon; *Trance and Dance in Bali*, Gregory Bateson/Margaret Mead; *Rituaes e Festas Borôro*, Conselho Nacional de Proteção aos Índios; *The Hunters*, Film Study Center of the Peabody Museum; *L'Hippocampe*, Cinégraphie Documentaire; *Cheese Mites*, Charles Urban Trading Company; *The Private Life of Plants*, MMC/TBS; *The Coming of the Dial*, GPO Film Unit; *Civilisation*, BBC; *The World at War*, FreemantleMedia; *The 1900 House*, Channel 4 Television Corporation/WNET Channel 13 New York/Wall to Wall Television; *Sounds and Silence*, Recycled TV; *Jazz on a Summer's Day*, Galaxy Films/Raven Film Productions; *The Debussy Film*, BBC; *Wonder Ring*, Stan Brakhage; *The Maelstrom* (1997), Peter Forgacs; *Paradox* (2004), Leandro Katz; *Lunch Love Community* (2010), Helen De Michiel and Sophie Constantinou; *Life in a Day*, © World in a Day Films Limited.